Imperialism, Race and Resistance

Imperialism, Race and Resistance

Africa and Britain, 1919–1945

Barbara Bush

LONDON AND NEW YORK

First published 1999
by Routledge
11 New Fetter Lane, London EC4P 4EE

Simultaneously published in the USA and Canada
by Routledge
29 West 35th Street, New York, NY 10001

Transferred to Digital Printing 2004

Routledge is an imprint of the Taylor & Francis Group

Typeset in Baskerville by Routledge
Printed in Great Britain by Biddles Ltd., King's Lynn, Norfolk

British Library Cataloguing in Publication Data
A catalogue record for this book is available from the British Library

Library of Congress Cataloging in Publication Data
Imperialism, race, and resistance: Africa and Britain, 1919–1945/
Barbara Bush. Includes bibliographical references.
1. Africa, English-speaking West – Politics and government –
20th century. 2. South Africa – Politics and government –
1909–1948. 3. Great Britain – Colonies – Africa –
Administration. 4. Africa, English-speaking West – Race relations
– History – 20th century. 5. South Africa – Race relations
– History – 20th century. 6. Great Britain – Colonies –
Africa – Race relations – History – 20th century. I. Title.
DT502.B87 1999
966'.09175217–dc21
98–55761
CIP

ISBN 0–415–15972–5 (hbk)
ISBN 0–415–15973–3 (pbk)

To Sarah and Matthew

Contents

List of illustrations   ix
Preface   xi
Acknowledgements   xv
Abbreviations   xvii

Introduction: why imperialism, race and resistance?   **1**

1 **Africa after the First World War: race and imperialism
   redefined?**   **20**

West Africa   **47**

2 **Britain's imperial hinterland: colonialism in West Africa**   **49**

3 **Expatriate society: race, gender and the culture
   of imperialism**   **72**

4 **'Whose dream was it anyway?' Anti-colonial protest
   in West Africa, 1929–45**   **101**

South Africa   **129**

5 **Forging the racist state: imperialism, race and labour in
   Britain's 'white dominion'**   **131**

6 **'Knocking on the white man's door':
   repression and resistance**   **157**

7 'Fighting for the underdog': British liberals and the
   South African 'native question'   **181**

Britain   **203**

8 **Into the heart of empire: black Britain**   **205**

9 **Into the heart of empire: the 'race problem'**   **228**

10 **The winds of change: towards a new imperialism in Africa?** **248**

   **Retrospective: Africa and the African diaspora in a
   'post-imperial' world**   **271**

   Notes and references   278
   Bibliography   344
   Index   375

Illustrations

Tables

Table 1	The non-African population of the Gold Coast, 1931	77
Table 2	Females as a proportion of the total non-African population of the Gold Coast, 1931	81
Table 3	The marital status of the non-African population, 1931	82
Table 4	Return of Africans in occupations other than industry	106
Table 5	The Gold Coast: occupations of Africans and the return of Africans engaged in industry	107
Table 6	Gold mining in the Gold Coast, 1921–31: general statistics	111
Table 7	Gold mining in the Gold Coast, 1921–31: the six major companies at work on 31 March 1931	111

Figures

Illustration 1	Cover illustration of *Empire Youth Annual*	26
Illustration 2	Rule Britannia	27
Illustration 3	On the banks of the Volta, Burifo, N.T.	32
Illustration 4	West Africa in the English imagination	50
Illustration 5	Captain Puckridge	62
Illustration 6	N.T.C. Trooper, Tamale	70
Illustration 7	Women travellers to West Africa: Lady Dorothy Mills	80
Illustration 8	Map of Princess Marie Louise's tour through the Gold Coast	83
Illustration 9	Bogged in the Nasia Swamp	85
Illustration 10	Lady on Nkole Ferry	91
Illustration 11	Palaver at Sunyani, Ashanti	96
Illustration 12	Minute by the Governor on the Criminal Code Amendment Bill, 1934	116
Illustration 13	Wartime loyalty	124
Illustration 14	Map of the approximate distribution of native areas in Southern Africa, *c.*1930	136

Illustration 15   Field-Marshal, the Rt. Hon. Jan Christiaan Smuts   139
Illustration 16   Bantu Men's Social Centre, Eloff Street Extension,
                   Johannesburg   154
Illustration 17   Letter with ICU logo from the National Secretary of the
                   Industrial and Commercial Workers Union of South
                   Africa   162
Illustration 18   Portrait of the Industrial and Commercial Workers'
                   Union Members   168
Illustration 19   Portrait of Clemens Kadalie and A.W.G. Champion   170
Illustration 20   Programme from the 34th Annual Conference of the
                   African National Congress, 1946   178
Illustration 21   Letter from Eslanda Robeson to Winifred Holtby   218
Illustration 22   Publicity leaflet for the International Africa Service
                   Bureau   224
Illustration 23   George Padmore, 'The British Empire Is Worst Racket
                   Yet Invented By Man'   260

Preface

You are not a country.
Africa, you are a concept, which we all
Fashion in our minds, each to each, to
Hide our separate years, to dream our separate dreams
(Abioseh Nicol, 1957)[1]

When Martin Luther King, in his emotive civil rights speech, declared, 'I have a dream', he evoked aspirations and longings of African diaspora peoples historically oppressed by racism. White dreams of power and black dreams of freedom have been in constant interplay since the age of slavery. Dreams of unbounded empire were paralleled by black visions of a world free from the nightmarish 'white terror' of racism and imperialism. Such dreams, however, were rooted in different world-views, ideologies and discourses that were transformed and reworked as the history of the 'West and the rest' unravelled. The symbolism of dreams provides a metaphor for different world-views on imperialism, race and resistance which translated into concrete actions, reshaping Africa's relationship to the West, represented before the Second World War, by the British Empire. The ways in which dreams of freedom disrupted and disturbed dreams of power, and the disjunction between dreams of freedom and lived experiences of power and oppression are the central concerns of this book. Paul Robeson, as the fictional African chief in the cover illustration, a still from the film *Sanders of the River* (1935), is a symbol of such oppression. But Robeson, the political activist, also encapsulates the essence of black dreams of freedom as a great and forceful opponent of racism and imperialism. I also chose the image because, through Robeson, it infers the complex links between Africa and its diaspora which thread through this study.

The origins of this book are in my long-standing interest in the African diaspora and black resistance which eventually drew me to African 'roots'. I have concentrated on the period from 1918–1945 – a rich and complicated epoch in imperial history which has not attracted the same outpouring of academic research as the pre-First World War era of 'new' imperialism. Fundamental to my study is an evaluation of W.E.B. Dubois' claim that 'the problem of the twentieth century is the problem of the colour line'.[2] It is informed by the exciting new developments in the study of imperial history which have adopted a more flexible and inter-disciplinary perspective and incorporated neglected areas, such as the crucial relationship between gender and imperialism. It also seeks to uncover what Kumari Jaywardena has termed 'underground' colonial history which incorporates the view from the colonised margins, as well as the imperial heartland.[3] As Linda Colley has pointed out, these 'untidy' edges of imperial history at the grass roots, in empire and 'at home', are important for they challenge and disrupt the 'monochrome' view of more orthodox 'top–down' studies of imperialism.[4]

My primary aims, then, are first to chart Africa's changing position in the world in the context of developments in imperialism and racism; second to provide insight into the workings of British imperial power and its impact on relations between white and black, coloniser and coloniser; and third to evaluate related developments in resistance to white supremacy in Africa and the African diaspora. The scope thus spans African, Imperial and British history, and highlights important imperial and pan-Africanist interconnections between West and South Africa and the British imperial heartland. My rationale for writing the book is that tensions between white dreams of power and black dreams of freedom, which emerged in the formal imperial era, are seminal to understanding Africa's still problematic relationship with the West. Four main questions are addressed. What was the link between the way Africa was conceptualised in the West and the nature of imperialist power? How were discourses of race and imperialism generated and translated into practice through British imperialism? What impact did this have on relationships between coloniser and colonised, and developments in resistance against racism and imperialism? Why is inter-war imperialism important in understanding the shattered dreams of African independence and the persistent problems of racism?

Such questions demand a broad canvas and I have therefore had to be selective in the sources and issues prioritised in order to establish wider trends. Wherever possible, I have utilised archival sources, but where there is a substantial secondary literature, I have combined a synthesis of central themes and arguments with insights from my own researches. The breadth of the study has necessitated an interdisciplinary approach, incorporating insights from cultural and literary studies. I have also drawn on fiction and film from the period. My concern is not with the intricate workings of colonial policy or British empire in Africa nor theoretical perspectives on race and imperialism as these have been ably covered elsewhere. I make no claims to any path-breaking approaches. Where this book differs from existing studies is in the way in which it tackles the gaps and silences exposed in the existing literature and interweaves economic, political, social and cultural developments to provide a more coherent, comprehensive and multifaceted analysis of relations between Britain and Africa in the crucial years between 1919–1945. It also addresses both men and women's experiences on the basis that women, black and white, have been marginalised in more orthodox studies of imperialism, and have been hived off into a separate 'gender and empire' category.

In developing my analysis, I have engaged with post-colonial perspectives, although I make no claims to furthering the debates and controversies which these have generated. As Kennedy (1996) and Darby (1998) have observed, many imperial historians, deterred by the theoretical excesses, have remained stubbornly resistant to incorporating 'post-colonial' insights.[5] This points to deep problems in the nature of orthodox imperial history. During the 1980s as an unknown post-graduate, I timorously criticised the gurus of orthodox imperial and African history for their Eurocentricism and failure to conceptualise the metropolitan centre and 'periphery' as indivisible. I was thus much heartened when my own hesitant challenges to conventional perspectives were validated by post-colonial insights, and more progressive historians began to explore the link between the imperial hinterland, the colonial 'others' who populated it and the development of British culture and national identity.[6] Pioneering 'post-colonial' studies have made important contributions to understanding the links between race, gender, culture, resistance and imperialism. They have critically interrogated the ways in which Western systems of knowledge have been constructed, including concepts of progress, and have generated a more nuanced understanding of culture and the crude dichotomy between 'tradition' and 'modernity', which was at the heart of contemporary race discourse. In sum, as Kennedy (1996) stresses, post-colonial theory has reinvigorated imperial studies and taken it in new directions, raising provocative questions about power, culture and resistance, concepts which are fundamental to this study.[7]

However, as Kennedy points out, there are also serious problems with post-colonial theory. Many historians, including myself, have felt tyrannised by theory and besieged by an anti-historicism. Our empiricist labours in the archives have been belittled as having insufficient theoretical depth and our jargon-free narratives dismissed as 'fiction'. Historians are now fighting a rearguard action pointing out the weaknesses of post-colonialism, particularly the high jargon and mystifying dense prose of much post-colonial writing. As an historian, one still treads warily in the minefield of deconstructionist history and discourse analysis. Perhaps the past is more diverse, chaotic and irrational than the orderings of conventional history have revealed. 'Facts' do have to be rigorously interrogated and historical 'truth' remains elusive, but, as Bill Schwartz and other critics have pointed out, the 'moment of post colonialism' has now passed. At some point 'the theoretically mundane ... obligations of a realist perspective' were reasserted, channelling the more useful post colonial insights more firmly down 'empirical and historical routes'.[8]

My main criticism is that the generalised, theoretical abstractions of post-colonial theory and discourse analysis obscured or mystified real structures of economic exploitation, globalised Western power and racial oppression. As this study will reveal, the 'discourse of imperialism' was expressed through tangible forms of power. Moreover, for people in many parts of the world, there is no 'post-colonial' condition. Global inequalities generated by capitalist expansion in the epoch of formal imperialism are still deepening, fusing the lived present with the past. As Giovanni Arrighi has stressed we need to analyse the dynamics of global capitalism in the 'longue-durée' in order to explain how it has structured relations between the poorer and richer nations of the world. How, asks Eric Hobsbawm, are we to make sense of these developments if not through historical enquiry which can make linkages and discover the patterns and mechanisms of historical change? It is for this reason that he defends the marxist perspective, despite all its failings, as still the 'best way' to understand the problems of an unjust world.[9] These 'global' perspectives on the dynamics of Western power provide the wider context for my more localised studies of colonial economies, 'cultures of colonialism' and the problematic formation of black resistance and political consciousness.

It has been impossible to deal with all the complex specificities in such a wide project, but I will have achieved my aims if I succeed in widening interest in the period and generating debate, controversy and further enquiry. In developing the conceptual building blocks of my book, I am indebted to pioneering studies into black diaspora history, African resistance, pan-Africanism, anti-colonialism, race and imperialism in the period which this book spans.[10] I have also drawn inspiration from the activities and writings of black men and women directly involved in resistance struggles. However, if my study appears biased towards 'white' sources, this reflects the difficulties of obtaining sources from the black perspective, particularly from the 'grass roots'. Moreover, as a white woman, I cannot claim to understand the history of black resistance as an integral part of black identity, or to understand the reverberations of imperialism from the position of the contemporary black experience. There are many fine studies acknowledged in this book which reflect on developments during the period from this 'insider' perspective. But black and white history is also interwoven in the ways in which 'black' and 'white' are defined and positioned in imperial and post-imperial societies. On a personal level, then, this book is also about exploring the constituents of my own 'whiteness' and the nature of the society in which I grew up.

I would like to extend my thanks to the School of Humanities and Social Sciences at Staffordshire University for enabling me to work on this book through funding a sabbatical leave, part-time help with teaching and a research visit to South Africa. Clare Midgley and Stephen Howe provided constructive and helpful comments on my manuscript. My special thanks go to Josephine Maltby, who ploughed through my drafts and gave me new inspiration and ideas. Many others have contributed to the production of this book, but I should like to acknowledge in particular the archivists in the University of South Africa's Documentation Centre for African Studies, Pretoria, Albert Bowyer for help with the illustrations and Pam Lowerson, who provided invaluable secretarial support. Staff and student members of the Colonial and Post Colonial Study Group at Staffordshire University also contributed with lively debate, constructive advice and interdisciplinary insight. I would also like to thank Heather McCallum, Senior Editor at Routledge, for her support throughout the preparation of the manuscript. Finally, this book would never have come to fruition without the support of my close friends and family, and the encouragement of Colin Holmes, who suggested I should tackle a PhD when, as a harassed young mother, the possibility had never crossed my mind. For better or for worse that PhD, after several years of metamorphosis, was transformed into this book.

Barbara Bush
November, 1998

Acknowledgements

Every effort has been made to contact copyright holders and we apologise for any inadvertent omissions. If any acknowledgement is missing it would be appreciated if contact could be made, care of the publishers, so that this can be rectified in any future edition.

Thanks to the trustees of H.R.H. Princess Marie Louise's estate for kindly granting permission to reproduce photographs from her book. Thanks also to Carlton International Media for the still for the cover.

Abbreviations

AAC	All African Convention (South Africa)
ACJ	Arthur Creech Jones Papers
ANC	African National Congress
APO	African Peoples' Organisation
ARPS	Aborigines Rights Protection Society (Gold Coast)
ASASP	British and Foreign Anti Slavery and Aborigines Protection Society
	British and Foreign Anti-Slavery and Aborigines Protection Society Papers
BMSC	Bantu Men's Social Centre
CAS	(British) Colonial Administrative Service (formerly Colonial African Service)
CDA	Colonial Defence Association
CIB	Colonial Information Bureau (Bulletin)
CO	Colonial Office
CP (GB)	Communist Party (of Great Britain)
CP (SA)	Communist Party (of South Africa)
CCP	Convention People's Party
CRB	Charles Roden Buxton Papers
CSU	Colonial Seaman's Union
CUP	Cambridge University Press
DJ	Duncan Johnstone Papers
DO	District Officer (Colonial African Service)
DC	District Commissioner (Colonial African Service)
FCB	Fabian Colonial Bureau (Britain)
FNETU	Federation of Non-European Trade Unions
FOA	Friends of Africa (Britain and South Africa)
IAFA	International African Friends of Abyssinia
IASB	International Africa Service Bureau
ICU	Industrial and Commercial Workers' Union (South Africa)
ICS	Indian Civil Service
IICU	Independent Industrial and Commercial Workers' Union (South Africa)

ILD	International Labour Defence
ILO	International Labour Organisation
ILP	(British) Independent Labour Party
ILP	(South African) Independent Labour Party
IRR	Institute of Race Relations
ITUC-NW	International Trade Union Committee of Negro Workers
LAI	League Against Imperialism
LCP	League of Coloured Peoples (Britain)
LGAA	London Group on African Affairs (Britain)
LPACIQ	Labour Party Advisory Committee on Imperial Questions
LRD	Labour Research Department
MUP	Manchester University Press
NAD	Native Affairs Department
NCCL	National Council of Civil Liberties (Britain)
NFRB	New Fabian Research Bureau (Britain)
NRC	Native Recruiting Corporation
NWA	Negro Workers' Association (Britain)
OUP	Oxford University Press
OUCRP	Oxford University Colonial Records Project
PO	Political Officer (Colonial African Service)
RILU	Red International of Labour Unions (Profintern)
SALP	South African Labour Party
SAIRR	South African Institute of Race Relations
SANNC	South African National Native Congress
SATLC	South African Trades and Labour Council
SATUC	South African Trade Union Congress
TUC	British Trade Union Congress
UDC	Union of Democratic Control
UDF	Union Defence Force
UNIA	Universal Negro Improvement Association
UNISA	University of South Africa (Pretoria, RSA)
WAYL	West African Youth League
WANS	West African National Secretariat
WASU	West African Students' Union
WEA	Workers' Educational Association
WH	Winifred Holtby Papers
WMM	William Macmillan Papers

Introduction

Why imperialism, race and resistance?

Not since the days of the Roman Empire has a single nation carried so great a responsibility for the lives of men and women born outside her shores as Great Britain does today. Within her forty or so dependent territories dwell eighty million people for whose welfare and enlightenment Britain is, to a greater or lesser degree, answerable.

(Winston Churchill, 1957)

Racism is the psychology of imperialism, the spirit of empire, because racism supplies the element that makes for the righteousness of empire. Hence racism is not simply a by product of empire, but ... part of the intestines of empire.

(Jan Nederveen Pietersie, 1990)

Though unintended by imperialists, the politics of colonialism have forever linked African peoples in their quest for freedom.

(William H. Watkins, 1994)[1]

Churchill was defending the record of colonial achievement against critics 'at home and abroad' during the era of 'popular decolonisation'. His sentiments encapsulate the meaning of imperialism to British national identity in the twentieth century: the implicit racism in the assumptions of subject peoples' need for 'enlightenment', but also the liberal concept of responsibility towards those in need of altruistic 'protection'. When I was a child in the 1950s and 'Two-Way Family Favourites' (a popular radio music request programme) still echoed the far-flung reaches of Britain's presence overseas, such images of empire suffused my education and provided the motif for pageants and projects. My conceptions of Africa were fragmentary and conflicting: thatched, round huts, altruistic white missionaries, but also terrified white families at peril from the 'savage Mau-Mau' in Kenya. Like the majority of the British working class whose families had no vested interests in empire and whose day-to-day preoccupations were deeply parochial, I remained largely oblivious of my 'imperial world-view' until I went to live in the Caribbean. Indeed, during the 1960s, my early memories of empire dissipated with the 'peaceful transition' to independence. New, 'modern' Britain was emerging, freed from the imperial shackles of the past and searching for new identities. Yet at the same time, race problems were moving into the heart of empire and images of Africa were now associated with chaos, violence and starvation in Biafra. During the 1960s and 1970s, imperialism became deeply unpopular, museums shelved their imperial artefacts, school curricula shifted towards liberal multiculturalism and academic research challenged orthodoxy on empire and Africa, prioritising resistance and the problems of the new nation states and redressing the racism and ethnocentricism in orthodox texts on empire. But the Falklands War and the revival of the Churchillian world-view by Margaret Thatcher, combined with the New Right's challenge to the liberal-reformism which had shaped the postwar world, revived interest in Britain's murky imperial past.

Imperialism

The 1990s is an apt decade for the reassessment of the historical relationship between Africa and Western imperialism. As Furedi (1995) has argued, the 'death' of socialism, Western disillusionment with the record of 'third-world' states and the emergence of a conservative, intellectual climate have arguably led to the 'moral rehabilitation of imperialism' and the resurgence of a 'more open imperial culture'. Thus recent humanitarian interventions in Africa are viewed by more scathing critics as 'recolonisation'. For Furedi, these developments represent a revalidation of Western identity and 'civilisation', a reassertion of Western values against the new 'barbarism' of the 'rest'. As with the nineteenth century partition of Africa, new interventionist discourse emphasises the chaos, poverty and inability of Africans to manage their own affairs. Distortions in African nationalism and the crises in 'post-colonial' African states have forced erstwhile staunch supporters of African independence movements to reassess their position.[2]

Furedi has been criticised by other historians for being strongly polemical and stressing only the negative aspects of imperialism, but his view of what is now an increasingly globalised imperialism is echoed in other recent studies.[3] In revisionist writings in the US and Britain there has been a 'whitewashing' of imperialism, and anti-imperialism is increasingly associated with a discredited marxism and failed African nationalism. In the new *Cambridge History of the British Empire* (1996), A.J. Stockwell asserts that 'the imperial legacy was skin deep' and the impact of imperialism on the non-Western world was exaggerated by apologists for empire and their nationalist critics. The editor, Peter Marshall, fails to take 'informal imperialism' seriously and persists in compartmentalising imperial history, arguing that empire hardly impacted on domestic history. Judgement on the imperial record, he concludes, is 'largely a fruitless exercise', as is moralising about whether it was good or bad. Attacking those who have painted a bleak picture of the imperial record, Max Beloff (1996) has made forceful arguments for the revalidation of Britain's imperial record, while Lawrence James (1994) extols the virtues of empire as 'a great civilising force' that swept away primitive rituals' – an 'empire to be proud of'. Even Denis Judd's lively study of the 'imperial experience' concludes that 'the British did their best'.[4]

These views raise important questions about how the imperial past is remembered. Memory involves forgetting, as well as remembering, and collective amnesia has comfortably erased more negative aspects of the imperial past. As Catherine Hall (1996) observes, the reconstructions of the remembered glories of the empire in 'heritage' experiences like Cadbury World (a 'theme' museum in Birmingham) have sanitised out racism and exploitation. Thus, in a 'post-imperial' age, empire still figures in popular consciousness. A recent *Daily Telegraph* Gallup poll carried out in 1997 suggested that many people still mourned empire and 70 per cent of Britons were 'proud of Britain's imperial achievements', although they 'knew little or nothing about imperial history'. To rectify this a Museum of the British Empire and Commonwealth was mooted to prevent empire fading from national consciousness as the history of the British Empire, 'proud or shameful', was 'indivisible' from the history of the English-speaking peoples. Such visions of empire suggest a nostalgic dream of past power, empire as 'bygone days', but, as Edward Said (1993) emphasises, 'imperial mentalities' still negatively impact on black minorities in the ex-imperial centres. British power may have waned, but imperialism 'still casts a shadow over the present' and Western domination of ex-colonised parts of the world persists.[5] Tomlinson (1991) and others have defined this ongoing process of 'globalisation' as less purposeful than imperialism, and characterised by 'one world' cultural fluidity and disintegration. Conversely, Harvey (1990) and Arrighi (1994) have both disputed the evidence for the disintegration of global capitalism, and Latouche (1992) has argued for an ongoing 'Westernisation of the world', built on assumptions of Western cultural and moral superiority and sustained by Western political, military and technological power. As Von Laue (1992) stresses, Westernisation carried the 'double thrust' of freedom, peace and justice, the best European traditions, but also the 'raw power to reshape the world in one's image'. Both Western liberalism and marxism embraced an evolutionary idea of culture which stamped the imprint of backwardness on 'non-European' cultures.[6] This is the 'cultural imperialism' that has been so central to the legitimisation of Western power.

Imperialism is extraordinarily hard to define and its meaning has produced a plethora of work. Imperial power relationships involve the interaction of economic, political, social and cultural 'imperialisms'. Thus, in practice, imperialism is complex and multifaceted and generates deep contradictions. Pietersie (1990) suggests that imperialism, like fascism is '... a phenomenon not yet understood, as if a theatrical performance still in motion'. If imperialism has been extensively documented and analysed, its actual character remains opaque, 'a situation conditioned by ... the ongoing realities of neo-imperialism and global hierarchy'.[7] The neutralisation of contemporary imperialism into the more benign concept of globalisation strengthens my case for re-evaluating the inter-war years, a period in British imperial history that remains curiously neglected compared to the extensive literature on the pre-1914 period. The reasons for this are threefold: the widely held view that the First World War was a watershed between a confident and expansive imperialism and decline leading to decolonisation; second, the refocusing of the centre of international developments to Europe with the rise of fascism and Stalinism; and, third, the economic depression in the 1930s, which prioritised domestic developments, and the 'weakness' and lack of direction in British politics. The concept of empire was also becoming more diffuse with three empires – the Dominions, India and Africa, the Caribbean and other more 'backward colonies'. However, although there were separate administrations, there were important linkages between the three empires.

Cain and Hopkins (1993) have argued most plausibly for the 'healthy continuation' of British imperialism fuelled by expansion and changes in the British economy, which remained strong relative to that of other Western states, even in the 1930s. Their research suggests that Britain was the 'only truly world power of consequence' before the Second World War, which was fought to defend the empire as well as to defeat fascism. Mounting international rivalries and growing nationalist resistance were symptoms less of the erosion of Britain's 'hegemonic status' than reactions to her continuing power. This is supported by other recent studies of the period.[8] Empire is thus central to understanding the positioning of British business in the global economy, although standard texts on British business history make only a cursory mention, if any, of these vital imperial linkages.

Whether 'orthodox' or 'post-colonial', studies of British imperialism have, in the main, concentrated on the pre-1914 era. I have concentrated on the interwar years, because, in contrast to the 'long nineteenth century' they represented 'modern times', a new cultural and political ethos, catalysed by the First World War.[9] Important trends emerged in the 'internationalisation' of imperialism and, as Lauren (1996) has demonstrated, racial inequality underpinned this 'New World Order'. This, in turn, helped to strengthen the 'colour bar' dividing Britain's 'white' and 'tropical' empires. British imperialism was extended, and 'Anglo-Saxonism' was strengthened through the white, imperial diaspora which was energetically promoted after the First World War. White settlers shared a diasporic consciousness, a common identity based on 'Anglo-Saxon' cultural roots, racial superiority and a sense of 'home' as the imperial centre. This white diaspora ensured that Western culture and liberal capitalism developed a global reach. White settlers and expatriate residents, in defining their own colonial identities through interaction with the particular economic, cultural and political configurations of their land of settlement, reworked and embellished a strong, white ethnicity with racism as a powerful, unifying bond. 'Imperial mentalities', home and colonial, will be explored in chapters 1, 2, 5 and 10.

Another feature of the 1918–45 period that makes it a rich area for study are the strong political tensions between marxism and liberal capitalism, complicated in the 1930s by fascism and the global upheavals of the Second World War, a 'good war' against fascist racism and forces undermining Western liberalism. These developments impacted on three areas central to this study. They generated new marxist discourses on race and empire, stimulated wider opposition to imperialism in Britain and catalysed the development of black consciousness in Africa and its diaspora. At the same time, the certainties of nineteenth century scientific racism and physical anthropology were challenged. It was also a seminal period in the development of anti-imperialism manifest in the emergence of anti-Western racial solidarity through pan-Africanism, black nationalism and anti-colonial nationalism. In turn, these strongly interlinked developments influenced official discourses on race and empire and resulted in policy changes which were subsequently implemented during and after the Second World War. Thus, taking the study up to 1945 also provides insight into the origins of postwar decolonisation and 'post-colonial relations' between the African diaspora, Africa and the West.

Africa and the African diaspora

During the inter-war period, there was a 'tranquil assumption' that colonial rule operated smoothly in Africa and self-government was regarded as so distant as to seem 'unimaginable'. The idea of Africa as a quiet 'backwater', until recognised as central to Britain's post-Second World War reconstruction, is still in common currency. The *Daily Telegraph's The British Empire, 1497–1997: 500 Years that Shaped the World* gives Africa barely a mention in the period 1914–45, and more academic, general works on empire also tend to sweep over the inter-war years, concentrating on the era of decolonisation.[10] While there are some important studies of colonial rule, research is still fragmentary. Yet, Africa remained central to Western race discourses and, although Africa had been 'tamed' and mapped by the 1920s, Englishmen's fantastic 'dreams of Africa' arguably remained as strong as when they were satirised by Jonathan Swift.[11] Moreover, as Cain and Hopkins (1993) stress, the international postwar settlement completed the pre-1914 partition of Africa and extended British power. The 'colonial moment' in Africa is thus central to understanding Africa's position in the international economy, Western concepts of Africa and the origins of African nationalism. Methods of consolidating British power, structural changes in the colonial political economy and international developments inspired new forms of protest which, argues Hopkins (1973) ensured that the 1930s were integral to the development of postwar nationalism.[12]

In exploring the impact of these developments, which contributed to an important shift in the relationship between Britain and Africa between 1935 and 1945 (Chapter 10), I have contrasted and compared West and South Africa. South Africa was chosen because of its central position in international race discourses as the fierce crucible of racial experiments in segregation. The *bête noire* of black and white critics of colonialism, it represented all the worst aspects of white settler rule and was used as a grim yardstick against which to assess developments in the fledgling, white settler colonies of Kenya and Rhodesia. However, South African historiography before the ending of apartheid developed a rather parochial and insular approach which tended to 'delink' the region from the rest of Africa and the British imperial orbit. South Africa was 'unique' in many ways, but developments also patterned those in other parts of Africa and contrasts with West Africa can yield fruitful insights. Moreover, British imperialism had a central role in the creation of the colony, and imperial ties were sustained through a resident High Commissioner, a large British–South African minority, financial interests and the proximity of the British Protectorates of Bechuanaland (Botswana), Swaziland and Basutoland (Lesotho). Important interconnections also existed between segregationist policy and structures of 'native administration' in South Africa and the development of colonial policy in other parts of British 'tropical' Africa. British West Africa provides an important contrast as a non-settler region, which, by the 1930s, was regarded as the 'most advanced' part of Britain's African empire and the potential centre of the 'African renaissance'.[13] West Africa was represented as a model of imperial rule in British tropical Africa and was fertile territory for the new 'cultural anthropology' and experiments in 'progressive' imperial policies.

Any discussion of Africa must also embrace the African diaspora in order to understand the complex chains of resistance linking colonial hinterland and imperial heart of empire. Racism fostered a greater consciousness of African roots among blacks in the diaspora, particularly in the US where 'one heard little or nothing about Africa'.[14] Africa provided a common sense of 'home', culture and history, forged through collective memories of oppression, which could inspire political unity against white oppression and express a strong African identity redeemed from Western racism. A stronger 'consciousness of Africa', expressed through pan-Africanism and Garveyism (see p. 14), thus forged tighter links between Africa and its diaspora. Although there are different types of diaspora as a 'dispersal from the original homeland', diaspora evokes peoples who are forced into exile by poverty and/ or coercion, as in the Jewish, Irish and African diasporas. Jews and diaspora Africans were both a people without a home, hence the term 'black zionism' to express the desire of an African 'nation in exile' for a homeland. Here lies the key difference with white diasporas. White diasporas, suggests Cohen (1997), may be seen as transitional, loosening bonds with the homeland as settlers progress and prosper. In 'victim diasporas' the emotional and cultural bond with the 'homeland' is strengthened through continued hardship or persecution.[15]

But there are also 'diasporas within diasporas', what Cohen terms 'cultural diasporas', exemplified by voluntary migration from the Caribbean to the US and Britain. Such voluntary 'exiles', who were actively searching for work, education, adventure or simply the promise of a new and better life, formed the transient and permanent black population in Britain in the inter-war years. In addressing the impact of such migrations, Homi Bhabha (1994) has evoked a 'diasporic consciousness', rooted in problems of displacement, but also the possibilities for resistance, collaboration and cultural negotiation created in the 'in between spaces' between different cultures. This cultural fluidity and physical mobility of diaspora Africans, which was so important in the development of black consciousness, are captured in Paul Gilroy's concept of the 'Black Atlantic' (1993).[16] This is my rationale for including a substantial section on the experiences of blacks in Britain (Chapters 8 and 9). As the centre of the most powerful empire, London provided a forum for a rich interchange of ideas between black intellectuals on imperialism and racism.

Race and imperialism

I have used the term 'race' in the title of this book to reflect contemporary usage and preoccupations. However, the term 'racism' also came into contemporary usage in the 1930s, marking greater awareness of racism as an ideological construct. Racism and imperialism have always been inseparable, although the nature and expression of racism has changed over time in form and content. As Memmi (1957) has stressed, racism is not an 'incidental detail' of colonialism (the practical workings of imperialism), but a 'consubstantial part' – the 'highest expression of the colonial system' and the basis of the 'fundamental discrimination' between coloniser and colonised. Analysis of the 'race problem' is crucial to understanding the nature of inter-war imperialism. A wide range of books on the 'race problem' were produced in the period and additional stimulus to these debates was provided by the development of national socialism which radically impacted on race thinking, strengthening analogies between the Jewish and the black diasporas. Lauren (1996) and Sowell (1994) both prioritise race tension as one of the most important features in contemporary history, at the centre of world conflicts, and thus needing a global perspective.[17] Like imperialism, racism has also had an ugly revival. Goldberg (1993) has linked this ongoing globalisation of 'racist culture' to the failure of the liberal discourse of racial equality, which has dominated in the West since the Second World War. In Britain, racism remains an essential ingredient of national identity, an 'inherent part' of what Anthias and Yuval Davis (1992) define as a 'hegemonic Anglomorphic ethnicity'.[18]

Reaching a consensus on the meaning of racism remains elusive. Attempts at definition have become even more complex, embracing race, gender, class, ethnic and national perspectives as they affect the identities of the post-colonial subject. As Miles (1996) points out, it is now very difficult to formulate a definition of racism.[19] With the emergence of identity politics and the emphasis on the politically correct usage of words and categorisation, it is easy to get sidetracked into complex justifications of terminology and abstract debates over being, identity and difference. The meanings of race and racism, black and black identity are currently heavily contested. In this study, where using primary sources, I will keep to the contemporary terms, 'coloured', ('Coloured' in South Africa), 'negro' and 'native', now discredited as racist, but in common usage at the time. 'Black' will be used in the sense that it is used by, for instance, Gilroy (1993) in establishing a certain shared diasporic cultural context and terrain of struggle against racism.[20]

The firm connection between racism, capitalism and imperialism made by the inter-war left will also inform my analysis, particularly in relation to the impact of marxism on black resistance and white anti-imperialism and the articulation of the race versus class debate (Chapters six and nine). As Miles (1996) argues, racism has 'threaded through the historical evolution of capitalism' and racial exclusion has not only created racialised class factions, but also generated resistance against racial inequalities. However, the dynamics of racism were given shape by specific historical contexts. Thus, Stoler (1989) argues that we must beware of homogenising the impact of racism, as the 'quality and intensity of racism' can vary widely in different colonial contests and at different historical moments. This is pertinent here to contrasts between West and South Africa. Men, women and members of different social classes also had variable experiences of, and reactions to, racism. Similarly, Anthias and Yuval Davis (1992) point out that the 'dichotomous categorisations of blacks as victims and whites as perpetrators of racism' is too universalising.[21] My study clearly demonstrates that whites did not articulate or express racism uniformly, and gender differences were particularly significant. Before analysing the discourses of race in more detail, it is important to establish why ideas about European racial and cultural superiority were so important in sustaining the culture of imperialism in Britain and its colonies.

Culture and imperialism

Imperialism, argues Said (1991), was as much a formative element in the development of metropolitan cultures as it was for colonised societies. 'Cultural imperialism' and 'popular imperialism' are very different, but they arguably constitute two prongs of the same hegemonic processes. The ideology and practice of imperialism was the domain of powerful groups and vested interests for whom empire brought tangible benefits. Working-class whites experienced empire as popular entertainment and spectacle, and also benefited as settlers in the colonies and through cheap products of empire. Such 'carrots', asserts Pietersie (1992), served to 'neutralise class struggle' and transform class solidarity and political unrest into national and racial solidarity. Thus, as John Mackenzie's pioneering work has demonstrated, popular imperialism (discussed in Chapters one and ten) relates to the cultural channels through which consent for empire and the discourse of Eurocentrism was secured in the imperial heartland.[22] Like popular imperialism, the concept of cultural imperialism is diffuse and difficult to define. As Tomlinson (1991) points out it is a composite of two highly problematic concepts which cannot be reduced to a single meaning. However, a key feature of cultural imperialism is that it operated through disrupting and changing 'the context within which people give meanings to their actions and experiences and make sense of their lives'.[23] In the colonial context, where strict racial boundaries and the expression of white expatriate culture confirmed white prestige and power (Chapter three), cultural imperialism was arguably essential to legitimising colonial rule and the racial orders that sustained it.

These links between culture and imperialism raise fundamental questions about the operation of power and knowledge in colonial societies. From an orthodox marxist perspective, capitalism is the most powerful force for cultural change and controls the channels of cultural imperialism through which the values and culture of the dominant power are spread at the expense of the dominated. But, argues Tomlinson, this implies passivity, whereas colonised subjects were actively engaged in complex cultural choices, interacting with the dominant culture, although 'not in conditions of their own choosing'.[24] Indeed, post-colonial studies have laid far more emphasis on how the colonised have subverted and actively appropriated aspects of 'Western' culture and melded them into their own culture creating new 'hybrid' forms. This has relevance to my study, particularly in the ways in which educated Africans and urban workers appropriated and subverted the discourses of democracy and modernity. However, this conceptualisation of cultural interaction on the 'borders', promoted by a variety of agents, black and white, must be tempered by the very real imbalance of power and the link between economic and cultural power.

Post-colonial theory has been influenced by the Foucaultian analysis in which culture in itself becomes a mechanism of repression through the operation of powerful discourses. These are expressed through representations of individuals and groups which have the power to include and exclude, to police and control every area of life, including sexuality.[25] But discourses of power work in the interests of powerful groups in Britain and the colonies, and are linked to other, more tangible, forms of power. As Chatterjee (1994) notes, colonisers were involved in a 'hegemonic project' that was powerful and long-lasting.[26] Here the Gramscian concept of hegemony is helpful in explaining the role of culture in securing consent to the colonial state without undue coercion. 'Hegemony' does not imply a complete system of ideological and political control – indeed, if this were so, there would have been no resistance or 'double consciousness' of black intellectuals generated by dynamic tensions between the 'hegemonic ideologies' of the colonisers, the indigenous pre-colonial ruling classes and the oppositional discourses of the African diaspora. To be successful imperial hegemony had to come to terms with, incorporate and transform African values. Thus, argue Marks and Engels (1994), direct violence, defined as state violence through soldiers and policemen, was the exception rather than the rule in the history of British imperialism in India and Africa. Control was more commonly maintained through 'gentle violence', which transformed colonial peoples' perceptions and changed the 'day to day reproduction of life under colonial rule in the name of civilisation and reason'.[27] In South Africa, however, the balance was tipped more towards coercion through state violence, whereas in West Africa subtler techniques of enforcing power arguably predominated, although it is important not to underestimate the extent to which direct violence was also used. These issues of hegemony and the operation of cultural imperialism are intimately linked to the relationship between knowledge and power as it affected the practice of imperialism. The discourse of colonialism has had a profound impact on the cultures of both Europe and Africa. How was this discourse constituted?

Discourses of power: race, liberalism and modernity

Stuart Hall (1992) has defined a discourse as 'a way of talking, thinking or representing a particular subject', which always operates in relation to power and is 'part of the way power circulates and is contested'. However, discourses of power are intimately linked to dominant ideologies, defined as modes of consciousness and ways of interpreting social reality, which may be taken for granted by those who have internalised them, and are durable and historically reproduced.[28] Discourse analysis, which heavily influenced post-colonial studies, is associated with post-modernist theory and philosophy and places great emphasis on language, meaning and symbolic representation. The problem with the 'discourse' of discourse analysis is that it can easily become bogged down in elaborate deconstruction and abstract debate. In scrutinising colonial discourse, it is also important to ask why discourses changed and how 'new' discourses were translated into changes in policy. For instance by the 1930s there was a noticeable shift in official discourse from 'native' to 'African', 'negro' to 'coloured', 'trusteeship' to 'partnership', and a new discourse of 'race relations' arose. In order to more fully concretise discourse in the real world, and establish firmer links between discourse and practice, it is important to examine how discourses of power are constituted. Three key discourses are pertinent here, race, liberalism and modernity.

Essentially, race discourses before the Second World War split into two camps: assimilationist (integrationist) and segregationist (separate development), although the precise terminology varied and they were interpreted in different ways by blacks and whites. Before the Second World War, assimilation into modernity through the spread of Western culture was the dominant 'progressive' discourse of the day, spanning liberal and left opinion. The segregationist position, which avowed 'respect' for traditional culture and the need to protect Africans from the evils of Western civilisation, dominated strategies for practical administration. However, there was never a clear demarcation line and contradictions emerged in the internal logic of both discourses when translated into practice. An either/or policy was deeply problematic and arguably unworkable and, as we shall see in Chapters two and five, although articulated differently, racism underpinned both positions. Partly as a result of these problems, a third discourse emerged, multiracialism, which emphasised the need to promote racial harmony through securing equality for the minority of Africans who were 'fit for citizenship', that is, had passed the 'civilisation test' (Chapters 8 and 9). This formed the basis of the liberal race discourse, which informed British policy and academic literature in the 'post-colonial' era.

Transformations in the liberal discourse of racial equality began in the interwar years, when nineteenth century 'scientific' racism was discredited and replaced by new 'cultural' definitions of race. Developments in anthropology also refined both segregationist and assimilationist discourses (Chapter 1). Turner (1994) argues that anthropological cultural relativism, which conceptualised cultures as 'porous, dynamic and interactive' and challenged the idea of a monolithic, homogenous Western culture, is a direct ancestor of contemporary multiculturalism, which stresses equal respect and rights for different cultures. The concept of 'plural' cultures, pioneered by the anthropologist, J.S. Furnivall, became increasingly popular with colonial governments during and after the Second World War when they were faced with the problems of nationalism and nation building in 'multiracial' colonial societies. Liberal multiculturalism also increasingly influenced official policy, reflected in Kenneth Robinson's 1962 Reith lectures on the 'Dilemmas of Trusteeship', which heavily promoted the liberal vision of 'good race relations' in Britain and its 'tropical' empire. Furedi (1998) has attributed this apparent shift towards a more egalitarian definition of race to the impact of the Second World War when the spectre of evil Nazism left Britain (and the West) uncomfortable with the racist past.[29] But how egalitarian and flexible was this new multiculturalism? With some irony, the 1997 Reith lectures were given by the black American academic, Patricia Williams, who argued problems of race had been buried by liberal multiculturalism and whites were still 'colour-blind' in assuming whiteness was the norm. As Malik (1996) has pointed out, there has been a conservative, anti-liberal backlash against multicultural discourses that have taken the US and Europe 'beyond the liberal hour'. The full circle has turned back to the beginnings of a dangerous, neo-scientific racism, linked to the 'new geneticism' and 'neo-Darwinism' of socio-biology.[30]

Clearly, many confusions and ambiguities emerged in the blurring of race and culture in liberal multiculturalism, which is why it is now heavily critiqued from the left, as well as the right.[31] When I sifted through the extensive literature for enlightenment, the debates became even more complex and opaque. As I see it, there are three main issues that are of relevance to my study. First, the distinctions between the assimilationist model and the multiracialist model are extremely fuzzy. Liberal multiculturalism, argues Mclaren (1994), remains rooted in imperialist 'Anglo-Saxonism' and aims to construct a 'common culture' a 'seamless web ... bent on annulling the concept of the border' between different cultures, with European culture taken as the norm. Second, liberal multiculturalism prioritised ethnic or cultural differences over racial difference, but culture or ethnicity became a polite euphemism for race (cultural racism) and, argues Stuart Hall (1992), 'a means of disavowing the realities of racism and repression'. Behind this rhetoric, racism became more firmly embedded in the structures of global power and what Goldberg (1994) has termed the 'conceptual orders' of Western thought. Thus, Eurocentric visions of the 'primitive' versus modernity and white fears of racial pollution through miscegenation and migration have remained inseparable from the continuing power of the West. Third, liberal multiculturalism as the 'politics of equal respect' assumes that equality can be achieved through reforms that remove cultural, political and economic barriers. But, as Goldberg (1994) has argued, the central paradox of modernity is that despite its commitment to the universal, liberal principles of equality, its link with capitalism has ensured continuing inequalities and racial exclusions. Western culture was thus 'Janus-faced': the public 'face' emphasised reason, freedom and equality, but hypocritically obscured racism, inequality and colonial oppression. This, argues Malik (1996), is the crux of the liberal dilemma.[32] As I shall be focusing on these contradictions in the liberal discourse of race, particularly in Chapters seven and nine, it is important to explore the nature of liberalism as it related to the discourse and practice of British imperialism.

Liberal ideals underpinned Britain's allegedly progressive imperial policy and informal pressure group activism on race and colonial problems (Chapters 1, 7, 9 and 10). Liberalism also defined itself in opposition to Marxist and fascist totalitarianism, and liberal values informed the reformist socialism associated with the British Labour Party and Trade Union Movement. As we shall see, even reformist critics of colonialism retained a faith in the liberal ideals and moral justification of empire. These inconsistencies and problems in the articulation of liberalism and its intimate link with liberal racial discourse provide a motif that threads through this study. As the dominant Western political discourse, liberalism has thus had enormous power in the twentieth century claiming to represent universal values even though these are, in effect, gendered (male) and culturally specific. This resulted in the exclusion or marginalisation of those who failed to meet the standards set for inclusion in the democratic processes, economic benefits and intellectual and cultural projects that define Western modernity.[33] The liberalism of the British empire allowed only for the advancement and 'inclusion' of Europeanised male Africans. This echoed the 'protective' and paternalistic liberalism of the early nineteenth century British utilitarians, such as James Mill, who argued that only those who were educated and thus 'civilised' were 'fit for citizenship', the role of government was to protect the interests of those who did not fulfil these criteria.[34]

Black intellectuals were quick to point out the contradictions between the twentieth century Western liberal commitment to full citizenship and democracy and the anti-democratic nature of colonial rule. Thus, during the Second World War, African nationalists demanded a more inclusive conceptualisation of rights and citizenship. The incorporation of liberal democratic discourse into anticolonial nationalism demonstrates that liberalism, like other 'isms', is not a monolithic discourse and can be interpreted both as a discourse of power and as a liberatory ideology. Fundamental to philosophical liberalism is a commitment to the universal principles of reason and moral value, which presupposes human rights and values. As Goldberg (1996) points out, such principles are not exclusively those of the dominant class, and may be contested and revised through political action.[35] This is an enabling concept that helps us to understand the ways in which black oppositional discourses reworked Western liberalism in articulating their grievances against racism and imperialism. It also explains the incorporation of liberal values, as an expression of progressive modernity, into more radical anti-imperialism or anti-racism, black and white. To understand more fully why this happened it is important to dissect more closely the complex relationship between race, culture and Western concepts of modernity.

In the imperial era, discourses of race and liberalism were rooted in the problems of 'culture contact' between different races (again race and culture are clearly conflated). The spread of modernity (capitalist organisation of the economy, liberal political values and Western culture) was double-edged and, as we shall see, opened up fierce debates over its impact on the colonised. Anthropologists and many colonial administrators assumed a simple dichotomy between tradition and modernity, and feared the negative and disintegrative impact of Western culture. But once change had been unleashed, dreams of preserving 'traditional African culture' in aspic were futile. Liberals and reformists criticised those who wanted to hold back 'progress', yet they also feared the potential for chaos which it unleashed. Post-modern theorists have been much engaged with the ambiguities of modernity. However, as Marshall Berman (1983) points out, the contradictions of modernity are in fact a much older preoccupation, reflected in the writings of the arch 'meta-narrator', Marx. In the *Communist Manifesto*, Marx and Engels argued that capitalist penetration through colonialism compelled 'all nations' to adopt the 'bourgeois' mode of production and 'what it calls civilisation', thus creating 'a world after its own image … '. Yet such expansion also destroyed 'archaic and feudal orders' thus:

> All fixed, fast frozen relations, with their train of ancient and removable prejudices and opinions, are swept away … All that is solid melts into air, all that is holy is profaned, and men at last are forced to face with sober senses the real conditions of their lives and their relation with fellow men.[36]

For Berman, Marx provided some of the most powerful insights into the nature of modernity and the links between modernist culture, economy and society. All men and women in the world, he argues, now share the experience of modernity, but, as in Marx's day, it is characterised by a 'maelstrom' of perpetual disintegration and renewal, of struggle and contradiction, possibilities and perils, unity and disunity. Modernity, concludes Berman, alters cultures irrevocably, but also offers a 'liberation of the spirit' from the constraints of 'tradition'. From this perspective, suggests Warren (1980), imperialism, as a 'pioneer' of capitalism, acted as a 'powerful engine of progressive social change' in Africa.[37]

Such views may be criticised for Eurocentricism in assuming irrevocable progress to Western modernity. They also pay insufficient attention to the uneven and frequently adverse impact of modernity on the 'non-Western world'. As we shall see in Chapters four, five and six, the penetration of modernity had devastating consequences for colonised societies and resulted in 'fragmented' forms of consciousness, which impeded and problematised black emancipatory struggles. But negotiating the complex impact of 'modernity' also constituted an important 'consciousness-raising' process for the colonised, which progressed the forces of resistance. Imperialism involved the imposition of bourgeois order and forms of production and exchange, but in unleashing modernity, the imperialist (the agent of bourgeois values) became like Marx's sorcerer 'who can no longer control the powers of the underworld he has summoned up'.[38] This is clearly manifest in the dilemmas of administration created when the 'rational' order, which colonial administrators tried to impose on African societies, was thrown into chaos by the conjunction of modernity with the 'irrational' and 'primitive'

(Chapter two). In this 'maelstrom of change', modernity also inspired new 'dreams of freedom' articulated through the oppositional discourses of Pan-Africanism and Garveyism.

Discourses of resistance: pan-Africanism and Garveyism

Pan-Africanism was a direct response to the imperialist annexation of Africa and Eurocentricism, and thus represented 'an exercise in consciousness and resistance'.[39] It was shaped through active intellectual engagement with the dominant discourses of imperial power. Different strains of pan-Africanist thought and activity have evolved with changing historical circumstances, but certain key concepts have unified the different strands – opposition to colonialism and imperialism, a revitalisation and promotion of African cultural ideals, the betterment and upliftment of black people and the importance of a free and united Africa for the furtherance of these ideals. Pan-Africanism began as an intellectual movement articulating a form of 'black nationalism' and, as Lemelle and Kelley (1994) point out, from its inception it was a hybrid discourse, originating in the African diaspora. It thus combined concepts of progress, civilisation and cultural nationalism, rooted in European rationalism, with Ethiopianism (the independent African church movements which emerged at the end of the nineteenth century as an assertion of cultural and religious autonomy and, thus, resistance to imperialism). By the First World War this intellectual black nationalism, which had been concerned with establishing a racial and cultural bond between Africa and its diaspora, had embraced more directly political objectives. In turn, the events of the 1930s and the influence of marxism led to a radical critique of liberal pan-Africanism. A merging of pan-Africanist and marxist ideas, shaping a radical pan-Africanism which had greater mass appeal, formed an important constituent of African nationalism.[40]

However, it was Garveyism (named after the Jamaican, Marcus Garvey) that first concretised the rhetoric of pan-Africanism into a populist movement with concrete objectives. Garvey's Universal Negro Improvement Association (UNIA) was the first pan-Africanist organisation to embrace Africans on the continent and overseas. Garvey spoke in a language that the poor understood, using the symbolism of Ethiopia as the source of liberation for Africans from Babylonian repression and as the cradle of an independent and proud culture, centred around a black God. Garveyism was a secular, political movement, but this religious symbolism was taken up and developed by Jamaican Rastafarianism.[41] Garvey built on the race consciousness that was fundamental to pan-Africanism, preaching black pride and the importance of diaspora Africans returning to Africa. African redemption from imperialism was thus fundamental to reclaiming 'Africa for the Africans'. He ran correspondence courses through the UNIA, teaching African history. He also advocated black self-help and industrial/vocational training along the lines developed by the black American, Booker T. Washington, (whose ideas on accommodationist 'negro' education were, ironically, highly influential among some colonial educators, as we will see in Chapter one).

Garveyism had a strong populist appeal in Africa and its diaspora. During the 1920s, it was seen as a serious threat in power circles in both the US and Britain. By the 1930s, however, Garveyism had fizzled out and was superseded by radical pan-Africanism. Leading pan-Africanists, like W.E.B. Dubois, thus dismissed Garvey as an 'impractical visionary' and a poor businessman, reflected in the failure of his Black Star Shipping Line, which was set up to return diaspora Africans to their African homeland.[42] Garveyism may have failed as a political movement, but Barbara Bair (1994) argues that, in its cultural manifestations, it had a far-reaching and radical impact, creating 'a powerful narrative of liberation' that reshaped black political consciousness, reversed white-defined constructions of cultural values and 'influenced the actions of a new generation of Africans who made anti-colonial independence movements a reality'.[43]

'Pan-Africanist' discourses of liberation thus embraced a broad political spectrum: black nationalism conceived as a cultural movement promoting race consciousness, the militant black nationalism of Garveyism with its intimations of separatist politics, the liberal Pan-African Congresses, which began in 1900 and promoted black political, as well as cultural unity, articulated grievances and lobbied for black rights and the radical pan-Africanism, which fuelled nationalism in Africa and inspired nationalist movements in the African diaspora. However, pan-Africanism in all its guises was a masculine discourse and this raises questions about the gendered nature of resistance (Chapters four, six and eight). For much of the period, with the exception of Garveyism, it was also predominantly an elite discourse. Given these limitations, pan-Africanism undoubtedly played an important role in stimulating race consciousness, which inspired resistance against colonial rule and white supremacy. For educated Africans, racial assertion was a response to feelings of humiliation, an expression of race pride and an important 'consciousness-raising' phase in the development of a more coherent political consciousness of the structural factors of oppression. Finally, the discourse of pan-Africanism was undoubtedly central to forging stronger links between Africa and diaspora, thus facilitating a more extensive, coherent and effective challenge to imperialism.

Imperialism and resistance

The foregoing discussion has illustrated intimate links between imperialism, racism and discourses of power and liberation, but how do I justify making resistance an integral part of this study? This is summed up by Pietersie (1991) who writes, 'We appear to know more about domination than about liberation', an indication, perhaps of the fact that history is always written to reflect the interests of the powerful whose copious sources are always available, unlike the fragmented and ephemeral records of the powerless. For Pietersie these are grounds for opening up a new perspective on imperialism that takes into account the interrelations of empire and emancipation as they changed and developed over time.[44] However, Pietersie's definition of emancipation as a 'humanising and civilising contribution' to imperialism is rather too generalised. It is important to distinguish between black resistance *and* white anti-imperialism, both of which arguably made a 'humanising contribution'. We must also distinguish between white anti-imperialists, associated mainly with the Marxist left, and liberal and reformist critics of colonialism, as both figure often in this study. Anti-imperialists opposed imperialism *per se* in contrast to critics of colonialism who directed their energies to reforming rather than abolishing colonial rule. However, white supporters of black causes, liberal of left, were not personally 'in resistance' to racial and colonial oppression. This is reflected in the differing content and language of white and black oppositional discourses.

Black resistance, white anti-imperialism and liberal and reformist criticisms of colonialism were stimulated by economic and political developments in the inter-war period. Networks of white opponents, critics of colonialism (the international humanitarian Quaker network was particularly influential here[45]) and pan-Africanists were oiled by the improvements in international communications, including the media, which also benefited colonial administrators. Marxist anti-imperialism was promoted through the Comintern and other international communist organisations. These expanding and interrelated networks were all seminal in the development of a mounting opposition to imperial power. However, the centre of these networks was in Europe, whereas the heart of resistance to imperialism was in the colonial hinterlands. Moreover, with the exception of the white left, as I shall argue in Chapter ten, the dissident discourse of reformist and liberal anti-colonialism was implicitly rooted in the dominant discourses of power.

Resistance has always been a feature of the colonial relationship between coloniser and colonised, but the First World War also catalysed new forms and levels of resistance which resulted in a growing crisis in relations between empire and imperial hinterland. Resistance may be defined as any action, individual or collective, violent or lawful, covert and overt, that is critical of, opposes, upsets or challenges the smooth running of colonial rule.[46] This definition embraces all forms of anti-colonial and anti-imperial resistance, but also the small acts of day to day non-compliance, which frustrated colonial administrators. However, the colonial relationship should not be conceptualised simply in terms of a simple dichotomy between the oppressing colonisers and the resistant oppressed. As Couze Venn (1996) points out, 'Power ... operates on the basis of both domination and seduction, such that sections of oppressed groups often collude in ... its exercise'.[47] Thus, African resistance and protest was also directed against individuals or groups who collaborated with the colonisers. However, collaboration could be transformed into resistance and vice versa, depending on changes in vested interests or colonial policy. Moreover, responses to colonial rule, accommodationist, survivalist or resistant, involved multiple strategies, which were mediated by gender, class, age, ethnicity, urban or rural residence and the nature of contact with whites.

Resistance represented an important point of interaction between the powerful and powerless and, argues Said (1987), created deep antagonisms between the coloniser and colonised, but also created '… an overlapping, inter-dependent relationship' which connected them in often unacknowledged ways.[48] From an Hegelian perspective, the essence of white power depended on the recognition and acceptance of colonial administrators by an inferior, colonised people; resistance thus threatened the self-image and identities of white men and women. Given this peculiar interdependency, Pietersie (1991) has argued for the relevance of the concept of the dialectic, in a more flexible form, in interpreting interaction between cultures on the unstable 'frontiers' of colonial societies. There is a fundamental dialectic, he argues, between imperialism and emancipa-tion, power and liberation, which operates at both a global and local level. The 'personification' of such dialectics is the racial 'synthesis' of the 'half-caste', dreaded as a 'monster … subversive of the foundations of race and empire'.[49] This fear of race-mixing as a threat to white identity is a theme which recurs throughout this book.

Dialogue, or active communication, between the colonisers and the colonised, albeit framed within a marked power imbalance, was arguably fundamental to working out these dialectics. Whatever the linguistic, conceptual and cultural distances created by colonialism, at certain points the two worlds had to collide and communicate. As Goldberg (1994) points out, 'dialogic exchange' presup-poses neither common style, nor a common set of values. As a starting point it requires only interaction, which may range from 'the flash of a smile, a scowl or a legal brief'.[50] The texture of such interaction will be discussed in the section on West Africa, where, for example, 'native lawyers' became a major irritation for the administration and 'surly natives' disturbed imperialist visions of an Africa grateful for white 'trusteeship'. In Britain, dialogue between white and black and between black colonial subjects from different parts of the empire generated new forms of resistance and political activity. White liberal and left-wing interest in the problems of imperialism resulted in important exchanges with Africans, which progressed the development of black political conscious-ness. But interaction with white 'sympathisers' and 'comrades' enhanced what W.E.B. Dubois termed the 'double consciousness' of black intellectuals; the sense of always looking at and measuring one's self 'through the eyes of [white] others'. Thus, black activists who straddled African and European worlds possessed 'two souls, two thoughts, two unreconciled strivings, two warring ideals'.[51] Greater awareness of this 'double-consciousness' led to the rejection of white political ideologies, help and 'guidance', and strengthened the arguments for black self-help. These interlocking, but contradictory spheres of dialogue and political activity around race and imperialism form an important conceptual framework for my analysis.

Exploring the links: imperialism, race and resistance

I have defined race, imperialism, resistance and related concepts in order to establish a firmer basis on which to explore the diverse responses of the real people, black and white, who lived through troubled, but exciting times – when indeed 'All that is solid' did appear to 'melt into air'. This introduction has also opened up my main lines of argument. To summarise briefly, these are: first, that British imperialism in Africa, rather than declining as a result of the adverse impact of the First World War, was expanded and strengthened, supported by the 'New World Order'; second, racism was fundamental to sustaining imperial power; third, the growth of African resistance, international events, white, anti-imperialist interventions and the changing intellectual 'mood of the times' resulted in important shifts in the discourse of race and re-adjustments in imperial policies; fourth, these important developments can only by fully understood through analysis of the interconnections between Africa, the African diaspora and the sinews of power which linked Britain's tropical and white settler dependencies. My final point is that the Second World War crystallised and amplified these important pre-war developments. However, despite the new liberal rhetoric of colonial self-determination and racial equality, white dreams of power persisted. Africa moved from the margins to the mainstream of British imperial policy, empire became even more firmly embedded in popular consciousness and this had important implications for both the future of African societies and black 'colonial subjects' who settled in Britain.

To develop my core arguments and themes, the book is divided into four main sections. Chapter one, 'Africa after the First World War: race and imperialism redefined?', sets the wider context and addresses the postwar settlement and 'empire strengthening', the concept of Africa in popular culture and imperial discourse and new threats to white power from 'Bolshevism' and black nationalism. Section two focuses on West Africa. Chapter two, 'Britain's imperial hinterland: colonialism in West Africa', explores the contradictions between the rhetoric and reality of imperial power though the eyes of the colonial officer. Chapter three, 'Expatriate society; race, gender and the culture of imperialism', analyses the texture of white colonial culture and the importance of gendered and racialised borders, real and symbolic, in shaping the identities of coloniser and colonised and sustaining imperial power. Chapter four, ' "Whose dream was it anyway?" Anti-colonial protest in West Africa, 1929–45', looks at the impact of 'modernity' on developments in race and political consciousness, and the ways in which the imperial government 'managed' these challenges.

The focus shifts in Section three to South Africa. Chapter five, 'Forging the racist state: imperialism, race and labour in Britain's "white" dominion', evaluates the contribution that British imperial policy made to the elaboration of segregationist policies, and considers key features in the development of the South African State. Chapter six, ' "Knocking on the white man's door": repression and resistance', charts the links between the strengthening of white settler state, outlined in Chapter five, and the problematic development of African resistance. Chapter seven, ' "Fighting for the underdog": British liberals and the South African "native question" ', explores the reasons for, and nature of, British white liberal intervention and its impact on black consciousness. Moving from the imperial hinterland to the centre, Section four addresses the impact of empire in Britain. Chapter eight, 'Into the heart of empire: black Britain', spot-lights Britain's expanding and diverse black community, state responses to this 'colour problem' and black action on race and colonial problems. Chapter nine, 'Into the heart of empire: the "race problem" ', critically evaluates the nature of white liberal and left involvement with the 'race problem' and its impact on black consciousness and activism. The final chapter, 'The winds of change: towards a new imperialism in Africa?', evaluates how evolving liberal discourse on race and empire, pressures from African resistance and interna-tional developments during the 1930s and the Second World War challenged the imperial certainties and orthodoxies analysed in Chapter one, redefining Africa's relationship with Britain and the West. My study concludes with a brief retro-spective analysis of the 'post-colonial' epoch in Africa, assessing continuities and disjunctures with the era of formal imperialism. It flags the enduring centrality of Africa to the search for black identity and dreams of freedom which, in a world where imperialism and racism are still the concrete manifestations of dreams of power, have yet to be fully realised.

1 Africa after the First World War

Race and imperialism redefined?

The welfare of Africa is a concern for the entire outside world.

(George Louis Beer, 1919)

History will note that the European interest in Africa ... was immensely increased by the war and the establishment of the mandates system.

(Margery Perham, 1931)

As colored men realised the significance of [the First World War], they looked into each other's eyes and there saw a light of un-dreamed hopes. White solidarity was riven and shattered [and] fear of white power and respect for white civilisations dropped away like garments outworn.

(Lotharp Stoddard, 1924)[1]

The First World War unleashed what Porter (1996) has termed the 'predatory imperialism' of Britain, France and Japan, but also Britain's white Dominions lending support for the left's arguments that it was an 'imperialist war', which could not have been fought and won without the colonial contribution. The Versailles Peace Settlement confirmed Britain as the supreme imperial power. Empire was vital to postwar recovery and economic survival in the troubled international economic climate between the wars. As Young (1997) points out, compared with the other great powers, Britain remained strong and successful up to 1939 and was fiercely competitive in trade, investment, shipping, insurance and new developments, such as radio and air transport. After 1929 a policy of imperial economic protectionism was pursued and Britain became increasingly dependent on imperial markets.[2] But this 'empire strengthening' on a global scale is barely acknowledged in more common trope of a Britain weakened by war and economic instability. For Lloyd (1995) the inter-war years saw the 'defeat of the imperial idea', and in *Tales From the Dark Continent* (1979) an ex-member of the African Colonial Administrative Service (CAS) looks back on the Great War as bringing an end to an era of imperialism characterised by 'supreme self-confidence' – a time when the British Empire was 'cock of the world'. His memories echo contemporary 'Decline and Fall' interpretations that emphasised the 'erosion of the collective image of the master race' and the 'general force of circumstances', including the ' … will of the oppressed' in undermining empire.[3]

During the 1920s, India and the 'white' Dominions, including South Africa, appeared to generate most interest. A greater priority was placed on creating a buffer of white Dominions, reflected in the Empire Settlement Act of 1922, and from 1919 soldiers were given financial support for emigration throughout the 'white' empire to minimise unrest created by unemployed, demobbed soldiers.[4] Africa is represented as a burdensome appendage and the 'cinderella' Colonial African Service (CAS), viewed as a financial 'millstone' round the neck of the Colonial Office, was unfavourably compared to the more prestigious Indian Civil Service (ICS). Recruits to the colonial service were described as 'hollow men' of the postwar 'straw generation' – disillusioned, materialistic and selfish – the anti-heroes of contemporary writers like Graham Greene and Joyce Cary.[5] Writing in the 1930s, the Africanist, William Macmillan complained of the 'abysmal ignorance' and lack of interest in African affairs across the political spectrum. African studies were a low priority in universities, reflected in the 'disproportionate' number of women experts in the field, and an 'abstention of masculine intellect' was apparent until the postwar era when Africa became more politically important.[6] But how accurate was this gloomy vision of the imperial mission in tropical Africa? As imperial uncertainties mounted in the Indian empire, Africa arguably became more important to sustaining Britain's imperial prestige. Colonial administration was extended and streamlined, and any resistance was counteracted by a fierce determination to continue to bear the 'burden' in Africa. The outpouring of writings on colonial policy and the race problem furnish testimony to the tenacity of the imperial vision of Africa. In this 'empire strengthening', the US was, paradoxically, a major stimulus as an important imperialist competitor, but also an indispensable ally in the strengthening of 'Anglo-Saxonism', the powerful discourse of racial superiority central to the extension of Western imperial power. Britain and the US were also in harmony in confronting the 'enemy without' and 'within' posed by the left's challenge to imperialism and capitalism.

A broader 'global' perspective, from the 'heart of empire', is thus crucial to interpreting the more localised and concrete interconnections between imperial policy, racist discourse and black resistance that are charted in the following chapters. This chapter, then, will first examine 'empire strengthening' strategies and Africa's role in sustaining a strong 'imperial consciousness' in Britain. Second, it analyses contemporary Western conceptualisations of Africa and evaluates the link between power, knowledge and racial discourses which underpinned British imperialism. I focus next on the postwar settlement, which strengthened the international racial and imperial order, endorsed British 'trusteeship' (paternalistic administration by a civilised nation of less 'advanced' peoples until they were able to manage their own interests) and affirmed global 'dreams of power', which centred on Africa. The final section explores the significance of war and 'empire strengthening' in shaping the parallel sphere of black resistance and anti-imperialism – new 'dreams of freedom' inspired by Bolshevism, black consciousness and intellectual 'anti-racism' that interpenetrated the imperial labyrinths.

'Empire strengthening': race and 'imperial consciousness' in inter-war Britain

Analysing empire between the wars is highly complex. As Hobsbawm (1994) points out, never had Britain's formal and informal empire been so extensive, but never had the rulers of Britain felt less confident about maintaining imperial supremacy. The spectrum of thought on empire ranged from deep pessimism to enduring optimism. Leonard Woolf, who had firsthand experience as an officer in the Colonial Service in Ceylon from 1904–11, argued that given the force of 'anti-Westernism', imperialism was no longer possible, and now the main question was whether it would be 'buried peacefully or in blood and ruins'. Conversely, the academic, Hugh Egerton, promoted the 'authoritative defence' of what he calls the 'sane imperialism' provided by Lord Lugard's *The Dual Mandate in British Tropical Africa*, (1922), the definitive elaboration of trusteeship. He acknowledges the 'disillusion and distrust of colonial subjects in the aftermath of war', but berates the 'strong prejudice' aroused in 'some minds' (particularly American) by the very words 'empire' and 'imperialism'. Although bright university undergraduates might 'sneer' at empire, imperialism still had a role in ensuring the ongoing 'orderly progress of native communities'.[7]

Imperialism after the war was more diffuse and complex, and neutralised by slippery concepts like 'trusteeship', 'Commonwealth' and 'self-determination'. It was shaped by what Hobsbawm (1994) has termed the 'Age of Catastrophe', which was marked by instabilities in the international system, increasing globalisation, the disintegration of old patterns of social relationships and fears that Europe would be eclipsed by the 'non-Western' world. Marxist-Leninism had changed the meaning of imperialism, and Leonard Woolf argued that the only people who used the term were the critics of Western policy towards 'backwards peoples'; many people, 'particularly the most patriotic of imperialists', now denied there was such a thing as imperialism, although the economic basis of imperialism had become 'even clearer'.[8] This was manifest in interconnections between political and economic power, which was reflected, for instance, in the extensive imperial economic interests of Conservative MPs. Strong defensive tactics were thus employed against new anti-imperialist challenges. The networks of power radiating from the influential Round Table Group were particularly crucial in this 'empire strengthening', but the powerful Freemasonry, which embraced members of the royal family, was also 'hostile to all subversive and disintegrating forces within the empire' and extended its influence among colonial elites.[9]

The Round Table Group (also called the 'Cliveden Set' or 'Milner Kindergarten' after Lord Alfred Milner, Colonial Secretary during the First World War) penetrated high politics and engineered important shifts in imperial thinking. Quigley (1981) suggests that the group evolved from a provision in a secret will made out by Cecil Rhodes in which he left a fortune to promote a 'Society of the Elect', modelled on the Jesuits. The journal, *The Round Table* (1910–), promoted Rhodes' ideal of a 'white commonwealth' – a world united into a federal structure around the United Kingdom, the apogee of Anglo-Saxon culture and the most grandiose dream of imperial power yet articulated. The Round Table Group convened 'imperial conferences' to help promote this vision of a new liberal empire. However, there was an implicit racism in Rhodes' 'moral view' of empire and liberal dictum of 'equality for all civilised men'. As Pietersie (1991) points out, his 'frontier mentality' of race, which conceptualised the native as a child subject to a superior Anglo-Saxon 'first race', was seminal in the formulation of segregationist South African native policies and the reinforcement of the imperial colour bar.[10]

The work of the group was supported by the Rhodes Trust (administered by Milner), and its influence grew steadily from 1922–39, spearheaded by an 'inner circle' including Philip Kerr, Lionel Curtis, Milner and Lord Frederick Lugard. Secretaries of State for the Colonies and Dominions and arbiters of knowledge, such as Lord Hailey, whose role in African affairs will be discussed at a later point, and Reginald Coupland were also connected to the group. A web of power was thus created, linking official and academic circles interested in colonial affairs. The group had considerable influence in the League of Nations Union and in consolidating the 'Anglo-Saxonism' which linked British and US imperial missions. Pietersie (1991) emphasises the importance of Quigley's neglected work in uncovering these powerful, but secret trans-Atlantic networks whose energies were channelled into strengthening Britain's liberal and democratic empire as a weapon against Marxist-Leninism.[11]

Africa, regarded as safe and quiescent, a balm to the troubled imperialist, was central to this 'empire strengthening'. During the First World War, African colonial economies were increasingly tailored to feed into world commodity markets, and royalties from mining companies became an increasingly lucrative source of income for colonial governments. By 1936, £1,222,000,000 was invested in Africa, £523,000,000 in South Africa, as opposed to £75,000,000 in Nigeria. Seventy per cent of all investments were in British Africa.[12] Cain and Hopkins (1993) argue that Britain received the 'lion's share' from imperialism in Africa, and by 1938 the tropical African territories contributed just over 3 per cent of Britain's total exports. Although this may seem insignificant, they point out that profits from Africa met the needs of special interest groups and made a 'useful if still modest contribution to settling Britain's international accounts'. 'Thus sustained', they argue, 'Britain demonstrated her determination not merely to keep her empire but also to enlarge it' and gained ground despite fierce international rivalries. The Round Table imperial visionaries ensured that Africa stayed in the public eye, and the elaboration of the Colonial Service provided opportunities for the 'gentlemanly' order of the middle and upper classes, from colonial officers to anthropologists.[13]

In the arena of domestic politics there was broad consensus on empire in Africa. Although the Labour Party was not as bombastic on imperialism as the

Conservatives, who represented direct vested interests, Labour had its own enthusiastic 'Empire Socialists'. Leslie Haden-Guest, for instance, advocated a socialist
'civilisation mission' in Africa, immigration controls and separate development to
prevent an uneducated and 'excitable' black proletariat succumbing to 'communist propaganda'. Left-wing critics scorned this notion of 'socialising' the empire
as on a par with 'socialising slavery', arguing that Labour was 'no friend' of colonial peoples.[14] As Stedman Jones (1983) has argued, the radical culture of earlier
working-class movements was neutralised in the latter part of the nineteenth
century and an 'enclosed and defensive' working-class culture developed, which
was reflected in virulent anti-Communism and passive acceptance of imperialism and the monarchy. The deep-seated racist attitudes which permeated all
levels of British society ensured a preference for the white Dominions and an
acceptance of the 'backwardness' of Africans.[15]

Such attitudes to race and empire were reinforced in popular culture. John
Mackenzie (1986) has forcefully argued against historians who compartmentalise
British and imperial history and claim that imperialism had no impact on the
British 'masses', particularly after the First World War. Here he is supported by
Cain and Hopkins (1993), who argue that the war 'enhanced the importance
and popularity of empire', and additions made after 1919 provided a continuing
sense of imperial mission. British national identities were still profoundly shaped
by reference to the imperial hinterland and its colonial subjects, and pioneering
research by Mackenzie and others has revealed how public awareness was
heightened and greatly extended by novel techniques of publicity and propaganda, such as film and radio. Imperial sentiment and the notion of 'citizens of
empire' was spread through the scouting and guiding movement, the imperial
curriculum taught in schools and children's books and comics.[16] Traditions,
including royal ceremonials, popular culture and the consumption of imperial
products (see Illustration 2) generated an 'imperial consciousness' and confirmed
racial and cultural superiority. Can we dismiss as ephemeral the continued
celebration of Mafeking Night into the 1930s, the Imperial Exhibitions and
Empire Games (first held in 1924) at the new Wembley Stadium, the increased
public interest in Empire Day, 24 May (a half-day school holiday in Britain and
marked by ceremony throughout the empire), and popular children's games, like
'Trading With The Empire'? Such 'empire propaganda', argued left-wing critics,
helped secure the 'patriotism and loyalty' of the working classes and led to ignorance and apathy about real conditions, while reproducing dominant stereotypes
about blacks.[17]

The new cultural power of film and radio was fundamental to imperial
'propaganda' in Britain and its colonies. In the 1930s, the media was mobilised
officially and through private enterprise (the Cable and Wireless Company was
formed in 1928). By 1939 there were nine million 'wireless' sets in Britain and,
argues Hobsbawm (1994), the importance of the radio as a medium of mass
information and propaganda was profound. From its inauguration in 1926, the
British Broadcasting Corporation gave unswerving support to 'monarch and
empire', and an empire service was started in 1932, the same year as the

Christmas Day royal broadcasts were started. Its chairman, Lord Reith, was a staunch imperialist and patriot, and Empire Day specials were *de rigueur*. The Empire Day Movement also sponsored broadcasts to 'children of the empire'.[18] The main centre for imperial film production was the Empire Marketing Board (which also organised shopping weeks around Empire Day) until it was axed in 1933 due to government cuts. In 1935 the Imperial Institute took over the Empire Film Library and in 1936 its audiences – mostly school children – reputedly totalled over 4,000,000.[19] Documentaries were shown to millions of people throughout the empire, although Hailey (1957) suggests that reactions of African audiences new to the medium were 'not always that desired' and film strips were cheaper and better understood. However, the establishment of the Colonial Film Unit in 1939, attached to the Ministry of Education in London, created local production units and prioritised films as a means of 'fundamental education'.[20]

In the 'Age of the Dream Palace' popular films were particularly influential and Hollywood was seminal in projecting imperial and racial superiority. American films about Africa and empire, argues Richards (1984), were also popular in the US as they reaffirmed the white supremacist basis of American culture. For film makers, the empire was 'good business' and a *Daily Express* journalist declared that films like *Sanders of the River* were 'far more successful at the box office than any equal amount of sophisticated sex nonsense'.[21] Stam and Shohat (1994) argue that 'Eurocolonial cinema', as the 'Eye of Empire', could transform white spectators into 'armchair conquistadors', affirming a sense of vicarious power, but also inducing a deep ambivalence among colonised spectators viewing offensive representations of themselves. As Mackenzie (1988) points out, cinema involved a 'world-view' explicitly and implicitly rooted in imperial perceptions. Anything reflecting adversely on the British army, the white race or the prestige of British rule that could 'inflame' the native population was cut or banned. Films dealing with sex between white women and black or Asian men were regarded as particularly dangerous, and race pundits warned that passionate love scenes in cinemas degraded white women in African eyes.[22]

Such attitudes reflected a morbid obsession with the evils of interracial mixing which created the ugly trope of the dangerous 'half-caste' who threatened the important racial boundaries of empire. A preoccupation with interracial sex, which drew heavily on eugenicist and biological racist discourse, became a powerful ingredient of popular racism which extended even to critics of colonialism.[23] This 'sexual dimension of racism' acted as an important trigger in the development of race consciousness in the US, Britain and the colonies, for it was white women, as the mothers of the race, and black men whose sexuality was policed, while the exploitation of black women by white men was condoned. In condemning the conduct of white men towards coloured women, black activists argued that the white 'bourgeois obsession' with interracial sex and miscegenation insidiously supported biological theories of racial superiority and was integral to consolidating economic and political dominance.[24] Control of sexuality thus became an important adjunct to 'empire strengthening'. As Foucault (1976) has argued, racism took shape through this 'biologising' of the

Illustration 1–Cover illustration of *Empire Youth Annual*
Source: London, P.R. Gawthorne Ltd., 1947.

Illustration 2–Rule Britannia
Source: Carson's Empire Chocolates advertisement from the Robert Opie Collection

state and a 'mystical concern' with protecting the purity of blood and superiority of the European race. This power found its ultimate expression in Nazism, but sexual power and racism were also interwoven into the mechanisms of British imperialism.[25] Although we must beware of over-prioritising control of the colonised 'body' through sexuality, as we shall see in chapters 3, 5 and 8, it was a dynamic point of contact between coloniser and colonised, and essential to confirming a white sexuality, rooted in repression and the control of animal instincts, and thus considered superior, civilised behaviour.

Although antipathy to sexual relationships between white women and black men remained strong, cruder racial discourse was muted by the new cultural explanations of race that emerged as a challenge to scientific racism. In Britain, this transformation is reflected in the writings of the scientist, Julian Huxley, a 'racist liberal' who, argues Barkan (1992), had supported Southern US racism and sympathised with racist scientific theories in the 1920s, but radically changed his views after confronting his own 'race complex' during a visit to Africa in 1931. In his important, co-authored text, *We Europeans* (1935), described by Barkan as a 'popular and influential anti-racist statement', Huxley replaced 'race' with 'ethnic group', but continued to oppose miscegenation and non-white immigration into white areas and to emphasise the natural genetic differences between classes which fitted them for different tasks.[26] Eugenics, the 'art and science of breeding better men' and a strong element of inter-war racism, remained popular, even with the left, and in the 1930s membership of the Eugenics Society and the Fabians (the 'think-tank' of the British Labour Movement) overlapped. Where Africans were concerned, all the basic assumptions of racial thinking were arguably left intact, despite the challenges to scientific racism. Malik (1996) suggests that Huxley was more preoccupied with fighting Nazi pseudo-scientific theory than challenging attitudes to negroes. This raises the question as to whether the problems of racism have been so forcefully tackled by intellectuals both sides of the Atlantic without the rise of National Socialism and allied anti-semitism.

However, the new emphasis on cultural, as opposed to 'race', explanations did change the etiquette of race relations and the language of racist discourse. The cruder racist language of the pre-war era now became unfashionable in educated, liberal middle-class circles who attributed race prejudice to the ignorant, lower-class whites in economic competition with blacks. However, this conveniently ignored the depth of institutionalised racism which still underpinned the empire. As Sir Alan Burns, a 'progressive' governor of the Gold Coast in the 1940s, admitted, the middle classes had 'allowed' working-class racism to exist and, in more 'educated' circles, racism was merely better and more hypocritically concealed. The Victorian hierarchy of races was still strongly ingrained in British and, indeed, Western consciousness. Leonard Woolf argued that the cultural gap between Africa and Europe was 'immense', but, in contrast to Africa, India also had an old and 'substantial' civilisation that gave Indians 'special status'.[27] Thus, Africans were accorded the lowest status in the colonial hierarchy, and Western imperial power in Africa was premised on powerful racial discourses which influenced both popular images of Africa and imperialist policies.

Britain's 'Wild West'[28]: racial discourse and the 'idea' of Africa

'Africans', remarked Margery Perham, 'have always suffered from being regarded as a huge, incomprehensible, vaguely menacing black mass' which 'denies individuality'. Yet, as a 'progressive', colonial expert, she continued to reiterate the trope of the 'raw pagan' or 'raw untutored native' in uneasy contact with 'civilisation'. Such images of savagery, including cannibalism, still peppered colonial discourse and, as Megan Vaughan (1994) and Jock Mculloch (1995) have pointed out, the new medical discourse and 'ethnopsychiatry', which developed with the elaboration of colonial administration, further pathologised Africans as mentally inferior, childlike, violent and unstable. Africa remained 'primitive' and 'backward', outside modern time – a conception also endorsed by critics of colonialism. While attacking the evils of economic imperialism in Africa, Woolf warned that the African was a 'completely helpless ... child', unable to resist Europeans, 'scrupulous or unscrupulous', and for this reason he favoured continued white 'trusteeship'.[29] This infantilisation disempowered the African colonial subject and even among liberal and reformist critics the debate was not about whether Britain should leave Africa, but what type of rule should exist during the civilising process from 'childhood' through 'troublesome adolescence' to 'adulthood'.

The Western vision of Africa has always been largely the product of its own imagination rather than a reflection of what actually happens in the continent. 'White mythologies' about Africa centred on the continent's ahistoric timelessness; its 'unity of culture' at 'virtually a single level of primitive savagery'.[30] Isolated in space and time, Africa was a world where 'tomorrow is yesterday and today is a thousand years ago', a 'dream-world come true'. Its music is repetitive and monotonous, 'eternal timeless music'.[31] MacCrone (1937) tied in such 'myths' to the formation of white racial identities through attributing negative traits to the 'other'. In the unconscious white mind, he argued, black still symbolised 'death, evil and misfortune' and the association between dirt, dark skin and the primitive was a strong element in physical aversion to blacks. Although MacCrone could himself be classed as a racist (Chapter 5), he foreshadowed post-colonial theory in arguing that in analysing such 'myths' it was not 'what things are but what they are believed to be that matters', even though all that is believed in is not, in the narrow sense, 'historical'.[32]

The 'idea of Africa' is thus a product of the West, conceived through conflicting systems of knowledge, myths, colonial mappings and one-dimensional African identities. It has a long history spanning back to the fabulous geographic mappings of the African interior and exotic imaginings that have captured the minds of Europeans from first contact with the continent. When Africa was 'opened up' it thus became a 'Wild West' of adventure, escape and exotic imaginings. The young Margery Perham found her interest in Africa aroused when she visited her married sister on the Somalia–Ethiopia border in 1921, fulfilling her 'romantic' childhood dreams, which were inspired by Rider Haggard. She experienced the continent 'at its wildest and most dangerous', the Africa which 'determined the character of much of Britain's early administration'. Europeans wanted to keep this Africa of their imagination – the 'pure flame of simple joy of the primitive' – free from the 'monstrous ... octopus of modernity'.[33]

Two powerful and enduring myths have shaped white visions of Africa: first, 'primitive' Africa had stagnated due to isolation from the outside world; second, Europe had redeemed this 'heart of darkness' through humanitarian intervention to abolish slavery. For the influential early nineteenth century German liberal philosopher, Hegel (who based his evidence on 'copious', second-hand missionary accounts), Africa was the 'unhistorical' only on the 'threshold' of the world's history:

> Africa Proper as far as history goes back ... has remained – for all purposes
> of connection with the rest of the world – shut up: it is the Gold-land

compressed within itself – the land of childhood ... beyond self-conscious
history ... enveloped in the dark mantle of night.

The 'sensual' negro represented man in his 'completely wild and untamed
state' and was therefore incapable of development or progress. On the eve of
independence this view still prevailed. 'In the race for progress', asks Elspeth
Huxley, chronicler of white colonisation of Kenya, 'why alone among the races
of mankind did [the Bantu] stand still ... building ... no permanent houses,
finding no means to improve their soil, evolving no industries, above all inventing
no written word and creating no form of art?' She conceded that independence
was inevitable, but that it was scarcely possible to believe that such Africans were
the 'inheritors' of Africa's future, a future that was an 'enigma'.[34] The Hegelian
'myth' of Africa, argues Said (1993), has proved powerful and enduring and was
absorbed into Western liberalism and marxism. However, Meisenhelder (1995)
argues that Marx and Engels, although they wrote comparatively little about
Africa, rejected the racist stereotypes of their age and disagreed with Hegel over
the static nature of African societies.[35]

On the surface, the second myth appears more benign, but it has arguably
proved equally damaging. It is rooted in Britain's abolition of slavery throughout
her empire in 1838. This confirmed Britain as the 'champion of the oppressed',
the most civilised, liberal humanitarian nation. The new paternalist concern,
which developed with abolitionism, viewed 'primitive' peoples as objects of pity
rather than contempt and the British State acknowledged its new role as
protector of the 'weaker races' or 'Aborigines' with a destiny to spread 'civilisation'. The abolitionist vision was recognised by enlightened imperialists, such as
Perham, as the first articulation of the concept of trusteeship and it had a
seminal influence on the rationale for British administration and international
interventions in Africa.[36] Both Britain and France used the suppression of
slavery as moral justification for intervention in Africa during the nineteenth
century, but Britain, as the first liberator of slaves, had the edge. During and
after the First World War, Britain's humanitarian image was greatly enhanced by
contrast with the cruelties of German colonialism. The ethical rationale for
British rule in Africa was consistently reiterated in literature from the inter-war
period, penetrating deeply into the national psyche through the popular media.
Sidney Olivier, described by Woolf as an 'extremist' in his criticisms of colonialism, argued that the 'liberal-thinking' British public was consistently duped
by this image of benevolent imperialism; philanthropic justifications were always
secondary to economic motives and to coerce Africans into subservience 'on the
pretext of doing them good' was 'obnoxious'.[37]

But the comforting myth of British benevolence held firm. Sir Andrew
Cohen, head of the Africa Division at the CO in the 1940s, reminded Americans that the anti-slavery movement enshrined a 'tradition' in British imperial
policy and 'public opinion' of 'deep and practical concern for the welfare of the
have-nots overseas'. Writing retrospectively, Perham warned that in the light of
the 'new African history and archaeology' that was reclaiming the old and varied

civilisations of Africa, it was easy to forget the 'harsh pagan Africa of slave raids, inter-tribal wars, witchcraft and twin-killing, poverty and disease.' The paternalist reinterpretation of Africa's past thus endorsed the Hegelian vision, erasing, for instance, records from the era of the slave trade when Africans were reported as 'shrewd businessmen' with whom British slave-traders had to deal with on terms of relative equality. Moreover, abolitionism redeemed Britain for the sins of the evil slave-trade. Elspeth Huxley argued that if the British had committed crimes against Africans, they had been more than cancelled out by Britain's abolition of the slavery, warfare and chaos which had 'kept Africa in a state of flux since the beginning of time'.[38] Africa's past was thus erased and its 'history' rewritten to begin only with the 'redemption' of colonial rule. Slavery continued to provide the rationale for intervention even in the so-called independent black states of Liberia, Haiti and Abyssinia, which was described by Arnold Toynbee as a 'byword for disorder and barbarity', with a culture that had stagnated 'at a level ... not much higher' than that of adjacent colonised areas. Liberia was also viewed as 'corrupt and inefficient' and the existence of domestic slavery in these two countries confirmed that blacks were not fit to rule themselves.[39]

A cluster of conflicting representations, derived from the period of slavery, had thus seeped deeply into British culture. The mass of British people may have been ignorant and vague about the finer points of imperial policy, but as Castle (1996) stresses, the 'fabulous' Africa was perennially popular in the entertainment media, while the written mass media and school curriculums reproduced crude African stereotypes, which emphasised the glories of empire and promoted cultural and national arrogance. As the restless and wealthy postwar generation, epitomised by Evelyn Waugh and 'emancipated' women like Lady Dorothy Mills, was seduced by the lure of the primitive and exotic, there was also an expansion of the popular travelogue.[40] The advertising and packaging of popular products used imperial and racist 'logos', and Africa continued to provide a 'colonial spectacle' to titillate the popular gaze in museum displays and 'exhibitionary narratives', such as the British Empire Exhibition held in London, 1926. 'Photographing the natives' remained popular, reinforcing images of the 'primitive' continent in popular consciousness (see Illustration 3).[41] Africa had a 'hypnotic' grip on the British as a wild and exotic adventure playground. Margery Perham noted how this interest in the 'romantic side' of Africa was 'ably' catered for by the British and American film industries.[42] Films like *Sanders of the River*, 1935 (based on the book by Edgar Wallace), *King Solomon's Mines* (1937), both starring the black American singer, Paul Robeson, and *Rhodes of Africa* (1936) proved highly popular. As Jim Pines (1997) argues, black representation in British cinema was inextricably bound up in colonial and race relations discourse and both black and white were portrayed in terms of colonial notions of cultural identity with no active voice for the colonised. In films like *Sanders*, Africans were nothing but a 'picturesque backdrop on a colonial stage'.[43] Such white fantasies of Africa persisted in mass entertainment films from the 1940s, like Abbot and Costello's *Africa Screams* (1946), re-released on video as a 'Cinema

Illustration 3–On the banks of the Volta, Burifo, N.T.
Source: Princess Marie Louise, *Travels in the Gold Coast*, Methuen & Co. Ltd. 1926

Classic'. In the film, Africa is represented as a big game adventure park, a source of easy riches (diamonds) and inhabited by dangerous cannibals, complete with the requisite cooking pot.

Africa also remained the adventure setting for children's comics and African characters were highly popular. Castle (1996) traces the expansion of commercial children's fiction, particularly for girls, depicting white female heroines who encountered 'natives' in adventures. As in the pre-1914 era, popular comics were replete with 'images of the happy, singing darky, the clown, the grave or sentimental brute' which, Castle argues, suggest relics of the slave-master relationship transposed into aspects of popular culture. But schoolboy heroes were also depicted as 'tolerant and protective of simple ... naive [and loyal] African chums'. Through comics and school texts, children were immersed in the national myths of the British redemption of Africa from slavery, or in images of Africans as noble savages, uncorrupted by white men's ways. Racism, Castle concludes, thus permeated this reading for the young, even if messages about empire were more subtle than in the pre-war period.[44] Such perceptions secured popular consent for colonial rule in Africa, but also underpinned official policies.

Power, knowledge and racial discourse: native administration and anthropology

Racism also underpinned the principles of native administration, which was premised on indirect rule, or administration by a small top tier of whites through 'native' authorities – the 'dual mandate'. This system of paternalist colonial administration, increasingly conflated with trusteeship after 1919, was based on the experience of Lord Frederick Lugard as governor of Nigeria, 1912–18, and became accepted as the best system for 'tropical', non-settler Africa. Lugard visualised an Africa where oppression and 'horrible cruelties' were replaced by 'order and justice', creating an efficient, bureaucratised society which was run with military precision and was based on 'sound accounting' as the foundation stone of economic, social and political development. Lugard's dreams of power reflected a cultural arrogance par excellence, which assumed British 'Victorian values' were best for Africans. Taxation, he declared, 'emancipates natives from indolence', promotes 'individual and collective responsibility', enhances 'self-respect', stimulates 'industry' and provides native rulers with 'fresh scope for their energies' and 'pride and progress' in their countries. This enabled the colonial government to further 'decentralise' power and 'push each community a step further up the ladder of progress'. Taxation buffered Africans from 'murdering traders and general lawlessness', brought tribes into contact with 'civilising influences', but was also 'of great importance' in securing recognition of British suzerainty and promoting 'confidence in Government'.[45]

The role of taxation in coercing African labour into the cash economy has long been acknowledged and Lugard clearly stipulates that taxes were to be paid only in cash. But its centrality to the wider culture of colonialism has received less attention. For Lugard, taxation also equalled civilisation and was a 'moral charter' for the independence of Africans in that it stimulated individual enterprise, emancipated the peasantry from oppression through slavery and forced labour, and moralised former slave traders. Taxation was a 'common burden [and a universal necessity] of civilisation' which African communities who aspired to be regarded as 'civilised' had to share.[46] His detailed memoranda on administration, observes Kirk-Greene (1970), tell us a lot about Lugard's own attitudes and beliefs. Lugard's writings reveal the tensions between the altruistic 'higher ideals' of administration and the pragmatics of colonial economics, between assimilation through progress and protection of native cultures. As Roberts (1991) has stressed, Lugard, like the other great empire builder, Rhodes, simultaneously extolled the liberal, imperial rhetoric of equality through civilisation while subscribing to ideals of race purity and white race pride. Implicit in 'trusteeship' was the 'divine right' of superior 'Anglo-Saxons' to rule the less civilised peoples through 'separate' development. But such attitudes endorsed white settler rule and confirmed the imperial 'colour bar' dividing dependent, non-white tropical colonies from self-governing 'white Dominions'. Behind the altruism and moral rhetoric was economic pragmatism and, thus, Lugard's memos on administration are riddled with logical inconsistencies and contradictions. His objective was to bring the 'benefits of civilisation' with as little interference as possible in African laws and customs, but he also stressed that it was the duty of colonial officers to 'encourage trade by every means in their power'.[47] However, British models of taxation (whereby the colonised paid for the benefits of white rule) also introduced the disruptive forces of modernity which threatened Lugard's bourgeois dream of order.

Concern over the impact of Western progress stimulated debates between 'assimilationists' and 'segregationists'. Segregationists defended separate development as the best means of preserving traditional African culture intact. Alien development on European lines, argued Elspeth Huxley, was harmful and the aim of British rule should be to 'create a good African and not a bad European'. Some humanitarians may have genuinely wanted to protect Africans from the more exploitative aspects of colonialism, but, in practice, as critics like Macmillan observed, this purist conception of indirect rule ignored African grievances and was 'inflexible ... doctrinaire ... and evasive of awkward realities' such as race consciousness'.[48] Faced with the problems of the 'detribalised' or educated natives, colonial officials retreated into exoticism, evoking nostalgia for the 'Spirit of the Old, Wild Africa – fascinating and terrible', which was lost when Africans tried to copy the 'baser' features of European culture. Sir Ralph Furse, who was in charge of recruitment at the CO, declared a preference for the 'man in the blanket' – the 'gloriously arrogant Masai' and dismissed African nationalism as 'emotional', thus treating the educated intelligentsia with contempt.[49]

Attitudes to the educated African differentiated French and British 'cultures of colonialism'. Whereas the British glorified the primitive, the French, argued the

American researcher, Raymond Buell, favoured the *assimile*, or educated African, who allegedly had less 'colour feeling' than the English and showed more 'tact and understanding' in handling black problems in Africa and France. Defending the superiority of their own policies, British imperialists argued that, despite greater use of ethnographic and anthropological studies in colonial governance, French administrators were 'harsh and cruel' to the mass of Africans. 'The Frenchman', wrote Margery Perham, 'does not preserve native culture because he does not share our respect for it ... to him it is barbarism in spite of an aesthetic appreciation of its externals.' From an African perspective, however, there was little to choose between the French policy of assimilation and British indirect rule.[50]

In practice, indirect rule proved unworkable and inspired strong resistance (Chapters 2 and 4). For black critics a cynical pragmatism lurked behind the altruistic facade of indirect rule, which was, in effect, simply the 'cheapest and easiest' method of rule.[51] The ideals of trusteeship conflicted with the development of the colonial economy and, as Porter (1996) notes, the British did little to justify their claim of disinterested paternalist trusteeship. Moreover, in implementing indirect rule whites deluded themselves into believing that they were preserving timeless African cultures when, as Ranger (1981) points out, they reinvented African 'traditions' through colonial codification to fit in with their own plans. Yet African societies could not be preserved in aspic and this generated new problems related to the penetration of modernity and how to control it. Faced with these problems, 'progressive' imperialists and colonial critics alike pushed for a streamlining of policies which allowed for 'social and material progress'. In *Ten Africans* (1936), Perham pleaded for the recognition of individual educated natives, although the mass of Africans remain primitive ciphers in her writings.[52] Conversely, 'conservatives' targeted the 'industrialised' and/or educated natives as the root cause of any unrest. Elspeth Huxley saw 'detribalised natives' as 'insolent and contemptuous', the native counterpart of the 'hooligan'. Missionaries and educationalists advocated a 'simple' education to counteract the 'cheeky' native, slow down the rate of change and bring about 'the moral regeneration' of African society.[53] Inspired by anxiety to avoid the 'dangerous results' of educational policy in India, educators like Sir Hans Vischer, an ex-colonial officer, and the missionary, Dr J.H. Oldham, helped set up the British Advisory Committee on Native Education in Tropical Africa in 1925, which opposed 'literary' education and pressed for a uniform, 'vocational' educational policy. Oldham and Visher had visited the Booker T. Washington Tuskagee Institute and were impressed by its work in vocational training for black Americans. Their policies were popular in official circles, but strongly opposed by the African intelligentsia who argued that they were geared to producing a 'malleable and docile African worker' and were rooted in deeply racist assumptions of African capacities.[54]

Dilemmas of indirect rule prompted academic studies of native administration funded through the Rhodes Trust. In 1937, the School of Oriental Studies established a separate African Department (instruction in African languages was introduced in 1917) and in 1938 it became the School of Oriental and African Studies to reflect the growing importance of African Studies. Applied 'scientific colonialism' also came into vogue, supported by the functionalist anthropology pioneered by Bronislaw Malinowski (who never personally carried out research in Africa) and his student, Lucy Mair, a lecturer in colonial administration at the London School of Economics. Anthropologists were the new actors on the African colonial stage and were primarily concerned with the disruptive effects of social change. Mair argued that anthropologists like herself glorified African tradition, resurrecting Rousseau's noble savage to counter the worst aspects of colonial rule. 'Progressive' imperialists, like Margery Perham, who was part of Malinowski's 'good set of young people', enthusiastically embraced the new anthropology arguing that 'only saints and scientists can know the very primitive'; her commitment to racial equality only extended to a favoured minority.[55]

Kuklich (1991) argues that British anthropology was simply a 'child of colonialism' and constructed a distinct identity dependent on its relationship with imperialism. It encouraged colonial officers to make more systematic studies of the language and culture of the peoples they administered, which were subsequently embodied into administrative strategy.[56] The establishment of an International Institute of African Languages and Culture in 1926, which represented a powerful alliance between anthropologists, missionaries and colonial officials concerned with the problems of 'culture contact' and which reflected Malinowski's influence in 'progressive' imperial circles, lends support for her views. Between 1931 and 1933 a group of anthropologists under Malinowski's direction set sail for West Africa under the Institute's anthropological fellowship scheme. Funding came through the Laura Spellman Memorial of the Rockefeller Foundation, founded in the memory of Rockefeller's wife in 1918 to address 'the more dangerous social concerns', pointing to a hidden agenda of US philanthropic foundations.[57] However, Goody, a 'second generation' African anthropologist, defends his mentors as detached empiricists who judged all cultures equally according to their relative value systems and who were often at odds with the more reactionary missionaries and administrators (1996). He argues that there was a high proportion of 'outsiders' involved in research in Africa who had 'disinterested' US funding and some, who were 'Left and Red', sought to modify or even abolish colonial rule and were not welcome in the colonies. Thus, Meyer Fortes, described by Goody as a 'South African Jew ... with strong left leanings', was only reluctantly allowed into the Gold Coast. In addition, he claims that anthropology was also one area where women were breaking through into academia, although they were heavily patronised and sometimes viciously attacked by their male mentors and colleagues. For such 'new' anthropologists, suggests Goody, colonial peoples were never simply research subjects and some, like Kenyatta, became Malinowski's students at the London School of Economics in their intellectual struggle against colonialism.[58]

Anthropologists did not sing with one voice. There were huge differences between the official anthropologists and the new generation of 'outsiders' who left Germany and South Africa after 1930, and were influenced by Marx, Freud and the intellectual challenges to scientific racism. Although some 'independent anthropologists' may have pioneered valuable studies, their overall contribution was limited and fragmented. With the exception of some South African anthropologists, the problems of the educated native, urban development and 'race-relations' between black and white were evaded. As Barkan (1992) points out, unlike their US counterparts – Franz Boas, Melville Herskovits, for instance – British anthropologists were not directly concerned with refuting scientific racism and physical anthropology. Even the justification of their research – to 'provide a full ethnographic record' of peoples 'without history' (still seemingly accepted as a valid defence by Goody) – suggests ethnocentrism and acceptance of dominant myths about Africa.[59] Thus British anthropologists were criticised by colonial critics, like William Macmillan, for romanticising the timeless 'primitive' and adopting an ahistorical approach that 'diverted' attention from 'the great problems of modern Africa'. They were also opposed by educated Africans who argued that it was not possible to preserve African societies against modernisation. In a wry comment on the patronising assumptions made by anthropologists, a Gold Coast student suggested young Africans should be trained in anthropology to study white society, an interesting proposition that was not well received, for middle-class British culture was the norm by which other societies were judged and not a 'problem'.[60]

Eslanda Goode Robeson, who studied with Malinowski at London School of Economics in the 1930s, argued that anthropologists were obsessed with the primitive. As a black American married to the famous Paul Robeson, she was seen as 'European' by her tutors. 'European', she notes, was loosely used among anthropologists and meant 'white' not only in colour, but also in civilisation. When she protested that she was a negro and identified with Africans, the response was that she could not possibly know the 'mind of the primitive' until she studied it. As a result she went off in 1936 to do her own field research in Uganda, producing a fascinating and rare travelogue by a black woman which reads very differently to that of her white contemporaries. Africans, she argues, did not trust white anthropologists and told them 'fantasic' answers to questions, via interpreters, 'in apparent seriousness'. Why, she asks, should they reveal their 'sacred histories' and the intimate details of their lives to whites who failed to show them the respect of learning their language and who were part of a more generalised oppressive white presence. This, she concluded, cast serious doubt on the validity of 'scientific data'.[61]

Anthropologists were largely a new extension to the 'gentlemanly order' and Africa was the key to their academic careers. They had the same approach to 'Darkest Africa' as 'Darkest England' (Fortes, for instance, had carried out work in London's East End before going to Africa). Both were alien territories with a perceived different and inferior culture. Academic anthropology thus did little to challenge existing conceptions of Africa. It validated the cult for the primitive in *avant-garde* European art, initiated by Picasso's 'borrowings', and seeped into C.J. Jung's psychoanalysis, inspiring his visits to Africa to seek the 'collective unconscious'.[62] More significantly, it informed popular amateur anthropological writings and ethnographic film, an important new medium, which snapped societies supposedly 'as they were' and which was extensively used in *Sanders of the River*. These representations of the primitive reached far wider audiences than studies from the small, enclosed, feud-ridden world of the academics. Finally, inter-war anthropoloists colluded with the colonial authorities in the 'creation of tribalism' and ethnic consciousness which, as Vail (1989) points out, is not rooted in the pre-colonial past, but is a twentieth century ideological construct. In the contemporary Western media, 'tribalism' is still represented as irrationality, an atavistic leftover emphasising African backwardness and explaining war and civil conflict. Anthropologists and postwar political scientists captured ethnicity at a 'moment in time' with no concern for historical roots or the dynamics of African cultures, and as Barrett-Brown (1997) has pointed out, this has led to consistent Western misunderstanding of indigenous culture and its potential strength in African development.[63] Thus, overall, anthropology supported rather than undermined the structures of knowledge and racial discourses which underpinned British imperial power and the Western conception of Africa. My discussion now broadens out to the articulation of this Western conception of Africa at the Versailles Peace Conference, which confirmed Africa's position in the postwar international racial and imperial orders and sustained Britain's position as the leading imperial power in Africa.

Dreams of power: Africa, race and the international postwar settlement

At the 1919 Versailles Peace Conference the British liberal 'higher ideals' rationale of imperialism was given international legality in the principle of trusteeship for less developed peoples. Under Article 22 of the League of Nations covenant member states, principally Britain, France or Britain's 'white' Dominions, were commissioned to administer mandated territories and a Permanent Mandates Commission was set up to ensure administrators conformed to the 'sacred trust' enshrined in the legal conception of the term mandate. The diplomatic negotiations were replete with high sounding cant about self-determination inspired by President Woodrow Wilson's 'anti-imperialism', which, as Louis (1977) points out, concealed a hidden agenda that promoted US economic interests. As an American diplomat observed, Wilson was 'jealous of his country's honour' at the postwar carve up of Africa and the 'colonial problem' was regarded as one of the most important questions to be dealt with at the conference.[64]

Seminal in the formulation of US and international policy on Africa was George Louis Beer's *African Questions at the Paris Peace Conference* (1923). Beer accompanied Wilson to Paris as chief of the Colonial Division of the US delegation. A businessman, as well as an academic, he had spent a good deal of time in London after 1903 and was a member of the powerful Round Table Group. Beer died in March 1920, but his 'plan for Africa', completed in 1918, coincided closely with the final recommendations of the Mandates Commission.[65] Beer stressed the need for intervention on humanitarian grounds but closer reading of his text reveals a pragmatic agenda of extending 'open door' trade policy with an eye on expanding African markets. Like all liberals of the day, British or American, he was advocating two essentially incompatible policies – 'progress' through Western capitalist expansion and 'rejection of all measures not in harmony with the welfare of the native'. Beer was thus far from being 'anti-imperialist'; on the contrary, he was endorsing the 'finer and sounder type' of imperialism that was advocated by progressive imperialists in Britain. He took as given (and good) that the 'gradual extension of European civilisation over all the continents of the globe' was a fundamental fact of the 'modern age'.[66] Deep contradictions in liberal thought concerning race and progress are embedded in the text. Beer embraced the dominant myths of African backwardness which defined Africa as a 'special case' for European 'tutelage', arguing that the negro was 'apparently incapable of advance by his own unaided efforts'. Any civilising influences had come from 'extraneous sources' and even in America the African had 'imitatively, and very imperfectly, acquired alien civilisation'. This dubiously endorsed American racial science theories that 'negro' brain structures resulted in arrested development in childhood preventing 'organic intellectual progress'. These racial theories influenced his mapping of Africa into three divisions, the 'Mediterranean Littoral', 'White Man's Africa', where a 'distinctly Western-type of civilisation' was developing, and 'Middle Africa', inhabited by 'aboriginal peoples in various degrees of development from the most primitive savagery and cannibalism upwards'. He acknowledged that in West Africa there were 'highly educated [civilised] natives', but these were only 'scattered exceptions' in an ocean of African backwardness.[67]

Given the durability of such negative conceptions of Africa, elements of the Peace Settlement suggest continuity with the pre-war period rather than the shaping of a 'new order'. Africa's position in the modern world was defined by the European imperial powers in the General Act of Berlin (1882) and the Declaration of Brussels (1895), which prioritised 'the moral and material welfare of the native populations', but also endorsed the 'equality of all nations' in a 'free trade' grab for Africa. The Anti-Slavery Conference in Brussels, 1889, confirmed the common Western commitment to stamping out slavery and controlling arms traffic and liquor imports to secure the 'benefits of peace and civilisation' for Africa. Lauren (1996) argues that international humanitarian conventions formalised the 'ironic marriage between anti-slavery and imperialism' and established the twentieth century moral standards for international responsibility for African welfare. In 1919 these 'general principles of civilisation' were incorporated into the General Act and Declaration of Brussels, which stipulated that no arms were to be exported to any part of Africa, bar the white settler areas, and the Saint Germain Convention, which banned imports of cheap spirits and outlawed the commercial distillation of spirits in the African colonies.[68] Olukoju (1996) and Akyeampong (1996) have both analysed how the racist paternalism of these liquor restrictions resulted in conflict between Africans and colonial governments, who were themselves torn between commitment to the international conventions and the need to raise revenue from duties levied on imported liquor.[69] There were also international agreements on the conservation of wild animals and the control of sleeping sickness (1900), which although undoubtedly well-intentioned, symbolised the European 'taming' of 'wild' Africa. Moreover, as Ryan (1997) points out 'conservation discourse' excluded Africans from their own lands through the creation of 'reserves' and helped to maintain boundaries between black and white, civilised and uncivilised, human and animal.[70]

This international paternalism justified the mandate system, first proposed by Beer in early 1918, and finally drafted by Lord Milner (Britain), Jan Smuts (South Africa), J.G. Latham (Australia) and Philip Kerr of the Round Table Group. Imperial interests were thrashed out by the British Empire Delegation, dominated by the white Dominions with no representation from the 'tropical colonies', bar token representation from high-ranking Indians who made little input into policy making. The British delegation were clearly in favour of 'empire strengthening' and this resulted in conflicts of interests over wider imperial issues between Lloyd George and Wilson, who did not want the world 'parcelled out by the Great Powers'. Wilson pushed for greater international control of the colonies, a proposal which found favour with the British reformist socialists, such as Woolf. In effect, though, there was little dissent over Africa, where, as Sidney Olivier noted, both Britain and the US had the edge over all other nations in evoking humanitarianism to justify imperialist intervention.[71] The structure of the mandate system has been amply dealt with in other studies. But to briefly reiterate, class A mandates were colonies that had reached a stage of development where their independence could be 'provisionally recognised' subject to 'assistance by the mandatory power'. This applied mainly to the 'liberated' parts of the Turkish Empire. Most of the ex-German colonies were class B Mandates, where mandatory trusteeship was essential. The final category of C Mandates, German Samoa and other small Pacific possessions, were deemed best administered as 'integral portions of the mandatory state'. The mandate system thus mirrored the hierarchy of 'civilisation'. Mandated territories were to be under the supervision of the League, but actual authority was to be exercised by one member, and the standard of government was set at 'roughly that which prevails in the British Empire'.[72]

There is something almost surreal about the way in which a small group of powerful men sat and pontificated about the future of a 'non-Western world' which had virtually no representation. Even Lord Hailey, who became a member of the Permanent Mandates Commission during the 1930s, conceded that there was little evidence of explicit support for colonial welfare; international law was limited to clarifying relations between 'civilised' states and securing 'equitable' trading and commercial opportunities for league members. As Alan Sharp (1998) has observed, the mandatory system served as little more than a convenient 'fig leaf' to enable visitors to acquire the spoils of war. Despite the high moral rhetoric, strong vested interests were at stake. Although there was some conflict of interest between the British and the US, there was a unified front over the threat of Bolshevism and the 'rising tide of colour' to Western interests. Although polite euphemisms had supplanted the blatant racism of the late nineteenth century, all delegates unquestioningly accepted the racial basis of mandate categories. Lauren (1996) points out that any attempts to discuss the race question at the Peace Conference were side-stepped by the US, Britain and the Dominions. Wilson, a Southerner in favour of segregation, had a 'lukewarm aloofness' to 'highly combustible' race questions. Japan became the 'standard bearer' for the coloured cause, but failed to gain support for a 'race equality' motion. Apart from the stimulus this rejection gave to Japan's own imperialist drive, argues Lauren, it also stimulated black race consciousness which was already sharpened by snubs to black delegations. Sensitivity to the 'coloured question' (generated by race consciousness) was mere 'moral wrapping paper'.[73] This was evident in the frustrated attempts of blacks to place their own grievances before the Peace Conference.

To press home the lack of black representation, the American pan-Africanist leader, W.E.B. Dubois organised the second Pan-African Congress at the Grand Hotel, Paris. Dubois, and other prominent blacks, initially placed great faith in the new League of Nations, seeing it as the beginning of a new age world forum on race issues. Demands were moderate and related to the welfare of blacks, favouring internationalisation of control, 'modernisation' and black representation in policy making 'under the guidance of organised civilisation'. But the US Government opposed the meeting and denied passports to those blacks and whites who wished to attend, although Dubois and sixteen other Americans who were already in Paris escaped US passport controls. The Foreign Office in London also denied permission for Africans from British colonies to travel to Paris. Despite these difficulties, the Congress met and passed a modest resolution in keeping with the liberal rhetoric underpinning the peace negotiations.[74]

The South African Native National Congress delegation evoked a similarly hostile response. The issue of the transfer of German South West Africa and the threat it posed to the South African British Protectorates was high on their agenda, combined with grievances related to segregationist legislation in South Africa. However, South Africa was now viewed as an embryonic 'sub-imperialist' power in the region and the delegation received short shrift. Beer argued that the 'Anglo-Dutch Dominion' was the 'paramount civilising force' in Southern Africa. An 'African Monroe Doctrine' was in the making and there was a distinct advantage in terms of economic development and native policy in having 'all white man's Africa South of the Zambesi' under one administration. As South African representative to the Peace Conference, Jan Smuts cultivated powerful connections with top British diplomats and politicians to push for mandatory power over South West Africa as 'an integral portion of the Union of South Africa'.[75] This was granted reflecting the uncritical acceptance of the 'civilising' influence of this white Dominion among delegates. South African ambitions included the admission of Rhodesia into the Union – a proposal seriously considered by the British Government. When Winston Churchill succeeded Milner as Colonial Secretary in 1921, he tried to persuade settlers in Southern Rhodesia to join

South Africa as a fifth province as a counterweight to Afrikaner nationalism. A delegation from Rhodesia attended a conference in Cape Town in 1922 on Churchill's advice to discuss the terms. In this context the South African proposals had a certain logic behind them, but they were rejected by Southern Rhodesian settlers who achieved self-government in 1923.[76] The CO took over the administration of Northern Rhodesia in 1924. All these developments merely consolidated the massive African land alienation that had marred the whole region since the late nineteenth century and confirmed international support for white settlers in Southern Africa and elswhere. Combined with policies to promote white settlement, 'Great White Walls' of immigration controls against 'non-Europeans' were erected to ensure that the white Dominions formed a 'white girdle of power and progress encircling the world.'[77]

The entrenchment of imperialism in the peace-making process drew criticisms from reformist critics like Woolf for whom the system was merely a 'cloak of fine [hypocritical] phrases' which covered the 'nakedness of the old imperialism' and internationalised economic exploitation. Yet there are deep inconsistencies in Woolf's attitude to Africa and race issues, reflected in his concern about the culture 'conflict' created by imperialism. In the interests of 'harmony and peace', he too advocated the control of migration which had created 'extraordinarily dangerous ... alien enclaves whether they be African in North America or white in Africa'. In challenging this 'inverse racism' Woolf echoed the black nationalist, Marcus Garvey, in his statement that if 'Europe was for the Europeans' let it also be 'Africa for the Africans'. Thus, while he attacked white settlement in Africa he implicitly endorsed separatism on the grounds of 'cultural' not race differences. Woolf was a highly perceptive critic of imperialism and, as a Jew, had personally experienced discrimination and racial slights, even within the Bloomsbury circle. He wanted a truly internationalised 'socialist' League as an 'antithesis to imperialism', but he implicitly accepted trusteeship and the liberal-humanitarian mission towards Africa, albeit freed of economic exploitation.[78]

This qualified position was accepted by other non-marxist critics, many of whom were initially optimistic about the role the League could play in improving 'native' conditions. This contrasted sharply with the unambiguous anti-imperialism of the marxist left, who attacked not only the mandates system in practice, but the whole moral basis of trusteeship, claiming that the League was a 'reactionary tool' of imperialist powers used to promote their own interests.[79] Although the left's overarching 'conspiracy' theory may be criticised as dogmatic reductionism, the alliance of US and British interests through the Round Table networks supports this view. The League remained a 'white male and middle-class' organisation with an almost total lack of black representation. A US woman delegate at a Save the Children Fund Conference on the African Child in 1931 noted that at international meetings only official spokesmen of colonial governments were allowed to speak; any real criticism of colonial conditions was received by delegates with 'ill-grace' and 'ignored', and British delegates were particularly sensitive to criticism.[80] As we shall see in Chapter 10, the League's record on

Africa in the 1930s proved dismal. This was understandable given that the prio-rities of the 'imperialist clique', which dominated the League, were 'empire strengthening' and the defence of Western interests against challenges from three interlinked sources – the 'rising tide of colour', colonial anti-imperialism and 'Bolshevism'.

Dreams of freedom: the 'rising tide of colour', Bolshevism and anti-imperialism

The spectre of race war and 'clashing tides of colour' haunted the privileged world of whites between the wars. However, white concern over the develop-ment of race consciousness had emerged before 1914. Woolf saw the 'savage Abyssinians' successful resistance against the Italians and the Japanese defeat of Russia in 1905 as the first serious challenges to Western imperialism. He argued that Japan's example provided evidence that 'the conquest of the world by Europe was now being followed by a world revolt against Europe'. After the War, the pace of Irish, Indian and Egyptian nationalism accelerated and helped to stimulate a 'determined agitation' for black rights. Woolf warned that 'a revolt of Africa against imperialism' would be 'far more terrible' than in Asia, particularly 'if the road taken by imperialism in South Africa and … Kenya were followed'. He tapped into a more general mood of the times when he gloomily summed up the 'menacing prospects of anti-Westernism' and its 'terrible and dangerous' consequences in terms of violence and conflict. The outcome was dependent on the 'folly or wisdom' of the US and Europe.[81] This 'rising tide of colour', linked to the 'red menace', caused deeper concern after the 'race' riots in Britain, the US and Jamaica in 1919. Race became a major preoccupation and a number of works dealing with the problem of the 'clash of races' or 'race war' appeared. The colonial authorities responded with greater repression and surveillance by using more sophisticated forms of colonial policing, including air power and improved communications technology.[82] But developments in communications and media also worked in the black cause. International cross-currents connecting educated black activists from different parts of the world multiplied, with London and Paris as the 'junction boxes' of anti-imperialist activity.

The oppositional ideologies of pan-africanism and black nationalism gener-ated a stronger race consciousness in Africa and the African diaspora. These developments in black consciousness were stimulated during the 1930s by ideological conflicts between marxism, fascism and liberal democracy and a new literature was aimed at 'debunking' scientific racism. Biologists, like Cedric Dover and Lancelot Hogben, influenced by socialism and anti-fascism, now refuted the Victorian concept of separate races (polygenesis) and eugenicist notions of the inferiority of 'half-breeds'.[83] The word 'racism', as opposed to 'race' or 'race prejudice', was used for the first time in the 1930s, locating the problem firmly in the political spectrum, and the inclusion of 'outsiders' – women, Jews, Leftists and blacks (like Dover) – 'infused a greater egalitarianism into scientific discourse'. Between 1934–8 anti-racist publications by individuals became more popular and from 1938 the scientific community in both the US and Britain declared itself against racism. Max Hirschfeld, a Jewish-German sociologist in exile in London, called for co-operation through an 'International Organisation for the Dispassionate Study of the Racial Problem' to avert the 'Great Race War' through international pressure, mainly from Jews. Anti-racist activity culminated in the Universal Race Congress in 1939 at the Chicago World Fair, although it was not until 1950 that UNESCO made its first statement on race.[84] Stimulated by these developments, black intellectuals debated differing explanations of racial inequality in formulating strategies to challenge racism. Cedric Dover argued that the absence of racism in the Soviet Union proved that racism was class-based and radical structural change was necessary to eradicate it. In contrast, J.A. Rogers adopted a 'melting-pot' theory of racial intermixing and pressed for recognition of black achievements to redress the imbalance caused by the 'whitening' of world history by racialist propaganda.[85]

Imperial governments, however, unwilling to accept the fact that the growth of race consciousness stemmed from real grievances against racism and imperial policies, targeted communist manipulation as a prime source of disaffection. 'Throughout the world', wrote the US biologist and race pundit, Lothrop Stoddard, 'Bolshevik agitators whisper in the ears of discontented coloured men their gospel of hatred and revenge'.[86] These conspiracy theories perpetuated the racist assumption that blacks were unable to act on their own initiative. However, in the sense that anti-colonial and civil rights movements found most of their support from the international left, there is a grain of truth in this paranoia. Moreover, marxism was attractive as an ideology of resistance. 'Nobody else within sight', writes Eric Hobsbawm of inter-war communists, 'offered both to interpret the world and to change it'. The Marx-Engels-Lenin Institute in Moscow became a global centre for the study of marxism and colonial liberation. This represented an important shift from the pre-war eurocentric focus in which 'uncultured negroes' did not warrant the same attention as the European working classes. Lenin opposed imperialism in all forms and called for the immediate self-determination of *all* colonial peoples which, in turn, would lead to the victory of the European proletariat. The major offensive was to be directed at the British Empire, as Britain was the leading 'colonial oppressor' (although Trotsky prophetically warned against a world imperialism under US leadership).[87]

The Communist International (Comintern) was set up in 1919 to co-ordinate national communist parties and promote world revolution. Like the parallel organisation, the League of Nations, the Comintern was committed to world peace, but argued that this was not possible while imperialism still existed. With increasing unrest in the African colonies, a 'Negro Propaganda Commission' was set up in 1924. It was comprised of representatives of the British and French Communist Parties, and black delegates attended Comintern congresses more regularly thereafter. Comintern organisations, like Red International of Labour Unions (RILU) or Profintern, were also directed to promote work among blacks. In 1922, International Labour Defence (ILD) was founded to give assistance to indicted black workers in the US and Africa.[88]

Initially, Comintern theoreticians believed they could build on the appeal of Garveyism. White marxists were also influenced by ideas of evolutionary development from 'primitive' to 'advanced' and thus targeted more 'advanced' US blacks, who already had a strong foothold in Africa through educational and missionary work, to develop anti-imperialist work in Africa. This intensified white fears about the subversive and conspiratorial role of US blacks in Africa. But tactics changed after 1928 when co-operation with 'bourgeois' black nationalists was dropped in favour of a 'united front from below' of workers and peasants in the colonies. The crisis in capitalism provided an 'unparalleled revolutionary opportunity', particularly in Africa, and communist papers and local parties were revamped to push this new line.[89] To further this strategy, the RILU set up the International Trade Union Committee of Negro Workers (ITUCNW), which published the monthly (often semi-monthly) *Negro Worker* in English and French from 1928–37. An important ITUCNW conference was held in Hamburg in 1930 to draw together the 'oppressed peoples' from all over the world and 'lay down a programme for practical work'. Seventeen delegates representing eleven trade unions attended, but nine elected delegates failed to arrive because of 'hindrances' placed in their way. Garveyism ('negro reformism') was rejected as a 'utopian illusion' that obscured a fundamental 'economic struggle' based on class, not race. The tone of the debates, which spanned colonial repression, racial discrimination and the barriers to trade unionism was strongly anti-imperialist.[90] The new League Against Imperialism (LAI), launched in Brussels in 1927, helped facilitate the conference by putting colonial delegates in contact with Comintern officials. In theory, the LAI was a non-party organisation with branches in the colonies and European imperial centres, but closely adhered to Comintern policies.[91]

Practical communist involvement in Africa was negligible, but, in ideological terms, marxism posed a remote but tangible threat to imperialist interests. Although white communists and imperialists shared a common conception of Africa as 'primitive', their solutions to this 'backwardness' differed radically. Black intellectuals viewed the Soviet Union's development of its own 'backward' peoples as progressive and enabling – in contrast to the policies in the British colonies.[92] In evoking the communist threat, colonial authorities avoided confronting the fact that unrest in the colonies was rooted in imperial policy. The spectre of communism was represented as the major threat to the British and French empires; Africa was 'overrun' by communist propagandists, an 'insidious deluge' that appealed to the 'emotionalism' of Africans. As Margery Perham noted, in the inter-war period the 'problem of colonialism' became inseparable from the rift between communism and the European powers.[93]

Summary

Faced by the combined threat of 'Bolshevik subversion' and the development of resistance and anti-imperialism in both Britain and in the colonies, 'empire strengthening' tactics were employed. These were rationalised by dominant race discourses which emphasised Africa's backwardness and need for white 'trustee-ship'. But behind the humanitarian rhetoric there were economic and political reasons for the expansion of British power linked to the changed global situation after the First World War. As Africa became a cause for international concern, British power in Africa was endorsed by the League of Nations and the US, who shared the same fears about the threat to Western power from the powerful cock-tail of 'the rising tide of colour' and Bolshevism. This extension of power resulted in the further elaboration and refinement of powerful discourses around race and empire – popular, official, academic and anthropological. At the heart of these discourses was a conception of Africa as 'primitive' and it was this image that remained embedded in popular consciousness. When I was a child, Africa was still represented largely as the Africa of the white imagination anal-ysed in this chapter. But there was also the dark and threatening Africa – the 'black bogeyman' of popular vernacular used to threaten children into good behaviour – intimating perhaps the fear of black retaliation against white supremacy. It is only when we turn to the colonial hinterland – the crucible of popular images and myths of Africa – that the contradictions between imperi-alist dreams of power and African 'dreams of freedom' emerge.

West Africa

2 Britain's imperial hinterland

Colonialism in West Africa

What is [West Africa's] spell? I cannot tell you, nor wherein lies its strange and unfathomable charm. It lays its hand upon you, and having once felt its compelling touch you can never forget it or be wholly free from it.

(Princess Marie Louise, Gold Coast, 1925)

You know, Africa is an old bitch; it gets you in the end.

(Assistant District Officer, Nigeria, 1938)[1]

As dreams of British power in India faded, the West African colonies of Nigeria, the Gold Coast, Sierra Leone and the Gambia, 'pacified' before the First World War, moved more firmly into the British imperial orbit. After the First World War, the British Togoland and Cameroon Mandates were incorporated into the region. The 'colonial myth' of the 1920s was that this process of incorporation into the British Empire and the international economy had been 'effected peacefully', with the exception of some small pockets of resistance, and 'amity' between 'pagans' and the British now prevailed. Colonial rule, argued Sir William Geary, a barrister in the Supreme Court in Lagos, would bring 'peace, trade, education ... justice and an equal chance for all' – a vision of progress where 'Labour pours into the railway track and a primitive people begin to learn the value of English silver and Manchester cloth'.[2] The inter-war years were marked by economic development. Most private capital invested in Africa, outside of the white settler areas, went to Nigeria, followed by the Gold Coast. This was reflected in the spectacular expansion of roads and the linked increase in the imports of cars, lorries, motorbikes and petrol.[3] In this economic dream, development would mutually benefit West Africa and Britain (Illustration 4). Development was promoted through the key principles of indirect rule, 'acceptance of the rudiments of law and order', the promotion of individual responsibility and a 'sense of discipline and respect for authority'.[4]

As the laboratory for paternalist trusteeship, the region attracted the administrator, businessperson, traveller, journalist and politician. Charles Allen, who was commissioned to interview ex-Colonial African Service (CAS) men and women for the BBC sound archives as a 'reconstruction of Britain's imperial past', found that there were was more said about West Africa than any other part of British colonial Africa.[5] But how was West Africa conceptualised through 'imperial eyes'? How did the Africa of the English imagination (explored in the preceding chapter) tally with real-life experiences and fit in with the economic dream of modern development? Who were the white men who carried the imperial burden and exercised power at the grass roots, and what motivated them? This chapter addresses the white 'vision' of West Africa, establishes the centrality of the colonial officer to the imperial mission and explores the tensions and ambiguities between the vision and realities of colonial rule as experienced through the trials and tribulations of 'duty' in the bush.

West Africa in the English imagination

A sense of unreality, of a hinterland 'at the back of once upon a time', suffuses contemporary representations of colonial society. West Africa is a 'mirage', a timeless world of adventure and exotic stimulation, outside modernity. Wealthy travellers revelled in the animal-like beauty of 'savages', their exotic customs and the emotional appeal of 'uncivilised' Africa, while colonial rule was justified on the grounds that natives were 'a thousand years away' from the district officer (DO) in the field.[6] Representations of Africa, which reached mass audiences in Britain, are epitomised in the film, *Sanders of the River* (1935). Based on the novel by Edgar Wallace, the film was made with the help of colonial governments.

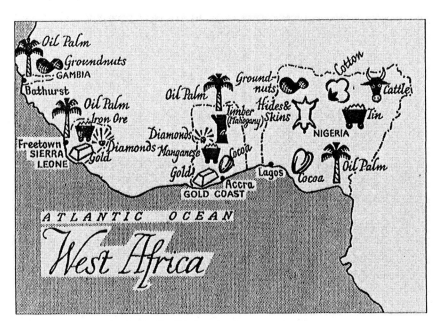

Illustration 4–West Africa in the English imagination
Source: Map of West Africa from *Empire Youth Annual*, London, P.R. Gawthorne Ltd., 1947

The ethnographic documentary film provides the 'authentic' African setting for the studio shots and a vision of the natural 'primitive'. 'Real members of the Acholi, Tefik, Juruba [*sic*], Mendi and Kroo tribes' were used, but 'Africa' is still transformed into a fantastic and unreal continent. All the Africans in the film magically understand English, including the evil, slaving king, and the main character, Bosambo, is played by the American actor, Paul Robeson. Bosambo is from Liberia, but he is allowed to become paramount chief of a tribe with whom he has no cultural or lineage connections by virtue of being given the 'Chain of Office' by the white District Commissioner, 'Lord Sandi' (Sanders). His respectability in white eyes is confirmed by his marriage to Lilongo, a 'beautiful Mohammedan' from the coast, who, unlike the bare-breasted women of the ethnographic scenes, wears a long Sari-like robe and has a perfect English accent.[7]

The narrative interest in the book and film comes through Sanders' heroic efforts to suppress slavery and sort out the problems of 'gin and rifles' – introduced via immoral white traders – and suppress the 'cruel' savages, who are nearly always slavers who oppose and even kill whites. There was, of course, a grain of reality in this distorted representation: Beer (1923) commented, for instance, on the liquor problem, particularly in West Africa, and *Sanders* clearly mirrored international humanitarian concerns reviewed in Chapter 1. Such preoccupations are also clearly evident in Lugard's authoritative *Political Memoranda* (1919). *Sanders* proved popular and Wallace produced a number of books on the same theme, including *Sandi the Kingmaker* and *Bosambo of the River*. Anthony Kirk-Greene, who joined the Colonial Service in Nigeria in 1949, claims that *Sanders of the River* was one of the main 'African readings' for many aspiring colonial officers before the Second World War. He argues that there was a 'degree of substance' in Sanders image as the archetypal DC in the bush – an image so powerful that even in the 1970s Sanders was alive and well – 'fiction sustaining a world that was lost'. Sanders, the old 'Africa hand', is the 'little brown man in immaculate white', drinking gin swizzles and keeping order with supreme control and confidence. 'There is only one type of man that can rule the native provinces wisely and that type is best represented by Sanders' writes Wallace.[8] The novel thus affords an entrée into the ultra-masculine world of the colonial officer at a time when the 'old style' District Commissioner was transformed from pacifier to civil servant.

Both the novel and the bowdlerised film version provide insight into the popular vision of colonial Africa. Sanders is responsible for some 'quarter of a million cannibal folk' in West Central Africa. He is aided in this mission by his native 'Houssa escort' and the maxim gun. He polices his area on his little steamer, 'Zaire', which evokes images of Conrad's *Heart of Darkness*. Lord Sandi has to deal with folk who are 'illogical' and believe in spirits, and he is immersed in an alien, forested world of 'violent death and horrid happenings' far from the civilised society 'beyond the lazy, swelling, blue sea'. But the novel also reveals the frustrations of the colonial officer whose autonomy is increasingly threatened (by, for instance, the extension of a more tightly ordered and bureaucratic Colonial Service). Sanders is scathing about ignorant whites and younger, better-educated district officers who wrongly believed that the native could be converted to 'good citizenship'. He is irritated by jumped-up black Christians, particularly those of the 'Ethiopian Mission', who 'preached the gospel of equality'. But his worst venom is directed at educated Africans, when the narrative clearly reflects the official discourses analysed in Chapter 1. The Reverend Kenneth McDolan, brought up by a white Christian family in Sierra Leone and speaking 'faultless English', buckles under Sanders' arrogant disdain, which shows 'how thumbnail deep is the civilisation of the cultured savage'. Such attitudes are more fully explored in his relationship with Bosambo. In the film, Bosambo is spirited, but deferential and loyal; in the book he is a far less straightforward character – a 'government-defying Krooman ... adventurer' from the coast who had been educated at a mission school and had worked as a steward on the Elder Dempster Line. By claiming to have white men's blood in his veins he 'libels' a British official in Sierra Leone and he is a known thief who has killed a man and escaped from prison in Monrovia. Despite this, Sanders takes him on because he is a 'clever man' and can manage his poor, 'defenceless' Ochori, the prey of evil African slavers.[9]

Beneath the racist distortions in *Sanders of the River*, the complexities and stresses of colonial society emerge, such as the duality and ambivalence of Africans and the problems with interpreters. Sandi has to pit his wits continually against cunning, duplicitous or 'wicked' Africans – even though his superior qualities always win. Whites and blacks lived in separate worlds, but where they collided there was a dynamic interaction that generated cultural change and conflict. The 'reality' of the mythologised colonial hinterland that shaped both popular and official impressions of Africa was in effect a complex intermeshing of different interests, white and African, that had its own peculiar dynamic. The 'real' (as opposed to fictional) Africa was a world where whites were literally and metaphorically on the edge, maintaining a precarious power that was undermined daily in small acts of resistance. The white colonial fiefdoms were trapped like amber in an idealised, English upper-class world, which was sustained by belief in the imperial mission, but engulfed by rapidly changing African societies. Colonialism impacted on the cultures and identities of both black and white people. Whites became expatriates, distanced from their own societies, fossilised anachronisms, obsessed with the lure of Africa while desperately clinging on to their Englishness and racial superiority. Africans in close contact with whites wore the 'white mask' and developed ambivalent responses to white rule and culture. Whites interpreted their responses as acceptance and were insensitive to the chameleon qualities of the colonised and the masks of subordination that concealed anger, resentment and hatred. As Sidney Olivier perceptively observed:

> The truth is different for different races ... they live to the same extent in different worlds. A conquered race that speaks two languages will tell the truth in its own language and will lie in that of its conquerors [giving] what he supposes to be the conqueror's truth, namely, what he desires.[10]

The records of 'the man [and woman] on the spot' illuminate a colonial society with all its contradictions. If we could move back in time into the minds of the coloniser and the colonised, we would find a world where imperial rule was accepted as a normal and rational phenomenon, unconsciously taken for granted by the majority of whites. Africans had an alternative, if tightly connected world, where the maxim gun, the bible and lucrative concessions made to some Africans had secured white hegemony. They were now confronted with alien beings with eccentric customs who had only a superficial understanding of their societies, but could wield enormous power. Elspeth Huxley conceded that European ideas often seemed 'strange and senseless to Africans', while Eslanda Goode Robeson claimed that Africans viewed colonial whites with suspicion on the grounds that in African societies only misfits and 'bad men' roamed, the good and respected stayed at home. For Africans, whites were alien and invasive, but also targets of humour and contempt in vernacular culture. A.W. Cardinall, a Gold Coast colonial officer, observed that Africans 'show disapproval or mock the acts of others in ways that are most shrewd and cunningly devised'. Drumming or whistling, even the way clothes were worn, could convey the deadliest of insults, but 'so subtle was the act' that the person targeted would remain oblivious.[11] Most whites were, of course, too arrogant to conceive that Africans would have opinions about them. As Hooks (1992) has pointed out, whites have always been oblivious to the fact that they have been watched by blacks with a critical, ethnographical 'gaze', but because of racism, black people have remained silent about representations of whiteness in the black imagination. However, African impressions of whites have been transmitted down the generations through oral family histories.[12]

With their obsession with the primitive 'other', whites were insensitive to the rich nuances of West African vernacular culture and complex urban cultures that stretch back to the European Middle Ages. Far from being backward and isolated from civilisation, West African societies have a long history of contact with the outside world through trade and diplomacy. Another hero of African 'pacification', Sir Harry Johnson, noted that prior to 1915 'almost unnoticed by Europe' there was a 'considerable traffic in sailing boats entirely manned by natives of Africa' transporting 'large quantities' of African produce across the short sea passage to Brazil. Johnson also alleged that the 'strange aristocratic, half-white indigene of West Africa, the Mohammedan Fula' travelled as merchants and were spreading Islam in Brazil. There were also 'Afro-Brazilians' who had returned 'home' when freed from slavery and worked as clerks in the Nigerian colonial service.[13] However, at times contemporary observers hinted at a deeper understanding of African culture and history, and here female observers could be more perceptive and open-minded than men. Although she revelled in the 'alien' exoticism of the colonial spectacle, Princess Marie Louise made imaginative connections between African and European culture (between, for example, 'Jack in the Green' and Ju Ju men) and was genuinely interested in Ashanti culture (Ashanti or Akan was the colonial term for the Asante State). She acknowledged the importance of talking drums in 'perpetuating tribal memory', traditions and genealogies of the Ashanti kings, and observed that in the 'wild' Northern Territories the chiefs were of a 'most ancient lineage' and 'in some strange and remarkable manner' had managed to preserve a 'fairly accurate' record of their descent. Sanders also notes how his fictitious Isisi kept 'extraordinary records' in their heads passed on from father to son.[14]

West African societies have long and rich histories, memories of which sustained resistance against white rule, but whites resident in West Africa minimised or erased earlier resistance to emphasise African loyalty to the British Crown and Government. Thus the Asante, who had fought sustained campaigns against the British in 1895 and 1900 and who were demonised as bloodthirsty barbarians, were transformed by colonial rule into Princess Marie Louise's 'gentle' and loyal subjects. Likewise, the militaristic and punitive 'empire builders', forced into endless 'little wars' with Africans, became the peaceful, dutiful administrators who ruled grateful natives whose interests they protected from the commercial carpetbaggers and the bloody savagery of aggressive slaving tribes. Lord Lugard, the first Governor of Nigeria, was described by George Padmore as a 'young military freebooter', who 'helped defeat ... fierce resistance' in imperial 'pacification', and Pakenham (1992) accuses him of sanctioning brutality against men, women and children during the 'pacification' of Nigeria. In the 'colonial moment', however, he was elevated to the progressive architect of humane trusteeship and, as Leonard Woolf pointed out, his contribution to bloody pacifications was forgotten.[15]

These transformations in the way both coloniser and colonised were represented is at the root of contemporary visions of inter-war West Africa as a tranquil colonial backwater where there was little unrest in contrast to turbulent and ungrateful India. Such generalisations became official orthodoxy in Britain, obscuring the complexity and diversity of colonial West Africa, as well as minimising African resistance and the more cynical economic reasons for colonial rule. This separation of the colonial 'mission' from the colonial economy has persisted in more recent research. Phillips (1990) has argued that colonial officials set themselves up as the 'guardians' of a romanticised, pre-capitalist order and the interests of capitalism were thus 'ill-served'.[16] But was there such a total schism between administration and commercial interests? Hopkins (1987) argues that 'big business' and government were indeed not always in harmony, as the government favoured free trade and competition. Moreover, at times, the profit motives of the merchants and entrepreneurs did conflict with the 'political' work of DOs, some of whom sincerely believed in their brief to protect vulnerable natives from such adverse influences. But, as we shall see in Chapter 3, the top end of the colonial hierarchy had their own vested interests in business. The 'King's peace', maintained by the Government, helped to sustain a colonial economy which paid for colonial administration and benefited private British citizens. Colonial governments, backed by the Colonial Office and the expatriate companies, all wanted to promote trade and primary commodity production and to integrate colonies into the international capitalist economy. As Yearwood (1998) concludes, we cannot take a conspiratorial view of colonialism, but this does not exonerate the role of government in exploitation.[17]

At the heart of the colonial project in Africa was the management and control of labour as Africa's 'chief asset'.[18] In West Africa, this was muted by the imperial commitment to the protection of native land rights and the encouragement of peasant production. There was no land alienation in Nigeria, but according to Hailey (1956), 5 per cent of the Gold Coast was under mining concessions and the United Africa Company had leases for rubber, palm oil and timber concessions in Nigeria. Throughout West Africa, commodification of peasant production had negative consequences as we shall see in Chapter 4. However, West Africa was viewed as a 'paradise' in contrast to East Africa or South Africa, and even critics of colonialism believed that British trusteeship was working well. On his visit to West Africa in 1934, the Labour MP, Charles Roden Buxton, described Nigeria as a 'model colony', full of 'happy and contented' natives and the finest achievement the British Empire had to its credit.[19] Some 'outsider' writers with firsthand experience of West Africa, Graham Greene and Geoffrey Gorer, for instance, did acknowledge the negative aspects of colonialism, but an element of pseudo-sociological exoticism runs through Gorer's work, while Greene stresses the 'hopelessness' and passivity of the African condition.[20]

Resident whites, however, were sensitive to the real problems faced by the 'man on the spot' and resented the intrusions of visitors who did not 'understand the native' and might misrepresent their work in England. Lugard alluded to the conflicts between the local administrator, accused of parochialism, and the 'casual traveller', known in the trade as 'Pagett MP', who after a short stay in a colony claimed to know how things should be done, although he 'never had the responsibility for carrying out his theories'. These conflicts are reflected in *Sanders of the River*, where Wallace satirises the self-professed experts who tried to interfere in his work, the 'upper-class gentlewoman', author of *Alone in Africa*, and the humanitarian son of an English newspaper proprietor who comes to investigate Sanders' cruelties against the natives. The play, *White Cargoes* (1926), which emphasised the horrors of life in West Africa and proved very popular in England, was described by Sylvia Leith-Ross as 'absurd' and condemned by Princess Marie Louise as a 'cruel libel' and 'utterly false and untrue'.[21]

Entering the world of West Africa in the English imagination can thus reveal much about the reality of power. Post-colonial writings have emphasised the fictional nature of white 'narratives' of colonial rule, arguing that they tell us less about the colonised than the 'imagined world' of the coloniser. But rooted in such 'fictions' is a tangible power expressed in economic exploitation, cultural oppression and power over the lives of the colonised. This power was not monolithic, nor did it operate uniformly, and the texture of colonial interaction was complex and multifaceted, reflecting the diversity of colonial 'subjects'. The colonial state was exploitative and autocratic, but communication with the colonised was not simply a 'monologue'; dialogue did exist even if this was 'circumscribed by the all too tangible violence of imperialism'.[22] The complexities of the relationship between coloniser and colonised exposed the stark mismatch between the discourse and the practice of trusteeship. The 'dilemmas' of indirect rule are clearly revealed in the everyday problems faced by the colonial officer 'in the field', who was at the cutting edge of colonial rule and had to cope on the hoof with the realities of the imperial mission. Who were these men and how did they make their stamp of power on West Africa?

'A Corps d'élite'? The colonial officer and the imperial mission

For new colonial officers travelling to West Africa, the first stage, after being kitted out at F.P. Baker, London, or Walter's and Co. Tropical Outfitters, Oxford, was the voyage on an Elder Dempster boat. Princess Marie Louise, the granddaughter of Queen Victoria, who made an official visit to the Gold Coast in 1925, wrote to her sister that on her voyage out there were no tourists, only men returning to work in the colonies and 'a dozen or so' women. The parochial nature of empire in Africa was underscored by the cummerbunds that the men wore at dinner, the different colours denoting identification with the different colonies and reinforcing an '*esprit de corps*'.[23] After negotiating the wild surf along the West African coast in the skil-fully manned local pirogues, their first contact with Africa was not with the wild and the primitive, but with the urban ports of Cape Coast, Lagos or Freetown. But behind that was the 'real Africa' in which colonial officers were to carry out their mission of trusteeship. New officers had been briefed for this role by official courses, Lugard's, *Political Memoranda* (1922), 'The Bible of West Africa' (required reading for new recruits until Lugard's ideas became outdated in the1930s) and novels like *Sanders of the River*.[24]

Why did they take on a job that involved discomfort, danger, risk of ill-health or even death from tropical diseases and isolation? A colonial officer in the Nigerian Service categorised the motives of Englishmen who went out to West Africa under three main headings – adventure, duty and profit. Some officers revelled in the 'huntin', 'shootin' and 'fishin'' and 'fun of the thing'; the aura of excitement and the 'indefinable, inexplicable fascination' of Africa, which compensated for the 'awful' conditions. For such men the imperial ideal combined adventure with public school values of duty, sportsmanship, self-discipline and male camaraderie. The 'raw pagan' areas were regarded as a chal-lenge to adventurous officers as they constituted the areas of the strongest traditional resistance.[25]

While the ultra-masculine ethos of the Colonial African Service attracted adventure seekers, there were also men, akin to the modern aid worker, who combined dissatisfaction from living in their own cultures with a belief that they were doing something to help the less fortunate. This in itself provided the job satisfaction that welded them to Africa. The Colonial Office (CO) ideal was a man who could give 'ideals and backbone' to the natives according to the guiding principles of 'honesty of purpose' and 'humanity'. But, as Margery Perham noted, there was a 'bewildering variety' of officers and it is doubtful if many recruits stood up to the 'supreme types' that she observed in Nigeria. For Princess Marie Louise, who had scores of sycophantic officers smoothing her way through sweat and toil in the baking sun, the 'very finest type' of colonial

administrator was represented by Major Walker Leigh, Chief Officer of the
Northern Provinces, Tamale, Gold Coast – a 'tower of strength in every emergency, courteous and charming with a sense of humour, beloved by all …
officials and … natives'.[26]

Service in Africa was 'very austere' compared to the sybaritic decadence of
the Indian Civil Service; the colonies were 'wretchedly poor' and officers were
paid less than in India.[27] The compensation was autonomy and power, which
even a very young assistant district officer (ADO) could wield, and the 'wild west'
ethos forged a distinct identity for the CAS in which they could take pride.
Colonial officers recruited before 1930 were often from a military background,
had few formal qualifications, but liked freedom and adventure. In *Sanders of the
River*, they are fondly attributed 'eccentricity and foibles of character', which
were 'admired by Europeans and Africans alike'. As 'little kings' in their districts,
they resented the 'professionalisation' of the service and increasing centralised
control from London during the 1930s, which diminished the power of individual officers.[28] The workings and ethos of the colonial service have been well
documented elsewhere by, for instance, Heussler (1963) and Kuklich (1979), but
certain key features are pertinent to this discussion. After an official Civil Service
inquiry in 1930, the whole service was rationalised, and in 1932 the two main
branches of the Colonial Services (African and Asian) were unified in the
Colonial Administrative Service, leading to improvements in pay and conditions
of service in Africa, more security of tenure and an increase in staff numbers.
During the 1930s, a greater emphasis on development led to an increase in technical officers and the introduction of women who reputedly did 'excellent work'
in education and welfare.[29]

Sir Ralph Furse was a 'paramount influence' in this reorganisation as
Director of Recruitment at the CO since 1910. His aim was to create a *corps
d'elite* of men, who, despite the difficulties of tropical service, would be attracted
by the 'challenge of adventure' and spiritual quest, and he personally vetted
thousands of young men up to his retirement in 1956. Administration in Africa
thus reached the peak of 'strength and excellence' in the 1930s as the public
image of the Africa Service in relation to the ICS was improved. Recruitment at
Oxbridge went up sharply and by 1939 over 80 per cent of candidates successfully completed courses in tropical administration at Oxford and Cambridge
compared with virtually none pre-1924.[30] This core one-year CAS course
included law, elementary surveying, colonial history, geography, anthropology,
agriculture, forestry, tropical hygiene and native languages. A degree was essential after 1930, and starting salaries averaged £500 per annum (rising to £1000)
at a time when only 4 per cent of Britain's population earned over that amount.
Colonial administration was well paid with generous fringe benefits and
pensions, although less prestigious technical staff did not fare so well.[31]

Like the ICS, the elite of colonial administrations, the Political Service, was a
'select club [of] hand-picked men of similar tastes and background' who
possessed initiative and commitment to public service, which was essential to
political work in the field.[32] Duncan-Johnstone, a Political Officer (PO) in the

Gold Coast, alludes to the 'strained relations' between the snobbish POs and the newer, technical officers from grammar school, 'redbrick' university backgrounds, who were regarded as more suited to 'routine' work. POs felt that technical and medical innovations upset the delicate balance of native society and this resulted in mutual hostility and lack of co-operation. But as the anti-imperialist, Leonard Barnes, noted, this 'exclusive aristocracy' of 'Officers and Gentlemen' was hardly equipped in 'social outlook' to handle the growing problems in the colonial economy.[33] Most civil servants at the CO, colonial 'experts' and officers in the field were products of the English public schools whose education was directed to maintaining the entrenched privileges of the English ruling classes and encouraging conformity and commitment to dominant values. Kenneth Bradley, whose *Diary of a District Officer* (1942) inspired the younger post-Second World War generation, equated indirect rule with the public school prefectorial system, where management was delegated to representatives of the subject people. Dealing with natives required 'physical presence', intelligence and 'imaginative sympathy', and the public school inculcated the valued qualities of 'integrity, fairness and firmness' and, above all, leadership. But, as J.A. Hobson pointed out, the public school had its dark side and also promoted 'imperialism masquerading as patriotism, militarism, chauvinism, arrogance and over-weaning self-confidence'.[34]

For Evelyn Waugh, colonial officers constituted a 'caste of just, soap-loving young men with public school blazers', middle-class aspirants for whom empire provided good job prospects. The Colonial Service was an export version of what Cain and Hopkin's (1993) have termed the strongly gendered culture of 'gentlemanly capitalism'. This was rooted in the service sector, which was centred in the City of London and the southern Home Counties, and reflected a shift in the imperial power base, analysed by Hobson before the First World War. Formed through a merger of the upwardly mobile middle classes and the aristocracy, it was characterised by preference for professional bureaucratic employment, supported by secure investment incomes rather than the hazards of business. The elite networks of the 'gentlemanly order', forged through Eton and Balliol, oiled the wheels of empire and ensured the 'continuing vitality of the gentlemanly diaspora'.[35] Thus, the Colonial Service in Africa was shaped largely by men and women from families who had prospered in colonial service, military and civil, in other parts of the 'tropical' empire, particularly the ICS, although by the 1930s there were also 'second-generation' officers and wives whose fathers had seen service in Africa in the official or business sector. The world of this gentlemanly diaspora was parochial and ordered through a rigid social hierarchy and 'excessive bureaucracy'. There was little communication between the different colonies and deep differences existed between the urban-based Secretariat (the Governor, Colonial Secretary and higher administrative staff), sheltered from daily contact with the governed, and the men on 'district duty' who resented the Secretariat's 'sense of superiority'.[36] On their career trajectories, the upwardly mobile colonial secretaries and governors moved about between Africa, the Caribbean and the Pacific and between different West African colonies. In contrast, the 'men in the field' tended to stay in one colony, working up through the hierarchy from ADO to a Provincial Commissioner in charge of a whole province.

'Good' or 'bad' postings were determined by the 'type' of African. As noted in Chapter 1, contemporary racial discourse romanticised the 'bush pagan', while the 'detribalised', urban worker, and what Graham Greene referred to as the 'trousered, bespectacled Coast clerk', were ridiculed and despised. Our 'hero', Sanders, derides 'Coast English' – the 'monkey talk' of the Krooboys and 'half-bred sailors' who 'have no language'. However, in practice, the more 'civilised' areas provided the higher status postings. The Sierra Leone Protectorate, for instance, was reputedly 'well suited to indirect rule in its most pure form' as 'natives' were 'untouched ... (by) the effects of civilisation' until gold was discovered in 1928. Yet Katherine Fowler Lunn, an American geologist, alleged that whites preferred Freetown, as in the 'backward' interior 'thieving' from Europeans was reputedly a 'lively evil' along all main routes and children, brought up to beware of 'white bogeymen', verbally abused passing Europeans as 'white debils' (*sic*). Similar distinctions existed in the Gold Coast between 'soft jobs' in Accra and the wilder, remote Northern Territories, which made some men 'very disgruntled' and 'took the heart out of a man'.[37] Moslem areas were particularly favoured. Duncan-Johnstone attributed this to the strict Islamic code of obedience, which was viewed as 'beneficial' to the smooth-running of colonial rule as it forbade alcohol, which was a 'great vice' among pagans, and Moslem pride 'saved natives' from the inferiority complex of the pagans and the Westernised 'mission boys'. In Nigeria, promotion came through the Northern Moslem Emirates, a plum posting where some sort of expatriate life was possible. The Hausa of Northern Nigeria were ideal 'natives' and the strong, centralised rule of the Emir facilitated the smooth workings of indirect rule. The southern, 'pagan' societies with more democratic, localised village administrations were far less easy to administer and a posting to the 'pagan' areas was regarded as a 'calamity' in a man's career.[38]

In this colonial pecking order, argues Kuklich (1979), conformists prospered, but renegade officers, 'bush-types' who had transgressed codes of behaviour and were unable to survive in 'polite' society or those who were too critical of the system, found their promotion to better postings blocked and could be relegated permanently to more remote areas.[39] At times, even officers whose career in the service was relatively successful, displeased their superiors and were punished by a spell in an unpopular area. After Duncan-Johnstone had allegedly 'mishandled' a riot in the Western Gold Coast (see p. 67), he was posted to the Togoland mandate in 1937 where the residency was the 'worst' he had seen, badly planned and 'full of sand-flies'. Although the posting was technically a promotion, it demoralised Johnstone and drained him of his earlier enthusiasm.[40]

Whether colonial officers were in 'backward', rural or more populous, rapidly developing areas, the vision of orderly administration was marred by the Pandora's Box of Western culture. Once opened, this unleashed dangerous and irreversible developments which threatened to become uncontrollable. Voicing the dominant view within the Colonial Service, Perham expressed deep concern about the impact of 'Europeanising forces' on a primitive people, marred by 'a dark stain' of paganism, who were 'so unready' for healthy development. But problems also emerged among the more 'advanced' Africans. For instance, the Yoruba of Nigeria – the 'most sophisticated and commercially enterprising people in Nigeria' – were making 'rapid progress', but, Perham warns, now also 'excelled in counterfeiting and illegal distillation, an art imported from America'.[41] To address these problems, prospective officers were encouraged to take an interest in anthropology in order to apply the 'scientific' principles of indirect rule. Colonial censuses became an important tool for collecting ethnographical data and some serving officers, including Duncan-Johnstone, also conducted their own research. Dr Charles Meek, a census officer in Nigeria and Captain R.S. Rattray, a Gold Coast colonial officer, became official government anthropologists. Rattray became renowned in England for popularising the 'wisdom and wit' of Ashanti proverbs at the 1924 Wembley Exhibition and Princess Marie Louise gained most of her information about the Gold Coast from his book.[42] 'Independent' anthropological expertise was also increasingly valued and research plans submitted to the International African Institute were clearly geared to the problems of colonial rule, even if anthropologists tailored them thus simply to secure funds. For instance, in 1932, the Austrian S.F. Nadel's proposed study of the Bauchi hill tribes (Jos Plateau) of Northern Nigeria (where 'primitives' had been sucked into the large scale mining of tin) was justified as being of 'political and colonial', as well as scientific interest.[43]

As African unrest grew, officers became more demoralised and complained of reduced leave, harder work and less leisure time. Although Lugard had stressed the importance of continuity of service, as Africans were 'naturally reserved and suspicious towards strangers', officers were frequently transferred between provinces, which, argued Duncan-Johnstone, took away the 'personal touch', broke continuity and served to 'bewilder' the native. Duncan-Johnstone's Gold Coast diaries record in meticulous detail the everyday problems of administration, staffing and dealings with natives, missionaries and police commissioners. Like most serving officers he was loyal to the imperial ideal, but critical of policies imposed 'from the top', which in the more remote areas resulted in inefficiency and an 'atmosphere of stagnation' masked by official complacence about the 'progress of the natives'.[44]

Colonial officers were expected to perform multiple, but vaguely specified, functions in an enervating climate which led to a high staff turnover. Some were as young as twenty, had often signed up in a 'very casual fashion' and were ill-prepared for the sudden immersion into a demanding and responsible job.[45] In addition to the psychological effects of isolation, housing conditions in the 'bush' were generally poor and there was a continual risk of malaria and other tropical diseases. We can but empathise with the lonely DO and ADO separated from their families for long periods, trying to maintain 'civilised' standards, dressing for dinner, listening to the gramophone in the evening and living for weeks without news from home. Princess Marie Louise provides us with cameos of such Gold Coast officers; Captain Eyre Smith at Lawra, Northern Territories, with only his wire-haired terrier for company, and District Commissioner Puckridge (see Illustration 5) laying out a garden 'in terraces with flagged paths bordered by [English] flowers and a sundial' around his 'little bungalow' in the heart of the forest. 'It struck me as fearfully pathetic', she wrote, 'how an Englishman will try to reproduce England, all that is English, in fact home, wherever he is'.[46]

Invalidity rates were higher for officials than non-officials, an indication perhaps of the strains of the job, which was often tedious and irritating. A substantial minority of officers developed nervous conditions ('neurosthenia', in the contemporary jargon, which was possibly a form of what is now known as ME). In the Gold Coast up to 9.2 per cent suffered from this as opposed to 14.2 per cent from malaria or black water fever.[47] The loneliness and fear of the bush with its 'infernal drums' also led to heavy drinking and short tempers. Under such conditions, trivial incidents could make a man go 'berserk' or even commit suicide, although Kenneth Bradley recalls that such men were 'exceptions'. Alone for eight months as an ADO in the Cameroons, without 'speaking a word of English', Richard Oakley recalls the common 'end of tourish' feeling: 'the climate, unending work with which one never catches up, and only one's company other than natives, all tend to undermine one's grip upon oneself, so that you find yourself going off at the deep end'.[48]

Too many officers became cynical and pessimistic and treated Africans in their charge shabbily and, while some developed relatively harmless eccentricities, others became dangerous megalomaniacs. (Our fictional Sanders is probably a combination of both.) These 'white chiefs' were trapped in a delusionary dream of relatively static and compliant societies that could be moulded gradually to their plans, when, in reality, like the Dutch boy with his finger in the dike, they were trying to hold back a flood of progress. How then did the colonial officer cope with the realities of life in the 'bush' and what was the texture of interaction between coloniser and colonised? Scrutiny of the day-to-day interaction between the colonial subject and the white 'man in the field' can offer valuable insight into mechanisms of coercion and consent.

'Wedded to his people': the colonial officer and the contradictions of duty

All the tensions between theory and practice inherent in indirect rule were encapsulated in the Political Officer's brief (laid down in detail in Lugard's *Political Memoranda*). As well as the 'guardian' of the people, he was also the tax-collector, local government treasurer and dispenser of justice. Certain minor services that were 'fairly sparsely distributed', such as education and hygiene, were his responsibility as were the construction of public works and public water supply. These were paid for through meagre Native Treasury funds, which also covered the 'salaries' of chiefs and other native officials. The Treasuries were nominally allocated to chiefs to promote responsibility and local government, but Political Officers were responsible for monitoring and assisting in the allocation of funds and kept a firm control over the accounts. POs were instructed to collect taxes to

Illustration 5 Captain Puckridge
Source: Princess Marie Louise, *Travels in the Gold Coast*, Methuen Co. Ltd., 1926

pay for government services and recruit labour, including female labour, to build roads which were seen as crucial to the 'spread of order', the promotion of trade and the acceptance of colonialism.[49] Britain had signed the Forced Labour Convention in 1930, but compulsory military service, convict labour, 'communal services' and 'emergencies' were excluded. Convict labour was used to tend the gardens of colonial officials and Africans could be required to perform work of a 'public nature' for not more than sixty days in a year.[50]

Regular tours of the district, Lugard stressed, were regarded as an essential part of the DOs job and of particular importance for 'taxation purposes'. In Lugard's vision, tax-collecting, the foundation stone of colonial rule, would 'promote intimate touch' between British officers and natives and would draw in 'inaccessible villages'. In reality, it proved a particularly 'disagreeable business' which provoked strong resistance and hostility.[51] Government-appointed chiefs were delegated to collect native taxes, but among 'primitive and pagan tribes', where there was no recognised central authority, this task fell to the DOs. Officers were instructed to make Africans pay something 'however poor they may appear to be', simply to uphold the principle, and tax-collecting was deeply unpopular, a 'strained and lonely job' where officers were permanently 'keyed up', unsure of when to relax authority or if unrest would erupt. Villages were found deserted, the inhabitants having fled to the forest with their livestock, in which case 'movable' property – for instance, yams and cloth – was distrained to the value of taxes owed (although Lugard stipulated that cash was to be insisted on even if it meant forcing Africans to market to sell goods).[52] In some parts, where more widespread guerrilla-type resistance was encountered, DOs would only travel with an armed escort. Oakley maintained that some 'tribes', like the Idoma of Nigeria, who had a bad reputation as 'disagreeable ... surly ... quarrelsome and dirty ... ', were 'openly hostile'. In particularly tense areas, officers carried loaded revolvers to warn Africans against taking 'unwise actions' or slept with a revolver by their beds.[53] Donald Cameron, as Governor of Nigeria, noted that 'scarcely a period of six months' passed without the need to call out the police or even an armed force. In 1930, after the 'assassination' by 'pagans' of an administrative officer in the political service in Northern Nigeria and the injury of six police constables, British MPs demanded to know what precautions the CO took to safeguard officers' lives. The Anti-Slavery and Aborigines Protection Society also protested against dangers to officers in the Gambia.[54]

Resistance to taxation was put down to the 'fundamental dishonesty' of natives and punished by collective or individual fines, or severe reprisals in the case of threats to officers' lives. In effect, as Walter Crocker, an Australian colonial officer who served in Nigeria in the 1930s and a critic of the administration, pointed out, the world recession had severely squeezed peasant communities. As Hailey (1957) observed, taxation was not only an 'oppressive novelty', but also a hardship and was undoubtedly used to force Africans into labour and cash crop production, altering the whole basis of pre-colonial African labour relationships. Wage labour represented 'white man's work' and deeper exposure to the racial discrimination in the modern labour sector (Asechemie 1997). Thus, colonial taxation constituted a deep cultural imposition of alien accounting practices and concepts of individual agency that assumed African societies were incapable of any logical management of resources.[55]

During the troubled depression years, the extension of direct taxation to untaxed regions combined with deteriorating economic conditions resulted in riots, which severely stretched the 'thin white line'. In February 1931 there was a serious armed uprising in the eastern part of Sierra Leone, led by a Moslem named Adara (Hydara) from French Guinea, whose objective was to free natives from the 'white man's oppression' and to distribute Crown lands among the landless peasants to compensate for the collapse of the palm kernel industry. Hydara called on peasants to refuse the payment of taxes and to drive out British officials. Soldiers were sent to quash the rebellion before it spread to the capital, which resulted in several dead, including Hydara and the English officer in charge of the mission. This important Moslem-inspired revolt contradicted the widely held view that Moslems were more manageable than pagans.[56]

In Nigeria and the Gold Coast, women were actively involved in anti-tax protests, posing additional problems for officers whose administrative 'bibles' said nothing about managing women. Duncan-Johnstone alleged that in the Gold Coast, rioting women were 'worse than men' and Cardinall commented how women 'did not hesitate to assert their rights and liberty'. As Vidrovitch (1997) shows, colonial interventions adversely affected women and threatened to undermine their marketing activities – an economic sector which they traditionally dominated.[57] In the southern Nigerian provinces of Calabar, Owerri (Warri) and the Igbo region, women were in the vanguard of opposition to the extension of taxation to market traders. Trouble began in Calabar in 1925 when the British imposed a market licence. This triggered more general protests over the erosion of women's political and cultural autonomy under colonial rule. Animosity was thus also directed against warrant chiefs who were the instruments of the British policies. Government troops were sent out, but nothing was resolved and trouble erupted again in December 1929 in what the colonial government called the 'Aba' riots (after one of the main towns involved), but which Africans called the 'Women's War'. The riots were sparked off by the orders of a warrant chief to begin a census for taxation purposes, renewing hostility to collaborative African men.

Women's grievances were part of a more generalised unrest resulting from the introduction of the Native Revenue Ordinance and a drop in the price of palm oil, the main export crop. Protest began non-violently with a general trade boycott, hostility to colonial officers and the closure of native courts, but events took a violent turn when police opened fire on angry crowds of women with the subsequent loss of life and the widespread arrests of 'agitators'. Punitive expeditions were sent out to administer a 'severe' lesson to the local population – provoking criticisms in the imperial parliament of the colonial administration.[58] The riots had reputedly caused £20,000 of damage. Fines were arbitrarily imposed and houses burnt down, despite the Governor's instructions that the emphasis was to be on 'pacification and reconstruction'. (Lugard argued that the burning of an African village was 'not a very severe punishment' as grass huts could be 'rebuilt in a few days'.) Order was only re-established in January 1930 and, according to Sylvia Leith-Ross, the South East Nigerian Service was in the 'doldrums' throughout the 1930s with no European sure 'whither he was going'.[59]

Concerns were voiced by British MP's about communist involvement in the 'peasant poll tax riots' and the Colonial Office set up a Commission of Inquiry. Critics of colonial policy, black and white, alleged that, without any formal warning, women armed only with sticks were shot at with rifles and machine guns, resulting in an official casualty list of forty-eight.[60] But for colonial apologists like Margery Perham, the riots constituted an 'extraordinary outbreak' when 'embarrassing mobs' of thousands of women 'destroyed native courts and looted government stations'. Perham attributed the riots to the 'populousness of Owerri province' where roads carried a 'constant stream of [people] on foot, bicycle or omnibus'; at each wayside market there was 'a dense crowd of women' who mobbed strangers with their 'frantic greeting', a 'semi-hysteria' easily converted into riot which could only be quelled by force. In the mythology of the Colonial Service, the colonial officers involved were subsequently vindicated. Sir Andrew Cohen relates the 'often-told story' of a young British officer who calmed a 'great and menacing crowd' of angry women by talking to them and 'turning their laughter against an old woman in the front'. Thus, did 'laughter' resolve many situations in Africa! In his 1956 survey, Hailey referred to the riots, but attributed them primarily to discontent with government warrant chiefs and does not mention any deaths.[61]

This growing unrest highlighted the grave problems of extending the general principles of native administration to more 'backward' areas, where native courts were allegedly weak and 'lacked force' and chiefs were 'disrespectful'.[62] Problems of the imposition of the building blocks of indirect rule, including taxation, were particularly severe in the Gold Coast Colony and Ashanti. In view of the powerful military resistance encountered by the British, argues Wilkes (1996), they could not dismiss the Asante as a 'savage race' and thus emphasised the need to crush the despotic and autocratic Asante state, which had expanded to incorporate non-Asante peoples. Thus, British colonial officials' attitudes to the Asante were a mixture of respect for their 'superior' qualities and anger and frustration over their failure to bend them to their will. After the military defeat of 1895, conflict with the Asante centred on the symbolic authority of the 'Golden Stool' and when Governor Hodgson, asserting his supreme authority, demanded that he should be given the stool to sit on, he was besieged in the fort at Kumasi, which precipitated the last Anglo-Asante war. Asante resistance was crushed and the Crown Colony of Ashanti and the British Protectorate of the Northern Territories of the Gold Coast were established in 1901 and merged with the older Gold Coast Colony, which was centred in Kumasi. However, throughout the colonial period, the three administrations, although united under one Governor, ran distinctive and sometimes divergent policies.[63]

Initially, the British administration tried to undermine the influence of the Asante stool system by promoting minor chiefs, but this policy was only partially successful. Both the Fanti and Asante had articulate intellectuals and well-developed political systems, and, in 1922, the government was forced to recognise the Golden Stool as the supreme symbol of office among the Asante. Chiefly authority, thus remained largely independent of government recognition and district officers had little control over native tribunals. Asante, argues Wilkes (1996), was a dynamic and 'highly politicised state'. Thus, areas which had been under Asante influence continued to assert their traditional democratic practices, which were centred on the symbolic authority of the wider 'stool system'. Local chiefs and headmen were chosen from a number of candidates and, like the occupant of the Golden Stool, could be destooled if their conduct displeased the people.[64] This was regarded as having a very disruptive influence on the smooth running of the administration. Thus, a system of 'paramount chiefs', whose authority was established by the government, not the people, was introduced, precipitating strong opposition. In 1928, a government-appointed *omanhene* (chief) allegedly forced people to carry out 'communal labour'. Duncan-Johnstone reported that, combined with his ' ... notorious quick temper together with his fondness for gin', this nearly resulted in a 'very serious riot [and] his forcible destoolment [removal from office]'.[65]

By 1930, the administration was subject to 'every form of attack' from 'without and within'; the stability of colonial rule was threatened not only by the 'agitators' and discontented educated class, but also by the 'disgruntled' chiefs, who were 'lazy' and unfit to hold office, and 'hordes' of (detribalised) alien labour.[66] The situation declined during the depression years when taxes were raised further to compensate for reduced budgets. As Hailey (1957) observed, until 1935 relations between the colonial government and the Asante and Fanti states were regarded as 'too delicate' for the imposition of direct taxes. With the exception of the Northern Territories, where taxation was introduced in the 1920s, it was some years before a system of direct taxation could be made to function 'with moderate efficiency'. Gold Coast Africans favoured duties on export products where part of the burden fell on the foreign purchaser, but the government was also forced to rely on indirect taxation. During the depression years, liquor imports became important as a source of revenue. However, this conflicted with the moral imperative placed on colonial governments by the international conventions, discussed in Chapter 1, directed at curbing liquor imports in tropical Africa. In the event, African temperance interests secured restrictive legislation and import taxes were raised, but Cardinall suggests that this merely increased the number of illegal stills.[67] Indeed, as Akyeampong (1996) has demonstrated, the widespread brewing of illegal *akpeteshie* (local gin) (which translated is ironically the 'whiteman's shame') as predominantly a working-class drink, became a site of popular struggles against the colonial government. Illegal distillation threatened government revenues, raised the spectre of crime and disorder and became a popular issue in nationalist politics in the 1940s.[68]

As a serving officer in the rapidly developing Western Province of the Gold Coast, Duncan-Johnstone was at the hard edge of these conflicts over extending the principles of native administration in the Gold Coast. He argued that the malfunctioning of indirect rule and discontent over unsuitable chiefs was the direct cause of unrest and provided 'fruitful and subversive soil' for the agitator. Natives would respect a 'firmer grip' and more direct rule would staunch the tide of discontent.[69] In November 1935, as Provincial Commissioner, Duncan-Johnstone had to deal with a serious riot in Wiawso, Western Province, in which four people died and forty-nine were seriously wounded. Trouble first erupted when an unpopular chief threatened to shoot anyone who tried to reclaim disputed property. The faction that opposed the chief was arrested and tension was so high that the local District Commissioner, A.F.C. Wilkinson, brought in police reinforcements and, after a stone fight, banned the sale of liquor. The situation deteriorated, shots were fired, the Riot Act was read and Wilkinson raided 'a number of houses', making two arrests. In an attempt to 'control the young men', a prominent elder who had been arrested earlier was released. More police reinforcements were drafted in, but tension was only finally defused with the ousting of the unpopular *omahene*, the first to succeed in the colony.[70] Both Wilkinson and Duncan-Johnstone were accused by the Governor of mishandling the riot and in Britain there were criticisms of the violent suppression of the riots. Official inquiries were still pursued when Duncan-Johnstone was on leave, although he ultimately came out unscathed and, somewhat ironically, was made Special Commissioner for Political Disputes and Unrest during the Second World War.[71]

The incident graphically illustrates British insensitivity to the strength of local feeling against 'puppet' chiefs, a factor conceded in retrospect by Duncan-Johnstone. The detailed post mortem revealed important differences of opinion between the Secretariat and the officers in the field. The Secretariat felt that Wilkinson was 'too fussy and prone to interfere' at a time of 'political chaos'. He had already been castigated by the Governor, Sir Shenton Thomas, about his clumsy interventions in a legal wrangle over a land dispute in 1933 when the Assistant Commissioner of Police and eighteen divisional chiefs had been prosecuted by the Queen Mother of Ashanti for 'wilful oppression of herself and her people'.[72] At the time of the riots, Wilkinson was under considerable stress and, on medical advice, Johnstone had requested that he should be transferred to a less lonely station. He had reputedly been destined for high office, but became known as a dangerous person, fanatically 'pro-native', who defended area chiefs and African workers against the excesses of the Ashanti Goldfields Corporation. Such actions effectively blocked his promotion and gave him the reputation of being 'aloof' and 'over-conscientious'.[73] Wilkinson was a useful scapegoat, but the real blame for the incident lay in the weaknesses of an unworkable policy imposed from the CO. This was the crux of the conflict between the 'pragmatists' in the colonies who had to actually carry out the imperial mission and the 'idealists' in London. In 1938, in an attempt to implement 'the full measure' of indirect rule', there was a major policy shift which allowed the 'educated community' greater participation in administration and placed more emphasis on development and welfare. However, Hailey argued that this was 'too late', and in trying to to impose 'order', the Gold Coast Government had succeeded to an even lesser extent than in other territories.[74] These acute dilemmas of indirect rule contributed significantly to the development of nationalism, as we shall see in Chapter 4.

The handling of riots throughout West Africa underscored the constant need for force and harsh punishments to maintain order. The law, argued Lugard, 'must be supported by force' to compel obedience and act as a deterrent to resistance. The fictitious Sanders was 'quick to punish', for the people whom he governed had 'no memory' and easily forgot the 'twenty-one with a pliable hippo-hide' and summary hangings. But in the 'real' world, too, individual offenders were exhibited in the stocks, publicly whipped (juveniles for any offence), sentenced to penal servitude in coastal labour colonies, chained in leg irons like the slaves of old and summarily executed without legal defence. There were at least sixty executions in Nigeria in 1929.[75] The government-created native courts had no jurisdiction over whites and any serious crimes relating to 'insurrection', murder, or threats to order where 'superstition' played a part were tried before the white Provincial Courts. These were headed by the Provincial Commissioner or Resident and exercised complete jurisdiction over all persons, native and non-native, and could sanction floggings of up to twelve strokes. In Nigeria, no legal practitioner was allowed to promote the 'fomenting of litigation by [native] lawyers' touts', which, Lugard stressed, was a 'public scandal' in the southern provinces. The ultimate crime, however, was 'exciting enmity against His Majesty', which was punishable by deportation.[76]

Within the Colonial Service, however, the need for such punishments was downplayed and, argued Oakley, the best respected officers were allegedly those who 'handled' natives 'properly' (that is dealt with them as 'naughty but likeable children'). Natives allegedly recognised two grades of white men – those who 'knew how to treat natives' and those who did not. The former were not necessarily 'weak and easy', but 'sympathetic' to pagan ways and keen to protect their charges against those who 'bullied' them. But the colonised were not grateful. Wallace's fictitious Bosambo related how in the 'upper districts' they called Sanders by a 'long and sonorous name', euphemistically translated as 'the man who has a faithless wife'. This 'little joke' was 'mightily subtle' because Sanders was 'wedded to his people'.[77] So how well did the colonial officer really 'know' the Africans in his patch? Whites had power over Africans in every area of their lives, but continued to fear the 'inscrutable' African, the unaccountability of the 'native mind', and the malign force of 'juju' (witchcraft) and other 'sinister' African practices (described by Gorer as 'anti-European' and 'consciously evil'), which interrupted their dreams of rational order. Secret societies, which had a 'mushrooming growth', constituted an area of African life that whites failed to understand and were seen as particularly problematic, heralding 'trouble and war'. Colonial officers recognised the power of African religion and magic, and felt it was 'judicious' to have witch doctors on their side to control the 'swirling tide of superstition that infects the African mind'.[78] However, they failed to stem the increase in witchcraft, cults and 'secret societies' that were, in effect, indicative of critical tensions in colonial society and the need to transcend the fragmented sense of identity resulting from colonial contact.

Anthropology did not aid the understanding of these developments as such practices were interpreted as stagnant, 'primitive' traditions rather than evidence of metamorphosising cultural practices in response to contact with modernity. In retrospect, Hailey (1957) concluded that anthropological studies had been useful in elucidating 'customary rules' of law, marriage and land tenure, but contributed little to understanding the problems of 'maladjustments' in African societies that were created by the extension of Western economic and political institutions.[79] Understanding was further hampered by the fact that many colonial officers remained ignorant of local customs and languages. As Roden Buxton pointed out, some refused to speak anything but English or to reply to Africans who used their own language. Misunderstandings and abuses of indirect rule were made worse by the use of interpreters who, Crocker alleged, had 'undue influence' and were given to 'insolence and sulking' when they received uncongenial orders. Use of interpreters, he argued, also resulted in mutual linguistic misunderstandings inherent in translation, an example of what Sidney Olivier called the 'imperfect … grammar of interracial intercourse', which adversely influenced how whites conceptualised blacks.[80]

White expatriate culture, explored in the following chapter, reinforced difference and distance between white and black to bolster white authority. Certain 'colourful' aspects of African culture – dancing, drumming (particularly the talking drums or 'native telegraph') were valued for their exotic content and 'mysteries', but serving officers were expected to maintain 'official decorum' and it was a 'very bad thing' to get swept away by enthusiasm for the exotic in front of natives.[81] Greatest contact was thus with collaborative Africans, clerks, interpreters, armed escorts (see Illustration 6) and native Government officials who acted as 'go-betweens' and without whom the colonial officer could not have executed the tasks of government. District messengers, argues Bradley, were regarded as the 'backbone' of the administration, 'hand-picked' local men, 'neatly uniformed and absolutely loyal' and were allegedly highly respected as experts in local customs. But 'semi-Europeanised' native clerks rattled whites by their ambiguous and inconsistent behaviour and, according to Kirk-Greene, this was compounded by the 'appalling gap' in competence between the white DO and the African clerk. The tensions in this relationship and insensitivity of whites to the conflicts behind the 'white mask', worn by the blacks who had to move back and forth between the public 'white sphere' and 'private' African sphere, have been skilfully depicted in Joyce Cary's *Mister Johnson* (1939), a novel based on his own experiences as a colonial officer in Northern Nigeria during the First World War.[82]

In this somewhat negative appraisal of colonial officers as the key agents of the imperial mission, I have, of course, looked into the past from a late twentieth century perspective. If we empathise with the mind of the colonial officer and the discourses which shaped his understanding of the world, there were undoubtedly those who respected African chiefs, made an effort to understand local

Illustration 6–N.T.C. Trooper, Tamale
Source: Princess Marie Louise, *Travels in the Gold Coast*, Methuen & Co. Ltd., 1926

cultures and/or had a genuine sense of mission to protect the 'underdog'. A small minority took the ideal of trusteeship literally, interpreting any damage or slight to 'their people' as a personal grievance and thereby became a 'joke' to their colleagues.[83] Kirk-Greene rejects the Sanders image of the arrogant, punishing DO and argues that after 1920 'new needs called for new breeds ... who had brains in their heads as well as fire in their bellies'. However, if the 'man in the field' did genuinely believe in the higher ideals of trusteeship, he found himself frequently frustrated by centrally imposed government policies over which colonial officers had little control. These policies were primarily about order and profit, and they remained at the heart of the imperial mission throughout the colonial era in Africa. As Andrew Cohen, a key figure at the CO during the Second World War stressed, 'Above all the District Commissioner is responsible for keeping law and order'.[84]

Summary

Violence was integral to the creation of colonial Africa and, although administration became more complex and subtle, during the inter-war years, force remained a defining feature of colonial rule. 'Uncivilised man', wrote Lugard, 'regrettably only recognises force and measures its potency by his own losses.'[85] The conflicts and strains faced by the 'man on the spot', which have been discussed in this chapter, highlight the tensions between the discourse of benevolent trusteeship and the imperatives of extending and securing imperial power in West Africa. At heart, the imperial mission was directed to the aggrandisement of white prestige and private profit rather than development in the best interest of Africans. This conditioned the texture of the interaction between the coloniser and colonised, and daily life, as experienced by white agents of empire at the sharp edge of contact with African societies, differed markedly from representations of West Africa in the English imagination. However, despite the recalcitrance of Africans to accept colonial rule, white power could not have been maintained solely through the threat of physical force and other forms of coercion; there was simply not the manpower available. Colonial rule was also sustained by the racist structures of colonial society, and consent was secured through the more subtle workings of cultural imperialism – what Franz Fanon (1966) has termed 'the colonisation of the personality'. Although such cultural power was not monolithic and culture also became a site of struggle, the distorting corset of colonialism trapped colonial societies in a rigidly gendered and racialised system which bolstered white power. It is to the wider expatriate community and the shaping of this 'colonial culture', both white and African, that we now turn.

3 Expatriate society

Race, gender and the culture of imperialism

No colony can be made by a benevolent theory of imperialism ... it is chiefly made by efficient and practical interest and by ... people who are capable of maintaining themselves as colonists.

(Lord Sidney Olivier, 1929)

Here were tin-roofed, concrete bungalows, and calling cards, and morning bridge for the ladies. There were at least a dozen women here; and afternoon teas and good roads and everyone had a car, and there were dances once a week and dinners that lasted till midnight every other day or so. And everyone was bored, and had malaria, and most of them drank too much, and all of them gossiped. And I loathed it.

(Erick Berry, colonial officer's wife, Zaria, Nigeria, 1930s)[1]

The last chapter explored the formal structures of imperial power and the masculine world of the colonial officer. But such power was also routinised into the fabric of everyday life, expressed through the spacial and social segregation of white and African and the diverse strategies of cultural imperialism. Colonial whites evolved an 'expatriate' culture which reinforced and amplified the cultural power gap between ruler and ruled, legitimising the imperial mission. Fundamental to the culture of imperial rule in West Africa were the rituals and bonding 'traditions' of the small, dispersed expatriate society which, argues Ranger (1983), were invented to make European activities in Africa more respectable and orderly.[2] It was a culture underpinned by strict codes of behaviour, but also one of anomie and decadence. Both men and women had more personal power than would ever have been possible 'back home'. They thus constituted 'a superior caste living an artificial life removed from all the healthy restraints of ordinary European society' who, Hobson argued, had a 'baleful influence' in both colony and metropole.[3] Racist discourse structured the texture of the interaction between the coloniser and the colonised, and expatriate identities derived from a gendered and racialised order which confirmed white superiority. In this chapter, I critically evaluate the nature of expatriate society and the 'white walls' it erected to preserve power and prestige. Through a comparison of white and African women, I confirm the importance of gender in articulating racial discourse and argue that, whereas white women were vital to 'civilising' the colonial frontier and strengthening the racial order, black women posed the major threat to the stability of colonial society. In the final section, I examine the ways in which the white rulers attempted to bond the colonised to the imperial project through 'invented traditions' and other forms of cultural imperialism.

Colonial racial attitudes did not develop in isolation, but were fostered by imperial discourse generated in the corridors of imperial power in Britain. However, on the imperial frontier, where it was vital to uphold white prestige, such attitudes were amplified. Any inexperienced colonial official could become a 'white chief' of a huge area and, in both the government and business sector, white men had inordinate power over African men and women. But in the 'model' West Africa colonies resident whites argued that the 'separate but equal' basis of indirect rule ensured that there was no race prejudice, unlike in India or South Africa, and relatively congenial race relations prevailed.[4] British West Africa was also favourably compared to French West Africa. French officers were drawn from the lower middle classes and were described by the writer, Geoffrey Gorer, as 'petit bourgeoisie turned Caesars' in contrast to the 'gentlemanly' British Colonial Service. Moreover, the French were not averse to employing 'men of half-blood' from the French West Indies or Indochina in their West African colonies at senior levels.[5] Contemporary accounts also allude to the low-class whites in the French colonies; the 'brutalised and degraded' poor, white women and prostitutes in Senegal and the cattle drivers, plantation overseers, shop hands and dockers living a hand-to-mouth existence in the Cameroons. This poor, white 'flotsam and jetsam', it was argued, was generally absent from British West Africa.[6] However, Graham Greene, who described himself as an 'innocent' in West Africa, presented a generalised picture of the disease, vermin and 'lethargy of daily life', where bored Europeans, slumped in 'squalor and unhappiness' consumed excessive amounts of alcohol 'from breakfast to bed-time'. Colonial officers also spoke of the 'routine boredom' and mercenary ethos.[7] The reality of 'non-settler', colonial societies was arguably somewhere between the bleak Hobbesian vision of chaos and decay, intimated by writers like Greene and Waugh, and the Panglossian utopia of colonial apologists. While the *corps d'elite* of the Colonial Service tried to 'keep up standards', there were dark undercurrents of miscegenation, degeneracy and violence. If the more obvious decadence and 'White Mischief' of white settler colonies like Kenya was muted in West Africa, racism, cruelty and aberrant behaviour were not uncommon among both government and 'business' whites.[8]

So what, then, was the texture of expatriate life? A veneer of 'normality' existed in the more sophisticated urban centres, where Europeans created a social life which revolved around dinner parties, clubs and sporting activities, such as tennis, polo, gymkhanas and cricket matches. Such social activities were regarded as important in maintaining morale and fostering the social integration of whites and, as Governor of Nigeria, Lugard had advocated the 'provision of a club house, recreation grounds (golf course, polo grounds) and parade grounds' where Europeans could meet regularly. White social networks were also oiled by the small European press and the introduction of the telephone and telegraph. Through such social activities, expatriate whites retained what Graham Greene termed 'a patriotism in the dust', centred on the clubhouse, their very own 'bit of England'. Back home, Africa 'hands' met in certain clubs to keep in contact while on leave or after retirement. The Corona Club (men only until 1937 when the Women's Corona Club was established), which had its own magazine, bonded together the expatriates of the Colonial African Service (CAS). Thus, in the English colonies 'going native' was the worst thing a white man could do. Although some 'rogues and outcasts' succumbed to Africa and 'went black', the majority distanced themselves from inferior African culture and tried to 'keep up standards' despite the lack of cultural outlets.[9]

Bonding rituals created a symbolic home away from home. British 'tribal ceremonies', 'Caledonian gatherings', Scottish dancing and 'various forms' of British sport were the 'compensations' of a tropical African posting – the 'lifelines of the British abroad'.[10] Social entertainment consisted of dances, fancy-dress parties, amateur theatricals, gymkhanas and dinner parties that were often followed by dancing to the gramophone, a precious link with 'civilisation', even in the bush. In 'Trousers over Africa' the fetish of 'dressing for dinner' is satirised by Beachcomber (J.B. Morton) in his *Daily Express* column when the political officer, 'Big White Carstairs', visits the residency and finds that his native servant had forgotten to pack his dress suit. Carstairs cannot come down to dinner as it is only 'Bolsheviks' or 'grammar school types' who dare to wear day clothes in the evening. After all, 'What would the natives think?'[11] At such dinners, English food, mainly out of tins, was the staple diet with African cooks pouring over the ubiquitous Mrs Beeton. However, the serving of certain foods culturally specific to the area was also important in forging a unique West African expatriate identity. Ground-nut stew or palm oil chop, described by the fictitious Sanders as 'a delicious kind of coast curry', was the West African equivalent of Indian curry and was usually eaten at Sunday lunch-times. As in India, the expatriate English language became spattered with a few 'native' words – usually from servant 'pidgin' – and was household-related. Food was 'chop' and 'small chop', and 'gadgets' were served as canapés before dinner.[12]

The anachronistic uniform of the tropics, seen as 'very old-fashioned' by younger officers in the 1930s – the spine pads, tropical suits and puttees, cholera belts and pith helmets – provided visual identity. The danger of the sun was an obsession and, if buildings were not 'sunproof', hats had to be worn even when inside. Erick Berry refers to an almost 'hysterical' belief that 'a shaft of sunlight no wider than a hatpin [could] strike ... through the brain'. Women wore the 'double terai', which was wide-brimmed and made of heavy felt and, literally, was one hat over another. The midday sun, however, required a pith helmet which was 'unpleasant' and unflattering to wear. Such hats were worn by colonial and 'business' wives alike. The tropical sun was supposed to have 'actinic rays' which occurred in the violet and ultra-violet parts of the spectrum, producing chemical changes in the brain. This susceptibility to sun differentiated the tender whites from the natives who, of course, did not suffer from the heat. The belief in sunstroke (which was, arguably, heat-stroke induced by all the heavy hats and clothing) persisted until the Second World War, when British soldiers walked about bare-headed with no obvious effect and thus exploded a major white myth.[13]

Historical 'sites of memory' were also important in furnishing a sense of continuity and reinforcing imperial myths of conquest and colonisation. In the Gold Coast, Kumasi Day was celebrated every 5 July to mark the end of the siege in 1900; photographs of officers, who were active in campaigns against the Ashanti, and the message sent from the besieged fort were 'treasured relics' of the Gold Coast Regimental mess. After visiting the mess, Princess Marie Louise reminded her sister of the photograph that always hung in 'Mother's room' of 'Christle' (her brother, Prince Christian Victor, who fought in the 1895 Ashanti wars) and a fellow officer seated on 'chop boxes' under the British flag at Kumasi. Such private memorabilia, from the highest to the lowliest British families, were also vital in sustaining a more general culture of imperialism.[14] The British monarchy was central to bonding expatriate culture. Members of the royal family had actively participated in the imperial project: the men as soldiers; the women as patrons of good works. 'Liko', Prince Henry of Battenburg, succumbed to malaria in the Gold Coast in 1896, while 'Christle' died in Pretoria during the South African War. The Princess Christian Hospital in Freetown, Sierra Leone, was a cause 'near to Mother's heart' and Marie Louise patronised the West African Nursing Service. When she visited the infants hospital in Accra, she distributed royal bounty with a prize from the Queen for the baby show.[15] Marie Louise followed her cousin, 'David', the Prince of Wales, who also toured West Africa in 1925. Such royal visits represented ritual confirmations of imperial power and the role of the monarchy as protectors of the native peoples.

While elements of expatriate society forged a common identity, there were also important differences between whites, which affected their perceptions of and relationships with Africans. The Colonial Service was strictly regulated by protocol. At the pinnacle was the Governor, representing the Crown, and his administrators in the Secretariat. These 'real rulers' were supposed to be there 'for the good of the ruled', although in Graham Greene's estimation they did not live up to their pious claims. Their cosseted lifestyles contrasted starkly with those of the isolated officers in the 'bush'. Princess Marie Louise recalls the luxurious comforts – electricity, soft carpets, fresh flowers, the lavish hospitality and the luxury car – at the residency in Kumasi. The elite of the lower ranks of the Colonial Administration were the political officers, who were regarded as 'Class A' whites. Technical or welfare officers and skilled white workers in government service only ranked 'Class B'. The tiny, expatriate white community also included businessmen, mining engineers, traders and employees of the Bank of British West Africa, but 'commerce and government' allegedly seldom mixed, except officially, and 'the missions kept aloof from both'.[16]

Colonial officials, argues Phillips (1990), luxuriated in an 'anti-capitalist bias', and the business and public sector maintained separate social spheres. There is some substance in this position given that the 'high culture' of the colonies was defined by the official ruling elites. But, as emphasised in Chapter 2, business interests were encouraged and protected by the colonial state, and at the top end of society there was arguably a convergence of interests and similarity of class backgrounds and lifestyles that led to more social mixing. Princess Marie Louise visited a number of private households, mainly in the mining areas of the Gold Coast, accompanied by Governor Guggisberg and his wife, Decima. The 'delightful' bungalow of Mr Holmes, the Secretary for Mines, and his 'charming wife' had the rare 'blessing' of electric light and fans and equalled the residency in comfort. While colonial officials and governors could not become directors of companies in which they had served until a specified period had elapsed, they often subsequently took up such positions, and governors and higher officials were recruited from the same social circles as directors of companies with imperial interests. Lord Lugard, for instance, reputedly had 'extensive interests' and was 'a well-known business man'.[17] The importance of the private sector to the colonial economy is also reflected in Cadbury Hall, a training college for agricultural students, which was built by the Gold Coast Government through the 'generosity' of Cadbury Brothers in appreciation of the 'energetic manner in which cocoa had been developed on the Gold Coast'.[18]

There were, however, differences between the ethos of business and Colonial service. Commerce in Africa was regarded as 'an escape', if only temporary, from the routine in Britain and, as with today's expatriates, a means of substantially increasing one's income and status. In Greene's estimation, the more instrumental businessmen and mining workers were more openly racist, but less hypocritical, in their attitudes to Africans than the administration. Yet, men in the private sector also shared the same pioneering spirit and sense of adventure as those in government service.[19] Moreover, all British whites constituted the superior caste within the small but diverse society of non-African residents, which developed with the expansion of colonialism. In Nigeria, for instance, there were 5,442 'non-natives', with 2,500 men in government service and 283 Syrian males. A similar profile, including a sprinkling of 'other Europeans' and black West Indians, usually missionaries and teachers, existed in the Gold Coast (see Table 1). Europeans were strictly differentiated from the inferior Syrian and Lebanese traders and shopkeepers who, in turn were regarded as superior to educated West Indians and Africans.[20] All these groups were superior to the mass of Africans.

Spatial segregation in urban and rural areas physically enforced racial boundaries and minimised 'racial pollution'. As Governor of Nigeria, Frederick Lugard justified a wide space (at least 440 yards) between the 'European reservation' and native dwellings on 'hygiene grounds' and to protect against disease and the noise of drumming. Segregation from the 'general African population' was also recommended by the Gold Coast Director of Medical and Sanitary Services. While the threat of disease was undoubtedly real (Cardinall recorded that in the Gold Coast, malaria and yellow fever were responsible for at least 50 per cent of white deaths), segregation was also justified on the basis of the undesirability of

Table 1 The non-African population of the Gold Coast, 1931

Nationality	Males				Females			
	1921	1931	Inc.	Dec.	1921	1931	Inc.	Dec.
British*	1480	1472	—	8	149	371	222	—
American	25	14	—	11	3	4	1	—
Arab	—	1	1	—	—	—	—	—
Austrian	—	1	1	—	—	1	1	—
Belgian	4	1	—	3	1	1	—	—
Bulgarian	—	1	1	—	—	—	—	—
Chinese	—	1	1	—	—	—	—	—
Danish	3	2	—	1	—	—	—	—
Dutch	7	38	31	—	2	5	3	—
French	73	138	65	—	6	19	13	—
German	1	68	67	—	1	18	17	—
Greek	7	24	27	—	—	2	2	—
Indian	14	56	42	—	—	—	—	—
Italian	59	98	39	—	—	5	5	—
Lithuanian	1	—	—	1	—	—	—	—
Norwegian	1	—	—	1	—	—	—	—
Romanian	—	1	1	—	—	—	—	—
Russian	—	1	1	—	—	—	—	—
Spanish	—	1	1	—	—	—	—	—
Swedish	—	1	1	—	—	—	—	—
Swiss	78	125	57	—	2	16	14	—
Syrian	72	390	308	—	44	180	136	—
Turkish	—	1	1	—	—	1	1	—
West Indian	—	17	17	—	—	3	3	—
Total	1825	2452	627	25	208	626	418	—

Source: A.W. Cardinall, *The Gold Coast, 1931*, Accra, 1932, p. 258
Notes
* Includes 541 civil servants

too much 'social intercourse' or familiarisation between European and African. For instance, the Nigerian Townships Ordinance (1917) stipulated that no natives, except bona fide domestic servants were to reside in the European reservation (at least fifty yards to the rear of white residences) and no European was allowed to live in non-European areas. Rest houses, which provided temporary accommodation for travellers, were also segregated and natives who used a house set aside for Europeans were 'liable to punishment'.[21]

White towns mapped out white space and arguably provided the model for the 'post-colonial', racialised western city. As urbanisation accelerated, it was even more vital to segregate the expanding 'colonial slum' from the European cities. An obsession with sanitation took hold of the colonial imagination which, argues Goldberg (1994), constituted a 'social metaphor' for the pollution of white urban space by uncivilised Africans.[22] Lugard was particularly concerned with the cleaning up and regulating of urban 'native' markets in order to exclude 'objectionable persons [thieves and prostitutes]' who frequently adopted the role of 'itinerant hawker' and were 'dirty and unsanitary'. (In the Gold Coast, for instance, the upward trend in the consumption of imported wheaten flour had resulted in an increase in female bakers who hawked their goods in markets or from door-to-door.)[23] Sexual and physical pollution, the spread of immorality and venereal diseases thus became associated particularly with African women.

White expatriate communities were visualised as enclaves defending the order of civilisation against the forces of disorder and degeneracy. However, at times, the complacency of these enclosed and parochial communities was threatened by potentially destabilising influences from the 'enemy within' – whites who did not wholly conform to the 'culture' of colonialism and/or the imperial dream of civilising mission or profit. Anyone critical of the administration, like Graham Greene (who was accompanied on his travels by a female cousin), were distrusted. 'Independent' anthropologists were also sometimes at odds with the colonial administrations. According to Goody (1995), the South African, Meyer Fortes, was nearly blocked entry into the Gold Coast in 1933 by the Governor, Sir Shenton Thomas, who described him as 'a particularly nasty type of Jew'. He was also 'undesirable' because he was associated with the Fabian left and reformist 'anti-colonialism'. In 1931, the International African Institute had to cancel the trip of another anthropologist, the German, Kirchhoff, on Colonial Office intelligence that his wife was a communist and that he had been involved in left-wing activities in Berlin before he had left Germany.[24] Whites who seriously deviated from the norm, particularly those suspected of communist sympathies, were ostracised by this highly conformist society. In Accra in 1930, the American Quaker, Anna Melissa Graves, who spent six months in West Africa, maintains that she was 'frozen out' of white society when she spent seven weeks in the Gold Coast, because she was too friendly with blacks. Even Alec Fraser, the liberal principal of Achimota College, who she had met at a 'Save the Children Conference' in Geneva in 1930 and with whom she had a 'lengthy correspondence', was 'cold' on her arrival. Graves eventually stayed with a coloured Accra family and declared that she found the Gold Coast a 'particularly bad place' for blacks, who were liable at all times to be insulted. In letters to anti-colonial activists in England, Graves complained about her 'persecution' and the Labour Secretary of State for Colonies, Drummond Shiels, sent a 'personal' letter to the Governor of the Gold Coast about the affair.[25]

Expatriate culture was defined through racial and cultural segregation, a sense of belonging and 'unbelonging'. Anthias and Yuval Davis (1992) assert that in the empire, 'Englishness was not threatened but glorified by the proximity of the colonised' – comparing this to the threat to English identity posed by the increase in black migrants in the 1950s.[26] But, arguably, the exaggerated Englishness of expatriate culture, the ultra-masculinity and stifling protocol of a society out of time with metropolitan Britain, suggests a threatened society that had to defend its culture. 'The typical colonial', wrote Eslanda Goode Robeson, 'seems to me weak, uncomfortably self-conscious, lonely, pathetic and frightened'. Such fear was reflected not only in the need to travel armed, but also in the fear of racial pollution, which was reflected in the strict policing of racial borders and white sexuality. This is where white women became important, acting as a moralising influence, tempering male behaviour, creating a more 'civilised' expatriate society and facilitating the expansion and retention of empire. As 'boundary makers of empire', women were thus fundamental to shaping the racialised culture of colonial society.[27]

'Colonial woman': civilising the 'Wild West' frontier?

'I am convinced', wrote Princess Marie Louise, 'that we do not sufficiently recognise the magnificent and unselfish part played by women in these distant and little known outposts of empire'. 'Colonial woman' was expected to be tough, plucky and healthy as opposed to the 'delicate flower' of Victorian representation. Yet, as Callaway (1987) argues, in the imperial model of gender relations white women remained constrained by rigid gender roles that confirmed the ultra-masculine ethos of the colonial 'gentlemanly order' and white men's eligibility to rule. A romanticised view of imperial masculinity is evident in the writings of Margery Perham, who as 'striking, attractive and athletic' would have made an ideal colonial wife. Although she never married, she had great admiration for her powerful imperialist patrons like Lugard and, argues Lavin (1991), always secretly hankered after marriage to a colonial 'hero' to 'fulfil her femininity'.[28] The presence of white women enhanced the glamorised image of the white male in contrast to 'dependent', 'child-like' African male, and white femininity was the reference point against which representations of African women were constructed. Visual contrasts between black and white women were starkly highlighted in snapshots of 'Native Beauties' and 'Belles' by women travellers like Lady Dorothy Mills (Illustration 7). Such stilted products of the 'white gaze' are very different from the more naturalistic snapshot of an African woman taken by the black American, Eslanda Goode Robeson (Illustration 10). Thus, as Ware (1992) argues, contrasts between black and white women were central to

Illustration 7 – Women travellers to West Africa: Lady Dorothy Mills
Source: Lady D. Mills, The Golden Land: A Record of Travel in West Africa, London: Duckworth, 1929.

articulations of whiteness and representations of white women as the very embodiment of civilisation.[29]

White women confirmed the permanence and vitality of expatriate society. From 1920, the Colonial Office encouraged married life in the African colonies as a stabilising influence and to cut down on 'moral lapses'. In the larger urban centres, argued Duncan-Johnstone, it was women who made it possible to recreate some semblance of a 'normal' social life, which centred around the club and the residency.[30] Overall, the gender balance remained noticeably skewed towards men. The 1931 Nigerian census recorded 1,066 'non-native' females – less than a quarter of the expatriate male population. Statistics for the Gold Coast reflect a similar pattern (Table 2) and the discrepancy between married men and women (Table 3) indicates that many men still left their wives 'back home'.[31] However, by the 1930s the numbers of wives joining their husbands, including 'business wives', had increased substantially in comparison with the early 1920s. There had also been an increase in professional women employed in the expanding 'welfare' branches of the Colonial African Service. However, married women remained in the majority and Callaway (1987) argues that single women, at the bottom of the expatriate hierarchy, needed to find a husband to gain acceptance in expatriate society. The lowest class of white women were nurses, first recruited into the Colonial Service in 1896, who, argues Birkett (1992), faced class prejudices by more 'respectable' wives who sometimes accused them of 'improper behaviour'.[32] Women's status in expatriate society thus depended on whether they were 'outside' or 'inside' the administration, married to a governor or a district officer, stationed in the 'remote bush' or the colony's capital. Apart from a small minority, however, most women were from the classes that constituted the 'gentlemanly diaspora' and shared common values and ideas about the imperial mission.

White women's writings on Africa reflect the power of a common imperial discourse relating to 'natives'. In addition to the memoirs of colonial wives who recorded their 'adventurous' lives in West Africa, transient visitors – wealthy travellers and explorers, anthropologists and colonial specialists – also wrote

Table 2 Females as a proportion of the total non-African population of the Gold Coast

	Male	*Female*	*Total*
Gold Coast Colony	1839	465	2304
Ashanti	491	133	624
Northern Territories	89	18	107
Togoland	33	10	43
Total	2442	626	3078

Source: A.W. Cardinall, *The Gold Coast, 1931*, Accra, 1932, p. 256
Note:
Of the 626 females, 425 were married. The remainder included 66 girls under 15 years and 141 females engaged in various work (including 9 doctors, 63 missionaries, 23 nurses, 19 teachers and 3 secretaries).

Table 3 The marital status of the non-African population

Province	Married		Unmarried		Widowed		Divorced		Total		Grand total
	M	F	M	F	M	F	M	F	M	F	
Western Province	332	92	233	11	9	2	5	—	576	105	684
Central Province	101	30	140	23	3	1	—	—	244	54	298
Eastern Province	453	206	547	92	13	8	3	—	1016	306	1322
Ashanti	234	81	249	46	7	6	1	—	491	133	624
Northern Territories	26	12	62	6	1	—	—	—	89	18	107
Togoland	11	4	22	6	—	—	—	—	343	10	43
Maritime	36	—	67	—	1	—	—	—	104	—	104
Totals	1193	425	1320	184	34	17	9	—	2556	626	3182

Source: A.W. Cardinall, *The Gold Coast, 1931*, Accra, 1932, p. 257

about their African experiences. Adventurous, wealthy British women had long been drawn to the 'Dark Continent', travelling alone with only native 'boys' to help them. The inter-war years saw a new genre of travel writing by independent, 'emancipated' women epitomised by Lady Dorothy Mills (see Illustration 7), who could afford to indulge in an increasingly popular exoticism of Africa which was reflected in the vogue for African dance and art. It was the emotional appeal of 'uncivilised' African music and the 'animal-like beauty of savages' that drew Mills to Africa, but her text consistently comments on and legitimises white rule. Princess Marie Louise fits into this category of modern women adventurers, but had additional kudos as an official royal visitor. She had travelled previously to the Congo and was in Kenya in 1928, but, as a direct descendent of Christian VII of Denmark, in whose reign Christianborg Castle had been built, the Gold Coast held a 'special appeal'. She was the first member of the royal family to visit some of the remoter West African areas and her letters to her sister, Princess Helena Victoria, provide rich insight into colonial society in the 1920s. Aged fifty-three, she enthusiastically trekked (by Lanchester and lorry) over 2,500 miles (see Illustration 8) without once getting ill, loved the 'wonderful roving life' in the African bush and had a keen interest in the customs of the people she met.[33]

Women were thus increasingly breaching the last frontiers of an ultra-masculine world and some men deeply resented women's presence as an intrusion on their freedom (including sexual freedom), particularly in isolated rural postings. District Officer Haig maintained that matrimony in Southern Nigerian 'bush society' was virtually an 'abhorred subject' and in some mining areas it was

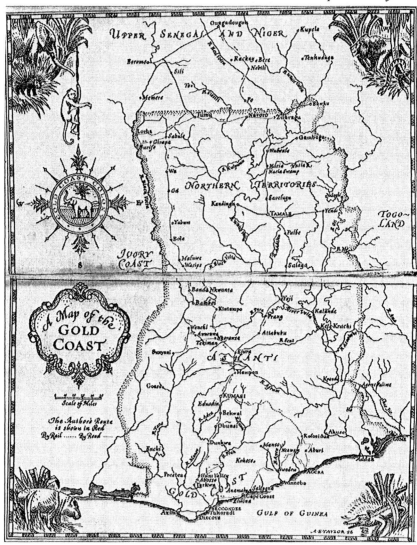

Illustration 8–Map of Princess Marie Louise's tour through the Gold Coast
Source: Princess Marie Louise, *Travels in the Gold Coast*, Methuen & Co. Ltd., 1926

believed that 'unoccupied' women were a serious liability and bachelor-only accommodation was provided. Wives were 'much left alone' with numerous male servants and became victims of boredom and a 'desolation that would drive many men to drink'.[34] Women also caused breaches in male comradeship. 'Unaccustomed to the freedom from household chores' they became involved in 'intrigues' at the club or committed adultery with their husband's colleagues. Duncan-Johnstone noted how the newly married wife of the DC at Tamale, Gold Coast, 'only had eyes' for another officer at the station. One ex-colonial wife recalled that Africa was a 'terribly tempting place' for a woman as there were many bachelors buzzing around women 'like bees round a honeypot'.[35] Such anecdotes depict colonial wives, immersed in the trivialities of expatriate life, as a liability in an ordered, masculine colonial society. Sylvia Leith-Ross argued that compared with earlier 'pioneering wives', like herself, such wives lived comparatively luxurious lives in the bigger expatriate centres, were prey to petty jealousies and 'small rumours' and were consumed with ambition for their husbands. However, the memoirs of other colonial wives suggest that their lives were far from easy; some women hated being in Africa, missed their children (there were few white children in West Africa before the Second World War) and never really fitted into the social life. Duncan-Johnstone observed that women 'quickly lost their looks' in the cruel tropical heat, suffered from ill-health (his own wife had malaria and paratyphoid) and some even paid the 'supreme sacrifice' for their country.[36]

Despite these drawbacks, Duncan-Johnstone and other officers maintained that a good wife, who saw marriage as a career, could be a considerable asset and an excellent 'all round' companion for her husband if she accepted her 'enormous responsibility' and kept her 'nerve'. The best wives were those with a strong constitution who were 'efficient – keen – and sensible', willing to go on 'treks' (or tour) and interested in the country and their husbands' work.[37] The trek was particularly appealing to the 'right sort of woman', although standards still had to be kept up and a comprehensive 'bush kit', which included 'hideous', but compulsory, mosquito boots had to be carried. Clothes retained importance in defining the borders between the civilised and the primitive, even in the 'far bush'. When on a trek, Decima Guggisberg, wife of the Governor of the Gold Coast, wore a 'Paris creation of spotless white drill', thin stockings and 'party shoes' which, suggests Princess Marie Louise, who wore her comfortable 'bush kit' of short skirt, shirt and high boots, was a 'trifle too impractical'.[38] Dressing for dinner by hurricane lamp and travelling through tropical rains sorely tested powers of endurance and ingenuity. Cars frequently became bogged down (see Illustration 9), and in Ouagadougou, French Upper Volta, a race meeting organised for the Princess was wrecked and the ladies 'soaked to the skin'. But, if they were the outdoor sort, women could enjoy themselves riding, shooting and hunting alongside the men. Marie Louise went on an expedition to the Volta and her escorts, Captains Eyre-Smith and Puckridge, desperate because there were no hippos, tried to out-do each other in colonial masculinity by both 'blazing away' at a poor crocodile. Afterwards they had a 'perfect English breakfast' of eggs, bacon, coffee and marmalade. In their memoirs many colonial wives referred to the 'special quality' of days touring the 'bush' when they could absorb themselves in the colonial spectacle of 'native performances' and African life.[39]

Whether on trek or at home, however, women were highly dependent on their male servants. The intimacy allowed between white women and African male domestic servants, who were 'feminised' as 'houseboys', is particularly illuminative of the gender/race order in colonial society. In an inversion of British

Illustration 9–Bogged in the Nasia Swamp

Source: Princess Marie Louise, *Travels in the Gold Coast*, Methuen & Co. Ltd., 1926

society, domestic help in the colonies was almost exclusively male and the West African 'Missus', who had sole responsibility for household management and entertaining, wielded considerable power over her indispensable 'boy'. 'Boys', who were often migrants from other areas and assumed to be 'dishonest', could sometimes be a 'great trial' and, as in other expatriate societies, the 'servant problem' was a perennial source of club conversation. Yet, if one had 'infinite patience', they could be made into good servants who produced some 'excellent' meals given the 'sameness' of the food available.[40]

White women had a strangely intimate relationship with African men as 'personal maids'. 'Boys' pulled baths for them and helped them with dressing and general toilette. On treks, Princess Marie Louise's 'boy', Malam, was indispensable – he washed clothes, sewed, kept her wardrobe tidy and helped her to hook up her dress and arrange her hair in the dark. Decima Guggisberg also had her favourite 'boy', James. When her 'boy' became sick, Marie Louise's lady-in-waiting, Alice Harrington Stuart, would have been left helpless and 'maidless', a serious plight in the 'bush', if Major Leigh Walker had not come to the rescue and offered one of his 'boys'. 'Zani' or 'Ali' (she could not get his name right), helped Alice in the 'mysteries of her toilette' and when she became unwell proved an 'excellent nurse' who looked after the 'small missus' in a most assiduous and 'touching' way.[41] Such 'boys' never posed a sexual threat to white women. Contemporary representations of the 'native' as safe, quiescent and completely under the power of white, male rulers neutralised black male sexual potency. White gender power relations were expressed through a strict double standard and, although white women/black men relationships existed in England, West Africa was 'no place for the wife of a black man'.[42] Powerful sexual taboos thus policed white female sexuality, which could only be broken covertly. We can but speculate if such sexual taboos were secretly breached; stories of bored white women furtively seducing black men are, however, well integrated into African folk mythology about the colonial period. The film, *Chocolat* (1989), set in the French Cameroons in the 1950s and based on real-life experiences, explores sexual power dynamics between a white, colonial wife and a black butler (who ironically resists the white woman's advances).[43] Such hints of suppressed and forbidden sexuality demonstrate the ambiguous responses of both men and women in close contact with Africans, although such relations tended to confirm rather than challenge the racism which sculpted colonial societies.

The relationship between white women and racism is a contentious issue. Octavio Mannoni (1964) in his classic study of colonial society in Madagascar suggested that racial superiority, particularly the domination of black men, could compensate for white women's subordination to white male power. But how relevant is this to West Africa? Sir Alan Burns, Governor of the Gold Coast, 1941–7, and J.H. Oldham both argued that women were 'always more prejudiced' than men and according to Macmillan (1938) some colonial administrators believed that the artificial nature of white women's existence in the non-settler colonies intensified racial segregation and 'race feeling' among African leaders.[44] Callaway (1987) rejects such views, maintaining that white women 'feminised' colonialism and were seminal in promoting greater racial tolerance and fostering 'mutual understanding' between whites and Africans.[45] Challenging the stereotype of the 'shallow, self-centred and narrow-minded' white woman, she argues for a more positive revaluation of women of the empire. However, Callaway is undoubtedly influenced by her own personal experience of Nigerian expatriate society during and after the Second World War when 'race relations' discourse became more acceptable. Callaway's research, argues Jane Haggis (1990), prioritises gender relations between white men and women, sanitises out the 'nasty aspects of colonialism' and exonerates white women from the racist character of colonial society.[46]

My own evidence suggests that 'colonial women' were tightly bound into the whole colonial project and vital to the development of a white supremacist, expatriate culture and broader discourses of race and imperialism. The 'feminisation' of colonial society did little to change negative conceptions of Africans and arguably the only difference between male and female colonial narratives was that women took marginally more 'maternalist' interest in the lives of African women. However, for white women, relations with African women were far more complex than those with African men. Margery Perham's novel, *Major Dane's Garden* (1925), a somewhat lengthy and mediocre novel written when she was twenty-four and based on personal experiences, illuminates the more problematic aspects of the gender order in 'tropical' Africa. The main theme of the book is the contrast between the slightly eccentric but 'good' officer, Major Dane, the 'man of action' and civilised integrity who is unselfish in his devotion to the natives, and Colonel Cavell, who is cold and distant towards his wife. While Cavell is away suppressing native unrest, Cavell's wife, Rhona, and Dane fall in love and when Cavell returns he admits to moral lapses, inferring sexual relations with black women: 'I've been no better and no worse than other white men ... Drink ... *and the other things* [my emphasis] ... even after our marriage.' The outcome is that Rhona Cavell returns to England and Dane, the perfect specimen of colonial masculinity, nobly disappears into the interior.[47]

Behind this colonial morality tale is an oblique criticism of white men's lust for black women, which was a threat to the moral fabric of expatriate society. Representations of black women as sexual temptresses contrasted starkly with the superior qualities of white women. As Haggis (1990) points out, studies of white gender relations have done little to challenge such representations and black women, argues Haggis, have remained invisible, 'buried deep beneath the weight of white women's vision'. Yet black women's presence liberated women from the 'good/bad' duality of metropolitan culture and was central to the construction of white women's privileged identities.[48] Thus, in analysing the relationship between white power, racism and the colonial gender order, it is also important to deconstruct white representations of African women.

'Dark rapture': African women and the colonial gender order

A contemporary observer, Felix Bryk, alleged that white men in Africa suffered from loneliness, were greatly tempted by drink and 'debauchery' and became 'strongly dependent' on the 'dark rapture' of native women.[49] White men's attitudes to African women epitomise most forcefully the simultaneous repulsion and fascination whites felt for 'mysterious' Africa. On the surface, white men declared that they found black women repulsive and made adverse comparisons between lustful black women, who desecrated the 'mystic quality of a woman's loveliness', and the 'English rose' admired for the 'implicitly superior' qualities valued by Englishmen. African women epitomised the 'dark' continent. Colonial officers stressed the 'debilitating' effect, mental and spiritual, of too close contact with the primitive, the unnerving 'ju-ju-worship and sensuality' of the African bush and the 'psychological curse' of black women's nakedness, 'flaunted' in a 'lustful and animal-like' fashion. This 'horrible desirability' of black women resulted in a dangerous sexual frustration.[50]

However, miscegenation breached the borders of the imperial colour bar, the basis of order and power, and 'half-castes' were synonymous with degeneracy and danger. In his epic, *Sex and Race* (1944), J.A. Rogers claimed that, in keeping with their disparaging attitudes towards black women, Englishmen ignored illegitimate offspring and underplayed the numbers of 'half-castes', in contrast with their counterparts in French West Africa, who openly took African wives and acknowledged children born out of wedlock. Such attitudes are reflected in *Sanders of the River* when 'Sandi' is forced to send two officers home after they have been seduced by a black woman (he breathes a sigh of relief when he discovers she is not pregnant). This inflammatory miscegenation was censored out of the film version and the temptress, M'Lino, was transformed into Bosambo's wife with the full blessing of 'Lord Sandi'. 'Half-castes' were represented as the worst element of the despised and 'troublesome' minority of 'Europeanised' natives. Carrying the most undesirable characteristics of both races, they were duplicitous and untrustworthy, or violent and criminal, the 'worst' material in Africa'.[51]

The colonial authorities were thus officially opposed to liaisons with native women. In 1909 the Colonial Secretary issued an order, 'Circular A', which prohibited officers from sleeping with African women, warning that officers who persisted in such behaviour would suffer 'disgrace and official ruin'. This was withdrawn in 1934 on the instructions of the Secretary of State for Colonies, Cunliffe-Lister, who believed it reflected adversely on 'the standard of good taste and conduct' prevailing in the CAS. Duncan-Johnstone argued that by now legislation was unnecessary; there was no 'real problem' as the low numbers of half-caste children indicated.[52] With the increase of white women and the development of an 'orderly' expatriate society, a veil of hypocrisy obscured the degree of interracial sex. White men continued to defy regulations and informal taboos, although this was attributed mainly to 'business' whites and lower-ranking technical officers, as opposed to the elite political officers, who were expected to lead exemplary lives. Evidence suggests, however, that the practice was widespread, although interracial liaisons were clandestine and discretion was the order of the day. Martin Lindsay, an officer in West Africa, recalled that although the convention was abstinence during a tour, ' … in the outposts most people probably had an African girl living with them' who would never be seen in the house with the officer and only came in 'after dark'. Black women could provide white men with an intimate and unique entrée into the local culture, as well as sexual comfort. An officer who had served in East Africa in the early 1930s noted that African women were known as 'sleeping dictionaries' because of their obvious advantages as 'language instructors'.[53]

White visions of 'dark rapture' have obscured the reality of African women's lives under colonialism. In his study of racial attitudes in South Africa, MacCrone (1937) noted how white men predominantly saw black women as more sensual than white women, full of 'primitive abandon' and freer in sexual relations. But embedded within male texts were real fears of powerful female sexuality and the resistant black woman who had to be firmly controlled as a threat to the stability of colonial society. As Bush (1996) has argued, colonial narratives constructed a 'fabulous fiction' of black women's identities, a confused composite of passive drudge, 'she-devil' and sexual temptress, which has endured through history. This duality of the sexual temptress/'she-devil' emerges clearly in the novel *Sanders of the River*. A 'shapely', fierce and defiant eighteen-year old girl poisons her husband and the siren, M'Lino, no average 'ugly' black woman, but attractive and fine featured, constantly defies Sanders, showing a contempt that 'no man would have dared to'. Accused of being a witch who has killed many men, she almost manages to weave her sexual magic over the 'woman-hating' Sanders before she is shot by his faithful 'Houssa', Abidoo. Another temptress, Dailila, a 'slim … tall' attractive girl, who is a 'trifle pert' for a native, also tries to seduce 'Sandi' through her irresistible 'dance of the three lovers'. Failing, she seeks revenge and Sanders is captured by her slave-trading father and made to 'dance on hot stones'. Once more he is saved by the faithful Abidou and, despite his 'aversion' to flogging women, Dailila is lashed.[54] In these anecdotes are intimations of real violence against women during colonial rule. Few whites spoke out against this (although Brigadier General Crozier was critical of the treatment of women during the pacification campaigns in Nigeria) and there is evidence that the ultra-masculine world closed ranks erasing violence against women from official records.[55]

Vaughan (1991) suggests that African women were seen by colonial officials as the 'repository of all that was dark and evil in African culture', as well as the central figures in fertility cults and 'traditional' religions. As late as 1931, whites wrote of the 'heathen grandmothers who held mothers and daughters in their power', leaving Christian husbands to stand by 'helpless and hopeless'. Vaughan (1991) and Cutrafelli (1983) both emphasise the rejection of Christianity by women, and Cutrafelli has argued that witchcraft was women's primary response to the cultural dislocations resulting from colonial rule which affected their position in the family and wider society. (Although there are some notable exceptions here, particularly in South Africa, where Christianity was a strong influence on African women as we shall see in Chapter 5). Colonial authorities and missionaries, she argues, thus encouraged the patriarchal authority of Christianised African men to 'control' women and curb their 'heathen practices'.[56] The colonial authorities were also keen to control the independent migration of women which, in the colonial mind, led to prostitution and moral degeneracy.

Underlying these moral panics were arguably real fears of the power of women. Market women, observes Coquery-Vidrovitch (1997) were particularly powerful as the Nigerian 'Women's Riots' indicated; they ruled market places, imposed fines and settled lawsuits. In south-east Nigeria, women consistently challenged the power of the United Africa Company, the largest seller of cloth which women traded in the remoter areas, and forced the company to listen to their grievances over inflated prices. There are cameos of powerful women who completely reverse the white stereotypes. Sylvia Leith-Ross, an old 'Africa hand' and ex-colonial wife, described a meeting with Madam Naomi, the first southeastern Nigerian woman to deal 'not only in palm kernels' (as women had always done), but also in the male preserve of palm oil. She found Madam Naomi 'magnificently swathed in her rose coloured velvet', sitting on a 'wooden chair ... knees wide apart, sipping neat whiskey'.[57]

Such insights point to the problems of generalising about the 'African woman'. Although women did share some common experiences, there were important class, ethnic and regional variations which affected African women's interaction with colonial cultures. However, whites interpreted the lives of African women from an ethnocentric position. Thus, they misunderstood the importance of women's institutions, particularly the secret societies, which helped to sustain women's identities in a time of cultural and economic change. Secret societies linked town and countryside and were important in women's protests against colonialism. For instance, the Igbo women's *mikiri* was crucial in the organisation of protest against both colonial and collaborative native authorities during the 'Women's War' in southern Nigeria in 1929.[58] This 'puzzling women's war' provided two rare early studies of African women by Sylvia Leith-Ross and Margaret Green. Green's study was a more considered, anthropological study, but both were funded on the basis of informing future administrative measures and retained a conceptual framework based on a crude dichotomy between 'primitive' and 'sophisticated' women. Leith-Ross's maternalist preoccupations and Eurocentric perceptions of civilisation are reflected in her later (failed) project in 1952 to set up a finishing school for the southern Nigerian elite to teach girls 'the correct way of laying table'.[59]

Although some white women showed a 'maternalistic' concern for African women, their perceptions differed little from those of men. However, whereas 'colonial man' was preoccupied with the sexualised African woman or 'she-devil', 'colonial woman', epitomised by Elspeth Huxley, tended to see women simply as beasts of burden, whose oppression under African male patriarchy contrasted with their own strength and freedom. Unaware of the rights of

Illustration 10–Lady on Nkole Ferry
Source: Eslanda Goode Robeson, *African Journey*, London, Gollancz, 1946

women in many African societies, claims Hayes (1996), white men and women saw the advent of colonialism as a positive event, liberating African women from the debasement of polygamy and agricultural toil.[60] Colonial discourse reconstructed both white and African gender identities and this was vital to sustaining white power. Colonial officers only dealt with male authority as family heads. African women were vague ciphers in the background, unless they became a threat to the authorities as they did in southern Nigeria in 1929. As Ranger (1983) points out, chiefs and the intelligentsia colluded in the colonial invention of African 'traditions' in order to keep women in their place, that is, as submissive mothers and primitive agriculturists. The construct of 'native' or 'colonial subject' in colonial discourses was a masculine trope and African women exist in colonial accounts as silent icons of the primitive – the ultimate 'others'. If any dialogue occurred with Africans, it was solely with the male elite – traditional or 'Westernised'. Thus, progressive imperialists like Margery Perham saw themselves as capable of 'friendship' with educated African men, but women were excluded from this privileged entrée into modernity. In effect, argues, Coquery-Vidrovitch, colonialism destroyed the fragile balance between dependency and autonomy in African gender relations. The intensification of cash crop production relegated women to subsistence production, but they still had to help men out with the cash crops and thus, under colonialism, had to work harder without compensation.[61]

African women were simultaneously damned by liberals for resisting progress and idealised by conservatives as the protectors of traditional culture. Conservatives saw women's mobility and education as threatening to traditional order and colonial rule, and before the Second World War only 1.5 per cent of African girls were in education as opposed to 5.3 per cent of boys. Sylvia Leith-Ross was appointed the first 'lady' Superintendent of Education in Lagos in 1926, but became generally disappointed with the lack of progress in girls' education and was invalided out of the service in 1931.[62] African women suffered from both white and African male prejudices against education and only a handful, like Adelaide Casely Hayford, made it into the new professional elites before independence. Hailey (1956) noted that after 1949 there was a 'striking increase' in the number of West African women going to the UK for further training, but the majority were nursing students. Women remained at the bottom of a well-defined gender, class and race hierarchy, with white men at the apex. As the Nigerian socialist and anti-colonialist, Mrs Fummilayo Annikulapo-Kuti, who mobilised market women in the 1940s, argued, women had lost far more under colonialism than men.[63] The gendered order thus intermeshed with the racial orders which sustained colonial rule. Central to the construction of both orders was white cultural power and the workings of cultural imperialism.

'Taming the wild': cultural imperialism and the colonial order

African awe and admiration of white culture was seen as essential to sustaining the dream of grateful subjects, which validated the existence of colonial rule. Mechanisms of cultural imperialism enhanced white prestige and facilitated the 'smooth' functioning of native administration. It was the male, educated African who experienced the most intense impact of cultural imperialism, and gender and class are important variables in evaluating white cultural power. However, the majority of colonised subjects who came into contact with whites experienced rituals bonding them to colonisers and empire. Pomp and ceremony accompanied all important imperial occasions, such as the arrival and departure of governors and VIP visits. English traditions, for instance Empire Day, St George's Day and Poppy Day, were celebrated with parades of ritual power and were enforced even in the bush. E.F.G. Haig recalled the ludicrous situation of Africans wearing 'poppies on their loincloths' when DCs were 'unable to explain its significance'.[64]

Loyalty, obedience and allegiance to the King and empire were paramount. The trope of the 'loyal subject' was invoked as evidence of the fact that most Africans welcomed British rule and was also used to secure support for the imperial power in wartime. For Hugh Egerton, the First World War was a test of the 'subject races' that had been 'more than passed' in West Africa with gifts, subscriptions to 'patriotic funds' and valuable military service. On her tour, Princess Marie Louise unveiled a war memorial to the 'very war-like and turbulent' Fra Fra of the Northern Territories who, having only been 'curbed' by the English after 1911, were transformed into 'peaceful and obedient people' who promptly showed their loyalty by fighting for the British in the Cameroons and Togoland. Loyal war veterans were focal points of imperial ceremonies in the inter-war years. In the Gold Coast, ex-servicemen were routinely inspected before palavers by 'His Excellency', the Governor, and during one such inspection, Princess Marie Louise spotted a veteran wearing 'Grandmamma's Jubilee Medal', having been part of the Gold Coast deputation at Queen Victoria's Diamond Jubilee. Others wore the Ashanti Star, which her brother 'Christle' had also been awarded for the 1895 'Ashanti War'.[65]

The motif of loyalty was impressed on chiefs, who were bought off with 'a large, round silver disc' bearing the King's head on a heavy silver chain. (Bosambo is given one in the film version of *Sanders of the River*.) On tour, Princess Marie Louise was asked to present these white-bestowed symbols of office 'in recognition of ... good chieftainship', adding that it was a 'much coveted and much prized honour', which proved that the wearer was a 'good and loyal chief' who cared about the welfare of his people. This again reflects Lugard's vision of an ordered Africa where chiefs were organised on military lines, from first down to fifth grade, and were sworn in by oaths of allegiance and insignia:

The formal recognition of the position of 1st or 2nd grade Chief is notified by the presentation of a 'Staff of Office' and in the case of a former by a Letter of Appointment on a parchment scroll. ... The Staff is surmounted in the case of a 1st class Chief by a silver and in the case of 2nd class by a brass head piece ... chiefs of the 1st grade may fly the Union Jack in their residences. ... A Chief of the 3rd grade may carry a short baton; lower grades may not carry any symbol of office.

Lugard also warned that 'official etiquette and ceremonial dress' were to be strictly adhered to as matters of 'great importance' to African chiefs (all assumed to be male, although as Coquery Vidrovich points out, there was a tradition of women chiefs in some parts of West Africa). Colonial administrators were thus warned to 'study native etiquette carefully' and 'prohibit the assumption of privileges ... by those not entitled to them by Native custom'. On the other hand, they were instructed to 'exact all proper courtesy' from Africans with whom they had dealings and to take prompt action on any signs of African 'discourtesy' or insulting behaviour towards whites, such as the offer of 'a contemptible present', 'despatch of a low-grade or dirty messenger', or lack of punctuality.[66]

Palavers (see Illustration 11) were particularly important in this bonding of colonial and 'traditional' authority, of monarchy and empire, and the pomp and ritual continued well into the 1950s. Elspeth Huxley argued that in the uncertain post Second World War years, palavers retained a 'mystical significance' and, although 'out of fashion' and supplanted by the 'doctrine of equality', appealed to some 'profound and enduring African emotion'. Writing of the Gambia, she evokes a vivid image of these invented traditions:

> On a dais sits a phalanx of officials in shining topees ... constrained by high collars most unsuited to the tropics ... beneath a Union Jack, flanked by two policemen, stands the Governor, addressing a gathering of chiefs. ... A curiously old-fashioned, Sanders of the River scene of British imperial power staging its little pageant beside this ancient, inimical waterway into the alien heart of Africa, and staging it well, with immaculate white men, loyal chiefs, orderly spectators, flags, bunting, bugles, the oath of loyalty, the Queen's message, the sense that this remote and uneventful little cluster of huts and bush is part of a greater fellowship from which it can draw nobility and purpose.[67]

Ranger (1983) has convincingly explained the importance of the invention of rituals and 'tradition' in gaining consent for empire from both the coloniser and the colonised and for creating a 'shared framework of pride and loyalty'. While this was arguably most successful in the colonial military and public school system, it was extended into the rural areas in the inter-war years. The monarchy was particularly important in the cementing of the 'shared' traditions of empire. During her visit, Princess Marie Louise opened roads, bridges and hospitals and visited colleges and schools. While on trek (itself an important ritual in confirming white presence, power and racial superiority) with Governor Guggisberg and his wife, she attended numerous palavers where the natives turned out in all their exotic finery and offered presents to the honoured white guests. Her role was to thank the chiefs for their welcome and offer to take back 'a message of homage and loyalty to their King'. Her tour extended the bounds of this imperial bonding and a District Commissioner in the northern provinces wrote to thank her as the first member of the royal family to visit 'this very out of the way corner of the empire'.[68]

The monarchy also provided visual symbols of empire. A letter from the 'people of Cape Coast' thanked the Princess for unveiling a bust of Queen Victoria, the monarch 'under whose auspices the empire had been built', in Victoria Park. The mythic benevolence of the 'Great White Queen', Victoria, was crucial to this benign representation of empire to the 'natives', and during Marie Louise's tour she was heavily promoted as Queen Victoria's grandchild. Of course, there was a huge amount of toadying to the Princess; for example, suitable letters from loyal 'natives' were clearly orchestrated by sycophantic DOs. Thus, a letter from chiefs thanking the Princess for the honour 'bestowed on them by her visit' adds that:

> Since we came under the white man's King, our people have prospered, sickness does not kill so many of our people, we are not raided for slaves. ... We want to tell our King we will always help him loyally.

The letter is signed 'Spoken by Nanweni, Chief of Lawra, Benni Lobi, Interpreter, St J. Eyre Smith, DC', who obviously influenced its content. In the realms of colonial fantasy, such sentiments reflect how colonisers *wanted* their subjects to think and behave, not the reality. But it is clear that Queen Victoria had become somewhat of a mantra to the colonised, representing the higher imperial ideals of justice and fairness (critiqued in Chapter 1) that would be carried on through the British monarchy.[69]

For the 'Westernised' elites, loyalty to King and country (Britain) was secured through an education which denigrated African culture. Chief Enahoro, who attended King's College for Boys, Lagos, the 'Eton of Nigeria', described his education as 'suited to an English gentleman'. He learnt about the imperial 'heroes' who had 'discovered Africa' and was strictly forbidden to speak in any language other than English. The important role of language in enforcing cultural imperialism has been emphasised by black intellectuals. 'To speak a language is to ... assume a culture' wrote Franz Fanon. Adopting the language of the coloniser was central to wearing the white mask which suppressed African culture and resulted in psychic stress and internalisation of racial inferiority. But it also opened up new forms of consciousness which stimulated nationalism as we shall see in Chapter 4.[70] Colonial administrators recognised early on the need to accommodate the developing bourgeoisie and safely channel their aspirations. Education, warned Lugard, 'has not brought happiness and contentment' to educated West African communities. 'African education', he argued, 'should be

Illustration 11–Palaver at Sunyani, Ashanti
Source: Princess Marie Louise, *Travels in the Gold Coast*, Methuen & Co. Ltd., 1926

for the advancement of the community and not used for 'the subversion of constituted authority'. To avoid the problems that had emerged in India, the 'primary object' should be 'formation of character and habits of discipline'. Religious and moral instruction was essential and 'reading books for girls' should be drawn up by 'a thoroughly qualified [white] lady'. Boys education should inculcate 'morals, truthfulness, courage, love of fair play and justice, respect for authority, cleanliness and the dignity of labour'. Biographies of 'good men' like General Gordon and David Livingstone were 'very useful' here.[71]

The flagship of 'new thinking' on African education was Achimota College which, in Hailey's estimation, was 'boldly conceived' as a 'comprehensive school for both sexes'. It was established in 1924 and, by 1929, the curriculum spanned 'industrial' and 'academic' education from kindergarten to college level. The first of its kind in West Africa, the college incorporated the ideas of influential colonial educationalists, discussed in Chapter 1, and was regarded as a showcase model of good colonial practice. The English staff were carefully selected (as recommended by Lugard) with only the 'highest degrees' and all became fluent in the various languages in which they had to teach. Fees of £50 per annum were charged, reflecting the ultimate vision of a tailored education for the minority elite, which would help with the Africanisation of the Civil Service.[72] From 1924–36 the college was run by its principal, A.S. Fraser, on the lines of a public school with playing fields and a gymnasium to encourage *esprit de corps* and a sense of 'high responsibility'. Fraser, a staunch Christian, was formerly head of Trinity College, Kandy, and his educational work, influenced by a visit to Booker T. Washington's Tuskagee Institute in 1912, was much admired. Achimota was Fraser's life's work, evidence that 'the glorious West African people' were gradually changing their conditions by 'evolving not revoluting [*sic*]'. He was a close friend of the important Gold Coast educator, Kwegyir Aggrey, and, as Wilkes (1996) points out, firmly believed that any respectable curriculum must also encourage students to value and understand their own cultures.[73] Sir Ralph Furse described Fraser's devices for reaching the African mind as 'brilliant and original' and, on his visit to the Gold Coast in 1934, the Labour MP, Charles Roden Buxton, was similarly impressed.[74]

Achimota was an inspired development and arguably reflected the unique relationship between the Gold Coast authorities and the Asante and Fanti (noted in Chapter 2). However, the Gold Coast also had technical schools run on 'boy scout principles' with drill and discipline. Scouting philosophy was seen as a valuable weapon in the 'moralisation' of African children and the movement had 'caught on tremendously', although numbers were small. Cardinall recorded that the total membership of the Gold Coast boy scout movement in 1930 was 1,982. Girl guides had even fewer numbers as they were restricted mainly to the coastal areas where there were enough 'European ladies' to act as officers.[75] Warren (1986) suggests that scouting in the 1920s offered a unifying multiracialist ideal and the reasons for local involvement were not primarily imperial. While this may have had some relevance for the 'white Dominions', as Evelyn Waugh cynically observed (if through his somewhat warped racist lens), the 'ten rules' of the Scouting Movement emphasised notions of white masculinity and bourgeois Victorian virtues, such as thrift, trust and 'cleanliness in thought, word and deed', which were clearly inappropriate in different cultural settings.[76]

African cubs and scouts, together with children at government schools attended Empire Day celebrations where they saluted the flag, sang 'Rule Britannia', paraded, marched in their best uniforms and played competitive games. In Accra, children sometimes gave scenes from their own history, but rituals involved were exclusively British.[77] Patriotism was instilled in schoolchildren from an early age. When Princess Marie Louise visited a convent of the White Sisters in Cape Coast, the children had been carefully coached for her visit and most of their writings consisted of 'simple explanations of the words empire, citizenship, patriotism, and a really excellent description of the origins of the Union Jack'. Everywhere Princess 'Mary Lewis' went there were schoolchildren waving flags and singing the national anthem.[78]

Educated Africans experienced the most intense cultural transformations, as well as the racial humiliations of being 'white', but not white. During the latter half of the nineteenth century, a small, Westernised African bourgeoisie emerged in the large urban centres. After the First World War, the numbers of locally educated Africans increased and the 'pioneer' work of European educators in the Gold Coast had resulted in an 'intelligent class' of Africans in Accra, Sekondi and other major centres. Contemporary studies estimated that 12,000 Africans were employed as clerks, teachers and clergymen, with an additional fifty lawyers, eleven doctors and a small number of cocoa brokers.[79] Africans in government employment were paid substantially less than their white counterparts, emphasising white superiority. In the Gold Coast, for instance, Africans recruited to the Civil Service under 'Africanisation' policies received only one-sixth of the European salary for the same work and were barred from the Political Service and higher administrative positions. In other colonies, no such 'ambitious and liberal' programme existed, a fact which Buell attributed to an absence of a class of 'capable Africans' such as existed on the Gold Coast.[80]

Commonly termed 'wogs' in West African slang, educated Africans were lumped together under the generic term of 'clerks' even though some were doctors and lawyers. The southern 'mission school graduates' in northern Nigeria were particularly despised and described as 'quasi-illiterates' or 'parasitic, ungrateful, showy, irresponsible and untrustworthy'.[81] In the Gold Coast, observed Graham Greene, African officials were accused of being 'venal and corrupt'. Even those in official positions who went to parties in Government House and were able to vote were a target of derision to the 'heartless perfect eye' of Europeans, scornful of their attempts to ape Western manners. During the inter-war years it was not considered appropriate to invite Africans into white homes and only a few rare and exceptional professional men, such as Dr Aggrey of Achimota College, were accepted as 'honorary Europeans'. Nigeria also had its 'Uncle Toms', such as Sir Akitoya Ajasa, a friend of Lugard who was the founder of the conservative *Nigerian Pioneer* and the first Nigerian to be awarded the British Peerage.[82]

The racially excluded African bourgeoisie, based mainly in the coastal towns, thus created its own parallel society which ironically 'mimicked' the culture of the group which despised it. In Lagos, Perham observed that the growing professional and trading elite, influenced by the model of US and West Indian blacks, lived in their own black suburb. The houses, which cost between £400 and £1,000, were built by native contractors and were part of a 'well-planned suburban housing scheme' which had been a 'rapid success'. Here, the African bourgeoisie created a superficially Western lifestyle with 'net curtains' at the windows and even tennis courts. Churches in Lagos were filled each Sunday with this black elite, who also attended 'literary clubs and social functions' where evening dress was worn. A similar modern, elite lifestyle was evident in Gold Coast towns. As Freund (1984) points out, 'ardent' Christianity, Western names and capitalist values promoted through missionary education became part of the 'cultural baggage' of the African bourgeoisie carried through to independence.[83]

Although the Colonial Office declared that no official colour bar existed, resentment over racial exclusions and humiliations intensified in the late 1930s. Colonial critics in Britain warned of the dangers of rigid class/colour boundaries and advocated new policies, including the introduction of interracial social clubs and Africanisation of the colonial administration.[84] But such policies failed to materialise and, as we shall see in Chapter 4, discontent grew. Wartime staff shortages finally led to a breach of the 'colour bar' – an acknowledgement of 'apparent' contradictions between Britain's 'political liberalism' and racial exclusions. In 1944, 'Africanisation' became formal policy, but opposition within the CAS persisted as did racial discrimination. The Governor of the Gold Coast, Alan Burns, admitted that blacks were barred from European clubs and residential areas and were refused accommodation in hotels.[85]

With the growth in African resistance, white prestige and imperial power were threatened, the complacency of expatriate society was shaken and fissures in colonial society deepened. According to Sylvia Leith-Ross, commercial whites now lived at a noticeably higher standard than 'government' whites. New recruits were viewed as upstarts who lacked ideals, were only interested in the money and would 'lose' the colonies. The 'old order' was challenged by 'progressive' governors who declared themselves opposed to racial segregation.[86] During and after the Second World War, the 'eventual' inevitability of independence forced a change in policies which reflected the new discourse of multiracialism, partnership and colonial development. By 1949, Sir Ralph Furse was reputedly asking recruits whether they were prepared to take Africans into their homes. Multiracial functions became commonplace at Government House, colour prejudice 'faded away' as Africans were reputedly seen 'as not only human but most charming human beings'.[87]

The war did lead to superficial changes in the culture of colonial rule. The 'tour' was shortened and revolutionised by improved communications, including air travel and the introduction of four-wheel drive cars. The expatriate white community expanded and became more diverse with a new model colonial wife determined to do 'as much as a woman is allowed in an African male society'.

There were dramatic improvements in living conditions with better drugs and refrigeration. But spatial segregation persisted and social contact with Africans only improved on the margins, although Sylvia Leith-Ross partly attributes this to the suspicion and hostility of Africans towards whites, which 'shocked' old hands. As imperial dreams faded with independence, colonial officers, retired on 'compensation terms', became an 'extinct species'.[88] But 'colonial' culture lingered on in the new expatriate communities of development advisers and businessmen, and returning colonial officials arguably impacted on English culture bolstering the forces of conservatism and the racist backlash against black migrants.

Summary

West Africa was ruled by a small minority of whites, and consent could not have been secured purely by force. The constant affirmation of cultural superiority was essential in sustaining the mystique of power. The 'culture of colonialism', premised on intermeshing race and gender orders, was fundamental to the workings of imperial power. At the heart of this culture was white expatriate society, a superior caste whose prestige and power was bolstered by seemingly impermeable 'white walls' segregating white and African cultures. However, this power could never be monolithic and was breached, by, for instance, miscegenation and the refusal of African men and women to conform to racist stereotypes. 'Prospero and Caliban', coloniser and colonised, were locked in complex spirals of power and dependence, collaboration and resistance.[89] The coloniser's 'reality' was shaped by dominant discourses generated at the heart of the empire, individual personality and class position, but also through interaction with the colonised. Conversely, African 'reality' was shaped by white racism and cultural oppression, but also the refusal to become the compliant 'colonial subject' of white 'imagination'. As this chapter has demonstrated, the nature and extent of interaction with the white culture of colonialism depended on whether you were a man or a women, a rural or urban dweller, a chief or a member of the 'Westernised' elite. The penetration of Western culture undermined and divided African colonial society, but it also stimulated new forms of organised protest against colonial rule and oppositional nationalist discourses through which African dreams of freedom were more forcefully articulated. This more concerted challenge to white economic, political and cultural power is the focus of my next chapter

4 'Whose dream was it anyway?'[1]

Anti-colonial protest in West Africa, 1929–45

The idea of nationalism is one of the most generally misunderstood in the modern world. The imperialists do not even try to understand it; they simply call it sedition and hand it over to the police.

(R. Lynd, 1919)

Nothing is more encouraging to the local agitator than the knowledge that they have the support of anyone in England and they are quite unable to discriminate between those whose support is of value and the obvious charlatan.

(Governor Jardine, Sierra Leone, 1939)[2]

From the contemporary imperialist perspective, the inter-war years were represented as a 'colonial honeymoon' with little sign of discontent and only a 'scanty vanguard' of politically-minded Africans.[3] But as dreams of power were concretised in the consolidation of the colonial political economy, the dream of freedom held strong. How were these dreams of freedom transformed into the reality of independence? As the preceding chapters have demonstrated, the extension of colonial rule generated a range of resistant responses which disrupted the imperial project and challenged white constructs of loyal and grateful colonised subjects. Pre-colonial African communities, argues Basil Davidson, provided the individual with an identity that was rounded and complete. This world was 'turned upside down' by colonialism and the traumatic impact has been explored in Chinua Achebe's classic novel about colonial Nigeria, *Things Fall Apart* (1962).[4]

Resistance was thus an enduring response to the imperialist penetration of West Africa. When annexation began in the 1880s, the British met with fierce opposition which included organised military resistance. West African merchants also hindered the colonisation process by refusing to give up economic rights in order that British firms could open up lucrative palm oil markets. Punitive expeditions were mounted against recalcitrant African leaders who refused to enter into trade agreements or organised armed rebellion and some, like King Prempeh of the Ashanti, were sent into exile. This 'traditional' or primary resistance ranged from formal military opposition to 'guerrilla' type warfare organised on a village basis.[5] After 'pacification', new forms of resistance emerged. These included the urban riot and strike, but also what Ajayi termed a 'politics of survival', which utilised more subtle 'indirect' forms of non-compliance. Memories of earlier resistance were sustained in families and communities and inspired the development of anti-colonial nationalist movements. The Nigerian nationalist leader, Anthony Enahoro, maintained that grievances he heard expressed as a child provoked the 'first stirrings of rebellion' in his heart. On the eve of decolonisation, Sir Alan Burns remarked on the deep suspicion of white justice and the depth of black solidarity. Although white revisionist histories of earlier resistance studies have questioned the degree of continuity in resistance, contemporary black historians continue to emphasise that nationalism had its roots 'deep in the African past'.[6]

However, African resistance strategies must be contextualised within the hegemonic power structures, analysed in the preceding chapters, and the diversity of African experiences of white power. Colonialism disorientated African societies and this affected the degree to which Africans could resist, otherwise a handful of whites would have been unable to hold on to power. Such wider problems raised by the concept of resistance were explored in the introduction. Since the 1960s, studies of resistance have moved on from anti-colonial narratives of generalised colonialist oppression and counter-responses associated with the reconstruction of a heroic past. As Beinart and Bundy (1987) have pointed out, resistance was fragmented and struggles between different classes, and rural and urban interests, precluded any coherent response. Collaboration was also nuanced and ambiguous and did not represent consistent and unswerving loyalty to the state, as the allegiances of groups and individuals shifted as the value of the alliance with the colonial state changed.[7] More importance has also been placed on 'hidden' rural struggles and the degree to which various points of rural and urban protest interconnected. While it is beyond the scope of this particular study to explore these interconnections in more depth, it is clear that urban and rural struggles overlapped. The divide between the 'traditional' rural areas, concerned with land rights, and the defence of hereditary authority rooted in 'ethnic' consciousness and urban 'nationalist' consciousness must also be challenged. Protest strategies, such as boycotts, petitions, use of lawyers, non-compliance with the law, strikes, violence and cultural assertions spanned rural and urban areas. Pan-Africanist ideas and news of international developments also penetrated into rural areas.

My main interest here is the development of more organised anti-colonial protest which moved resistance on from localised struggles against the penetration of colonial rule. Peasant farmers and urban workers now had to fight to secure better terms as they were more fully incorporated into the colonial economy. The key catalyst was the encounter with 'modern', Western culture through a monetised economy, primary commodity production, Christianity and education. This generated important changes in African consciousness which varied depending on ethnic, religious, gender and class backgrounds. Improved communications, the expansion of the African press and linkages across the African diaspora, as West African students in London established contact with activists from other parts of the British Empire (Chapter 8), also stimulated race and political consciousness.With these developments, the African intelligentsia were able to articulate grievances more coherently and adopt leadership roles in political organisations. Initially, these were directed at securing a better deal from colonial rule, but, ultimately, their goal was independence.

This underscores an important gender dimension in analysing resistance that has, as yet, not been fully explored. Women have been left out of the more orthodox narratives of resistance, although as Coquery-Vidrovitch (1994) shows, West African women were often particularly formidable in challenging the colonial state and collaborative traditional elites in defence of their interests. Women's resistance was a vital part of the more generalised resistance and popular struggles which continuously taxed the colonial authorities. The last two chapters have reflected on the diverse ways in which women challenged the colonial state, and it is clear that they interpenetrated the 'modern' sector as traders, cocoa farmers and retailers of illegal gin. As Akyeampong (1996) points out, their struggles for survival in a male-orientated colonial economy frequently led to victimisation by the authorities. However, the class configuration of women, argues Coquery-Vidrovitch, differed from that of men and was characterised by a minuscule, educated elite comprised mainly of teachers, who adopted their husbands' political concerns, a minority of wealthy market women, who were generally illiterate, but astute and pro-active in airing grievances against colonial rule, and the mass of poor peasant women marginalised in the informal sector and subsistence production. Only the first two groups, in very small numbers, joined in the politics of independence movements and there was little cohesiveness between the three groups of women.[8] The organised struggles and discourses of liberation which are analysed here were thus articulated primarily through men who dominated the modern sector as cash crop producers, urban workers, miners or the educated bourgeoisie.

In focusing primarily on the modern sector, this chapter engages with the marxist conceptualisation of capitalism and Western culture as simultaneously oppressive and liberating. While the last two chapters focused on the articulation of white power at the 'local' level, the context now broadens out to take into account the 'global' economic and political influences that also shaped resistance. I argue that as African protest became more vocal, colonial governments responded with tougher repressive policies and few concessions were made to African demands. This further stimulated African political consciousness and generated more forceful criticisms of colonialism in the imperial heartland. This complex interplay between colonialism, repression, resistance and political consciousness is analysed in relation to three major areas – the articulation of economic and political grievances, the suppression of 'dangerous ideas' and contraction of colonial civil liberties, and the development of nationalist consciousness.

The 'negro toilers': contesting the colonial economy

In imperial discourse, the colonial economy worked smoothly to the mutual benefit of both coloniser and colonised but, as Boahen (1990) notes, the destabilisation of local African economies ensured that Africans suffered economic defeat as well as social humiliation. For contemporary British critics, the colonial administration in West Africa clearly subordinated its altruistic aims of more pragmatic economic contingencies, sanctioned labour policy, and condoned the use of forced or coerced labour.[9] As stressed in the foregoing chapters, although the interests of private capital and government were not always in harmony, the colonial and imperial governments favoured capitalist development. Conservative MPs and ministers influential in formulating colonial policy had financial interests in companies operating in Africa and, although the imperial government was against compulsory acquisition of land, 'scientific' plantation production was regarded as superior to peasant production. Mining was particularly important as royalties were a valuable source of revenue to colonial coffers.[10] The overriding priority of the colonial administration was the establishment of a viable colonial economy, and in the inter-war years local West African economies were more tightly harnessed to the global economy. The autonomy and wealth of native merchants was gradually whittled away as British proto-multinationals like United Africa Company (UAC), Elder Dempster, Lever Brothers and Cadbury Brothers gained increasing control over peasant commodity production, West African trade and markets for imported goods.[11]

The related proletarianisation of African peasants led to greater dependency on wage labour, migration and urban growth. The 1930 Gold Coast census noted how the development of the cocoa export industry was marked by 'land-lordism', a move from collective to individual ownership, greater use of hired, as opposed to family, labour and the concentration on cash crops to the detriment of food production. This widened class and gender differences between Africans and had important implications for poorer farmers and workers.[12] The commercialisation of peasant production in Southern Nigeria had a similar impact. Migrant labour, including large numbers from the surrounding French territories, filled labour shortages in the expanding mining areas in the Gold Coast and Nigeria. Newberry (1983) argues that such migration was not always 'voluntary', although Hailey maintains that any coercion was 'definitely forbidden' in 1924 and recruitment agencies developed, with shopkeepers as the main agents (here there are parallels with South Africa, as we shall see in Chapter 5). Proletarianisation led to shifting ethnicities, new class alignments and conflicts which became important in the articulation of nationalism. Freund (1988) argues that the African working class were seminal in challenging colonial rule as grievances against labour conditions mounted.[13]

The more 'respectable' public sector employment also expanded in the 1920s, particularly in transport, but state employees were treated little better than Africans working in private industry and commerce. Workers employed by the state received between nine-pence and one shilling and six-pence per day. The

American researcher, Buell, remarked that all West African rates during the 1920s were considerably lower than those paid in South Africa. Africans were generally restricted to low paid, low status jobs. This is exemplified in Cardinall's breakdown of African employment patterns in the Gold Coast (see Tables 4 and 5). The overwhelming majority of African 'railway workers' were labourers. There were 6,500 'clerks', the majority in commerce, but, noted Cardinall, the term 'clerk' indicated a very menial, non-manual occupation. Where Europeans and Africans were engaged in similar occupations, such as mining, there was a gross disparity in wages.[14]

From the employers' perspective such inequalities were justified by the low productivity of African workers in contrast to European workers, although as Hailey conceded 'poor diet … chronic disease' and 'disincentives' such as poor housing and low wages increased rapid turnover and inefficiency. What he omits to add is that allegations of laziness and inefficiency may also have reflected 'day-to-day' individual resistance to working for the white man. Cardinall observed that Africans did not lack enterprise and the ability to work hard when they benefited from the profits. He cites, for instance, African lorry owners who bought motor vehicles on hire purchase and, by combining European and African methods of business (including the use of family labour and barter), were able to undercut and thus healthily compete with European transport firms. However, for the majority who were dependent on wage labour, economic development brought few benefits. Labour legislation was inadequate: there were penal sanctions for breach of contract by employees and accident compensation was virtually non-existent. Discontent increased after 1929 and the depression years were marked by anti-government riots, strikes, demonstrations and fledgling trade union protest, reflecting the influence of Western political ideas. Such unrest was sparked off primarily by deteriorating economic conditions, but also reflected a deeper dissatisfaction with colonial rule. As Hobsbawm (1994) argues, the slump marked the 'effective beginning of the indigenous political and social discontent', even where political nationalist movements did not emerge until after the Second World War.[15]

After 1929, prices for West African crops dropped 60–70 per cent, colonial budgets and wages were cut and control over local economies intensified as private companies also rationalised their operations to buffer themselves against the world depression. Conditions of labour deteriorated as expatriate firms and government departments reduced their labour forces and cut wages. Graham Greene, who toured West Africa in the 1930s, observed that the economies which assisted colonial governments through the depression 'were nearly all at the expense of the coloured man'. Pressures were placed on peasant producers throughout the region to expand cash crop production, which undermined the subsistence economy and increased dependency on food imports. Proletarian-isation accelerated as multinationals reorganised and extended their grip over production, leading to acute African suffering.[16] In the wealthier Gold Coast and Nigeria the large European firms managed to keep afloat by rationalising their operations and securing a monopoly over the purchase of cocoa and palm oil,

Table 4: Return of Africans in occupations other than industry

Occupation	Gold Coast Colony			Ashanti	N.T.	Togo	Total
	W.P.	C.P.	E.P.				
Auctioneer	2	7	8	4	—	—	21
Banker	3	—	—	—	—	—	3
Blacksmith	193	234	601	75	50	26	1179
Boatman	124	43	848	—	—	—	1015
Bookbinder	3	—	3	—	—	—	6
Bricklayer	259	628	1372	279	30	105	2673
Brickmaker	4	6	37	10	1	—	58
Butcher	51	122	551	101	65	12	902
Cocoa-broker	69	261	944	259	1	21	1565
Carpenter	890	1164	2892	554	59	57	5216*
Corn-grinder	6	23	217	52	—	—	298
Doctor	45	52	85	4	—	—	186
Dom. servant	1627	1355	4162	1305	442	23	8913**
Druggist	13	10	83	23	2	—	131
Electrician	53	5	83	13	—	—	154
Farmer	2028	10271	21814	1900	3028	788	39829
Fireman	70	—	—	—	—	—	70
Fisherman	2363	5047	—	—	4	—	7414
Goldsmith	197	291	1059	234	3	23	1807
Gov. social servant	703	171	1681	483	51	18	3107
Hawker	280	206	2750	8	385	6	3635
Herdsman	22	6	98	32	21	—	179
Labourer	3990	1345	9292	2587	738	46	17998
Lawyer	5	13	32	—	—	—	50
Leatherworker	11	12	33	1	64	2	123
Licensed trader	17	17	127	13	886	—	1040
Miner	30	5	—	—	—	—	35
Minister	21	41	130	44	100	2	338
Native tribunal employee	71	66	316	88	8	3	552
Painter	101	33	265	52	7	—	458
Photographer	40	50	—	18	—	6	114
Platelayer	11	4	3	—	—	—	18
Policeman	330	201	831	233	110	31	1736
Porter	18	58	303	4	—	—	383
Printer	15	13	117	2	3	—	150
Sawyer	62	50	511	23	1	22	669
Shoemaker	72	190	575	129	9	10	986
Soldier	—	2	344	606	175	—	1127
Surveyor	13	36	78	18	2	2	149
Tailor	368	359	1912	484	69	53	3245
Teacher	115	274	878	134	31	42	1474
Telegraphist	15	5	34	—	1	—	55
Trader	934	3105	4395	890	1286	79	10698
Washerman	216	112	814	129	10	9	1290
Weaver	43	58	373	69	51	13	607

Source: A.W. Cardinall, *The Gold Coast, 1931*, Accra, 1932, p. 171
Notes:
* Probably includes apprentices and those 'dabbling' in woodwork
** Registered when in the service of non-Africans

Table 5: The Gold Coast: occupations of Africans and the return of Africans engaged in industry

Occupation	Gold Coast Colony			Ashanti	N.T.	Togo	Total
	W.P.	C.P.	E.P.				
Clerks							
Commerce	546*	1488	3,105*	813	28	30	6010
Manufacture	9	—	—	—	—	—	9
Mining	—	—	15	—	—	—	15
Municipal	493	—	66	—	—	—	559
Contractors							
Building	—	—	61	—	—	1	62
General	40	31	63	22	17	—	173
Haulage	—	—	1	—	—	—	1
Firewood	—	—	—	—	—	—	—
Painting	5	—	—	—	—	—	5
Road-making	14	—	19	—	—	—	33
Driving							
Motor	360	743	2234	813	51	59	4260
Railway	39	—	3	—	—	—	42
Stationery	7	—	—	—	—	—	7
Mechanics							
Motor	371	—	685	287	5	4	1352
Railway	43	—	14	—	—	—	57
Other	55	116	13	—	—	—	184

Source: A.W. Cardinall, *The Gold Coast, 1931*, Accra, 1922, p. 170
Notes:
* This figure includes 54 female clerks in the Eastern Province and Western Province.

often with government consent, severely depressing prices at the expense of the local African producers. In the Gold Coast this resulted in a considerable reduction in cocoa prices paid to peasant producers, a two-thirds drop in the importation of sugar, flour, canned rice and fish and a 98 per cent drop in gin imports. Moreover, food, agricultural tools and other manufacturing commodities could only be purchased through stores owned by British trading companies, although a Labour Party circular noted that peasants could 'barely' live on their reduced income much less buy British goods.[17]

Appeals through the Gold Coast Aborigines Rights Protection Society

(ARPS) – formed in 1897 to defend African land rights – for an inquiry into the actions of the European companies fell on deaf ears. An alliance of brokers, drivers, market women and chiefs, who were united around common grievances against the private companies, led to a series of boycotts on cocoa sales and imported goods. Some colonial officers, like Duncan-Johnstone (the Provincial Commissioner for the Western Province), who worked in areas affected by the boycott were highly critical of the private companies. However, African critics alleged that in 1937 the governor, 'considerably concerned' by the loss of revenue, urged his staff in the field to persuade Africans to drop the boycott. As Hargreaves (1996) observes, the boycotts were not directed against the government, but official reactions were conditioned by wariness of the involvement of urban nationalists.[18]

The Nowell Report, published in 1938 after an official inquiry, criticised both expatriate firms and the colonial authorities for failing to protect native producers. It noted the 'widespread feelings of injustice' among natives and recommended improvements, such as the establishment of producer co-operatives and the improvement of credit facilities for farmers (Hailey recorded that there were eighty-two thrift and credit societies by the late 1940s). As African brokers had no chance of bargaining with the big companies who controlled 98 per cent of the export trade, the report favoured the establishment of a state-run Cocoa Marketing Board, which stabilised prices, but retained European control.[19] Hopkins (1973) thus suggests that the boycotts had slim, concrete results and disinterest in Britain, combined with the power of the expatriate companies, led to a further erosion of the independence of peasant producers. However, for Africans the boycotts represented a spirited, morale-boosting and novel from of resistance against white power and private foreign interests. They were also arguably important in building more widespread support for the nationalist movement as the actions of the government and private companies radicalised conservative chiefs.[20]

Serious economic problems, precipitated by the economic depression, resulted in a more general growth of discontent in the larger towns and the mining areas. By 1931, the Trinidadian political activist, George Padmore, reported that Nigeria was 'aflame', while the headmistress of the government girls' school in Accra noted that many families were reputedly on the verge of starvation and people were 'furious' over the rise in unemployment and high cost of living. In the Gold Coast, new forms of urban taxation, such as the 1934 Waterworks Ordinance, which levied a rate for water from street taps, were deeply resented as they imposed 'very real hardship' on the poorest section of the community and represented a 'violation' of promises made by the former 'progressive' Governor Guggisberg that taxation would not be extended. In a mass demonstration in Cape Coast, stand pipes were damaged, policemen assaulted and the police station 'razed to the ground'. Soldiers and police reinforcements rushed to the scene, but were 'impeded by the people of neighbouring Saltpond' who had blocked the road in sympathy with the demonstrators.[21] In the ongoing struggle to impose direct taxation an ordinance was also passed in 1935 authorising the raising of revenue by 'annual levies', which deprived Africans of any control over local revenues, stipulating that they could not 'spend a penny' without the permission of the district officer.[22]

In response to these deteriorating economic and social conditions, fledgling trade unions sprang up throughout West Africa, although numbers were small and activities often spontaneous and uncoordinated. But this 'tendency towards trade unionism', noted by Cardinall, was viewed by the imperial government as a perturbing development reflecting communist influence. West African delegates attended the 1930 International Trade Union Committee of Negro Workers and testified to the 'distressing situation' of workers and the 'growing militancy of the rising generation'. As Raymond Buell shrewdly observed, the colonial authorities in West Africa were faced with the development of 'the same type of industrial problem' which had 'tormented' Europe and America for so many years. Here was the spectre among 'good' and deferential 'pagans' of the working-class 'mob-rule' which had so terrified the British ruling classes before they tamed 'the wild beasts of the forest' with promises of social reform.[23]

Between 1928 and 1930 there were a number of serious labour disturbances in West Africa. Left critics accused the colonial authorities of 'indifference' to the plight of strikers, victimisation of trade unionists and support for the private companies who wished to 'break the spirit' of the new trade unions.[24] Imperialist discourse became preoccupied with the dangerous consequences of 'culture contact' with modernity. Africans in the urban areas were represented as violent and unstable, their real grievances diminished by colonial 'ethnopsychiatry' as flaws in the African personality resulting from detachment from traditional values.[25] Problems of colonial management became particularly severe in the Gold Coast, where urbanisation was most advanced. Slums had developed around Accra, Kumasi and the mining towns of Tarkwa and Obiasi, where, argues Akyeampong (1996), immigrant urban workers had begun to construct a unique urban popular culture, a creative synthesis of African and Western influences, which was centred on working-class bars and highlife music. From the white perspective, however, these developments were further evidence of the disintegration of traditional values and controls, and the new industrial areas were associated with prostitution, the spread of venereal diseases, illegal liquor and crime.[26]

In the Gold Coast, workers' grievances centred on the poor conditions in the mines. After the First World War, gold, manganese and diamond mining expanded and there was an increase in iron ore exports. The 'model' colony was visited in 1925 by the Prince of Wales, followed by Princess Marie Louise and the Under Secretary of State for Colonies, Ormsby-Gore, and presented a glowing report to Parliament on progress in the mining areas. However, by 1931 Cardinall reported that the colony was advancing faster 'than may seem good to the Government' which 'on occasion had to act as a brake rather than an accelerating force'. Problems were acute in the Western Province, particularly in Kumasi, where the area of greatest agricultural production coincided with mining and forestry development. The mining areas, noted Cardinall, were rapidly expanding and constituted the largest concentration of labour 'under direct [European] control and influenced by European thought and the 'industrial work ethic.' As the local natives were reputedly 'of very little use' for mining, 'alien' migrant labour constituted 29.9 per cent of the total mining workforce of 12,380, although statistics were unreliable because of the transient nature of migrant labour and the high death rate.[27]

Princess Marie Louise, accompanied by the Governor's wife, Decima Guggisberg, went down the mines at Obuasi, headquarters of the Ashanti Goldfields Corporation, in 1925. She described conditions thus:

> the cage was rather small and very wet with a big iron bar running down the centre … a steady stream of very dirty water poured down from somewhere upon us and, in spite of the dreadful heat, we had to be muffled up in our mackintoshes to keep dry.

The heat at the level at which the men worked was even more intense. There were deep holes full of water to fall into and she hit her head every ten yards on a projecting rafter. The two visitors walked for miles to watch the men work, sometimes 'lying full length along slippery beams'. After an hour in the stifling heat, they emerged 'in such a state of dirt and heat' that the Princess had to cancel further planned engagements. Yet, she made no comment on the impact such conditions may have had on the men who worked there every day. In contrast, miners lives were described by African observers as 'worse than hell'.[28] Miners worked seven days a week on a three shift basis, and a daily rate of one shilling to one shilling and three-pence was paid on completion of a thirty day 'ticket'. The average age of underground mineworkers was twenty-six. The length of service varied from ten months to three years and labour turn over was high. Most miners dwelt in company housing and food prices were high. Such conditions were arguably comparative to those of South African miners (Chapter 5), if on a lesser scale. Buell had drawn attention to the poor conditions of work in the 1920s, but the myth still prevailed in Britain that conditions were far better than those in Kenya.[29]

During the 1930s, the gold mines were rationalised and labour-saving technology was introduced, resulting in a greater unemployment of miners, but an *increase* in the value of gold produced (see Tables 6 and 7). The mines became restive places and in 1933 the authorities of the Ariston Gold Mines Ltd. opened fire on African mine workers after they had demanded payment of overdue wages. However, Duncan-Johnstone recommended that the ringleader, Paul Kraa, should receive an 'exemplary sentence' as a 'very serious' situation might arise if the 'idea of labour intimidation' should spread to the whole mining area. The following year an accident caused the death of forty-one Ariston miners and the Secretary of State for Colonies, Philip Cunliffe-Lister, was asked to support claims for compensation. A sum of £12 was set for bereaved families, but in 1938 the radical activist, Isaac Wallace Johnson, complained that little compensation had been paid out.[30] There was little improvement in labour conditions, and in 1939 sixty migrant workers died in mining accidents. Labour MPs registered concern, but, like the private companies, the government's main preoccupation was the suppression of 'agitation and subversion' in the mines. The colonial critic, Norman Leys, intimated that this policy may have been linked to vested interests as 'many high officials on pension and some still in government employment' had taken service with the mining companies.[31]

Table 6: Gold mining in the Gold Coast, 1921–31: general statistics

	No. of companies		No. of labourers		Fine oz. won	Value (£)
Year	Mining	Producing	European	African		
1921	14	10	252	10313	203395	868979
1922–3	15	12	265	10083	259,738*	1,103,326*
1923–4	16	12	257	10025	200703	852548
1924–5	15	9	229	10338	210301	893359
1925–6	13	11	190	9135	198083	841394
1926–7	11	9	195	8240	189117	803369
1927–8	10	8	202	7831	168933	711833
1928–9	9	7	209	7792	167115	709903
1929–30	9	5	200	7386	218494	928161
1930–1	6	4	181	7121	246075	1045327

Source: A.W. Cardinall, *The Gold Coast, 1931*, Accra, 1932, pp. 76–7
Note:
* Covers a period of 15 months (1 January 1922–31 March 1923).

Table 7: Gold mining in the Gold Coast, 1921–31: the six major companies at work on 31 March 1931

Company	Area working	Tons crushed	Fine oz. won
1. Akoon Syndicate, Limited	Abontiakoon	48255	19552
2. Tarkwa and Aboso Mines Limited[a]	Aboso & Adjah Bippo	118589	44884
3. Ariston Gold Mines (1929) Limited	Prestea	57637	22619
4. Ashanti Goldfields Corp. Limited	Obuasi[b]	133284	159019
5. Bibiani (1927) Limited	Bibiani	—	—
6. Lyndhurst Deep Level, Limited	Konongo	—	—

Source: A.W. Cardinall, *The Gold Coast, 1931*, Accra, 1932, pp. 76–7
Notes:
a. Tarkwa was first opened by the French in 1880.
b. The mine at Obuasi was one of the richest gold mines in the world.

Active protest by African workers was sporadic and haphazard, but the authorities viewed it as part of a wider scheme orchestrated by 'subversives' and feared mass organisation and the spread of unrest to non-mining and urban areas. Duncan Johnstone recorded that the government had stipulated that to prevent further agitation, 'no unauthorised person' was to be admitted to workers' quarters. In 1938, African activists complained that packets of the *African Sentinel*, the mouthpiece of the nationalist West African Youth League (see p. 118), were seized by the local police on the instruction of the manager of Ariston Gold Mines Ltd. who had threatened to dismiss any employee in possession of any such literature.[32] After 1937, protest also began to spread to other sectors; the colony's motor drivers, who had formed a union, and the 'boatboys' in Accra were on strike and nationalists described the situation in the colony as 'tense'. The authorities attributed these developments to the ARPS or 'Sekyi's mob' (after the nationalist leader, Kobina Sekyi).[33]

After 1936, there was also renewed strike action, because of poor social conditions, in southern Nigeria. The government was forced to implement more direct rule to gain a grip on growing opposition, but, as the medical missionary, Walter Miller, observed, such measures failed to address the poverty, exploitation, dominance of 'cartels' and 'miserable cinderella' of agriculture. In 1938, unrest spread to Sierra Leone when employees of the Elder Dempster shipping line demonstrated against the lack of accident compensation and 'very desperate' conditions. According to the Labour MP, Reginald Sorensen, there was also widespread discontent over the use of floggings and the 'administration of pepper' to extract taxes. In 1939, this unrest culminated in a series of strikes and demonstrations, leading to clashes with the police, arrests and prosecutions for unlawful assembly.[34] Repression intensified and, in May, a strike by the Marbella Coaling Workers and War Department Amalgamated Workers was allegedly 'ruthlessly' crushed by armed police, and a written protest was handed to the Governor in the presence of an estimated crowd of 15,000.[35] Later in the year, 3,000 labourers at the Marampa Mine (owned by the Sierra Leone Development Company) protested over low pay, but the Secretary of State for Colonies, Malcolm MacDonald, rejected their grievances on the basis that it was a mistake to compare labour rates in the colonies with British rates and conditions – a racist 'civilised labour policy' that also extended to black workers in Britain, as we shall see in Chapter 8.[36]

Parliamentary pressure intensified for new measures to deal with the problems of the 'growing army' of Africans in 'industrial occupations' outlined in Orde Browne's influential study, *The African Labourer* (1932). However, this had little impact as the dominant view 'back home' was that in contrast to East or South Africa, labour conditions in West Africa were 'generally good' and there was still no labour department in the Colonial Office as late as 1937.[37] MacDonald continued to maintain there was little unrest and gave his full support to governors when any criticism was made of their policies and actions. However, labour unrest in the West Indies in 1938 jolted the Colonial Office out of its complacency and minor concessions were made, including the recognition of trade

unions, to prevent the spread of further unrest. With war approaching, the imperial government recognised that it was vital to placate the colonies. In 1939,
British advisers were sent out to 'guide' the emergent African trade unions along
the moderate path of British trade unionism.[38] However, such reforms were only
introduced under extreme pressure, and the repressive and punitive responses
which had emerged in the 1930s continued as labour unrest persisted during and
after the Second World War.

After 1935, the development of nationalism, spearheaded by the intelligentsia, channelled the diverse rural and urban protests into a more widespread
agitation against colonial rule. Duncan-Johnstone selected three main reasons for
the growth of unrest. First, the long-term world depression, which had impoverished Africans who were once relatively prosperous; second, the introduction of
indirect rule, which had given 'uncontrolled' power to those as yet 'completely
unfitted' for it; and third, the growth in the influence of educated Africans as
both chiefs and colonial officials lost the 'respect and obedience' of the mass of
Africans. Younger colonial officers, he argued, were increasingly pessimistic
about the existing system, while old 'Africa hands' were left bewildered by the
rapid development of nationalism, 'unrest and disaffection'.[39] The 'native',
argued the ARPS, was no longer prepared to accept the colonial officer as 'ruler,
father, judge ... and friend' when he was patently none of these things. Indirect
rule was anti-democratic 'direct rule' and, as we saw in Chapter 2, many rural
Africans resented the 'puppet' native chieftaincies, which the Nigerian nationalist, Nnamdi (Ben) Azikiwe, described as 'the velvet glove on the iron hand of
British power'.[40]

Given the power of the colonial administration, lawsuits and journalism were
the only 'legitimate' means of criticising colonial rule and venting racial humiliations. Many future nationalist leaders and 'active seditionists' were at some stage
lawyers, journalists or newspaper proprietors. The traveller, Geoffrey Gorer,
observed that there was 'a plague of litigation' in the Gold Coast and 'almost
every development of public works' was held up by lawsuits, while in Nigeria the
'native lawyer' was arousing Africans' aspirations. African lawyers, who were
supported by a 'scurrilous' native press which indulged in an 'orgy of insults and
abuse', took legal action against government officials, which further reduced
white prestige. Such 'obstructionism', warned Duncan-Johnstone, was 'typical of
the modern negro' – the 'race-conscious' minority who had been educated to
think 'individually' instead of collectively (tribally).[41] As it became increasingly
vocal and 'inflammatory', the lively and well-established African press became a
particular target of government repression. Described as 'unprincipled and
undisciplined', the press allegedly made 'blatant appeals to race-consciousness'
and its 'lying propaganda' had an 'evil' effect on an impressionable and uneducated people.[42] This combination of attacks from the intelligentsia, labour
protest and rural discontent fuelled white paranoia and put colonial governments
on the defensive. Even the mildest criticisms were now regarded as 'Bolshevist'
and colonial rule became increasingly autocratic. This was reflected in the introduction of the Sedition Ordinances and other legislation directed at curbing

'agitators', suppressing the press and controlling the 'dangerous ideas' which were supposedly at the heart of the growing unrest. Such legislation generated strong protest from the African intelligentsia and stimulated new debates around colonial civil liberties in Britain.

'Dangerous ideas' and the suppression of colonial civil liberties

'Dangerous ideas' were more difficult to control than sporadic riots and strikes, which could be contained by policing, and the intensification of Comintern activities in Africa produced anxiety and paranoia in both colony and the metropole. A secret memo to the CO from Governor Thompson in 1930 reported, on the basis of police intelligence, that 'Tunisian Bolshevik organisations', who were 'out to destroy European power', were intending to stir up trouble in northern Nigeria. Although the threat comprised eight men who did not speak the local language (Hausa), the authorities took it seriously enough to contact the French authorities. A similar paranoia was evident among Gold Coast officials. Duncan-Johnstone advocated a bond of 'Christian Ashanti States' as a 'bulwark' against Communism, and the governor, Sir Shenton Thomas, demanded that tabs be kept on 'known subversives'.[43] In response to the communist threat, amendments were introduced to the existing Criminal Codes to 'protect' colonial subjects from Bolshevism through press controls, bans on imported subversive publications and control of undesirable 'agitators'. Modelled on legislation that was introduced in Cyprus in the mid-1920s, these became known as the 'Sedition Ordinances'. The first sedition amendments were implemented in Nigeria after serious riots in 1929.[44] After pressure on the CO from Governor Thompson, the Nigerian Sedition Ordinances were tightened in 1932 and the communist *Negro Worker* and other 'suspect' publications were banned from Nigeria and other colonies. This was followed by a crackdown in Lagos on 'agitators' like I.T.A. Wallace Johnson (see p. 117), which prompted the British branch of the League Against Imperialism (LAI) and the Labour Party to write letters of protest to the CO.[45]

Initially, the CO had reservations about extending legislation to the Gold Coast for fear of provoking 'greater public criticism of the administration', but the mood hardened in the face of growing anti-colonial protest and the financial constraints of the depression years. The academic, William Macmillan, who visited the Gold Coast in 1933, maintained that the Governor, Shenton Thomas (a 'pleasant and friendly man'), had a preference for the 'more easily ruled' Islamic peoples and was nearly in despair over his 'intelligent and prosperous people'. Shenton Thomas was an advocate of 'strong government' and had the ear of the Conservative Secretary of State for Colonies, Sir Philip Cunliffe-Lister, alerting him to the 'considerable volume of subversive literature' encouraging 'sedition' that was entering the colony. He emphasised that the majority of people in the rural areas were contented and 'absolutely loyal', but farmers and the despised urban intelligentsia could be 'difficult'. Cunliffe-Lister fully endorsed the new legislation on the grounds of the need to control 'filthy, blasphemous seditious stuff' and curb the intelligentsia.[46] The new Gold Coast Criminal Code Amendment Ordinance No. 21 (Sedition Ordinance) was announced in the official *Gold Coast Gazette* in February (see Illustration 12) and received the assent of the Governor on 31 March 1934. Under the new legislation, Governors were given wide powers and considerable autonomy of judgement as to what constituted 'sedition'. Individuals could be charged with conspiring to 'seditious enterprises', engaging in seditious writing, publication of such writings or importation or possession of proscribed newspapers or books. Customs and post officers could forfeit or destroy seized literature and police had wide-ranging powers to 'examine packages'. 'Seditious intention' was defined as attempting 'to bring about hatred and contempt or to excite disaffection' or 'promote feelings of ill-will and hostility between different classes'. Such offences risked imprisonment of up to seven years or heavy fines and those not born in the colony could be deported.[47]

These repressive measures aroused the concern of the newly-formed British-based National Council of Civil Liberties (NCCL), which had established a British Overseas Committee in the colonies and Dominions. The organisation noted that many people were 'gravely disturbed' by the Sedition Ordinances and viewed them as 'symptomatic' of an 'increasing repressive tendency' in both home (the 1934 Incitement to Disaffection Act) and colonial legislation. The NCCL argued that such measures were 'bound to undermine' native confidence in British law and cause more general 'disaffection' among a 'simple and law abiding people'. This was reflected in the public outcry against the legislation. The ARPS demanded Thomas' 'immediate recall' and more generalised protest was aired at a 'monster meeting' of Accra residents, which was accompanied by 'rioting and stone throwing'. Geoffrey Gorer noted that there was a 'very constant and palpable' anti-white feeling in the colony.[48] For the administration it was a 'critical time' and Duncan-Johnstone, who blamed the 'chaos' on 'artificial agitation, by the ARPS, requested an extension of his tour of service, as the situation was too 'delicate' to leave to the 'inexperienced'. The Governor of the neighbouring French Ivory Coast, fearful of the spread of unrest, issued a confidential circular to his administrators, warning them of *a movement de rebellion* in the western province which bordered on French coffee plantations that employed migrant and conscript labour. The French allegedly saw the Gold Coast as a 'political plague spot' and listed the names of leading agitators.[49]

The ARPS organised a Central National Committee to co-ordinate opposition to the new laws. The committee split into a 'radical' faction led by Samuel R. Wood, Secretary of the ARPS, and George Edward Moore, who had served a term in jail for 'provoking a riot', and a more conservative 'Ashanti' faction supported by chiefs. Despite Shenton Thomas' assertions that they would not be able to raise funds, two ARPS delegations travelled to London in July where they received support from West African students and other black activists, the NCCL, Labour MPs and the British left.[50] In November 1934, they presented their petition to the King and in May 1935 they presented it to the House of

Gold Coast

Gazette

Extraordinary

Published by Authority.

WEDNESDAY, 21st FEBRUARY, 1934.

MINUTE BY THE GOVERNOR.

The Criminal Code Amendment Bill, 1934.

As it has been suggested in the local Press that there may be reasons for clauses 4 and 5 of this Bill which have not yet been stated, I propose to tell the public, who are entitled to know the facts, why the necessity for such legislation has arisen.

2. Everyone knows that there are in the world certain seditious organisations, whose aim appears to be the destruction of law and order. These organisations are very active, and hardly a country in the world is free from their attack. In consequence, most countries have found it necessary to protect themselves by law against such attack.

3. A few years ago the importation of seditious literature into the Gold Coast was unknown. But there is no law in this country to prevent it, and the organisations to which I have referred have begun to take advantage of this weakness. Seditious literature has been sent to this country for the last two years at least, and it is increasing rapidly in quantity. For a definition of sedition, see paragraph 12 below.

4. The people of this country are perfectly loyal, and they have a right to expect the Government to protect them in its capacity of trustee.

5. The Bill, therefore, is designed to protect the public against the importation of seditious literature. I want it to be clearly understood by everyone that, if the Bill is passed, the people of this country will be more safe and more secure than they are to-day.

6. It has been suggested that the Bill will affect adversely the ancient rights and liberties of the Gold Coast people. I shall, therefore, now state WHAT THE BILL WILL NOT DO.

7. It will not alter the Constitution in the slightest degree. The basis of British Trusteeship will remain unchanged.

8. It will not affect the liberty of the Gold Coast people under the trusteeship of Great Britain.

9. It will not affect the right of the Press or of any person to make a fair criticism of the Government or any Government proposal.

10. It will not affect the right of any person to make a fair criticism of the Executive and Legislative Councils or to suggest reforms or changes in those bodies or in the Supreme Court or any Government Department.

11. It will not enable this Government to pass any legislation which otherwise it would not have been within its power to pass.

12. It has been suggested that the word "sedition," as used in the Bill, will be used to mean that the right of free speech will be destroyed. There is no truth in this suggestion. The definition of "sedition" in the dictionary is, "Conduct or speech inciting to rebellion," i.e. an attempt by force to overthrow law and order.

13. It has also been suggested that the word "sovereignty" in the Bill means the local Government. This suggestion is incorrect. The definition of "sovereignty" in the dictionary is "sovereign power," i.e. the power of the Sovereign. So, when the Bill says that it is sedition to attempt to bring about a change in the sovereignty of this Colony, it merely means that an attempt to alter the position of the people of this Colony in their relation to the King is an offence.

14. It has been said that the Bill casts doubts on the loyalty of the Gold Coast people. This is totally untrue. I know full well that the people are, and always have been, loyal. I know that they venerate the Crown. To define "sedition" is not to say that a people are seditious any more than to define "murder" is to say that a people are murderers.

15. I say that the people of this country are being threatened to-day by a danger of which they know little or nothing, and it is my bounden duty to protect them against it. To be fore-warned is to be forearmed.

16. I deny absolutely any suggestion that the people of the Gold Coast will be injured by the provisions of the Bill. They need not be afraid. Their rights and privileges remain as they have always been, and in addition they will have a safeguard against attempts from outside sources to undermine their loyalty. Even if they regard this as unnecessary for themselves, they ought to welcome such protection for the sake of their children and their children's children.

F. S. W. THOMAS,
Governor.

Illustration 12–Minute by the Governor on the Criminal Code Amendment Bill, 1934
Source: *Gold Coast Gazette Extraordinary*, 21 February 1934, Public Records Office

Commons. Both delegations claimed to represent most chiefs and 'enlightened
… educated citizens' and cited their main grievance as the 'oppressive' infringe-
ment of individual liberties and increasingly autocratic government. They
declared their 'staunch loyalty' to the empire and argued for the repeal of the
Sedition Ordinance on the grounds that it 'reflected adversely on Gold Coast
peoples', who were not interested 'in foreign or Soviet aspirations or teachings'.
However, to prevent further 'grave' disorder, the ARPS recommended that the
government should curb the 'flagrant abuse of power' by government-appointed
chiefs, allow educated Africans more representation and improve elementary
education and other welfare facilities which were 'completely inadequate'.[51]

Despite these protestations of loyalty, CO officials, who regarded ARPS delegates as 'anti-white and anti-government', refused at first to see the delegation
and turned down their demands for a parliamentary inquiry.[52] In August 1936,
the ARPS was finally granted a personal interview with Malcolm MacDonald,
the new Secretary of State for Colonies, but maintained that 'contrary to all
precedents', the delegates were refused permission to take their legal counsel
along and 'no detailed reply' to the petition was given. The Government was
allegedly arrogant and discourteous in its treatment of the delegation, and guilty
of 'discrimination against black men', although this was fiercely denied by CO
officials who 'could not understand' what 'all the fuss' was about. [53] Given these
obstructions, the petition had little impact. Shenton Thomas was replaced by the
more 'liberal' Arnold Hodson, but he, too, soon hardened his line against the
'Bolshevik' press. The delegation and its British supporters failed to reverse the
repressive thrust of colonial policy and Sedition Ordinances were introduced
into other African colonies, with slight variations depending on local circumstances. In the Gold Coast, legislation was further amended to detain and
remove 'unsatisfactory' native rulers without the benefit of *habeas corpus*.[54]

After the Italian invasion of Ethiopia in 1935, the West African press became
even more strident. As editor of the Gold Coast *African Morning Post*, Nnamdi
Azikiwe wrote strong editorials criticising indirect rule and the barriers to
African progress, and circulation rose to 10,000 (a record for West Africa) across
Sierra Leone, Nigeria and the Cameroons. In 1937, Azikiwe launched his own
newspaper, the *West African Pilot* – a 'pop' family paper which claimed to be 'the
most sensational, sophisticated and important' West African newspaper of the
1930s. It capitalised on the heightened political awareness that followed the invasion and declared itself as 'one of the foremost mouthpieces' of the new radical
nationalism of the later 1930s. In 1936, charges of seditious libel were brought
against Azikiwe and the Sierra Leonian, I.T.A. Wallace Johnson, who was
regarded by the Gold Coast authorities as particularly dangerous – an 'ex-
convict' and a 'professional agitator' who had 'graduated from Moscow in the
art of subversive propaganda'.[55] The excuse for arrest was the publication of an
article, 'Has the African a God' (an attack on indirect rule) in the *African Morning
Post*. Written under the pseudonym, 'Effective', Wallace Johnson's authorship
was disclosed after the police intercepted packets he had posted to the LAI and
Negro Worker's Association in London. Johnson was convicted and the case

against Azikiwe, as the newspapers' editor, was dropped. The NCCL argued that the article 'merely expressed' the bitterness that Africans felt over the 'cynical betrayal' of Ethiopia by the European powers and even the CO felt that Governor Hodson had 'overreacted' as the 'wild rhetoric' of the article hardly constituted sedition.[56]

Wallace Johnson left the Gold Coast in March 1937 to pursue an appeal to the Privy Council. A court order obliged him to keep a low profile, but on his arrival in London he worked at the London office of the LAI, became involved in founding the International Africa Service Bureau (IASB) and edited the Bureau's bulletins, *Africa and the World* and the *African Sentinel*, which was a 'left-wing and lively' publication founded in 1938. Wallace Johnson thus used his stay in London to publicise West African grievances and win the support of the NCCL and sympathetic Labour MPs.[57] His conviction, rather than suppressing agitation, generated renewed protest in West Africa and strengthened developing pan-Africanist and anti-imperialist links connecting Britain and her 'tropical' empire. In 1938, he returned to West Africa and founded the Sierra Leone branch of the nationalist West African Youth League (which he had helped set up in the Gold Coast in 1934) with the aim of building a 'mass movement' across class lines. As strike action escalated, WAYL propaganda was accused by the colonial authorities of inciting 'bitterness ... and enmity [against] constituted authority [and] the white race'. WAYL's newspaper, the *African Sentinel*, and other 'subversive' papers, such as the *New Times and Ethiopian News*, edited in London by Sylvia Pankhurst, were banned. In 1939, an Incitement to Disaffection Bill, Deportation Ordinance, Undesirable Literature and Trade Union Bill were introduced by the Governor, Sir Douglas Jardine, with the full support of the CO.[58] The West African Civil Liberties and Defence League in Freetown (affiliated to both the WAYL and the NCCL) sent a cable of protest to the NCCL and the Secretary of State for Colonies, Malcolm MacDonald, was challenged in the House of Commons about colonial peoples' 'right to free expression of opinion'. The NCCL pointed out that the *Sentinel*, which was 'freely sold' on railway bookstalls in England, advocated only 'peaceful methods' of advance for coloured people, but MacDonald upheld the ban.[59]

In June and July, the CO received written protests from the British Labour Party and trade union organisations demanding the immediate withdrawal of the legislation, which opponents in Sierra Leone described as 'totalitarian' and 'fundamentally un-British' – a betrayal of a loyal people's trust.[60] Governor Jardine, however, was arrogant and dismissive of black organisations and blamed all 'strikes, mutinies and disaffection' on 'hostile agencies' (WAYL) who were 'inspired and partially financed' by London communists. After he gave an inflammatory speech in June, the WAYL (which now had a Women's Auxiliary section) and the Sierra Leone branch of the British-based League of Coloured People (LCP) organised a demonstration in Freetown (photos of which are enclosed in the relevant CO file) demanding Jardine's recall.[61] The colonial authorities pinpointed Wallace Johnson as the main instigator of political and industrial unrest. In early 1939, legal aid granted for his appeal against his earlier conviction under the Gold Coast Sedition Ordinances, which had still not been resolved, was stopped and his case was dismissed. Renewed pressures from the NCCL and sympathetic MPs forced the CO to reconsider his case, but the onset of war ended any hope of success. Wallace Johnson was arrested in Freetown on 1 September 1939 and charged with criminal libel. Despite the lack of supporting evidence he was convicted and officially interned in a camp for aliens under the Sierra Leone Defence Regulations.[62]

In protest against the contraction of civil liberties in Sierra Leone, the London-based League of Coloured Peoples organised a deputation to the CO, which included African nationalists based in England and white sympathisers like Sylvia Pankhurst. The deputation argued that the colonial authorities failed to recognise that 'genuine economic hardship', poor living conditions and harsh treatment were the root cause of the 'legitimate' unrest and warned that Britain would 'lose the colonies' unless it adapted to changing conditions in Africa. However, the CO backed up Governor Jardine, who had taken steps 'on his own initiative' to improve labour conditions. It was argued that new legislation was 'well within the spirit of British justice' and necessary to safeguard 'peace and good order' and secure the strategic importance of Freetown as a garrison.[63] Labour MPs continued to protest Wallace Johnson's detention, but the government was adamant that his detention order could not be revoked without 'injury to public safety'. His length of detention thus remained at the 'Governor's discretion'.[64]

Thus, with tacit CO support, colonial governments were able to consistently ignore legitimate grievances and introduce repressive legislation to defend the imperial project in Africa. Samuel Wood of the ARPS argued that the authorities were deaf to reasoned demands for greater equality and met them with 'arrogant ... [and] unscrupulous exercise of force'.[65] Any protest against colonialism was trivialised as a problem restricted to a small minority of troublemakers manipulated by communists. In practice, communist contact with West Africa was fractured and sporadic, although the *Negro Worker*, edited by George Padmore, had a limited circulation. Comintern insight into West Africa was generally hazy and practical political work was directed to more promising areas, such as South Africa and India. The group most exposed to communist influence were the well-travelled seamen. Padmore estimated there were only 4,000 Nigerian and Sierra Leonian seamen ploughing between Liverpool and the West African ports in the 1940s. Adi (1997) argues that the only significant marxist-oriented organisation in the inter-war period was WAYL and, although there was some communist influence in Nigerian organisations after the Second World War, overall the influence of communism was minimal.[66]

Although colonial officials were justified in their concerns over the WAYL, as Furedi (1995) points out, in representing Africans who opposed colonialism as fanatics, criminals or dupes of communism, ostrich-like imperialists were able to keep their heads firmly in the sand, denying the ultimate futility of imperial domination. African nationalist 'mobs' were tarred with the same moral degeneracy as the nineteenth century English working-classes and deemed unworthy of democracy.[67] However, despite physical violence and contraction of civil liberties, protest against colonial rule became more widespread. Colonial administrations now changed tactics and targeted the colonial intelligentsia in order to neutralise any potential radicalism and steer emergent nationalist sentiments into a more malleable form. This was facilitated by the lack of ideological consistency among the educated elite, the problems of the 'double consciousness' of black intellectuals and the myriad ethnic and class divisions in the West African colonies. So how real was the threat of 'dangerous ideas', in effect the development of race and political consciousness, and what part did they play in bonding the diverse threads of African protest into a mass nationalist struggle against colonial rule?

Bonding the threads of protest: black consciousness and the development of mass nationalist struggles

During the 1920s, the nationalist aspirations of the African, educated bourgeoisie remained moderate and directed toward reforms within the colonial state. In 1926, the Nigerian Democratic Party (DP) laid a memorandum before the Under Secretary of State for Colonies, Ormsby-Gore, on his visit to West Africa, which was directed primarily at legal and electoral reform and the abolition of segregation in the European and native sections of Lagos. In his official report, Ormsby-Gore concluded that rather than there being any suggestion of 'sedition or non-cooperation' in West Africa, there was a 'dominating sense of loyalty ... to the empire'. Buell made similar observations about the Gold Coast. But pan-Africanism and Garveyite black nationalism had also stimulated race consciousness and awakened a 'floating discontent', which found expression through younger political agitators.[68] Garveyism was a powerful influence on the development of African nationalist consciousness and, during the 1920s, was regarded as a threat on a par with communism. Its populist appeal extended beyond the new urban elites. Garvey's manifesto, wrote Joyce Cary, 'went all through Africa', despite the fact that US Garveyites were banned by colonial governments and Garvey was ridiculed in white papers as a 'comic figure'. For Cary this demonstrated that the 'root fact' of African politics was 'colour and race', hence the appeal of Garvey's powerful slogan: 'Africa for the Africans'.[69]

For Europeans it was education that had opened up this Pandora's box of black consciousness, and the colonial authorities thus implemented new policies to 'control' the 'aggressiveness' of the intelligentsia. Meyer Fortes was invited to join the staff of Achimota College in 1933 as 'anthropological help' was needed 'to deal constructively with the restless spirits of the students who found themselves between two worlds' – a recognition that 'inbetweenness' is a potential site of liberation, as well as identity conflict. In 1934, the Nigerian authorities established Yaba Higher College. However, the College only offered diplomas that were inferior to British awards ensuring that Africans would remain 'permanently subordinate' to Europeans.[70] Colonial education was now seen as a bitter chalice that provided Africans with the intellectual tools to challenge their position as colonial subjects, but failed to gain them full equality with whites.

Western education provided Africans with the language of democracy and rights, but affirmed white cultural superiority and excluded educated Africans from full citizenship. Younger, educated West Africans criticised the black bourgeoisie who mimicked their colonial masters, arguing that they were still treated as inferior and had been given the 'worst of both worlds'. Experiences of race prejudice in Britain (Chapter 8) fuelled this race consciousness. Rejecting this 'white manning' and allied cultural conflict, Kobina Sekyi, the Gold Coast nationalist, called for a return to the 'rationality and dignity' of the old order and a reassertion of the traditional cultural identity against an imposed culture which alienated Africans from their roots. J. Ayo Langley (1974) describes Sekyi as 'the foremost' exponent of a new, radical race consciousness, but for colonial officers, like Duncan-Johnstone, he was 'obsessed by an inordinate ambition coupled with a blind hatred of all things European'.[71]

A major stimulus to emergent black consciousness was the Italian invasion of Ethiopia in 1935, which stirred the 'communal feelings' of blacks throughout the diaspora, led to an upsurge of radical pan-Africanism and coalesced the emerging strands of West African nationalism. Africans lost faith in Europeans and argued that they had a 'ruinous effect' on the development of Africa, which could now only be saved by Africans themselves.[72] There was a new sense of the interconnectedness of the problems of Africans throughout Africa. Eslanda Goode Robeson remarked on how ordinary Africans she met were keenly interested in outside events. Margery Perham warned that Britain should not make light of her obligations to the Southern African Protectorates (Chapter 7) as any negligence would 'send a shock wave through West Africa where all such matters were keenly watched … and discussed in their numerous newspapers'. These developments challenged the trope of the passive, 'primitive' others of the English imagination. Writes Cary:

> I was like other whites. I knew nothing of what was going on in the native mind. … I assumed that [as] their ideas of the world were primitive … they were isolated also in mind. But they were not. In a continent still illiterate; where all news goes by mouth and every man is a gatherer, news of any incident affecting the relations between black and white, a strike in South Africa, a war with Abyssinia, spreads through the whole country in a few weeks. It is the most exciting news [for] it tells of a black victory.[73]

Anti-colonialism and pan-Africanism was also stimulated by links with the black colonial diaspora in Britain. A key organisation here was the London-based West African Students' Union (WASU), established in 1926, under the leadership of the Nigerian, Lapido Solanke. This organisation was closely linked to the National Congress of British West Africa, founded in 1922 to channel nationalist and pan-Africanist aspirations and to forge unity across the region. After 1930, the WASU was increasingly influential in encouraging opposition to colonial rule through political discussions held at its London hostel (Chapter 8) and branches of WASU were formed in the four colonies.[74] Some of the West

African intelligentsia in London also came into closer contact with the British anti-imperialist left and became more familiar with marxist ideas. Marxism provided the more radical African nationalists with a 'world-view' analysis of imperialism and racism, which enabled them to articulate a harder-hitting anti-imperialist stance, and marxist ideas were incorporated into the radical pan-Africanism which emerged in the late 1930s. The majority of African nationalists, however, had only a crude and fuzzy grasp of marxist–leninism as a 'political fashion' to be superficially absorbed and then discarded. The Nigerian, Enahoro, conceded that he had 'plodded through' the *Communist Manifesto*, the 'greatest drudgery' he had ever known, because it was 'required reading in the company of budding intellectuals and politicians [and] fashionable in Lagos ... '. Enahoro spent several spells in prison in the 1940s because of his 'left-wing' views, but aspired only to building a political organisation of the 'character and composition of the British Labour Party'. Communist influence, concluded the academic, William Macmillan, was probably 'no more than a ferment' and 'American Negro teaching on race' was of equal importance in the growth of anti-colonialism.[75]

By the late 1930s, the colonial authorities were forced to acknowledge this growing nationalist sentiment, but blamed it on anti-European race-consciousness. Anti-colonial movements, argues Furedi (1995), were thus pathologised as 'maladjustment' to the penetration of Western culture, and African nationalism was represented as unstable and dangerous, a reflection of the African's own failure to cope with 'the too quick pace of change and the indigestibility of great chunks of Westernism'. However, more progressive imperialists recognised the importance of economic factors and the validity of nationalist aspirations. As the new 'star' in the imperial firmament (Chapter 10), Malcolm Hailey was shrewd enough to realise the potential of this nationalist sentiment and thus argued that it was the 'positive modern elements' that should be cultivated rather than the 'reactive' anti-Europeanism of the 'absurd Garvey movement' or the baleful influence of Communism. African consciousness, he argued, was no threat to European authority if 'moderation was ensured'.[76] Hailey recognised that the key to this upsurge of nationalist consciousness was the 'co-option' of elite Africans into imperial governance, which would drive wedges between moderates and radicals, undermine any potentially dangerous movements. The co-option of the moderate Western educated minority became official policy during the Second World War.

White interventions intensified problems of forging coherent nationalist ideologies out of the conflicting ideologies of marxism, pan-Africanism and the liberal democratic values fundamental to the Western education of the African intelligentsia. Strong differences emerged between Azkikiwe Nnamdi, whose 'Renascent Africa' was a combination of liberal welfare capitalism, Christianity traditional values, Garveyite self-help and black enterprise, and Nkrumah, who developed a more radical brand of pan-Africanism which incorporated marxist perspectives.[77] Radicals accused leaders like Azikiwe of opportunism, 'lack of integrity' and selfish race pride, but Azikiwe was reluctant to be 'tarred with the same revolutionary brush' as Nkrumah because affiliation with communism would 'damn' the nationalist movement.[78]

Despite these problems, the Second World War catalysed the undercurrent of broad-based protest that had been developing during the 1930s and transformed nationalist movements into mass political parties with a clear anti-imperialist agenda, influenced by the stress on freedom, self-determination, racial equality and civil liberties articulated in the Atlantic Charter. As in the First World War, African soldiers were deployed, many in North Africa, and mostly in non-combatant roles as labourers, drivers, guards and orderlies, although there were also a spattering of West African pilots in the Royal Airforce. As Killingray and Rathbone (1986) point out, African troops were generally loyal and effective, but there were a few mutinies towards the end of the war.[79] However, the ethos of the war was entirely different from that of the First World War, and West African 'loyalty to empire' was firmly linked to expectations of change and greater self-rule at the end of the war. Moreover, colonial policy during the war intensified rather than diffused mounting grievances during the 1930s. Sylvia Leith-Ross, who worked in the Information Service in Lagos during the war, recalled that an insulting recruiting poster in Lagos, which depicted African soldiers in Khaki with the 'bright scarlet lips of a Nigger Minstrel on Brighton beach', was interpreted as a 'premeditated insult'. New forms of taxation were introduced, there was greater direction of labour, including use of forced labour, for the war effort and a rise in food costs.[80]

At the end of the war, civilians and demobbed soldiers had high expectations for the future (Illustration 13). However, these were soon punctured and grievances were expressed in serious strikes and riots. A general strike in Nigeria in 1945 was supported by seventeen unions representing 150,000 workers, many of whom were government employees. The strike was over wage demands to meet the rising cost of living, but was strongly anti-government and anti-colonial in character. The British government re-introduced wartime regulations, arrested strike leaders and suppressed the local press. A public rally was held at Conway Hall, London, attended by British anti-imperialists and African nationalists, reflecting the increasing diasporic dimension to African struggles.[81] Indian independence in 1947 charged this tense situation and in 1948 there were serious riots in the Gold Coast in which twenty-nine people were killed. Nkrumah, regarded as the most dangerous nationalist leader, was imprisoned on the orders of the Governor, Gerald Creasy, but was released as a result of popular pressure and formed the Convention People's Party, which ultimately led the Gold Coast to independence in 1956. Although Nkrumah was against violence and favoured Gandhian tactics of civil disobedience, the Gold Coast Government believed his populist nationalism was 'communist inspired'.[82] The success of the CCP was indicative of the catalysing effect of the Second World War on mass, as opposed to elite, political consciousness.

The authorities were deeply perturbed by this 'seething unrest' and British residents in the colonies sensed a 'tense and hostile feeling' and were 'stung' by the lack of gratitude on the part of Africans whom they had treated with

Illustration 13–Wartime loyalty
Source: *Empire Youth Annual*, London, P.R., Gawthorne Ltd., 1947

'disinterested kindness and generosity'.[83] Sylvia Leith-Ross accused educated Africans, in contact with 'white sympathisers' in England, of fomenting this unrest. For the first time, her 'faith in the black man was shaken' and she condemned the 'deliberate ... falsifying' of words and actions and the 'daily sneers' and 'fantastic' accusations of the press. This suggests the growing influence of African newspapers, which, observed Hailey, reached a wider audience than the literate minority as it was 'common for those who cannot read them to listen to those who can'. Thus, the press fostered developments in mass nationalist consciousness and the further 'intrusion of politics' into the Trade Union Movement, which, argued Hailey, was the real threat to imperial power.[84]

With the onset of the Cold War, the CO, which had centralised colonial administration during the war, responded to this unrest with some urgency. The media was a vital weapon in this struggle for the hearts and minds of Africans during what Killingray and Rathbone (1986) have termed 'the second colonial occupation' of Africa. The press, particularly in the vernacular, was regarded as essential to development, and more control over content was ensured by a government-controlled London Press Service, which provided free news and, maintains Hailey, was 'widely used'. A wide-ranging cultural offensive was launched to extend government information services and train journalists to counteract the 'deplorably low standard' of the press, which was too political and spread 'inaccurate information' that could do 'untold harm' among 'unsophisticated' populations.[85]

Once Britain accepted that decolonisation was inevitable, particularly in the advanced colonies of Nigeria and the Gold Coast, efforts were made to ensure change with the 'minimum of prejudice' to the interests of imperial power. Private interests also adapted and rapacious companies, like the UAC, now cultivated better relations with Africans, promoting them to higher positions and providing scholarships and special training in England. The British still clung to their myths of benign rule and reformist concessions to the demands of the intelligentsia, demonstrated that West Africans possessed more rights than their counterparts in East or South Africa.[86] Decolonisation avoided the more widespread violence that darkened the transition to independence in Kenya, but this peaceful decolonisation was not accidental; it was the product of policies devised before the war to contain the groundswell of discontent. However, in the longer term, British 'divide and rule' colonial policies and the cultivation of 'moderate' elites had important implications for independent African states. In Nigeria, for instance, rivalries developed, based on ethnic nationalisms, which mirrored the colonial mapping of the colony. These emerged with the development of nationalist parties, but intensified after independence as political power became increasingly intermeshed with access to the economic resources of the new state. This resulted in appeals to 'tribal' loyalties by political leaders to advance their own economic interests. Regional competition for access to state resources, combined with ethnic rivalries, erupted into factional violence which culminated in the Nigerian Civil War (the 'Biafran War' of 1967–1970). While the problems of the post-colonial Nigerian state cannot be attributed solely to imperialism, colonial rule created the conditions for conflict by sharpening class, ethnic and regional divisions in Nigeria. In Ghana, Nkrumah's more radical regime also disolved into corruption, widening the divisions between the political elite and the masses. Both states succumbed to military coups.[87]

Interrogating the reasons for the failure of African nationalism in the post-independent period is a challenging, controversial and complex task that is beyond the scope of this present study. However, the workings of imperialism in West Africa undoubtedly enhanced social cleavages between rural and urban classes, the elite and the masses, and made it difficult to form bonds that would survive the immediate transition to independence. Cultivation of the moderate, bourgeois elite secured a continued base for Western financial interests, while, argues Lauren (1996), the manipulation of the communist threat deflected the just grievances of the masses.[88] The manipulation of ethnicity and 'tradition' under colonial rule also had important consequences. As the masses had been excluded from modernity under indirect rule, the nationalist intelligentsia appealed to ethnic as well as pan-African consciousness in building nationalist movements. The attraction of ethnic identity, points out Vail (1989), was that it cut across class lines and prioritised culture and 'traditional values' in a time of change. Ethnicity, he argues, is dynamic, not static, and thus may also by viewed as 'another form of popular consciousness' which emerged with the political struggles against colonialism. However, progressive imperialists saw such 'ethnic consciousness' or 'tribalism' as regressive and divisive. Malcolm Hailey (1957) defined it as closing ranks against the 'alien forces of Western ideas and techniques' and contrasted it with the 'constructive nationalism' influenced by Western ideals of self-determination.[89]

Colonial experts thus downplayed ethnic consciousness and the force of African culture in their management of the transition to self-rule. Hailey argued that the 'doctrine of identity', based on the development of 'European' social and political institutions, was 'a decisive preference of Africans themselves'.[90] However, this 'doctrine of identity' assumed the Westernised male elite as the conduits of 'progress' and excluded the mass of men and women whose protest and resistance since the inter-war years had, arguably, ended colonial rule through *force majeure*. As yet, the link between gender, resistance and nationalism in West Africa remains under-researched. As Coquery-Vidrovitch (1994) argues, market women were an important force in opposing colonial rule and were early supporters of nationalist movements. The West African Youth League actively recruited women and had five educated women on its central committee in the 1930s, and political parties in the run up to independence recognised the utility of women, establishing women's sections, which were presided over by the wives of leaders. However, with rare exceptions, bourgeois women failed to make links with working-class or peasant women thereby widening social divisions.[91] Although women had token representation in nationalist organisations, African and white patriarchal attitudes ensured that women were marginalised in nationalist organisations, with rare exceptions like Adelaide Casely-Hayford and Mabel Dove-Danquah, who both belonged to the tiny Europeanised West African elite and were married to leading African nationalists.[92]

There is a huge literature on the meaning of nationalism and decolonisation (a problematic and much contended concept) that is beyond the scope of this work.[93] Orthodox studies of African nationalism, however, have tended to focus too narrowly on nationalist movements after 1945 and erased the important earlier resistance struggles. Hailey's 1956 study, for instance, barely makes any mention of strikes or other forms of resistance during the 1930s. Similar criticisms can be made of more recent Eurocentric studies of decolonisation. As emphasised in this chapter, anti-colonialism was diffuse and widespread, and articulated in a variety of ways by all classes of Africans, rural and urban, male and female. Thus, Thomas Hodgkin (1956) associated anti-colonial nationalism with any group that 'explicitly [asserted] the rights, claims and aspirations of a society'.[94] It was arguably the myriad resistance struggles of inter-war years, rather than the verbal challenges of the intelligentsia, which seriously disrupted imperial rule and punctured the dreams of British imperial power. As demonstrated in Chapter 2, subtle everyday acts of non-compliance and cultural resistance, sometimes not even perceived as resistance by whites, also persistently demonstrated that white rule was not welcome. Nationalist leaders could not have achieved power without mass grass roots support, male and female, but after independence they lost out to the greed and corruption of the new African leaders. Colonial hegemony was arguably replaced by the hegemony of the new African rulers who manipulated ethnicity and 'invented' their own nationalist traditions and myths to retain power. But the dreams of independence were also marred by the very real poverty and nature of the colonial economy. In 1941, Rita Hinden of the Fabian Colonial Bureau noted that even the most 'advanced' and potentially rich colony, the Gold Coast, was hampered by lack of capital investment, monoculture and dependency on food imports. Thus, the links which continued to bond West Africa to Britain and the international economy perpetuated the economic dependency and poverty of the colonial era.[95]

Summary

To understand fully the nature of the challenge to imperialist power in West Africa we must move away from narrow nationalist narratives and explore broader patterns of resistance. This chapter has focused on protest in the 'modern sector', but it is implicitly linked to the previous two chapters, which explore a range of resistant responses. I have argued that the colonial authorities were faced with a mounting tide of popular discontent and protest during the inter-war years, which they tried to suppress through mechanisms of cultural imperialism, but also increasingly repressive policies. When these myopic policies stimulated a more concerted opposition to colonial rule in Africa and Britain, there was some damage limitation with cosmetic reforms in colonial policy. These changes were linked to a broader shift in Britain's relationship with Africa after 1935, which resulted from international developments and important changes in discourses on race and empire in the imperial heartland (Chapters 9 and 10). But 'dangerous ideas' that stimulated race and political consciousness proved difficult to police and, in 1939, West Africa, in particular the Gold Coast, had become the powerhouse of radical African nationalism and pan-Africanism. The war further catalysed mass nationalist consciousness and, in order to hold on to power, new imperialist strategies were deployed to win the 'hearts and minds' of African subjects. This ensured the 'peaceful transition' to independence with all the structures of the colonial state intact. The majority of nationalist leaders were finally steered away from more radical ideologies and the Commonwealth continued to bind ex-colonial subjects to the 'higher ideals' that had underpinned the empire – a reflection also of the success of more subtle workings of cultural imperialism during colonial rule. In 'radical' Ghana, at the independence celebrations in 1957, which was captured on newsreel, 'African statesmen and elegant black and British ladies danced the beguine … and pictures of Nkrumah and the Queen of England stood [illuminated] side by side'.[96] This image of a peaceful and democratic transition was a carefully constructed British myth that was soon shattered by the rapid failure of democracy, which led to a resurgence of the broader forces of resistance, now in opposition to African rulers. However, it has persisted as a comforting myth that sustains Britain's image as a benign and beneficial imperial presence in West Africa – an image that becomes far more tarnished when we turn to the murky role of British imperialism in the white settler colony supreme, South Africa.

South Africa

5 Forging the racist state

Imperialism, race and labour in Britain's 'white dominion'

The white vermin, my Lord
Invades the lands of our forefathers
They, the adolescents who defecate
In the house like infants
The white man carves the land
With blood drenched knives,
From North to South the sun bleeds …
(traditional poem).

Blessed be the rulers of this land
Who make the laws to suit their own purposes in life …
They rule their natives with a firm hand
Caring not whether God sees
Days and nights the Children of Africa
Are reminded of their defeats in the battle fields
Their colour of skin remains a stigma in their life time
(A.W.G. Champion, 1928)[1]

A seamless web of imperial and racist discourses connected South Africa to the rest of Africa and Britain, the imperial centre. As Mamdani (1996) has provocatively argued, segregation and Apartheid was a concentrated and formalised form of practices that were developed by all colonial states in Africa. Many of the developments which occurred in West Africa in the inter-war period were replicated in the Union of South Africa. Black consciousness was permeated by the same diasporic influences and was triggered by the depression, increasing state repression and the two world wars. After 1935, the invasion of Ethiopia and the acceleration of nationalism in West Africa boosted black South African nationalism, articulated through 'youth movements' and fired by dreams of African regeneration. But in South Africa, imperialism, racism and African struggles for freedom were complicated and intensified by white settler rule. South Africa was arguably not 'unique', but possessed 'in miniature most of the great problems with which the world has been confronted during the twentieth century'.[2]

When the British academic Ifor L. Evans visited South Africa in 1933, he concluded that although the methods of 'native' policy were essentially the same

as elsewhere in British tropical Africa, the context in which they were developed
was 'utterly different'.[3] A key point of difference was the proletarianisation and
landlessness of substantial sections of the African population as opposed to the
'peasantisation' of West Africa. South Africa also possessed a tenacious white
ruling minority, a rapid rate of industrialisation and capital accumulation, and
an indigenous communist and liberal opposition to state policies. As the white
settler colony supreme, it became the model for settlers in East Africa and the
Rhodesias. The South African state's vicious racial policies were arguably
matched only in French Algeria. South African race policies, however, did not
develop in isolation. Australia was also a deeply racist state, although the
majority status of whites and international focus on South Africa deflected attention.[4] Analogies based on points of convergence at critical points in their
histories and shared 'race problems' have also been made between South Africa
and the southern states of the USA. In South Africa, however, as Leonard Woolf
pointed out, the 'Negro problem' was 'embittered by imperialism'.[5]

Imperialism is fundamental to understanding developments in South Africa.
As the liberal historian, Cornelis de Kiewiet, stressed, South African history must
be written as both local and imperial history, part of a vast network of influences
linking the different parts of Britain's empire. Before the Second World War, as
Britain's prime African settler colony, South Africa had greater international
acceptance and, 'although a small power', it played a 'respected [and] constructive
international role'.[6] South Africa was also seminal to contemporary international
debates over race problems. Britain and other international powers, however,
ignored the development of segregation. 'Race problems' were represented as a
purely internal domestic problem arising mainly out of conflict between 'Boer
and Briton'. The South African historian, William Macmillan, warned against
the localisation and isolation of South African race problems from wider trends
in world history.[7] The isolation of South Africa under Apartheid tended to rein-
force this parochialism.

Since the end of Apartheid serious questions have emerged about which
version of history should be taught and how history can be delinked from the
culture of oppression which sustained white supremacy. The histories of the
oppressed were rendered invisible or distorted to fit in with the myths of the
powerful. South African history is thus a minefield of conflicting historical
visions of the past and the intersection of ethnicity, nationalism, class and gender
presents a particular challenge to historians. White and black people have their
own sites of memory – the Afrikaner Voortrekker monument in Pretoria, the
graves of the Zulu kings in Natal. In Cape Town, the Cape Malays have the
graves of their Moslem saints, which are rooted in memories of their rebellious
slave past. Some sites converge, but have different meanings to blacks and whites
– as in the 12 December African commemoration of 'Dingaan's Day', which, as
the day of the defeat of Dingaan's Zulu army at Blood River in 1838, is also
sacred to Afrikaners. There is a huge and stimulating literature on all aspects of
South African history and racial policy which I do not intend to duplicate here.[8]
My interest here is in the wider context of developments in imperialism, racism

and resistance in South Africa. This chapter, then, will evaluate the role of British imperialism in the forging of the South African state, the development of segregationist ideology and the implications this had for whites and blacks in South Africa. Chapters 6 focuses on the development of black resistance, while Chapter 7 assesses the impact of British liberal interventions in South African 'native' problems.

'Bantu, Boer and Briton': British imperialism in South Africa

The Act of Union in 1910, which granted South Africa internal self-government as an imperial 'white dominion', was represented as a 'signal example of Britain's political wisdom and justice' when, for the first time in history, a victorious nation surrendered power 'of its own free will' to the vanquished, Smuts, 'the greatest of Boer Guerrilla leaders', and General Louis Botha.[9] From this point onwards, however, the tensions intensified between Afrikaner republicans and those groups that favoured continued bonds with Britain. By the outbreak of the Second World War, South Africa acted as an autonomous state which operated a form of 'internal colonialism', but which was also an embryonic sub-imperialist power acting as proxy for Western imperialist interests in the region. These developments arguably occurred with the collusion of Britain and the English-speaking minority in South Africa.

Up to the 1970s, historians like de Kieweit attributed the consolidation of the segregationist state to the 'frontier' racial attitude of Afrikaners, whose ascendancy had eclipsed the liberal, moderating traditions of nineteenth century British liberalism.[10] Britain's benevolent and liberal image was fortified by the abolition of slavery in the Cape in 1838 and the liberal constitution conferred on the Cape in 1854, which secured limited franchise for Africans who possessed suitable property and salary qualifications. Such measures established the principles of 'Cape liberalism', which became the 'beacon of hope' for educated blacks and secured their loyalty to the British Empire until they were 'sorely disillusioned'.[11] It was this rhetoric of liberal imperialism which prompted Bechuanaland, Swaziland and Basutoland to 'voluntarily' become Protectorates of the British Empire. However, Magubane (1994) has argued that the Round Table Group was seminal in promoting this sanitised version of humane British imperialism and Legassick (1995) and Keegan (1996) have both demonstrated that the origins of segregation were rooted in British imperial policies. For Keegan, the pre-industrial, 'liberal' Cape was the 'original seedbed' of the processes of dispossession and accumulation out of which the racial state emerged and, as Evans emphasised, the British were initially responsible for the development of 'native' policy.[12]

The expansion of British imperialism in South Africa had an irreversible impact on African societies. Differing degrees of collaboration with, or resistance against, the British Crown or the Boers, sometimes capitalising on pre-existing antagonisms, had driven wedges between African peoples and between African and 'Coloured' people, facilitating the expansion of white power. The African nationalist Sol Plaatje's remarkable novel, *Mhudi* (1930), which draws on Barolong oral traditions, vividly depicts the diverse relations that Africans had with Boer trekkers and British missionaries and settlers. The Barolong fight the Matabele (Ndebele) alongside the Boers in revenge for the Matabele ruthlessly wiping out their people. Indeed, the book offers a rare insight into the geographical mapping of Southern Africa and social relations between different African peoples before the white settlers had irreversibly transformed the landscape.[13]

With accelerated economic development, Africans were drawn further into the white world and their lives became more tightly controlled by British 'Randlords' who introduced the first Pass Laws to control migrant labour in 1894. From this point on, blacks and whites were subjected to the same processes of proletarianisation. British economic penetration and tighter integration into the global economy resulted in the reorganisation of agriculture into larger farms, depopulation of the countryside and the creation of a 'poor white' class, intensifying economic competition between black and white labour. The establishment of British sugar plantations in Natal led to the introduction of Indian indentured labour, which complicated the race/class divisions. With industrialisation, European migrants poured in, diversifying the white ethnic base and further entrenching divisions between black and white labour. Thus, for the poor and dispossessed, argues Cammack (1990), the extension of British imperialism, consolidated by the 1899–1902 South African (Boer) War, brought a new and more concentrated oppression.[14]

The South African War was rooted in the British greed to exploit South Africa's rich mineral reserves and cheap 'native' labour and sealed the conquest and incorporation of the African societies into an evolving settler (British and Afrikaner) society. Defined as a 'white man's war', it marked the completion of the British conquest, which was begun in the 1870s, of South Africa and was represented as the triumph of liberalism and modernity over backward, Afrikaner racist forces. But the war left a bitter heritage: the treatment of women and children in the British concentration camps and the defeat of the Afrikaner commandos stimulated nationalist and republican aspirations. Africans had also fought on both sides and suffered in the camps; those who had aided the British believed that the war had been fought to 'free the oppressed natives' from Afrikaner cruelty, but found that it was such men that the British subsequently 'entrusted with the destinies of our race.'[15]

After the South African War, new legislation was introduced to further control migrant labour and secure white supremacy. From 1902–5, the Governor-General, Viscount Milner, launched a period of reconstruction which involved tighter control over African land and labour. Measures were also implemented to subdue the 'troublesome native', particularly the 'mission-educated' native, who was the unwanted product of imperial development. British missionaries, liberals and administrators were in agreement with Afrikaners on the racially exclusive occupation of land, separate political representation and education, and the need to preserve tribal cultures through separate development.[16] By 1905 all the elements of segregation were in place and in 1909 the South Africa Act created the Union of South Africa. In an attempt to secure rights for Coloured minorities in the ex-Boer republics during this period of transition, the African Peoples' Organisation (APO), founded in 1902, sent deputations to Britain in 1906 and 1909, headed by Dr Abdurahman, a British-educated Cape Town Moslem who became leader of the APO in 1906. However, the APO delegations failed to reverse the tide of segregationist legislation.[17]

The foundation stone of segregation was the 1913 Land Act, passed with the full support of British South Africans, and only repealed in 1991. Under the new legislation, less than 10 per cent of land was set aside for the majority of the African population as 'native reserves', which formed the basis of the later 'homelands' and Bantustans (Illustration 14). The creation of the reserves reshaped and compartmentalised African ethnicities and accelerated the trend of migration to the towns. In the early years, some Africans, supported by sympathetic government officials, used loopholes to circumvent the legislation and in 1918, argues Evans (1934), the Governor-General granted several thousand applications for land.[18] But for the mass of Africans, the Act, which curbed the development of a more prosperous African farming class, had deeply negative consequences (akin to the impact of the Highland clearances in Scotland). Sol Plaatje forcefully itemised the great social distress caused by the eviction of over one million black tenants and their livestock from white farms, which was facilitated by the extension of the pass system to prevent squatting. Overall, concludes Plaatje, 1913 was a 'fateful year' for Africans, marked by disasters, the deaths of leaders and unprecedented drought. These adverse conditions also posed new threats to whites as 'native mine boys' rioted in the gold fields, calling for the intervention of imperial troops.[19]

The Act and other policies implemented by the British shook black faith in British liberalism and catalysed a new consciousness of democratic rights. For Plaatje it demonstrated definitively that 'English colonists can be just as devilish as Boers on questions of colour' and some had even 'out-Boered the Boer'. Pressure groups emerged to articulate black grievances, led by the mission-educated Westernised elite, who had established a buoyant black press.[20] In 1914, the South African Native National Congress (SANNC), formed in 1912 to fight the proposed Land Act, also sent a deputation. Sol Plaatje, a key member of the deputation, stressed:

> This appeal is not on behalf of the naked hordes of Cannibals who are represented in fantastic pictures displayed in the shop windows of Europe, most of them imaginary; but it is on behalf of the five million loyal British subjects who shoulder 'the black man's burden' every day …

This burden included labouring for whites, 'beautifying' the white quarters of the towns, while the black areas were neglected, and paying heavy taxes. But the imperial government and the South African High Commissioner, Lord Gladstone, failed to respond to the SANNC's appeal for imperial protection.

NOTE

The map shows the approximate distribution of Native areas South of the Zambezi, except in Swaziland, where it would be difficult to indicate their limits on so small a scale. Particular thanks are due to the South African Institute of Race Relations for permission to incorporate data from an outline map of the Union: and to the Mandates Section of the Secretariat of the League of Nations for similar assistance with regard to South West Africa.

This map of Native areas should, of course, be compared with others showing rainfall, physical features and population density, which are more easily available.

The numbers in the map refer to the following areas:

Union

1. Glen Grey
2. Fingoland
3. Tembuland
4. Pondoland
5. Zululand
6. British Bechuanaland

H. C. Territories

7. Basutoland
8. Bamangwato Res.
9. Bakwena Res.
10. Bangwaketse Res.
11. Batawana Res.
12. Bakhatla Res.

S. W. Africa

13. Rehoboth Gebiet
14. Bondelzwarts country
15. Ovamboland

In South West Africa the shaded portions represent the Native leases and the Treaty Reserves as they existed in German days, including the Rehoboth Gebiet. The additional Reserves, including Ovamboland, created under the administration of the Mandatory are shown in black. Elsewhere all the Native areas are in black. In the case of Southern Rhodesia, the Native Reserves alone are indicated.

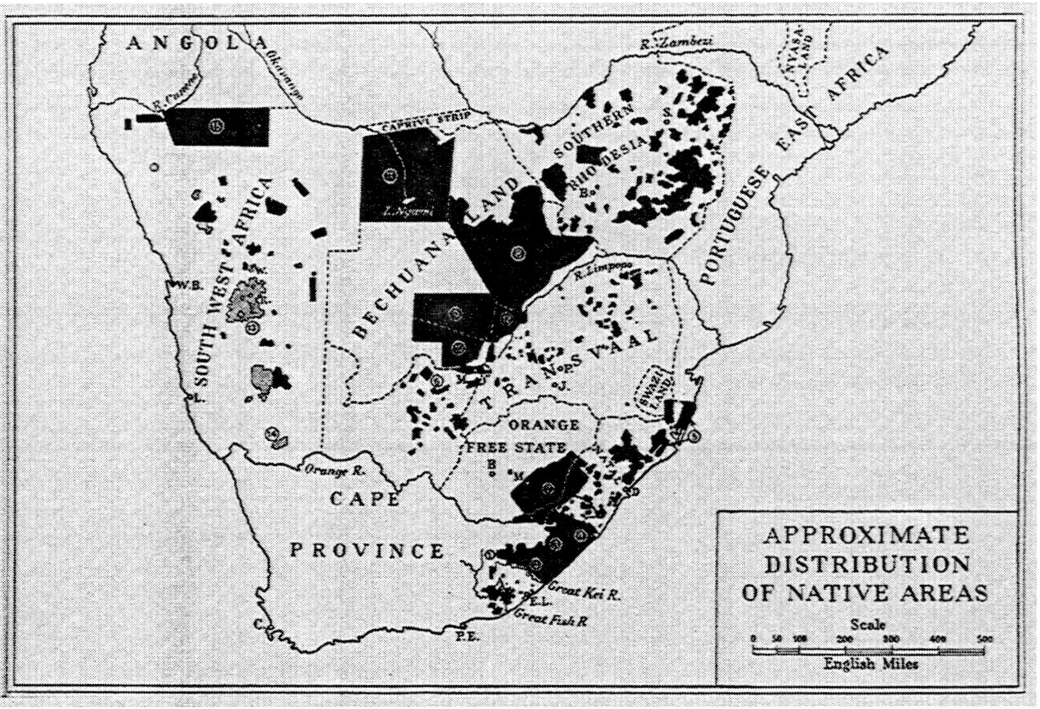

Illustration 14–Map of the approximate distribution of native areas in Southern Africa, *c.*1930
Source: I.L. Evans, *Native Policy in Southern Africa: An Outline*, Cambridge, Cambridge University Press, 1934

The Anti-Slavery and Aborigines Protection Society (ASAPS) also discouraged people from supporting the deputation on the basis that segregation was in the 'best interests' of the natives.[21]

At the outbreak of the First World War, the SANNC, 'prompted by loyalty to the British Empire', sent a representation to the Governor-General volunteering African help. (Ironically, this African loyalty contrasted with the serious Boer rebellion in 1914, led by General de Wet, a supporter of the nationalist leader, General Herzog, which took loyal Afrikaners several months to quell).[22] After the war, the SANNC renewed its petitioning to secure British imperial intervention to reverse segregationist policies in reward for African loyalty. The SANNC pointed out that Africans had contributed to the war effort in South West Africa as drivers and labourers and also taken part in the German East African Campaign, under Lieutenant-General Smuts, many of them suffering hardship and dying of malaria. In addition, 25,000 Africans had worked in the French docks and 'behind the trenches in Flanders'. Africans had contributed in money and kind to support various war funds, and chiefs and leaders had exhorted their people to remain 'quiet and loyal' and had ensured a continued output of gold and cyanide through encouraging labour recruitment.[23] Mendi Memorial Day, commemorating 615 black South Africans who sank in the SS Mendi in the service of the empire, came to symbolise African war sacrifices and, during the Second World War, a Mendi Memorial scholarship fund was set up to commemorate this major African disaster.[24]

But compensation for those injured and killed was 'extremely inadequate' and the failure of the imperial government to reward Africans through reversals in the segregationist legislation rekindled African grievances. At a special session of the SANNC, held in Johannesburg on 16 December 1918, it was agreed that a 'memorial' should be sent to King George V outlining these grievances, and a deputation was sent to London to petition the imperial government. A letter to Milner, now Secretary of State for Colonies, emphasised the timeliness of the mission as the world was 'on the threshold of an era of freedom, justice and peace' and requested that the memorial should be placed before the Peace Conference. 'Will Britain', wrote Selope Thema, 'after fighting for the liberation of the World ... from Prussian militarism and tyranny, allow tyranny and autocracy to flourish in one of her Dominions?'[25] The SANNC called for amendments to the South Africa Act to abolish the colour bar and extend the franchise to Africans, and petitioned against the incorporation of German South West Africa and the British Protectorates into the Union. They were vehemently opposed to any suggestion of South Africa becoming a 'white republic'. The organisation also complained about pass laws, unfair taxation and the failure of the state to provide for education, except by helping missionaries with 'little sums'. The Coloured Soldiers Association and the APO, representing the Coloured minority, articulated similar grievances and also petitioned Milner to use his influence at the Peace Conference.[26] The major grievances were eloquently summed up in Sol Plaatje's, *Some of the Legal Disabilities Suffered by the Native Population*, (1919).

A SANNC deputation arrived in London in June 1919. Although the SANNC had planned for eight delegates, only three, L.T. Mbaza, R.F. Selope Thema and the Reverend A.L. Ngcayiya, 'a member of the Ethiopian Church', travelled to England on the 'Voronej' on the 22 March. The ASAPS were asked to find them lodgings as they were mostly 'honest natives' and reputedly 'well supplied ... with funds'. Other delegates followed, including L. Mvabaza and Dr Rubusana (APO), who were classed as 'doubtful characters'.[27] The Union Government conceded that the SANNC had a 'considerable following', but stressed that it was not representative of the 'various native tribes' and had 'no authority to speak on ... behalf ... [such] tribes'. Although superficial differences existed between the imperial and the Union Government, they were essentially 'entirely' in agreement over the response to the deputation. The British position was that any alteration to the South Africa Act by the British Government would probably 'make the position of natives worse not better' and Milner strongly advised the King not to receive the deputation.[28]

The deputation initially had hopes that they could petition the new League of Nations. However, the ASAPS were advised by the South African High Commission that it was 'very difficult to see what these good men [could] accomplish' in Paris and that the very serious shortage of accommodation and 'general unwillingness to receive Coloured men will add greatly to their difficulties'. Both the British and the Union Government agreed that the administration of the Protectorates and SANNC grievances were domestic and should not be taken up by the League. According to Egerton (1922), Smuts was 'deeply impressed' and offended by the 'humiliating sight' of a native deputation in Paris bearing an 'appalling document' animated by a spirit of distrust of South African whites.[29] When the deputation returned home, Plaatje stayed on in London in the hope of influencing the peace negotiations. He attended the Pan-African Conferences in Paris and London in 1919 and 1921, and petitioned South African delegates to the Peace Conference, but without noticeable success.[30]

As Union delegate to the Peace Conference, Smuts was the linchpin in communications between the Union and British Governments over the SANNC deputation. Although an Afrikaner, he believed that South Africa needed the support of Britain to develop. He was cultivated by the best society in England and had close contacts with influential liberal imperialists. His modest house in Irene, near Pretoria, now a museum, is full of memorabilia of these powerful connections. The pro-English, Cambridge-educated Smuts, who was twice prime minister of the Union of South Africa, was thus seen as a political counter force to Afrikaner republicanism, which remained a threat to Britain's visions of a powerful, white Commonwealth. He is attributed with coining the phrase, 'the British Commonwealth of Nations' at an imperial conference in London in 1917 and has been described as one of the world's 'few illustrious men'.[31] A charismatic figure, he commanded great loyalty and maintained a high profile in international diplomacy up to the Second World War. Yet, as Beinart (1994) notes, despite many biographies, Smuts remains an elusive figure who often spoke with a 'forked tongue', but also had a capacity for compromise that enabled him to navigate successfully the troubled waters of white South African politics until after the Second World War. Like his close friend Denys Reitz (a South African Party MP and government minister in the inter-war years), he was passionate about the environment and protection of South African wildlife (Illustration 15). Unfortunately, such concern did not extend to Africans. Despite the hopes of British liberals, who banked on Smuts to keep the stifled flame of Cape liberalism alive, he did nothing to prevent the deepening of segregation. As Winifred Holtby noted, for Smuts and his contemporaries, English and Afrikaner, the 'human horizon' did not extend to the 'Coloured races'.[32]

The British imperial behemoth flicked off the SANNC deputation like an irritating fly. What could a few poor and weak Africans do no matter how articulately they stated their case? Internal problems in South Africa were no longer Britain's concern: South Africa was now conceptualised as a 'White Man's country', part of Britain's 'white commonwealth' and a major 'civilising influence' in the region. The Highveld, free from malaria and other tropical diseases, stretched up to Rhodesia and formed a solid block of territory 'within the British Empire', which was eminently suited to white settlement.[33] The peace settlement had also endorsed South Africa's mandate over ex-German South West Africa

Illustration 15–Field-Marshal, the Rt. Hon. Jan Christiaan Smuts
Source: *Empire Youth Annual*, London, P.R. Gawthorne Ltd., 1947

(Chapter 1). Thus, in the inter-war years, South African settler society was well placed to consolidate the racist state with the tacit blessing of Britain and the League of Nations. However, orthodox British interpretations of inter-war South African history have attributed the forging of the South African state to the rise of Afrikaner nationalism and downplayed the continuing importance of British imperialism.[34]

The rise of Afrikaner nationalism is seminal to understanding the conflicts between 'Bantu, Boer and Briton'. The Afrikaner National Party was founded in 1914 by Generals Botha and Herzog to counteract the dominance of the South African Party (SAP), which fostered unity between the British and Afrikaners, accepted imperial links with Britain and thus protected British financial interests. The Nationalists were first elected to power in 1924 with the goal of cementing white unity against imperialist control. Perhaps it is no coincidence that J.H. Thomas, the Labour Secretary of State for Dominions, chose to visit South Africa in the run-up to the elections with a delegation of British MPs who were connected with the British Empire Parliamentary Association.[35] After the National Party and the SAP formed the United Party in 1934 to tackle the deep problems created by a combination of depression, drought, and floods the 'purified' nationalists (*Gersuiwerde Nasionale Party*) split away in 1934 under Dr Malan (described by Reitz as a 'tight-lipped Covenanter with no sense of humour'). Malan placed far greater emphasis on the mobilisation of Afrikaner ethnicity through organisations like the Afrikaner *Broederbond*, formed in 1918 with the aim of establishing an independent Afrikaner government and promoting Afrikaner culture. This inspired even greater concern over the need to defend British interests, represented in the foundation of the Dominions Party, led by Colonel Stallard, and mostly consisting of the 'ultra-British' of Natal.[36]

Afrikaners were of mixed Dutch, French and German descent. Some felt a closer cultural affinity with Germany than Britain and, during the 1930s, the more extremist Afrikaners embraced fascist ideas. Para-military greyshirts became more noticeably active against communists and Jews, but pro-German sentiment also extended to mainstream politics. The British Left thus alleged that by 1937 fascism was 'solidly established' in South Africa and militaristic tactics were employed to suppress black protest and end industrial disputes.[37] The developing trend towards fascism was given impetus by the 1938 centenary celebrations of the Great Trek and the formation of the Nazi-modelled *Ossewa Brandung* (the ox-wagon picket), which glorified the Afrikaners' pioneering heritage and a mystical creed of purity of race and white destiny. It was only in 1939 with the outbreak of war that the tide of Afrikaner nationalism seemed to be reversed. When Herzog's neutrality motion was defeated, Smuts became head of the National Government and South Africa again affirmed its support for the British war effort.

Segregation was associated exclusively with this rise of Afrikaner nationalism, and British South Africans and investors in Britain were exonerated from any responsibility for the oppression of the African labour from which they benefited. British interests and profits were protected by the imperial government, whose main objective was to keep valuable South Africa within the Commonwealth. The British Government thus did little to challenge 'Boer native policy' and endorsed white supremacy in the 1931 Statute of Westminster. This granted the Union greater freedom of legislation and stipulated that members of the House of Assembly must be of European descent.[38] Arguably, Britain's economic interests were the paramount interest of imperial representatives in South Africa and even the British 'Protectorates' became a *de facto* part of the Union through the migrant labour system. Since the mineral revolution, South Africa had a central role in the imperial economic system and the international monetary system and, as Ally (1994) has noted, South African gold was important in sustaining the global supremacy of sterling and London's gold markets. As Deborah Lavin's study of Lionel Curtis has revealed, the Round Table and the Royal Institute of International Affairs fervently promoted imperial interests through links with Round Table members in South Africa, aided financially by South African magnates like Abe Bailey. Even when British influence over the internal politics of South Africa weakened in the 1930s, British capitalists were still extracting large profits from South Africa, which the Left regarded as the prime factor in the poverty and oppression of Africans.[39] While British imperialism may not be directly responsible for the segregationist legislation and racist ideology that underpinned African oppression, it had laid the foundation stones. In designating South Africa as part of the 'white Commonwealth', the imperial government implicitly endorsed the rise of the racial state and white supremacy.

Constructing the racial state: white South Africa

South Africa, argued Leonard Woolf, was always 'on the brink of some huge catastrophe' because of the intractable 'native problem'.[40] Policies established before the First World War were fleshed out and consolidated in the inter-war years, culminating in the Native Trust and Land Act, 1936, and the Representation of Natives Act, 1936, which consolidated separate development and took away the limited African franchise in the Cape. Dubow (1995) argues that these two bills were essential to forging political consensus around segregation as the legitimising ideology in South African politics. As Hailey (1957) conceded, there was little difference between English and Afrikaner support for these segregationist policies. At the root of the daily practice of racial segregation, justified as a sound policy on economic and 'hygienic' grounds, was scientific racism. Segregation was implemented by an armoury of legislation and backed up by anthropology as an organising principle. Academic liberals who advocated greater equality were accused of 'floppy sentimentalism' that, if allowed to prevail, would bring about the 'ultimate downfall' of European civilisation in South Africa.[41]

In the elaboration of scientific racism, anti-miscegenation became a 'primary article' of faith linked to a deep fear of being racially diluted or 'swamped'. The Immorality Act, passed in 1926, made extra-marital miscegenation a criminal offence and Buell (1928) observed that illicit intercourse was declared 'as serious an offence as bestiality' with a penalty of five years' imprisonment. Anti-miscegenation laws were essential to social control and the 'defence of civilisation' had become dependent on black respect for the virtue of white womanhood as the embodiment of the white race. White women who transgressed these racial borders were 'completely abandoned to immorality' – even white prostitutes would not 'stoop so low'. So tightly were these borders policed that any breach unleashed moral panic. Under the front page headline, 'White Women and Black Men – Horrible Sex Depravity in Johannesburg – English Girls go Native', a 'sensational weekly' reported how 'low class white sirens openly played Delilah to the blackest of black Sampsons' threatening 'the integrity of the whole white race'.[42]

But what was denied the white goose remained sauce for the gander and the old practice of white men having black mistresses persisted, a fact much resented by black men and a central theme of Sol Plaatje's, *The Mote and the Beam: An Epic on Sex Relationship Twixt White and Black in South Africa* (1921). As racial attitudes hardened, such practices went firmly underground. Large Coloured populations existed in the Cape and Natal. Children of such unions were placed in an invidious position: identifying with whites, yet suffering discrimination on the grounds of colour.[43] These attitudes extended to liberals who rejected the biological basis of scientific racism. They argued that the 'sex barrier' was worth maintaining as only the elimination of the fear of race mixing would encourage South Africans to endorse a more liberal race policy. Emotionally unstable and 'embittered half-castes ... despised by whites and Africans' (or 'half-breeds' as they were known in less polite circles) demonstrated that miscegenation was a bad thing, which neither race desired, and thus the whole problem called for 'careful investigation'.[44] However, racists blamed liberals for making the problem worse. In the novel *Bayete? 'Hail to the King'* (1923), written by the Natal planter, George Heaton Nicholls, a drunken houseboy tries to press his sexual attentions on a golden-haired mistress. Another character, Nelson, an educated black leader, reveals his true colours when he tries to shower 'hot bestial kisses' on a woman liberal whom he believed was in love with him. The 'Black Peril Outrage' was thus a combination of 'mission boy aspirations' and white liberalism.[45]

In 1937, I.D. MacCrone, a lecturer at Witwatersrand University, published a pioneering and comprehensive study of race problems that cast a 'baleful influence on race relations ... in sunny South Africa'. His study incorporated 'historical, psychological and psychoanalytical perspectives' and had general relevance to 'race contacts ... race relations and the problems ['the rising tide of colour'] which follow in their wake'. There are deep flaws in his research – the study was limited to 400 English, Afrikaner and Jewish students at Witwatersrand University – and his emphasis on 'scientific' attitude testing minimises the importance of class and capitalism in the generation of racism. But, as an historical text, MacCrone's study sheds valuable insight into contemporary racial thought. Psychological attitude testing and social science 'fact finding' informed the research carried out by the South African Institute of Race Relations, established in 1929, of which MacCrone later became a director. However, only white attitudes were addressed, black attitudes were ignored until the 1970s when studies revealed that such 'attitudes' in effect constituted the self-same grievances that had existed since the First World War.[46]

The erection of psychological and physical borders between black and white, argued MacCrone, could be traced to changes in 'psycho-sexual' dynamics from the earliest settlement of the Cape. Racial attitudes were thus central to social identities and the preservation of group interests and were rooted in popular myths and tradition, the economic, political and social structure, the black threat to social order and 'pseudo-scientific' beliefs. MacCrone is seductively 'modern' and plausible on first reading, but his own racism is given away by use of terms like 'raw untutored native' and in the way his questionnaire is constructed to emphasise the problematic aspects of the African population. He was 'in sympathy' with segregationist policies and clearly distanced himself from more radical liberal academics at Witwatersrand, such as William Macmillan.[47] Thus, MacCrone offers no solutions to race problems, but his study does reveal the fear at the heart of South African (British and Afrikaner) racism. Contradictory stereotypes emerge of the docile 'happy carefree black', but also of the dark threat where blacks had the monopoly on violence, theft and house-breaking. The most interesting aspect of the study is the way in which MacCrone pre-empts post-colonial theory by articulating the process of 'othering' – whereby whites project characteristics onto blacks that they simultaneously despise and envy. Thus, whites 'envied' black sexual freedom and the fact that they were 'free from worry and responsibility' and 'satisfied with so little'. Yet they were also physically repulsed by black body odour and black skin, which was 'dirty' to touch and could contaminate and 'pollute', and revealed fearful dreams about a 'second Blood River', being chased by blacks or becoming victims of black violence. Attitudes of male and female respondents differed only marginally in that women expressed sexual fears of black men and, in labelling black women 'prostitutes', distanced themselves from identification with their problems.[48]

In keeping with orthodoxy of the day, MacCrone attributes racism primarily to the Afrikaner's 'frontier mentality' and their Calvinistic creed of the elect; his English-speaking respondents were reputedly more 'pro-native'. Comparative studies of the American and South African frontiers have suggested that in both white settler societies, the closing of frontiers, which represented the triumph of Western civilisation and progress through the suppression of savagery, hardened racist attitudes. However, De Kiewiet (1965) argued that whereas the American frontier was closed and the 'enemy' (the Native American Indian) relegated to 'forgotten and inoffensive' reservations, in South Africa no such 'closure' occurred. In the US, the Native American Indians were romanticised, whereas in South Africa frontier 'enemies' remained as 'desperate social problems' in towns and European kitchens, 'unheroic and unromantic'. This, he argues, explained why white schoolboys played at 'Cowboys and Indians' not 'Zulus and Boers'. Thus, for Afrikaners, the metaphorical frontier remained an area of struggle against both African and British threats to their culture, which produced a rest-lessness where 'Utopia always lies beyond the next horizon'.[49]

In their critiques of these earlier conceptualisations of the frontier, Keegan (1996) and other contemporary historians have prioritised class and industrialisation as the root of modern racism. The 'frontier', argues Beinart (1994), was a defensive line between whites and blacks who resisted conquest before they were incorporated and transformed into reservoirs of cheap labour. In this context, the frontier was not the exclusive province of the Afrikaners, who were defending their autonomy against a predatory British imperialism. English settlers also fought indigenous people and developed a 'frontier mentality'. The crucial difference was that British settlers brought capitalism and trade to the frontier, the success of which was premised on greater militarisation.[50] These are valid points. However, the 'frontier' as a metaphor for chaos and racial disintegration arguably remains relevant in understanding the siege mentality of a white settler (British and Afrikaner) society. At the fringes there were threats from hostile 'natives' and racial dilution through 'bastard half-castes', and opportunities for individuals to cast aside the restraints of civilised life. Though rooted in different interests, a culture of racism united the British and Afrikaners in defence of threatened racial boundaries and defined a new South African national identity as formal fetters with Britain were loosened. With the elaboration of segregationist ideology and the use of 'legitimate' state violence, the 'frontier' was stabilised and tamed. But, in the inter-war years, enemies within and without, communists, liberal 'negrophiles' and 'inferior' Southern European and Jewish migrants posed new threats to this racial order. The poor white problem threatened to blur racial borders, which were only sustained through economic and social superiority. The fear of racial 'swamping' also persisted and white emigration was heavily encouraged, supported by English emigration societies, to counteract growing disparities between white and black birth rates.[51]

By the Second World War, white South Africans had created an enclosed white world from which they tried to erase black South Africa. A travel book written in the early 1950s to attract both tourists and settlers waxes lyrical about the perfect climate, the wildlife, the beaches and verdant suburbs, sanitising South Africa into a white paradise with only a passing reference to plentiful 'reserves of native labour'. The 'colour problem' is only touched on briefly at the end of the book and is downplayed as similar to anywhere else in the empire where the primitive nature of blacks justified the need for segregation and 'benevolent tutelage'. Descriptions of the Cape centre on the neat Mediterranean-style villas and genteel English south coast lifestyle of English South Africans. Only the 'African' exotica of the flora and fauna intrudes into this 'European' landscape.[52] In the physically more 'African' areas of the highveld, white cities had carved their myopic niches. Outside the 'native reserves', imperial mappings referred only to white settlements, omitting the larger, shadow black cities of the African locations and nourishing the fantasy of South Africa as a 'white man's country'. 'Real' Africa was located in game reserves, which also became the province of whites as they pushed Africans out in their 'appropriation' of nature and wildlife. As Mackenzie (1991) has argued, the creation of nature reserves had serious consequences for African cultures and socio-economic structures.

However, wealthy whites were obsessed by 'nature' and Denys Rietz described his estate in the Kruger National Park, ironically named Sandringham, as a 'terrestrial paradise'.[53] Physical prowess in sport, hunting and outdoor pursuits defined pioneering, hyper-masculine 'colonial man' as a heroic husband to 'colonial woman', the bearer and protector of the white race. In contrast, black men were emasculated and infantalised as 'boys', while black women were represented as drudges or prostitutes. This articulation of gendered white identities was vital in sustaining racial supremacy.

Segregation was thus the result of complex forces at work in white South African society, including a defensive culture of racism, which was shared by the British and Afrikaners, but the outcome was a complex class/race system that mirrored racial categories. Defence of economic interests and the management of the 'native labour problem' arguably underpinned the elaboration of white racist ideology. The black majority consistently threatened white dreams of building 'a white man's country', and fear and paranoia were translated into repressive legislation and violence. There are clear parallels here with other colonial societies, settler and non-settler (as we have seen in the section on West Africa). A complex debate has emerged since the 1970s over the relationship between capitalist development and segregation/apartheid and there has been more emphasis on understanding racial ideology as a discourse of power that predated industrialisation. While these intellectual interrogations are important, we should not lose sight of the degree to which the control of black labour was a central feature of the construction of the racial state and the maintenance of white supremacy in a period of massive social, cultural and economic change. How, then, did the racial state affect the lives of black South Africans?

Constructing the racial state: black South Africa

Until the late 1930s, 80 per cent of the African population lived in rural areas. English academics, like Egerton (1922), justified segregated reserves on the basis that 'indirect' rule in British Basutoland and neighbouring South African Transkei had been 'successful' in preventing racial deterioration, preserving race integrity and providing the 'opportunity to build and develop ... separate racial types'. The principle of segregation was enshrined in the 1920 Native Affairs Act, and the 1927 Native Administration Act extended the principles of 'indirect' rule. Although South Africa was unique in the extent of land appropriation, policies implemented by the Native Affairs Department (NAD) bore close similarities with those other parts of British Africa. On his visit to South Africa, Ifor Evans noted the similarities with British indirect rule in West Africa: the administrators of the 'native reserves' were predominantly English-speaking and the discourse of white 'trusteeship' paralleled that in West Africa in its commitment to the preservation of traditional culture. However, Evans, who believed that a more equitable solution to the question of land was preferable to segregation, emphasised that the reserves, with the exception of the Transkei, were too scattered and fragmented to make indirect rule work (see Illustration 14).[54]

The contradictions between 'trusteeship' and the imperatives of the expanding colonial economy were most starkly highlighted in South Africa, where economic development was dependent on labour from the 'native reserves' and wider 'foreign' recruitment from the Southern African region. Although as Rich (1996) points out, the NAD struggled to secure its status as a 'state within a state', the reserves, interpenetrated by the migrant labour system, could never be 'autonomous'.[55] By the 1920s, William Macmillan reported that rural conditions were 'dismal'. Africans had been pushed into marginal lands where meagre resources and population pressure caused severe distress. Environmental deterioration, the low productivity of farming and taxation forced rural African males into labour for whites, primarily as miners or farm labourers. Traders, mostly white, became the conduit for African commerce as well as the recruitment of migrant workers, which further reduced the autonomy of South African peasant farmers who, argues Bundy (1979), had responded positively to the new opportunities and markets created by Western penetration in the nineteenth century.[56]

As in West Africa, taxation was used as a 'soft' coercive force. In 1925, the various systems of taxation were rationalised into a general poll tax for all adult males, including urban migrants. 'Native' education, development, prisons and policing in the reserves was charged to Africans. (In the 1930s, 14.5 per cent was spent on education as opposed to 29 per cent on prisons.) Men had to travel to distant places to pay taxes (in a lump sum), involving the loss of earnings and, until 1939, default was a criminal offence, involving fines or imprisonment. Hailey (1956) observed that Africans who received the lowest incomes were 'heavily taxed' in comparison to non-Africans and they also made a major contribution to the general revenue through indirect taxation. However, as Evans (1934) observed, although their labour in mines and on farms was indispensable to the national income, they received little back from the State.[57]

The model 'native republic', the 'Red Blanket Republic' of the Transkei, named after the ochre-dyed blankets worn in the region, provides an excellent case study of contradictions between 'indirect' rule and the needs of the South African economy. Even in the 1950s, whites still represented the Transkei as a rural, if somewhat overpopulated, idyll of 'green rolling hills speckled with round thatched huts, cattle, goats and sheep'.[58] Hailey (1957) observes that the Transkei had always been viewed as a 'purely African area' that was populated by 'tribes' whose presence in the Cape colony was 'embarrassing'. As 'the most successful system' of indirect rule, trainee administrators were sent to the Transkei to learn in order to extend the system elsewhere. The veneer of indirect rule was so skilfully applied that even politically conscious Africans cited the 'excellent work' of the United Transkeian General Council (*Bunga*) based in the native 'capital', Umtata, and housed in 'new and commodious buildings' after 1928 as proof that the 'natives' were capable of governing themselves.[59] But it was the white authorities who held ultimate power. Although chiefs retained a powerful symbolic standing as guarantors of African land and culture, they had to work under white magistrates (restyled 'native commissioners' after 1927) and the *Bunga* was chaired by the white chief magistrate, who was responsible for all administrative functions. Native administration, including the salaries of Europeans, was paid for through the Native Development Account, which was raised through local taxation, and, as in West Africa, Europeans kept tight control over finances.[60]

The colonial discourse of the administrators echoes that of their counterparts in West Africa. Natives had 'undoubted ability' and were 'great speakers and clear thinkers', but had 'no executive ability' and were 'carefree and happy-go-lucky'. They were also fond of lengthy litigations and there were three wealthy solicitors in the district 'doing very well'. As in other parts of Africa, the legal profession was one of the few outlets for educated blacks, who were barred from the upper ranks of the civil service and restricted to clerking, agricultural demonstrating and court interpreting. Similarly, native clerks were belittled as 'uppity', demanding equal pay even though they were 'not as good' as whites.[61] But there the similarity ends for 'indirect' rule in the Transkei was an even more impossible ideal than in West Africa. The overriding poverty pushed men into work in the Rand mines or cane-cutting on the Natal sugar plantations. The chiefs and traders, with the acquiescence of the administration, became deeply implicated in labour recruitment. A Transkei magistrate estimated that in 1929 up to 50 per cent of able-bodied men were away at any one time. The Transkei was 'absolutely dependent' on the mines and recruiters could 'quite easily' earn £1,500–2,000 per year. If recruited via an agent, migrant workers were advanced £3, which was taken out of their first two months pay. Transkeian men learnt from their experiences: mines had good and bad reputations and an increasing number of men tried to go 'independent' as this gave them more freedom and choice. But poverty had them stitched up. They still needed loans (made at an 'exorbitant rate of interest') to migrate, and traders were reluctant to provide them as they did not want to lose capitation fees.[62]

Despite the pressures of poverty, the Native Recruiting Corporation (NRC), which was under the control of the Director of Native Labour, and also recruited from Basutoland and Swaziland, admitted to the academic and liberal activist, Margaret Hodgson (Ballinger), that it was difficult to induce men to go to the mines and a 'voluntary system without contract could not work'. Men would not go unless forced to, in order to pay taxes, and coerced recruitment was 'common'. There were also heavy penal sanctions for breaches of the Native Service Contract Act, which was introduced in 1932. The consciousness of migrant mine workers was split between two worlds. Rhythms of rural life influenced attitudes to contract work and the 'best recruiting months' were January to March. 'After that', a recruiter noted, 'circumcision rites come on in April and men stay behind to join in beer drinks' only joining up again in August. The men objected to the long, nine-month contract as it interrupted the reaping of crops, but a reduction to six months was not feasible as the mine owners would have to pay more commission to recruiters. Administrators also reported that this culture of migration had made 'native management' more difficult as natives became less law-abiding and easy to 'manage'. Native customs and institutions were under pressure, undermining the principles of indirect rule, at a time when young, inexperienced and transient administrators were replacing the 'old-timers' who knew 'their people' and understood their languages.[63]

Margaret Hodgson observed that in a 'backward' coastal area of the Transkei, which she visited during her researches, natives were 'hopelessly' exploited by traders, but also 'very suspicious' of white men, closing ranks about any enquiries from the authorities. Africans devised strategies to make the best of their deteriorating situation. They 'knew the value of things', sold wool as well as mealies to traders, lent money to each other, combined resources to buy sheep and would 'pool their experience over the fire at night'. Because of the heavy taxation they could lose their lands if in arrears, but 'they always manage to find the money for the native land'. Strong resistance in the Transkei influenced its developing political culture and shattered the white myth of an 'essentially acquiescent and loyal' reserve, where 'Khosa, Pondos, Tembus and Fingos, once hereditary enemies, now lived amicably under European laws'.[64] Bundy and Beinart (1987) have argued that militancy can be traced back to the unrest created by inflation after the First World War, when a new, militant urban consciousness fed back into the rural districts. Resistance was particularly strong in the Herschel district of the Ciskei (birthplace of the feminist writer, Olive Shreiner), which was viewed as a notoriously 'backward area' with marked divisions between the 'red' (that is, 'red ochre peoples' associated with 'tradition') and 'school' (the collaborative educated elites). Deep economic problems resulted in strong mass protest movements, influenced by external ideologies, particularly Garveyism, which bridged Christian and traditionalist classes. Women had a high level of participation in these movements. But these 'hidden struggles' of rural Africans, including their support for organisations like the Industrial and Commercial Workers' Union (Chapter 6), were continuously undermined by segregationist policies.[65]

Conditions deteriorated further in 1929 with the onset of the depression. To add to the misery of the populace, new taxes were imposed, including one which doubled the cost of blankets, an important article of clothing due to the cold South African winters. Africans were now increasingly dependent on traders for clothing as, with the penetration of British trade, women had adopted cotton print dresses and blankets, transformed into 'traditional dress' replaced hides. A trader informed Margaret Hodgson that the tax on blankets and 'German prints' hit the Africans harder than the hut tax. A similar tax was also introduced in Basutoland where a 'small cotton square' was all people could buy for their children as warm woollen blankets were now double in price. In the high altitude of Basutoland this allegedly led to an increase in child mortality. Rural conditions in this British Protectorate were, if anything, worse than in the Transkei. A liberal visitor noted that the Basotho were suffering from malnutrition and medical services were 'hopelessly handicapped' by lack of funds. Transkei magistrates reported that they were inundated with applications from Basutoland and other parts of the Union to enter the Transkei. The Union Government also made the High Commission authorities responsible for Basotho paupers in the Union.[66]

With the onset of the depression, additional poll and health taxes were levied on the black population throughout South Africa. The ICU reported that the lives of urban and rural workers were wretched: 'Their food is only mealie pap and salt. The quarters in which they live are not fit for pigs ... they work from sunrise to late at night'. A combination of drought and economic crisis caused a sharp upturn in the drift to urban centres. Numbers were swollen when official recruitment from Nyasaland (Malawi), Bechuanaland and Mozambique (suspended in 1914) was resumed in 1932 through the Witwatersrand Native Labour Association. In 1936, Eslanda Robeson described the crowded 'mine trains' carrying workers back and forth, and everywhere she went she noted families on the move, the women 'carrying all their worldly possessions on their heads'.[67]

Unemployment rose, but went largely unrecorded as Labour Exchanges were closed to African workers who were supposed to return to their reserves. No social insurance existed, although poor whites had access to inadequate assistance from charitable organisations. In 1932, a commission (funded by the US Carnegie Foundation) reported that an estimated 300,000 whites were living at, or below, a minimum level that was essential to a 'European standard of living', leading to fears of racial degeneracy.[68] From 1927, the government had pursued a policy of substituting poor whites for blacks in the lower grades of jobs on the railways but, argues Evans, this had proved expensive and had failed to solve the perennial poor white problem. 'Civilised labour' policies were thus extended to municipal and public works, further legislation was introduced to control the flow of black labour into the cities and police operations were widened to arrest 'illegal' natives in the locations.[69] These government policies, combined with social distress, led to increasing urban unrest. In 1930, in the Carnarvon location in the Cape, there were riots over land and labour at which 'Professor' James Thaele, representing the ANC, made a speech saying that South Africa would 'never be a white man's country' and was arrested for sedition. The same unrest was happening 'all over the country' and the Carnarvon trouble had been 'brewing for years'.[70]

Social researchers drew attention to the serious consequences of urbanisation – over-crowding, immorality, crime, prostitution and venereal diseases. There was a rising death-rate from tuberculosis in the urban areas and miners suffered from a high incidence of silicosis and pneumonia, which was caused by the sudden change from the hot air of the mines to the cold air of Rand winters. Rand miners lived in 'appalling' slum conditions and the American researcher, Buell, recorded that sodomy was common in mining compounds and illicit liquor trade resulted in widespread drunkenness (although this was allegedly encouraged by the employers as a form of social control). Alcohol was seen as a particular curse, the main cause of the rising crime rate, and laws were introduced in the Transvaal against the sale of alcohol which, argued the ICU, simply increased illicit liquor drinking.[71] Such moral panics obscured the real causes of urban malaise. Conditions of life were little better for the urban Coloured community. After dining with Dr Abdurahman, who lived in Cape Town's

District Six (now cleared), Margaret Hodgson described the area as 'very terrible'.[72]

As is the lot of the poor everywhere, Africans and poorer members of the Coloured community become the prime victims of violence and theft in survival struggles on the urban margins. In Alan Paton's *Cry the Beloved Country* (1948), the naive Zulu pastor is robbed on arrival in Johannesburg, his son has turned to crime and the city corrupts male and female. Racists attributed crime and 'black on black' violence to the disintegration of 'traditional' African society and the 'inherently lower morality' of blacks. Violence and lawlessness were thus displaced onto blacks and, as Marks and Trapido (1987) point out, official policies of casting a blind eye to black crime encouraged vigilante groups and ethnically informed gang warfare. However, urban Africans were also the target of routine state violence. Violence was inherent in segregation and conditioned the experiences of both blacks and whites. 'The only shared culture in South Africa is the culture of violence' wrote Breyten Breytenbach and, sadly, this violence has intensified with the ending of apartheid.[73]

The trope of the streetwise African ripping off his own kind provides a powerful cameo of the violent and soul-crushing life of the migrant in the city – the 'blanket kaffir' disorientated by the streets of Johannesburg. But migrant workers did not lead an atomised life and formed their own associations, which provided practical support and a sense of identity. Ethnic identification was important here, but argues Vail (1989), this was rooted in a need to maintain positions in rural societies rather than in animosity towards other workers. Cultural identification was also an expression of resistance. The *Amalaita* gangs in the Transvaal and Durban, for instance, built on Zulu culture creating an 'anti-authoritarian and powerfully masculine' culture, which evoked militarist symbols of defiance.[74] When she visited the mining compounds on the Rand, Eslanda Robeson observed how Zulus danced in their traditional costumes. Pondos wore their hair in regular 'corn rows', sometimes 'wrapped' in a style that blacks in the Southern US would 'recognise immediately', Swazis wore their hair long, dressed with red-brown clay and Basuthos wore their typical blankets. In the spirit of resistance, miners chanted 'grievances' to visitors, but their dances were suppressed.[75]

However, migration was also a gendered experience and one of the great dangers to society was the 'alarming ... influx of native females into large towns'. Women were a 'positive danger to the whole community they invaded' and the authorities defended the degrading and humiliating medical examinations that women moving to urban areas had to undergo.[76] These compulsory medical examinations were included in the grievances of the 1919 SANNC deputation and were taken up again in the 1940s by the newly formed women's section of the ANC in a memorandum to the Minister for Native Affairs.[77] As in West Africa, women had no place in the formal urban economy and were forced to survive in the informal sector through, for instance, beer brewing and running shebeens. African women also moved into domestic service, formerly dominated by Coloured women (who were now shifting into factory work), transforming relations between white and black women into 'maids and madams'. Domestic service also increased the vulnerability of black women to white male lust. As Marks (1989) stresses, this intensified 'the pain of people whose ruthless exploitation was not only economic but also sexual' and contributed to the increase in venereal disease, the 'white man's disease', unknown among Africans before the mineral revolution. [78]

These transformations in African women's lives resulted in shifts in gendered identities as African patriarchal controls over women weakened, often with painful consequences. Lauretta Ngcobo's novel, *And They Didn't Die* (1990), charts the experiences of one such woman, married to a migrant worker, who moves to the town as a domestic and is raped by her white boss. After she has a child, her other children are returned to her husband's family according to Zulu tradition, and she is left to eke out a precarious rural existence. At the bottom of the economic and racial pyramid, few women made it into the ranks of the educated bourgeoisie, except as wives, with the exception of a tiny minority of teachers and black nurses. Yet migrant women found strength in adversity and Belinda Bozzoli's *Women of Phokeng* (1991), which draws on oral memories, reveals their consciousness of oppression and assertions of identity within the 'structured brutality' of South African society.[79]

As Stasiulis and Yuval-Davis (1995) have pointed out, imperialism created 'new sites for gender struggles and relations between and within communities of indigenous peoples and Europeans'. Under segregation, black and white women were both carefully policed to ensure they did not 'unsettle' settler society. Unfortunately, their empowerment (with the ending of apartheid) has intensified the violence that is inherent in racism and related distortions in black and white patriarchy, leading to frightening increases in murder and rape.[80] However, under segregation and apartheid the pressures on black women were far more intense than those experienced by white women. The endless pressure of racism and poverty embellished the worst aspects of African patriarchy, taking away whatever protective elements there were. Black men channelled their own anger and confusion into misogyny and violence against black women, many of whom found solace in Christianity. As modernity disrupted traditional gender relations, missionaries targeted women, providing an education based on Western ideals of domesticity, and such strategies appear to have been far more successful than in West Africa. Deborah Gaitskell (1982) argues that African women saw missions as a refuge from 'gender specific tribulations', but also as a means to material advantages in the form of land, training and employment. Church membership provided women with a network, peer support and an outlet for organisational talents that were frustrated by racial, patriarchal and class mechanisms of control. In the urban areas, they creatively adapted their Christian beliefs and networks to meet new challenges and changing moral codes.[81]

Urban Africans thus created their own communities that were sustained by the expanding black independent churches and the vibrant urban working-class 'Marabi' culture, which developed in the 1930s. Migrant culture, centred around the shebeens of the Rand and Pretoria, was distinct from the settled urban

Christian communities. New forms of music, dance and the 'creolised' street language of the cities created an urban hybrid identity. A melange of traditional forms, US jazz and blues, the music of the independent black churches and the choral music of trade unions and worker organisations created the 'rhythms of resistance', which expressed resentment over unfair taxes, police harassment and segregationist legislation. These new urban community identities were vital in developing and sustaining a culture of defiance and feelings of collective pride and solidarity. Self-help initiatives like the *stokvel* and burial societies helped to deal with poverty through the pooling of meagre funds.[82]

The relationship between power, culture, language, music and historical memory is crucial to understanding African resistance. African resistance was glorified in poetry (as demonstrated in the quotes at the beginning of this chapter), and African oral traditions and literature transmitted the bitter memory of white invasion down through the generations. Thus, cultural struggles centred on white attempts to destroy African 'creative instruments and products' and devalue African culture as of 'no relevance to modernity'. The cultural reworkings of the inter-war African townships testifies to the irrepressible vitality and dynamism of oppositional cultures that prevented the transformation of African men and women, rural and urban, into cowed victims. 'With segregation', wrote a later ANC activist, 'impenetrable walls' developed between black and white cultures; sympathetic whites could imagine hunger and observe from 'outside the fence', but could 'never get inside a black skin and feel ... what it is like to be black'. This gulf of consciousness between blacks and whites was revealed in the psychiatrist Wulf Sachs' 1937 study of a Johannesburg slum dweller, 'John', a healer-diviner keen to learn about European medicine. Sachs' pioneering study provided rare insight into the inner world of the urban African trying to navigate between two diametrically opposed cultures and a racism that inferiorises all that makes sense and meaning to his existence.[83]

The new urban culture, argues Coplan (1982), emphasised continuities of experience and communication between town and countryside, and blurred the divisive white categories of rural 'pagan', urban 'blanket kaffir', 'mission school' African and urban 'criminal'.[84] But the elements of urban culture, which strengthened black resistance, were also feared by whites whose response to urban development was threefold: slum clearances and legislation; anthropological studies of 'culture contact'; and projects initiated by liberals, philanthropists and missionaries to direct the new urban consciousness into 'safe' channels and to improve race relations. The government also censored films, although, paradoxically, film was also seen as a potentially useful propaganda medium in 'Bantu education'.[85] However, the response of the state was overwhelmingly repressive and geared to tighter control of migration and pass laws through the Native Laws Amendment Act 1937. As 'native problems' could not be resolved exclusively through repression and violence, the government relied increasingly on the voluntary sector of missionaries and philanthropists to develop cultural initiatives in education and welfare (where government spending was minimal) to help stabilise African societies in flux.

Philanthropic initiatives were backed by American foundations and clearly directed to 'social control'. Strategies to undermine potential African resistance from 'detribalised' natives were directed almost exclusively towards African men and depended on fragmenting solidarity by cultivating ideas of individual advancement combined with identification with the dominant culture. The American missionary, Ray Phillips, arrived in South Africa in 1918 to help develop the social welfare programme that was initiated by the American Board Mission. He saw his role as twofold: to awaken whites to the problems of urbanisation and to counteract the work of agitators and 'Moscow emissaries' through 'moralising' the leisure pursuits of Africans. Central to this project was the suppression of 'evil literature' in circulation, and in 1930 the Carnegie Corporation offered £1,000 for the establishment of a non-European library at Germiston (Transvaal), where books were carefully selected and censored.[86] Reputedly an 'expansive' and sociable man, Phillips had considerable influence over the black bourgeoisie who saw him as 'one of the very few men all natives ought to know and respect'. In contrast, another American sponsored by the Carnegie Foundation, Dr Charles T. Loram, was regarded by black activists as a government lackey who was of 'no use to the native peoples'.[87] A protégé of Smuts, Loram was strongly influenced by US racial science and advocated the model of 'negro education', which was favoured in the Southern US, and a 'scientific solution' to the native question. Appointed Chief Inspector of Native Education in Natal in 1920, he was influential in early philanthropic initiatives to 'tame the restive, newly mobile Bantu' and his Native Welfare Societies (whites only) were the forerunner of the more progressive, 'interracial' Bantu Men's Social Centres.[88]

The Bantu Men's Social Centre (BMSC) in Johannesburg represents a white vision of 'taming' the Bantu people through 'Victorian values'. The driving forces behind the project were the American missionary, F.B. Bridgeman, and Howard Pim, an English Quaker. The first centre was opened in 1920 under the patronage of the Governor-General of South Africa, the Earl of Athlone. The BMSC provided social and games rooms, a tea and coffee counter, a Gamma Sigma Club Room for debating and lectures, classrooms and reading rooms, a gymnasium and hall, lavatory facilities and bath and dressing rooms – health in body and mind (see Illustration 16). The centre ran night school classes for beginners (including bookkeeping, emphasising the Victorian obsession with the link between sound accounting and morality), ran a musical glee club, had nightly 'radio wireless programmes' and a free weekly 'bioscope show'. Under its first resident superintendent, Frederick Livie-Noble, Pathfinder Scout work was also developed.[89] The BMSC's objectives were to help African men develop 'physically, mentally and spiritually' and to promote 'worthy character' through 'healthful recreation and good citizenship'. The annual fees were ten shillings for non-Europeans and all applications had to be vetted by the executive. The organisation was multiracial, but whites kept a firm, paternalistic control and the organisation reflected the segregation of the wider society. There were thus two classes of members who paid different fees and separate annual general meetings of European and native members were held to elect separate executive members. Whites dominated the executive committee by nine to six, which ensured white control. Black officials were always subordinated to an 'assistant capacity' and the president and the treasurer was always white. Prominent Africans who were associated with the centre from the early 1920s include the ANC activist, R.V. Selope Thema, the trade unionist, A.W.G. Champion, and Richard William Msimang, one of the only two English-educated Bantu attorneys practising in Johannesburg, who had represented the SANNC deputation in 1919.[90]

In 1933, the BMSC affiliated to the South African Institute of Race Relations (founded in 1929). The night school was reported as 'popular' with men continuing advanced study at the Methodist Men's Institute, and the bioscope had been extended to children and was 'very popular' with up to 700 children attending. A Bantu School of Arts had also been started and one of the protégés was Moses Tladi, who had been discovered some years earlier as 'a garden boy with a love of drawing' and who had later successfully exhibited his work. The centre also hosted the Third Transvaal Eisteddfod in December 1933 and the Bantu Dramatic Society played 'She Stoops the Conquer' to a 'European and

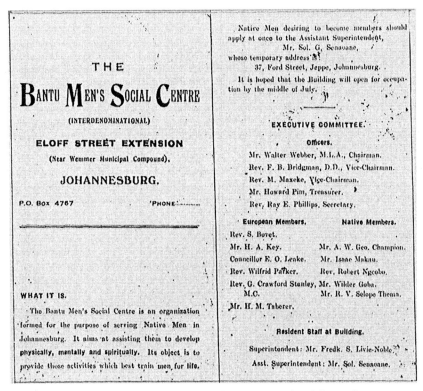

Illustration 16–Bantu Men's Social Centre, Eloff Street Extension, Johannesburg
Source: A.W.G. Champion Papers, University of South Africa Archives

Bantu' audience – supposedly to rave reviews. The first 'native' play was also staged in the same year, although white culture was clearly prioritised. However, the centre suffered from a 'want of consistent membership' (341 members of whom only 236 were active) and the failure of members to keep up subscriptions.[91]

It is hardly surprising that so few Africans were attracted to the centre: the philosophy behind the initiative was paternalistic, patronising and clearly influenced by American race relations thinking. When Eslanda Robeson visited South Africa in 1936, the BMSC held a party in her honour. Members, she noted, were 'quite European', although a 'real African ballad' was sung and she was given a present of 'African records' for Paul. The centres struggled on into the 1940s, but with very small numbers. In a positive vein, Couzens (1982) suggests that BMSC libraries and cultural initiatives introduced members and visitors to black American culture and politics, stimulating race awareness. He cites the writer Peter Abrahams, who, when he was sixteen, walked into the BMSC in Johannesburg and was inspired by hearing 'for the first time' a record of Paul Robeson singing 'Ol' Man River'.[92] However, the BMSCs were carefully steered by whites who wanted to mould African members to their own image as their 'well-behaved' protégés. As we shall see in the following chapter, African trade unionism, communism and the ideals of liberal democracy provided a more liberatory, but to whites an infinitely more threatening, path to African advancement.

Summary

British imperialism in South Africa laid the foundations of racial segregation in South Africa and 'native policies' mirrored those developed in other parts of British Africa. In many ways, Africans in South and West Africa shared similar experiences of white rule and the impact of capitalism. However, in South Africa, change was more rapid, the tentacles of the state more extensive and oppression more intense. After the First World War, argues Rich (1996), white South Africa established its autonomy and identity through the 'modernising' of the colonial state.[93] However, 'modernising' implies progress towards democratic citizenship as well as economic growth. The 'modernisation' of the South African white settler state was accompanied by retrogressive segregationist legislation and an elaboration of scientific racism. This entrenchment of segregation widened the economic, political and cultural gulf between black, white and Coloured people. Although South African settlers now had political autonomy, such policies were developed with the complicity of the imperial government whose main priority of imperial policy was to hold on to its valuable white dominion and to secure British economic interests. However, deep contradictions existed between the ideology of segregation and the imperatives of the expanding economy. As William Macmillan, a vigorous opponent of segregation, stressed, blacks and whites were part of the same process of proletarianisation and formed part of one 'complex South Africa'. Poverty and oppression in the 'native reserves' stimulated migration and the development of black urban cultures. As in West Africa, the cultural fluidity of the urban areas and the breakdown of 'traditional' values and controls was interpreted as a threat to the stability of society. The government responded mainly with repression; liberals responded with moralising educational and cultural initiatives. However, these measures could not stem the tide of African resistance, the focus of my next chapter, which developed into more organised resistance struggles in the inter-war years.

6 'Knocking on the white man's door'

Repression and resistance

> The goal is one, namely freedom for all. ... We realise that for the African this is only a beginning of a long struggle entailing great sacrifice of time, means and even life itself. To the African people the [UN Declaration of Human Rights] is a challenge to organise and unite themselves under the mass liberation movement, the African National Congress.
>
> (A.B. Xuma, President General, ANC, c.1946)

'The White population' wrote Leonard Woolf, 'already hears the black man knocking on three entrances to his house ... economic ... political ... social, [an] unpleasant and terrifying experience'; the more blacks developed and 'adapted to civilisation', he warned, the greater the danger of revolt.[1] White repression stimulated a vigorous resistance, which bent and undermined the structures of segregation. As Bonner, Delius and Posel (1993) have demonstrated, popular struggles and countless atomised acts of non-compliance were among the most defining influences on the development of apartheid. Edward Roux's classic early text, *Time Longer Than Rope* (1964), charted this long history of African resistance, from the pre-First World War organised armed resistance and tax rebellions to later political action against segregation and apartheid. However, such pioneering studies, associated mainly with the South African left, tended to concentrate on organised resistance in the urban areas, thereby marginalising the rural struggles. More recent research has emphasised how rural and urban struggles, and mass and elite protest were intertwined in a broader culture of resistance to white supremacy.[2] As in West Africa, this broader pattern of resistance, which was manifest in a myriad of ways, was seminal in the development of the organised resistance, which is the main focus of this chapter.

Essential similarities existed between the pattern of resistance in West and South Africa, but there were also important differences related to the degree of industrialisation in South Africa and the specific nature of the interaction between colonialism and indigenous cultures. For instance, Christianity and the tensions between liberal capitalism and communism played a far more prominent part in the development of black consciousness. Moreover, the oppression experienced by the mass of the African population was more intense, as were the strategies to undermine resistance. Opposition to segregation was fragmented and undermined by contradictory ideological influences, ethnic consciousness and African collaboration. Recent studies have thus provided a more nuanced insight into the dynamics and complexities of resistance, survival and collaboration. As Beinart (1994) has pointed out, resistance was not uniform and the South African state had its non-white allies – the 'bossboys' in the mining compounds, rural headmen and teachers who helped maintain order, black policemen, labour recruiters and undercover agents who infiltrated black political organisations. Unterhalter (1995) has also emphasised the importance of challenging binary notions of oppression and resistance, and argued that the complex intersection between gender, race and imperialism is important in understanding the problems of conflict and fragmentation within resistance movements.[3]

These challenges to orthodox studies have revealed the problematic gender dimension of the discourse of resistance. The trope of the resistant African was male and women, particularly working-class women, were rarely visible in earlier resistance narratives. Black female activism did not gain any recognition until the 1950s, when the pass laws were extended to women, and, as Beall, Hassim and Trades (1989) have pointed out, tensions between the male-defined aims of the general liberation struggle and specific women's grievances were to prove an enduring debate in the post-Second World War years. For both black and white men, argues Cheryl Walker (1994), women represented 'tradition' as opposed to the 'modernity' that informed organised black politics. Black consciousness movements and ethnic nationalism also established women as the icons of 'traditional' culture.[4] Bozzoli (1991) has challenged assertions of the passivity and conservatism of African women and a number of pioneering studies have now revealed the indispensable contribution that African women have made to cultural struggles, anti-pass law campaigns, trade unionism and, indeed, all forms of resistance. In the inter-war years, however, politics was arguably forged in the cities where numbers of women were low which, suggests Coquery-Vidrovitch (1997), explains the greater prominence of women in rural struggles.[5] Although there was some nominal female involvement in black politics, black organisations and their white supporters focused almost exclusively on male African rights or generalised rights, which muted women's specific gender struggles.

This chapter, then, focuses primarily on organised protest and the ideological influences that shaped the discourse of resistance. It parallels my study of organised resistance in West Africa in Chapter 4, analysing the development of black consciousness and the tensions between 'Africanist' and 'Western' frameworks of political action and thought. My analysis also highlights the dialectic between repression and resistance. As in West Africa, state repression, rationalised by the need to control subversive influences, particularly communism, stimulated more widespread resistance. But in South Africa, repression was much harsher and effectively crushed any movements that seriously threatened white supremacy. However, the resistance struggles of the inter-war years were arguably not in vain as they established the patterns and processes of resistance that ultimately made apartheid unworkable. I have charted these struggles through the developments in race consciousness after the First World War, the mobilisation of protest by the Industrial and Commercial Workers' Union (ICU) and the Communist Party of South Africa (CPSA) and developments after 1935 stimulated by changes in the international and local political environment.

The aftermath of the First World War: Bolshevism and Garveyism

In the last chapter, I discussed the early initiatives of the South African National Native Congress (SANNC) in challenging segregationist policies. Such initiatives were associated primarily with the educated bourgeoisie. Colonialism, Christianity and capitalism had opened up avenues for advancement during the nineteenth century which, suggest Marks and Rathbone (1982), stimulated a class coherence and self-consciousness only rarely achieved by the African working classes. Segregation 'stunted and repressed' this advance and stimulated organised polit-ical movements through which the bourgeoisie claimed to speak on behalf of all Africans.[6] After the First World War, the educated bourgeoisie were strongly influenced by the multiracialist ideals of the Reverend Dr James Kwegyir Aggrey, who visited South Africa in 1921 with the African Education Commission (funded by the US Phelps Stokes Foundation) and was enthusiastically received by black and white liberals.[7]

However, communism and populist Garveyism refigured the way grievances were articulated and exposed conflicts of interests and consciousness between the African petty bourgeoisie and labouring masses. During the 1920s, the SANNC (renamed the ANC in 1923) remained firmly wedded to liberal values, promoting 'unity of the races' and agitating ' ... by just means ... for the removal of the colour bar ... and ... equitable representation of natives in Parliament'. The moderate leadership was thus opposed to the 'socialist subver-sion' that influenced the more militant ICU and the divisive race politics of Garveyism.[8] In *The Black Problem* (1920), the moderate Professor D.D.T. Jabavu, lecturer in Bantu Studies at Fort Hare Native College, warned that 'Bolshevistic and Nihilistic' doctrines were gaining ground and that while such great inequali-ties between black and white existed, 'agitators' could exploit the situation.[9] With these developments in race consciousness, rifts between moderates and 'extrem-ists' began to widen resulting in splits and weaknesses within the ANC.

'Professor' James Thaele, a leading figure in the Cape Town branch of the ANC, attacked the faith of the ANC moderates in 'British Justice' and Garveyite ideas gained in popularity during the early 1920s, fanning out from the Cape, where it had a strong impact, to other parts of the Union. Branches of Garvey's Universal Negro Improvement Association (UNIA) also flourished in the Transkei where Garveyite influence was reflected in the millenarian Wellington Movement, named after its leader, Elias Wellington Buthelezi. Buthelezi believed black Americans would shortly arrive in aeroplanes to liberate black South Africans which, suggest Hill and Pirio (1987) may reflect the power of Garvey's announced intention in 1923 to visit Africa, which fired rumours of liberation

throughout Africa. The Wellington Movement also forged links with the independent black churches, organised practical schemes for self-help and had
connections with the Industrial and Commercial Workers Union (ICU). Hill and
Pirio claim that Garveyist ideas continued to mobilise support in the Transkei
long after the ICU and the ANC collapsed.[10] Paul Rich (1996) maintains that
Garveyism never constituted as serious a threat to the state as organised labour
unrest and communism. However, Hill and Pirio claim that the impact of
Garveyism has been underestimated by historians and that Garveyite ideas were
a 'potent expression of mass-based nationalism'. Garveyism was influential in
the Industrial and Commercial Workers Union (ICU), and Marks and Trapido
(1987) contend that this mix of Garveyism and black trade unionism was a
'particularly potent brew'. Garveyite ideas, they argue, drew on black consciousness and 'Africanism', which had long been a response to colonialism and
coexisted alongside a continued belief in the 'bounty' of Queen Victoria as
'protector' of African Rights.[11] From this broader perspective, Garveyism
undoubtedly contributed to the emergent race consciousness that raised government alarm in the 1920s.

Whites blamed this new race 'awareness' on the 'constant intercourse'
between the United States and South Africa since the late nineteenth century,
which had helped spread Ethiopianism and given blacks a 'peg' on which to
hang their discontent, a 'positive formula' to soothe their pride and enhance
'racial self-consciousness'.[12] In his novel *Bayete* (1923), the British Natal planter,
George Heaton Nicholls, raises the spectre of a black take over sparked off by a
'kaffir' mine strike. The instigator is a Bishop of the Ethiopian Church, a
'striking and handsome Arab', educated in the USA, who preached subversion,
pressing the black 'proletariat' to resist and strike for the franchise. Order is
finally restored by a white *coup d'état*, but the moral of the book is clear:
American black separatist ideas, which argued that Africa should be rid of
whites, could not work.[13]

Some black American race 'agitators', such as Max Yergan, who arrived in
South Africa in 1921, were suspected of communist links, emphasising the
dangerous slippage between the 'black' and 'red peril'. Yergan had previously
worked for the international YMCA in East Africa, Egypt and India and had a
wide and enigmatic 'reputation'. Margery Perham claimed that, like other
American missionaries, he had been sent to deflect the educated Bantu away
from 'materialism and political education' through Christianity.[14] However,
David Anthony (1994) suggests that in Yergan's case the initial suspicions of the
authorities were 'completely justified'. Yergan, he argues, was influenced by both
Christian radicalism and left-wing ideas by the time he arrived in South Africa,
where his experiences pushed him further to the left. He vigorously opposed
capitalist and racialist oppression (although he and his family lived very well at a
higher standard than they could have achieved in the US). Based at the 'native
University' of Fort Hare, Eastern Cape, Yergan travelled around South Africa as
an organiser for the 'native' branch of the Student Christian Association and,
despite constant surveillance, continually outmanoeuvred the police. When he

returned home in 1936, he became highly visible in the US left. Yergan ultimately became a virulent anti-communist and an 'unabashed apologist' for the apartheid regime. However, in the 1930s he cultivated 'a coterie of disaffected students' at Fort Hare, including the communist ANC leader, Govan Mbeki, who was imprisoned after the Rivonia treason trials.[15]

Other outside influences were influential in the development of black organisations and political consciousness. Passive resistance to poll taxes and pass laws was inspired by Gandhi, who developed his *satyagrapha* (soul force) in Natal before the First World War when, as a young lawyer, he defended the rights of Indian indentured workers. African diaspora connections and pan-Africanist consciousness were further strengthened after the Italian invasion of Ethiopia in 1935. But communism was regarded as the most important threat to the state. Margery Perham recorded that in official circles (which included British diplomats), the manipulating 'hand of Moscow' inspired 'dangerous ... anti-white feelings' and was behind all native unrest.[16] The involvement of the Communist Party of South Africa (CPSA) in black struggles simultaneously stimulated and fragmented black consciousness as black activists were pulled in different directions between the competing ideologies of liberalism, reformist socialism, marxism and pan-Africanism. The catalyst for these developments was the entrenchment of segregation.

Workers of Africa unite?: the Industrial and Commercial Workers Union and the Communist Party of South Africa

'Civilised labour' policies, combined with the deteriorating conditions of African workers led to the foundation by Clements Kadalie in 1919 of the ICU – the first African trade union (see Illustration 17). Communists helped draft the constitution and the ICU adopted the slogan 'Workers of Africa unite – you have nothing to lose but your chains'. However, the major formative influences were arguably pan-Africanism and reformist socialism. The founding principles emphasised that the organisation was non-racial, non-sectarian and non-political and that the ICU's socialism was based on the 'fundamental principles of Christianity' and commitment to a form of 'co-operative commonwealth' instead of capitalism.[17] In 1920, the new ICU co-ordinated an African mineworkers' strike on the Rand, which, for white South Africans represented a dangerous trend in the 'modernisation' of African thought. After the strike, the Native Affairs Department (NAD) warned that race consciousness and the spread of education among South African 'natives' was leading to a '[growing] realisation of disabilities ... and an ability to formulate schemes for ... emancipation'.[18]

However, the first serious challenge to the state came from white, not black, labour. The 'Rand Revolt' in 1922 was instigated by 'very dangerous revolutionaries', including two Australian miners and a secretary of the Afrikaner Nationalist Party, and resulted in 'anarchy' in Johannesburg. These developments aroused grave concern on the part of the Prime Minister, Smuts, and his

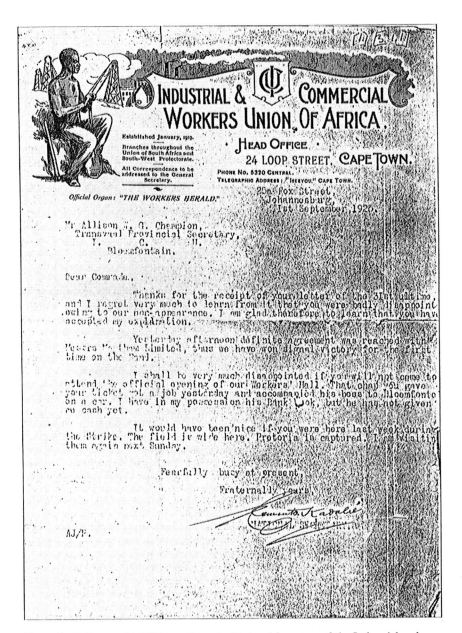

Illustration 17–Letter with ICU logo from the National Secretary of the Industrial and
Commercial Workers Union of South Africa
Source: A.W.G. Champion Papers, University of South Africa Archives

Afrikaner and British allies.[19] Troops were ordered in, backed up by air strikes, and over 200 strikers were killed. Ringleaders were hanged and government responses to the strike intensified opposition to Smut's South Africa Party. After the 'Revolt', the British-dominated South African Labour Party (SALP), founded in 1916, entered into an electoral pact with the Afrikaner Nationalists. This paved the way for the introduction of 'civilised labour' policies aimed at providing sheltered employment for unskilled whites in competition with blacks. The American researcher, Buell, saw this as a key factor in heightening racial tension.[20]

The Communist Party of South Africa (CPSA) was seen as the prime instigator of both black and white unrest. Formed in 1921 as a result of a merger of a number of radical offshoots of the SALP, founder members included David 'Ivon' Jones, a Welsh migrant and active trade unionist in the gold fields, and Sidney Bunting, a practising Johannesburg solicitor from a wealthy British liberal, non-conformist background. In the early 1920s, the CPSA concentrated mainly on organising white labour, leading to accusations of racism in the party. However, in 1925, in keeping with international communist (Comintern) directives, the CPSA abandoned co-operation with the racist SALP and work with white labour in favour of increasing African membership.[21] After this date, the gulf between communists and the white labour movement deepened as the SALP continued staunchly to defend 'civilised' labour policies.

This shift in CPSA policy, combined with the rapid spread of the ICU, resulted in a hardening of white South African attitudes. By 1925, the ICU was claiming 'signal victories' in organising labour on the Rand.[22] The organisation had expanded rapidly and General Herzog, who became Prime Minister in 1924, confirmed his commitment to stamping out black political movements, particularly when communist influence was suspected. The South African state thus developed the most sophisticated apparatus of state repression in Africa. Under the 1927 Native Administration Act, anyone found guilty of promoting a 'feeling of hostility' between natives and Europeans was liable to a £100 fine, one year's imprisonment, or both. In May 1930, the new Minister of Justice, Oswald Pirow, amended the 1914 Riotous Assemblies Act, which had been directed against militant white trade unionists, to suppress the growing black discontent. Critics of these measures argued that white lawyers (British and Afrikaner), who had often been educated abroad and were more likely to be 'open-minded' and liberal, were now marginalised in the legal system. As a result, Pirow, described by liberals as a dangerous Afrikaner 'fanatic' who 'scared' the natives, had extensive power over the movement of suspects and could ban agitators without the sanction of the Supreme Court.[23]

A broader-based opposition to government policies began to emerge after 1928. Mass demonstrations and protest against the pass laws were organised, attended by ANC and ICU supporters, and the CPSA co-ordinated joint black and white May Day demonstrations against unemployment. But any protest against segregationist policy was swiftly and, at times brutally, suppressed. At a passive resistance campaign organised in Durban by the CPSA on the symbolic

Dingaan's Day, 12 December 1930 (which was supported by moderates like Professor Jabavu), leaders were arrested, the black communist leader, Johannes Nkosi, was shot dead and many more were seriously wounded. Several Africans were also killed during a battle with armed police at an ANC meeting in Worcester (Western Cape Province) and left-wing sources maintained that during the years 1929–31, forty-three black workers were killed, 100 imprisoned and hundreds deported to their native reservations. Leaders of black workers were exiled and white communists also suffered – Edward Roux and Douglas Wolton were sentenced to hard labour in 1932 and Wolton was jailed in 1933 for allegedly inciting transport workers in Cape Town to go on strike.[24]

The ICU was also harassed by the authorities, despite the fact that after 1926 there were concerted attempts by British liberals to steer the organisation away from communism, including the sponsorship of an adviser, William Ballinger, to work with the ICU (Chapter 7). For instance, in 1930 a member's house ' … was raided at 2.10 a.m. … for poll tax'. Police broke in, dragged the clothes off the bed where he and his wife were sleeping and 'generally misbehaved'. Ballinger protested and the police apologised, claiming, somewhat unconvincingly, that they did not know the victim was an ICU member. Ballinger recorded in 1932 that 'two of the best secretaries' in the Transvaal were 'in trouble': one had been given five weeks hard labour for 'seditious utterances', the second had been banned under the Riotous Assemblies Act. Kadalie was 'waiting sentence' in East London. If there was any 'agitation', complained Ballinger, workers were threatened with the sack or replacement with unemployed whites. A man, who had worked in the Johannesburg Blue Train Office for forty-two years, was given twenty-four hours notice in 1933 to make way for a 'white lad'.[25]

By 1930, the ICU had split into three factions: Kadalie's Independent ICU (IICU) centred in East London; the ICU Yasé Natal, based in Durban and led by Allison Wessels George Champion; and Ballinger's Johannesburg branch. But the groundswell of popular protest against government policies continued. Kadalie led a serious mass strike in East London, in the Eastern Cape Province. Beinart and Bundy (1987) argue that the IICU had 'considerable success in reaching and recruiting the fragmented and variegated proletariat [including women] in East London'. Pass-burning and 'kaffir beer boycott' campaigns against municipal beer halls, which provided a healthy revenue for city councils, were also launched in urban centres throughout the Union. The boycotts were triggered when the authorities introduced the Kaffir Beer Act, which closed down illegal shebeens, – a bitter blow to African women who earned a living by running shebeens. These struggles over beer brewing reflected women's increasing contributions to popular struggles in the townships. Opposition was particularly strong in Durban where the ICU Yasé Natal supported the boycotts and women's attacks on the beer halls. At a meeting in the ICU hall, Champion addressed a crowd of approximately 5,000 Africans and protested against collaborative Africans who were attempting to 'disorganise' the boycott. ICU officials in Durban clearly linked the suppression of the shebeens as part and parcel of the wider government repression. The meeting was described as 'peaceful', but local whites tried to break it up, resulting in the death of two blacks and two whites as well as numerous injuries. ICU offices were 'wrecked' in what Perham, who visited Durban shortly after the incident, described as 'anti-native riots'. Champion was deported from Natal for three years.[26]

Even the most cautious African leaders now acknowledged that native policies and state repression were leading to a new 'spirit of discontent'. Delegates at the 1930 Non-European Conference, founded in 1929 under the chairmanship of Professor Jabavu, acknowledged that African leaders had been 'good boys' for too long and urged more practical action against poll taxes and 'militaristic' police actions through passive resistance. But problems of unifying the black opposition persisted. Margaret Hodgson warned that the conference was differentiating into conservative versus radical, middle class versus proletariat. Kadalie wrote a 'bitter sneering reply' when asked to attend, although Champion was sent to 'look in'. Dr Abdullah Abdurahman, the representative of the Coloured population, who had been 'fobbed off' by Smuts with promises of a Coloured franchise, 'had no sympathy with the native' and had a 'hearty contempt for the stupidity of the Bantu members'. Thus, argues Hodgson, the conference became merely a glorified debating forum.[27]

Splits between Coloureds and 'natives', reflecting the 'divide and rule strategies' cultivated by the government, were particularly damaging. Since its inception, the APO had arguably been dedicated to the reconstitution of a distinct Coloured identity and, under the leadership of Abdurahman, played to white fears of an alliance between Coloureds and Africans and refused to open membership to Africans. Golden (1989) argues that Abdurahman wanted to secure benefits for the Coloured bourgeoisie by distancing Coloureds from 'barbarous natives' and emphasising common causes with the white polity. This elitist strategy led to splits within the Coloured community as poorer Coloured activists, left with no political platform, developed a working class, as opposed to ethnic, identity and became prominent in the ICU and the CPSA.[28] Cape 'Coloured consciousness', forged through segregation, remains problematic despite the end of apartheid and some Afrikaner speaking Coloureds still prefer to vote for white political parties for fear of being swamped by the 'Africanism' of the ANC.

Changes and errors in communist tactics also deepened splits in the black opposition. After 1928, in accordance with Comintern directives, the CPSA began to build its own 'revolutionary' organisations. The CPSA was purged of 'right deviationists' and leadership was taken over by Douglas Wolton, an English communist, and his wife Molly, a Lithuanian migrant. To attract more popular support, a new paper, *Umsebenzi*, ('Worker' in Xhosa) was launched and sold at ANC and weekly Fabian meetings in Cape Town.[29] The South African Federation of Non-European Trade Unions (FNETU) was set up in 1929 as a direct challenge to the ICU. A similar counterpart to the ANC, the League of African Rights, was established in the same year. Robin Cohen (1979) argues that the League embodied an 'inchoate but powerful national consciousness', but was suddenly disbanded on the 'disastrous' advice of the Comintern in 1931. It was replaced by *Ikaka Labasebenzi* (Worker's Shield), a branch of International Labour Defence, set up to provide defence, 'legal or otherwise', for those suffering in the struggle against 'imperialist oppression'.[30]

These changes heralded the CPSA's contentious 'Black Republic' phase where the revolution in South Africa was to be led by the black proletariat in two stages – a preliminary struggle for 'self-determination' in an 'independent native republic', followed by a revolutionary movement to create a United Socialist Republic of Africa. The US Communist Party also adopted a 'Black Republic' strategy for the Southern States and the new policy stimulated lively debates around race versus class in international revolutionary circles in the 1930s. The 'Black Republic' strategy suggests that white marxists, like white liberals had problems grappling with the thorny issue of segregation versus integration. The older integrationist Bunting faction, which had dominated the party in the 1920s, interpreted the strategy as a return to Garveyism, although the advocates of the policy now fiercely rejected Garveyism as 'petty bourgeois'.[31] As Alison Drew (1997) has pointed out, most histories of the CPSA have been written from an 'insider', Left perspective and, thus, the CPSA's own view of the past remains largely unchallenged. While it is clearly simplistic to see the party solely as an instrument of Comintern or Soviet policy, she argues, it is also naive to see the party's behaviour as solely a reflection of African conditions. However, the ultra-Left phase, initiated by the Comintern after 1929, arguably led to the loss of the most accomplished leaders, like Roux who became increasingly marginalised and left the party in 1936.[32]

Given these internal problems and its political isolation, the CPSA's activities before the Second World War reached only a small number of Africans. The party's 'education programme', started in 1928, consisted of little more than 'shoestring' evening classes held in the Johannesburg party office by black CP members, such as T.W. Thibedi, the African secretary-organiser of the FNETU, and Albert Nzula, both of whom were kept under close surveillance by the authorities. Like their liberal counterparts, white communists had an ambivalent relationship with black party members and complained of general illiteracy and lack of politicisation. They thus eventually washed their hands of Thibedi as 'useless' and accused him of 'mishandling' funds. When he was expelled from the party, Roux, a white man took over his job. Similar allegations were made about other 'native Union secretaries', who were described as 'weak from every point of view'.[33] A handful of Africans who attended the Lenin School in Moscow (established in 1926 to train Communist Party activists) – Moses Kotane, J.B. Marks, Edwin Mofutsanyana and Albert Nzula (who died in obscure circumstances in Moscow in 1933) – managed to climb up the hierarchy. Most Africans, however, found it difficult to adapt to the culture of the party. Communist night schools provided only a rudimentary education and most African members were at a severe disadvantage to more educated whites in developing leadership confidence.

Despite official paranoia, communist influence was never very strong in the major black organisations. However, struggles between white liberals and communists to guide the direction of black resistance resulted in ideological confusion and dangerous factionalism. In conjunction with the increase in state repression, this weakened black organisations. The ICU was purged of communists in 1926 and in 1930 the moderate Pixie Seme replaced Joseph Gumede, who had communist sympathies, as President General of the ANC. The liberal academic, Margaret Hodgson, described the 1930 elections as chaotic and the Congress as 'hopeless'. She alleged that Seme, an attorney who had been associated with a 'bogus land scheme' in 1929 for which another man had reputedly gone to prison, was 'not a man to be trusted'. Some black activists, she argued, would rather have had Gumede, who was one of the few who regularly attended meetings and was not corrupt, unlike 'Seme and others', who 'always got what they could' from the Congress.[34] Thus, these schisms in the ANC and ICU paved the way for individualistic opportunists, who were more likely to collaborate with the authorities, and encouraged greater personal corruption.

By 1929, the ICU was 'standing at the gate of hell' after fragmenting into three strands. State repression and white liberal and communist intervention contributed to this, but, argued Champion, in Natal black solidarity was also undermined by collaborative ANC moderates like the Reverend, 'Mr Facing-both-ways', John Dube. Dube and other members of the educated African bourgeoisie were opposed to the ICU and had backed the revival of the Zulu chieftancy and the establishment of Inkatha KaZulu in 1922–3 (forerunner of the present Inkatha Freedom Party) as an alternative conservative political force.[35] In Natal (now KwaZulu Natal), as Shula Marks (1987 and 1989) has demonstrated, complex alliances of ethnicity, race and class interpenetrated relations between Africans and the dominant white minority. 'Tradition' was regarded as a counterweight to more radical influences and the revival of ethnic organisations in Natal was welcomed by the state, the black middle classes and white Natalians, like Heaton Nicholls.[36]

The ICU Yasé Natal (see Illustration 18) allegedly attracted much support and a large income, but its leader, Allison Wessels Champion, was regarded as 'violent' and the police recommended deportation. Champion, remarked Margery Perham, had formerly been a 'spy for the Chamber of Mines' (the main recruiter of migrant labour) in Johannesburg, but was now regarded as dangerous and an 'egotistical' arch agitator ... clever ... embittered and reckless', who refused to placate white authority and made vicious attacks on white interventions in the ICU. Despite his criticisms of Dube, Champion adopted a populist style and increasingly asserted his ethnic identity as the self-styled 'lion-hearted young Zulu'. He built his fiefdom around the African Workers' Club, the first of its kind that was independent of white patronage, and carved his power niche by tapping into the particular social configuration of Natal, cultivating the support of the *Amalaita*, the unruly and sometimes violent urban youth gangs of Durban and the Transvaal. The *Amalaita* were apolitical, but could be mobilised through appeals to Zulu ethnicity and were active in the ICU beer hall riots in 1929–30, singing regimental Zulu anthems at ICU meetings.[37]

Illustration 18—Portrait of the Industrial and Commercial Workers' Union Members

Source: Champion Papers, University of South Africa Archives

Ballinger, however, described Champion as the 'leader of the [native] middle classes'. From a petty bourgeois background and named after an American missionary who had adopted his father, he served two years in the police in the 1920s and had a brief, unsuccessful spell as a diamond digger before working in the mines as a timekeeper. During his banishment from Natal, he worked in a Johannesburg bank and, on his return to Durban, began to develop his own business.[38] Communism, he believed, was 'hopeless' among natives and unless an African 'boss class' developed, there was 'no hope for anybody'. Champion thus advocated liberation through 'black capitalism', which avoided confrontation with white power structures. Margaret Hodgson, noted that both Champion and the Coloured leader, Dr Abdurahman, were concerned primarily with fostering entrepreneurialism as the prime means of uplifting their own ethnic groups.[39]

After the split in the ICU, the titanic clash of egos and conflicting individual interests of Kadalie and Champion (depicted together in Illustration 19) arguably contributed to the further decline of the organisation. Whereas Champion was influenced by US concepts of black entrepreneurialism and embryonic ethnic nationalism, Kadalie had a Garveyite pan-Africanist vision of the 'consolidation of the African races into one gigantic movement'. He wanted to establish ICU branches throughout the continent and blamed Champion's secession for the break up of the organisation. The 'great Zulus', he warned, wanted to stand alone and 'have nothing to do with greater South Africa'.[40] His Africanist sentiments intensified after his humiliating contact with white liberals (Chapter 7). He now aspired to be 'the great African Marcus Garvey' and declared the IICU's intention to build a 'free black nation', drawing on Xhosa tradition and myths, as well as Christianity in building support in Transkei and the Eastern Cape.[41] However, in *Mehlomadala* (1928), written in Zulu and English, Champion accused Kadalie of being an outsider from Nyasaland who could not speak 'the language of Tshaka (*sic*), Moshoeshoe and Hintsa' – the great early resistance heroes. At the nub of the bitterness and rivalry between the two 'comrades' was Kadalie's 'treachery' in turning against Champion under guidance from the ICU's white 'advisers'. Champion also alleged that as a result of his visit to Europe, funded by £800 from the ICU, 'Comrade Kadalie' had lost nearly all his old friends. He had come back from Europe with a 'revolutionised mind' and now wanted 'a European private secretary, [and] white girls as shorthand typists'. When the visit was debated at the Kimberly conference, argued Champion, two 'lady delegates' told Kadalie that he 'went away a black man and came back a white man'.[42]

After the brief successes of the IICU in East London, Kadalie's star declined as Champion's moved into the ascendant. By 1934, Champion was no longer seen as a threat and the authorities had 'no objections' to his organising meetings of 'natives'. He joined the executive of the ANC in 1935 and became president of the Natal branch in 1946. By 1951, he was regarded as too conservative and lost his seat on the executive, but continued to be active in local politics.[43] In contrast, Kadalie was accused of corruption and heavy drinking, which

Illustration 19–Portrait of Clements Kadalie and A.W.G. Champion (standing)
Source: A.W.G. Champion Papers, University of South Africa Archives

contributed to new splits in the IICU. Embittered and politically marginalised, he was described by Ballinger in 1933 as a 'physical wreck … slightly paralysed on one side [reputedly] due to syphilus [sic] and heavy drinking'. Kadalie thus became the main scapegoat for both communist and reformist failures to effect change through the ICU, which arguably detracted from his contribution to black struggles in the 1920s. However, he remained active in trade union affairs in the Cape until his death in 1951.[44]

In assessing the contribution of the ICU to black struggles, Bradford (1987) argues that whereas the ANC was cut off from the mass of Africans, the ICU tapped into the popular community struggles of the new African proletariat and dispossessed peasantry. As the first African trade union the ICU pioneered the black trade union movement, which has been so central to the liberation struggle. The organisation expanded rapidly in the 1920s, although Bradford's research indicates that it found most of its support in rural areas by campaigning about local community issues. However, Beinart and Bundy (1989) argue that while the ICU had the potential to unite the struggles of urban workers, farm labourers and black peasants, it collapsed because it failed to cement these links with the rural areas. Rural movements, they add, possessed their own 'internal logic' and were not always assimilable into the liberal norms of the black urban intelligentsia who, like Kadalie, viewed them as parochial.[45] Channelling the fragmented consciousness of migrant labour on an organised basis also proved very difficult for both the ICU and the communists. Similar problems of forging a more unified opposition dogged black political initiatives to challenge new segregationist legislation and white repression, which intensified after 1930.

Hope and despondency: state repression and black protest, 1930–39

Between 1930–2 the activities of the ANC and the ICU sunk into a nadir. The authorities had also severely clamped down on the CPSA, particularly in Durban, where there were further disturbances in 1931. Ballinger reported that the Party had 'crashed' and membership had declined to 150 by 1933. However, resistance to growing repression and violence continued. The accelerated drift to the cities led to stricter policing of locations and large numbers of Africans were imprisoned for violation of pass and liquor laws. Police raids on the Rand became more frequent and protests were organised against the police 'pick-up van', the prototype of the dreaded Caspars of the apartheid era, which cruised the locations in search of 'illegal' migrants.[46] Violence, allegedly provoked by Fascist Greyshirts, erupted at an organised protest against police pick-up raids at the Vereeniging location in September 1937 and resulted in the death of three policemen and the arrest of 450 Africans. A subsequent Commission of Inquiry concluded that the riots were not solely due to communist influence, as was alleged, and the pick-up raids were toned down.[47] Anti-white sentiment intensified. The missionary, Ray Phillips, reported that in the locations there was 'intense resentment and hostility' towards the police and that Africans were bitter, defiant and resentful. Mission-educated Africans, he warned, were 'exceptionally discontented' and lacking in respect for white missionaries who were faced with 'bitter antagonism' and 'bombarded with questions'. He was deeply concerned about communism's potential to supersede Christian education and promote 'racial strife'.[48]

The prime cause of discontent among educated Africans was the passing of the 1936 Native Representation Bill (described by radical blacks as the 'Slave Acts'). This legislation removed the slender citizenship rights of a small minority of educated Africans in the Cape and remained in place until the end of apartheid, which explains why the first democratic elections in 1994 were such an emotional and charged event. For educated Africans, the act was the culmination of a steady erosion of their rights. The 1853 liberal Cape Constitution had extended the franchise to all her majesty's subjects 'regardless of colour', but African rights were eroded in 1892 when a property and educational qualification was introduced to keep out the 'blanket kaffir'. In 1927, there were 16,480 Africans on the electoral roll, but this was whittled away after 1930 when all white adults, including women, attained universal suffrage.[49]

The 1936 Act catalysed suppressed African anger and revived black political organisations. There was a new militant mood in the air, reflected in a resurgence of pan-Africanism and even moderate black leaders now warned against reliance on white help. In a renewed attempt to unify the fragmented opposition, the All African Convention (AAC) was formed in 1935. The symbolic first meeting on Dingaan's Day in December of the same year, attended by delegates from rural and urban areas and the British Protectorates, was reputedly the biggest Coloured and black conference ever held. In his 1936 presidential address to the Convention, Professor Jabavu, an erstwhile advocate of racial integration, argued that blacks had remained 'loyal and patient ... like asses' for too long, depending on white 'friends'. He emphasised that 'nationalism and race pride' was a necessary preliminary step in black development and recommended greater self-help to develop 'political and economic power'.[50]

This new militancy was fuelled by the 1935 Italian invasion of Ethiopia and even moderates now predicted that, unless white attitudes changed, there would be 'an outbreak of revolution' in South Africa.[51] AAC leaders strongly condemned the invasion and began to link their cause with Indian nationalism and the struggles of 'all people of African descent'. Jabavu equated the loss of the Cape franchise with Italian aggression against the Ethiopians, arguing that both developments had exposed the 'savagery' beneath the European veneer. The Cape ANC accused Britain of helping to betray Ethiopia and reneging on her 'protection' of the Protectorates.[52] The CPSA also recognised the potential of the Ethiopian crisis to fire black consciousness. Its newspaper, *Umvikeli Thebe*, adopted the slogan 'Freedom in Africa' and the CPSA bookshop in Johannesburg carried educational articles and books on Ethiopia and the US race problem. The Union Government was deeply concerned about these developments and warned that the 'new partition of Africa' was a 'menace' to white civilisation as the 'long memory of Africa ... never forgets or forgives ... an injustice'.[53] South

Africa took a strong line at the League for sanctions against Italy and was critical of the inertia of Britain's failure to act, indicating the widening divergence of interests between the settler state and its imperial centre.

Margaret Ballinger (née Hodgson) commented thus on this new fighting spirit:

> The natives ... as a result of hardening Government policy ... seem to have been shocked into a measure of self-consciousness. ... [They] give the impression [of finding] a new purpose ... [but] it is too early to say whether it will be more than a flash in the pan ... [they] will either stand together and plump for a solid forward policy [or] ... go into the wilderness for years ... [54]

But the wilderness it was. The momentum generated by the Ethiopian invasion and opposition to the abolition of the Cape franchise quickly evaporated. Despite its strong rhetoric, the AAC was never regarded as a major threat by the authorities. The 1935 convention was officially opened by the Mayor of Bloemfontein and the majority of delegates remained staunchly anti-communist, rejecting communist calls for strikes and passive resistance and accepting liberal pleas for compromise.[55] More radical pan-Africanists argued that the authorities capitalised on continuing divisions within the African leadership in order to weaken opposition to state policies. Max Yergan, who was the AAC's US-based Secretary for External Relations and co-founder with Paul Robeson of the US-based Council on African Affairs (1937), stressed the need for unity, but rifts between moderates and radicals widened. Like the ICU, the AAC was potentially a powerful, unifying force, but, as one radical black critic pointed out, it arguably failed to integrate the conflicting pan-Africanist, nationalist and class consciousness within the movement.[56]

Through white eyes, liberal and communist, Africans lacked a coherent political analysis and there were 'few indicators' of an advance in African political consciousness after the collapse of the ICU. The Reverend Phillips saw both the AAC and the ANC as useless organisations, riven by divisiveness and tribalism. Writing in retrospect, Edward Roux condemned African political leadership as 'immature' and suffering from a 'childish individualism', while Jack Simons contrasted the divided black movement to the 'more cohesive and politically mature' Indian community.[57] However, Africans were in an impossibly weak position and many showed great bravery and fortitude in continuing to resist despite the threat of police brutality. There were insuperable barriers facing black organisations, including lack of funds and organisational expertise. African activists also found it difficult to travel abroad in view of tight official restrictions and had to rely on white representation at international forums, liberal or communist. Mobilising the masses was also very difficult. In the climate of fear created by the white state, individuals risked harsh punishments for even the most minor act of protest or 'insolence' to whites. As in other violent and repressive societies, many men and women were preoccupied simply with surviving, although they also engaged in small acts of non-compliance.

White interventions and cultural imperialism also fragmented and weakened the educated black leadership, who developed a divided consciousness, which was reflected in 'ambiguity and equivocation'.[58] The educated minority had great influence within the ANC in the 1920s and was cultivated in both South African and British liberal circles as a 'steady and law abiding influence' that was committed to co-operation with whites and moderate change. Jabavu was particularly admired as 'one of the foremost Bantu leaders', a 'highly educated ... intellectual pioneer' whose contribution to improving the relationship between blacks and whites could 'hardly be overestimated'.[59] However, the ambivalent attitudes of educated Africans who wore the 'white mask' irritated their white patrons. Even Jabavu at times displeased his white, liberal patrons, who were concerned at his ability to manipulate blacks and arouse 'racial feeling'. William Macmillan argued that another ANC activist, Selope Thema, wavered between willing co-operation and 'bitter antagonism'. White visitors to Fort Hare Native College and Lovedale College also sensed an underlying 'envenomed hostility' on the part of students they met.[60] Educated Africans occupied the dangerous and unstable space between white and black cultures, and this sharpened race and class contradictions, raised consciousness and inspired resistance. However, cultural ambivalence, combined with constant racial humiliations, could also destabilise the psyche. Serious drinking problems were not uncommon among black leaders like Kadalie, Thema and, the communist, Albert Nzula, arguably an indication of such stresses, but also of despondency over crushed hopes of reversing segregation.

Most of the black bourgeoisie were educated at Lovedale and Fort Hare, which was the only institution of university rank for Africans. Both institutions were situated near Alice, in the Eastern Cape, and described in the South African propaganda literature of the 1940s as 'the black man's Eton and Oxford'. Lovedale College was attached to the Lovedale Mission Station of the United Church of Scotland and was founded in 1838 to provide vocational instruction for both boys and girls. In 1868, it opened a boarding school where advanced studies could be pursued. Females were still mainly restricted to 'domestic' skills, but could also study nursing and teaching after 1900. Males were trained for the church and teaching. Lovedale thus provided a colonial education that was similar to that in other parts of Africa and designed to repress discontent and inculcate Christian, liberal-democratic values. Fort Hare was established in 1916 through the co-operation of the Union Government, Transkeian Territories General Council and missionary societies. The British High Commission Territories made an annual grant.[61] The College prioritised vocational skills and 'Bantu Studies', which in segregationist discourse were supposed to help preserve African culture. However, with the entrenchment of segregation, opportunities to study in Britain dwindled and Fort Hare was the only access that Africans had to higher education. These strategies effectively stifled the development of the African intelligentsia and professional classes.

Among the mass of rural and urban Africans different, but equally problematic, barriers to a coherent and politically effective mass consciousness existed.

Contemporary political activists attributed problems of organising migrant labour to 'tribal feelings'.[62] As Marks and Rathbone (1982) observe, the formation of working-class consciousness was complicated by the rural roots of migrant workers. Connections between workers and peasants, they argue, were 'intimate and continuous' and they were often the same people at 'different but ... closely juxtaposed periods of their lives'. Lack of class solidarity has been blamed on ethnic divisions rooted in this rural consciousness. However, Vail (1989) suggests that ethnic self-identification may also be interpreted as a dynamic and complex cultural response to social dislocation.[63] A sophisticated literature has developed since the 1970s, stimulated by the problems of 'ethnic violence' in KwaZulu Natal, which explores the complex relationship between ethnic, class and nationalist consciousness. However, certain key points pertaining to ethnicity and class consciousness are relevant here. As Van Onselen (1973) observes, the rural roots of migrant workers and the lack of 'working-class consciousness' did not prevent them at times from exhibiting a keen understanding of their position within the labour market. In the same vein, Marks and Rathbone (1982) suggest that the newly proletarianised had a sharper awareness than the black petty bourgeoisie, that 'the black man is poor and the white man is bad'.[64] The state feared the potential mass strength of the urban proletariat and rural peasantry, which constituted the greatest threat to the state, hence the violence and other tactics, including deprivation of education and the cultivation of ethnic and status divisions among African, Coloured and Indian, workers to prevent a more coherent consciousness emerging.

In spite of these manifold barriers to the formation of mass movements, which could reverse segregation, important developments occurred between the two world wars that helped to advance the struggle for African liberation, even if the main pattern was 'one step forwards, two steps back'. The complex system of legal and ideological repression fragmented black opposition, but it also stimulated a more concerted resistance from all sections of the non-white population. When Eslanda Robeson visited South Africa in 1936, she found black South Africans politically sophisticated, including women, who were involved in community projects and attended AAC conferences (although, as in West Africa, women remained marginal to African political movements, except in a supportive role through women's branches).[65] The main lines of struggle that African organisations were to adopt after the Second World War period were clarified through the interplay of conflicting ideological influences, namely: a unifying non-ethnic nationalism, ethnic nationalism, pan-Africanist black separatism and marxism. The Second World War catalysed these developments and brought new hopes for the organised mass struggle against white supremacy.

Towards the future: the impact of the Second World War

During the Second World War, optimism grew as the Afrikaner nationalist ascendancy was temporarily halted when Smuts once again became Prime

Minister. Rapid industrial growth and the importance of African labour in the war economy raised living standards of black urban workers and led to a resurgence of trade unionism. The ICU was rekindled in the rural towns and played its part in the Alexandria (Johannesburg) bus boycotts in 1943 in protest against a rise in fares. There was also renewed ANC militancy against the pass laws, spearheaded by radicals like J.B. Marks, which culminated in anti-pass campaigns in 1944.[66]

These wartime developments, in conjunction with the surge of nationalist optimism throughout Africa and the African diaspora, boosted morale and led to a rejuvenation of the ANC and AAC. The growth of mass African nationalism inspired a vision of 'a new [young] Africa, an Africa reborn … rejuvenated'. Radical pan-Africanism with its emphasis on black unity, rejection of white patronage and anti-imperialism is reflected in the rhetoric of the 'youth movements' centred in the 'Bantu' colleges of Lovedale and Fort Hare, where Nelson Mandela was a student. The AAC's 'Sons of Young Africa' and the ANC Youth League were founded in 1943. Older black leaders were optimistic about these developments, sensing an important 'turning point' in the fortunes of black organisations.[67] The ANC, which had almost been eclipsed by the AAC in the 1930s, was now transformed into the main nationalist movement. At the annual ANC conference in December 1946 (see Illustration 20), President General A.B. Xuma emphasised that there was no room for division or personal ambition in building the ANC as a 'mass liberation movement'. The conference endorsed a Bill of Citizenship Rights for South African blacks, which reiterated the main grievances outlined by the SANNC in 1919, but also reflected the new influence of the discourse of universal human rights. The document also recognised common claims and grievances with other Africans, but stressed that the situation was 'most urgent' in South Africa.[68]

The war also rekindled links with Britain as South Africans, black and white, enlisted as soldiers of the empire and Commonwealth in the 'good' battle against fascism. Smuts' premiership reaffirmed membership of a wider international community and hopes for a reversal of segregationist policies as extremist Afrikaner nationalism appeared to lose force. Beinart (1994) argues that Smuts' skills at political compromise permitted a period of relative openness during the Second World War, and white liberals and welfare planners briefly had more influence than at any other time in the country's history. However, Smuts remained resistant to African and liberal pressures to reverse segregationist policies and his cabinet was drawn from pre-war politicians who had firmly supported segregation, even if they opposed Afrikaner republican nationalism.[69] When amendments to industrial legislation were proposed in 1941, he ignored ANC requests to persuade the Minister of Labour, Walter Madely, the long-time leader of the racist SALP, to abolish discrimination on colour lines and recognise African trade unions. Margaret Ballinger was asked to intervene, but was 'sorely disappointed' by Smuts' 'efforts' and concluded that 'despite the loyalty and co-operation shown by Africans' in the war effort, the government had chosen to listen to the Afrikaner opposition rather than heed African pleas. Smuts nominally supported African 'agitation', but only if it was around pressing issues of 'native' welfare.[70]

The wartime experiences of black soldiers also stimulated race consciousness. Grundlingh (1986) argues that initially blacks were reluctant to enlist as they still retained vivid memories of the sinking of the S.S. Mendi (Chapter 5) and harsh treatment meted out to the Native Labour Contingent in the First World War. Anti-war feeling among literate Africans, he argues, was 'rife' and, as in West Africa, the contribution of the black bourgeoisie to the war effort was linked more to furthering black rights than loyalty to imperial Britain. For the majority of the South African population, propaganda calls to fight for freedom did not square with their experiences of state repression and Grundlingh suggests that economic factors, particularly rural poverty, may have been a major factor in recruitment (80 per cent of recruits were from rural areas). Ultimately, 80,000 enlisted, which was 25 per cent of the total Union Defence Force (UDF) manpower. Initially, black soldiers were barred from bearing arms, but by 1944 the UDF included blacks and Coloureds in combatant roles, although segregated corps still existed.[71] At the end of the war, demobbed African soldiers, whose racial and political awareness was heightened by their experiences in Europe, nourished the new political radicalism. Student militancy increased and there were riots at Lovedale College in 1946. White (1995) argues that after the relative isolation of the inter-war period, black South Africans once more felt part of momentous international developments and rejected moderation for stronger tactics and a more confrontational position.[72]

Given these developments, the ANC had high hopes that a postwar peace settlement would support their claims for African rights, but were only to be disappointed yet again. Smuts represented South Africa in international forums and was unlikely to press African claims. Despite its humanitarian and anti-racist rhetoric, the new United Nations offered little support for black South Africans until the balance was changed with the admission of the non-aligned bloc of ex-colonial states. However, the ANC delegation's visit to New York, facilitated by Max Yergan, did raise international recognition for South African problems and widen black American support. Xuma also raised African grievances, including the continued Union mandate over South West Africa, in a petition to the UN.[73] Despite these efforts, South West Africa remained a mandate under the nominal trusteeship of the United Nations and was absorbed more tightly into the South African state – only gaining independence as Namibia after a protracted liberation struggle.

In evaluating these developments, Rich (1996) argues that the ANC could have been more pro-active in fostering links with other nationalist organisations or pan-African initiatives before 1945. He cites the rather poor performance of ANC delegates (Mark Hlubi and the writer, Peter Abrahams) at the important 1945 Pan-African Congress in Manchester (Chapter 8).[74] However, in criticising the ANC we must allow for the fact that South African blacks had less freedom of travel than colonised subjects from other parts of Britain's 'black' empire. 'Bantu' education policies fostered a parochial consciousness and cut the African

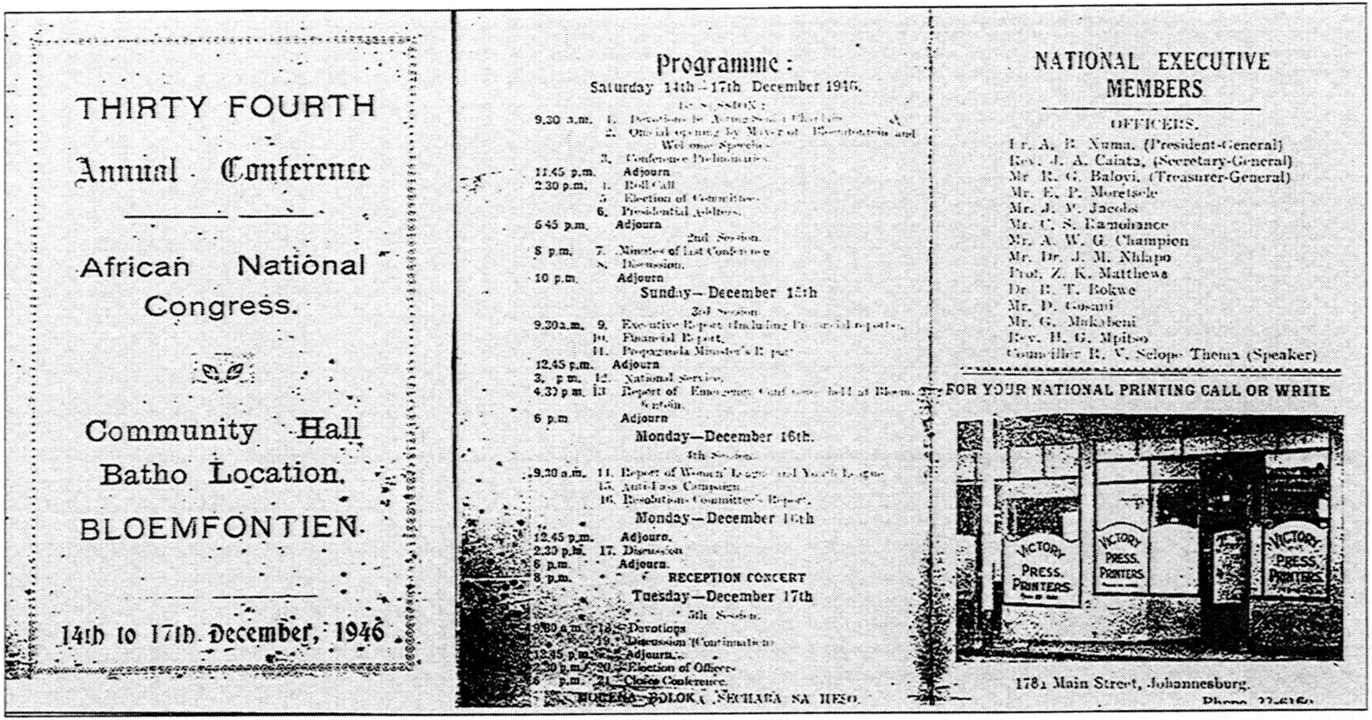
THIRTY FOURTH

Annual Conference

African National Congress.

Community Hall

Batho Location.

BLOEMFONTIEN.

14th to 17th December, 1946

Programme:

Saturday 14th–17th December 1946.

[illegible]

9.30 a.m. 1. [illegible]

2. [illegible] and Welcome Speeches

3. Conference Preliminaries

11.45 p.m. Adjourn

2.30 p.m. 4. Roll Call

5. Election of Committees

6. Presidential Address.

5.45 p.m. Adjourn

2nd Session.

8 p.m. 7. Minutes of last Conference

8. Discussion.

10 p.m. Adjourn

Sunday—December 15th

3rd Session

9.30 a.m. 9. Executive Report [illegible]

10. Financial Report.

11. Propaganda Minister's Report

12.45 p.m. Adjourn

3. p.m. 12. National Service.

4.30 p.m. 13. Report of Emergency Conference held at Bloemfontein.

6 p.m. Adjourn

Monday—December 16th.

4th Session.

9.30 a.m. 14. Report of Women's League and Youth League

15. Anti-Pass Campaign

16. Resolutions Committee's Report.

Monday—December 16th

12.45 p.m. Adjourn.

2.30 p.m. 17. Discussion

6 p.m. Adjourn.

8 p.m. RECEPTION CONCERT

Tuesday—December 17th

5th Session.

9.30 a.m. 18. Devotions

19. Discussion (Continuation)

12.45 p.m. Adjourn.

2.30 p.m. 20. Election of Officers

6 p.m. 21. Close Conference.

[illegible] BOLOKA SECHABA SA HESO.

NATIONAL EXECUTIVE MEMBERS

OFFICERS.

Dr. A. B. Xuma. (President-General)
Rev. J. A. Calata. (Secretary-General)
Mr R. G. Baloyi. (Treasurer-General)
Mr. E. P. Moretsele
Mr. J. V. Jacobs
Mr. C. S. Ramohanoe
Mr. A. W. G. Champion
Mr. Dr. J. M. Nhlapo
Prof. Z. K. Matthews
Dr. R. T. Bokwe
Mr. D. Gosani
Mr. G. Makabeni
Rev. H. G. Mpitso
Councillor R. V. Selope Thema (Speaker)

FOR YOUR NATIONAL PRINTING CALL OR WRITE

VICTORY PRESS. PRINTERS

178½ Main Street, Johannesburg.

Illustration 20–Programme for the 34th Conference of the African National Congress, 1946
Source: A.W.G. Champion Papers, University of South Africa Archives

intelligentsia off from contact with the stimulating anti-colonialist climate of the international community of students and activists in Britain. Rich also makes insufficient allowance for the cultural oppression and physical violence of the state, which constantly undermined black organisations, and it is an extraordinary tribute to the tenacity of African spirit that resistance was consistently sustained.

Despite these barriers, the war had stimulated black consciousness and revived links between communists, black trade unionists and nationalists, which had important implications for future developments in black resistance. But, if the war renewed hope and optimism, there were also countervailing forces. Urbanisation and the rise in strikes and squatter movements had enhanced white fears of black crime and 'swamping'.[75] The trend was thus towards greater repression and, in August 1946, an African miners' strike, led by the communist, J.B. Marks, which brought twelve mines to a halt for three days, was brutally repressed. In a swing to the right in 1948, the 'purified' Nationalists under Dr Malan were elected, apartheid became the official policy of the new Nationalist government and Smuts, and the sad remnants of South African liberalism went into the political cold. The Cold War deepened the rift between the communists and any remnants of white liberal and reformist opposition, and, in 1950, the Communist Party was legally banned. Thus, the patterns of repression and segregationist policies established in the inter-war years persisted in an even more intense form. This repression ultimately pushed the ANC, in tandem with the CPSA, into a more radical position in the 1960s when the armed liberation struggle was launched.

Summary

What, then, was the balance sheet of inter-war organised resistance? Progress was made and the growth of race consciousness in the 1920s, combined with the populist appeal of the ICU, raised African hopes. During the 1930s, these hopes were mingled with greater despondency as the further consolidation of white power, combined with poverty and social dislocation generated by the international economic depression and severe drought, reduced the ability of Africans to mobilise politically in both urban and rural areas. Black consciousness was fractured along class and ethnic lines, which also hindered the development of black political organisations. After 1935, black activists moved closer to the pan-Africanist orbit, which stimulated black consciousness. The Second World War revived black trade unionism and transformed the ANC into the main nationalist movement. Yet these hopes were crushed once more with the implementation of apartheid in 1948 and the subsequent intensification of repression. Throughout this period, South Africa was part of the 'liberal' British empire, but the imperial government had colluded with, rather than opposed, white South African policies. Belonging to 'British South Africa' had done little to help black South Africans as ANC delegations in 1913, 1919 and 1933 had proved. However, the failure of the imperial government to protect 'native rights' in South Africa led to the informal interventions of British liberals, which had implications for both black resistance and imperial policy. Thus, a fitting conclusion to this analysis of imperialism, race and resistance in South Africa is an assessment of these British liberal interventions.

7 'Fighting for the underdog'
British liberalism and the South African 'native question'

> Criticism of South African policy and practice by peoples overseas arouses deep resentment in the minds of Afrikaans and English-speaking peoples alike [because] of its frequent failure to show a sympathetic understanding of their problems or the recognition of the work being done for native welfare.
>
> (Society of Friends, 1938)[1]

South Africa presented the biggest challenge to British liberalism, but also the most spectacular erosion of its ideals. Underlying the above statement, issued by a deputation of British Quakers to South Africa in 1939, is an admittance of the failure of British liberal interventions into South African problems in the preceding years and a recognition of the growing gulf between South African and British-based liberals. Before the First World War, the ideal of Cape liberalism was still sustained in official British rhetoric, and voluntary sector connections were forged primarily through missionary links and the international Quaker network, which centred on the Anti-Slavery and Aborigines Protection Society (ASAPS). As the imperial government was increasingly loath to interfere in internal South African politics, the South African 'native cause' was more consistently taken up by British-based pressure groups, which embraced a broad spectrum of opinion from liberal to reformist (democratic) socialist. Although opinions differed about the causes and solutions to the 'native problem', a broad consensus existed on the need to counteract segregation and to keep the flame of British liberal ideals alive in Southern Africa. In Britain, activists concerned with South African problems had links with the British Labour Party, Independent Labour Party and Trade Union Movement and there were a smattering of Labour MPs who provided access to the imperial parliament. The older philanthropic ASAPS also had influential parliamentary connections. In South Africa, however, liberals worked in a political vacuum, which was outside the arena of mainstream politics, as all three political parties, including the South African Labour Party (SALP), were committed to segregationist policies.

Loose-knit, 'pan-liberal' links developed between London-based pressure groups and South African liberal organisations, which were bonded by a shared compassion for the 'underdog', a liberal position on race and commitment to the higher ideals of imperial trusteeship, but also, as Vera Brittain stressed, the need to counteract communist influence.[2] 'Liberal', as defined in my Introduction, is thus broadly used here to define all non-communist British initiatives. However, serious divisions emerged over practical solutions to the 'native problem' between the paternalistic, but implicitly racist, 'protective' liberals, including missionaries and philanthropists, and the reformist socialists, who developed a more incisive economic and political critique of segregation and black poverty. In the 1930s, rifts also widened between the diminishing constituency of South African liberals, immersed in an increasingly isolated and hostile political environment, and British-based activists, some of whom were pushed further to the left as conditions within South Africa deteriorated. These rifts between 'conservative' liberals and 'radicals' deepened when the more radical British South African critics of segregation, like William Macmillan, left South Africa in the 1930s.

My analysis widens out recent critiques of the 'Cape liberal tradition' (Chapter 5) and seminal studies of liberal interventions in South African politics. I have not included missionary activity and developments within established South African liberalism during the inter-war years as these have been ably covered by, for instance, Rich (1984) and Elphick (1987).[3] Moreover, the secular political involvement of British activists was stimulated by the perceived conservatism of this older liberal constituency. Although some continuities with the pre-First World War period existed through, for instance, the ASAPS, postwar British liberal and reformist intervention was characterised by a broader activist constituency, with more female and working-class participation, and shaped by the political ethos of the inter-war period, particularly the ideological conflicts between liberalism, communism and fascism. Reformist activists had links with the Labour Party and were influenced by Fabian socialism with its emphasis on careful research, which could inform the gradual implementation of social and economic reforms. Problems in South Africa were now viewed from a wider 'internationalist' perspective and in relation to race problems in other parts of the empire – Kenya, Nigeria, Australia – and the United States. South Africa was also regarded, 'rightly or wrongly', as the 'centre of world race conflict' where urbanisation had cancelled out tribal differences and led to a new 'political solidarity' that challenged white supremacy.[4] Intersecting these concerns was the intensification of state violence, the retreat of nineteenth-century 'protective' Cape liberalism with the ascendancy of Afrikaner republicanism and the threat of the absorption of the British High Commission Territories (Protectorates) of Bechuanaland, Swaziland and Basutoland into the South African white settler state.

British liberal-reformist interventions in the South African 'native problem' were arguably significant in two key areas: in initiatives to neutralise the more destabilising trends in blacks resistance and in generating critiques of 'native policy' and related discourses of empire, race and culture in the imperial heartland. My examination of key areas of intervention suggests that practical initiatives were undermined simultaneously by the fusion of white interests in a segregated South Africa, the ideological rifts that fragmented the opposition to segregationist policies in Britain and South Africa, and the desire of black activists for political autonomy. Implicit to this study is the 'liberal dilemma' of how to tackle racism and oppression, admirable humanitarian motives, while remaining committed to a capitalist system that sustains oppression. My arguments are developed through an analysis of practical initiatives in relation to the Industrial and Commercial Workers Union (ICU), the multicultural Joint Councils and 'native' development in South Africa and, finally, the British High Commission Territories (Protectorates). I conclude with a retrospective evaluation of British liberal interventions.

Industrialisation and the 'helpless Africans': the Industrial and Commercial Workers' Union

While on a lecturing tour of South Africa for the League of Nations Union in 1926, Winifred Holtby, the English writer and feminist, had made contact with members of the 'university circle', who were active in the Johannesburg Joint Council, including William Macmillan, Professor of History at Witwatersrand University, and the writer, Sarah Gertrude Millin. The Johannesburg liberals had already penetrated the ICU to counteract communist influence. Holtby was thus able to meet Champion and Kadalie, the 'Zulu Bolshevists', and was converted to the 'native' cause. The 'native' situation, wrote Holtby to her close friend, Vera Brittain, was 'desperately serious' with 'really bad' strikes and riots. Back in England, she set out to canvass the support of the British Labour Movement and to alert liberal opinion about the 'terrible' conditions in Johannesburg, where there was a 'huge mass of absolutely helpless people', led by inexperienced black leaders, who were 'bewildered by modern industrial conditions'. Although motivated primarily by humanitarian sympathy for the underdog, she was concerned over the developing cleavage between Africans and moderate European opinion, which allowed a 'crude ... undiluted ... brand of vehement Communism' to impose itself on native ignorance.[5]

After 1928, practical activities polarised around finding a suitable trade union adviser to send to South Africa to keep the ICU on a firm reformist path. The trade unionist, Arthur Creech Jones (who became Secretary of State for Colonies in 1947), wrote to Kadalie advising caution and moderation and warning him to avoid 'bitterness' against whites. But finding an advisor proved more difficult than anticipated – a reflection of the deep parochialism within the British Trade Union Movement.[6] Creech Jones' early interest in the affair soon began to wane and, in the absence of more suitable candidates, the choice was finally narrowed down to William Ballinger, a 35 year old Scot from a respectable working-class background, a bookkeeper by trade who had Independent Labour Party (ILP) and Workers' Educational Association (WEA) affiliations. Ballinger was inexperienced, but Creech Jones argued that he was 'cautious and level-headed' with an enthusiasm for work in South Africa. Support for a 'Ballinger Fund' was mobilised by the ever-energetic Holtby, and Ballinger was in South Africa by July 1928, funded by the Noel Buxton Trust, which was administered by John Fletcher of the Quaker Society of Friends and the ASAPS.[7]

From the outset, Ballinger made it clear to the ICU that his aim was to improve the living standards of natives through 'non-violent methods' and in a short time he had succeeded in alienating the black leadership, who accused him of trying to take over the running of the ICU. Kadalie, who had initially welcomed the help, alleged he was 'more of a dictator than an adviser', while Champion, who had always been circumspect about Ballinger, claimed that he became an adviser against the wishes of ICU officials. Ballinger's British sponsors encouraged greater intervention in the ICU as they became increasingly disenchanted with their protégé, Kadalie, described by Holtby as sincere, but also 'a vain ... extremist' and 'heavy-drinking womaniser'. His trip to Europe in 1927 (Chapter 6), sponsored by British liberals, had not improved his image in white eyes. He was increasingly accused of corruption and in 1930 Ballinger reported that he had tried to keep Kadalie 'on the rails', but Kadalie did not dare to come to the ICU headquarters because £500 of funds had vanished.[8]

White sponsors alleged that ICU officials were 'only in it for the money'. Mabel Palmer, a former member of the British Fabian Society and friend of Beatrice and Sidney Webb, who had emigrated to Durban to lecture in English, wrote a patronising letter to Champion berating his 'injudicious' refusal of Ballinger's advice and failure to clear himself from suspicion of financial 'slackness'. She withdrew her support for the ICU and stressed that she could not invite him to join the Joint Council, despite his 'leading position among the natives'. Distrust of black abilities is reflected in her seemingly well-intentioned request that she would be glad to have 'any *important* (her emphasis) documents' in Champion's possession 'for her College library' to keep safe for future historians. This assumption that Champion could not be relied upon to look after historical sources underestimated the value that Africans attached to their own history of struggle. As Beinart and Bundy (1987) observe, ICU documents were a vital part of the 'historical legacy of resistance'. Thus, when Champion addressed a meeting of the Independent ICU (IICU) in East London on the 12 December (Dingaan's Day) 1930, he exhorted listeners to 'keep your native Cape history – it must be written and kept for future generations'.[9] Like other white liberals, Mabel Palmer failed to appreciate the sensitivity of Africans to white criticisms. Black male pride may also have been scorched by the superior attitudes of women liberals like Mabel Palmer, who saw themselves as 'emancipated' women. Hence, Champion replied that he was not at all interested in Palmer's 'most disturbing' letter, nor did he care to win the favour of her friends. Most of all he did not want her telling him what she thought of him. He wrote:

> You should always try to respect my feelings, Mrs Palmer, whether you are a European and I, a native ... I want no favours from all who think like you. If I am such a bad character let it rest at that.[10]

Schemes to sponsor Africans to study in Britain also proved a disappointment to well-intentioned liberals. Alex Hlubi, an ICU member, studied trade union education at the Quaker Fircroft College, Birmingham, from 1930–2. However, when he showed signs of being 'too political', funding was withdrawn and Ballinger and his other South African sponsors decided that he should return to South Africa. A research and complaints officer of the ICU was rejected outright, on Ballinger's advice, as candidates for sponsorship had to be of 'good character' and suitably deferential to their white patrons.[11] Irresponsibility, incompetence, opportunism and 'fiddling the books' is common to the discourse of white communists and liberals, and is reflected in a general lack of trust in placing blacks in positions of authority. However, liberals placed more emphasis on white deference and, like colonial officials, tended to equate morality and civilisation with sound accounting. Such allegations, however, need to be contextualised within the mismatch of cultural values between blacks and whites and the ambivalent, dependent and sometimes humiliating situation of black activists. Yet how could blacks and whites share equal standards? The personal accounts kept by Champion in his diaries reflect the huge gulf in living standards between African activists and their white patrons. Poverty, combined with exposure to an alien culture of financial accountability, undoubtedly resulted in some corruption, but morally righteous whites conveniently overlooked the fact that corruption was not restricted to the less 'civilised'. They also failed to acknowledge the existence of African systems of communal organisation and related alternative systems of accounting.

The splits in the ICU were thus blamed on black incompetence, although state repression and white interventions were equally, if not more, to blame.[12] Ballinger's role in these developments is ambivalent as his activities displeased both black and white. His work with the ICU continued into the 1930s, but his white sponsors were increasingly alienated by his perceived left-wing leanings. A brief *rapprochement* with communists as state repression intensified was interpreted as evidence of a 'dangerous radicalism' and incensed the more cautious liberal elements in South Africa and Britain, who now regarded Ballinger as a 'monster [and] renegade to his country and his colour'.[13] The police kept tabs on him. His correspondence with the communists, Sidney Bunting and Edward Roux, was intercepted and right-wingers, like Dr Malan, were convinced that he was a communist agent. In 1930, he founded the short-lived South African Independent Labour Party (ILP) as an alternative to the racist South African Labour Party (SALP), which resulted in a (failed) attempt to 'buy his principles' with an offer of a lucrative salary to reorganise the SALP.[14]

As Margaret Hodgson (who married Ballinger in 1934) has pointed out, Ballinger was arguably the only European with 'firsthand' knowledge of native conditions, but he was regarded as an extremist because he was openly critical of the timidity and conservatism of South African liberals and had links with communists and left-wingers in the British ILP. Macmillan saw him as a 'catfish' who disturbed liberal complacency, gaining him the negative epithet 'white kaffir'.[15] Yet Bradford (1987) argues that far from being radical, Ballinger always did the bidding of his liberal backers, some of whom, she alleges, were members of the Chamber of Mines. In retrospect, her assertions are valid. Ballinger certainly became more conservative over time and although Mouton (1997) has revived his memory in his detailed and extensive study, he is regarded as an irrelevance by many scholars of the period.[16] For the purposes of my analysis, however, Ballinger's relationship with his sponsors is pertinent to understanding the divisions that dogged liberal initiatives and the gulf in perceptions between British and South African-born liberals.

Ballinger's class background, as well as his political views, complicated his relationship with middle-class liberals. Because of his working-class background and financial dependency, his bourgeois patrons saw him as their protégé who, like the black bourgeoisie, was expected to unquestioningly follow their advice. His relations with Howard Pim, who as a partner in the firm of Pim and Hardy, Accountants, in Johannesburg, administered the 'Ballinger Fund', were particularly delicate. Pim was a liberal of the old Cape tradition, 'an old friend of Rhodes and Jameson', and thus highly cautious. He also allegedly enhanced Ballinger's sense of insecurity by keeping him 'in the dark' about finances.[17] But, as Mouton (1995) points out, Ballinger was a prickly character and his 'indifference, vanity and emotional undemonstrativeness' ultimately put a strain on his marriage as well as his relations with liberals. Although he did make some positive contribution to the ICU, he could be arrogant, tactless and insensitive to African trade unionists and he underestimated their real achievements in developing black trade unionism.[18] Despite his alleged radicalism, he was wedded to the pragmatic and essentially anti-communist position of British reformism and his Johannesburg branch of the ICU continued to fight for better working conditions with the support of the Joint Councils and the South African Institute of Race Relations (SAIRR).

Challenging segregation: the Joint Councils of Europeans and Natives

Political differences and personality conflicts between 'radicals', like Ballinger and Macmillan, and the conservative 'garden party set' also emerged in the multiracial Joint Councils, the parallel prong of liberal intervention. The Joint Councils were part of a package of new liberal 'philanthropic' multracialist initiatives, which included the Bantu Men's Social Centres, discussed in Chapter 5, and the South African Institute of Race Relations (SAIRR). Set up in 1921 in response to mounting African grievances, the councils were composed of African leaders who were 'chosen by Africans' and 'leading white people'. Charles Loram, the Chief Inspector of Native Education in Natal, and his close friend, David Rheinnalt Jones, were prime motivators behind the early councils. Modelled on US interracial councils, they promoted racial integration as the best way forward for Africans. The leading members of the early Joint Council Movement were long-standing Christian-humanitarians who had been active in the older Native Welfare Societies. They were joined by the 'University people', such as Mabel Palmer and William Macmillan, who were interested in academic aspects of the native problem and hopeful that the councils would prove more dynamic than the Johannesburg Bantu Mens' Social Centre, which Holtby described as an ineffective 'experiment in reconciliation'. Unlike the ICU, with an unpredictable and inflammatory black membership, the councils engaged in moderate political agitation against the Union Government's native policies in co-operation with the mission-educated African bourgeoisie, providing an acceptable 'buffer institution' to channel African grievances and liberal criticisms of official policies. By 1930, there were thirty councils.[19]

From the outset, the councils had close links with the British-based Anti-Slavery and Aborigines Protection Society. In 1927, the Johannesburg Council was involved in a UK appeal, co-ordinated by the chairman, Howard Pim, for funds to fight against segregationist legislation. During the 1920s, argued Margery Perham, the councils received good publicity in the British press and acted as a 'wonderful education and stimulus' to liberal-minded people. British liberals regarded them as 'one of the most helpful things in South Africa' in challenging segregation and an important point of contact between blacks and whites.[20] In 1930, the London Group on African Affairs (LGAA), which became the leading pressure group in Britain on African affairs until the Second World War, was set up to further assist the work of the councils on the suggestion of Rheinnalt Jones, who was visiting Britain.[21] Most activity, however, centred around the Johannesburg Council where William Macmillan headed a small radical faction, which was opposed to the conservative clique led by Rheinnalt Jones, Adviser on Race Relations at the SAIRR from 1930 and Director of the Bantu Studies course at Witwatersrand University.

Macmillan held an ambivalent position in South African liberal politics. An 'insider', who had lived in South Africa since he was six, he became more closely allied to the 'outsider' British liberal-reformists as he became more critical of state policies. In 1929, a report he produced on conditions in the native reserves for the Union Government was suppressed and published in Britain as *Complex South Africa* (1930). Influenced by Fabian socialism, Macmillan described himself as a 'lib-lab', but he was frequently accused of being a marxist because, like the journalist, Leonard Barnes, he saw the problems of South African natives as largely economic. Margaret Ballinger (née Hodgson), who before her marriage in 1934 was a junior lecturer in his department and knew him well, described him as a 'liberal radical'. He made regular trips to Britain to seek new allies, publicise South African problems and strengthen his contacts with like-minded critics of colonialism, such as Norman Leys. A prolific academic and pioneer 'Africanist', his intellectual contribution to African studies is now increasingly recognised.[22]

Macmillan opposed segregation on moral and economic grounds, and directed his research and writing to publicising African problems in South Africa and Britain. However, as he began to adopt a more radical position, he clashed with the 'establishment' British liberals, like Lionel Curtis, who 'pinned their hopes on Smuts' and his stock among South African liberals declined. His closest colleagues after 1930 were William and Margaret Ballinger and the young Fabian, Julius Lewin, who worked for the *Cape Times* and helped to get Ballinger's articles published. Leonard Barnes was also part of this small radical clique.[23] When the Joint Councils merged with the SAIRR after it was established in 1929, the conservative Christian liberals gained more control and the radicals were increasingly marginalised. The 'paralysed conservatives' of the SAIRR were influenced by American race-relations philosophy, with its emphasis on preventing race conflict, and the British school of anthropology, which, in Macmillan's view, failed to address the dynamics of change and, in emphasising separate (plural) cultures, reinforced rather than challenged segregation. Under the chairmanship of Professor Albert Hoernle, argued Macmillan, the SAIRR, which became the main forum for liberal race issues in the 1930s, refrained from expressing any 'political' views and thus failed to recognise that all issues relating to blacks were 'quintessentially' political.[24]

The SAIRR had the support of the London-based ASAPS and British South African liberal benefactors, such as the Quaker Maurice Webb. Howard Pim, a prominent member of the Joint Councils, and manager of Ballinger's ICU funds, was a founder member of the SAIRR. Funding came initially from the Phelps Stokes Fund and the Carnegie Foundation, which was administered by Charles Loram, who became Professor of African Education at Yale in 1931. For the 'radicals', Loram was a 'very cautious civil servant and educationalist', who 'alarmingly disposed' of research funds which could have been used to finance Ballinger's more practical schemes in native development.[25] A key bone of contention was the SAIRR's use of Carnegie funding to support the Witwatersrand University Bantu Studies course for administrators, which had been set up in 1921. The development of Bantu Studies reflected the influence of British anthropology. Arthur Radcliffe-Brown was at the University of Cape Town from 1920–6 where he taught Hoernle, the first chairman of the SAIRR, and other prominent liberals, and stimulated the development of South African anthropology.[26] By 1931, Bantu Studies, in which the SAIRR had a close interest through its Director, David Rheinnalt Jones, were given precedence over Macmillan's courses. Macmillan was deeply disturbed by this development. In his estimation, Bantu Studies relegated Africans to a 'special and inferior category' rather than including them as a common part of humanity, and thus effectively 'drew the political sting' from the study of African disabilities. He doubted that the Joint Councils would have any success while the 'missionary clique' held sway, 'in cahoots' with the anthropologists of the SAIRR, who had an 'amazing grip' on British opinion (Margery Perham, for instance, attended the Bantu Studies course in 1931 and was suitably impressed).[27]

These developments precipitated further rifts in the Johannesburg Joint Council. Meetings were stormy and the radicals accused the conservatives, who dominated the councils, of favouring the 'social welfare' approach, which was 'safe' for the government. Ballinger and Macmillan wanted to foster developing black political awareness and self-reliance through adult education and co-operative development. They argued that blacks had been 'spoon-fed' for too long by wealthy philanthropists who regarded the native problem as a 'fashionable cause' and were ignorant of the 'real issues' that concerned the mass of Africans, thus alienating 'incipiently political natives'. When he went to address the Durban Bantu Men's Social Centre on co-operative development in 1934, Ballinger was rudely rebuffed by a Natal Quaker, Maurice Webb, and forced to hold the meeting in a local Indian school. 'I was appalled', he wrote, that a man who knew 'so little about Native affairs [presumed] to make decisions for Africans as to whom was allowed to speak ... in their own premises'.[28]

In this atmosphere of bitterness and rancour the early optimistic buoyancy of the Joint Council movement evaporated and in 1931, Ballinger described the councils as 'sadly inept' and the blacks as 'lifeless and repressed'.[29] Macmillan became 'despondent and cynical'. His 'growing views of a revolutionary kind' alienated the influential Smuts, who Macmillan disliked and distrusted and, according to Perham, he expressed a desire to leave South Africa as early as 1929. His eventual departure came after a disagreement with the 'liberal' Principal of the Witwatersrand University, H.R. Raikes, over 'strong' letters he had written in 1932 to government officials and the *Rand Daily Mail* on the subject of native rights.[30] His voicing of this strong opposition to state repression and his radical stance on the native problem precipitated difficulties in both his private and public life. Thus, he arrived in Britain with a suspect political reputation and the additional stigma of divorce. For six years he was kept out in the cold, earning a precarious living from freelance writing. During his last years in South Africa, Macmillan had also alienated powerful 'establishment' liberals, like Lionel Curtis, which may have also contributed to his difficulties in finding a job in England.[31]

With the departure of Macmillan, Barnes and Lewin in 1932 and 1933, the conservatives were further able to consolidate their position. In 1933, Oliver Schreiner (the advocate nephew of the writer, Olive Schreiner) took over as chairman of the Johannesburg Council in Macmillan's absence, which, for Ballinger, marked the 'death blow' of the council.[32] However, the political toothlessness of the Joint Councils cannot be blamed solely on the policies of the conservative liberals. Liberal opposition comprised a small and fragmented minority who were powerless to hold back the tide of segregationist legislation, which the majority supported. Even at the height of activity in the 1920s, liberal activism was limited to a tiny enthusiastic minority, centred in the Johannesburg Council, consisting mostly of people who were British born and who were 'scarcely more than voices crying in the wilderness'. The Cape and Durban Joint Councils were far less active as no-one with similar 'expertise' and contacts was available.[33]

By 1930, British liberal support for both the ICU and the Joint Councils was flagging as other worthy causes competed with South Africa for wealthy liberal patronage. The Quaker, John Harris, complained about trade union and parliamentary apathy back in England, blaming Ballinger whose speeches had alienated 'certain people'. 'I am sorry', he wrote to a colleague, 'but I expect you know how often one has disappointments in fighting for the underdog ... '. Funds from England had virtually dried up by 1933. The Joint Councils continued under South African liberal guidance, but were engaged primarily in welfare work and reputedly maintained 'cordial relations' with 'responsible' government officials.[34] As his supporters in Britain ebbed away, Ballinger prudently entered into a *rapprochement* with the SAIRR and reaffirmed his commitment to a gradualist approach, acknowledging that it 'was one thing to accept the principle of equal rights [but] another to apply it'. No longer ostracised, he became more optimistic and continued with his co-operative and trade union work throughout the 1930s. By 1934, most South African liberals attested to his 'good work' and support from British liberals revived in response to his exposure of conditions in the Protectorates.[35]

In 1930, William Ballinger, Margaret Hodgson and a few other committed British liberals who were resident in South Africa, such as Jean Ross, a senior mistress at the Girls' High School in Pretoria, began to research conditions in the Protectorates, where, argues Rich (1984), they could test out ideas on developments that were blocked in South Africa. Co-operation and credit societies had first been promoted in the Transkei in the 1920s, but, argued Hailey (1957), co-operative societies in the Union had refused to lend support.[36] Drawing on his WEA experience, Ballinger now attempted to set up 'study groups' and develop education on co-operation in the Transkei and the Protectorates. His 'native development' work was regarded as less controversial than his trade union activities and gained a wide cross-section of support, which included trade unionists, humanitarians, progressive missionaries, colonial experts with establishment connections, and representatives of the British Co-operative Movement. Ballingers' new focus on the Protectorates also raised wider issues relating to British imperial policy in the region. Practical action on Southern Africa thus became more broad-based and evolved in two directions – pressure group activity against the transfer of the British Protectorates to the Union and fund-raising and publicity for Ballinger's work in native development.

The 'Protectorates Question' and 'native' development

When she visited Southern Africa in 1929, Margery Perham was appalled by the conditions in Basutoland. Official reports on Bechuanaland and Swaziland, undertaken in 1932–3, confirmed the extent of neglect and underdevelopment in the Protectorates which, argued Hailey (1957), the British had never really wanted.[37] In Bechuanaland, which had a population of only 150,000 as compared to half a million in Basutoland, indirect rule, argued Ifor Evans (1934), was so indirect as to be 'no rule at all', which was reflected in the fact that the protectorate was administered from Mafeking in the Union of South Africa. Whites controlled trade and held important timber and mining concessions. The development of a monetised economy had begun to destroy the old subsistence economy and pushed Africans into wage labour in the Union. In 1931, there were 3,419 men employed in the Rand mines. Migration had resulted in serious social problems, including family breakdown, drunkenness and venereal disease, but failed to alleviate poverty as little money was sent back.[38]

Similar conditions existed in Swaziland and Basutoland. Swaziland, the smallest protectorate, had passed to British 'protection' in 1906. Europeans held mining concessions, including asbestos deposits, and 49 per cent of land was alienated to whites, mostly absentee owners in the Transvaal, although there was also a poor white problem. In his 1932 report, Sir Alan Pim (brother of Howard Pim) observed that land alienation had engendered 'a mistrust of European intentions', which had hampered European efforts to establish a more effective system of administration. Taxes were higher than in the Union or the other Protectorates, and Evans (1934) argued that sums spent on law and order seemed 'very high for a small territory'. Administration, which was devoted largely tó the concerns of Europeans, was 'very backward' and run by white magistrates drawn from the police and clerical staff in the Union who, unlike colonial officers working in other parts of Africa, had no training. Salaries were low and there was little interchange of officers, creating a parochial mentality.[39]

The Protectorates were administered by the Resident Commissioner, who was responsible to the High Commissioner of the Union of South Africa, and were hence under the Dominions as opposed to the Colonial Office. In the depression years, the administration's main priority was to cut expenditure. The British High Commission depended on the migrant labour system to boost the meagre finances in the Protectorates and thus objected to any criticisms of worker conditions on the grounds that they could 'imperil' good relations between the Union and the imperial government.[40] In 1931, the imperial secretary, Captain Clifford, used his influence to block the publication of several critical newspaper articles on Basutoland by Leonard Barnes. He also warned Tshekedi Khama, the regent of the Bangwato, who comprised 50 per cent of the population of Bechuanaland, that it would do the regent 'no good' to have William Ballinger in Bechuanaland, despite the fact that the latter had done 'a great deal for the natives' in the Union of South Africa. This discreet 'collusion' with the Union Government, combined with British maladministration, argued Barnes, had 'betrayed' the trust that African rulers had placed in the imperial government when the High Commission Territories were annexed as 'protection' from Afrikaner expansionism.[41]

Dire conditions in the Protectorates nourished African grievances and the British administration reacted swiftly to suppress any potential 'agitation'. During the 'Black Republic' phase, the South African Communist Party (CPSA) made contact with the Basutoland organisation, *Lekhotla-la-Bafo* (League of the Poor), which had been formed in 1928 to defend the rights of peasants against the educated elite and conservative chiefs. The CPSA's long-term strategy was to bring about a federation of native republics and drive British imperialism out of the Protectorates.[42] *Lekhotla* was suppressed by the authorities with full support from the chiefs (although this was officially denied by the Dominions Office). The organisation was allowed to hold meetings only if no 'seditious matters' were discussed or calls for financial donations made and, in London, the legality of such actions was questioned by ASAPS.[43]

Circulation of the communist publication, *African Defender*, in Swaziland resulted in the victimisation of native workers, and William Ballinger and the Swazi king, Sobhenza, met with 'obstructional' tactics in promoting co-operation. In

Bechuanaland, Chief Sebele was banished in 1931 from the Bakwena reserve as a 'danger to peace'. The ban was still in force in 1933 and the Secretary of State for Dominions, J.H. Thomas, refused to institute a Commission of Inquiry or to reveal his whereabouts on the basis that Sebele had been 'repeatedly warned' about maladministration.[44] Tshekedi Khama, the influential regent of Bangwato, also alienated the Bechuanaland authorities in 1930 by opposing draft legislation that was aimed at setting up native authorities and courts, based on the West African model, and was temporarily suspended. However, liberal champions of the African cause had conflicting sentiments about the actions of these traditional chiefs. Ballinger believed the Swazi king, Sobhenza, to be the 'most enlightened king in South Africa', while Margaret Hodgson saw him as an example of oppressive African patriarchy, 'an autocratic heathen' only concerned with his harem and hunting.[45] In the main, however, critics of colonialism and progressive pro-imperialists regarded the traditional authorities in the Protectorates as 'autocrats' who blocked progressive modern reforms, which were the key to development.

British liberal concern over the Protectorates was compounded when the Union of South Africa was granted full internal autonomy in 1931, and the Afrikaner Nationalist Party, led by General Herzog, renewed demands that the Protectorates should be transferred to the Union. Evans argued that support for these demands was provided by the fact that the Protectorates were viewed as a nuisance to the British taxpayer and were dependent economically on South Africa, hence reducing the control that the British administration had over the territories.[46] Within the 'liberal' imperial establishment there was considerable sympathy for the Union's proposals and, between 1933–5, the 'Protectorates Question' generated much interest in Britain, with opinion polarised between the pro- and anti-transfer lobbies. Opposition divided into two broad camps: the moderate liberals and progressive colonial experts, like Margery Perham, who advocated an improved system of indirect rule and colonial critics, like Barnes, who were deeply critical of British policy, but still held that British liberal ideals could be a 'powerful influence' for social good. In contrast, the Left condemned British imperialism outright on the basis that its main function in South Africa was to provide a secure base for British capitalism.[47] The kernel of the mainstream debate over transfer is summed up in Margery Perham and Lionel Curtis's, *The Protectorates of South Africa: A Question of their Transfer to the Union* (1935), which is based on a collection of letters in the *Times*, 1933–5. Ultimately, Herzog's proposals were rejected, but the Union Government persisted with its claims. Herzog visited London in May and June 1937 and, as a result, a Joint Advisory Conference was set up, which was comprised of the Resident Commissioners of the three Protectorates and the Union Secretaries for Native Affairs.[48]

Wider public interest in Britain was also aroused by the 'Tshekedi incident'. In October 1933, Tshekedi Khama was temporarily deposed after he had sentenced a (clearly disreputable) young white man, Phinehas McIntosh, to a public flogging in Serowe, the largest African (as opposed to European) town in British Africa with a population of 30,000. Michael Crowder's absorbing investigation into the incident reveals that the flogging was a culmination of several such assaults (often drunken) on Africans in Serowe by MacIntosh and his friends. The Bechunalaland administration and white settlers, he argues, despised poor whites like McIntosh, a wagon builder who lived with an African girl and had 'gone native', on the grounds that his behaviour reflected badly on their self-image as rulers.[49] However, the flogging represented a loss of white control and whites feared that it would spark off a native uprising. The British High Commissioner, Lieutenant Charles Rey, thus swiftly retaliated and called for reinforcements from the Union. Two hundred royal marines, backed by air power, were sent from Cape Town to Serowe to 'maintain order' and ensure that the Bechuana people would remain 'more loyal' than ever.[50] The expedition was under the command of the popular First World War military hero, 'Evans of the Broke', who was acting High Commissioner in South Africa and Commander in Chief of the Africa Station of the British Navy and close friend of the pro-Nazi, Oxford educated, Oswald Pirow. The outcome of this colonial 'pacification' was that Tshekedi was suspended and sent down 'the road to Rhodesia' into exile (McIntosh was also exiled as an undesirable resident). In the broader context, the incident raised important issues relating to attitudes to interracial sex, diplomatic relations between Britain and the Union of South Africa and, most importantly, serious questions that were pertinent to the relationship between colonisers and colonised. However, in the short term, argues Crowder, the incident provided the British authorities with a perfect excuse to depose Tshekedi, who was viewed as 'obstacle to development'.[51]

Tshekedi Khama had become regent in 1925 when Seretse, the real heir, was a minor. Educated at Lovedale and Fort Hare, he was a 'sore point' among South African whites and even Ballinger, who complained about his 'obstructiveness' on his visit to Bechuana in 1930–1, described him as a 'thinly disguised barbarian' who committed injustices against his people. To the British Left, however, he was an anti-imperialist and for Africans, a symbol of resistance, an 'intelligent ... determined ... and ... popular young man ... with a forceful personality' who became a legend to blacks for daring to flog a white British subject.[52] Tshekedi feared that commercial penetration and mining claims made by the British South Africa Company would lead to annexation by the Union and, in an attempt to secure the British Government's backing against transfer, he wrote two pamphlets and entered into a vigorous correspondence with prominent 'friends of the native', such as Charles Roden Buxton. Despite these efforts, the Dominions Office refused to invite him to London, maintaining that any representations regarding problems in the Protectorates would have to be submitted through the Resident Commissioner to the Governor-General.[53] In contrast, British liberals and reformists condemned his deposition and mounted a campaign to influence public and parliamentary opinion. The LGAA and ASAPS lobbied Parliament and the Dominions Office, and pressed for reforms in the Protectorates, including the promotion of native development through the establishment of co-operatives. Tshekedi was reinstated on the basis that he disclaimed any jurisdiction over whites in the future. However, he continued to express concern over the delicate nature of relations with the Union Government and the problem of increased native unrest.[54]

The campaigns in London may have had some minor impact on the Tshekedi affair, but, by and large, the imperial government did little to improve conditions in its Protectorates. Despite pious reassertions of trusteeship, they were regarded mostly as a 'nuisance' and as useless possessions that were 'barely solvent without subsidies'. The government continued to recognise the 'legitimate' demands of the Union Government and stressed that transfer was the 'ultimate aim'.[55] This official apathy, combined with increased African unrest in both the Protectorates and the Union, resulted in wider British support for native development schemes. 'Progressive' imperialists and missionaries believed co-operation could deflect a 'dangerous potential for ... revolution and law-breaking' as well as improve native conditions and help preserve native areas as 'inviolable sanctuaries'.[56] While Ballinger and his supporters were opposed to indirect rule 'purists' and 'antiquated schemes' of missionaries, they also argued that co-operation would protect 'natives' from the adverse influence of industrialisation. Practical schemes to encourage adult education, co-operation and self-reliance were thus mooted as the best way of protecting Africans from economic exploitation and the adverse influence of communist agitation.[57]

However, after the ICU fiasco, British-based liberals were concerned that Ballinger's new initiatives on co-operation would become 'too political'. Leonard Barnes was also criticised for his analysis of the native problem as a struggle against economic imperialism, and both Barnes and Ballinger were warned against 'alienating' the potential support of influential South African liberals and the British Co-operative Wholesale Society. Despite these reservations, tactical moves by fund-raisers, who emphasised the practical aspects of Ballinger's work, met with some success and by 1933 he was fully involved with Native Co-operative Development. When he visited England in 1934, Ballinger found the 'co-op people' in Manchester 'kind and very sympathetic'.[58] In order to co-ordinate fund-raising, the 'Friends of Africa' (FOA) was formed in London in September 1934. Founder members included the Ballingers (then visiting London), Frederick Livie-Noble, Julius Lewin, Holtby and Creech Jones. General members included William Macmillan, Margery Perham and a representative of the Co-operative Guilds. The 'Friends' offered 'practical encouragement and aid to 'native' development in South Africa and 'guidance of movements for social, economic and educational progress'. Leonard Woolf acted as an adviser to the group. The FOA's aims reflected the most up-to-date Fabian ideas on native development. A South African branch was subsequently set up in Cape Town in 1935, which included prominent liberals, such as Sir James Rose Innes and Howard Pim.[59]

In the long term, it was hoped that Ballinger could extend his work to the Rhodesias and possibly West Africa, ultimately co-ordinating 'Co-operative and Industrial movements' throughout the continent. In practice, the 'Friends' brief never extended further than South Africa. Ballinger continued with his co-operative and trade union work throughout the 1930s as the FOA's Southern

African adviser on Native Industrial and Co-operative Movements. In 1939, he became organising secretary for the South African 'Friends'. By 1940, however, London-based African work was reported to be 'rather out of the picture' as active intervention of British liberals petered out.[60] As the new 'Society for the Friends of Africa', the South African Committee took over as the central co-ordinating body and became increasingly dominated by the cautious liberals of the SAIRR. Ballinger became more isolated and Mouton (1995) argues that he became lazy and disinterested, and the SAIRR decided once more that it was impossible to co-operate with him. He became a senator for the Transvaal in 1948, but, argues Mouton, his political star had been waning since 1936 and he was eclipsed by his wife, Margaret Ballinger, who in 1938 was elected one of the first Native Representatives to speak for disenfranchised Africans in the Union Parliament.[61]

In retrospect, attempts to encourage co-operative development had a negligible impact. Co-operative schemes had met with a modicum of success in the Transkei, but as late as the early 1950s, notes Hailey (1957), there were still no co-operative society in Bechaunaland. By the 1940s, economic conditions in Bechuanaland had arguably deteriorated: migrant labour continued to be drawn to the Union and 60 per cent of adult male taxpayers were resident outside Bechuanaland.[62] Yet, despite shoddy treatment by the imperial government, Bechuanaland reputedly sent more troops per head than any other British colony to help the war effort. Such loyalty was not rewarded. When Tshekedi Khama applied in 1947 for a visa to raise grievances before the Trusteeship Council of the United Nations, he was refused by the British authorities, despite protests from the ASAPS and the Fabian Colonial Bureau. As Smuts believed that South Africa deserved to be rewarded for its 'considerable contribution' to Britain's war effort, the Protectorates were again threatened by renewed campaigns for the annexation of the High Commission Territories and the Rhodesias into the Union.[63]

However, Bechuanaland was once more put in the spotlight in Britain when Seretse Khama married a British woman, Ruth Williams, in 1948. His uncle, Tshekedi, had a strong aversion to interracial relationships and would not accept Seretse's marriage. For once, he was supported by the Dominions Office (now renamed the Commonwealth Relations Office), which argued that Seretse's return to Bechuanaland as chief of the Bangwato would 'inflame' white South African opinion.[64] Seretse was exiled from Bechuanaland in 1950, but found support for his cause in Britain. The British Left, angered by this appeasement of South Africa, formed the Council for the Defence of Seretse Khama and the Protectorates. According to Howe (1994), the struggle over Seretse, who was seen as an enlightened, modernising African leader, was 'emblematic' of the wider struggle for racial equality and resistance to Apartheid. It assumed 'massive symbolic importance' in the rapidly growing British anti-colonial movement. As links between African nationalists and London-based anti-colonial activists strengthened, any residual support for South African liberals evaporated. With the implementation of Apartheid, the transfer of the Protectorates to South Africa, seriously considered by the imperial government before the war, now became a dead issue. By 1961, even British officials saw the Protectorates as the 'last bastion' of the Commonwealth and its 'non-racial' policies.[65] The Protectorates thus remained British, but, after independence, imperial policies pursued before the war left the independent states of Botswana, Swaziland and Lesotho still vulnerable to a predatory South Africa.

Retrospective: British intervention and the 'liberal dilemma'

In retrospect, 'pan-liberal' initiatives were doomed from the start. The imperial government had abnegated responsibility and liberal critics within South Africa constituted a small and increasingly muffled voice, unable to curb the repressive and segregationist policies, which were supported by 'Boer and Briton' alike. In a letter to Smuts in 1930, Margaret Ballinger noted how the liberal spirit had become more 'diffused' and intimated that hopes that the pro-British Smuts would act as a bulwark against settler policies had been misplaced. 'Through drifting', she wrote to him, 'you ... seem to acquiesce in what is reactionary'. Hopes were further dashed when Herzog's National Party and Smuts' South Africa Party merged into the United Party in 1933 to tackle serious domestic problems. In the estimation of younger generation liberals, like Leonard Barnes, this 'fusion' of interests ended any nominal hope that the ideals of British justice and 'fairplay', which had motivated the old Cape liberals, would prevail.[66]

By the 1930s, observed Barnes, the 'humanitarian' faction was essentially an incursion from without and South African born sympathisers with African problems could be 'counted on one hand'. British South Africans were as strongly committed to segregationist ideology as Afrikaners. The prominent Natalian, George Heaton Nicholls, was one of the major architects of the 1936 Native Representation Act and, as chairman of the Native Affairs Commission and Honorary Member for Zululand, fully supported segregation. Margaret Ballinger argued that in Natal British hypocrisy provided a veneer of sophistication that concealed 'as strong a belief in superiority of blood and race as the Afrikaners'. This 'most English province' was 'a desolation of the spirit, [less] than half educated, led by social and political climbers ... its unctuous self-satisfaction and pious liberalism ... a constant vexation to the soul ... '. The finer 'English tradition' had been so distorted and betrayed that a 'black Veld Free State' was preferable.[67]

The liberal spirit was further undermined by the departure of British residents as the economic, racial and political climate deteriorated. By 1930, more British, including prominent liberals, were leaving South Africa than entering. Returnees took their investments with them, and, in 1932, Howard Pim wrote: 'We are steadily bleeding to death ... times are [very difficult] ... millions of capital have left the country [but] the stream continues'. The South African activists felt demoralised and abandoned. Margaret Hodgson 'lacked energy for African Affairs' and wanted to leave the Union 'as others had done'. By 1936, support for Ballinger from England was only intermittent. 'Life is really disheartening', she wrote, 'every day we miss more and more the people who have drifted [away].'[68]

South African liberals became more critical of the lack of commitment and 'insensitivity' of their British supporters, who treated them like parochial colonials. Howard Pim complained of the poor support for Ballinger and Macmillan, and found the English 'Friends of Africa' – with the exception of a few dedicated individuals – 'cold, detached and patronising'. British-based liberals were accused of being insensitive to the difficulties that South African liberals encountered in dealings with the Union administration. Alfred Hoernle's *South African Native Policy and the Liberal Spirit* (1939) defended the South African liberal response to the 1936 abolition of the Cape franchise and, argues Rich (1988), Hoernle hoped the book would be read widely in the UK to counteract the criticisms of influential 'radicals' like William Macmillan.[69]

This widening gulf between British and South African based activists was not restricted to liberals. The CPSA, as part of the international Left, also had 'outside' advisers who were criticised for not understanding the problems faced by party activists in South Africa. Roux had built up contacts with British communists and reformists when he was at Cambridge in the 1920s. A British Comintern expert, George Hardy, a founder member of the British Communist Party, was sent to South Africa as the CPSA's 'British adviser' in 1936 on the basis of experience in Canada and the US. But, argue Simons and Simons (1969), 'like many radicals from abroad', he proved idealistic and ignorant of local conditions, claiming to have found a 'great revolutionary force in the medley of races and classes', which did not exist.[70]

By the late 1930s, the gulf between 'home and colonial' had widened further, deepening the isolation of South African liberals. Ballinger had to work more closely with the SAIRR and by 1948, when he was elected Senator for the Transvaal, his cautiousness alienated younger, black radicals. In contrast, Margaret ('Peg') Ballinger became a respected political figure. Her advice was actively sought by black activists and, in Mouton's estimation, she proved a 'brilliant parliamentarian and an uncompromising opponent of racial oppression'.[71] In many ways, Margaret Ballinger was the more interesting character. She did most of the research and writing (she had to give up her academic career on her marriage to Ballinger in 1934) and comes over in her diaries as unpatronising and non-judgemental in her dealings with Africans. A fellow liberal, Ellen Hellman, described her as 'transparently sincere and always challenging' with a warm personality and a 'fine intellect' – a 'voice in a million'. Among other achievements, she founded the first Association for European and Bantu Women and the Margaret Ballinger Home for convalescent African children.[72] But opting to remain in South Africa tarred the Ballingers with the white colonist brush. When Margaret Ballinger was proposed in 1961 as the first visiting Professor of Race Relations at the University College of Rhodesia and Nyasaland, she was rejected as unacceptable because she was a 'South African Colonial'.[73]

In Britain, committed activists now faced an uphill struggle to sustain interest in South African 'native' problems. Macmillan tried to rectify the great lack of knowledge in British circles about 'native' conditions throughout Africa, but outspoken criticisms only alienated him further from the more conservative opinion he most wished to influence. He, too, became disillusioned and, in retrospect, advised his close colleague and friend 'Peg' Ballinger, who was writing her autobiography, 'one can't do much more than show how often Smuts and Co. missed buses'.[74] Frustrated by the ineffectiveness of liberal initiatives to effect any change in South Africa, British 'Africa activists' turned their attentions to West Africa. Arthur Creech Jones became increasingly interested in West African labour problems and before her untimely death in autumn 1935, Winifred Holtby had also planned a visit to West Africa. This new interest was pioneered by Macmillan, who had proposed as early as 1933 that the 'African Renaissance' would come from West Africa, comparing the 'sturdy independence' of the 'resentful' West Coaster to the crushed spirit of the black South African. Change in West Africa, he argued, would bring about a 'new outlook' in Britain, which would in turn help combat racism in South Africa. As disillusionment set in, the Ballingers likewise became convinced that the future lay in West, not South, Africa and expressed a desire to settle in the Gold Coast.[75]

The unsuccessful revival of liberalism in opposition to the 1936 Native Representation Act, which confirmed the principle of white representation of blacks with the creation of four new native representative seats in the Senate, was almost totally indigenous.[76] British-based liberal interest was reduced to the perennial Quaker minority. In 1938, British Quakers sent a deputation to South Africa and their cautiously worded report endorsed some of the 'good work' that the Native Affairs Administration had done '*in loco parentis*', and recorded that the Native Trust and Land Act and the Native Areas and Slum Acts had actually helped to improve the lot of natives. The deputation did not agree with the politics of segregation and acknowledged native 'resentment', but, like the imperial government, was careful not to criticise the South African government too strongly on the grounds that it had been faced with a 'stupendous task', with little precedent, and its policies were bound to be 'experimental'. As the anti-colonial activist, Reginald Reynolds – a Quaker himself – pointed out, although Quakers had done some 'splendid work' for race relations, they were cautious and hesitant and avoided any association with organisations or ideas that could be construed as radical.[77]

The 'liberal dilemma', wrote Leonard Barnes, lay in the unwillingness of liberals to threaten the *status quo* of which they were an integral part.[78] Unlike communists, liberal-reformists, with perhaps the exception of the 'extremist' Ballinger, did not take personal risks before the Second World War, although this arguably changed with the full implementation of Apartheid. They may have been seen as an irritation by the authorities, but never dangerous and were consistently opposed to any *rapprochement* with the Left, precluding the development of a more coherent opposition. Humanitarian concern for the 'underdog' and a belief in the higher ideals of British paternalistic liberalism arguably concealed implicitly racist attitudes. Michael Scott, who visited South Africa in the 1930s, noted that it took him some time to discover the 'full strength' of colour prejudice that surfaced even among the most 'enlightened' Christian humanitarians at moments of 'extreme exasperation'. Although white communists were not free from patronising attitudes to blacks (Chapter 6), liberal discourse was suffused with the prevailing dominant representations of African culture and assumptions that it was 'natural' for Africans to look for a 'paternal bearing' in the white man.[79] When blacks failed to match up to expectations, liberals complained about their lack of gratitude.

The discourse of liberalism (and reformist socialism) was shaped by white middle-class men who held implicitly superior attitudes to every group they regarded as inferior and less rational than themselves, including women. Liberal 'rationality' and superior intellectualism was most highly refined in the writings of Fabian socialists, like Leonard Woolf, where it achieved a 'worthy' arrogance. Africans were sensitive to the concealed racism of European 'sympathisers'. On first arriving in England, Kadalie, one of few South Africans to travel to Europe, encountered strong prejudice on the train to Waterloo and had serious difficulties in finding accommodation, but he was subsequently flattered by the Holtby clique into regarding himself as an equal.[80] Arthur Creech Jones remarked that Kadalie had ' ... much disturbed the friends of the native races' by making demands for white secretarial help, calling on them in a 'nauseatingly ... over-dressed manner' and making 'grotesque allegations' about the harsh treatment of blacks in mining compounds. Embarrassed by this 'inappropriate behaviour', he informed Kadalie that he was his 'own worst enemy'.[81] But the myth of British liberalism held strong and African intellectuals continued to blame Afrikaner, not British racism, for holding blacks back, although they were aware that British 'niceness' was rarely translated into action.[82]

It was the liberal faction within South Africa that had the greatest stake in maintaining the *status quo* and exhibited the most acute form of the 'liberal dilemma'. The kernel of this liberal dilemma was what Albert Memmi (1958) defined as the problem of the 'coloniser who refuses'. Memmi argued that such an individual does more harm to himself (or herself) by consciously rejecting the position that he subconsciously assumes as a result of his colour, heritage and religion. In this context, Memmi concludes, it is futile for the coloniser to reject his position. Living within the system exalts him to the status of the coloniser and if he refuses and takes action accordingly he is left in limbo.[83] This illuminates the shifting positions of William Ballinger – an 'outsider radical' who filtered to the Right to gain respectability and, in so doing, arguably became more fully incorporated into the colonising society. The opposite relates to Macmillan, who moved closer to 'limbo' as he framed a more radical analysis of the situation in South Africa.

Liberals sat perpetually on the fence between whites, with whom they identified culturally but also condemned for transgressing liberal principles, and oppressed blacks, with whom they sympathised but could not identify, except in the case of the black elite who 'wore the white mask'. British-based liberals also found it difficult to reconcile their high ideals with their privileged position as citizens of an imperial state, and this was manifest in a polite obscurantism on questions of racial equality. Most prominent liberals came from comfortable bourgeois backgrounds and thus had a vested interest in the existing system. Some even benefited from shares in South Africa, ironically gaining personally from a system of labour exploitation that they criticised.[84] However, their dilemmas were muted by distance and the absence of the pressures of living in a colonial society, conveying the impression that they had more incisive and progressive solutions to the 'native problem'. One can arguably sympathise more with the vacillating South African liberals than those comfortably distant in Britain. South African liberals were undoubtedly in an invidious position between segregationists and Africans and, weak and divided, had restricted scope for action with no base in mainstream politics. Moreover, Afrikaners had always resented British South Africans because of their identification with the British 'Motherland' as home, which they interpreted as an indication of split loyalties and a lack of commitment to an autonomous South Africa.[85]

How then do we judge the record of liberal and reformist interventions in South African 'native problems' in comparison to white Left initiatives? In the inter-war years, neither communists nor liberals had much success in challenging segregation, although the selfless commitment of the few dedicated individuals in both camps must be acknowledged. However, the CPSA had a larger working-class constituency, including East European Jewish migrants, who had also suffered oppression and were not part of the culture of British imperialism. Communists, who risked assault and imprisonment, were often under constant police surveillance and were the only whites to take an uncompromising stance on racism. Liberals, argues Rich (1996), were important as the 'liberal conscience' and, unlike the communists, had some access to the state. But they became increasingly marginalised and ineffective, and it was the CPSA that forged an alliance with African nationalism, founding a more radical tradition of struggle against segregation and Apartheid. A Liberal Party was founded in 1953 with Margaret Ballinger as President, but it only endorsed qualified franchise and its policies reflected the eternal liberal dilemma of trying to find a middle way. It was thus 'too advanced' for most white settlers and not advanced enough to win mass support.[86] For Macmillan, the party was 'too late', lacked a 'cutting edge' and only attracted support from 'Africanist' members of the ANC, whose rejection of communism was stronger than their commitment to a common struggle. Yet the very fact that the Liberal Party remained critical of Apartheid was sufficient to make it a danger to the state. Nearly fifty of its leaders, black and white, were banned and the party was forced into dissolution in 1968. Thus Vigne (1998), who was actively involved in the party, has defended its record, arguing that liberal struggles have now been vindicated in the democratic consti-tution of the new South Africa.[87]

With the implementation of Apartheid in 1948, South Africa became the pariah state, and the role of British imperialism and British South Africans in the oppression of black South Africans became even more submerged. Yet, Britain's self-image as a champion of racial equality and African rights concealed a deep hypocrisy. As Padmore (1948) pointed out, while 'apologists' for British imperialism condemned Apartheid in South Africa, they continued to condone the white settler regime in Kenya. Britain remained the premier investor in South Africa, and the 'liberal and tolerant' British Government was still encouraging white settlement of South Africa and Rhodesia, the 'latest and one of the brightest jewels in Britain's colonial diadem' in the 1950s.[88] White dreams of Africa thus continued to erase Africans, except as a plentiful source of 'adaptable labour'. Macmillan (1949) noted that South Africans still expressed 'an almost proprietary interest' in the Southern African region and beyond. When the royal family visited in 1947, the itinerary mapped the pre-war vision of a white 'African Monroe doctrine' extending to Southern Rhodesia. However, liberal smugness about British tolerance and lack of racial prejudice was challenged when Britain developed its own 'race problem' after 1945. While the British state condemned Apartheid, it implemented harsher measures against black immigration.[89] Dilemmas over race, culture and equality, which South African liberals had grappled with in the 1930s, had now reached the heart of empire.

Summary

In the absence of any official criticism of South African policies, British liberals and reformist socialists championed the native cause in South Africa and their interventions offer insight into how Southern African problems were conceptualised within a 'global' as opposed to a 'local' context. But the liberal emphasis on compromise, combined with ambivalence over the pace and direction of African progress, reduced black faith in the liberal pledge of 'racial equality'. As illustrated in Chapter 6, Africans ultimately lost faith in their liberal supporters. The 'betrayal' over Ethiopia led to an 'immeasurable' increase in race feeling and a 'bitter resentment towards whites' and they increasingly rejected white 'guidance'.[90] As the white settler state established its autonomous identity, the gulf between British and South African liberals widened, and South African liberals entered the wilderness years. The postwar implementation of Apartheid, which culminated in the withdrawal of South Africa from the British Commonwealth in 1962, symbolised the ultimate triumph of Afrikaner nationalism and the final demise of British liberal influence. But lessons had been learnt from pre-war liberal interventions and when outside pressure-group activity resurfaced in the 1950s, it was in a supportive, as opposed to a directing, role in black struggles against Apartheid. The balance sheet of pre-war involvement may not have been impressive, but it did generate new dialogues between blacks and whites, which sustained and stimulated blacks dreams of freedom and generated wider interest in imperial and race questions in the imperial centre. Practical initiatives on race relations, tested and refined in South Africa, informed liberal initiatives in Britain's own emergent race problem and it is to developments in the metropolitan heartland that we now turn.

Britain

8   Into the heart of empire

Black Britain

We have noticed an unwillingness or inability on the part of coloured people
to talk to white folk with … candour. … This one can only assign to distrust
of the white man which is definitely increasing [and] is a prime factor which
should be borne in mind in our work with coloured seamen.

(London Group on African Affairs, 1931)

London hotels are quite prepared to receive coloured visitors from the East
as guests either to sleep or take meals but … in the present state of public
opinion … did not feel able to receive persons of the Negroid race, [though]
they would not refuse them meals if accompanied by someone they know.

(The Joint Council to Promote Understanding Between White and Coloured
People in Great Britain, 1933)[1]

Eric Walrond, a talented West Indian writer, observed in the 1930s that a
'peculiar negro problem … complex and varied' had developed in London and
other major centres with black populations.[2] There had long been a 'black presence' in Britain, but after 1870 the demands of the imperial economy, combined
with irreversible changes in colonial societies, made 'colonisation in reverse'
inevitable and brought imperial race problems into the heart of empire. The
majority of blacks arrived in Britain as the flotsam of imperial trade, but, during
the First World War, colonial workers and seamen filled labour shortages.
Numbers of 'coloured' colonial residents, including demobbed colonial soldiers,
expanded further after the war, generating white hostility, but also increasing
white consciousness of 'black Britain'.[3] Racism in England was inseparable from
the racism that underpinned the empire, and the imperial dimension within
Britain itself is fundamental to any analysis of changing relations between
Britain and Africa. Liberal-reformist groups, which were active in South Africa,
were also involved in the emergent race problem in Britain. Howe (1993) notes
that British political discourse usually categorised issues of race relations and
immigration as colonial subjects until at least the late 1950s.[4]

Through the eyes of white Britain the mass of poorer 'coloured colonials'
had a diffuse identity, which embraced Africans, West Indians and Asians and

represented an 'alien' and problematic presence. These marginalised outsiders were defined primarily by their powerless status as colonial subjects who were barred from British citizenship. But the black community was far from homogenous. In addition to the tiny, but expanding, resident population of middle-class professional blacks and colonial students, there were the flamboyant folk characters like 'Ras Prince Monolulu', the 'Abyssinian Herbalist' and 'Professor Edgar B. Knight', who earned their livings as race course touts, 'crocusers' (quack doctors) and market sellers. Knight was reputedly 'well known' on the Yorkshire market circuit and was buried 'in style' in Wombwell, Yorkshire, in 1930. Other notable blacks included the American actor, singer and political activist, Paul Robeson, and the Manchester boxer, Len Johnson, of Sierra Leonian origin, who joined the Communist Party in the 1930s. There was also a small number of black American entertainers – a reflection of the British fad for African-American jazz music.[5]

There were thus important differences in class, culture and consciousness, tempered by temporary or long-term residence, which affected the experiences of black men and women in Britain. The mass of poor blacks felt the main force of repressive state policy, while educated blacks had to negotiate the discrete pitfalls of 'interracial' contact with white Britain. For 'Westernised' blacks, contact with the imperial culture and blacks from other parts of the empire resulted in identity shifts, which were related to a growing sense of the diasporic dimension to race and imperial oppression. But working-class blacks also developed a stronger sense of identity as an oppressed resident minority. The dynamics of race, class and culture, and inclusion and exclusion from white society affected individuals differently, but there was a growing awareness of a shared bond of racism, which stimulated the formation of black organisations. Through an analysis of diverse black experiences, this chapter will argue that black experiences of racism in the imperial heartland were important in the fuller articulation of grievances against racism and imperialism in Africa and the African diaspora.

'Inverse imperialism': the 'colour problem' and the racial state

'Inverse imperialism' – the creation of non-white minorities in the white world of Europe and the USA – was as dangerous as white settler imperialism in Africa, argued Leonard Woolf. 'Culture clashes' and the problems of assimilating minorities, black or white, were at the heart of the 'race problem'. Before 1914, there was already growing concern about the welfare of destitute black seamen and racial antagonism between blacks and whites.[6] After the war, tensions finally erupted in the anti-black riots in Liverpool, Cardiff and other ports in June 1919. The government linked these 'race riots' to the widespread unrest in the US, Jamaica and Africa, as well as to unstable post-war economic conditions, and pressed for further control of 'subversive' Bolshevism and Garveyism in Britain and the colonies.[7] The fundamental causes were the scarcity of jobs and the fears of returning white soldiers of economic competition from black workers (although the popular press blamed the riots on sexual competition between black and white men). The latter problem was attributed to the presence of French Senegalese soldiers, the 'Black Scourge in Europe', in the occupied Rhine zone, which posed a threat to white women and had stirred up 'race consciousness' among returning white soldiers.[8]

The riots impressed race issues upon popular consciousness and established a pattern of state responses throughout the inter-war period, which were based on restrictive legislation, repressive policing, and calls for repatriation. As Spencer (1996) has pointed out, Britain's immigration policy was already racialised before the Second World War. To check any further influx of 'alien' workers and to reduce unemployment, the 1919 Aliens Restriction Order (extended in 1920) was introduced, amending the 1905 Aliens Order, which had been designed to stem Jewish immigration. The police were given broad powers to enforce the new legislation and to quell any potential disturbances. Where the worker was clearly an imperial subject, the main solution was repatriation. 'coloured labourers' could not be 'compelled' to go home, but were to be offered 'every opportunity' with transport provided by the Ministry of Shipping.[9]

The Special Restriction of Coloured Alien Seamen Order (1925) was the first legislation directed solely against coloured migrants. Evans (1995) argues that it was clearly racist in intent, if not letter, and fitted into the well established pattern of colonial legislation. The distinction between 'alien' and 'colonial subject', who technically had free right of entry, was ill-defined and, armed with the new legislation, the police could arrest seamen indiscriminately without warrants or could close down black clubs and cafés. When further amendments were introduced in 1927, the Labour MP, Charles Roden Buxton, described the new powers given to the Home Secretary as 'dangerously wide' as he could deport any alien without giving good reasons if he judged that it was 'conducive to the public good'.[10] Although Lane (1995) argues that Yemeni seamen were the prime target, all coloured seamen had to register with the police. Tabili (1994) has meticulously charted the impact of the orders, combined with the discriminatory employment and trade union policies, which affected the lives of all coloured seamen.[11]

The depression in the shipping industry in the 1930s and '20,000 British unemployed seamen' led to accusations that coloured seamen were evading supervision and making illegal landings. The government was accused of failing to deal with the problem and asked to take action on the 'undesirable results' of 'colonies' of coloured seamen, particularly unemployable 'half-castes'. Labour and Conservative MPs made emotive speeches accusing ship owners of taking on 'curry and rice' blacks as 'cheap labour' and demanded that the Home Secretary should secure 'the protection of the British Race' by dealing with the black problem. The Home Secretary made assurances that 'all practicable steps' were being taken to remove 'coloured aliens' and to step up the 'prosecution and ... deportation of coloured boarding house keepers', who supplied forged documents and profited out of the employment of aliens. But 'the most effective remedy', he argued, was for 'ship owners to give preference ... to British over coloured seamen', that is, 'civilised' labour policies. The Home Office now defined British subjects as 'mainly Indians or Lascars'; other coloured seamen were 'aliens' and this caused grave problems with respect to registration with the police.[12] Harassment of 'alien', coloured seamen under the Aliens Orders thus intensified, discrimination against blacks in employment became more frequent and economic insecurity fuelled latent racism in the Labour Movement. A report compiled by the London Group on African Affairs (LGAA) in 1931 drew attention to white hostility to blacks in over eleven ports, which was promoting a 'markedly unhealthy spirit' among 'stranded seamen' who were living in 'piteous conditions'.[13]

After its formation in 1934, the National Council for Civil Liberties (NCCL) made appeals to the Home Office in the defence of colonial seamen, who 'had served in the army and merchant navy' and 'passed for so long as British subjects' only to be reclassified as aliens and 'stranded by an ungrateful country'. In addition to problems of nationality, wrongfully accused British-born coloured seamen had to pay the expenses of detention and were refused any compensation.[14] Problems of nationality became even more pressing with the introduction of the 1935 British Shipping Assistance Act, which subsidised British ship owners providing that they gave preference to seamen of British nationality. This allegedly led to a 'wilful misapplication' of the Aliens Orders when seamen of undisputed British origin were classified as aliens. In Cardiff, where local officials were urging repatriation, black bitterness, compounded by economic distress, culminated in a riot on 16 April 1935, which was sparked off by the 'flagrant actions of a labour delegate' who refused the right of a captain to rehire his coloured crew. The League of Coloured Peoples (founded in 1931) funded an investigation which concluded that official policy in Cardiff constituted 'a new monument to economic ignorance' and prejudice, and recommended restitution of the full rights of colonial seamen and the removal of illegal classifications as aliens.[15] White liberals, evoking the impact of the Italian invasion of Ethiopia on pan-African race-consciousness, warned how the plight of seamen in Cardiff was 'carefully watched' in Africa. Predictably, their solution to the problem was improved social welfare to ward off future unrest and they organised a deputation to the Home Secretary to press for a 'full [Government] inquiry' into the 'many disabilities' of an estimated 10,000 coloured people in Britain.[16]

Liberal concern, however, skirted around issues related to wider economic problems and concentrated on the 'moral aspect' of the problem, particularly the 'evil effects of cohabitation between white women and coloured men'. Labour and Conservative MPs expressed strong concern that the employment of half-castes might 'lower the standards of the rest of the community' and continued to press for repatriation of unemployed coloured seamen.[17] The government finally responded in December 1936 by setting up an 'Interdepartmental Committee on Coloured People in the United Kingdom', which included representatives from the Colonial Office (CO), India Office and the Board of Trade and was briefed to make 'special enquiries'. Such measures, however, proved merely cosmetic. Ministers prevaricated on the 'colour problem', the coloured population still had difficulty in obtaining passports and nationality certificates, and responsibility was shunted between departments, with no-one willing to take direct responsibility.[18]

The government thus continued to condone 'civilised' labour policies. Poverty and distress among the black population persisted. A report produced in Liverpool in 1939 maintained that 75 per cent of non-white males were unemployed. In 1937, there were allegations of discrimination by the Unemployment Assistance Board (UAB) against coloured seamen in Cardiff and the NCCL drew attention to the continued harassment of blacks by the police. In its 'roast beef' policy, the UAB distinguished between rates of assistance given to single, coloured men who lived communally (twelve shillings per week) and single men who lived at home (fifteen shillings per week) on the grounds that coloured men's standard of living was lower than that of other British citizens. These dual rates still operated in 1939 when 'very serious complaints' were made by coloured seamen.[19] The main concern of the Government was to eliminate the problem rather than to alleviate poverty. The Aliens Orders were renewed in 1938 and were only abolished in 1942 when colonial workers and servicemen once again became vital to the war effort. The 1948 British Nationality Act finally attempted to clarify the status of colonial subjects and opened up the way for the laissez-faire period of migration before the state clamped down again in the 1962 Commonwealth Immigration Act. As Tabili (1994) concludes, this state manipulation of the Aliens Orders, which were so important in determining definitions of race and nationality, was linked primarily to the needs of the imperial system in war and peace.[20]

Between the wars the black 'presence' was thus redefined as a racially excluded minority up against a barrier of prejudice and hostility, which hardened during the depression years. Yet the perceived 'colour problem' related to very small numbers. In Liverpool, the coloured community numbered approximately 5,000 – mostly people of West African origin. Cardiff had approximately 3,000 coloured seamen, of which 2,000 were African or of African descent, but only 200 families had black fathers. The population in other ports was even smaller.[21] However, the racialised state associated areas like Cardiff's Tiger Bay and Liverpool with poverty, vice, venereal disease and tuberculosis – an intermeshing of physical and moral pollution. Tiger Bay was described as a 'coloured ghetto', where 'no respectable people' ventured except by day on business. African and Somali seamen mixed with the 'lowest people' and were crowded thirty to forty people to a lodging house with a single white landlady/ cook. A.M.E. Huggins, the chaplain attached to the Missions to Seamen, Cardiff, maintained that coloured seamen were unwelcome in white lodging houses and were harassed by the police who closed down 'Negro clubs'. It was 'common' for blacks to be pushed off the pavements and a 'strong sexual antagonism' existed towards black seamen. A 1934 study of Cardiff thus concluded that poverty, miscegenation and the black threat to white unemployment were firmly linked in the popular consciousness and intermarriage was of 'paramount' importance.[22]

In the popular white imagination, black men were sexual predators who mixed only with the 'lower types' of white women. But intermarriage was important to building their lives in an alien society. Little (1948) argued that poorer black men were often hard-working and good to their white wives and Tabili (1994) suggests that marriage or cohabitation with white women, who were mostly respectable working-class women, conferred benefits as it was the single men who were targeted as 'transients' and harassed under the Aliens Orders. White women also helped to sustain interracial settlements, operating cafés and boarding houses, which were important in the development of hybridised cultures, and through intermarriage became 'critical participants' in the challenge to racial barriers.[23] Whites had no understanding of these inner lives of 'coloured seamen'. 'Gathering verifiable facts', argued Frederick Live-Noble of the LGAA, was impeded by black reluctance to talk to white researchers, which resulted in a 'wealth of generalisation' and 'great divergence of opinion among people working with coloured men'.[24]

Working-class black men insulated themselves from a hostile society by retreating into their closed and defensive communities and forming strong attachments to fellow countrymen. Informal friendly societies, like the 'Sons of Africa', promoted self-help and 'black brotherhood' and performed important social and cultural functions, including funerals. In Liverpool, the African Churches Mission, run by Pastor Daniels Ekarte (a young mission-trained African from Calabar, Eastern Nigeria), promoted black self-help, helped African seamen fight for equal wages and provided pastoral care, religious guidance and aid for unemployed youth. But, as in South Africa, white philanthropists did not like blacks who took an independent stance and Ekarte was accused of using the mission to enrich himself; a claim dismissed by Sherwood (1994) who asserts that he lived and died a poor man.[25]

Black responses to racism, however, are difficult to assess. With the exception of Ernest Marke, few black residents from the pre-Second World War period left written records (or few have as yet been unearthed by researchers). We have only the rare ephemera kept as family mementoes – photographs, passports, and other material fragments of black workers' lives and long-distant homelands to which many rarely returned. Family memories also provide glimpses into the 'hidden' lives of the inter-war black community, recording fierce opposition to black men's marriages to local women, prejudice against their children at school and social ostracism. As Little (1948) observed, such men passed down to their families a legacy of bitterness and a deep suspicion of whites based on their own experiences.[26] The British black community looks through a different window into the past. This is clearly revealed in Neil Sinclair's oral history of Tiger Bay where the 1919 riots are still valorised as the 'First War of Tiger Bay', a landmark in resistance struggles, marked by the organisation of a communal defence against white mobs. Blatant prejudice towards blacks and their white wives in police handling of the riots stoked bitterness in black folk memories of the riots and, argues Sinclair, helped bond a close-knit, supportive and cosmopolitan community built on intermarriage. Identities were forged by experiences of racism, but also by African cultural influences, which contributed significantly to

Tiger Bay's noted musical talents (not restricted solely to Shirley Bassey). Cardiff blacks also identified increasingly with the diaspora and anti-colonial nationalism during the 1930s. To the residents the 'Bay' thus became a fortress against white hostility. However, in white eyes it was demonised as a centre of crime, prostitution and violence. In the 1950s, the area was redeveloped and renamed Butetown (after the Marquis of Bute, a 'local' landowner), an erasure of history that compounded the grievances of Cardiff's black population.[27]

Black and white: interracial London

The harrowing experiences of poorer, black settlers and transient colonial seamen are central to understanding the dynamics of race, class and culture in Britain, but they comprised only one element of the black population. In London there was a more diverse black community, including colonial students and activists and American and West Indian entertainers. Social life and black political activity centred around 'coloured' clubs and 'Spade' cafés. The politicised socialite, Nancy Cunard (heiress to the Cunard shipping fortune), met the London docker and activist Chris 'Jones' in 'Walker's Café' in the London Dockland, and the Florence Mills Night Club, co-owned by Amy Ashwood Garvey, the first wife of Marcus Garvey, became the 'haunt of black intellectuals'. Novels from the period, such as Keate Weston's *London Fog* (1934) and Humphrey Gilkes' *Black* (1935) indicate heightened white awareness of the 'darkside' of the city.[28] Black experiences in the imperial 'heart of a heartless world' (to paraphrase Marx) were shaped by the racism that permeated every level of British society, but also through novel social contact with whites. This took two forms: socialising in the fashionable London clubs and other social venues, where blacks were an exotic adjunct to the hedonistic and sexually liberated lifestyle of the 'fast' set, and the inclusion of educated, 'civilised' blacks in white liberal 'interracial' initiatives. Although these represented very different social spheres and forms of social contact between black and white, they were interconnected through general white assumptions of the 'otherness' of black culture and constituted important sites of cultural intermix, transforming black identities in Britain.

However, the dominant perception of black culture in Britain remained negative. Black clubs in Soho, Notting Hill and the East End of London laid the foundations for the postwar culture of the 'dark side of the city' and, in white eyes, they were associated with vice and the corruption of white women. In the film *Piccadilly* (1929), scripted by Arnold Bennett, the exotic Chinese dancer, Shosho, from the lavish white Piccadilly Club, drags her white lover into a seedy club in Limehouse where black and Chinese men dance with drunken white women. Evelyn Waugh's sybaritic London (and Paris) of the 1920s is peppered with 'niggers' ('negroes' when he is being polite). Blacks were also associated with the decadent sexuality of the period, including bisexuality. Waugh noted having cocktails with Nancy Cunard and her 'negress' and refers to homosexual orgies with black male prostitutes.[29] Representations of black London as an 'underworld', into which whites, like Orpheus, are dragged down into moral corruption, endured well into the post-Second World War era, as Colin MacInnes' novel, *City of Spades* (1958), demonstrates. Attracted to the excitement and dangers of this 'underworld', 'chic' women went 'slumming it' in black clubs – a fad which persisted into the 1950s when socialites like Sarah Churchill, grand-daughter of Winston Churchill, frequented black circles in Notting Hill. Pilkington (1988) interprets this as a 'bid for escape from high society prudery', but it may also be seen as part of a long history of white appropriation of aspects of black culture which, argues Maycock (1997), tends to perpetuate racist stereotypes.[30]

For society women, 'socialising' with black men also included interracial sex. Both Waugh in *Decline and Fall* (1928) and Holtby in *Mandoa, Mandoa* (1933) have satirised rich, white women who had black 'toyboys' as scheming, shallow and decadent characters for whom black men were simply a short-lived whim. But whereas Holtby was attacking white decadence and racism, Waugh openly ridiculed the 'flashily dressed' American black boyfriend, insinuating the 'uncontrollable passions and animal nature' of blacks. Waugh had plenty of real life models, including his close friend, Olivia Plunket Greene, who 'could talk about nothing but black men' and an illegitimate daughter of a wealthy art dealer, who lived with 'another nigger', Leslie 'Jiver' Hutchinson, an accomplished Jamaican trumpet player and band member. The scene, writes Waugh, of the art dealer entertaining 'his illegitimate daughter … her black lover and her black lover's black wife and baby … might seem improbable in a book'.[31] In contrast to colonial Africa, where strong taboos existed barring relationships between white women and black men, in Britain women of all classes 'consorted' with blacks. Garvey maintained that the media was preoccupied with the strange fascination of white women with black men, who reputedly 'gathered in cafés' and seemed to do 'no honest work'. Even the aristocracy were caught in 'compromising situations' with 'coloured' men (evidenced in the 'Lady Mountbatten Scandal' which was blasted all over the popular press in 1932). The 'coloured' man was allegedly Leslie 'Jiver' Hutchinson. Another 'scandal' involved Paul Robeson, who was implicated in an affair with Peggy Ashcroft when she played Desdemona to his Othello.[32]

Nancy Cunard's Bohemian lifestyle, left-wing associations and passion for jazz music and African exotica (in a Man Ray photograph her arms are covered in African bangles) made her an easy target for caricature as a 'nigger lover'. In 1931, her controversial liaison with Henry Crowder (a black American composer) was luridly exposed. A high society friend of her mother, Emerald, quipped on enquiring about Nancy, ' … what is it now, drink, drugs or niggers?' and the conductor, Sir Thomas Beecham, reputedly wanted Nancy 'tarred and feathered'. Cunard wrote a spirited defence of her relationship and the socialite, Doris Garland Anderson, who was married to a black American 'celebrity', also bitterly criticised the 'smart set' who treated black men like toys and devalued genuine relationships. Most 'respectable' middle-class women, she argued, associated with blacks 'purely for political reasons'. Her book *Nigger Lover* (1937) touched on an important issue in liberal interracial circles and was 'strongly recommended' by the LCP.[33]

Miscegenation threatened metaphorical frontiers of race and nation, but, suggests Pilkington (1988), also challenged the control white men had over white women. The complex psycho-sexual relations between white women and black men were rooted in the contrasting conceptions of black and white masculinities, which were integral to the power relations of imperialism and institutionalised racism. In assessing the extent and nature of racism in British society, the sexual element cannot be ignored. British society developed a lurid preoccupation with the breaching of racial borders by white women, but black male residents were also keenly aware of the 'sexual politics' of imperialism. For educated blacks, relationships with white women were bound up with struggles over power and status, and it was tempting and flattering for black men to 'sleep with the enemy'. Margery Perham, who had contact with West African students, argued that blacks entered into liaisons with white women as the 'supreme ... compensation' for the 'severe racial humiliation' they suffered in Britain. Black activists maintained that this sexual assertion was a 'revolutionary act ... to get their own back on Europe', although they criticised the 'gigolos' and 'Europeanised missionary boys' who capitalised on rich white women's 'fascination' for black sex ('sexual imperialism') merely for 'prestige value'.[34]

However, educated white women were also the catalysts of more positive interracial contact, and black activists praised the many 'devoted' women who were 'above scandal' and gave practical help and support to black causes. Such women, they argued, perceived a 'close relationship' between racial and sexual oppression (for Jewish women this link was particularly significant) and were able to develop a more empathetic and 'egalitarian' relationship with black men. Members of the Gold Coast Aborigines Rights Protection Society (ARPS) delegation to London in 1934 (Chapter 4) noted how the attitudes of such women were the reverse of those in the colonies, where white women were reputedly more racist than men. Their stay in England would have been 'almost intolerable' without the 'sympathy, kindness and assistance' of Englishwomen as 'landladies and organisers'. White women's reputation for kindness, as 'the only sympathetic people who reached out to black men', persisted after the Second World War'.[35]

Political and social interaction between white women and black men was an integral part of the interracialism cultivated by well-meaning liberals. Such 'friends of the black man' organised interracial garden parties, tennis club teas and similar events to which black professionals and popular black artists, like Robeson, were invited. Black intellectuals were also welcomed in the left-wing literary circles satirised in Ethel Mannin's novel *Comrade O' Comrade* (1945) where the Trinidadian intellectual, C.L.R. James, is the handsome, 'eminent young Trotskyist', who was invited to tea at the house of Mary Thane, an earnest liberal whose name was 'a byword throughout British Africa' (possibly a caricature of Winifred Holtby). Women like Holtby were key social facilitators in these interracial salons. In addition to her 'Africa work', Holtby threw herself enthusiastically into interracial initiatives, counting resident blacks in her circle of friends and welcoming 'a string of native visitors' at her flat in Maida Vale. At a 'tea party' attended by Eric Walrond, who was now in London, writing for Garvey's *The Black Man*, and the Jamaican playwright, Una Marson, 'the colour question, miscegenation, birth control and race prejudice' was heatedly thrashed out.[36]

Black students and 'celebrities' also mixed with the *avant-garde* London set in the 'interracial' Harlem-style West End nightclubs which, argued Nnamdi Azikiwe, the Nigerian nationalist, created a 'false illusion of equality'. Black Americans, male and female, were particularly favoured on the basis that they came from a 'unique and cultured world' far apart from that of the 'primitive African'.[37] The revue, *Blackbirds* (1926, 1936), pioneered by the popular black American singer and dancer, Florence Mills, was a big success among the wealthy 'London set'. The 'blackbirds' were enthusiastically taken up by Waugh's circle providing entertainment and 'intimate gossip' at parties. Waugh described one such 'studio party', hosted by a 'black man', as 'all very refined ... with hot lobster and champagne cup'. Florence Mills and other favoured blacks who attended sang songs to entertain the guests. Perhaps the most well-known celebrities were the black American stars of British cinema in the 1930s, Elizabeth Welch and Paul Robeson.[38] Robeson's first appearance in Britain was in the mediocre American show *Voodoo* (*Taboo* in the US version) at the Blackpool Opera House in 1922 where, according to Brown (1997), he gained an early favourable impression of ordinary British people. Robeson's great success in Eugene O' Neill's play, *Emperor Jones* (1925), *Showboat* (1928) and *Othello* (1930) made him a star. In his autobiography, he recalls that he was readily accepted in 'aristocratic circles' where he was treated as a 'gentleman and a scholar'. Like other black Americans, Robeson felt that his 'intelligence and ability' was respected in Britain, which he regarded as 'infinitely better' for blacks than the USA.[39] The Robeson's lived in Hampstead Heath 'next to Ramsay MacDonald' and Robeson embraced the British way of life, for example 'watching cricket matches with his son at Lords'. When Essie Robeson went to Uganda she was given VIP status and (remarkably for a black woman) stayed at the Ugandan Governor's Residence in Entebbe.[40]

Such apparent acceptance and social recognition was highly seductive. But individual blacks were only deemed 'equals' because they were 'cultured' and educated and had passed the 'civilisation test'. As Nancy Cunard pointed out, Europeans seemed to want to reform the world in their own 'dreary and decadent image', and failed to recognise black achievements that were not based on having attained 'honorary white' status.[41] White patronage was thus dependent on conformity to white standards, political moderation and dissociation at the mass of blacks in Britain and the colonies. Robeson found this out at deep personal cost in his later, more politicised years. The implicit assumptions that their white patrons held about the superiority of white culture ultimately alienated educated blacks. Race consciousness was also stimulated by a greater awareness of the widespread racism in British society and the common experiences that linked Africans and blacks in the African diaspora.

Racism and race consciousness

Aware of the covert racism, which framed their interaction with 'liberal' Britain, more race-conscious blacks challenged the deceptive veneer of racial equality. Eric Walrond argued that blacks in the colonies tended to see England through a 'romantic and illusory' veil and, given their vast black empire, the English were 'surprisingly inexpert' in race relations. No official segregation existed, but blacks were not welcome in certain districts and university students were subtly discouraged from settling in England. Una Marson, the Jamaican poet, who was one of the rare black women trying to make a name for herself in literary circles, was enraged by the racist insults she had to endure in addition to sexist attitudes from both black and white men. Other contemporary accounts testified to widespread discrimination in housing, hotels, nursing and other professions.[42] Multiracial organisations, such as The Joint Council to Promote Understanding Between White and Coloured People in Great Britain, and the League of Coloured Peoples (LCP), both founded in 1931, carried out research that revealed that the deepest prejudice was directed towards students and professionals from Africa and the Caribbean. However, when the need for legislation to prevent discrimination was finally raised in Parliament in 1938 by a sympathetic Labour MP it fell upon deaf ministerial ears.[43]

Most whites shared deeply ingrained prejudices and, argued Little (1948), stereotyped views of blacks were widespread among all sections of the population. Even the friends of the black man, like Holtby, were not free from such attitudes. When Holtby saw *Emperor Jones*, she commented on how skilfully the 'magnificent creature', Robeson, had depicted 'the return of the Negro to his primitive, dark fears ... superstitions, childishness and charm'.[44] Racism was nourished by the 'light entertainment industry [and] ... lurid novels', the school curriculum and the enduring popularity of the exotic attraction and colonial spectacle in popular culture. In the early 1930s, for instance, the public were invited to pay three-pence to take a look at a 'pygmy woman' on show in a draper's shop in Peckham – a spectacle described by the ASAPS as an 'objectionable exploitation' of a 'helpless' native. However, the main concern raised in the organisation's correspondence with government officials was that the woman was an 'alien' from the Belgian Congo, who could therefore be repatriated (although she proved to be a 'British subject' from Cape Colony).[45]

The African intelligentsia complained bitterly about the adverse effect such displays of African 'savages', at exhibitions and elsewhere, had on racial attitudes in Britain. In a similar vein, Marcus Garvey criticised newspaper photos of 'sharp-dressed Harlem Negroes ... lazily playing dice' and cinema images of 'naked and savage' Africans, which 'insidiously strengthened prejudice'.[46] As stressed in Chapter 1, the powerful new medium of film created the 'celluloid colonial spectacle for voyeuristic mass audiences'. Film-makers used black students and residents, male and female, as 'exotic' extras. 'We all knew that the witch doctor in *Sanders of the River* (1935) was Mr Graham, the "Bengal Tiger" from Sophia Street', recalled one Tiger Bay resident. With little chance of other employment, 'coloured' girls also sought roles as film extras or made their way to the clubs of Piccadilly and Soho to become chorus girls and exotic female dancers. The popularity of black 'exotics' in British popular entertainment persisted during wartime. In Alfred Butts *Showboat*, 1940, Makumalo (Mark) Hlubi, a 'tall, well-built, brown-skinned South African student', who was one of the South African ANC representatives at the 1945 Pan-African Congress, had a 'special part' in the show performing the dance of a Zulu warrior, 'dressed in animal skin and fiercely brandishing a spear', to 'tremendous' applause.[47]

Entertainment, even if only as 'bit players' and film extras, was one area that blacks in Britain could gain some recognition and, given the barrier of discrimination in employment, earn some money. However, the emphasis on the 'exotic', sexual and/or 'primitive' appeal of both black men and women in popular entertainment contributed to a more general inferiorisation of black morality and culture, and confirmed the dominant view that the majority of black colonial subjects were 'unfit' for citizenship. It was for these reasons that Robeson came under attack from more race conscious blacks for his role in *Sanders of the River* and other films. Why did Robeson accept the role of the African chief in *Sanders*, given that he was already politicised by this time? It is possible that Robeson was attracted to the film's strong 'anti-slavery' theme or, as Duberman (1989) argues, because he believed that it would portray Africans in a positive light. However, as revealed in Chapter 2, the film proved a 'colonial spectacle' par excellence, prompting Garvey to accuse Robeson of 'discrediting his race'. Incensed by the 'anti-black propaganda' promoted in the cinema industry, Garvey complained to the BBC, the Moving Picture Board and the Colonial Office Film Committee, but failed to get any of Robeson's films banned. Ironically, argues Bourne (1998), *Sanders* has been the most consistently shown of Robeson's films, resurfacing in the 1950s, re-screened on Channel 4 in 1993, described as 'Korda's celebrated production' and now released on video.[48]

Robeson subsequently repudiated *Sanders*, and his wife, Essie, admitted that when she met 'real Africans' she 'blushed with shame for the mental picture my fellow negroes in America have of our African brothers [as wild black savages]'. There would be 'no sequel to ... perpetuate such misconceptions' she emphasised. Yet contact with Africans in *Sanders* also made a lasting impression on Robeson, and both he and Essie moved 'closer' to Africa and dedicated themselves to restoring African culture to a respected position. Robeson enrolled at the School of Oriental Studies (which became the School of Oriental and African Studies, or SOAS, in 1938) to study African languages and Essie studied anthropology at the London School of Economics. Admitting his former 'lack of responsibility', Robeson began to 'feel more Negro in spirit', reflected in the inclusion of new arrangements of negro spirituals in his concert repertoire.[49] He continued to star in British films, but in 1938 *The Keys* reported that he had decided not to take on any more roles unless the script had a 'cast iron' story. Reflecting his increasing commitment to left-wing causes, in the film *Proud Valley* (1939) he (quite plausibly) plays a black American who has pitched up in Cardiff as a sailor and, because of a lack of work, is forced to move inland to become a miner. The film prioritised the class solidarity of black and white workers over race, which was demonstrated in the black miner's acceptance as an equal by his Welsh co-workers. In retrospect, Robeson's politics may seem naive and ideal- istic, and Cripps (1977) argues that black audiences could not identify with his role in the film. However, in *Proud Valley* Robeson broke the mould of negative stereotypes of blacks, and the film did attempt to address the more serious prob- lematic of race and class.[50]

As his politics shifted to the Left, Robeson became increasingly suspicious of his former middle-class patrons and rebuffed, for instance, Winifred Holtby's overtures (made via his wife, Eslanda) to 'get him to South Africa' to help publi- cise Ballinger's trade union work discussed in Chapter 7 (Illustration 21). He cultivated links with the working classes, particularly the Welsh miners with whom he formed an enduring bond, and the Scots, a 'friendly and democratic people, with … honest minds … and warm hearts'.[51] Lloyd Brown (1998) argues that Robeson became a militant anti-imperialist through living in the heart of empire and his experiences helped to develop his socialist ideals. After visiting the Soviet Union in 1934, Robeson became involved in 1937 with the working- class Unity Theatre in London and committed himself to fighting against fascism and oppression in South Africa.[52] He also developed important contacts with anti-colonial activists in Britain, which helped to smooth Essie's African trip, and, although he never visited Africa, he was sufficiently well known there for whites to register concern about his political impact on the 'natives'. Thus, in this wider context, Robeson's political odyssey reflected the impact of dialogues between black and white activists in the heart of empire, which stimulated pan- Africanist solidarity and the growth of organised black activism.

The colonial intelligentsia in Britain were seminal to these developments, particularly African and West Indian students, who became more race-conscious as a result of the ubiquitous racism that they encountered. Black students in London, for instance, were forced to live in 'inferior' districts and their problems were compounded by the poor scholarships that were provided by colonial govern- ments. As Eslanda Robeson pointed out, African students in British Universities studied in the 'medium of a strange language, under trying conditions of strange customs … [and suffered] from loneliness and social ostracism'. They made an effort to understand white culture and 'adapt', but were never accepted as equals in academic circles and, argued the Gold Coast nationalist, Kobina Sekyi, were still treated as 'savages' by the working classes. Only approximately 300 of the total of 4,000 colonial students were African or West Indian, but, argues Adi (1998), they had a marked impact on black politics through the West African Students' Union (the WASU), founded in 1925 by the Nigerian, Lapido Solanke, as a forum for the nationalist aspirations of African students in Britain.[53] As future African leaders, their experiences in Britain and dialogues with other activists were central to the development of anti-imperialism.

19 Buckingham Street,
Adelphi,London,Mar.3.

My dear Miss Holtby:

Thank you so much for your letter of
February 28th. I have talked the matter over with Mr.
Robeson, and we are so sorry to have to refuse your request. Mr.Ballinger has already caused us so much trouble
in South Africa by his interview with the press on his
arrival there,that the last thing we would want to do
is to have Mr.Robeson's name linked with his work! He
told the press that Mr.Robeson is now "politically
minded",and is coming to South Africa to find out conditions for himself,and do something about them! Of course
nothing could have been more reckless,nor more harmful
for us. I know that Mr.Ballinger said all these things,
quite unconscious of the difficulties they would make for
us;but we have been flooded by letters from the press,
from white people and Negroes in South Africa,protesting
that they supposed Mr.Robeson was an artist and not a
politician. And of course,he is an artist and not a politician. I can imagine nothing more dangerous for him,
especially when he visits Africa,than to be considered a
politician!

Mr.Robeson joins me in sending you
greetings and regrets.

Sincerely,

Eslanda Goode Robeson

Mrs.Paul Robeson.

Illustration 21–Letter from Eslanda Robeson to Winifred Holtby
Source: Winifred Holtby Papers

Articulating black grievances: resistance in the heart of empire

Although pioneering pan-Africanist organisations had been established before the First World War,[54] new organisations to publicise black grievances against racism and colonial injustices emerged in the inter-war years. Black activism was complicated, however, by the gulf between educated and working-class blacks, Africans and West Indians, which was manifested in differing levels of consciousness and perceptions of white society. The black working-class, highly fragmented along ethnic lines, was transient, frequently unemployed and particularly difficult to organise. Activism thus took different forms and varied according to the aims and ideology (radical or liberal) of the movement or organisation, as well as the position of individual activists within the movement. 'Colonial' activists, who had no base in mainstream British politics, engaged in pressure group activities, lectures, lobbying and the production of pamphlets and political writings. As in the African context, women were marginalised from the discourse and practice of resistance or were mostly in subservient roles within organisations. There was a smattering of female students, mostly from Sierra Leone, who joined black organisations, especially the LCP,[55] but the only black female activists of any prominence in the 1930s were Una Marson, who became Secretary of the LCP in 1932, the formidable Amy Ashwood Garvey, Marcus Garvey's first wife, and Eslanda Goode Robeson.

Fierce debates developed over the degree of collaboration with whites and whether race or class was the primary cause of black oppression. The epochal events of the 1930s sharpened these debates. Some black intellectuals, like Robeson, moved closer to Marxism and adopted a class analysis of imperialism and racism; others, like the Trinidadian, George Padmore, a key black Comintern agent in the early 1930s, took an increasingly 'race conscious' position as he became disillusioned with white communist politics.[56] The militant race position was represented by Garvey, who argued that there was no difference between white communists and capitalists in their assumptions about the 'eternal' inferiority of blacks. Pointing to 'Jewish solidarity', he accused radical pan-Africanists and black communists who opposed his exclusivist line of 'selling out on racial loyalty' and undermining black unity.[57] However, Garvey's views appeared increasingly eccentric and irrational to black intellectuals, who were moving towards a radical pan-Africanism that incorporated elements of the Marxist analysis of imperialism. For instance, C.L.R. James, arguably the leading black intellectual of the period, a 'sage decades ahead of his time' who 'fired black liberation', acknowledged the importance of race and the need for a pan-Africanist black struggle independent of white control, but continued to stress the primacy of class over race and the need for black and white unity in the struggle against capitalism.[58]

While black intellectuals articulated a more coherent ideology of anti-colonial nationalism, 'Garveyism' degenerated into a form of 'black imperialism', which emphasised the need for racial purity and incorporated a romanticised and impractical ideal of African nationalism. *The Black Man*, established in Jamaica in 1933 and published erratically until Summer 1939, declared Garvey's commitment to the US system of democratic government and black capitalist enterprise on the basis that blacks were neither 'Communists' nor 'rebellious'. In 1937, he started his School of African philosophy (Universal Negro Improvement Association Training College), which involved correspondence courses that were examined solely by Garvey, who issued 'degrees'. Whites now saw him as the 'lone champion of the Negro Cause' who aroused the 'curiosity and amusement' of an 'uncaring' Sunday crowd in Hyde Park.[59] Although he addressed public meetings and had links with the Kilburn Liberal Association, Garvey was politically isolated from the powerhouse of black intellectual developments. Garvey's emphasis on self-help, 'African redemption' and black pride has had a powerful, long-term resonance throughout the diaspora and was a formative influence on radical pan-Africanism and African nationalist leaders. However, the black Left regarded Garvey as a 'deluded' and 'reactionary' demagogue, preaching a dangerous 'inverse racism' and black separatism that supported white segregationist ideology, obscured economic realities and was no real solution to imperialist exploitation.[60] Increasingly isolated and marginalised, Garvey died in relative obscurity in London in 1940.

In addition to the divisions between Left intellectuals influenced by Marxism and the Garveyite black separatist position, there were also black activists who favoured moderate, liberal integrationist strategies, which were represented by the League of Coloured Peoples (LCP). The LCP was founded in 1931 by the staunchly anti-communist Dr Harold Moody, a long-term Jamaican resident from a conservative, Christian background. Centred mainly in London, the organisation was committed 'to improve relations between the races' and attracted the support of white liberals, including progressive pro-colonialists like Margery Perham.[61] Until the late 1930s, the LCP had more white than black members and shared its membership with the London Group on African Affairs. The title of its magazine, *The Keys*, drew on the imagery of the black and white keys on the piano playing together in harmony – a metaphor for interracial co-operation first evoked by Dr Kwegyir Aggrey. The organisation held interracial social functions and engaged in charitable work among poor blacks, but also organised conferences on the race question in Britain and the empire, and was committed to 'the welfare of coloured people in all parts of the world', reflecting the influence of pan-Africanism on the black membership. *The Keys* provided a lively forum for debate over 'race and colonial questions'. Contributors ranged from black radicals, such as C.L.R. James, to white conservatives, like Dame Catherine Furse of the World Bureau of Guides and Scouts. [62]

Black LCP membership overlapped with the WASU, but relations between the two organisations were always uneasy. Moody, who retained strong editorial control over the *The Keys* until 1935, believed in the 'civilisation test' and the need for educated negroes to help the less articulate. He was thus viewed by radicals like Padmore as an 'Uncle Tom' who capitulated to the Colonial Office.[63] Rifts deepened in 1934 when a bitter dispute erupted over Aggrey House, a proposed Colonial Office hostel for African students, which Moody welcomed.

The WASU argued that Aggrey House represented a Colonial Office strategy to secure firmer control over student political activities in order to counteract 'left-wing' influences. The Aggrey House proposal also posed a threat to the autonomy of the WASU's Africa House, a hostel established in 1933 with West African funding and run by students. Aggrey House was thus boycotted and an Africa House Defence Committee was set up with the support of both white and black sympathetic organisations. Adi (1998) argues that Colonial Office reports indicate that the boycott had some success, although the WASU was finally forced into a grudging acceptance of Aggrey House. Moody, however, had strongly opposed the boycott, resulting in a WASU boycott of the LCP that had a 'serious' impact on LCP membership (never more than three hundred). Bitterness between the two organisations intensified when Moody joined the Management Committee in 1935, the year the hostel was officially opened.[64] However, the WASU's opposition was arguably vindicated. The hostel reflected a new official strategy of encouraging multiracial dialogue with Africans, providing an illusion of participation in decision making in order to steer African nationalism into 'safe channels'. Thus Ivor Cummings, a Sierra Leonian, who became the Secretary of Aggrey House, was a member of a number of Colonial Office Advisory Committees on African Education and other matters, and included in imperialist forums on developments in the empire.[65]

The diversity of cultural and class backgrounds, compounded by differing political perspectives, thus fragmented the black community and undermined any consistent solidarity. It was difficult, for instance, to reconcile the gulf between the bourgeois LCP and working-class organisations who had different aims and interests. For instance, the Negro Workers' Association (NWA), whose Secretary was a Barbadian communist, Arnold Ward, rejected liberal interracialism, refused to 'bow to philanthropic aid' and stressed international solidarity of black and white workers. Ward, an active speaker at political meetings in London, described the NWA as 'a fighting organisation of class conscious workers' dedicated to improving the lot of the poor black population of Britain of whom 'comrades abroad … even negro comrades, were largely unaware'. However, such organisations were also dependent on white support, albeit Left rather than liberal, and their existence and rhetoric arguably reflected the broader strategies of the white Left. Funding for the NWA came through the League Against Imperialism and the Co-operative Guilds. Reginald Bridgeman of the LAI was chairman and, predictably, the treasurer was white. Communists were also influential in organising the short-lived Liverpool Negro Association (1930) and the Colonial Defence Association (CDA), set up in Cardiff in 1937, which campaigned against cuts in benefit payments to unemployed colonial seamen and unfair methods of recruitment.[66] Such organisations saw the problems of British blacks as one facet of the wider problem of imperialism and, given their radical stance, attracted little support outside the Communist Party. However, they did address issues that affected the majority of the black population in Britain, who had little representation in organisations like the LCP, and established a precedent for later black trade union activism.

The Colonial Seaman's Union (CSU), a 'welfare and propaganda' society of blacks and Arabs rather than a trade union, was arguably more acceptable to both white and black moderates. It had branches in London, Cardiff and other major ports and was led by a London docker, Chris Braithewaite, alias 'Jones', a pseudonym adopted to avoid discrimination at work as a result of his political activities. Braithewaite had come to Britain at the end of the war and lived with his white wife in Stepney. Despite a lack of formal education, he had reputedly read widely while in the Merchant Navy and was 'passionate' about black disadvantage, speaking frequently at socialist meetings and gaining a reputation as a 'fiery orator'. In the 1920s, he was an organiser for the NUS (National Union of Seamen) where, according to Tabili (1994), he had heated exchanges with white officials. Although Braithewaite had some links with the Communist Party during the early 1930s, his closest links were with the non-communist Left, particularly the Independent Labour Party activist, Reginald Reynolds, and his wife, the writer Ethel Mannin, who both helped to organise a relief committee to provide support for his wife and six children when he died of pneumonia in September 1944.[67]

In 1936 Chris Braithewaite's daughter presented flowers to Emperor Haile Selassie at an emotional 'royal welcome' ceremony when Selassie and his family arrived in London in exile. The Italian invasion of Ethiopia, the last independent relic of 'African greatness', fostered a stronger sense of pan-Africanist unity among London-based blacks, which was reflected in greater concern for events in the colonies and South Africa. Growing economic discontent in the West Indies and the 'inspiring example of India' gave additional immediacy to this new radicalism. Bonds between London-based activists and the colonies were strengthened. Articles in *The Black Man* and *The Keys*, edited from 1936 by the more radical Peter Blackman, exposed the dangers of fascism and imperialism demanding 'nothing less than complete freedom for Africa' through mass action.[68] Previous bitter rifts were temporarily forgotten and moderates and radicals co-operated in 1935 in setting up a new 'umbrella' organisation, the International African Friends of Abyssinia (IAFA), which grew out of an *ad hoc* group that was formed to aid the 1934 Gold Coast ARPS deputation to London. The aim of this 'all Negro organisation' was to help maintain the 'territorial integrity of Abyssinia' and alert the British public to the threat of fascism in African colonies.[69] It was supported by the white Abyssinian Association, formed in 1937, and the anti-imperialist, anti-fascist *New Times and Ethiopian News* (1936), edited by Sylvia Pankhurst. Although white support was welcomed, the political activity generated by the Ethiopian crisis prioritised black self-help, reflecting a growing disillusionment with white interventions.

In May 1937, radicals in the IAFA founded the International Africa Service Bureau For the Defence of Africans and Peoples of African Descent (IASB) whose aims were 'to support the demands of colonial peoples for democratic rights, civil liberties and self-determination', press for 'constitutional reforms' and educate British public opinion on the 'true' conditions in the colonies. (see Illustration 22). Executive members included C.L.R. James, Isaac Wallace

Johnson, Nnamdi Azikiwe, Gilbert Coka (South Africa), George Padmore, Jomo Kenyatta and Ras Makonnen with Amy Ashwood Garvey as Vice President. The IASB was influenced by Marxism and a radicalised pan-Africanism, and much of its dynamism may be attributed to the veterans of radical black politics, George Padmore and C.L.R. James. Although 'active' membership was restricted to blacks, the IASB encouraged the support of sympathetic whites, who were allowed associate membership, and provided interested white organisations with speakers. The IASB's newspaper, *International Africa Opinion*, launched in 1938 and sold at left-wing meetings, was regarded by the authorities as 'inflammatory' and was suppressed in London and West Africa (Chapter 4). Special branch officers also allegedly kept tabs on known IASB activists.[70] There was some justification for official concern as, with the formation of the IASB, African and British activism on race and imperialism fused, strengthening links between the colony and the heart of empire, and stimulating the growth of pan-Africanism and mass anti-imperialist sentiment in Africa and the West Indies. These important developments were further catalysed by the Second World War.

Wartime developments

The Second World War, as Lauren (1996) has noted, was itself a 'race war' and brought about a revolution in race consciousness.[71] It also resulted in a sharp increase in the numbers of black men and women resident in Britain as armed services personnel or workers. In official rhetoric, tolerance and welcome prevailed – a recognition of the importance of the colonies to the war effort. However, there was no 'immediate abolition' of the colour bar throughout the empire, as demanded, for instance, by the long-standing critic of colonialism, Norman Leys, and only token measures to improve race relations were implemented, such as, the appointment of Ivor Cummings as first black officer of the new Welfare Department of the CO. As Spencer (1996) points out, the Home Office was consistently opposed to black and Asian settlement on the grounds that it would lead to social unrest and the growth of communist influence.[72] Smith (1986) also points to conflicts of interest between the Home Office, War Office and Colonial Office which were reflected in differing attitudes to 'coloured' residents in Britain. These debates over official policy were influenced by the presence of large numbers of black American GIs in a segregated US army, which, in the wider public domain, also led to an increase in racist incidents against all blacks resident in Britain, including 'race bans' from 'white' dance halls. Sir Alan Burns conceded that the treatment of blacks deteriorated during the war 'even in England', although he partially blamed this 'problem' on the 'shortcomings' of blacks and their 'aggressive anti-white stance'[73] However, these new developments provided a further stimulus to black initiatives against racism. For instance, the famous West Indian cricketer, Learie Constantine, discriminated against by the Imperial Hotel in Russell Square in 1943, challenged the hotel for 'personal distress and injury' and his case set a precedent in civil law against the colour bar when he gained token damages. The LCP also

The INTERNATIONAL AFRICAN SERVICE BUREAU

For the Defence of Africans & Peoples of African Descent

All communications must be addressed to the General Secretary.

Head Office:
94 Gray's Inn Road,
London, W.C. 1.

Telephone:
HOLborn 6117

WHAT IS THE INTERNATIONAL AFRICAN SERVICE BUREAU?

The I.A.S.B. is an organisation representing the progressive and enlightened public opinion among Africans and Peoples of African descent.

It supports the demands of Africans and other colonial peoples for democratic rights, civil liberties and self-determination.

WHY SUCH A BUREAU?

For centuries, from the time of the trans-Atlantic Slave Trade period down to the present, the black peoples of the world have been the victims of the most ruthless forms of oppression and exploitation. But never since the emancipation of the slaves have Africans and other subject races been so awake to a realisation of the wrongs and injustices inflicted upon weak and defenceless peoples as since the brutal Italian fascist war against Abyssinia.

This cold-blooded organised act of imperialist aggression against a people who had been led to place their security in the League of Nations and the Kellog Peace Pact, demonstrated as never before that the world is still dominated by the philosophy of might over right. It has also opened the eyes of Africans the world over, that they have no rights which the powerfully armed nations are bound to respect. And precisely because of this, they have decided to close their ranks and place their hopes for their future, not in imperialist statesmen, but in the organised will of the common people and progressive forces of all lands who are passionately devoted to the cause of peace.

With this object in view, representative leaders of African and peoples of African descent, with the assistance of English friends of subject races, have organised the Bureau in order to co-operate with all peace-loving, democratic and working-class forces who desire to help the advancement of Africans.

EDUCATING PUBLIC OPINION.

One of the chief functions of the Bureau will be to help and enlighten public opinion in Great Britain, especially the working and middle classes, as to the true conditions in the various colonies, protectorates and mandated territories in Africa, the West Indies and other colonial areas. In this way we hope that the people of England will be in a better position to raise their voices in protest against abuses and injustices which obtain in many colonies.

The Bureau will also attempt to gain the support of all Britons, regardless of party affiliation, in agitating for constitutional reforms, such as the granting of freedom of speech, press, assembly and movement, and other democratic rights which are at present denied to millions of loyal black subjects.

In carrying out such a mission, the Bureau will be allowed to supply speakers to Labour Party branches, Trade Unions, Co-operative Guilds, League of Nations Union branches, Peace Societies and Religious organisations, in order to explain the present conditions under which native races in various parts of the Empire live.

MEMBERSHIP.

The International African Service Bureau is a non-party organisation, which owes no affiliation or allegiance to any political party, organisation or group in Great Britain.

(a) *Active Membership* is open to all Africans and peoples of African descent, regardless of nationality, political creed or religious faith, who accept its aims and abide by its Constitution.

(b) *Associate Membership* is open to Europeans and members of other races who sympathise with the aims and objects of the Bureau and desire to demonstrate in a practical way their interest in Africans and peoples of African descent.

(c) *Affiliated Membership.* There is no conflict between the Bureau and other existing organisations which have for welfare of the African race at heart. The Bureau does not attempt to usurp or in any other way monopolise the activities of such organisations. Rather it aims to co-ordinate and centralise the activities of the various organisations—be they political, trade union, co-operative, fraternal, cultural, etc.—which at present exist in different parts of the black world, and in this way bring them into closer fraternal relation with one another, as well as sympathetic organisations in Great Britain and other countries, so as to arouse concerted action upon all questions affecting the common economic, political, social and educational well-being of the Africans and peoples of African descent.

For further information about the Bureau, please write to the General Secretary, International African Service Bureau, 94 Gray's Inn Road, London, W.C. 1.

CONTRIBUTION FORM.

In order to show my sympathy with your cause and the excellent work which the Bureau is conducting on behalf of Africans and other subject races of the Empire, I enclose the sum of:—

Name:..

Address:..

C.A. Press,
Crawley, Oxford.

Illustration 22—Publicity leaflet for the International Africa Service Bureau
Source: Arthur Creech Jones Papers

became more militant, although bitter power struggles between moderate and radical elements persisted, even after Moody's death in 1947, contributing to the League's final disintegration in 1950.[74]

As the war ended, however, rapid developments in African nationalism threatened to relegate the plight of black workers in Britain to a secondary position, although more radical nationalists were keen to integrate working-class grievances into the wider anti-imperialist movement. Nkrumah, appalled by the living conditions of London blacks, which he had observed during the war, helped establish a Coloured Workers' Association with Ernest Marke. He was critical of the lack of interest of the student class in Britain who were generally 'aloof' from the mass of coloured people whom they 'distrusted' and 'despised'.[75] Radical attempts to reconcile differences between workers and intellectuals were evident in the agenda and organisation of the anti-imperialist Fifth Pan-African Congress, which was organised by the new Pan-African Federation and held in Manchester in October 1945. Whereas earlier congresses were restricted mainly to bourgeois intellectuals, this path-breaking congress brought together the black British community, American pan-Africanists, like W.E.B. Dubois, colonial activists and trade unionists. Altogether over 200 delegates attended, including representatives of all coloured organisations in Britain with the exception of the LCP. The Manchester-based black entrepreneur, Ras Makonnen, one of the organisers, was able to organise accommodation with sympathetic black and white residents, and the American Red Cross (coloured section) held a pre-conference dance for delegates, resident hosts and black GIs.[76]

The congress thus represented a new 'militant' stage in the anti-colonial struggle, which sought a 'third road', firmly rejecting liberal patronage and organised communism. However, the support of the 'minority of the European Left' who had 'not failed the black cause' was welcomed and a number of sympathetic whites attended. Reflecting the impact of the Second World War, the 'Principle of the Declaration of Human Rights' laid down in the Atlantic Charter was endorsed in a 'Declaration of Colonial Peoples', which demanded total political and economic freedom from imperialist control. Specific resolutions were passed on East Africa, South Africa and the British South African Protectorates, reflecting the degree to which events in 'white settler' Africa had stimulated black consciousness. The 'colour problem' in Britain was discussed at the first session (chaired by Amy Ashwood Garvey) and delegates drew attention to the increase in prejudice during the Second World War. A resolution was passed protesting the treatment of coloured seamen and 'immediate action' on the 'colour bar' demanded, with discrimination made a legal offence throughout the empire.[77]

Marika Sherwood's archival research indicates that the CO dismissed the event as of little importance, but for Africans and people of African descent, the congress was arguably highly significant and represented a watershed in the development of black political consciousness. After the congress, the Pan-African Federation continued its activities at both a parochial and an international level and was active in 1946, for instance, in the defence of Donald Beard, a Jamaican airman accused of murder (Michael Manley, the Jamaican nationalist, won his acquittal at the Manchester assizes).[78] But, as the locus of political ideas and action shifted to the colonies, the upsurge of British black political activity petered out, leaving black British residents without any coherent representation. As 'coloured' migration to the 'mother country' accelerated in the 1950s, racism became more deeply entrenched and this uncomfortable elision of the imperial centre with its colonial hinterland generated 'post-colonial' problems before formal colonialism ended. Moral panics about 'floods' of immigrants and the 'colour problem' intensified as English identities, rooted in the stability of empire, were threatened by decolonisation.[79] The new 'commonwealth' migrants were once more transformed from 'empire' citizens to undesirable aliens and rapidly became disillusioned with the imperial 'motherland'.

Bitterness intensified with the 1958 Notting Hill riots, which, as in 1919, were 'anti-black' riots fuelled by sexual competition over white women, housing short-ages and economic factors. For Evans (1991) the riots marked the 'last gasps' of the British Empire, which had done so much to shape race relations in Britain. However, they also spurred a revival of black politics, inspired by new activists such as the communist, Claudia Jones (a remarkable Trinidadian woman who is buried next to Marx in Highgate Cemetery), who played a key part in the organ-isation of the Notting Hill Carnival.[80] These postwar black struggles drew on the legacy left by the pre-war pioneers and reconnected with black oppositional discourses that had been honed and sharpened through pan-Africanist intercon-nections in the heart of the British Empire.

Summary

While the poorer, resident black community have retained bitter memories of the inter-war period, time-mellowed, educated black activists have 'rose-tinted' reminiscences of British 'fairness' and the relative freedom of blacks in London before the Second World War.[81] This arguably reflects the fact that between the wars, black experiences and the nature of political consciousness and activism were differentiated by cultural background and class, with educated blacks finding more favour in white liberal or left-wing circles. Despite these differences, black experiences of British racism, in all its complex forms, stimulated black consciousness and, in terms of 'mental liberation' from white patronage and practical organisational activities, quantum leaps were made. The experience of migration enhanced black feelings of occupying the 'in-between space' in British society and, as Homi Bhabha (1990) has pointed out, this space of potential subjugation and exclusion could also become a potential space for cultural (and political) liberation. Experiences of life in Britain had a marked impact on African students, activists and intellectuals, who pioneered a resurgent pan-Africanism which fuelled African nationalism. For African diaspora blacks, racist exclusion engendered closer identification with Africa, progressing more gener-alised struggles against racism and imperialism. As in the case of South Africa, dialogue between blacks and whites, and the intersection of black ideologies of pan-Africanism with competing white ideologies of liberalism and Marxism were central to the emergence of a more radical black consciousness. It is to this complex dialogue between whites and blacks around 'race and colonial questions' that we now turn.

9 Into the heart of empire

The 'race problem'

Both West Africans and West Indians ... feel very strongly that British professions of liberalism should be expressed in prompt and positive action. There is a great deal of impatience with English attitudes which deplore colour prejudice ... but envisage no alteration ... to the existing situation.

(Kenneth Little, 1948).

[As] a 'suppressed minority' you are not just a person: you are a problem and every crusading crank imagines he knows how to solve your problem [but] you are not supposed to criticise your [white] friends or you will be called mean and ungrateful.

(Claude Mackay, 1970)[1]

Intervention into the 'race problem' in Britain followed a similar pattern as in South Africa, involving a broad spectrum of activists embracing progressive imperialists, liberal humanitarians, academics, reformist socialists who were active in the Labour Movement and members of Left organisations like the League Against Imperialism (LAI) and the Communist Party (CPGB). A fertile and frequently vituperative dialogue developed over causes and solutions to 'race and colonial questions', which fostered 'new thinking' on race in Britain. Initiatives on the 'race problem' also generated innovative dialogue between blacks and whites, and thus contributed to important developments in black consciousness. Both liberal-reformist and Left responses were influenced by developments in Africa, which was reflected in the fact that individuals worried by the new race problems in the heart of empire were often also active on African issues. However, a marked divergence in approach existed, which correlated with liberal and Left political positions. Liberals tended to skirt around issues relating to wider economic problems and focused on improving 'race relations' or ameliorating social problems resulting from 'culture contact' between different races. Furthermore, underpinning liberal 'sympathy for the underdog' was an implicit political agenda influenced by fears of Left infiltration in fledgling black organisations. In contrast, the Left viewed race problems as part of the wider class and anti-imperialist struggle. This chapter will critically assess liberal-reformist and Left involvement in race problems in the heart of empire and the implications this had for black resistance to racism and imperialism and related developments in liberal discourse on race.

Liberal initiatives on the 'colour problem'

Liberal initiatives on the 'race problem' filled a vacuum left by the state, which relied largely on restrictive legislation and policing. Activities which engaged the energies of individuals and organisations, ranged from charitable provision for impoverished blacks and social research to interracial social events and pressure group activity to tackle the more superficial aspects of the colour bar. Older, all-white, philanthropic 'welfare' organisations were involved primarily with the problems of poor 'coloured' seamen, while newer pressure groups, such as the Joint Council to Promote Understanding Between White and Coloured People in Great Britain, cultivated a 'multiracial' membership, which included the educated black minority. The white constituency interested in race issues was so small that concerns and membership of organisations frequently overlapped. However, more progressive reformists, who were committed to the emergent discourse of multiracial equality, were critical of the conservative, philanthropic 'do-gooders' and their localised and piecemeal, paternalist interventions.

Philanthropists continued the Christian charity of the Victorian bourgeoisie and were initially involved with the white poor, transferring their attention to the black poor when they became a visible 'problem'. One of the most prominent welfare organisations was the Liverpool Association for the Welfare of Half-Caste Children, founded in 1927 as successor to the Liverpool University Settlement, which had been established in 1908. In addition to charitable aid for 'distressed' blacks, the Liverpool Association (which later became the Liverpool Association for the Welfare of Coloured People) also sponsored research and, in 1930, published M.E. Fletcher's 'Report on the Investigation into the Colour Problem in Liverpool and Other Ports'. Barkan (1992) suggests that this report reflected the influence of anthropological studies of 'race-crossing' sponsored by the Eugenics Society. This intimates that charitable interventions into the poor black problem may have been spurred by fears of the adverse effects of miscegenation as much as by altruism. Paul Rich (1986), who has carried out an extensive study of such organisations, has aptly dubbed these initiatives 'philanthropic racism' and, as they arguably made a negligible contribution to tackling the problem of race prejudice, I have no further interest in them here.[2]

The first national liberal organisation to draw attention to the wider ramifications of the race problem was the respected and influential British and Foreign Anti-Slavery and Aborigines Protection Society (ASAPS), which was formed through an amalgamation of the two leading British anti-slavery societies in 1909. Quakerism was a seminal influence in the Anti-Slavery Society and the organisation had wealthy and influential Quaker international connections, which facilitated practical initiatives throughout the British Empire. In 1911, the ASAPS was instrumental in organising a 'Universal Races Congress' at the Imperial Institute in London to discuss relations between 'so-called whites and coloureds' with a view to encouraging 'a fuller understanding'. From this point onwards the ASAPS became an important non-governmental organisation working in the new area of liberal race relations while retaining its long-standing commitment to the 'protection of natives' and the global eradication of slavery.[3] Although concerned primarily with the welfare of 'natives' in the empire in 1913, the ASAPS organised a London conference on the 'Welfare of Africans in Britain', which reflected growing concern over social and political problems stemming from black poverty.

After the First World War, the organisation administered the Welfare of Africans in Europe War Fund. Set up by the League of Nations in 1921, this fund was originally designated to 'control African labour contingents in France', but was extended to cover 'all black imperial subjects whom [the war] had brought to Europe'.[4] John Harris, secretary of the ASAPS from 1910–34, was Honorary Secretary of the British branch of the Committee for Welfare of Africans in Europe War Fund and was thus able to exert considerable influence over financial resources and allocations until the fund petered out on the eve of the Second World War. The annual reports indicate that most of the income from the invested fund money was spent on loans to individual students and colonial seamen in economic distress, with a preference for 'those who had served in the Great War'. The fund also supported the 'benevolent work' of white and black welfare organisations, such as the Cardiff 'League of Goodwill' and Pastor Daniels Ekarte's African Churches Mission (although the trustees were not so comfortable with black self-help initiatives). Local trustees were also empowered to provide 'passages to Africa for natives and their dependants' if they felt it was 'expedient', and, it was noted that 'more and more destitute seamen and students required assistance in this area' as the depression deepened.[5]

Files from the early 1930s contain numerous letters from individual Africans and organisations acting on their behalf requesting financial help with educational and legal fees, loans, travel arrangements and 'general welfare'. In assessing cases, the Welfare Committee tempered moral and humanitarian concern with more practical 'political' considerations and the trustees were generally reluctant to give support to 'political' activities. For instance, when Kenyan Kikuyu leaders came to England in 1930 to speak before the Joint Parliamentary Committee Upon Closer Union in East Africa in defence of African interests, Harris was loath to provide support for the deputation. He was deeply concerned that the fund would have to foot the bill and warned that 'exceeding care' would have to be taken over the conditions in which natives were 'encouraged' to come to England. The following year a South African delegation to London, led by Dr D.D.T. Jabavu, was refused funds on the grounds that such delegations were generally 'sufficiently provided for'. Yet when the Kenyan nationalist, Jomo Kenyatta, found himself in 'straightened circumstances' in London in 1933 and applied to the fund for aid to return to East Africa, despite his 'suspect' politics, a loan was granted as he had always repaid previous loans.[6] This suggests that although the politics of applicants undoubtedly influenced the allocations of funds, the trustees were equally concerned with the prudent management of scarce resources.

The administration of the fund, which was the only substantial source of financial aid for Africans in Britain, thus provides revealing insights into liberal attitudes to blacks and the 'black problem'. In their dealings with blacks, the trustees proved patronising and parsimonious, and money was lent, not given. Where students were concerned, only 'worthy' Africans – those who had an 'earnest desire' to improve themselves through a British education – were considered. However, such students were also regarded as a somewhat heavy moral responsibility, and a Lagos contact was warned that African students arrived 'very raw and ignorant of [British] ways and customs' and it was 'not an easy task' to 'guide' such youths and watch over their welfare.[7] Despite their caution, the trustees were consistently disappointed by the fact that certain Africans aided by the fund were insufficiently 'grateful' and defaulted on their loans. A Lagos resident, for instance, had debts outstanding for 'feeding, clothing and educating' his child at Pathway College, Reading. After a 'member of staff' had allegedly been the victim of a 'serious fraud', the fund refused to lend money without a 'person of substance' acting as guarantor. Like South African liberals, they regarded most Africans as financially naive and inherently corrupt.[8]

Destitute sailors, who were regarded as particularly bad risks, found it extremely difficult to obtain loans. When Moses Quaker applied for money to redeem pawned clothing before returning to Sierra Leone, Harris informed the Crown Agents that the trustees were 'not very happy' at lending for such purposes, although they did contribute 'a small amount … essential to [Moses] health'.[9] In dealing with coloured seamen, the committee was keen to establish the nationality of 'distressed natives' to avoid having to bear any unnecessary financial burden for 'alien' applicants. 'Uncivilised natives' (such as the 'pygmy of Peckham' mentioned in Chapter 8) could only be restored to their homes if they were British subjects.[10]

In 1934, in reply to a request on behalf of an African medical student in Edinburgh, John Harris noted that the committee would like to help, but that there had been 'so much destitution' that funds were momentarily 'quite exhausted'. This may reflect a keen desire to make accounts balance (a major preoccupation of the controlling committee), but also a growing wariness about the 'worthiness' of applicants. Although Harris pleaded poverty, the 'Report for the Year ending 31st May, 1934' indicates that the fund's balance stood at over £12,000 – only £35 less than the previous year and greater than the original 1921 sum. In fact, the only time the fund fell below the 1921 level was between 1922–4 (presumably on account of the aid given to colonial soldiers and seamen immediately after the war). During the slump there was a net increase in the fund's resources.[11] This anomaly may reflect the disappointment of the trustees in the outcome of their work. They continued to make grants towards the 'valuable work' of welfare organisations in Liverpool and Cardiff, but conceded that the situation of blacks was deteriorating rather than improving. By 1939 the committee reported that many cases of distress had been 'extremely complicated' and had involved 'a considerable amount of time and correspondence'. The trustees were also disappointed by their attempts to help African students and were deeply perturbed by black protest over official plans for Aggrey House, the Camden Town hostel for African students (Chapter 8), which the ASAPS had always supported. The fund's 1939 report noted that the hostel had been made 'very comfortable'. However, it added that this had not been achieved without 'considerable difficulty' as it was 'almost impossible' even for educated Africans to understand the importance of 'meticulous care' in the handling of public property and funds.[12]

Given such attitudes and the piecemeal allocation of meagre funds, it is hardly surprising that the all-white Committee for the Welfare of Africans failed to make any significant impact on the quality of life of blacks in Britain. The paternalism of the conservative liberals who administered the fund only served to humiliate blacks racially, further stimulating race consciousness. As blacks in Britain began to articulate their own grievances more forcefully, new organisations emerged which combined concern for 'coloured' welfare with multiracial initiatives that were directed at placating the black intelligentsia. Whereas the philanthropic welfare societies were all-white, the newer 'multiracial' organisations, such as the Joint Council to Promote Understanding Between White and Coloured People in Great Britain, paid lip service to racial equality by encouraging black membership and social interaction between blacks and whites. The Joint Council (modelled on the South African Joint Councils) was set up in 1931, on Quaker instigation, to co-ordinate the different groups interested in 'overcoming' colour prejudice with the aim of encouraging 'wider appreciation of ... the contribution of coloured people to human welfare'. At the inaugural meeting, concerned white activists argued that the colour problem had become 'more tangible' with the growth of modern communications. There was an urgent need to improve race relations, they argued, to avert the 'political dangers of the colour bar' and race consciousness, which was 'undermining the empire'.[13]

In aims and composition, the Joint Council was thus very similar to the League of Coloured Peoples and Harold Moody, who was also a member of the Joint Council, warned of the danger of overlap. But, whereas 'coloured' membership of the LCP was predominantly Afro-Caribbean, the Joint Council set out to ensure representation of all non-white minorities, including Indian and Chinese students. However, most of the council's interracial work was directed towards coloured students, with the bias in favour of Indians rather than Africans. This arguably reflected the need to placate the grievances of the Indian intelligentsia, enhanced by experiences of racism in Britain, in view of the more immediate dangers of Indian nationalism. The emphasis was on placating the grievances of educated blacks rather than tackling the wider causes of racial inequality, and John Fletcher stipulated that references to prejudice should be confined to 'specific incidences'. Members became preoccupied with the etiquette of the language of race relations – debating the use of offensive terms like 'nigger' and 'native' and whether negro should have a capital letter.[14] This clearly reflected the problems of racial terminology, which became more politically loaded as black consciousness developed. Practical activities reflected a continued emphasis on welfare work among poorer blacks. The Joint Council, in conjunction with the LCP, also took over the running of the annual 'Coloured Children's Party', begun by John Fletcher, in 1928. In November 1932, it was involved in a 'Negro service' for First World War soldiers, which was organised by the Elks Negro Friendly Society in Westminster Cathedral. Wider political and economic issues were thus generally avoided, prompting criticisms from more radical black organisations.[15]

While the Joint Council was arguably a forerunner of the race relations organisations that mushroomed in the postwar era, the London Group on African Affairs (LGAA) had a wider brief, namely 'to assist in the improvement of race relationship in Africa' and I have already discussed the organisation's involvement in the South African 'native problem'.[16] However, the LGAA's concerns also extended to race problems relating to Africans in Britain, emphasising the inseparability of race questions in Britain and the empire. As a 'non-political and non-sectarian' pressure group, the organisation sought to recruit 'Conservative and Liberal' members with 'progressive principles' on race. The chairman was the ubiquitous John Fletcher, and the secretary, Frederick Livie-Noble, formerly Honorary Secretary of the Pretoria Joint Council. Dr Harold Moody was also a member, representing a token black involvement in the organisation. In addition to a strong interest in South Africa, the new organisation had links with the Kikuyu Central Association and other 'correspondents' throughout black Africa, and offered 'hospitality and kindness' to individual Africans visiting Britain. For the LGAA the key to 'sound progress' was improved welfare and 'mutual understanding' between the races which would counteract the 'dangers of Communism and Indian nationalism' among 'unguided' Africans.[17]

From its formation in 1930, the LGAA was deeply concerned about the growth of race consciousness in Britain, where dissatisfaction was 'rife' and had spread to coloured seamen 'who had not seen war service' and whose claims to British citizenship were 'highly doubtful'. Livie-Noble alleged that in London and Liverpool such men were influenced by 'alien agitators' and, although he was against enforced repatriation, supported the removal of 'known agitators'. In a letter to Winifred Holtby, for instance, he referred to a Sierra Leonian named Bassey, who had contravened the Aliens Orders. 'Steps must be taken to have him repatriated', he wrote, ' ... I shudder to think what will be his influence in his own country ... '. He also recommended that Bassey's 'voluminous correspondence' should be destroyed.[18]

In 1931, the LGAA organised a meeting to draw attention to the 'enormous proportions and urgency' of the 'colour problem'. Livie-Noble was asked to prepare a draft document, detailing socio-economic conditions and cases of discrimination, in consultation with the Joint Council and prominent blacks like Eslanda Robeson (who promised to 'have tea' with him to discuss the problem).[19] Research revealed that the plight of colonial seamen constituted a 'permanent problem' which was racial as well as economic, but no practical initiatives emerged and the LGAA transferred responsibility to the Joint Council as 'the

best body to deal with the matter'. By 1935, however, support for the Joint
Council had dwindled considerably and, although members maintained that it
had been 'of considerable value' at a time when 'so many events were making
for racial friction', they admitted that its successes were not 'spectacular'.[20] How,
then, do we evaluate these white, liberal interventions in the race problem in
Britain? What motivated activists? Were they well-intentioned 'champions of the
oppressed' or was multiracialism simply a new strategy to rebalance the imperial
and racial status quo which was threatened by black consciousness?

Liberals and race: champions of the oppressed or closet racists?

Christian conviction, moral conscience, guilt, and zeal for good causes motivated
liberal activists, as well as the desire to control the emergent political consciousness of African activists in the heart of empire.[21] Liberals were highly suspicious
– suspecting communist influence – when blacks adopted an independent stance.
Thus, John Fletcher strongly opposed a counter organisation to the Joint
Council, The Council for Promoting Equality and Civil Rights Between White
and Coloured People, established in 1933, on the basis that it was 'firmly' under
the influence of the LAI and had a 'strong objection' to imperialism.[22] In maintaining that most of its black members were in 'communist pay' and manipulated
by white communists, Fletcher not only fell prey to crude conspiracy theories,
but reinforced the paternalistic belief that blacks were incapable of organisation
without white help. However, in assessing individual motives and practical
involvement with black residents in Britain, it is important to differentiate
between philanthropists and reformist socialist activists, whose involvement with
race problems was informed by political conviction as well as a 'passion of pity'
for the underdog. We must also consider an important gender dimension to
political activism around race and colonial issues. Women were strongly represented in race relations and 'Africa work' and, as noted in Chapter 8, black men
appreciated their dedication, although few female activists expressed any interest
in, or understanding of, black women's problems. The archetypal female activist
was Winifred Holtby. Close male colleagues claimed that she was the 'stoutest
warrior of all' and 'a constant source of inspiration' to others working in the
African cause. In Holtby's satirical, 'anti-imperialist' novel, *Mandoa, Mandoa:
A Comedy of Irrelevance* (1933), Jean Stanbury, the main female character who was
'bound to a life of duty and self-sacrifice', foregoing marriage for 'independence
and work for the native', was arguably modelled upon herself.[23] Like many
younger, 'modern' women involved in the 'cause', Holtby's attitude to blacks was
less patronising than those of her white, middle-class male co-activists. Her
commitment and selflessness was acknowledged by South African and Nigerian
students, whom she helped financially in their studies in England.[24]

Holtby saw herself as a progressive radical. In *Mandoa, Mandoa* she was acid
about humanitarian do-gooders who had 'grown fat on reform', but were basically
patronising philanthropists, prigs and cynics. 'Mandoa' was a fictitious indepen-

dent African country loosely akin to Ethiopia, and the book is essentially a critique of the commercial interests that were trying to open Mandoa up to tourism and, ultimately, imperial domination. But, she also satirises the humanitarian delegation, which was trying to stamp out slavery, and the Labour Party establishment (Lord and Lady Lufton, arguably modelled on Sydney and Beatrice Webb), who had 'abandoned' the cause of true socialism and embraced imperialist values. A rather mediocre novel, if a refreshing change from the masculine genre of fiction about Africa, *Mandoa* was praised in Holtby's 'Africa' circles where it was seen as a 'ruthless satire on imperialism', which had 'propaganda value'. The novel clearly links race, colonial issues and reflected contemporary debate at the heart of empire. *Mandoa* also provides an interesting contrast to Evelyn Waugh's far more popular *Black Mischief*, which was published in the same year. Whereas Waugh's novel, based on his travels in Ethiopia, reproduces the dominant racist representations of African 'backwardness' and barbarity, Holtby's book is informed by progressive, liberal discourse on race, attacks anthropologists, and portrays her main black character as a man of intelligence, culture and sophistication.[25]

However, Holtby, like her close colleague, Norman Leys, never developed a coherent, theoretical analysis of colonial or racial oppression, retained an emotional commitment to empire and the higher ideals of trusteeship and was deeply suspicious of communism. (She had visited the Communist Party's offices and concluded that the whole argument against communism was summed up in the state of the toilet!).[26] From a well-connected background, she was universally popular and accepted in more conservative circles – regardless of her 'radical' views. Although a professed socialist who linked race questions to 'capitalist exploitation', Holtby's response to racial injustice was emotional and empathetic. A feminist friend noted that Holtby had become a 'martyr' to the cause and that her zeal verged on developing into an 'unwholesome ... complex'.[27]

In contrast, the pragmatic male reformists avoided over-sentimentalising Africans and had colder and more clinical relationships with blacks resident in Britain. Although genuinely dedicated to the improvement of race relations, they were unable to transcend an ingrained belief in black inferiority. An apt example here is the prominent activist, Charles Roden Buxton, the great grandson of Thomas Fowell Buxton (the 'Emancipator' of slaves). As a lawyer and Labour MP, Buxton wrote copiously on African and race problems, but his attitude to blacks remained essentially aloof and arrogant. At his 'interracial parties' he saw himself as an 'agent of culture' helping blacks to pass the 'civilisation test'. Male liberals and reformists also never managed to divest themselves of the fear of race-mixing, which was at the heart of popular racist discourse, and thus racial equality and integration stopped short of 'mixed marriages' – a thorny problem which was consistently evaded and fudged.[28]

For middle-class white liberals, the 'colour problem' was only one of a number of 'worthy causes'. Differences in political opinion, strong individualism, personal animosities and divisions within the broad umbrella of activism on race and African issues prevented the emergence of a more forceful and influential lobby. Arguably, the most fundamental weakness in liberal initiatives on race was in the very nature of liberal, multiracialist discourse. Racial equality and integration into white society was premised on the degree to which blacks accepted white culture and values and, thus, excluded the illiterate majority who, as yet, were not sufficiently 'civilised'. Liberal and reformist 'champions of the oppressed' were constrained by their class and cultural perceptions and, although committed in principle to racial equality, were unable to transcend assumptions of cultural inferiority and an ethnocentricism, which prioritised whiteness and Western culture as the norm.

As in South Africa, liberals criticised racial prejudice but not the fundamental reasons why it persisted – a 'liberal dilemma' which resulted in inertia and vacillation. William Macmillan blamed the ineffectiveness of Joint Councils in both South Africa and Britain on the fact that the 'race relations' idea, imported from the US, had instilled a strong distrust of anything 'political'. Liberals, he argued, saw blacks as objects of 'reform', offering cosmetic measures only and failing to challenge the structural roots of racism. Paternalism and lingering doubts about an independent black potential limited their intellectual and practical contribution to race issues. Radical black intellectuals and the white Left also criticised the charitable, piecemeal basis of the British Joint Council and its role in 'pacifying' colonial students, and attacked the moderate black bourgeoisie who co-operated in interracial initiatives.[29]

Ultimately, liberal vacillations and the failure to include blacks in active roles in multiracialist organisations led to black disillusionment. Blacks resident in Britain, argued Marcus Garvey, sensed a latent racism behind the liberal mask of 'false niceness' and commitment to multiracialist ideals, and, as noted in Chapter 8, suspicion of white 'do-gooders' was widespread in poorer black communities. The move towards black self-help in the wake of the Ethiopian crisis led to a further rejection of liberalism, which extended to previously co-operative organisations like the LCP. The younger generation of radicalised blacks became more discerning about which whites they were prepared to co-operate with. They were still prepared to accept white support, but only if it was not directed towards manipulating or directing black movements. Some now argued that only communism could throw down the 'barriers of race', reflecting the appeal of the alternative ideology of Marxism to black intellectuals across the diaspora. 'Goodbye Christ ... ' wrote the American poet, Langston Hughes, 'Make way for a new guy with no religion ... Marx ... Lenin ... Worker ... Peasant ... ME'.[30] What, then, did the oppositional ideology of Marxism and Left-inspired organisations do to tackle racism?

'Blacks turn Red':[31] the British Left and the 'colour' and 'colonial' questions

The broad Left included the Communist Party of Great Britain (CPGB), certain factions within the Independent Labour Party (ILP) and organisations like the NCCL. There were important political differences between the social democrats in the ILP and the revolutionary Marxists in the CPGB, but they shared in common an anti-imperialist position and critique of the more cautious liberal-reformist approach to race problems. For the Marxist Left, represented primarily by the Communist Party of Great Britain (CPGB), 'race hatreds' could only be resolved with the overthrow of capitalism and, thus, analyses of the race problem in Britain were firmly located within the wider struggle of the 'toiling masses', in colony and metropole, against imperialism and capitalism.[32] In contrast to the practical 'welfare' schemes and race relations initiatives of the liberal-reformists, the Marxist stance on racial equality and colonial freedom tended to be abstract and theoretical, although practical campaigns over specific issues were mounted with varying results.

During the 1920s, the new CPGB was slow to respond to race problems in Britain as members arguably held deeply ingrained ethnocentric views. Delegates to Communist International (Comintern) forums were reluctant to endorse complete colonial independence or sever imperial connections on the grounds that the 'rank and file' British worker would consider it 'treasonable' to help the 'enslaved' nations rise against British rule.[33] However, the 1919 riots did prompt the party to condemn the exploitation of colonial blacks, stressing the connection between race and colonial questions and linking the liberation of the colonies with the fight against 'capitalist immigration laws'. Under the editorship of Rajani Palme Dutt, *Labour Monthly*, which was founded in 1921 with Comintern support (although it was not an official CPGB publication), developed a strong internationalist slant to counteract the parochialism of rank and file members. Leading party members emphasised links between the British worker and the empire, although India, Ireland and Egypt remained the main overseas preoccupations.[34] Like the Communist Party of South Africa, the CPGB's policies clearly reflected the theoretical and tactical shifts in Comintern policy. In 1925, the Agitation and Propaganda Department of the Comintern sent the CPGB a lengthy summary of its theoretical deficiencies and failure to take a 'world-view'. In response, the party's Labour Research Department expanded propaganda and research work aimed at exposing the evils of British imperialism.[35]

Following the Comintern's Left turn in 1928, the party was purged of 'rightists' and was directed to step up work with the 'negro toilers'. The CPGB's 'New Line' prioritised revolutionary work in the 'backward' areas of Africa and the organisation of colonial workers in Britain.[36] Anti-imperialist propaganda and education work was expanded, but the CPGB was still heavily criticised by the Comintern's Red International of Labour Unions (RILU) for 'insularity'. The party was thus directed to: concentrate practical work on fighting racial prejudice within the trade unions; organise Britain's 'toiling Negroes, Hindus and Arabs'; and 'vastly strengthen' its poorly developed colonial work by sending 'organisers' to the British colonies and fostering closer links with the International Trade Union Committee of Negro Workers (ITUC-NW), formed in Hamburg in 1930.[37] There is some evidence that the CPGB's Minority Movement was active in organising pickets in support of colonial seamen's grievances during the South Shields' 'Arab Riots' in 1930, but, on balance, practice failed to match up to theory. Comintern analysts continued to complain about stagnation in colonial work in Britain, although this was partially blamed on the 'inertia' and 'lack of initiative' of blacks. A British Communist noted that resolutions on the colonial struggle were dutifully passed, but were mostly of a 'philanthropic character', liberal in tone and glossing over important class issues.[38] By 1932 domestic problems had almost completely overshadowed colonial work, although Left involvement in race and imperial issues continued through the British branch of the LAI.

Technically speaking, the LAI was an international 'non-party mass organisation' and the British branch was the liveliest in Europe, reflecting Britain's position as the pre-eminent imperialist power. In 1928, a 'broad working-class conference' was organised to launch the new British branch, which was attended by 308 delegates. The LAI acted as a forum for the interchange of radical ideas on race and empire, and black members included Arnold Ward of the NWA and the Indian activist, Shapuri Saklatavla, the Communist MP for Battersea, 1922–4 and 1924–9.[39] The leading activist was Reginald Bridgeman, an enigmatic, upper-middle-class left-winger, who had influential contacts in Parliament and the Colonial Office and gave the League an aura of respectability. A 'moral radical' and 'fellow traveller', his CP membership was never convincingly established, although he maintained an unswerving commitment to Comintern policies until he was re-admitted to the Labour Party in 1938. Reformist socialists regarded Bridgeman as the arch-communist ringleader in the LAI as he had a key position in the co-ordination of African work and liaisons with black activists, and was able to forge cross-links with kindred organisations like the NCCL, of which he was also a member. Under Bridgeman's direction, the LAI's London office became a rendezvous for black activists and a 'clearing house' for information and assistance.[40]

Until 1929, the organisation enjoyed support from Labour Party and ILP sympathisers. After 1928, however, the CPGB, in keeping with the Comintern's 'New Line', rejected further co-operation with social democrats. In September 1929, Conrad Noel, the Anglo-Catholic 'Red Vicar' of Thaxted, Essex, took the chair of the British section and the LAI and became responsible for implementing the CPGB's 'New Line' policy on race questions. Accusations that the LAI was communist inspired soon led to the resignation of Labour Party members. The ILP continued to participate in forums like the LAI, but this led to defections by more resolutely anti-communist members, like Holtby and Leys, to the splinter group, the Socialist League, set up by Stafford Cripps in 1932. Thus, by 1932, LAI membership was predominantly pro-communist, with the exception of staunchly anti-imperialist ILP members like Fenner Brockway.[41]

At its 1931 conference in London (where delegates from colonial countries allegedly took a 'very active part'), the LAI pledged that it made 'no distinction of colour, race or sex' and would take up the struggle against 'all colour bar restrictions' in Britain. It was reported that the CPGB had now delegated the organisation of colonial seamen and students in Britain to the LAI, which had established new branches in Manchester, Birmingham, Edinburgh and Liverpool, where a 'Negro comrade' (Arnold Ward) 'had established good connections with colonial workers' and was active in opposition to the Alien's Registration Scheme. Adi (1997) argues that the LAI and affiliates, such as the NWA, were 'extremely active' among West Africans in Britain and maintained important contacts in West Africa. The LAI supported the grievances of the Gold Coast Aborigines Rights Protection Society delegation to Britain (Chapter 4), whose leaders addressed the annual LAI conference in 1934. The organisation was allegedly also instrumental in co-ordinating Left protest against Colonial Office control of Aggrey House (Chapter 8) in co-operation with the CP.[42] However, any Africans associated with the LAI were tarred with the 'Moscow brush' and regarded by liberal-reformists as dangerous agitators. Jomo Kenyatta, for instance, was described by the Labour Party International Department as 'a well-known … native from Kenya, who had been repudiated by the Kikuyu Association for … visiting Moscow' and acting as Bridgeman's 'co-partner' in the LAI.[43]

Counteracting empire propaganda was regarded as a key aspect of the LAI/CPGB's anti-imperialist work. For the Left, prejudice against colonial workers in Britain was part of the 'colour bar', which had been built up 'to preserve the economic subjection' of black people throughout the world.[44] This subjection was reinforced through ideological channels which promoted 'false patriotism', extolled the virtues of the white race and empire and facilitated colonial exploitation. Similarly, colonial education was designed to 'lure' the exploited peoples away from their own traditions, render them 'submissive' and thus ensure their defence of the empire against Bolshevism.[45] The LAI thus campaigned against 'reactionary teaching' and Empire Day celebrations in British schools and organisations that 'gloried in empire', such as the Boy Scouts, although the impact of such campaigns was arguably extremely limited. In its opposition to Empire Day celebrations, the CPGB and the LAI were supported by a minority of reformist socialists, such as the novelist H.G. Wells, who also strongly opposed the 'arrogant flag-waving class' and the promotion of imperialism and militarism. Propaganda pamphlets were issued and demonstrations were organised to 'counteract' the pro-imperialist position of the 'Thomas School' (named after the influential Labour MP and Minister, J.H. Thomas) and to 'clear the minds' of the working class of their 'imperialist allusions'.[46]

The campaign to free the 'Scottsboro Boys' widened the base of left-wing agitation, highlighted the ugly threads of a common racial oppression throughout the African diaspora and strengthened trans-Atlantic links between black activists. The 'Scottsboro Boys' were nine young blacks (the youngest was 14) who were charged with the rape of a white girl in Scottsboro, Alabama, in 1932. The evidence was dubious and the *New York Times* declared them innocent, but the case dragged on for seven years. The 'Scottsboro Affair' drew attention to the fact that for US blacks, the threat of lynching was ever-present and the case became internationally famous, rousing liberal and Left opinion on both sides of the Atlantic, which arguably saved the defendants from execution. In 1932, the International Labour Defence, LAI and NWA merged to form a Scottsboro Defence Committee under the chairmanship of Mrs Carmel Haden-Guest. The president was Professor Hymie Levy, and Eleanor Rathbone, Naomi Mitchison and Cobina (Prince) Kessie (A Gold Coast student who was active in the West African Students' Union) were vice-presidents. Reginald Bridgeman was financial secretary and Jomo Kenyatta and Mrs Gladys White were joint secretaries. Other organisations represented in the broad-based committee included the CPGB, NCCL and the LCP.[47]

On 6 June 1932 a large meeting was held outside Shoreditch Town Hall in Stepney. The meeting was addressed by Mrs Ada Wright, the mother of one of the defendants. Later the same year, Chris 'Jones' (Braithewaite) of the Colonial Seaman's Union addressed a meeting in Trafalgar Square and in the 1933 London May Day march was reputedly joined by a 'large Scottsboro contingent' which carried a banner with the slogan 'Races Unite Against Imperialist Oppression'.[48] During 1934 the Scottsboro Defence Committee organised speeches, demonstrations and protests, and the ILD co-ordinated a 'world-wide petition'. Eventually, five defendants were freed, but four were given heavy sentences (death in one case, although this was later commuted to life). Anti-communist opinion continued to maintain that the 'Boys' were guilty, claiming that the campaign to free them was simply a 'Communist Conspiracy'.[49]

Not all black activists welcomed the campaign and the pan-Africanist, Ras Makonnen, argued that many blacks were 'embarrassed' by the 'artificial' imposition of American 'race positions' during the British Scottsboro Campaign.[50] However, George Padmore argued that the 'Scottsboro Affair' was significant in flagging a greater awareness of the international dimension of racism. It also inspired Nancy Cunard's *Negro Anthology* (1934), which includes a substantial section on Scottsboro, and sharpened the agenda of the Council for Promoting Equality and Civil Rights between White and Coloured People. This organisation was set up in late 1933, shortly after the controversy over Tshekedi Khama (Chapter 7), as a new collaborative initiative between the LAI and black activists. The council incorporated remnants of the disbanded ITUC-NW and members included Kenyatta, Cobina Kessie, Bridgeman and Natalie Koutane of the German Refugee Committee. Through organising lectures, issuing pamphlets and 'exploring channels of publicity', the council aimed to expose the iniquitous 'Bar of Colour' and 'the grave injustices of African people'. After the Italian invasion of Ethiopia in 1935, the council was merged into the International Association of the Friends of Abyssinia (IAFA).[51]

For the CPGB, Ethiopia was the 'cockpit' of the colonial struggles and a 'symbol' of the independence of African people. It was argued that the Ethiopian crisis illustrated the 'evils' of worldwide imperialism – the root cause of fascism and war. The LAI was active in the protest against the invasion, which led to accusations by non-communist critics that Bridgeman was the main instigator of the black unrest precipitated by the crisis.[52] But, the white Left failed to sustain interest in Ethiopia and the CPGB's 'anti-colonial' specialist, Rajani Palme Dutt, accused both Right and Left in Britain of having a 'largely unconscious, deeply ingrained … imperialist outlook' and reacting negatively to Ethiopia. Such attitudes led to growing black cynicism.[53]

By this time, however, a new organisation had emerged which spanned the communist and non-communist Left. The National Council of Civil Liberties (NCCL) developed a more consistently radical approach to race and colonial problems, which centred on the defence of the civil rights of blacks in Britain and the colonies. A 'non-political and non-religious organisation' formed in 1934 to 'promote democracy [and] assist in the maintenance of civil liberties, including freedom of speech, propaganda and assembly', founder members included E.M. Forster, the lawyer, D.N. Pritt, and Ronald Kidd, the secretary, who handled colonial issues. Other prominent members included Rebecca West, H.G. Wells, J.B. Priestley, Rose Macaulay, A.A. Milne, Bertrand Russell, Ethel Mannin, Arthur Creech Jones and Vera Brittain.[54] Groups affiliated to the NCCL were set up in the colonies, co-ordinated by the British Overseas Sub-committee, and black activists recommended the organisation to individuals seeking help and advice. Of all the British pressure groups concerned with Africa, the NCCL was arguably the least patronising and most consistently respected by black activists. Its progressive stance and strong opposition to the erosion of civil liberties in Britain and the empire led to accusations that it was a communist 'front' organisation. Although some NCCL members, like Reginald Bridgeman, had communist links, the organisation had parliamentary links and, in essence, remained fully committed to liberal democratic values.[55]

This broader, left-wing interest in imperialism was fuelled by German imperial aspirations. At a conference held in Battersea Town Hall in February 1937, attended by leading academics such as G.D.H. Cole and Harold Laski, a resolution was presented by S. Alley of the Colonial Seamen's Union calling for the unity of colonial and British workers in a 'Popular Front' against imperialism and fascism to oppose the German claims.[56] In July 1939, communists shared a platform with Leonard Barnes, Reginald Reynolds (ILP) and NCCL delegates at a 'Conference on the African Peoples, Democracy and World Peace', which was organised in London by the LCP, NWA, Coloured Film Artistes Association and the Gold Coast Students' Association. Speakers included Haile Selassie, Dr Harold Moody, H.G. Wells, Arthur Creech Jones and Stafford Cripps of the Socialist League. A resolution was unanimously passed against the appeasement of Germany in respect of demands for the return of her colonies (Chapter 10). The conference also condemned methods of colonial rule and the denial of civil liberties.[57]

By this time the LAI had lost its former momentum. Recalling the organisation in the later 1930s, Julius Lewin described it as a 'small outfit' which was a 'CP front organisation'.[58] Policies mirrored shifts in Comintern policy and *Colonial News*, which replaced *Anti-Imperialist Review* after 1934, placed more emphasis on anti-fascism and concern for the security of the Soviet Union. The International League had virtually collapsed in 1937 and the LAI merged with the new Colonial Information Bureau (CIB), which continued to co-ordinate activities and propaganda on race and colonial issues. From Spring 1937, the

CIB published a short, fortnightly journal, the *Colonial Information Bulletin* (CIB). CIB members attended a 'World Congress (Assembly) Against Racialism and Anti-Semitism' held in Paris at which Ronald Kidd of the NCCL delivered a speech on racial discrimination.[59] However, much black support had ebbed away by 1938 as African activists, like Kenyatta, became increasingly alienated from communism.

There are conflicting views about the links between black activists and communists after 1935. Howe (1993) maintains that a loose alliance of the ILP, Socialist League and IASB, centred around Reginald Reynolds, Diana Stock, George Padmore and Chris Braithewaite, was operating in rivalry with communist organisations from the late 1930s. Adi (1997) suggests that, after Comintern promptings, the CP stepped up its colonial work and, through the NWA, recruited its first West African member, J. Desmond Buckle, a Gold Coast medical student. However, the Comintern's 'Popular Front' against fascism undoubtedly marginalised colonial affairs and resulted in the liquidation of black organisations. The foremost black Comintern agent of the early 1930s, the Trinidadian, George Padmore, was expelled in 1935, although he remained a dangerous agitator in the eyes of the British Government as a radical pan-Africanist.[60] Such twists in policy led to accusations that communists had 'betrayed' the colonial people's struggle and that blacks were mere pawns in Stalin's cynical manoeuvres to defend the Soviet Union. Disillusionment was compounded by the CP's uncritical stance on the Nazi-Soviet Non-Aggression Pact, signed on 28 September 1939.[61]

The CIB, however, struggled on, maintaining a nominal black membership. Desmond Buckle, Kenyatta and Peter Blackman continued to attend 'inner cabinet meetings'.[62] The *Colonial Information Bulletin* was replaced in 1940 with *Inside the Empire*, a monthly review edited by Ben Bradley, which continued the *Bulletin's* dual emphasis on problems of colonial workers in both Britain and the colonies and anti-colonial propaganda. In 1945, it was changed again to *Inside the Empire Quarterly*, which focused on the 'welfare and liberation' of subject peoples. The CPGB Colonial Committee expanded and in 1944 a new policy document, *Colonies: The Way Forward*, was produced. But membership of the CIB rapidly dropped off after the outbreak of war and when, Arthur Clegg took over directorship, it was virtually defunct. In Howe's estimation, Left anti-colonialism did not really revive until the formation of the Movement for Colonial Freedom, which reconstituted the alliance of Left-imperialist elements established during the early days of the LAI. Fenner Brockway was prominent in this new organisation, but Bridgeman had disappeared from the scene and, in the new cold-war climate, communists and fellow travellers were not welcome.[63] Given the chequered nature of Left involvement in race and colonial questions, how did the white Left fare, in contrast to liberals, as 'champions of the oppressed'?

In evaluating the British Left response to race and colonial problems, it is important to recognise the deep-seated parochialism and apathy, which was revealed in a 1934 survey of trade unionists, co-operative societies, ILP members and academics. Attitudes to 'colonial liberation movements' proved to be 'extremely disappointing' even among the more 'politically advanced'. Moreover, like the reformists whom they so bitterly attacked, white communists had a tendency to label black activists as politically ignorant, unreliable opportunists who used CP funds for their own organisations or, worse still, personal gain.[64] In a decade when it was fashionable to adopt political causes, other issues vied for the commitment of the intellectual Left – Spain, China, Palestine, unemployment – while the rank and file, preoccupied with domestic issues, were unenthusiastic about the 'Negro question'. In comparison to the 'expatriates', with firsthand experience of African conditions, who acted as advisers for the reformist organisations, CPGB colonial analysts lacked direct experience and arguably adopted a stereotyped approach to African problems which failed to allow for the diversity of the colonial experience. A class analysis of racism was arguably more incisive and challenging than the woolly interracialism of liberal-reformists, but communist activists were also products of the ambient imperial culture. Recalling his expulsion from the Comintern, Padmore was scathing about British and American communist 'opportunists' and 'hypocrites' who were 'not entirely free' from prejudice and had alienated blacks from communism.[65]

Balanced against these weaknesses is the uphill battle that communist activists had in a hostile anti-Communist climate, with virtually no parliamentary support and subjected to regular police harassment. Pre-war CP membership never exceeded more than 18,000 and only reached *c*.55,000 at its peak in the Second World War. Thus, there was never any serious possibility of reversing the powerful tide of reformist and imperialist ideology which 'profoundly influenced the mental attitude of the British worker'.[66] In retrospect, radical black activists acknowledged the efforts of the British Left to tackle racism and colonial problems, despite the depth of racism among its own ranks. As Howe (1993) has pointed out, given the Labour Party's ambivalent record on colonial issues, many African nationalists who came to Britain turned to the CPGB which, 'for all its doctrinal shifts, seemed forthright in its anti-colonialism'.[67] While black intellectuals and activists rejected official communist organisations in the 1930s, they did not reject Marxism, conceding that it had some good points. Those who had visited the Soviet Union, like Robeson and Padmore, were impressed by the apparent lack of racism. Even after his break with communism, Padmore continued to admire some of the progress on literacy and development which had been made in the Soviet Union. Arthur Clegg recalls being shown around a Soviet Exhibition in London in 1941 by an enthusiastic Padmore.[68]

During the Second World War and the postwar period, Marxism arguably had a wider impact on black intellectuals. In 1947, the CPGB held a conference on the British Empire. Adi (1997) maintains that the party began to take a more active role in recruiting West African members. Several Gold Coast members of the London-based West African National Secretariat, including Nkrumah, were party members and during its brief life (1945–7) WANS was extremely active and worked closely with the British Communists in pursuing its goal of 'absolute independence for Africa'. These developments were reflected in growing Home Office concern that communists were 'a large element in the coloured population'.[69] The cold-war climate of the 1950s, in which many activists wrote their retrospective accounts of the period, may have induced a distorted picture and downplayed the importance of Marxism as a formative influence.

Marxism, liberalism, race and resistance: the balance sheet of the 1930s

In contrast to liberalism and reformist socialism, only Marxism offered a truly anti-imperialist perspective and a consistent and unqualified commitment to racial equality and colonial freedom from the pre-war period through to the present day. However, the orthodox Marxist interpretation of racism as inherent in, and subordinate to, class exploitation had deep flaws, which was recognised by the black intellectuals of the day and incisively critiqued in postwar academic literature. There are also deep inadequacies in the crude 'race versus class' dichotomy. As Anthias and Yuval Davis (1992) have demonstrated, this fails to account for the complex interactions of gender, ethnicity, class and nationalism which mediated social relations in both the colonial and metropolitan context. Despite these weaknesses, as Miles (1994) has pointed out, Marxist insights facilitated a reconceptualisation of racialism and race as ideological forces which, 'in conjunction with economic and political relations of domination, located certain populations in specific class positions' and structured the exploitation of black labour. Marxist perspectives facilitated a deeper understanding of what Pietersie (1990) has termed 'the domain of racial conflict', where racism was a 'function of [dialectical] struggle', generating resistance which, in turn, hardened racial perceptions and identifications.[70] Thus the most crucial difference between liberalism and Marxism was arguably in responses to black resistance. Where liberal-reformist multiracialism was directed towards minimising any potential conflict generated by resistance, Left-initiatives saw resistance as fundamental to challenging racism. This explains liberal fears that communist influence among blacks would generate further resistance and racial conflict. But how valid were these fears?

Black intellectual contact with Marxism was seminal in forging what Robinson (1983) has termed 'the black radical tradition'. For activists like Nkrumah, Marxism was crucial to their intellectual and political development. But, ultimately, neither Marxism nor liberalism provided black activists with an adequate ideological framework for political action. As stressed in Chapter 4, there is evidence that many African nationalists engaged only superficially with Marxist ideas or took advantage of communist support during a time when their causes were unpopular in Britain. This undoubtedly contributed to white communist allegations of black 'opportunism'. However, although Marxism was ultimately rejected by many black activists and intellectuals as culturally and theoretically inappropriate, in the process of elaborating an adequate theory of 'revolution for black people' there was an equal rejection of 'white' liberal democracy. As Paul Gilroy (1993) has demonstrated, black activists and intellectuals have always had an uneasy and complicated relationship with these competing 'white ideologies', which were both rooted in Western cultural and political development since the Enlightenment. As black activists became disenchanted with both liberal and Left support for their 'cause', they turned increasingly to a more culturally relevant pan-Africanism. This incorporated elements of Western liberalism and Marxism, but articulated a discourse of resistance which had wider mass appeal for blacks for whom theoretical discussions were meaningless.[71]

From a wider perspective, Marxism only attracted a small minority of black intellectuals, and Garveyist ideas have arguably had more widespread, long-term populist appeal. In the inter-war years, as Tabili (1995) has demonstrated, the mass of working-class blacks expressed resistance to imperial inequalities through practical, everyday practices, not intellectual debate.[72] The same could be argued for the majority of Africans. However, dialogue between black and white activists, liberal and Left, arguably widened and deepened the scope and possibilities of resistance. The ideological triad of liberalism, Marxism and pan-Africanism which framed black resistance strategies in the inter-war years remains relevant today. It informs stimulating and sometimes bitter debates over the nature of contemporary racism, the primacy of race or class in analysing racial oppression and whether the way forward is through black separatism or integration into 'white politics'. This underscores the fact that neither Marxism nor oppositional black discourses of liberation are monolithic and, as in the inter-war years, retain diverse and contradictory strands. The plethora of works, and the density and complexity of contemporary debates around race and racism, indicate that many issues raised in the inter-war years through dialogue between white and black activists remain unresolved.[73]

Whereas Marxism was arguably important in shaping the discourse of resistance, the significance of inter-war liberal initiatives on race is located primarily in the elaboration of a liberal, multiracialist 'race relations' discourse. Unlike Left initiatives, which arguably added greater urgency to 'safer strategies' to quell black discontent, multiracialist initiatives posed no threat to existing power structures. 'Race relations' discourse was thus 'respectable' and acceptable in imperial power circles. By 1941 the need for Britain to improve imperial race relations to secure the loyalty of the colonised for the war effort was accepted in principle by the British Government. Britain cherished its image as a liberal and tolerant country. Liberal commitment to racial equality became official policy, although, as suggested in Chapter 8, deep contradictions existed between rhetoric and reality. Thus, argues Holmes (1986), it is vital to challenge the 'much vaunted and often trumpeted virtues of liberty and tolerance' celebrated by many historians. As Malik (1996) points out liberal race discourse emerged when blacks became more race conscious and cruder racial arguments could no longer be openly expressed – a point clearly illustrated in my own analysis of liberal initiatives. Assessing the significance of this shift in official policy and discourse, Tabili (1996) concludes that the main outcome was that the liberal establishment could now blame racism on the white working classes, thus deflecting attention from the continuing role of the state in the institutionalisation of racism.[74]

Inter-war 'race relations' discourse, with its stress on assimilation of those 'fit for citizenship', was clearly a product of the imperialist ethos of the time, but it paved the way for the liberal multiculturalism of the 'post colonial' era articulated through academic sociology and the 'race relations industry'. This emerged in the 1950s when it became apparent that the philanthropic welfare initiatives in the paternalist, voluntaristic tradition of the pre-war era were inadequate to tackle the problems created by the new 'alien wedge' of postwar migration from the Caribbean. However, as Miles (1994) has pointed out, until 1958 race relations continued to be viewed as a 'colonial problem' in that problems festering in the colonies had been transferred to the 'mother country'. This was reflected in the pioneering studies of 'dark strangers' in Britain by, for instance, Shiela Patterson (1962) and Elspeth Huxley (1964), which were clearly influenced by the authors' experiences of 'race problems' in the empire.[75] As Malik (1996) has demonstrated, implicit assumptions about the superiority of Western culture remained embedded in postwar 'race relations' discourse. Thus, early liberal academic race relations literature emphasised the need for the assimilation of black migrants into white society. The goal, emphasised Patterson, was to minimise conflict and to promote racial 'harmony' through cultural integration, which would ensure a 'peaceable society'. A migrant group, which refused to accommodate the 'receiving societies' norms', presented the 'receiving society' with an 'insoluble problem'.[76]

The Institute of Race Relations (IRR), founded in 1958 under the directorship of Philip Mason, also reflects links with the pre-war era. Like the South African Institute of Race Relations (founded in 1929), IRR research was heavily influenced by US theories and anthropological perspectives. Moreover, the organisation was an offshoot of the Royal Institute, which had been prominent in imperial affairs before the war, and continued to locate race problems in Britain in the wider international context. Between 1958–68, the IRR dominated the liberal 'race relations industry' until the directorship was ousted by a Left 'coup' in 1968. Under the new direction of Archie Sivanandan, a more radical perspective on racism and resistance was adopted which reprioritised links between institutionalised racism, capitalism and the legacy of colonialism which had been erased from contemporary liberal sociological analyses. But Marxist approaches to race have remained marginalised. Miles (1994) argues that influential academics like Michael Banton, one of the original architects of the 'race relations paradigm', continue to reject the concept of racism, and focus on the eradication of particular practices of discrimination.[77]

Critiques of liberal 'race relations' or multiculturalist discourse have tended to focus exclusively on the post-Second World War era. However, the origins of the discourse, which borrowed heavily from US race relations theory, are clearly rooted in an imperial context when practical liberal initiatives were arguably primarily directed to defusing black resistance through mild reforms. From its inception, liberal race discourse made problematic assumptions about race, culture and equality, and evaded the root causes of racism. The involvement of liberals in race problems thus arguably had as much to do with defining their own whiteness and defending the status quo as tackling black problems. In this context, race relations initiatives and institutions, argues Katznelson (1984), acted as 'buffer institutions' between the state and black minorities, which were directed to preventing conflict and defusing black protest and resistance. Such institutions, observes Goldberg (1993), also perpetuated racist beliefs by the very nature of their 'formative principles'.[78] The incorporation of the 'race relations paradigm' into official policy on race during and after the Second World War was arguably the legacy of inter-war liberal initiatives on the race problem, a legacy that has perpetuated rather than resolved the problem of racism in 'post-colonial' societies.

Summary

The emergence of a pressing 'colour problem' in Britain pushed both liberal-reformists and the Left into taking action. For both political constituencies the colour problem was seen as inseparable from the 'colonial problem'. However, the Left adopted a global perspective which hitched initiatives on race to anti-capitalist and anti-imperialist struggles. Liberals adopted a more fudged and piecemeal approach that was informed by humanitarian concern and evolving liberal race discourse, but also by the need to ward off communist and other extremist influences in black organisations. Although black activists and intellectuals had serious criticisms of the white Left and problems with the Eurocentric basis of Western Marxism, they arguably found the paternalistic and implicitly racist approach of liberal-reformism more problematic. Given their implicit assumptions about assimilation into white culture, liberal-reformists may indeed be seen as 'closet racists'. In the context of the era, however, the ideas and attitudes of a minority were genuinely progressive. Blacks had to find their own path to liberation, but activists from the 1930s acknowledged that certain individuals, liberals and left-wingers, had championed the black cause – denouncing racism and colonialism when it was not 'fashionable'. These included E.D. Morel, John Harris, Norman Leys, Sylvia Pankhurst, Ethel Mannin, Fenner Brockway, Creech Jones, Dorothy Woodman of the Union of Democratic Control, Roden Buxton, Reginald Bridgeman, Nancy Cunard and Diana Stock, editor of the *Socialist Review* and, for a time, a companion of Jomo Kenyatta.[79] Furthermore, dialogue with whites of all political views stimulated important developments in black consciousness and African nationalism. In the later 1930s, developments concerning the 'race problem' at the heart of empire coalesced with the growth of resistance in Africa and the Caribbean into a more forceful clamour of diverse black and white voices that challenged imperialism. Winds of change blew more strongly, threats to empire mounted and the imperial government was forced to re-orientate policy towards its African empire, which is the focus of my final chapter.

10 The winds of change

Towards a new imperialism in Africa?

In England ... there is news of Africa everywhere: in the press, in the schools, in the films, in conversation. English people are actively interested in Africa. Members of families are out in Africa in the Civil Service, in the military, in business; everywhere you go, someone's uncle, brother or cousin is ... teaching, administering, or 'serving' in Africa. Women go out to Africa with their men. ... There are courses on Africa in every good University ... Everywhere there is information about Africa.

(Eslanda Goode Robeson, 1936)

The British Empire is the only 'bloc' of countries which stands four-square against Chaos, in a world rapidly growing madder and madder ... racked between rival ideologies.

(*Empire Problems*, 1938)

The political ferment ... in Africa ... cannot now be arrested ... it must be channelled into constructive purposes.

(Arthur Creech Jones, Colonial Secretary, *c*.1948)[1]

As stressed in Chapter 1, after the First World War, both official and popular discourse assumed that British rule in Africa would endure into the distant future. These dreams of imperial power were premised on a belief in African 'backwardness', representations of the non-settler colonies as a tranquil colonial backwater and support for white settler rule in South and East Africa. The foregoing chapters have demonstrated how this dream of power was consistently challenged by black resistance in both the colonial hinterland and heartland. I have also traced the allied interventions of white communist activists, liberal 'friends of the black man' and anti-colonialist critics in emergent 'race and colonial questions'. However, before 1935, African problems were rarely included in the political agenda of the imperial parliament and criticisms of the principles and workings of colonial rule generally went unheeded. This situation changed during the late 1930s as the growth of resistance in the colonial hinterland, combined with developments in international imperialism, refocalised

Africa at the crux of debates over imperial policy. Africa was brought into the heart of mainstream politics in the imperial parliament.

These interrelated developments forced the pace of change as the Second World War approached, resulting in a perceptible shift in colonial policy towards development and progress towards self-rule. The Lugardian vision of trusteeship and indirect rule was now viewed as anachronistic and the criticisms of the 'dissident' liberal and reformist 'African activists' were increasingly incorporated into official discourse. But, while these changes represented a marked shift in the imperial relationship, imperial policy makers held on to their dreams of power in Africa through new 'empire strengthening' strategies. As British power in India was more consistently undermined and, the 'have nots', Italy, Germany and Japan, demanded a slice of the global imperial pie, retention of the African Empire became essential to the continuation of Britain's great power status. Strains of empire deepened further during the Second World War, compounded by the growth of US power, but dreams of imperial power persisted through 'inter-imperial' co-operation on African development.

This chapter, then, examines how Africa was transformed from a 'tranquil backwater' to a continent which, as Eslanda Goode Robeson observed, was 'news' everywhere. It charts the influences that redefined the relationship between Africa and the West, confirmed in the post-First World War settlement (Chapter 1), and thus grounds my analysis once more in the wider context of global power relations. The main focus is on discourses of power in the imperial heartland and why and how these changed in response to international developments and African demands for self-determination and racial equality. It addresses the key question of how the imperialist mission was sustained in an era of global instability, war and clamorous pressures for change in the imperial hinterland. The complexities of decolonisation are beyond the scope of this study. However, this concluding chapter does address the domestic, colonial and 'inter-imperial' conflicts of interests which led to the dismantling of Britain's formal African Empire. In charting these developments, I focus first on the contribution of Britain's liberal and reformist 'Conscience on Africa'[2] in shifting the agenda on race and imperialism. Second, I assess 'empire strengthening' tactics that were deployed to offset the potential 'chaos' of new global and imperial uncertainties and the challenge of African resistance. I conclude with a review of developments during the Second World War when Africa impinged even more persistently on official and popular consciousness as 'the end of the jolly old empire' became more of a reality. I argue that the growth of mass African nationalism strengthened trends towards colonial development though 'partnership' between Britain and her dependencies, but behind the liberal rhetoric, racist perceptions of Africa remained strongly ingrained in popular and official consciousness. This facilitated postwar 'empire strengthening' in Africa, now supported by the US, which continued to interrupt African dreams of freedom.

I begin my analysis with the dissident voices of the broad spectrum of critics of colonialism, because, like a Greek chorus, they have echoed through the previous chapters, commenting 'in the wings' on imperial problems. Although their practical campaigns arguably failed, African activists were well-connected and their ideas were ultimately smoothly incorporated into official discourses. In contrast to Marxist anti-imperialism, which constituted a direct threat to imperialism and was an important stimulus to 'empire strengthening', the dissident discourses of the critics of colonialism and 'friends of the native' were famed within the broader discourses of imperial power and posed no threat to empire. Most critics of colonialism retained a belief in the 'higher ideals' of empire and trusteeship and, thus, differed from the post-Second World War anti-colonialist constituency that supported African independence, the main focus of Stephen Howe's study.[3] Inter-war critics did not want to dismantle empire, but wanted to transform it into a British Commonwealth – premised on liberal values of progress towards modernity and 'equality for all civilised men' – a vision that was also shared by progressive liberal imperialists. Differences did exist, but dialogue between progressive imperialists and 'dissidents' was an essential formative phase in the reorientation of imperial policy.

'Britain's conscience on Africa': challenging imperial orthodoxy

Until the mid-1930s, critics of colonialism were voices in the wilderness. Individuals who championed the 'native cause', mainly earnest, middle-class intellectuals and 'doers', dubbed the 'Foreign Legion' by contemporaries, faced a formidable task and admitted that there was still 'great public ignorance' about African affairs.[4] As stressed in Chapter 1, the mainstream Labour Movement was arguably as committed to imperialism as the Conservative Party. The main link with parliamentary politics was through the few sympathetic Liberal and Labour MPs, who would raise questions in Parliament, or via the Labour Party Advisory Committee on Imperial Questions (LPACIQ), whose members included Leonard Woolf, Charles Roden Buxton, Sidney Olivier, Henry Polak, Norman Leys, William Macmillan and Julius Lewin – 'Africa activists' who have figured prominently in foregoing chapters.[5] In this climate of apathy, initiatives on Africa were fragmented and piecemeal, and the only major campaign of significance was the support for the trade unionist William Ballinger's work in South Africa (Chapter 7). Arguably, the only British organisation to maintain a substantial and consistent interest in the 'native problem' in Africa was the Anti-Slavery and Aborigines Protection Society.[6] From 1926 onwards, however, there was growing criticism of 'white settler policies' in East and South Africa. With great foresight, Leonard Woolf argued that the idea that South Africa or Kenya could be 'permanently converted' into a white man's country was 'a dream of political insanity', an insanity which could be delivered upon the heads of settlers' children in the third or fourth generation. However, 'no acute problem' was perceived to exist in West Africa, except in the 'relatively unimportant mines and plantations'. With only minority dissent, the concept of trusteeship was fully endorsed, as was the need to prevent 'subversive ideas' from replacing traditional values as modernity impinged on African societies.[7]

The election of a Labour Government in 1929 brought new hopes and the Prime Minister was urged to maintain a 'high standard of justice' in colonial territories in view of a 'healthy and growing public opinion'.[8] In 1930, the LPACIQ created a forum for Labour activists interested in colonial issues and the National Fabian Research Bureau (NFRB), established in the same year, was steered towards greater interest in Africa by the trade unionist, Arthur Creech Jones. Despite these initiatives, in office, Labour proved a disappointment and the bulk of MPs, with the exception of individuals like Ellen Wilkinson and Drummond Shiels, who was Under Secretary of State for Colonies, 1929–31, remained indifferent to African affairs. There was a deterioration of conditions in black Africa as the economic downturn, precipitated by the Wall Street Crash, kicked in. In 1932, the ASAPS registered its 'grave concern' over the 'growth of repression', which was 'without precedent'.[9] However, with developments in the 1930s the fragmented 'conscience on Africa' merged into a more consistent and vocal minority. How was this concern over African problems transformed into practical action and what impact did it have on official policy, if any?

During the 1920s, most individuals and organisations interested in colonial affairs had co-operated with, or worked through, the official Labour Movement. After 1930, there was more independent action. The Union of Democratic Control (UDC), which made a clear link between the 'colonial problem' and issues of peace and democracy, began to take a more active part in African issues when Dorothy Woodman became secretary in 1931.[10] With its good parliamentary connections it proved a useful ally to new pressure groups specifically focused on Africa, like the London Group on African Affairs (LGAA) and the 'Friends of Africa', whose interventions in race and colonial problems have already been discussed in previous chapters. Such groups paralleled the larger India-focused groups, which were established in the early 1930s, like the moderate India League and the more radical 'Friends of India'. However, West Africa still aroused little interest in Parliament and 'Africa activists' continued to focus their energies on the South African 'native problem' and the entrenchment of white settler rule in East Africa.[11] The imperial government had continuously supported white settlers not only in Kenya, but also in Nyasaland (now Malawi) and Northern and Southern Rhodesia (now Zambia and Zimbabwe). Critics of government policies protested this erosion of native rights in South and East Africa, and stressed the urgent need to reassert the moral basis of empire. The settlers had powerful parliamentary allies, who sympathised with the problems they faced, and it was still widely believed that only vigorous white settlement could develop East Africa. The imperial government, argued Hailey (1956), thus found it increasingly difficult to reconcile its commitment to the 'paramountcy' of native interests with its recognition of the important role white settlers played in developing the East African colonies.[12]

Hailey rejected the idea that the government was biased towards settlers, but contemporary critics took a different position. Bias, they argued, was clearly evident in a proposed BBC series on East Africa and controversy over the content of the programmes channelled concern into concrete action. Winifred Holtby and

Norman Leys, who had worked for the medical services in Kenya and Nyasaland before retiring to England in 1918, mounted a publicity campaign and wrote to the liberal press. They argued that programme content was biased towards white settlers and presented a 'misleading picture' of the lives of modern Africans. Furthermore, proposed speakers, who included the South African Prime Minister, General Herzog, were mainly opponents of native rights, suggesting that the BBC endorsed segregation. In consultation with LGAA members a letter was finally sent to *The Times*, although it still had not been published by November – a factor attributed to the 'strong public opinion' in favour of the white settlers.[13]

The series, 'Africa and the Dark Continent', was finally broadcast in December 1930. General Herzog was excluded, but there were no other modifications, highlighting the role of the media in reinforcing dominant values about empire and the superiority of white culture. However, the campaign against the entrenchment of white rule persisted and the UDC, supported by other organisations, sponsored a visit to England by the Kenyan Kikuyu activists, Parmenas Githendu Mockerie and Jomo Kenyatta, to speak before the 1931 Joint Parliamentary Committee Upon Closer Union in East Africa in defence of African rights. Mockerie and Kenyatta attended a Fabian summer school and Mockerie's book, published in 1934 and described by Julian Huxley as 'a rare indictment of British administration from the native perspective', allegedly had a strong impact on liberal opinion, strengthening campaigns against white settler rule.[14]

After 1930, the liberal 'conscience' began to prick more consistently at the imperial power centre, which placed African issues more firmly on the political agenda. By the mid-1930s, Africanist networks had expanded and good crosslinks were established with the Royal Geographic Society, the Royal African Society and 'progressive' liberal imperialists. Macmillan and other African 'experts' spoke at monthly meetings of the 'African Circle' (connected to the Royal Empire Society, which was refounded in 1928 out of the older Royal Colonial Institute).[15] However, the 'Circle' remained essentially conservative, as did the other 'empire strengthening' cliques that were influenced by Round Table liberalism (Chapter 1). It was thus mainly the more cautious liberals of the LGAA who had connections with the progressive imperialists of the 'African Circle'. The more trenchant critics of colonialism were thus frequently at odds with the more cautious liberals in the LGAA and 'progressive' imperialists, such as Margery Perham. They had initially supported the LGAA in the belief that its 'nucleus of influential people' lent an aura of respectability to the African cause, but now argued that the organisation's cautious approach rendered 'concerted political action' impossible.[16] These divisions led to the foundation of the Friends of Africa (FOA), which was formed in 1934 to consolidate the more *ad hoc* African Group, which had focused primarily on South African problems (Chapter 7). The FOA tried to revive flagging interest in the 'native problem' and, although co-operation with the LGAA continued on certain important issues, adopted a more openly political perspective, maintaining contacts with the Socialist League and the left-wing publishers, Gollancz.

Small advances were thus made before 1935 in the articulation of criticisms of colonial policies and in forging links with black activists. But activism was fragmented, lacked ideological coherence and failed to win the support of any mainstream political forums. After the brief flurry of interest in the early 1930s, any wider interest in African problems waned. In 1932, Geoffrey Dawson, the editor of *The Times*, wrote to William Macmillan that the paper had 'so much hay on its fork' that it did not want to revive the 'native problem' for the present time. By 1936 the 'African Circle' was abandoned due to 'paucity of attendance'.[17] Veteran activists were disillusioned and depressed. Norman Leys warned another 'outcast', William Ballinger, of the danger of 'sticking your hands' into politics and retrieving them 'empty and burnt'. Segregation became more deeply entrenched in the white settler colonies, the government encouraged further migration and settlers, an 'island in a sea of black', were given greater autonomy in implementing measures to prevent the erosion of 'the white shores'.[18] So where did the critics of colonialism make an impact? Arguably, in the less controversial area of colonial development in West Africa and other 'non-settler' colonies where their ideas on colonial reform were more compatible with progressive imperialist discourse.

Dialogues between critics of colonialism, pioneering academic Africanists and progressive imperialists intensified during the 1930s with a greater awareness of emergent race consciousness in 'non-settler' colonies. Such dialogues were germane to the framing of new agendas on Africa, which began with the growing scrutiny of the system of indirect rule. Summing up the key areas of debate, the LGAA's *Africana* pointed out:

> There is at present a great divergence of opinion as to whether Africans should be encouraged to develop along the lines of their own culture or to be assimilated into a European system of civilisation. A great deal of unnecessary difficulty has arisen through regarding these two policies as mutually exclusive. This problem is of course fundamental to race relations.[19]

The main points of difference between the critics and progressive imperialists arose over the pace and nature of African development. Until the late 1930s, 'trusteeship' and the need for Europeans to act as 'political midwives' in Africa was not seriously challenged, even by the most radical critics. The Labour Movement continued to endorse the League of Nations mandate system (Chapter 1) and even left-wingers, like Leonard Barnes, defended the 'man in the field' for having 'lightened the burden' of the African. Fabian 'modernisers' were critical of colonial 'backwardness' and poverty, but their proposals to develop 'habits of industry' among natives through education, trade unions and co-operative organisations added little to the paternalist discourse of progressive imperialists.[20] The main dilemma for both progressive imperialists and critics was how to reconcile the need for some kind of European tutelage with the liberal principle of equal rights for educated blacks.

This raised thorny questions relating to the 'colour question', which was the

cause of much colonial unrest. For Leonard Barnes, the colour problem was a 'crucial test' of empire which had received inadequate consideration in informed circles. He linked racial oppression to economic oppression, but it was the liberal, progressive, imperialist analysis, as advocated by Margery Perham, that was incorporated into official policy. This prioritised 'individual race humiliation', not colonial oppression, as the cause of heightened race consciousness – a situation that could be harmoniously redressed by placating the intelligentsia.[21]
Perham's stature as a 'progressive' colonial expert grew under the patronage of powerful men like Lugard and she became a leading authority on Africa, as well as an accomplished BBC broadcaster, with an easy access to *The Times* and other influential publications denied to more critical voices. The vision of enlightened liberal imperialism, promoted by the Round Table Group, arguably appealed to the sympathetic 'feminine nature' of women colonial experts, and Perham was more open to new ideas and dialogue with educated Africans than her male counterparts. She reputedly had a 'passionate concern for progress towards racial equality' and 'a strong consciousness of race', condemning the popular representation of Africans as 'a huge, incomprehensible, vaguely menacing mass'. However, her prime concern was to avoid 'Indian difficulties' in Africa through placating 'frustrated' nationalism. As Gertzel (1991) notes, her concern was mainly for the African intelligentsia and her 'candid' descriptions of Africans were not always complimentary.[22]

Perham was arguably instrumental in catalysing new thinking about the problems of indirect rule. Many imperialist 'eminents', including Lord Lugard, attended an address she gave to the Royal Society of Arts in 1934. Critics, like Macmillan, and representatives of the African intelligentsia, including a Nigerian woman, 'Miss Thomas ... the first African woman to be called to the bar', also participated in the discussion, which revealed 'the spectrum of ideas on African administration held in 1934'. Here we have clear evidence of a shift from a white colonial monologue to an 'interracial' dialogue with privileged blacks. Such reappraisals of colonial policy had little impact on the Colonial Office, but African issues began to figure more prominently in parliamentary debates. In 1935, a conference on African Groups brought together 'experts' of all political persuasions to press for more research, improved welfare and better information to counteract public ignorance. Difference of opinion existed over policy between reformist socialists and more conservative delegates, but a Consultative Committee on African Affairs was set up to co-ordinate action and liaise between different groups.[23]

After 1935, the dissident discourses thus moved more firmly into the mainstream orbit of imperial affairs. An important trigger to new thinking on Africa was the serious labour disturbances in the West Indies in 1937–8, which aroused more widespread concern over the poor conditions and lack of development in Britain's 'tropical empire'. The Caribbean had long been marginalised from British consciousness, but now there was a shift towards analysing Africa and African diaspora problems as interrelated. This approach was pioneered by William Macmillan, who, during a visit to the West Indies in 1934, observed that the 'groundswell of discontent' in Jamaica was a warning for Africa. He found the Jamaican peasantry 'scandalously exploited' – a 'shattering' commentary on the capitalist system'. 'I was trying to find a model colony', he wrote to Norman Leys, ' ... I'm sadly dashed and much more unrepentantly socialist'.[24] The record of his visit was published in a neutralised format in Macmillan's *Warning From the West Indies: A Tract for Africa and the Empire* (1936), which was recommended by *Labour Monthly* for its 'conscientious exposure' of poverty and exploitation. However, he was no radical at heart and opposed Left idealists who wanted to push self-government too soon onto 'helpless' people.[25] His emphasis on gradualism and empirical research found particular favour in Fabian and Labour Party circles from 1937. With the growth of labour unrest there was more careful social research into colonial problems. Fabians advocated improved welfare and concessions to colonial trade unions and the African intelligentsia as a 'safety valve' to prevent extremism and rebellion.[26]

Arguably, a combination of pressure from concerned individuals in Britain and African resistance was beginning to shift the agenda on race and empire. This was reflected in a greater number of publications devoted to African problems. As Howe (1993) notes, it is difficult to estimate the impact of dissident or anti-colonial discourse on changes in imperial policy as such discourses are not dealt with in any depth in relevant historical studies. The small minority of 'African activists' have been dismissed as 'voices in the wilderness' or simply cranks and eccentrics. Yet, the critics of imperial orthodoxy arguably had a more significant long-term impact than has previously been acknowledged. In retrospect, Perham acknowledges the 'seers and prophets', such as J.A. Hobson, E.D. Morel and Leonard Woolf, to whom British public opinion should have been more 'responsive'. This contrasts with her predictably antagonistic assessment of Marxist anti-imperialists whose ideas, she argues, were regarded as 'utterly inapplicable' by those concerned with bringing civilised development to 'the gross poverty and disorder of tribal Africa'. She thus concludes that 'Liberal and Socialist politicians and writers' played a major part in the forward movement of thought and productive dialogue with Africans, although, she added, it should not be forgotten that 'there was [also] a liberalism of this kind on the Conservative side ... [which included] some men of high authority in the colonial service'.[27]

Ultimately, it was international events and the quickening of the pace of African nationalism that forced a more comprehensive reappraisal of Britain's relationship with Africa. With these wider developments, ideas that had been thrashed out by the critical minority arguably became more influential as African problems permeated more widely into public consciousness. In 1935, Sir Edward Grigg, a Conservative MP who was Governor of Kenya from 1925–31, attacked the 'ceaseless propaganda' in circulation which alleged that the colonial system was 'pure exploitation', dangerous ideas that were 'infiltrating' the universities, influencing 'larger numbers of our younger men' and could 'undermine' the peace of the empire. Perham also remarked on a 'growing body of informed opinion in England' which watched colonial problems 'keenly'.

From the left-wing perspective, there was now an 'increasing number', drawn from all sections of Britain, who, while not prepared to stand out for complete independence, were 'willing to give their support to ... the struggles of colonial peoples to achieve elementary rights'.[28] The key to wider recognition of the minority views of pioneering critics after 1935 was the dovetailing of imperialism, fascism and colonial unrest, which threatened the old imperial certainties and brought Africa firmly back into the mainstream imperial agenda. Responses to these new challenges to empire were twofold: a more clamorous criticism of existing colonial policies and new 'empire strengthening' tactics.[29] These contradictory responses fused in a creative tension that culminated in a reorientation of imperial policy.

1935 to 1939: empire in Africa redefined or undermined?

Troubled times rendered imperial policy a political quagmire. The government became more reactionary and vacillating, adding extra bite to widening divisions over Britain's imperial role in Africa.[30] In 1936, Perham identified three major problems in Africa: how to give space to educated Africans in a system designed for 'backward masses'; how to reconcile the clashes between white settlers and blacks who had been 'detribalised though industrialisation'; and finally, how to respond to the demands of the 'have nots', Germany and Italy, which posed threats to the existing imperial system. These threats were manifest in the 1935 Italian invasion of Abyssinia (Ethiopia) and German claims for the return of colonies lost in the peace settlement after the First World War. Any recommendations that Britain and France should freely share the advantages of trusteeship with the 'have nots', argued Perham, would be the 'first stage to the internationalisation of imperialism' which could 'deprive' it of its present attractions.[31] The new imperialist scramble of the 'have nots' was an ugly harbinger of war and revealed the more naked economic basis of imperial expansion. The primary concern of the British Government was the defence of empire. Cain and Hopkins (1993) thus see the 1930s as a period when the 'imperial problem' became acutely mirrored in a renascent imperialism in Africa, South America and China. Where Africa was concerned, they argue, the problem was not so much African nationalism, but how to accommodate the 'have not' nations and the increasing intervention of the 'anti-colonial' US without weakening the empire. Although Cain and Hopkins perhaps underestimate the importance of African resistance in compounding Britain's imperial dilemmas, international imperial collusion over the Italian invasion of Ethiopia supports their analysis of British responses to the internationalisation of imperialism.[32]

'See no Abyssinia, hear no Abyssinia, speak no Abyssinia' blazed a cartoon caption in the *Evening Standard* in summer 1935 – an ironic comment on the high media profile of the crisis. 'Abyssinia was news' declared Evelyn Waugh. Waugh, who had attended Emperor Haile Selassie's coronation in 1930, was sent as a correspondent to cover the invasion and found himself part of a 'mob of the worlds' press' in Addis Ababa, the imperial capital. Though his representations of the country are viewed through his own cultural prism, his writings are alive and vivid, charting the collapse of the only independent African state (Liberia was basically an informal US colony). The violation of this deeply symbolic state, remarked Macmillan, aroused a 'tremendous awakening' throughout the black diaspora. Everywhere the 'old, cheerful subservience' was giving way to 'a new touchiness … to suspicion [of whites] verging on hostility' as Africans entered a 'troublesome adolescence'. In 'native' newspapers linkages were made between the oppression in Ethiopia and South Africa, with cartoons equating Mussolini with General Herzog.[33] The profound impact of the invasion on black resistance in Africa and Britain has already been covered in previous chapters. How did these developments impact on imperial discourse? In pro-imperial circles, India still remained a top priority, but Africa was placed much more firmly on the political agenda as fears grew that 'nascent race feeling', inspired by the invasion, 'would arise faster in Africa … than in Asia'. Reginald Coupland, Beit Professor of Colonial History at Oxford, warned that unless European notions of biological superiority were abandoned, there would be a major 'conflict of colour'.[34]

However, the response of the League of Nations and the British Government to the war between the Italians and Ethiopians, which broke out on 3 October 1935, disappointed black critics and their British supporters. The League of Nations imposed ineffective sanctions against Mussolini and Anthony Eden, the Secretary of State for Foreign Affairs, evaded any clear statement on policy. The British Government was embarrassed rather than sympathetic when Selassie fled Ethiopia to plead his case at the League of Nations and, supported by the French, tried to secure a commitment that he would not engage in any 'political or diplomatic action'. As the Labour MP, Eleanor Rathbone, observed, Selassie was expected to visit Britain 'incognito' rather than as a 'visiting sovereign or a monarch in exile'.[35] Such responses were conditioned not only by alleged fears of the conflict escalating, but by contemporary racist discourses. In contrast to 'barbaric' Ethiopia, the Italians were a civilised power who had been humiliated by their defeat by Minilik II in 1896, an event that Lauren (1996) argues was a general 'blow to Western pride'. Although reluctantly admitted to the League of Nations, as stressed in Chapter 1, Ethiopia was represented by Europeans as a backward state that still practised slavery. Thus, pro-imperialists argued that for the exploited non-Amharic people, who had been absorbed into the Ethiopian Amharic empire, a change from Ethiopian 'misgovernment' to rule by a 'civilised power' would be a 'merciful deliverance'.[36]

Ethiopia may have been the last African empire, but it was no match for the Western, imperial powers. Both Italy and Britain had carved out spheres of influence within the country since 1919 and, despite protests from the Ethiopians, had violated their obligations under the Treaty of Versailles. The country had thus long been vulnerable to the penetration of Western technology and capitalism. Sbacchi (1985) argues that the Italians simply exploited these weaknesses, including ethnic tensions within the empire, and berates the cynicism, expediency and racism of the European powers in failing to act against the brutality of the Italian invasion. Rather than opposing the invasion, Britain formally recognised Mussolini as 'Emperor of Abyssinia' in November 1938. British interests in Ethiopia were strengthened after 1941 when the British Army liberated both Ethiopia and Italian Somaliland from Italian Fascist rule. At this point, Perham argues, there was a temptation for Britain to annex the country and British political officers were dispersed through the provinces. However, imperial policy makers were now more sensitive to Ethiopia's significance to Africans and 'caution prevailed'.[37]

In the absence of a positive response from the government, sympathetic liberals established an Abyssinian Refugees Relief Fund, which was set up to aid individual victims of the invasion.[38] Some progressive imperialists, like Margery Perham, were also shocked by the invasion and consideration in official circles of a re-division of the colonies to satisfy the 'have nots'. At a conference held in London in October 1935, organised by the National Peace Council, these problems were discussed by an important cross-section of African 'experts', including Lord Lothian, representing the Round Table clique, Barnes, Macmillan, Roden Buxton, the anthropologist, Lucy Mair, John Harris (ASAPS) and Reginald Bridgeman of the LAI. However, a black delegate, Arnold Ward of the Negro Workers' Association accused liberal delegates of being preoccupied with peace in Europe and showing little real concern for the problems of Africa and the threat to Ethiopia.[39] There was some justification in these criticisms, given the fact that responses to the German Fascist threat, seen as particularly threatening to colonised people, were also overwhelmingly concerned with placating Germany and the defence of empire.

Claims for the return of German colonies lost through the 1919 Treaty of Versailles stimulated important new debates about the value of colonies. Hitler had been initially disinterested in reclaiming the colonies, but after 1936 German claims were voiced 'with ever-increasing emphasis'. Hitler now demanded 'unconditional surrender' to Germany of her pre-war colonies and the German imperial dream of 'Mittel-Afrika' was revived.[40] British imperialists were forced to justify why Britain should have colonies when Germany (and Italy and Japan) also had valid claims based on access to raw materials and markets. This focalised the economic benefits of empire to Britain. 'The African colonies', declared Sir Edward Grigg, were a 'valuable asset' – a field of 'absolutely safe investment'. Out of total revenues from African colonies, 75 per cent was spent in a manner that 'directly' benefited Britain. As an 'integral part' of its policy of appeasement, the government was now prepared to discuss concessions to 'other powers', who believed 'undue restrictions' had been placed on international trade through Britain's system of imperial preference. Another powerful reason for concessions, argued Leonard Barnes, was that the government and powerful establishment intellectuals saw Hitler as a 'bulwark to Communism'.[41]

In December 1938, there was a major parliamentary debate on the future of the colonies. This was prompted by a motion proposed by the Labour MP, Philip Noel Baker, who warned that Hitler's treatment of the Jews was a 'grave warning' on how the 'inferior races' would be treated under German rule and proposed an extension of the international mandate system. The Secretary of State for Colonies, Malcolm MacDonald, acknowledged a growing anxiety in the African colonies, where rumours of proposed transfer had resulted in 'mass protests' and a 'paralysing insecurity' which had affected development. The motion was defeated, although MacDonald later affirmed that the British Government was not contemplating any transfer without giving 'full attention to the views of the inhabitants'.[42] The radical black activist, George Padmore, condemned this 'hypocritical cant', which extended to 'Labour imperialists', and claimed that the British Empire was the 'Worst Racket Yet invented by Man' (see Illustration 23).[43]

Writing in 1956, Hailey assessed the German claims as one of the most disturbing features of European politics before the Second World War, and argued that proposals for the internationalisation of colonies gained widespread support in Britain. However, this support was not unanimous, even in imperialist circles. The conservative Colonial League, whose members included Leo Amery and Lord Lugard, which was founded to promote to the public the importance of the British Empire, was opposed to any concessions to Germany. They disagreed with the government's policy of 'retreat' and advocated strengthening Britain's defences and, thus, the empire in which many members had personal vested interests. Leo Amery demolished the economic and moral arguments for considering the German claims, arguing that any concessions would constitute a crime against 'helpless peoples', and alienate the Commonwealth, France and the US. The Union of South Africa also opposed the claims, although this was linked to demands that South West Africa should be administered as a fifth province of the Union.[44]

Similarly, the 'German colonies question' widened rifts between more radical African experts and the Labour Party, who advocated concessions to Germany as a policy of appeasement. Leonard Barnes was deeply critical of Arthur Creech Jones' proposals that colonial territories should be pooled and managed by an international civil service to safeguard equal access to trade and raw materials for all [civilised] countries. Like communist critics, he argued that colonies should be 'freed not pooled' and warned against the spectre of 'international imperialism' and more 'systematic colonial exploitation.'[45] Barnes' earlier writings retained a faith in the moral duty of empire and the trusteeship of the League of Nations, but when this was violated he shifted towards a more openly anti-imperialist position, rejected Empire Day 'bunk' and became more sympathetic to the Marxist-Leninist analysis of colonial oppression, although he rejected Bolshevik tactics. Pointing to the 'mutual interdependence of fascism and imperialism' he was against any appeasement to fascism and warned that the main threat to peace was capitalist rivalry in the colonies.[46]

Historians are now divided over the extent to which the claims were seriously considered. Howe (1993) argues that proposals to provide outlets for the colonial ambitions of Italy and Germany were never incorporated into government policy. Cain and Hopkins (1993) draw attention to the conflicts of interest

"IF IMPERIALISM MEANS A CERTAIN RACIAL SUPERIORITY, SUPPRESSION OF POLITICAL AND ECONOMIC FREEDOM OF OTHER PEOPLES, EXPLOITATION OF RESOURCES OF OTHER COUNTRIES FOR THE BENEFIT OF THE IMPERIALIST COUNTRIES THEN I SAY THOSE ARE NOT CHARACTERISTICS OF THIS COUNTRY."

Last week we described this statement by the Prime Minister as

Britain's Biggest War Lie

This week, George Padmore, the Negro Socialist Leader, shows, in the article he has written below, how Britain treats her native colonials as helots. He says:—

The British Empire Is Worst Racket Yet Invented By Man

By GEORGE PADMORE

AS a piece of humbug this statement cannot be beaten. How is it possible to maintain an empire without imperialist methods? This is just a contradiction in terms, and Mr. Chamberlain certainly knows better. For his father in collusion with Cecil Rhodes annexed more territory in Africa for British Imperialism than Hitler has yet succeeded in grabbing in Europe for German Imperialism. But all who knew British imperialists are not surprised at Mr. Chamberlain's statement, for they are the most hypocritical ruling class in the world.

NEVILLE'S FATHER

Space will only permit a very brief reference to the manifestations of racial superiority and suppression of economic and political freedom within the British Empire, and, since South Africa and the Rhodesias are associated with the name of Joseph Chamberlain, I will confine myself to these territories.

The policy of "no equality between black and white either in Church or State" is the official doctrine governing interracial relations in Africa. It is the most blatant expression of racial superiority. In South Africa and Rhodesia the natives are treated as social pariahs. Politically they are completely disfranchised, and economically they have been reduced to the status of helots.

Robbed of their lands, deprived of all means of independent economic existence, taxed in order to compel them to go and work for the Europeans at starvation wages, herded into reserves and compounds, the lot of the South African natives is more tragic even than that of the Jews under the swastika. Not without reason Professor Haldane recently declared that he would prefer to be a Jew in Germany than a Kaffir in Johannesburg.

This state of affairs is not confined to South Africa but constitutes the general sociological structure wherever Europeans have settled, Rhodesia, Kenya, etc.

NO EXPLOITATION

When Mr. Chamberlain talks about the absence of economic exploitation, he consciously disregards the facts. The Rand mines, for instance, make such large profits that they are able to pay out more than £20,000,000 in dividends annually and to contribute £14,000,000 in taxes to the Union revenue.

Whence comes this profit? Only from the ruthless exploitation of the 300,023 African miners, who are paid a wage of 1s. 6d. per day as compared with the 20s. per day paid to the white miners. This wide difference in wages between the white and black miners is legalised by the Colour Bar Act, with the full endorsement of the Labour Party and the trade unions.

The copper mines of Rhodesia in 1937 paid out £5,000,000 in dividends, while to 17,000 African wage-earners it paid £344,000. Another set of parasites—this time the South Africa Company—also benefited to the tune of £500,000 simply for the privilege of having titles to these mineral lands which Cecil Rhodes had filched from the African chiefs. The British Empire is the biggest racket that the infamnity of man has yet conceived. Hitler and his gang are just amateurs at empire racketeering.

South Africa, Rhodesia, Kenya—these names are synonymous with all that is

worst in racial oppression and economic exploitation. As the well-known colonial authority, Dr. Norman Leys, has most aptly put it: "When the historian of the future looks for examples of the moral result of the capitalist system of society, where avarice allied with racial pride and domination showed least sign of shame, where the common people were most despised and poorest, where the law was least regarded and loyalty least possible, he will point to South Africa and Kenya."

British imperialist methods are as ruthless as those of their rivals. But having had longer experience they have developed a technique of cleverly masking their exploitation. Moreover they have been able to enlist in this conspiracy of silence the support of the leaders of organised labour by sharing with them some of the spoils of their colonial exploitation.

LABOUR IMPERIALISTS

This united front between the imperialists and the trade unionists constitutes the historic basis of reformism in the British Labour movement, which makes the Labour defender of British imperialist interests in the present war. Whenever the Empire is threatened Labour is compelled to rally to its support, since it is the junior partner in John Bull, Ltd.

Thus, it is no accident that we have Major Attlee denouncing Red Imperialism on the one hand, and collaborating with Red, White and Blue Imperialism, on the other!

It is only when there is some riot in Jamaica, or shooting in Palestine, or unrest on the North-West Frontier, that the average Briton is made even remotely conscious of his responsibility toward the hundreds of millions of coloured people over whom the British ruling class speciously claim to be exercising a benevolent trusteeship.

This consciousness, however, is only momentary, and explains why a British Prime Minister is able to make such a false statement as the one quoted at the beginning of this article without being challenged even by the leaders of His Majesty's Opposition.

HYPOCRITICAL CANT

Africans and peoples of African descent who have been the victims of "those evil things—brute force, bad faith, injustice, persecution and oppression," practised upon them from the days of Queen Elizabeth's slave system to the present form of modern capitalist-imperialist slavery can well sympathise with the Jews and other victims of Nazi oppression, but we repudiate all this hypocritical cant of Mr. Chamberlain.

We want deeds not words. If the honour of the British people is ever to be retrieved and amends made for the injustices committed in their name, then this is the time for the British working class to come forward boldly in support of the demands of the colonial peoples for justice and freedom.

The job of the British working class is

not to play the rôle of watchdog for a cynical ruling class, but to try and straighten out the mess that their "betters" have landed them into. Unless they turn their attention to this essential task they will find themselves every decade or so taking up arms "in defence of democracy."

It is time for the British working class to set about changing the colonial system by assisting in the complete liquidation of capitalist-imperialism. Only by taking the lead in this all-important task will they show the colonial peoples and the German workers that they stand in a different camp from the imperialist robbers.

THE ONLY HOPE

We do not demand national freedom as a means in itself. We are internationalists, as such, want to see a World Federal Union, with colonies as free units, part of such a Union. We know, however, that this will remain a utopian dream until such time as Imperialism has been liquidated and mankind released from the yoke of capitalist bondage. Federation, yes! But federation on the basis of free collaboration of all peoples, backward as well as advanced. Socialism plus Federation is the only hope of mankind!

Wells Rejects Half-way House

WITH H. G. Wells the I.L.P. has often differed, but the speech which he delivered to the P.E.N. Club last week on the "Federal Union" proposal was sound Socialist sense.

"I am quite ready to sign my name to a federal, free Socialist World State," he said, "but I will not play with any of these time-wasting half-measures."

"Half-measures are no good at all. We are in the presence of a world revolution, one of the greatest changes in the world, and that is either ending of war.

"These half-way houses are refuges for the mentally indolent.

"If you were to attempt federation, as now planned, it would be more disastrous than the League of Nations failure."

WHAT IS SOCIALIST PEACE? Meeting at Unity Hall, Quex Road, Kilburn, Friday, Dec. 15, 7.45 p.m. Speakers: C. A. Smith, Reg. Groves, Chris. Jones, G. Flemm.

between the Colonial Office, who opposed any transfer, and the Foreign Office, who gave 'serious consideration' to colonial appeasement.[47] It is easy to debate these finer points of international diplomacy, but, in the context of the epoch, British consideration of fascist claims was perceived as a very real threat from the perspective of the colonised. As Havingdon and Meredith (1993) point out, the fact that plans to redistribute colonies did not go through, was not so much due to considerations of the moral duties of trusteeship, but the unwillingness of Germany to enter into negotiations for a general settlement in Europe. The response of the British Government, they argue, did tremendous damage to British prestige in the African colonies. This is reflected in the criticisms of black organisations based in Britain, which passed strong resolutions condemning any possible deals with Germany. International diplomatic parrying with the lives of colonial peoples, who were mere pawns in the game, crystallised colonial grievances mounting since the early 1930s, and Leonard Barnes observed that a 'great resentment was smouldering' throughout Africa. German racial policies, absent in Italian Fascism, and the apparent universal eclipse of democracy in the 1930s, combined with 'broad social forces', also regenerated concern over repression of colonial civil liberties (Chapter 4) and resulted in a common bond of 'anti-imperialism', a 'colonial chartism' which demanded improved welfare, better education, freedom of speech and greater political representation.[48]

For those with vested interests, the uncertainties of the age intensified paranoia about the 'disintegration' of the Empire and the defence of Empire was paramount. At a conference organised in 1938 by the Cambridgeshire branch of the Royal Empire Society a participant warned that no previous Empire had ' … so many problems before it at once'. Though never previously defeated, the empire now 'faced grave dangers' from communist enemies within the 'nerve centre of empire' and threats from without, including US ambition, appeasement of fascism and colonial nationalism. Although the content of the conference speeches would now be construed as the ranting of right-wing cranks, it arguably reflected the fears of well-connected and influential imperialists. The conference was well attended by brigadiers, admirals and representatives from the pro-empire Victoria League and a message from Queen Mary was included at the beginning of the published conference proceedings. Reflecting the shift over the 1930s to liberal multiracialism, the organisers acknowledged the importance of dialogue with educated Africans and the Sierra Leonian, Ivor Cummings, chaired sessions as a representative of African students in Britain. Key questions which were discussed illuminated the main establishment preoccupations of the day, particularly the defence of the empire. But concern was also expressed about threats to the 'British race' and culture from 'very foreign' Eastern European refugees.[49] This expresses a fear of 'swamping' and loss of 'Englishness' which presages responses to black migrants in the 1950s when the formal empire was, indeed, disintegrating. Given these fears, empire strengthening was the prime consideration of the delegates.

The media was also actively engaged in counteracting any disintegrating tendencies and ensuring that the empire remained constantly in the hearts and minds of the mass of the British population. In the debates about decline of empire, there is a common assumption that the dark clouds of fascism and unemployment led to a loss of popular support for empire in the 1930s. Cain and Hopkins (1993), however, argue that the British Government mounted an 'extensive publicity campaign' in defence of empire, a 'process of moral rearmament' that helped to prepare both Britain and its empire for a war that would 'carry forward the imperial enterprise, as well as end the threat of Fascism'. The media, particularly the BBC, also continued to support vigorously the monarchy and the empire, the most powerful unifying traditions in the construction of British national identity, at a time when enemies from within and without were threatening to fragment and divide. As Cannadine (1983) stresses, the 'outstandingly successful [royal] tours' cemented bonds between Britain and her empire, and royal rituals, particularly the Coronation of George VI in 1937 (where Walton's two coronation marches were entitled 'Crown Imperial'), provided public displays of the greatness, wealth and power of empire, generating emotive imperial sentiment across the political spectrum. The appeal of monarchy and empire acted as a distraction from internal problems, but also reaffirmed the comforting belief that, in a newly competitive world, Britain and her empire 'remained at the forefront'.[50]

Events in the 1930s had thus given a clear message to imperialists: adapt or die. Arguably, they took the former option with a degree of success. In addition to the empire strengthening tactics already outlined, there were important intellectual developments in imperial discourse which were also arguably directed towards 'empire strengthening'. A new discourse of development emerged which built upon the dissident discourses of the early 1930s and incorporated them into imperial policy. How did progressive thinking on race and imperialism move from the margins to the centre, changing the imperial relationship with Africa? According to Malcolm Hailey, the architect of the monumental *African Survey* (1938), a key factor was the growth of African resistance. This had rendered a paternalist trusteeship that would endure into the far distant future patently unworkable. Africa now occupied a 'more intimate place' in European affairs than did India. As Pearce (1982) observes, the late 1930s were the real 'turning point' in Africa, not the Second World War era, as more orthodox studies of decolonisation have assumed. Colonial governments now faced the political gymnastics of managing 'agitators' while maintaining imperial power. There was thus greater recognition that the time had come to 'accelerate development' in Africa and promote the 'gradual spread of freedom among all colonial subjects', although officials still clung to the belief that this would be a 'slow, evolutionary process'.[51] Over the next decade the imperial agenda shifted from indirect rule and Lugardian trusteeship to greater self-rule. However, this was directed towards ensuring a continued British imperial presence in tropical Africa rather than independence.

In this reformulation of British responses to Africa, there were two seminal intellectual influences, Fabian research and Malcolm Hailey's *African Survey* (1938). Labour Party demands for improved colonial welfare and development was strengthened by 'new thinking' and activity in the imperial establishment. Academics played an important part in dethroning Lugard and elevating their own imperial pundit, Sir Malcolm Hailey (1872–1969). The pro-active Round Table clique were 'largely responsible' for appointing Hailey to carry out the African survey. This was first suggested by Smuts in 1929. In 1930–1, an African research scheme, centred at the Royal Institute of International Affairs, Chatham House, was initiated which helped to secure Carnegie funding for the survey. A former Governor of the Punjab (1924–8) and the United Provinces (1928–34), Hailey had no direct experience of Africa. Roberts (1986) argues that the survey represented a growing trend to depend on expertise from India rather than South Africa. As an 'outsider', Macmillan, who had firsthand experience of Africa, was passed over when the Africa survey post was mooted in 1935, receiving a mere £100 for a draft of 'Africa Emergent' to brief Hailey.[52] In contrast, Hailey, a Round Table member who had sat on the League of Nations Permanent Mandates Commission from 1935–9, was an establishment insider. Macmillan's considerable research on Africa was not even acknowledged in the list of contributors to the survey, even though his recommendations for greater social and economic development formed the key theme of Hailey's survey.

Drawing on his experience of Indian nationalism, Hailey recommended 'limited' official acknowledgement of African grievances to minimise the challenge to European authority. In 1938 a policy to tackle the 'colour bar' was adopted by the CO with proposals to extend it to the Dominions Office. Hailey's survey, particularly the updated 1956 version, reflected new thinking on race and racial difference. He rejected the use of the 'cranial index' and intelligence testing, which was still in vogue in the 1930s, and concluded that there was no biological basis to differences between ethnic groups. Yet, he still surmised why sub-Saharan Africa had not shown 'greater initiative' in the 'mechanical arts' or other developments to improve conditions of life.[53] Such attitudes beg the question as to how much Hailey related to Africa? Pearce (1982) alleges that he greatly missed India, complaining, for instance, about the standard of African servants (although he 'marvelled at the physical attributes of African women'!) and, argues Roberts, his survey simply perpetuated the trope of the 'African' and Africa as a 'laboratory for controlled social experimentation'.[54]

Macmillan conceded that Hailey was 'able enough', but so cautious of 'offending conservative opinion' that his report would 'say nothing'. In imperial circles, however, Hailey was regarded as a 'star of dazzling brilliance' whose *African Survey* represented the end of the *laissez-faire* period in Africa.[55] This massive study undoubtedly shifted the agenda on Africa towards 'partnership', greater development and welfare. 'The assumptions of trusteeship', concluded Hailey, 'though possessing a moral influence' had been 'basically negative' as they 'failed to place on the colonial power any direct obligation to assist in the material or social development of the indigenous population.'[56] Written with authority and the neutral 'objectivity' of a trained civil servant, his survey (republished in revised form in 1957) borrowed heavily from relevant secondary sources. The survey is comprehensive and detailed, covering the whole of Africa and including political, economic and social profiles of African societies. *African Survey* thus constituted a new mapping of the continent which enabled Britain to achieve some hold on Africa throughout troubled times, including independence.[57]

Hailey's memorial in Westminster Abbey, that veritable temple of empire, immortalises him as the 'Ruler of Great Provinces in India. ... In Africa, no less renowned for labours which gave shape to African freedom'. With perhaps the exception of Smuts, who, according to Flint (1988), dismissed it as 'merely an encyclopaedia with little guidance or illumination', Hailey's *Survey* was regarded across the political spectrum as a 'tremendous contribution' to knowledge of Africa.[58] In many ways, Hailey simply renovated old discourses of white power in a more subtle form and gave respectability to the colonial reforms, which a minority had pressed for since the early 1930s. However, the wide acclaim for his survey reflects the growing reformist and official consensus on empire, which deepened with the new threats, but also new imperial possibilities that emerged with the onset of the Second World War.

The end of the 'jolly old empire'? the Second World War and after

As Malik (1996) has noted, fascism and the war entrenched the ideal of good-ness, decency and tolerance of a humane British nation, which, as emphasised in Chapter 1 was deeply embedded in national mythology.[59] The more consensual and egalitarian concept of 'Commonwealth', underpinned by liberal multira-cialist discourse, filtered into official and popular discourse. Pressure for colonial reform was stepped up by the influential Fabian Colonial Bureau (FRB), founded in 1940 with Creech Jones as chairman and Rita Hinden (a South African economist) as secretary. The Bureau carried out detailed research and initiated dialogue with nationalist organisations, such as the West African Student's Union, to win them over to moderation and gradual reform, consolidating reformist work with black organisations which had begun in South Africa in the late 1920s.[60] In recognition of the indispensable contribution of the colonies to the war effort, the 'colonial lobby' also stepped up the pressure for change. Margery Perham stressed the need for a move from 'power to service' and greater sensitivity to the 'offence' caused by use of terms like 'black' and 'primi-tive'. Erstwhile outsiders like Macmillan, who was asked to join the Empire Intelligence Section of the BBC, became incorporated into this 'remaking' of imperialism and toned down their criticisms of official policy. The emphasis was now on the management of change, and research funding was placed on a firmer basis with the founding of the Colonial Social Science Research Council in 1944 (the forerunner of the Social Science Research Council, which replaced it in 1965). Anthropologists were thus in greater demand as advisers to colonial governments and as the 'chroniclers of the transition to independence' many students of Malinowski and Evans-Pritchard, such as Audrey Richards, became influential in postwar African studies.[61]

Rapid changes in the CO occurred between 1940–3 and the 'spirit of dictation', which had characterised earlier colonial policy, was rejected in favour of 'partnership' and 'mutual consultation'. In 1940, the Colonial Development and Welfare Act was passed as a measure, which, as Havinden and Meredith (1994) stress, was vital to keep the colonised committed to the war effort, but also to impress public opinion in Britain and the US. For Morgan (1980) the act represented a real change of attitude at the CO – a 'heart-searching' in response to outside criticisms which inspired reform.[62] A more cynical view is that reforms consolidated the 'empire strengthening' tactics advocated by Hailey and others before the war. Although some extra finance and support was made available, the colonised were still expected to pay for their own social development. Developments funds were firmly linked to capitalist interests, setting a precedent for the future.[63] A Colonial Development Corporation (subsequently the Commonwealth Development Corporation), set up by the CO in 1945, was chaired by Lord Trefargne, a former Director of Barclays Bank. George Padmore complained that there was not 'one single black man' on the board, which comprised city bankers and ex-governors. Barclays Bank also set up its own Overseas Development Corporation with Sir Bernard Bourdillon, the ex-governor of Nigeria, as a director. This 'new economic imperialism', euphemistically described as 'colonial development and welfare' was the inspiration for Padmore's *Africa: Britain's Third Empire* (1949), a forceful critique of imperialism from the African point of view to counteract the 'plethora of apologists for empire'.[64]

Despite fine-sounding statements on progress, there was a reluctance to move forward. In *Soviet Light on the Colonies* (1944), Leonard Barnes claimed that the backward nations of the Soviet Union had made more progress since the 1917 revolution than Africans had after a century of British 'trusteeship' and Parliament threatened to ban the book in the armed forces. (This was prevented by NCCL intervention, although the book was subsequently erased from the 1937–45, Penguin Special Edition files).[65] Governors dragged their feet on Africanisation and argued that development was hindered not only by adverse physical conditions, but also by the 'lack of character and courage' among blacks, as well as the weak, divided and inefficient leadership. Citing the spectre of 'independent' Liberia, the 'progressive' Governor of the Gold Coast, Sir Alan Burns, warned of the potential 'chaos' that would result from white withdrawal without a 'long and careful preparation'. Civil liberties were also further curtailed with the outbreak of war and delegates at a conference, organised by the NCCL in 1941, demanded a 'minimum programme' of civil liberties and the abolition of racial and religious discrimination 'for all British subjects without distinction'.[66] The 'colour problem' was still recognised as a barrier to progress, even by progressive imperialists like Perham, and, as Pilkington (1988) stresses, racist stereotypes, reflected, for instance, in the publication of Enid Blyton's *The Three Golliwogs* (1944), persisted in the 'liberal' war years and after, perpetuating an imperial mentality of superiority. Although there were black pilots in the RAF, the mascot of the crack dam busters squadron, the hero Guy Gibson's black labrador, was called 'Nigger'. [67]

In official rhetoric, however, the war opened up the 'Liberal Hour' and a mood of dynamic optimism. 'On the way! That is the keynote today in the empire' wrote Margery Perham in 1945. This optimism also extended to the African colonies and the sweeping return to power of a 'humane' Labour Government, which understood the aspirations of colonial people, raised 'great hopes ... in the hearts of colonial people'.[68] Colonial people also had high hopes for the new United Nations, which established an International Trusteeship System to act as the 'conscience of mankind' and passed a Universal Declaration of Human Rights in 1948. But, like its predecessor, the League of Nations, the UN failed to sustain the new hopes of Africans and African diaspora people, who became rapidly disillusioned with the new organisation.[69] African nationalist leaders were also quickly disillusioned by the imperial policies of the new Labour Government. Arthur Creech Jones, now Secretary of State for Colonies, reaffirmed the advantages that colonial rule had brought to Africans and was criticised by more radical black and white activists for his extreme caution and steadfast refusal to give a target date for independence. Pearce (1983) suggests that Creech Jones' trip to West Africa in 1944 'profoundly shocked him' and he feared 'disintegration' and 'chaos' if the British did not continue to exercise control. Here his position differed little from that of the defenders of empire, like Perham, who also emphasised the 'restlessness, disruption [and] demoralisation' which emerged as 'raw tribesmen turned proletariat'. Never had there been so many apologists and defenders of the 'jolly old empire', even on the left, observed Padmore.[70]

During the war, Churchill had stressed the importance of Africa to Britain's continuing imperial credentials and, with the loss of India, the African empire became central to Britain's postwar reconstruction. Sir Bernard Montgomery, chief of the Imperial General Staff, made a tour of Africa in 1947 and, invoking the spirit of Rhodes, argued for the 'immense possibilities of African development' to help Britain maintain its standard of living and provide a reserve of military manpower. For Montgomery, the African was a 'complete savage', and as Kent (1993) points out, his vision was 'in the realms of fantasy'. However, his report impressed the Cabinet, reflecting the importance that the new Labour Government attached to the economic value of the African empire.[71] To further the new imperial policy, Andrew Cohen, as head of the African Department at the CO and 'Emperor of Africa', continued the policy of co-opting moderate nationalists with a vested interest in collaboration with the authorities and private companies. The industrialisation of West Africa and the cultivation of an African working-class was now favoured in some circles to demonstrate that Britain was a progressive imperial power, although, argues Butler (1997) 'obstacles' in the imperial system impeded economic 'modernisation'. As Cooper (1996) has demonstrated, the growth of African labour militancy, which subverted the representation of Africans as primitive rural tribesman, precipitated these changes in colonial discourse. The labour question, he argues, is fundamental in understanding the precipitate character of decolonisation in Africa.[72]

With the new commitment to African development there was an expansion of academic research. In his 1957 *Survey*, Hailey praised the establishment of an African Studies Branch at the CO and the expansion of teaching and research at SOAS to give 'direct assistance to colonial governments'. He noted that US universities and foundations now expressed greater interest in Africa and there was more 'intercolonial and international co-operation' on development initiatives.[73] To gain consent for the new imperial policies in Africa, colonial propaganda was stepped up. A government report, *The Colonial Territories, 1948–1949*, stressed the need to combine defensive policies to retain the empire with 'pro-active policies' directed towards the expansion of higher education, an enhanced role for the British Council (founded in 1934) and information services to spread the 'British way of life', and the training of colonials in journalism and film making to aid the expansion of a 'less inflammatory' media. Development funds were vital to ensure that the African colonies did not become 'subjugated' by another 'less liberal' power, which was clearly an anti-communist statement. As Kent (1992, 1993) points out, with the onset of the Cold War, Britain clutched more tightly at 'African straws', promoting inter-colonial co-operation with France and, with the help of the US, initiating reforms to prevent the spread of communist influence.[74]

US criticisms of British colonialism had initially put imperialists on the defensive, but towards the end of the war the US was increasingly seen as an important ally in forestalling 'attacks on the empire' by 'Negro intellectuals ... inspired by Communist doctrine'.[75] After the war, as Louis and Robinson (1994) point out, the British imperial mandarins found themselves caught between their vision of the 'third British Empire' and dependence on the US for financial support to implement colonial development. The Cold War resulted in greater recognition of the need for Anglo-American co-operation to defend common interests. By the 1950s, Sir Andrew Cohen reported that the US was providing 'valuable help' to African territories in capital and personnel. These interlocking power networks, argues Pietersie (1990), ensured important continuities between British and American imperialism and helped sustain the 'myth' of continuing British influence as decolonisation transformed empire into commonwealth.[76]

Historians, writes John Kent (1993), 'all agree' that the Second World War dramatically undermined the empire. However, as his detailed research reveals, it took a long time dying in the minds of policy makers. Empire also remained deeply embedded in popular consciousness. As Mackenzie (1987) observes, during the war the BBC heavily promoted Empire and Commonwealth. A Festival of Empire was held in 1946 and 1,000 schools remained affiliated to the Empire Day Movement. Empire Day continued into the 1950s (I remember the pageants of my own childhood) and the empire remained prominent in Christmas Day programmes into the 1950s.[77] The British Commonwealth, formally instituted in

1948, was actively promoted at home and abroad, and the royalty continued to play a symbolic role in securing the loyalty of imperial and Commonwealth subjects – reflected in Princess Elizabeth's trip to South Africa in 1947. The coronation of Elizabeth II in 1953, observes Cannadine (1983), continued the imperial motif of great state occasions: trees were planted throughout the British Empire, the Queen's dress contained embroidered emblems of the Dominions and regiments of Commonwealth, and colonial troops marched in the procession emphasising that Britain was still a great imperial power.[78] Empire thus remained central to defining British national and racial identities and, as Webster (1998) demonstrates, imperial decline and the increase in 'colonial' migration into the heart of empire threatened these 'imperial identities'. Books which evoked nostalgia for empire now proved popular. In this genre were Elspeth Huxley's autobiographical memoirs of Africa, which validated white settler societies and the imperial mission and, argues Webster, endowed colonial men and women with the 'most exemplary qualities of Britishness'.[79]

Western representations of Africa, discussed in Chapters 1 and 2, also proved highly durable. In the *Empire Youth Annual* (1947), directed to 'boys and girls of the British Empire and Commonwealth' (see Illustration 1), South Africa is presented as a white paradise and the achievements of the great white pioneers lauded. The Gold Coast is given short shrift and it is noted that the Northern Ashanti were 'reluctant to give up their unsavoury practices of human sacrifices, sorcery and slave dealing' and were 'yielding only slowly to civilising influences'. *Arthur Mee's Book of the Flag* (1941), which firmly linked imperial and British history in the formation of British national identity and patriotism, conveyed a similar message. Emphasising the benefits of the British civilising mission, the book points out that Africa was the 'dark continent' within living memory, but 'today a man might walk five thousand miles from the Cape to the pyramids in the shelter of the flag'. During the 1950s and 1960s, images of 'primitive' Africa were popularised by the South African, Laurens Van der Post and the Belgian documentary makers, Armand and Michaela Denis, who, argues Birkett (1997), manipulated the media to promote their own career interests and perpetuated a paternalistic and romanticised, but implicitly racist view of Africa which downplayed the importance of nationalism and other 'modern' developments. Yet, Van der Post became a 'guru of international repute' with his appeal for people in a consumerist age to find their 'dark, imaginative, feminine African inner being'.[80]

The immediate postwar years, then, were marked by strong continuities in imperialism and racist conceptions of Africa. Despite liberal rhetoric, Britain's key aim was to hold on to empire in Africa. Decolonisation was not seriously on the agenda until the growing unmanageability of African nationalism, combined with the 1956 Suez crisis, forced decolonisation. Thus, African resistance continued and was supported in the metropolitan centre by the new anti-imperialist Movement for Colonial Freedom, which was founded in 1954 and was arguably the model for War on Want and Anti-apartheid, which both started as offshoots of the MCF.[81] The dissident white 'conscience on Africa' had merged into official orthodoxy on African development and a new, more radical anti-colonialism emerged, expressed by activists like Leonard Barnes, whose writings reputedly had a 'tremendous' influence on young Africanists in the crucial years from 1936–52. Although in later years, Barnes' writings arguably became less radical and more pessimistic about African potential for self-government, he was lauded on his death as a 'left-wing humanist' and a 'staunch supporter of African rights before it became a popular cause'.[82]

Thus, the turbulent decade from 1935–45 reshaped both official and dissident discourses on Africa. The different political parties and vested interests moved to greater consensus over the future role of Britain in Africa and 'empire strengthening' tactics in Africa arguably sustained British influence throughout the momentous upheavals of the war and its aftermath. In this sense, as Hargreaves (1996) observes, when decolonisation was finally achieved it represented the completion rather than the abandonment of the imperial mission in Africa. Imperialism arguably continued, repackaged in a new, more insidious form. Although defending the British imperial record, Margery Perham warned of a new inter-imperialism replacing British 'imperial pride and sense of obligation'. Foreign investment, she argued, although welcome, could lead to a situation in which 'a weak people might be politically independent and yet economically subject', as well as prey to debt and the 'despoliation' of their lands. However, this Western economic and cultural stranglehold on Africa continued to be justified on a moral and humanitarian basis. The internationalisation of Africa had thus come full circle, but the language of imperialism was now transformed into a more neutral discourse of aid and development which sanitised the past. In this new humanitarianism, colonial oppression and resistance was erased and the inter-war period represented as 'a long period of peaceful and constructive progress'.[83]

Summary

Before 1935, little attention was paid to African grievances or the wider problems of imperial policy, despite African protest and the stirring of 'Britain's conscience on Africa'. Between 1935–9, fascism and allied international developments in imperialism, combined with growing unrest in the colonies, resulted in 'empire strengthening', but also the recognition of the need to amend imperial policy to defuse any threats from African nationalism which could undermine the empire. This resulted in greater consensus between progressive imperialists and reformist critics over the future of the African colonies. During the war, the discourse of global democracy, equality and human rights blossomed and, for Africans, this heralded an era of hope and optimism. But, once again, dreams of power intruded into these dreams of freedom. As Hobsbawm (1994) emphasises, there was a seamless web between the two world wars during which capitalism acted as a 'permanent and continuous revolutionising force of globalisation', which strengthened rather than undermined imperialism.[84] The Second World War stimulated the ongoing internationalisation of imperialism in which the

USA emerged as the supreme imperial power. Racism and imperialism thus survived the upheavals of the global wartime abyss. The colour bar persisted in the 'white settler' colonies and white settlement in Rhodesia and South Africa was actively encouraged by the British Government in the 1950s. Other parts of sub-Saharan Africa remained locked in the economic clutches of the West, even after formal independence had been granted and the British imperial star had waned. This begs the question as to what the long resistance struggles in Africa achieved. The prime achievement, as with the resistance struggle against slavery, was undoubtedly the assertion of autonomy from white rule. African resistance and protest also stimulated reforms in colonial policy and hastened the end of formal empire in Africa. Challenges to the 'colour bar' were also seminal in the elaboration of liberal, multiculturalist discourse. However, the struggles of the oppressed against the powerful are always 'one step forward and two steps backwards'. Considerable advances have been made since the 1920s, but 'dreams of freedom' from Western racism and cultural and economic oppression have yet to be fully realised.

Retrospective

Africa and the African diaspora in a 'post-imperial' world

Is ours then a world of power, of capital, or a world of emancipation? Surely it is both, although collective memory records the achievements of empires and imperial civilisations much more readily than it does the humanising and civilising contributions of emancipation movements. ... The issues [relating to empire and emancipation] are complex, large in scope and ever in motion. The post-imperial age has begun but the age of empire is not over.

(J. Nederveen Pietersie, 1990)

We dare to dream the same dream that has always filled the villages, ghettos, townships and slave quarters with hope, that has always animated the spirit of resistance, that has united the dispossessed. ... We, the African people are our own liberators and thinkers, whose task it is to take a mighty stride towards genuine freedom, by any means necessary.

(Kampala Declaration: Resist Recolonisation! 7th Pan-African Congress,
Kampala, Uganda, 1994)[1]

The relationship between Africa and the West is still unravelling and the dialectic between Western dreams of power and African dreams of freedom is arguably as relevant today as during the period explored in this book. As Melville Herskovits remarked on the cusp of independence, African resistance and movements for racial, economic and political self-determination must be projected against 'the broader screen of relations between Africa and the outside world since the earliest times'.[2] Colonial rule was a brief interlude yet, as my study has demonstrated, the years from 1918–45 are fundamental to understanding the nature of Western power in Africa and discourses of twentieth century racism. In my analysis of the indivisible links between imperialism, race and resistance, I have continuously emphasised the interconnections between the imperial hinterland and the heart of empire in stimulating resistance and redefining Africa's relationship with Britain and, ultimately the Western world, in the prelude to independence. These developments were catalysed by the unique cultural, economic and political ethos of the times, including polarisations between liberalism, communism and fascism. A new sense of a common experience of racism and colonial oppression was forged across Africa and the African diaspora, strengthening black resistance. The discourse of freedom and human rights generated during and after the Second World War opened a wider window of hope for the colonised. Dreams of freedom now seemed attainable with the acceleration of nationalism. But dreams of power did not fade with these new challenges and imperialism and racism were re-interpreted and strengthened in the postwar global order.

In remembering the 'colonial interlude' in Africa, we should not forget the African men and women who consistently challenged cultural, political and economic oppression. We must also acknowledge the 'metropolitan conscience' which emerged as conditions in Africa worsened, particularly in South Africa, and the dedication of individuals who championed the African cause. In the context of the time, moreover, many cautious liberals and 'grass-roots' colonial officers genuinely believed they were helping Africans. Looking back on the era, George Padmore also distinguished between anti-imperialism and anti-Britishness, and testified to the 'sterling qualities' of the 'common people of Britain', which 'Africans and other colonial peoples could emulate to great advantage', such as 'integrity, fair play, justice and tolerance', which set Britain apart from other imperial powers. The British liberal conscience lives on, represented in the Coalition for Jubilee 2000 pressure group, formed in 1995, which aspires to a mass mobilisation of humanitarianism on a par with the Anti-Slavery Movement to release Africa from its crushing debt burden.[3] Liberal 'champions of the oppressed', however, faced the problem of how to secure change without damaging the structures of capitalism and their liberal interracial vision only acknowledged the equality of a minority of 'civilised' blacks. Liberalism was arguably motivated by conscience rather than commitment to a real equality. As the radical US journalist Andrew Kopkind noted, liberalism must have its 'victims' to sympathise with and this becomes a problem in that the victim finds this patronising. Moreover, gulfs in race and class mean that the sympathiser does not really know the victim. In this sense liberal sympathy and support can be as much related to defining whiteness as trying to understand the problems of the victim. The oppressed, concludes Kopkind, do not need sympathy, but solidarity in a common struggle. [4]

How then do we assess the imperial record in Africa? The writer, Joyce Cary, argued that British rule was bad in economic terms, but good in terms of culture and civilisation.[5] While there may have been some benefits in terms of health, communications and education, development under colonialism was limited, uneven and haphazard in its impact. Britain and other imperial powers had a surreal dream of taming 'wild' people and ruling acquiescent and grateful subjects. But instead of producing order, imperialism intensified economic and cultural oppression and generated disorder and resistance. Would Africa have been better off if it had never been formally colonised? We have little tangible evidence to test this counter-factual hypothesis, although Walter Rodney tried to argue the case in *How Europe Under-Developed Africa* (1975). Such speculations are futile as Africa's contact with Western 'modernity' preceded colonial rule and, once the dynamic of change built up momentum, there was no turning back. The problem, therefore, is not development *per se*, but what kind of development, for no society can ever remain unchanging and free from cultural interchange with other societies. As one African academic put it, Africans recognised the positive benefits of Western knowledge and Africa would have embraced modernity and integrated with the West, but on its own terms and time-scale.[6] However, the West imposed its own model of change on Africa and thus distorted development.

While the impact of imperialism was mostly negative in terms of economic exploitation and racial oppression, contact with Western modernity through Christianity and liberal democracy also inspired dreams of emancipation and a better future. The failure of these dreams cannot be blamed solely on imperialism. As Warren (1984) points out, the new ruling elites continued to exploit and oppress the majority of Africans while blaming all the problems of post-independent states on colonialism and neo-colonialism.[7] African states have degenerated into 'lootocracies' characterised by 'spoils politics' or the 'politics of the belly'. An all pervasive corruption robs the poor and rewards the already wealthy, a case of what Steve Riley (1998) calls 'Robin Hood in reverse'. The mass of poorer Africans, particularly women, have been marginalised and the raised expectations of the decolonisation period remain unfulfilled. However, centuries of Western intervention created the conditions for the corruption and conflict which now blights Africa. One of the most important legacies of the colonial period, argues Mamdani (1996), was the way in which the autocratic structures of 'indirect rule' were absorbed into the post-colonial states, impeding the development of democracy and civil society.[8] Colonial states also inherited the artificial boundaries and 'traditional' ethnic groupings, mapped out in the colonial era, which has resulted in war and state disintegration.

From the early 1980s, Africa was subjected to the new Western ideological folly of development through the 'hidden hand' of the international market place. Neo-liberal (or neo-imperial?) policies placed African economies at the mercy of global market forces, which led to greater immiseration of the masses and deepened the African crisis. Harnessing African cash crops and mineral production to global capitalism, arguably the prime aim of British imperial rule, remains the essence of the modernising project in Africa. African states are now increasingly vulnerable to 'recolonisation', as 'smart white boys' (from the International Monetary Fund) are sent in to run their countries.[9] However, these new Western interventions are veiled in a humanitarian discourse of 'good governance', democracy and human rights. Aid has become increasingly dependent on democratisation, but is this insistence of the grafting of Western liberal capitalist democracy onto African societies not simply another example of the West knowing what is 'good' for Africa? Democracy cannot be imposed from without and must evolve within the culture of any given society. As Bayart (1993) argues, we cannot understand contemporary African problems without moving away from Western perceptions and taking into account the long-term development of African political thought and social action within an African cultural context.[10]

Other global developments that have implications for Africa include the revolution in global communications. While there is a benign post-modernist vision of this globalisation, which stresses hybridisation of cultures, it may also be interpreted as heralding more powerful cultural imperialism. As Pietersie (1990) points out, it was the British who first developed a sophisticated expertise in information management and propaganda, and the US global communications grid built on and strengthened Britain's imperial 'All Red Routes' which encircled the world. As the new imperial superpower, the USA also has its own visions of Africa as a continent of 'enchanting darkness'.[11] The US-dominated international media remains Eurocentric, privileging the West against the rest – a discourse rooted in the colonial past. For the Kenyan writer, Ngugi Wa Thiongo, the cultural impact of imperialism has been the most damaging and persistent. The West still controls the production of knowledge and, argue Stam and Shohat (1994), Eurocentricism can only be counteracted by a 'decolonisation' of global culture which empowers the dispossessed.[12]

Western discourse on Africa thus still devolves on a generic Africa and visualises the continent in a two-dimensional, standardised monochrome that glosses over the enormous diversity within the continent. Since the 1970s, the West has arguably witnessed 'a craze for the primitive' which continues to depict African cultures as static and backward. As a result of this 'craze', African art and artefacts have become big business. The plundering of Africa's past, initiated under colonialism, persists, removing the very sources that can redress the distorted Western visions of African history and culture.[13] Africa is still represented in museums as a 'colonial spectacle' and critics argued that the *Africa: The Art of a Continent* exhibition at the Royal Academy in 1995, mounted as part of the *africa95* celebrations in London, was little more than a display of exotic objects 'looted' during colonial rule that reproduced static visions of Africa as 'past, pagan and primitive'. This 're-traditionalisation' of African society emphasises the tribal and exotic, and denies the creative and dynamic fusion of African and other cultures in contemporary African cultural life.[14] White 'dreams' of Africa also persist in imagery in the international media which perpetuates visions of backwardness, difference and exoticism. This is particularly prominent in advertisements that play on global signifiers and cultural 'hybridity', which, argues Henry Louis Gates (1994), has degenerated into a commodified post-modern mystification, a seductive vision of 'all the colours of the world, with none of the oppression'. Contemporary academic preoccupations with ethics, philosophy and psychoanalysis, he adds, have avoided political analysis and elided economic realities. 'What's wrong? Racism, colonialism, oppression, cultural imperialism, patriarchy, epistemic violence … we lost the facts'.[15]

In the 1940s the journalist, Alexander Campbell, raised the important question of the future of Africa and concluded that unless there was 'reorganisation', there would be a 'great collapse, famine and bloodshed'. If things remained the same, he argued, 'Africa will remain a great slum among nations'.[16] From the Western perspective, his prophecy seems to have been realised. Since the collapse of communism, Africa has been relegated to 'fourth world' status, forgotten and marginalised in the 'New World Order', and images of chaos and disease have reinforced existing negative images of Africa. With the exception of countries of strategic or economic value, the continent is now of little interest to the West and even humanitarian interventions are suffering from 'doner fatigue'. The UN and governments will now only help those who 'help themselves'. African problems are blamed on the inability of Africans to 'pull themselves up by their boot-strings'.[17] However, we must avoid these universalising and negative visions that stem from the colonial era and beyond. Africa is as diverse as Europe in its people and cultures, and the pattern of post-colonial development has been far from uniform. Positive developments have also occurred, and, as Michael Barratt Brown emphasises, Africa still has choices and the potential to reverse the bleak trends of recent decades. As Patrick Chabal (1994) has argued, the Western vision of Africa, honed through British imperial rule, has always been 'largely a figment of its own imagination rather than of a serious interest in what actually happens in the continent'. Framed by this 'politics of the mirror', African culture and development is consistently judged from Eurocentric perceptions. The reality of Africa can thus never match Eurocentric expectations, which leads to perennial disappointment.[18]

Africa has never generated the same fond nostalgia for empire as India, which remains the main focus of recent popular reassessments of empire. In this new climate, revisionist historians have resurrected the benefits of British rule in the inter-war years, emphasising how African colonies have been worse off since independence. The uglier facts of colonial rule have effectively been erased.[19] Negative visions of Africa have arguably contributed to the resurgence of racism in Europe, which is linked to the conservative backlash against liberal multira-cialism. 'Fortress Europe' now wants to protect itself from the hordes of economic refugees bringing disease and problems. Since the 1980s, incidents have been reported where African stowaways have been thrown overboard, echoing the horrors of the slave trade and starkly reminding us of the long conti-nuities in Western racism that have sustained Africa's position in the international order.[20] Racial violence is now increasing in Europe. In Britain, this was highlighted by the racist murder in 1993 of Stephen Lawrence, and his parents', as yet fruitless, long struggle to bring his murderers to justice. This durability of racism is rooted in an imperial consciousness that has remained a central part of British identity, surviving what Stuart Hall (1978) terms the 'profound historical forgetfulness' about race and empire during the 1960s and 1970s, when liberal mulitculturalism came into its own.[21]

In this gloomy reappraisal of the legacy of the imperial era in Africa, post-apartheid South Africa, the new 'rainbow nation', shines out as a beacon of hope. South Africa was central to this analysis as the crucible of the most intense debates over race and a clear example of the problematic construction of Britain's 'white empire'. As a 'new', or, more aptly, reformed imperialism was forged in non-settler Africa during the transition to independence, British and South African 'native' policies grew further apart and white settler supremacy became more deeply entrenched. The end of Apartheid in South Africa was thus an epic moment in history – the last African 'decolonisation'. However, democratisation has been accompanied by deepening economic and social inequalities and the expansion of an entrepreneurial and professional black bourgeoisie. The dreams of ordinary people of a decent life after decades of oppression have yet to be realised. Ethnic divisions which were encouraged in the colonial era still threaten to fragment the new South Africa. In the wider context, Sub-Saharan Africa could now become prey to white South African capital and investment, a new danger since the end of Apartheid.[22] The direction of South Africa is still not clear. The Truth and Reconciliation Commission alone cannot heal all the ugly wounds of almost a century of segregation. However, there is still room for optimism. The ending of Apartheid has acted as a great moral boost to those still experiencing racism and oppression and, as it emerges from its enforced isolation, black South Africa can now engage in a fuller cultural, economic and political interaction with the rest of Africa, which could help to regenerate the continent.[23]

It is in this ongoing resistance to racism and Western economic and cultural power where we find the hopeful signs and the endurance of 'dreams of freedom'. The alternative pan-Africanist vision of Africa remains as relevant today as during the inter-war period and, argues Tunde Zack-Williams (1995), Africa and African diaspora identities and struggles are still intimately linked.[24] Pan-Africanism is now a far stronger force in the diaspora than in Africa, dominated by African Americans, who African critics accuse of 'reinventing Africa'. Yet, argues Horace Campbell (1994), pan-Africanism now has an even more vital role in confronting the falsification of African history and negative media images of Africa and is a humanist force, that is part of a 'new universal culture of emancipation'. 'Liberate yourself from mental slavery' sang Bob Marley – a rallying cry of Rastafarianism, which has had resonance throughout the globe, including among native American Indians and New Zealand Maoris.[25]

However, if dreams of freedom in Africa and the African diaspora are to be fully realised, there must also be a change of heart in the West. Africa still reels from the impact of Western imperialism and the racist discourses that have defined Western modernity since the Enlightenment. Perhaps the last people to be liberated from imperial mentalities are those who had (or still have) the greatest stake in empire. A more positive and constructive conceptualisation of Africa and the restructuring of the grossly unequal economic relationship is fundamental here. Africa does not want to be condemned to a fossilised world of 'tradition', but neither does it want an imposed modernity transplanted from the West that denies the validity of its own history and culture. Africa needs to decide its own destiny and there are hopeful signs in the enduring vitality and ingenuity of ordinary African men and women in the face of adversity. In Britain too, while racism is still a strong factor, there are trends towards a cultural hybridity and a more positive and constructive multiculturalism. The mixed marriages which seemed such a threat to the stability of empire and the integrity of 'white culture' are now increasingly common, and there is more tolerance of black/white social interaction than in the US, a fact noted by black British visitors to the US and vice versa.

Many important changes have thus occurred since the period charted in this book. However, in weighing up the balance sheet of imperialism, the negative arguably outweighs the positive. Given the endurance of racism and imperialism, albeit in evolved forms, it is easy to become a Cassandra prophesying doom. What is the future for Africa? Will it become further marginalised or more intensely internationalised by global capitalism? Or will it be increasingly claimed by its diaspora as a source of cultural renewal and an alternative to white culture and power? We must avoid 'Afro-pessimism' and cling to the hope of a more optimistic future. Once more, resistance is the key to this. Sympathetic support in the West is vital, but change is dependent on continued resistance to Western racial and economic oppression in Africa and the African diaspora. Important advances have already been made. The US inherited a world shaped by British imperialism, but also the contradictions inherent in the dialectic between race, resistance and imperialism. Resistance will thus continue and, ultimately, the place of Africa in the world will be determined by Africans.

Notes and references

Preface

1 D.A. Nicol 'The continent that lies within us' reprinted in O. Bassir (ed.) (1957) *An Anthology of West African Verse*, Nigeria: Ibadan, cited in M.J. Herskovits (1962) *The Human Factor in Changing Africa*, New York: Alfred A. Knopf, p. v.
2 W.E. Burghardt Dubois *The Souls of Black Folk: Essays and Sketches*, first published in Chicago, 1902 with a new introduction by Herbert Aptheker, New York, 1973, p. 54.
3 K. Jaywardena *The White Woman's Other Burden*, London, Routledge, 1995, p. 262.
4 This important point was made by Linda Colley on 'Start the Week', *BBC Radio 4*, 9 March 1998.
5 P. Darby, 'Taking Fieldhouse further: post-colonising imperial history' in *Journal of Imperial and Commonwealth History*, 1998, 2: 323–50; D. Kennedy, 'Imperial history and post-colonial theory', ibid., 1996, 24 (3): 345–63.
6 See, for instance, S. Marks 'History, the nation and empire: sniping from the periphery' in *History Workshop*, Spring 1990, 29: 111–19.
7 Kennedy, 'Imperial history and post-colonial theory', p. 365.
8 B. Schwartz 'Conquerors of truth: reflections on post-colonial theory' in B. Schwartz, (ed.) *The Expansion of England: Race, Ethnicity and Cultural History*, London, Routledge, 1996, pp. 9–31, p. 21. See also G. Prakash (ed.) *After Colonialism: Imperial Histories and Post Colonial Displacements*, Princeton, Princeton University Press, 1995.
9 E. Hobsbawm 'To see the future look at the past' in *The Guardian* 7 June 1997; G. Arrighi *The Long Twentieth Century: Money, Power and the Origins of Our Times*, London and New York, Verso, 1994, Introduction.
10 For example, P. Gilroy, *The Black Atlantic: Modernity and Double Consciousness*, London, Verso, 1993; S. Howe, *Anti-colonialism in British Politics: The Left and the End of Empire*, Oxford, Clarendon Press, 1993; P. Rich, *Race and Empire in British Politics, 1890–1960*, Cambridge, Cambridge University Press, 1986; J. N. Pietersie, *Empire and Emancipation; Power and Liberation on a World Scale*, London, Pluto Press, 1990; P.G. Lauren, *Power and Prejudice: the Politics and Diplomacy of Racial Discrimination*, New York, Westview Press, 1996, second edition; F. Furedi, *The Silent War: Racism, Imperialism and Ideology in the Twentieth Century*, London, Pluto, 1998. Other seminal literature is discussed in the Introduction.

Introduction: why imperialism, race and resistance?

1 Foreword by the Rt. Hon. Sir Winston S. Churchill to P. Abrahams, *Jamaica: An Island Mosaic*, London, Corona Library, 1957, p. vii; J.N. Pietersie, *Empire and Emancipation: Power and Liberation on a World Scale*, London, Pluto Press, 1990, p. 223; W.A. Watkins, 'Pan-Africanism and the politics of education' in S.J. Lemelle and R.D.G. Kelley (eds)

Imagining Home: Class, Culture and Nationalism in the African Diaspora, London, Verso, 1994, p. 238.

2 See, for instance, B. Davidson, *The Black Man's Burden: Africa and the Curse of the Nation State*, London, James Currey, 1992; F. Furedi, *The New Ideology of Imperialism: Renewing the Moral Imperative*, London, Pluto Press, 1995, pp. 84–94. For a critique of 'recolonisation', see J. Hanlon, *Mozambique: Who Calls the Shots?* London, James Curry, 1991.

3 See, for instance, H.J. Kaye, 'Imperialism and its legacies' in the introduction to V.G Kiernan, *Imperialism and Its Legacies*, London and New York, Routledge, 1995; I. Wallerstein, *Historical Capitalism with Capitalist Civilisation*, London, Verso, 1996. For a criticism of Furedi, see Anthony Clayton's review of *The New Ideology of Imperialism* in the *Journal of Imperial and Commonwealth History*, 1995, 23: 185–7.

4 D. Judd, *Empire: The British Imperial Experience, from 1765 to the Present*, London, Harper Collins, 1996. See also: A.J. Stockwell, 'Power, Authority and Freedom' in P.J. Marshall (ed.) *The Cambridge Illustrated History of the British Empire*, Cambridge, CUP, 1996, p. 184; Marshall, Introduction, ibid.; M. Beloff, 'The British Empire' in *History Today*, 1996, 46 (2), February; L. James, *The Rise and Fall of the British Empire*, London, 1994 and 'An empire to be proud of', *The Daily Mail*, 5 May 1994.

5 E.W. Said, *Culture and Imperialism*, London, Vintage, 1993, pp. 4–6, 32–7; N. Darbyshire, 'Darkness over empire' *Daily Telegraph*, 26 August 1997; A. King 'Pride and a fall in knowledge of empire', ibid.; C. Hall 'The ruinous ghost of empire past', *The Times Higher*, 18 March 1996.

6 T.H. Von Laue, *The World Revolution: the Twentieth Century* in *Global Perspective*, London, 1989, Ch. 1; S. Latouche, *The Westernisation of the World*, London, Polity, 1996, pp. 5–8; J. Tomlinson, *Cultural Imperialism: A Critical Introduction*, London, Pinter Publishers, 1991, p. 175. See also D. Harvey, *The Condition of Post-Modernity*; G. Arrighi, *The Long Twentieth Century: Money, Power and the Origins of Our Time*, London and New York, Verso, 1994. For a straightforward overview of debates over globalisation, see B. Axford, *The Global System*, London, Polity Press, 1995.

7 Pietersie, *Empire and Emancipation*, p. 22.
So much has been written on theories and explanations of imperialism that it would be impossible to include even a sample of the literature here. However, a good recent summary of debates can be found in ibid., Part One, 'Theoretical overtures'. Also useful is Stephen Howe's summary of current debates in 'David Fieldhouse and imperialism: some historiographical revisions' in *Journal of Imperial and Commonwealth History*, 1998, (26) 1: 213–32.

8 P.J. Cain and A.G. Hopkins, *British Imperialism: Crisis and Deconstruction, 1914–1990*, London, Longman, 1993, pp. 234, 315. See also J.R. Ferris, 'The greatest power on earth: Great Britain in the 1920s' in *International History Review*, 1991, 14 (4): 739; B. McKercher, 'Great Britain pre-eminent in the 1930s', ibid., p. 751. Though coming from a very different perspective, A. Clayton's *The British Empire as a Superpower, 1919–1939*, London, 1989 is also relevant here.

9 E. Hobsbawm, *The Age of Extremes: The Short Twentieth Century: 1914–1991*, London, Michael Joseph, 1994.

10 *The British Empire 1497–1997: 500 Years that Shaped the World*, London, Telegraph Group, 1997 (with Lawrence James as a major contributor). For the contemporary view, see M. Perham *Colonial Sequence, 1930–1949: A Chronological Commentary upon British Colonial Policy, Especially in Africa*, London, Methuen & Co. Ltd., 1967, pp. xii–xiii, 1.

11 A. Little, Johannesburg, 'From Our Foreign Corespondent', *Radio 4*, 27 September 1997. For the centrality of Africa to the elaboration of global racism, see D.T. Goldberg *Racist Culture*, London, Blackwell, 1993, p. 174. The classic works on colonialism are Louis H. Gann and P. Duignan (eds.) *Burden of Empire: An Appraisal of Western Colonialism in Africa South of the Sahara*, New York, 1968 and Louis H. Gann and P. Duignan (eds.) *Colonialism in Africa, 1870–1960*, London, 1970, 2 vols. For a

summary of the literature, see R. Oliver and J.D. Fage, *A Short History of Africa*, London, Penguin, 1988, 6th edn, pp. 274–79.

12 A.G. Hopkins, *An Economic History of West Africa*, London, 1973, pp. 171, 291; Cain and Hopkins, *British Imperialism: Crisis and Deconstruction*, p. 213. Andrew Roberts is one of the few historians to deal with the 'colonial moment' in a more multi-dimensional framework embracing black resistance and shifts in official attitudes at the centre (*The Colonial Moment in Africa: Essays on the Movement of Minds and Materials, 1900–1940*, Cambridge, CUP 1986).

13 See, for example, W.M. Macmillan, *Africa Emergent: A Survey of Social, Economic and Political Trends in British Africa*, London, 1938.

14 E. Goode Robeson, *African Journey*, London, Victor Gollancz Ltd., 1946, p. 3.

15 R. Cohen, *Global Diasporas*, London, UCL Press, 1997, pp. 31, 81. Cohen provides a useful typology of diasporas, including commonalities and differences, which I have drawn on here.

16 'The Black Atlantic', which embraces Africa, America and Europe, is both a geographical and metaphorical concept. Gilroy borrows from William Blake's phrase 'All the Atlantic mountains shook', a metaphor for the upheavals of the enlightenment and the trans-Atlantic slave trade (*The Black Atlantic*, pp. 12–19). See also H. Bhabha, *The Location of Culture*, London, Routledge, 1994, pp. 1–6.

17 P.G. Lauren, *Power and Prejudice: the Politics and Diplomacy of Racial Discrimination*, New York, Westview Press, 1996, 2nd edn, pp. 2–3; T. Sowell, *Race and Culture: A World View*, New York, Basic Books, 1994; A. Memmi, *The Coloniser and the Colonised*, London, Earthscan, 1990, first published, 1957, p.140.

18 F. Anthias and N. Yuval Davis, *Racialised Boundaries: Race Nation Gender, Colour and Class and the Anti-Racist Struggle*, London, Routledge, 1992, p. 40; Goldberg, *Racist Culture*.

19 R. Miles, *Racism after Race Relations*, London, Routledge, 1994, p. 85.

20 Gilroy, *The Black Atlantic*, pp. 32–3. Problems of terminology relating to South Africa are discussed in D.E.H. Russell, *Lives of Courage: Women for a New South Africa*, London, Virago, 1989, p. 6.

21 Anthias and Yuval Davis, *Racialised Boundaries*, p. 15; A.L. Stoler, 'Rethinking colonial categories: European communities and the boundaries of rule' in *Comparative Studies in Society and History*, 1989, no. 31, pp. 135–6; Miles, *Racism after Race Relations*, pp. 51, 104–5.

22 J. Mackenzie, *Propaganda and Empire*, Manchester, MUP, 1988, Introduction; J.N. Pietersie, *White on Black: Images of Africa and Blacks in Western Popular Culture*, New Haven and London, Yale University Press, 1992, p. 77 and Chapter 5, 'Colonialism and Western popular culture'; Said, *Culture and Imperialism*, pp. 4–6, 32–7.

23 N. Thomas, *Colonialism's Culture: Anthropology, Travel and Government*, London, Polity, 1994, pp. 2–3; J. Tomlinson, *Cultural Imperialism: A Critical Introduction*, London, Pinter Publishers, 1991, p. 7.

24 Tomlinson, *Cultural Imperialism*, pp. 3, 140.

25 See, for instance, L.A. Stoler's acclaimed *Race and the Education of Desire: Foucault's History of Sexuality and the Colonial Order of Things*, London and Durham, Duke University Press, 1995.

26 P. Chatterjee, 'Was there a hegemonic project of the colonial state' in D. Engels and S. Marks (eds) *Contesting Colonial Hegemony: State and Society in Africa and India*, London and New York, British Academic Press, 1994, p. 79.

27 D. Engels and S. Marks (eds) *Contesting Colonial Hegemony: State and Society in Africa and India*, London and New York, British Academic Press, 1994, pp. 1–2.
    Cultural imperialism has arguably become more powerful and sophisticated as the twentieth century has progressed and now operates primarily through powerful multi-nationals like the Coca Cola Corporation. These corporations assert 'soft power' through marketing techniques to change culturally determined consumer tastes.

However, they are backed by the potentially omnipotent political and armed force of the US ('The Coca-Cola conquest', Channel 4 Television, 6 August 1998).

28 S. Hall, 'The West and the rest: discourse and power' in S. Hall, *et al.* (eds) *Formations of Modernity*, London, Polity Press/Open University, 1992, p. 295. For discussions of the link between ideologies, power and the state, see E. Laclau, *Politics and Ideology in Marxist Theory*, London, 1977, pp. 1–10. Modern discussions of ideology derive from Gramsci's refinement of Marx's concept of ruling class ideas (*The German Ideology*, pp. 57, 64).

29 F. Furedi, *The Silent War: Racism, Imperialism and Ideology in the Twentieth Century*, London, Pluto, 1998; K. Robinson, *The Dilemmas of Trusteeship: Aspects of British Colonial Policy Between the Wars*, London, 1965; T. Turner 'Anthropology and multiculturalism' in D.T. Goldberg, *Multiculturalism: A Critical Reader*, Oxford, Blackwell, 1994, pp. 411–13. For the challenge to scientific racism, see E. Barkan, *The Retreat from Scientific Racism: the Changing Concepts of Race in Britain and the United States between the World Wars*, Cambridge, CUP, 1992.

30 K. Malik, *The Meaning of Race: Race, History and Culture in Western Society*, London, Macmillan, 1996; p. 174; P. Williams, *Seeing a Colour Blind Future*, London, Virago, 1997. For a provocative discussion of the 'new' geneticism, see M. Kohn, *The Race Gallery, The Return of Racial Science*, London, Cape, 1996.

Patricia Williams' lectures unleashed accusations from those unwilling to listen that the lectures were too 'politically correct' (N. Lacey 'Perspective: Grace under fire', *The Times Higher*, 7 February 1997).

31 See, for example, Miles *Racism after Race Relations* and various articles in Goldberg (ed.) *Multiculturalism*.

32 Malik, *The Meaning of Race*, p. 6; Goldberg *Racist Culture* 1994, pp. 4–5; S. Hall, 'The new ethnicities' in D. and A. Rattsani (eds) *Race, Culture and Difference*, London, Sage, 1992, p. 256; P. Mclaren 'White terror and oppositional agency: towards a critical multiculturalism' in Goldberg, *Multiculturalism*, pp. 45–75. For stimulating critiques of Eurocentricism, see Z. Sardar, A. Nandy, M. Wynn Davies, *Barbaric Others: A Manifesto on Western Racism*, London and Boulder, Colorado, Pluto Press, 1993; S. Amin, *Eurocentricism*, London, Zed, 1989.

33 For a fuller discussion of these issues, see Goldberg, *Racist Culture*, Chapter two, 'Modernity, race and morality'.

34 D. Held, *Models of Democracy*, London, Polity, 1987, pp. 66–71.

35 Goldberg, 'Multicultural conditions', in Goldberg, (ed) *Multiculturalism*, pp. 17–18.

36 K. Marx and F. Engels, 'The Manifesto of the Communist Party' in *Selected Works in One Volume*, London, 1968, pp. 39ff.

37 B. Warren, *Imperialism: Pioneer of Capitalism*, London, 1980, pp. 3, 125; M. Berman, *All That is Solid Melts into Air: The Experience of Modernity*, London, Verso, 1983, pp. 15, 34–5, 90.

38 Marx, cited in Berman, *All That is Solid Melts into Air*, p. 101.

39 W.A. Watkins, 'Pan-Africanism and the politics of education' in Lemelle and Kelley (eds) *Imagining Home*, p. 223.

40 Lemelle and Kelley, Introduction, *Imagining Home*, p. 3. For background to the early development of pan-Africanism, see W.J. Moses, *The Golden Age of Black Nationalism, 1850–1925*, New York, 1978 and for a more general analysis, see V. Thompson, *Africa and Unity: The Evolution of pan-Africanism*, New York, 1969; I. Geiss, *The Pan-African Movement: A History of Pan-Africanism in America, Europe and Africa*, New York, 1974. For the black radical perspective, see C.L.R. James, *A History of Pan-African Revolt*, London, 1938.

41 G.A. Nelson, 'Rastafarians and Ethiopianism' in Lemelle and Kelley, *Imagining Home*, pp. 69–71. For a fuller study of Garvey, see R.A. Hill and B. Bair (eds) *Marcus Garvey: Life and Lessons*, Berkeley, California, UCLA Press, 1987; L. Mackie, *The Great Marcus Garvey* London, Hansib Publishers, 1987. For a firsthand insight into Garveyism, see

Amy Jacques Garvey (ed.), *The Philosophy and Opinions of Marcus Garvey*, reprinted in London, Frank Cass, 1967.

42 C.J. Robinson, 'W.E.B. Dubois and Black Sovereignty' in Lemelle and Kelley, *Imagining Home*, p. 151. Booker T. Washington founded the Tuskegee Institute which provided vocational and manual training for blacks and advocated racial upliftment through self-help and black entrepreneurialism.

43 B. Bair, 'Pan-Africanism as a Process: Adelaide Casely Hayford' in Lemelle and Kelley, *Imagining Home*, p. 123.

44 Pietersie, *Empire and Emancipation*, p. xii, iv.

45 See, for example, A.M. Bak Rasmussen, *A History of the Quaker Movement in Africa*, London, British Academic Press, 1994.

46 Engels and Marks, *Contesting Colonial Hegemony*, p. 2.

47 C. Venn, 'History Lessons: Formation of Subject, Post Colonialism and an Other Protest', in B. Schwartz (ed.) *The Expansion of England: Race, Ethnicity and Cultural History*, London, Routledge, 1996, pp. 32–60, p. 32.

48 E. Said, cited in Pietersie, *Empire and Emancipation*, p. 353.

49 Pietersie, *Empire and Emancipation*, pp. 356–61, 378. See also G.W.F. Hegel, *The Phenomenology of Mind* with an introduction and notes by J.B. Baillie, London, 1949, 2nd edn, pp. 234–6. Hegel was talking about the master/slave relationship, but his ideas are also arguably relevant to the colonial context.

50 Goldberg, 'Multicultural Conditions', *Multiculturalism*, p. 25.

51 W.E. Burghardt Dubois, *The Souls of Black Folk: Essays and Sketches*, first published in Chicago, 1902, with a new introduction by Herbert Aptheker, New York, 1973, p. 45.

1 Africa after the First World War: race and imperialism redefined?

1 G.L. Beer, *African Questions at the Paris Peace Conference*, edited and with an introduction, annexes and additional notes by Louis Herbert Gray, London, Dawsons of Pall Mall, 1923, p.280. M. Perham, 'The future of East Africa' in *The Times*, August 1931, cited in *Colonial Sequence, 1930–1949: A Chronological Commentary upon British Colonial Policy, Especially in Africa*, London, Methuen & Co. Ltd., 1967, p. 41; L. Stoddard, *The Rising Tide of Colour*, London, 1935, first published 1924, p.4.

2 A. Porter, *The Lion's Share: A Short History of British Imperialism, 1850–1995*, London, Longman, 1996, 3rd edn, first published in 1976, pp. 265, 272; J.W. Young, *Britain and the World in the Twentieth Century*, London, Arnold, 1997, pp. 80–7, 100. For contemporary left analyses of the war, see V.I. Lenin, *Imperialism: The Highest Stage of Capitalism: A Popular Outline*, London, 1939, first published in 1916; H.N. Brailsford, *The War of Steel and Gold*, London, 1914; F. Brockway, *How to End War – the I.L.P. view on Imperialism and Internationalism*, London, I.L.P. Publication Department, 1922.

3 See for instance, R. Briffaut, *The Decline and Fall of the British Empire*, New York, 1938, pp. 11, 17, 20–2; Angus Gillan cited in C.Allen, ed. *Tales From the Dark Continent: Images of British Colonial Africa in the Twentieth Century*, London, Futura, 1979, p.39; T.O. Lloyd. *The British Empire, 1558–1995*, Oxford, OUP, 1996, Second Edition 1995, p.293. Psychological weaknesses and insecurities are also heavily stressed in N. Mansergh, *Survey of British Commonwealth Affairs: Problems of External Policy; 1931–1939*, London, 1942, pp. 415–7.

4 For further background to white settlement, see K. Fedorowich, *Unfit for Heroes: Reconstruction and Soldier Settlement in the Empire Between the Wars*, Manchester, MUP, 1995.

5 Sir R. Furse, *Acuparius: Recollections of a Recruiting Officer*, London, 1962, pp. 32–3; C. Parkinson, *The Colonial Office from Within, 1909–1945*, London, 1947, pp.100–2.

6 Furse, *Acuparius*, p. 286; W.M. Macmillan, *Africa Emergent: A Survey of Social, Political and Economic Trends in British Africa*, London, 1938, pp. 207, 269.

7 H.H. Egerton, *British Colonial Policy in the Twentieth Century*, London, Methuen & Co., 1922, preface; L. Woolf, *Imperialism and Civilisation*, London, Hogarth Press, 1928, pp. 17, 27; E. Hobsbawm, *The Age of Extremes: The Short Twentieth Century: 1914–1991*, London, Michael Joseph, 1994, p. 211. Egerton was a fellow of All Souls College and a former Beit Professor of Colonial History at Oxford.

8 L. Woolf, *Imperialism*, pp. 29–30; L. Woolf, *Empire and Commerce in Africa – A Study in Economic Imperialism*, London, 1920, p. 34; E. Hobsbawm, *The Age of Extremes: The Short Twentieth Century: 1914–1991*, pp. 14, 87.

9 H. Harper, 'Disintegrating forces in the Empire', in H.E. Harper (ed.) *Empire Problems* (Report of the Third Cambridge Empire Conference, 28–30 October 1938), London, Frederick Muller Ltd.,1939, p. 131. For the imperial interests of Conservative MPs, see S. Haxey, *Tory MP*, Left Book Club Edition, London, Gollancz, 1939, Chapter V, 'Tory Stake in the Empire', pp. 89–116. Pietersie also discusses the importance of Freemasonry in *Empire and Emancipation; Power and Liberation on a World Scale*, London, Pluto Press, 1990, p. 141.

10 Pietersie, *Empire*, pp. 253–4. See also C. Quigley, *The Anglo-American Establishment: From Rhodes to Cliveden*, New York, 1981, pp. 19–20, 130–5, 192, 254; and H.A. Wyndham, *Problems of Imperial Trusteeship: The Atlantic and Emancipation*, London, 1937, for the contemporary 'Round Table' view on race.

11 Pietersie, *Empire*, p. 271; Quigley, *The Anglo-American Establishment*, pp. xiii, 63–4, 156–8, 168–9, 181–3, 311–4.

12 S. Frankel, *Capital Investment in Africa*, London, 1938, p. 159. Hailey (1957) also provides a wealth of detail about the economics of empire in Africa.

13 P.J. Cain and A.G. Hopkins, *British Imperialism: Crisis and Deconstruction, 1914–1990*, London, Longman, 1993, pp. 201–4, 213–4, 233. For Africa and commodity markets, see D. Rothermund, *The Global Impact of the Great Depression, 1929–1939*, London, Routledge, 1996. Havinden and Meredith also argue that trade was a major reason for continued imperial expansion (M. Havinden and D. Meredith, *Colonialism and Development: Britain and its Tropical Colonies, 1850–1960*, London, Routledge, 1993, pp. 4, 20).

14 R. Palme Dutt, *Empire Socialism*, London, CPGB, 1926, pp. 6–7, 10, 14; L. Haden-Guest, *The Labour Party and the Empire*, London, Labour Party, 1926, pp. 7, 17, 24, 83–4. Ironically, Haden-Guest's daughter was a member of the CPSA in the 1930s and he himself moved sharply to the left in the late 1930s.

15 P. Sarathi Gupta, *Imperialism and the British Labour Movement, 1914–1964*, London, 1975, pp. 52–6. See also G. Stedman Jones, *Languages of Class: Studies in English Working-class History, 1832–1982*, Cambridge, CUP, 1983, p. 238.

16 J.M. Mackenzie (ed.), *Imperialism and Popular Culture*, London, MUP, 1987; J. Mangan (ed.) *Benefits Bestowed? Education and British Imperialism*, Manchester, MUP, 1988. See also Cain and Hopkins, *British Imperialism*, pp. 213–4.

17 *Colonial Information Bulletin*, 1 (7), July 1937, p. 3. Empire Day was the brainchild of the Earl of Meath who, in 1896, suggested the Queen's birthday, 24 May, should be a day of patriotic celebrations, and founded the Empire Day Movement in 1903 (Mackenzie, 'In Touch with the Infinite; the BBC and the Empire, 1923–53' in Mackenzie (ed.) *Imperialism and Popular Culture*, pp. 165–85, p. 165).

18 Mackenzie 'In Touch with the Infinite'; Hobsbawm, *Age of Extremes*, p. 195.

19 J. Richards, 'Empire and Cinema in the 1920s and 1930s' in J. Richards (ed.) *The Age of the Dream Palace*, London, 1984, pp. 134–6; R. Smyth, 'Movies and Mandarins: the Official Film and British Colonial Africa' in J. Curran and V. Porter (eds) *British Cinema History*, London, Wiedenfeld and Nicholson, 1983, pp. 78–94.

20 Sir M. Hailey, *An African Survey; A Study of Problems Arising in Africa South of the Sahara*, London, OUP, 1957, p. 364. See also p. 1254.

21 Paul Holt in the *Daily Express*, 1938, cited in Richards, 'Empire and Cinema', pp. 1, 34. See also ibid., pp. 34–6.

22 B. Matthews, *The Clash of Colour: A Study in the Problem of Race*, London, 1924, p. 43; J. M. Mackenzie, *Propaganda and Empire*, Manchester, MUP, 1988, pp. 68–9; R. Stam and E. Shohat, 'Contested Histories: Eurocentricism, Multiculturalism and the Media' in D.T. Goldberg (ed.) *Multiculturalism: A Critical Reader*, Oxford, Blackwell, 1994, pp. 296–34, 303–4. Government policy on censorship is outlined in *Report of the Colonial Films Committee, 1929–30*, Cmd. 3630, London, HMSO, 1930.

23 See, for instance, Lord S. Olivier, *White Capital and Coloured Labour*, London, 1929, p. 37.

24 C.L.R. James, 'A History of Negro Revolt' in *Fact*, September 1938, 18: 64–6. See also C. Dover, *Half-Caste*, London, 1937, pp. 14–6, 70, 107–8; W.E.B. Dubois, *The World and Africa: An inquiry into the part which Africa has played in world history*, New York, 1965, first published 1946–7, p. 25.

25 M. Foucault, *The History of Sexuality*, trans. from French by Robert Hurley, London, 1978–1979, first published, Paris, 1976, vol. 1, *An Introduction*, pp. 84–5, 148. Although his arguments are not always convincing, Roger Hyam provides useful detail here in *Empire and Sexuality*, Manchester, MUP, 1991.

26 J. Huxley and A.C. Hadden, *We Europeans: A Survey of Racial Problems, with a chapter on Europe Overseas, by A.M. Carr Saunders*, London, Jonathan Cape, 1935, pp. 7–8, 89, 167, 281; E. Barkan, *The Retreat from Scientific Racism: The Changing Concepts of Race in Britain and the United States between the World Wars*, Cambridge, CUP, 1992, pp. 179–82, 297.

27 Woolf, *Empire and Commerce*, pp. 33–4; Sir A. Burns, *Colour Prejudice with Particular Reference to the Relationship Between Whites and Negroes*, London, 1948, p. 15.

28 This term was used by Peter Brook, 'Beyond the Blue Horizon', *BBC Radio 4*, 3 March 1994, in exploring popular culture and Africa in the inter-war years.

29 Perham, *Colonial Sequence*, p. 89; Woolf, *Imperialism*, p. 34. See also M. Vaughan, *Curing their Ills: Colonial Power and African Illness*, Cambridge, Polity Press, 1991; J. McCulloch, *Colonial Psychiatry and the African Mind*, New York, CUP, 1995. Cannibalism, as a common trope in European popular culture, is discussed in J.N. Pietersie, *White on Black: Images of Africa and Blacks in Western Popular Culture*, New Haven and London, Yale University Press, 1992, pp. 113–22.

30 Beer, *African Questions*, pp. 179, 282. For a critique of the Western view of Africa, see V.Y. Mudimbe, *The Idea of Africa*, London, James Currey, 1995; R.C. Young, *White Mythologies: Writing History and the West*, London, Routledge, 1990.

31 G. Hoyningen-Huene, *African Mirage: The Record of a Journey*, London, B.T. Batsford, 1938, pp. 8, 17, 27.

32 I.D. MacCrone, *Race Attitudes in South Africa: Historical, Experimental and Psychological Studies*, London and New York, OUP, 1937, pp. xvii, 179.

33 Hoyningen-Huene, *African Mirage*, pp. 26–7; biographical data from a BBC talk in the series 'The Time of My Life', Radio 4, 11 January 1972, quoted in M. Perham, *African Apprenticeship: An Autobiographical Journey in Southern Africa, 1929*, London, 1974, 'Prologue'.

   Perham was a leading exponent of the progressive indirect rule school and close to Lord Lugard. She travelled extensively in Africa and became a lecturer on native administration at Oxford. Throughout her career, she maintained 'a close nexus ... with the ideas of the Colonial Service' (ibid.).

34 E. Huxley, *East Africa*, London, published for the Penns in the Rock Press by William Collins, 1941, as part of the promotional British Commonwealth in Pictures series, pp. 16–7; G.W.F. Hegel, *The Philosophy of History*, with an introduction by C.J. Friedrich and translated by J. Sibree, New York, Dover Publications Ltd., 1956, pp. 91–9. Interestingly, the Sibree translation was first published by the Colonial Press, 1899. Hegel's original text was based on a series of lectures given in the 1820s.

35 E.W. Said, *Culture and Imperialism*, London, Vintage, 1993, p. 168; T. Meisenhelder, 'Marx, Engels, and Africa', *Science and Society*, Summer 1995, 59 (2): 197–205.

36 Perham, *Colonial Sequence*, pp. 35–7. For the impact of anti-slavery on British policy and Western thought see D.B. Davis, *Slavery and Human Freedom*, London and Harvard, Yale University Press, 1986.

37 Olivier, *White Capital and Coloured Labour*, pp. 41–2; Woolf, *Imperialism and Civilisation*, p. 108.

38 Huxley, *East Africa*, pp. 35–6; Sir A. Cohen, *British Policy in Changing Africa*, London, Routledge & Kegan Paul, 1960, first printed, 1959, with a foreword by Adlai E. Stevenson, 1958, pp. 7–8; Perham, *Colonial Sequence*, Introduction. For insight into relations between Africans and Europeans in the era of slavery, see N. Tattersall, *The Forgotten Trade: Comprising the Log of Daniel and Henry of 1700 and Accounts of the Slave Trade from the Minor Ports of England, 1698–1725*, London, Jonathan Cape, 1991.

39 M. Perham, 'Education for Self Government' in *Foreign Affairs*, October, 1945, reproduced in *Colonial Sequence*, pp. 263–76, p. 272; A.J. Toynbee, *A Study of History*, London, 1935, 2nd edn, 3 vols, vol. 2, p. 365.

40 K. Castle, *Britannia's Children: Reading Colonialism through Children's Books and Magazines*, Manchester, MUP, 1996. Waugh's travels and his motives for travel are summarised in *When the Going Was Good*, London, Penguin, 1968. Mills wrote of the 'vexed black problem' in books such as *Episodes from the Road to Timbuktu*, London, Duckworth, 1946, first published in 1927. Her books successfully popularised official policies and were republished in the 1940s by Duckworth's School Library.

41 J.R. Ryan, *Picturing Empire: Photography and the Visualisation of the British Empire*, London, Reaktion Books, 1997; A.E. Coombes, *Reinventing Africa: Museums, Material Culture and Popular Imagination*, Yale University Press, New Haven and London, 1994, particularly Chs 5 & 6; and Pietersie, *White on Black*, pp. 188–212 for advertisements.

42 Perham, 'East Africa', *The Times*, 1931, cited in M. Perham, *Colonial Sequence*, p. 41. See also Brook, 'Beyond the Blue Horizon'.

43 J. Pines, 'British Cinema and Black Representation' in R. Murphy (ed.) *The British Cinema Book*, London, British Film Institute Publishing, 1997, pp. 207–16, p. 207.

44 Castle, *Britannia's Children: Reading Colonialism through Children's Books and Magazines*, pp. 105, 115, 170–3.

45 Lord Lugard, *Political Memoranda: Revision of Instructions to Political Officers on Subjects Chiefly Political and Administrative, 1913–1918*, edited with an introduction by A.H.M. Kirk-Greene, London, Frank Cass, 1970, pp. 9, 168–9, 200–1, 208. See also Lugard, *The Dual Mandate in British Tropical Africa*, London, 1922. For a more in-depth study of imperial discourse during the inter-war years, see P. Hetherington, *British Paternalism and Africa, 1920–1940*, London, 1978.

46 Lugard, *Political Memoranda: Revision of Instructions to Political Officers on Subjects Chiefly Political and Administrative, 1913–1918*, pp. 166–7, 208, 319.

47 Ibid., pp. 9, 30. See also, Kirk-Greene, Introduction to ibid., p. xx; Roberts, 'The imperial mind' in A. Roberts (ed.) *The Colonial Moment in Africa: Essays on the movement of minds and materials, 1900–1940*, Cambridge, CUP, 1990, pp. 24–62, p. 60.

48 Macmillan, *Africa Emergent: A Survey of Social, Political and Economic Trends in British Africa*, pp. 16–17, 22, 87, 375; Huxley, *East Africa*, pp. 56–8. For humanitarian arguments for separate development, see A.S. Cripps, *An Africa for the Africans: A Plea on Behalf of Territorial Segregation Areas and of their Freedom in a South African Colony*, London, 1927, pp. 100–1, 115–8, 142–3.

49 Furse, *Aucuparius: Recollections of a Recruiting Officer*, pp. 145, 264, 292, 306.

50 G. Padmore, *Africa: Britain's Third Empire*, New York, Negro Universities Press, 1969, first published in 1949, pp. 258–9. See also M. Perham 'France in the Cameroons' in *The Times*, May 1933, reproduced in *Colonial Sequence, 1930–1949: A Chronological Commentary upon British Colonial Policy, Especially in Africa*, p. 74; R.L. Buell, *The Native Problem in Africa*, New York, 1928, 2 vols, vol. 2, pp. 77, 79–85. For French cruelty, see also G. Gorer, *Africa Dances*, London, 1935, pp. 42–5, 77, 115. For fuller comparison

between French and British policy, see P. Gifford and W.R. Louis (eds) *France and Britain in Africa: Imperial Rivalry and Colonial Rule*, New Haven and London, 1971.

51 Padmore, *Africa: Britain's Third Empire*, p. 112.

52 M. Perham, *Ten Africans*, London, 1936, pp. iv–xii; Porter, *The Lion's Share*, p. 265: T.O. Ranger, 'The Invention of Tradition in Colonial Africa' in E. Hobsbawm and T.O. Ranger (eds) *The Invention of Tradition*, Cambridge, CUP, 1983, pp. 211–63, p. 250.

53 B. Matthews, *Consider Africa*, London, 1935, pp. 17–18, 95–6, 100–3, 125, 130–2; E. Huxley, *East Africa*, p. 41.

54 Z.K. Matthews 'An African View of Indirect Rule in Africa' in *Journal of the Royal African Society*, 1937, 36 (3): 433–7. See also *Memorandum by the Advisory Committee on Native Education in the British Tropical Dependencies, 1924–5*, Cmd. 2374, London, HMSO, 1925, pp. 1–5. Oldham's ideas are outlined in J.H. Oldham and B.D. Gibson, *The Remaking of Man in Africa: on Christian Education in Africa*, London, 1931. Vischer was a Swiss person who became a British citizen.

55 Perham, *Ten Africans*, Introduction; L. Mair, *Anthropology and Social Change*, London, 1969, pp. 45–6, 89, 110 and 'A Science of Colonial Government' in *Contemporary Review*, 1934, 145: 80–8. For comments on Perham, see correspondence between Malinowski and Oldham, cited in J. Goody, *The Expansive Moment: Anthropology in Britain and Africa, 1918–1970*, Cambridge, CUP, 1995, p. 26.

56 H. Kuklich, *The Savage Within: The Social History of British Anthropology, 1885–1945*, Cambridge, CUP, 1991, pp. 50–2. For the compatibility of Malinowski's theories with indirect rule, see Porter, *The Lion's Share: A Short History of British Imperialism, 1850–1995*, p. 287.

57 Goody, *The Expansive Moment: Anthropology in Britain and Africa, 1918–1970* , pp. 17–18. Also relevant is E.H. Berman 'Educational Colonialism in Africa: The Role of American Foundations, 1910–1945' in R.F. Arngrove (ed.) *Philanthropy and Cultural Imperialism: The Foundations at Home and Abroad*, Boston, 1980, pp. 185–7.

The IIA (International Institute of African Languages and Culture) provided seventeen Rockefeller funded fellowships between 1931 and 1939, all but three in British territories. The recipients included six South Africans and four German/Austrians (Roberts, 'The Imperial Mind', pp. 50–1).

58 Goody, *The Expansive Moment: Anthropology in Britain and Africa, 1918–1970*, pp. 39–43, 75–7, 85, 106, 125–7. For misogyny of male anthropologists, see, for example, Evans-Pritchard to Fortes, 1937, 19 July 1940, cited in ibid., pp. 69–71. Key women anthropologists included Audrey Richards, who became a Smuts Reader at Cambridge and subsequently Director of African Studies in the 1940s, Edith Clarke, a Jamaican who went out to the Gold Coast in 1931, and Lucy Mair at LSE.

59 Goody, *The Expansive Moment: Anthropology in Britain and Africa, 1918–1970*, p. 3; Barkan, *The Retreat from Scientific Racism: The Changing Concepts of Race in Britain and the United States between the World Wars*, pp. 57, 67, 91.

60 Discussant's comments (including William Macmillan) in M. Perham, 'Some Problems of Indirect Rule in Africa', Address to the Royal Society of Arts, 24 March 1934, reproduced in *Colonial Sequence, 1930–1949: A Chronological Commentary upon British Colonial Policy, Especially in Africa*, pp. 91–119, p.115. African students that attended included a West African law student, S.J. Thompson and Joseph T. Sackeyfio (Gold Coast).

61 E. Goode Robeson, *African Journey*, London, Victor Gollancz Ltd., 1946, pp. 10–12, 163. Eslanda (Essie) Robeson travelled with her nine-year-old son, Pauli, as a VIP, a reflection of Robeson's 'film star' status. However, she still found difficulty obtaining visas, particularly for South Africa. Her explanation is that they wanted to keep educated negroes out with the exception of a few missionaries (p. 15). Essie was fair skinned and highly educated, but had a strong sense of her African 'roots' through her father who was interested in 'Negro' history (p. 21).

62 Roberts, 'The Imperial Mind', p. 60. For the influence of African art on Picasso's work, see J. Richardson, 'A Perfect Image of Savagery', in *Guardian Weekend*, 19 October 1996, pp. 4–23, p. 22.

63 M. Barratt Brown, 'An African Road for Development: Are We All Romantics?' in *Leeds African Studies Bulletin*, December 1997, 62: 13–41, 30. L. Vail, Introduction, in L. Vail (ed.) *The Creation of Tribalism in Southern Africa*, London, James Currey, 1989, pp. 1–7.

64 Louis Herbert Gray, 'Introduction' in G.L. Beer, *African Questions at the Paris Peace Conference*, p. xv. See also W.M. Louis, *Imperialism at Bay: The United States and the Decolonisation of the British Empire, 1941–1945*, Oxford, OUP, 1977, p. 188.

65 Gray, 'Introduction' in *African Questions at the Paris Peace Conference*. Gray, who was Secretary to the US Colonial Division at the talks, updated the manuscript for publication after Beer's death.

66 Beer, *African Questions at the Paris Peace Conference*, pp. 45, 73–6, 414. For further insight, see W.M. Louis, 'The United States and the African Peace Settlement of 1919: The Pilgrimage of George Louis Beer' in *The Journal of African History*, 1963, 4: 413–33.

67 Beer *African Questions at the Paris Peace Conference*, pp. 72, 112, 193, 179.

68 Ibid., pp. xvi, 85–6, 105, 168–70, 279. Annex F, 'Convention Relating to the Liquor Traffic in Africa and Protocol', pp. 501–6; P.G. Lauren, *Power and Prejudice: the Politics and Diplomacy of Racial Discrimination*, New York, Westview Press, 1996, 2nd edn, pp. 31–3. For a fuller background to international settlements in this period, see H. Wesserling, *The Partition of Africa, 1880–1914*, translated by A.J. Pomerans, London and Westport Conn., Praeger, 1996.

69 A. Olukoju, 'Race and Access to Liquor: Prohibition as Colonial Policy in Northern Nigeria, 1919–45' in *The Journal of Imperial and Commonwealth History*, 1996, 24(2): 218–43; E. Akyeampong, 'What's in a Drink? Class Struggle, Popular Culture and the Politics of *Akpeteshie* (local gin) in Ghana, 1930–67' in *Journal of African History*, 1996, 37: 215–36.

70 Ryan, *Picturing Empire: Photography and the Visualisation of the British Empire*, pp. 125–6.

   Conservation discourse is a relatively new area of interest and there is not space to discuss the nuances here. The main debates and issues are admirably summed up in J.M. Mackenzie, *The Empire of Nature: Hunting, Conservation and British Imperialism*, Manchester, MUP, 1988.

71 Olivier, *White Capital and Coloured Labour*, p. 44. See also Lloyd George, 'Peace Conference: British Empire Delegation', 5, minutes of the meeting held at the Hotel Majestic, Paris on Thursday, 28 January, 1919, marked 'Secret' and 'Property of His Majesty's Britannic Government', Smuts Papers. H 5, vol. 13; ibid., 'British Empire Delegation', 1, minutes of the meeting, 13 January 1919.

   The delegation met at the Hotel Majestic in Paris with Lloyd George as chair. Delegation members included A.J. Balfour, Secretary of State for Foreign Affairs, the Chancellor of the Exchequer, Austin Chamberlain, E.S. Montagu, the Secretary of State for India, a General and a Rear Admiral, Philip Kerr, the Prime Ministers of Canada and New Zealand, Louis Botha, the Prime Minister of South Africa, Jan Smuts as the Union's Minister of Defence and official representative at the Peace Conference, Major-General His Highness the Maharaja of Bikaner, Sir Bahadur Ganga Singh and the Right Honourable Lord Sinha K.C., Parliamentary Under-Secretary of State for India.

72 Memorandum by Lord Milner, 'Appendix' in 'British Empire Delegation', 13, minutes of the meeting held on 13 March 1919. See also 'British Empire Delegation', 5, minutes of the meeting held on 28 January 1919 and the general survey of minutes from January to March. For general background to the mandates, see A. Sharp, *The Versailles Settlement: Peacemaking in Paris, 1919*, London, St Martin's Press, 1991; B. Digre, *Imperialism's New Clothes: The Reparation of Tropical Africa, 1914–1919*, New York, 1990.

73 Lauren, *Power and Prejudice*, pp. 73–4, 89–98, R. Segal, *The Race War: The World Wide Clash of White and Non White*, New York, Bantam, 1967, p. 58. See also A. Sharp, 'The Mandate System in the Colonial World' in W.R. Keylor (ed.) *The Legacy of the Great War: Peacemaking, 1919*, Boston, New York, Houghton Mifflin, 1998, pp. 169–86, p. 170; Hailey, *African Survey: A Study of Problems Arising in Africa South of the Sahara*, 1956, p. 431.

74 Dubois, *World and Africa: An inquiry into the part which Africa has played in world history*, pp. 83–9, 237–43 and 'Memoranda on the Future of Africa', cited in Keylor, *The Legacy of the Great War: Peacemaking, 1919*, pp. 224–27.

75 'Order of Executive Council: Appointment of Smuts', 15 April 1919, Smuts Papers A1, band 115, vol. 13; Beer, *African Questions*, pp. 60–1, 72, 112, 465 and Annex L, 'Mandate for German South West Africa', pp. 545–6.

76 'Terms of Admission of Rhodesia into the Union of South Africa', 21 July 1922, Smuts Papers, A1, band 115, vol. 32; 'Proceedings of the Rhodesian Conference' (Secret, no. 5), ibid., vol. 31. At this time, both Southern and Northern Rhodesia were governed by the British South Africa Company and its paramilitary arm, the British South African Police, under a charter obtained by Rhodes in 1889 (Roberts, 'The Imperial Mind', p. 45).

77 Contemporary source, cited in Lauren, *Power and Prejudice*, p. 59.

78 Woolf, *Imperialism*, pp. 82, 127–9, 133 and *Empire and Commerce*, pp. 354–7, 360–7.

79 See, for instance, Briffault, *The Decline and Fall of the British Empire*, pp. 203–9; Dover, *Half-Caste*, p. 238. For the view of reformist critics, see N. Leys, 'The Tropics and the League of Nations' in *Socialist Review*, January to March 1921 2 (1): 28–35.

80 A.M. Graves (ed.) *Both Deeper than and above the Mêlée – Letters from Europeans*, Baltimore, privately printed, 1945, Appendix 5, p. 406 and *Benvenuto Cellini had no Prejudice against Bronze: Letters from West Africans*, Baltimore, privately published, 1943, pp. 102, 160–6.

The 'Save The Children Fund' was set up originally to take care of Armenian and Greek children displaced from Turkish Armenia during World War One, but by 1931 had turned its attention to Africa. Anna Melissa Graves was an American Quaker who was on the Executive Board of the Women's International League for Peace and Freedom until 1934 and visited Geneva often.

81 Woolf, *Imperialism*, pp. 13–4, 16, 19, 60, 92.

82 D. Killingray, 'A Swift Agent of Government: Air Power in British Colonial Africa, 1916–1939' in *Journal of African History*, 1984, 25 (2): 125–48. For general background to developments in colonial control, see D.E. Omissi, *Air Power and Colonial Control: The Royal Airforce, 1919–39*, Manchester, MUP, 1990.

83 C. Dover, *Half-Caste*, London, 1939, with a preface by Lancelot Hogben, pp. 38, 48, 52, 226 and *Know of this Race*, London, 1939, pp. 9–16, 67. Hogben, a Fabian mathematician and friend of the anthropologist, Meyer Fortes, was in South Africa between 1927–1929 and made himself unpopular with the authorities by accepting coloured students in his classes and holding Saturday night 'open' houses, which were seen as a 'hotbed of radicalism' (Goody, *The Expansive Moment*, p. 230).

84 Barkan, *The Retreat from Scientific Racism*, pp. 9, 284–92; M. Hirschfeld, *Racism*, translated and edited by Eden and Cedar Paul, London, 1938, pp. 28, 112–5, 256–63.

85 J.A. Rogers, *Sex and Race: Negro Caucasian Mixing in All Ages and All Lands*, New York, 1942–1944, reprint, Helga M. Rogers, 1972, 3 vols, vol. 3, pp. 138–142; C. Dover, *Know of This Race*, London, 1939, p. 35.

Rogers was brought up in the West Indies where he became interested in issues related to inter-racial sex. He began writing for the black press in the US in 1920, and during the inter-war years travelled extensively, scouring libraries for data on race and sex. In 1930 he was elected to membership of the Paris Society of Anthropology. *Sex and Race* was published privately and provides a wealth of detailed information (Rogers, op. cit., 1, pp. 302–4, 3). Lemelle and Kelley see Rogers as a forerunner of Afrocentricity who failed to adopt a critical stance towards capitalism and the class struggle (S.J. Lemelle and R.D.G. Kelley (eds) *Imagining Home: Class, Culture and Nationalism in the African Diaspora*, London, Verso, 1994, p.3).

86 L. Stoddard, *The Rising Tide of Colour Against White World Supremacy*, New York, 1921, p. 22.

87 *National and Colonial Questions: Theses adopted at the Second Congress of the Comintern*, Moscow, August 1920, London, CPGB, 1920, pp. 21–4; Hobsbawm, *Age of Extremes*, pp. 55–6.

88 G. Padmore, *The Life and Struggles of Negro Toilers*, London, RILU, 1931, pp. 121, 123; T.A. Jackson, 'The I.L.D. and The Negro Peoples' in *Negro Worker*, Feb–March 1933, 3 (2/3): 12. By the 1930s, I.L.D. had members in South Africa and contacts in Kenya, Sierra Leone and Senegal.

89 *The Revolutionary Movement in the Colonies and Semi-Colonies: Thesis… Adopted by the Sixth World Congress of the Communist International, 1928*, London, 1929. For white fears, see D. Thwaite, *The Seething African Pot: A Study of Black Nationalism, 1882–1935*, London, 1936; and for general background, see E.T. Wilson, *Russia and Black Africa Before World War II*, London, 1974, pp. 113–39.

90 'A Report of the Proceedings and Decisions of the First International Conference of Negro Workers at Hamburg, Germany, July, 1930', Hamburg, ITUCNW, 1930, pp. 1–5, 12, 30–40. See also 'Report of the 4th Congress of the RILU', London, CPGB, 1928, p. 187; 'Report of the 5th Congress of the RILU', London, CPGB, 1930, p. 164.

ITUCNW delegates represented 20,000 workers, 7 countries and 11 different unions. The provisional executive committee included James W. Ford (USA), W. Thibedi (South Africa), Johnstone Kenyatta and George Padmore (at that time a Comintern agent). I.T.A. Wallace Johnson (Sierra Leone), E. Small (Gambia) and Frank Macaulay (Nigeria) also attended. The conference was to have been held in London, but was blocked by the British Government.

91 The main organisers of the LAI were Munzenberg, a German Comintern agent, and Vitandath Chattopadhaya, an academic and India nationalist. Clements Dutt, a British communist, made an 'important theoretical contribution' (W. Munzenberg, 'The Frankfurt Conference of the LAI', *Imprecorr*, 9 August 1929, 9 (38): 813–15). For a fuller discussion of the LAI, see S. Howe, *Anti-colonialism in British Politics: The Left and the End of Empire, 1918–64*, Oxford, Clarendon Press, 1993.

92 Wilson, *Russia and Black Africa*, pp. 99, 108–9.

93 Perham, *The Colonial Reckoning*, pp. 98–9. See also Thwaite, *The Seething African Pot*, pp. 156–7, 198 and F. Coty, *Contre le Communism: Le Peril Rouge En Pays Noirs*, Paris, 1930.

2 Britain's imperial hinterland: colonialism in West Africa

1 Princess Marie Louise, *Letters from the Gold Coast*, London, Methuen and Co. Ltd., 1926, p. 233; A.D.O. Nigel Cooke, cited in C. Allen (ed.) *Tales from the Dark Continent: Images of British Colonial Africa in the Twentieth Century*, London, Futura, 1979, first published in 1979 in conjunction with the BBC, p.193.

Princess Marie Louise of Schleswig-Holstein (but British to the core) was the granddaughter of Queen Victoria and daughter of Edward VII and Queen Alexandra (daughter of Christian IX of Denmark). She recorded her official visit to the Gold Coast in 1925 through letters to her sister, Princess Helena Victoria.

2 Sir W. Geary, *Nigeria Under British Rule*, London, 1927, p. 272. See also Brigadier General F.P. Crozier, *Five Years Hard: Being an account of the fall of the Fulani Empire and a picture of the daily life of a Regimental Officer among the peoples of the Western Sudan*, London, 1932, p. 99.

3 Sir M. Hailey, *An African Survey: A Study of Problems Arising in Africa South of the Sahara*, revised in 1956, London, OUP, 1957, p. 1322; A.W. Cardinall, *The Gold Coast, 1931*

... *based on figures and facts collected by the chief census officer of 1931*, Accra, Government Printer, 1932, pp. 107–12.

4 Lord Lugard, *Political Memoranda: Revision of Instructions to Political Officers on Subjects Chiefly Political and Administrative, 1913–1918*, edited with an introduction by A.H.M. Kirk-Greene, London, Frank Cass 1970, p. 273.

5 Allen, *Tales from the Dark Continent*, 'Introduction'.

6 E.F.G. Haig, *Nigerian Sketches*, London, 1931, p. 233; G. Hoyningen-Huene, *African Mirage: The Record of a Journey*, London, Batsford, 1938, pp.16–7. 'Hinterland' is from the Scottish word, 'behind', but may be used in a metaphorical sense to denote cultural 'twilight zones'. I am indebted here to inspiration from Cairan Carson's *Last Night's Fun: A Book About Irish Traditional Music*, London, Jonathan Cape, 1996, Chapter 1.

7 *Sanders of the River*, London Film Productions, 1935, producer: Alexander Korda, directed by Zoltan Korda and starring Leslie Banks as Sanders. Lilongo was played by the American actress, Nina Mae McKinney. Thanks were given to the co-operation of B. Bourdillon, Governor of Uganda, and 'other colonial Governments'. Wallace's African experience was primarily as a journalist in the Boer War. After the Sanders novels, he turned to writing popular crime fiction.

8 E. Wallace, *Sanders of the River*, London and Melbourne, Ward, Lock and Co. n.d., p. 5; and A. Kirk-Greene in the Introduction to Allen, *Tales From the Dark Continent* and 'Sanders of the River' in *New Society*, 1977, 788 (42): 308–9.

9 Wallace, *Sanders of the River*, pp. 5, 14–15, 48–61, 90, 134.

10 S. Olivier, *White Capital and Coloured Labour*, London, Hogarth Press, 1929, pp. 41–2.

11 A.W. Cardinall, *The Gold Coast, 1931 ... based on figures and facts collected by the chief census officer of 1931* Accra, Government Printer, 1932; E. Goode Robeson, *African Journey*, London, Victor Gollancz Ltd., 1946, p. 77; E. Huxley, *East Africa*, London, published for the Penns in the Rock Press by William Collins, 1941, p. 37.

12 B. Jewsiewicki and V.Y. Mudimbe, 'Africans' Memories and Contemporary History of Africa' in *History and Theory*, 1993, 32 (4) 1–18; B. Hooks 'Representing Whiteness in the Black Imagination' in L. Grossberg, C. Nelson, P.A. Treichler (eds.) *Cultural Studies*, London and New York, Routledge, 1992, pp. 338–46, 339.

13 S. Leith-Ross, *Stepping Stones: Memoirs of Colonial Nigeria, 1907–1960*, edited by M. Crowder, London and Boston, Peter Owen, 1983, pp. 83, 180; Sir H.H. Johnson, 'Africa and South America' in *The Nineteenth Century and After*, July, 1918, XXV: 181–94, 187. See also R.S. Smith, *Warfare and Diplomacy in Pre-Colonial West Africa*, Madison, University of Wisconsin Press, 1989. West Africa and Brazil were initially linked through the slave trade and the two regions remain linked through Yoruba culture, which is a strong element of certain religious sects throughout much of the Caribbean and Latin America.

14 Princess Marie Louise, *Letters from the Gold Coast*, pp. 41–3, 56, 58, 99; Wallace, *Sanders of the River*, p. 171.

15 L. Woolf, *Imperialism and Civilisation*, London, Hogarth Press, 1928, p. 273; G. Padmore, *Africa: Britain's Third Empire*, New York, Negro Universities Press, 1969, first published in 1949, pp. 49–50; T. Pakenham, *The Scramble for Africa 1876–1912*, London, Abacus, 1992, p. 68.

16 A. Phillips, *The Enigma of Colonialism: An Interpretation of British Policy in West Africa*, London, James Currey, 1990, pp. 2–3, 156.

17 P.J. Yearwood, 'The Expatriate Firms and the Colonial Economy of Nigeria in the First World War' in *The Journal of Imperial and Commonwealth History*, 1998, 26 (1): 49–71, pp. 49–50; A. G. Hopkins 'Big Business in African Studies', *The Journal of African History*, 1987, 28 (2): 119–140, p. 129.

18 G.L. Beer, *African Questions at the Paris Peace Conference*, edited and with an introduction, annexes and additional notes by Louis Herbert Gray, London, Dawsons of Pall Mall, 1968, first published in 1923, p. 27.

19 C.R. Buxton, 'An Onlooker in West Africa', Part 2, *Labour*, March 1935, enclosed in C. Roden Buxton Papers, 5/4, p. 42. See also Hailey, *An African Survey A Study of Problems Arising in Africa South of the Sahara*, p. 723. In Kenya, land alienation was 7 per cent and in Southern Rhodesia, 49 per cent.

20 G. Gorer, *Africa Dances*, London, 1935; G. Greene, *Journey Without Maps*, London, 1946; first published in 1936, pp. vi, 27. Gorer was described by left-wing critics as 'intellectually honest', but 'politically naive' (Review of *Africa Dances* in *Labour Monthly*, 1935, 17 (11): 711–12).

21 Leith-Ross, *Stepping Stones*, p. 99; Princess Marie Louise, *Letters from the Gold Coast*, p. 37; Lugard in discussion after M. Perham's talk on 'Some Problems of Indirect Rule in Africa', 1934, reproduced in M. Perham, *Colonial Sequence, 1930–1949: A Chronological Commentary upon British Colonial Policy, Especially in Africa*, London, Methuen & Co. Ltd., 1967, p.107. 'Pagett MP' is a generic term coined by Kipling. Here it depicts the interference of the metropolitan government in imperial issues of which it had no firsthand experience.

22 A.E. Coombes, *Reinventing Africa: Museums, Material Culture and Popular Imagination in Late Victorian and Edwardian England*, New Haven and London, Yale University Press, 1994, p. 6.

23 Princess Marie Louise, *Letters from the Gold Coast*, p. 12.

24 Ex-DO, K. Bradley, in C. Allen's *Tales from the Dark Continent*, p. 55.

25 R. Oakley, *Treks and Palavers*, London, 1938, 'Introduction' and pp. 8–9, 18, 60, 118, 207–8 .

26 Princess Marie Louise, *Letters from the Gold Coast*, p. 141; M. Perham, *African Apprenticeship: An Autobiographical Journal in Southern Africa, 1929*, London, 1974, pp. 232–3 and 'Nigeria Today' in *The Times*, 1932, reproduced in Perham, *Colonial Sequence*, pp. 64–5; For the ideal job specification for a political officer, see C. Jeffries, *The Colonial Empire and the Civil Service*, Cambridge, CUP, 1938, pp. xxiv, 24–8.

27 Duncan-Johnstone, Diaries, 31 July 1929, A.C. Duncan-Johnstone Papers (DJ), 1/7, p.12.

28 W.R. Crocker, *Nigeria: A Critique of British Colonial Administration*, London, George Allen and Unwin, 1936, pp. 152–3, 159, 165; and C. Allen, *Tales from the Dark Continent*, p. 17.

29 K. Fowler-Lunn, *Gold Missus: A Woman Prospector in Sierra Leone*, London, 1938, p. 34; R. Heussler, *Yesterday's Rulers: The Making of the British Colonial Service*, Syracuse, 1963 and H. Kuklich, *The Imperial Bureaucrat: The Colonial Administrative Service in the Gold Coast 1920–1939*, Stansford, UCL Press, 1979.

For changes in the service, see the introduction of *Report of a Committee on the System of Appointment in the Colonial Office and the Colonial Service, 1929–30*, Cmd. 3540, London, HMSO, 1930, conducted by Sir Warren Fisher.

30 R. Furse, *Aucuparious: Recollections of a Recruiting Officer*, London, OUP, 1962, pp. 189–90; C. Parkinson, *The Colonial Office from Within*, London, 1947, pp. 25–6.

31 L. Barnes, *Empire or Democracy: A Study of the Colonial Question*, London, Victor Gollancz Ltd., 1939, pp. 87–91, 93.

32 Oakley, *Treks and Palavers*, pp. 8–9.

33 Barnes, *Empire or Democracy*, p. 91. See also Duncan-Johnstone, Diaries, 14 March 1928, DJ, 1/4, p. 15.

34 J.A. Hobson, *Imperialism: A Study*, London, 1988, edited and with an introduction by J. Townshend, first published in 1902, p. 43; K. Bradley, *Once a District Officer*, London, Macmillan, 1966, p. 15.

35 P.J. Cain and A.G. Hopkins, *British Imperialism: Crisis and Deconstruction, 1914–1990*, London, Longman, 1993, pp. 25–6, 131–2, 201, 233; Hobson, *Imperialism*, pp. 150–4; E. Waugh, *When the Going Was Good*, London, Penguin, 1968, first published by Duckworth in 1946, p.158.

36 Crocker, *Nigeria*, pp. 325–9. See also Duncan-Johnstone, Diaries, 2 August 1929, 31 August 1929, DJ, 1/6. For backgrounds of men and women in the CAS, see C. Allen, *Tales from the Dark Continent*

37 Duncan-Johnstone, Diaries, 6 August 1929, DJ, 1/6; K. Fowler-Lunn, *The Gold Missus: A Woman Prospector in Sierra Leone*, London, 1938, pp. 25, 298, 301; *Sanders of the River*, p. 191; Greene, *Journey Without Maps*, pp. 33, 40–1, 54–7. Fowler-Lunn was married to a British geologist in The Gold Coast Colonial Service.

38 Crocker, *Nigeria*, p. 53; Duncan-Johnstone, Diaries, 16 February 1928, DJ, 1/3, p. 24.

39 Kuklich, *The Imperial Bureaucrat*, pp. 94, 203–4.

40 Duncan-Johnstone, Diaries, 4 May 1938, DJ, 3/6, p. 26.
    Duncan-Johnstone began his career in 1913 as an Assistant District Commissioner (ADC) in the Eastern Province and was promoted to Provincial Commissioner of the Eastern, Southern and Western Provinces during the 1930s, retiring in 1942.

41 Perham, 'Nigeria Today' in *The Times*, December 1932, cited in *Colonial Sequence*, pp. 61–3.

42 Princess Marie Louise, *Letters from the Gold Coast*, p. 41; A.C. Duncan-Johnstone and A.C. Blair, *Enquiry into the Constitution and Organisation of the Dagbon*, Accra, 1932.
    After school in Scotland, Rattray served in the South African War, became an elephant hunter and moved through Africa recording languages and folklore on his way. He became a DC in the Northern Territories of the Gold Coast, Provincial Commissioner and then a government anthropologist and was reputedly one of the 'great characters' in West Africa. (C. Allen, *Tales from the Dark Continent*, pp. 50–1).

43 Nadel's research plan, presented to the International African Institute, London, via Malinowski, 12 December 1932 and other research proposals made between 1932–33, reproduced in J. Goody, *The Expansive Moment: Anthropology in Britain and Africa, 1918–1970*, Cambridge, CUP, 1995, 'Appendix 1' and pp. 52–4.
    Nadel was also interested in African music, which was possibly what he really wanted to research. Other proposals addressing general problems of social control and cohesion included the place of individuality and leadership in primitive communities, individual variations in successful adaptation to new conditions, the family as the pivot of social organisation in West Africa and the psychic stresses of Western education on the African child.

44 Duncan-Johnstone, 'Reflections After Two Months Sojourn in Tamale', (Northern Province), DJ, 1/7, pp. 36–9; Diaries, September 1930, ibid., 1/4, p. 5; Lugard, *Political Memoranda*, p. 14.

45 F.B. Carr, 'Reminiscences' (unpublished manuscript describing the Nigerian Service, 1919–1949), OUCRP, Rhodes House, p. 6.

46 Princess Marie Louise, *Letters form the Gold Coast*, pp. 51, 123.

47 Cardinall, *The Gold Coast*, p. 264.

48 Oakley, *Treks*, pp. 207–8; Bradley, cited in C. Allen, *Tales From the Dark Continent*, pp. 91, 138.

49 Lugard, 'Duties of Political Officers and Miscellaneous Subjects' in *Political Memoranda*, pp. 9–41.

50 Hailey, *An African Survey: A Study of Problems Arising in Africa South of the Sahara*, pp. 1366–8. See also Lugard, *Political Memornada*, p. 205.

51 Duncan-Johnstone, Diaries, March 1928, DJ, 1/3, p. 6. See also Lugard, *Political Memoranda*, p. 169.

52 Crocker, *Nigeria*, pp. 65–6, 72–9, 69, 235. See also Haig, *Nigerian Sketches*, pp. 60–4, 110–1; Oakley, *Treks*, pp. 50, 59–67, 151, 195; and Carr, 'Reminiscences', pp. 30–1, 43.

53 Haig, *Nigerian Sketches*, p. 72; and Oakley, *Treks*, pp. 60–3, 194–5.

54 J. Harris, Secretary APS, to Secretary of State for Colonies, J. MacDonald, 9 November 1935, Anti-Slavery and Aborigines Protection Society Papers, D1; W.T. Lunn (Lab), *Hansard*, (Commons), fourth series, vol. 235, col. 930–1, 17 February

# #

1930; and Sir D. Cameron, *My Tanganyika Service and Some Nigeria*, London, 1939, pp. 284–5.
55 D.P.S. Asechemie, 'African Labour Systems, Maintenance Accounting and Agency Theory' in *Critical Perspectives on Accounting*, 1997, 8: 373–92; Hailey, *African Survey: A Study of Problems Arising in Africa South of the Sahara*, p. 680; and Crocker, *Nigeria*, pp. 25, 69.
56 Crocker, *Nigeria,*, p. 139. See also G. Padmore, *The Life and Struggles of Negro Toilers*, London, 1931, pp. 97–8.
57 C. Coquery-Vidrovitch, *African Women: A Modern History*, Boulder Colorado, Westview Press, 1997, p. 38; Duncan-Johnstone, Diaries, 24 May 1930, DJ, 1/11, p. 15; and Cardinall, *The Gold Coast*, p. 169.
58 *Report of a Commission of Inquiry into the Disturbances at Aba and other Places in South Eastern Nigeria in November and December 1929; 1930–31*, Cmd. 3784, London, HMSO, 1931, pp. 4–5. See also Coquery-Vidrovitch, *African Women*, pp. 164.
59 Leith-Ross, *Stepping Stones*, p. 99; Lugard, *Political Memoranda*, p. 249; R. Kedward to D. Shiels, *Hansard*, vol. 234, col. 1014, 29 July 1930; J. Horrabin to K. Lunn ibid., vol. 244, col. 845, 5 November 1930.
    Leith-Ross's brother, Upton Fitzherbert Ruxton, was the Lieutenant-Governor of the southern provinces at the time of the riots and was responsible for introducing the Native Revenue Ordinance.
60 R. Kedward to D. Shiels, *Hansard*, vol. 234, col. 1013, 29 January 1930; R. Kedward to W.T. Lunn, ibid., vol. 239, col. 2480–9, 5 June 1930. For black protest, see G. Padmore, 'Africans Harassed by Imperialists' in *Negro Worker*, May 1929, 2 (2): 3; B.N. Azikiwe, 'Murdering Women in Nigeria' in *The Crisis*, May 1930, 7: 164. For Parliamentary concern over communist interest, see Sir K. Wood to A. Henderson, Secretary of State for Foreign Affairs, *Hansard*, vol. 245, col. 272, 24 November 1930.
61 Sir A. Cohen, *British Policy in Changing Africa*, London, Routledge & Kegan Paul, 1960, p. 65; Hailey, *African Survey*, p. 466; and Perham 'Nigeria Today', pp. 61–2.
62 Crocker, *Nigeria*, pp. 74–5.
63 I. Wilkes, *One Nation, Many Histories, Ghana Past and Present*, Accra, Ghana Universities Press, 1996, pp. 38, 53–4.
64 ibid., pp. 30–1.
65 Duncan-Johnstone, Diaries, 31 March 1928, DJ, 1/3, p. 36; Hailey, *African Survey*, pp. 518–26. According to Cardinall, *Omanhene* is an Akan word which means 'lord of' or 'one who has power over the Oman or tribe' (Cardinall, *The Gold Coast*, pp. 72–3). Again, we must be cautious of the ways in which colonial officials used African terms. The occupant of the Golden Stool was the *Asantehene* (Wilkes, *One Nation*, p. 29) and there may have been some blurring of terms here.
66 A.F.C Wilkinson, DC Axim to Commissioner, Western Province, 17 March 1930, Wilkinson Papers (unpaginated); A.C. Duncan-Johnstone, P.C. Southern Province and Northern Territories, 'Policy and Standing Orders to Political Officers', 1930, DJ 1/11, pp. 30–4.
67 Cardinall, *The Gold Coast*, pp. 237–41: Hailey, *African Survey*, pp. 660–7. Contrary to prevailing white views, Cardinall maintains that there was 'very little drunkenness' among Gold Coast Africans (p. 240).
68 E. Akyeampong, 'What's in a Drink? Class Struggle, Popular Culture and the Politics of *Akpeteshie* (Local Gin) in Ghana, 1930–67' in *Journal of African History*, 1996, no. 37, pp. 215–36.
69 Duncan-Johnstone, Diaries, 1 November 1930, DJ, 1/8, p. 18 and 'Notes on Native Administration, 1936–1942', 13 July 1936, DJ 5/8, pp. 1–2.
70 'Wiawso Riot, 1935' marked 'Confidential' and addressed to the P.C.'s Office, Sekondi at Wiawso, 20 November 1935; 'Sefwi-Wiawso Native Affairs' signed A. Duncan-Johnstone, Provincial Commissioners Office, Sekondi, 20 November

1935, to Colonial Secretary, Accra, marked 'Confidential', DJ, 5/5, pp. 1–5, 8, 10–11.

71 Colonial Secretary, Accra, to Duncan-Johnstone, Sekondi, 8 April 1936; Letter addressed to Duncan-Johnstone at the RAC Club, London, 20 May 1936, DJ, 5/5, pp. 21–3. For criticisms see R. Kidd, NCCL, to Creech Jones, 8 July 1936, Arthur Creech Jones Papers, 18/3, pp. 9–10 and W. Lunn (Lab) to J. H. Thomas, Secretary of State for Colonies, *Hansard*, vol. 308, col. 1772, 19 July 1936.

72 Colonial Secretary, Accra, to Duncan-Johnstone, Sekondi, 8 April 1936, DJ, 5/5, pp. 21–2. See also 'Minute on Political Disputes' by Sir Shenton Thomas, 25 October 1933, DJ, 5/5, pp. 1, 3; Wilkinson's report enclosed in Duncan-Johnstone, Sekondi, to Colonial Secretary, Accra, marked 'Private and Confidential', 12 June 1936, DJ, 5/5, pp. 22–4, 33; Duncan-Johnstone, P.C.'s Office, Sekondi, to Colonial Secretary, Accra, 12 June 1936, marked 'Confidential', DJ, 5/4, p. 82.

73 Duncan-Johnstone, Sekondi, to Colonial Secretary, Accra, 12 March 1936, DJ, 5/5, pp. 33, 35, 38. For Wilkinson's relations with the Ashanti Goldfields Corporation, see Governor Slater to Wilkinson, 8 January 1929; Wilkinson to W. Eaton Turner, Manager of the Ashanti Goldfields Corporation, 25 March 1929; and Wilkinson's memo as DC., Obuasi, on 'Rights of the Ashanti Goldfields Corporation, Ltd.', Wilkinson Papers.

74 'Memorandum on the Introduction of the Full Measure of Indirect Rule', circulated with a letter from A. Duncan-Johnstone, Commissioner, Eastern Province, to D.C. Kpandu and all districts, Eastern Province, P.C.'s office, Koforidua, 9 September 1938, marked 'Strictly Confidential', DJ, 5/8, p. 24; and Hailey, *An African Survey*, p. 1152.

75 R. Kedward to W. Lunn, *Hansard*, col. 2408–9, 5 July 1930; Lugard, *Political Memoranda*, pp. 252–6; and Wallace *Sanders of the River* pp. 195, 184, 191.

76 Lugard, *Political Memoranda*, pp. 83–8, 116–7.

77 Wallace, *Sanders of the River*, p. 192; and Oakley, *Treks*, pp. 38, 45, 204.

78 DO, Nigeria, cited in C. Allen, *Tales From the Dark Continent*, pp. 102–3; and Gorer, *Africa Dances*, p. 241.

79 Hailey, *African Survey…1956*, pp. 60–61.

80 S. Olivier, *White Capital and Coloured labour*, pp. 26, 41; Roden Buxton, 'An Onlooker in West Africa'; and Crocker, *Nigeria*, pp. 74–5, 83, 235.

81 Oakley, *Treks*, pp. 95–6, 204. See also Crocker, *Nigeria*, p.94.

82 K. Bradley and A. Kirk-Greene cited in C. Allen, *Tales from the Dark Continent*, pp. 64, 80; J. Cary *Mister Johnson*, 1939. Cary was from an Anglo-Irish background, fought in the Nigerian Regiment in the 1914–18 War. He was forced to retire from the colonial service in 1919 because of ill-health.

83 Kuklich, *The Imperial Bureaucrat*, p. 10

84 Cohen, *British Policy in Changing Africa*, p. 197; and Kirk-Greene, 'Introduction' in C. Allen, *Tales From the Dark Continent*, p. xiv.

85 Lugard, *Political Memoranda*, p. 249.

3 Expatriate society: race, gender and the culture of imperialism

1 S. Olivier, *White Capital and Coloured Labour*, London, Hogarth Press, 1929, pp. 30–1; E. Berry *Mad Dogs and Englishmen*, London, Michael Joseph, 1941, p. 178.
  Erick Berry was an American journalist from New York who married Hubert Best, an English DO in Northern Nigeria.

2 T.O. Ranger, 'The Invention of Tradition in Colonial Africa' in E Hobsbawm and T.O. Ranger (eds) *The Invention of Tradition*, Cambridge, CUP, 1996, first published, 1983, pp. 211–63, p. 219.

3 J.A. Hobson, *Imperialism: A Study*, London, 1988, edited and with an introduction by J. Townshend, first published, 1902, pp. 150–1.

4 W.R. Crocker, *Nigeria: A Critique of British Colonial Administration*, London, George Allen and Unwin, 1936, pp. 200, 207; and R. Oakley, *Treks and Palavers*, London, 1938, p. 41.

5 M. Perham, 'France in the Cameroons' in *The Times*, May 1933, reproduced in *Colonial Sequence, 1930–1949: A Chronological Commentary upon British Colonial Policy, Especially in Africa*, London, Methuen & Co. Ltd., 1967, p. 75. See also G. Gorer, *Africa Dances*, London, 1935, pp. 42–5, 77, 115.

6 Lady D Mills R.M., *The Road to Timbuktu: The Record of a Woman's Adventurous Journey*, London, 1927, p. 57; E.F.G. Haig, *Nigerian Sketches*, London, 1931, pp. 184–9.

The texture of colonial life in French West Africa in the 1930s is evocatively satirised in the French black comedy, *Coup de Torchon*, (1981, Director Bernard Tavernier).

7 Haig, *Nigerian Sketches*, p. 193. See also G. Greene, *Journey Without Maps*, London, 1962, first published in 1936.

8 There have been few academic studies of expatriate society, although more popular works like James Fox's *White Mischief*, London, 1982, are illuminating. Waugh also provides a vivid, if depressing, vision of expatriate society on his trip through central Africa in 1930–1. His descriptions of a hell-raising, hedonistic Kenyan society are particularly good (*The Diaries of Evelyn Waugh*, edited by Michael Davie, London, Penguin, 1976, 3 December 1930 to 16 February 1931, pp. 345–53).

9 Duncan-Johnstone, Diaries, 24 May 1930, A.C. Duncan-Johnstone Papers, (DJ), 1/11, p. 15; and Mills, *Timbuctu*, p.7. See also Greene, *Journey Without Maps*, pp. 42, 55; Lord Lugard, *Political Memoranda: Revision of Instructions to Political Officers on Subjects Chiefly Political and Administrative, 1913–1918*, edited with an introduction by A.H.M. Kirk-Greene, London, Frank Cass 1970, pp. 31–3.

10 Sir A. Cohen, *British Policy in Changing Africa*, London, Routledge & Kegan Paul, 1960, p. 74.

11 J.B. Morton, *The Best of Beachcomber*, selected and introduced by Michael Frayn, London, Penguin, 1966. 'Beachcomber's' articles were published between 1924–63 and draw frequently on 'imperial' themes.

12 D. Ruston (Nigeria 1920s) cited in C. Allen (ed.) *Tales From the Dark Continent*, London, Futura, 1979, p. 133; E. Wallace, *Sanders of the River*, London and Melbourne, Ward, Lock and Co. n.d., pp. 247, 272.

13 Cohen, *British Policy*, p. 74; and C. Allen (ed.) *Tales of the Dark Continent*, pp. 52–3. See also Berry, *Mad Dogs and Englishmen*, p. 36, 135–7 and for similar comments, Princess Marie Louise, *Letters From the Gold Coast*, London, Methuen & Co. Ltd., 1926, p. 106.

14 Princess Marie Louise, *Letters from the Gold Coast*, p. 37–8. The concept of sites de memoire is more fully developed in P. Nora, 'Between Memory and History: Les Lieux de Memoire' in *Representations*, Spring 1989, 26: 7–24.

15 Princess Marie Louise, *Letters from the Gold Coast* pp. 24, 37–8, 106, 225.

16 S. Leith-Ross, *Stepping Stones: Memoirs of Colonial Nigeria, 1907–1960*, edited by M. Crowder, London and Boston, Peter Owen, 1983, p. 85. See also Princess Marie Louise, *Letters from the Gold Coast* pp. 171–9.

17 S. Haxey, *Tory M.P.*, Left Book Club Edition, London, Gollancz, 1939, pp. 108–9. See also A. Phillips, *The Enigma of Colonialism*, London, James Currey, 1990, pp. 11, 125.

18 Princess Marie Louise, *Letters from the Gold Coast*, pp. 201, 35.

19 C. Allen (ed.) *Tales From the Dark Continent*, pp. 5–6; and Greene, *Journey Without Maps*, pp. 33, 40–1, 54–7.

20 A.W. Cardinall, *The Gold Coast*, Accra, Government Printer, 1932; and *An Economic Survey of the Colonial Empire 1936*, London, HMSO, 1936, p. 188. For attitudes to Syrians, see Mills, Lady D., R.M., *The Golden Land: A Record of Travel in West Africa*, London, Duckworth, 1929, p. 23.

21 Lugard, *Political Memoranda*, pp. 416–20; and Cardinall, *The Gold Coast*, p. 262.
22 D.T. Goldberg, *Racist Culture: Philosophy and the Politics of Meaning*, Oxford, Blackwell, 1993, pp. 190–2.
23 Cardinall, *The Gold Coast*, p. 176; and Lugard, *Political Memoranda*, pp. 33, 419.
24 Personal correspondence between J.H. Oldham and Shenton Thomas, 1933, Malinowski to Oldham, 3 November 1933, cited in J. Goody, *The Expansive Moment: Anthropology in Britain and Africa, 1918–1970*, Cambridge, CUP, 1995, p. 47.
25 A.M. Graves (ed.) *Benvenuto Cellini Had No Prejudice Against Bronze: Letters from West Africans*, Baltimore, privately printed, 1943, pp. lxv, lxii–lxiii, xlix–lxvi.

   Graves was born in Maryland in 1875 into a wealthy confederate family and began her 'personal odyssey' in 1919, aged 42, when she was shocked into pacifism by the First World War. She travelled widely, visiting Russia in the 1920s and was suspected of communist sympathies. During the Second World War, she was denied a US passport. (*Benvenuto*, pp. ixiv, 57–8, 167–75.) She earned the respect of blacks (Dubois, *The World and Africa*, p. ix) and also had contact with British critics of colonialism – Fenner Brockway, Frank Horrabin and Barrett Brown, Principal of Ruskin College. Her letters to contacts in West Africa and elsewhere provide a useful insight into the period. However, black academics have condemned Graves as an interfering 'white missionary' whose publication of her correspondence with Adelaide Casely Hayford and her daughter, Gladys, was a 'voyeuristic invasion into … privacy' (B. Bair, 'Pan-Africanism as a Process: Adelaide Casely-Hayford' in S. Lemelle and R.D.G Kelley (eds) *Imagining Home: Class, Culture and Nationalism in the African Diaspora*, London, Verso, 1994, p. 133.
26 D. Stasiulis and N. Yuval-Davis (eds) *Unsettling Settler Societies: Articulations of Gender, Race, Ethnicity and Class*, London, Sage, 1995, p. 56.
27 A. McClintock, *Imperial Leather: Race, Gender and Sexuality in the Colonial Contest*, London, Routledge, 1995, pp. 24–5; and E. Goode Robeson, *African Journey*, London, Gollancz, 1946, p. 184. For white women's vital role in empire, see C. Midgley (ed.) *Gender and Imperialism*, Manchester, Manchester University Press, 1998; N. Chaudhuri and M. Strobel (eds) *Western Women and Imperialism: Complicity and Resistance*, Bloomington and Indianapolis, Indiana University Press, 1992; and V. Ware, *Beyond the Pale: White Women, Racism and History*, London, Verso, 1992.
28 D. Lavin, 'Margery Perham's Initiation into African Affairs' in A. Smith and M. Bull (eds) *Margery Perham and British Rule in Africa*, London, Frank Cass, 1991, p. 54; H. Callaway, *Gender, Culture and Empire: European Women in Colonial Nigeria*, London, MacMillan, 1987, p. 15; and Princess Marie Louise, *Letters From the Gold Coast*, London, Methuen & Co. Ltd., 1926, p. 202.
29 Ware, *Beyond the Pale*, pp. 11–16; illustrations of African women in Mills, Lady D., R.M., *The Golden Land: A Record of Travel in West Africa*, London, Duckworth, 1929, pp. 32, 64, 124.
30 Duncan-Johnstone, Diaries, 29 February 1928, (DJ), 1/3, p. 31. Official policy is outlined in Sir F.D. Lugard, *The Dual Mandate in British Tropical Africa*, Edinburgh and London, William Blackwood and Sons, 1922, p. 142.
31 *An Economic Survey of the Colonial Empire*, 1932, HMSO, 1934, p. 142; and Cardinall, *The Gold Coast*, p. 257.
32 D. Birkett, 'The White Woman's Burden in the White Man's Grave: The Introduction of British Nurses in Colonial West Africa' in Chaudhuri and Strobel (eds) *Western Women and Imperialism*, pp. 177–91; and Callaway, *Gender, Culture and Empire*, pp. 47, 140–4.
33 Princess Marie Louise, *Letters from the Gold Coast*, p. 205; Mills, *The Golden Land*, pp. 39, 71, 120–1. For Princess Marie Louise in Kenya, see 'Letter to Ingeborg Dinesen', 20 May 1928, in I. Dinesen, *Letters From Africa, 1914–1931*, London, Picador, 1981, p. 391.
34 Mills, *Episodes from the Road to Timbuktu*, pp. 57–8; and Haig, *Nigerian Sketches*, pp. 27–32.

35 Oral testimonies from ex-colonial wives cited in C. Allen (ed.) *Tales From the Dark Continent*, pp. 141–2; Duncan-Johnstone, Diaries, 4 August 1929, DJ, 1/7, p. 49.

36 Diaries, January 1934, DJ, 3/1. Leith-Ross, *Stepping Stones*, p. 84. See also the oral testimonies from ex-colonial wives cited in C. Allen, *Tales from the Dark Continent*.

37 Haig, *Nigerian Sketches*, pp. 27–32. See also Duncan-Johnstone, Diaries, January 1934, DJ, 3/1.

38 Princess Marie Louise, *Letters from the Gold Coast*, pp. 201–2.

39 Callaway, *Gender, Culture and Empire*, p. 63. *Letters from the Gold Coast*, pp. 94,111–2.

40 Princess Marie Louise, *Letters from the Gold Coast*, pp. 32, 201. See also Cardinall, *The Gold Coast*, p.173. In the Gold Coast, 50 per cent of the 4,855 domestic servants working for Europeans were from other parts of West Africa, hence they had to be licensed and Cardinall argued that this acted as a powerful deterrent, which was reflected in the crime statistics.

41 Princess Marie Louise, *Letters from the Gold Coast*, pp. 52, 75, 87–8, 101. Princess Marie Louise who took her own English maid, Annie Picknett, with her to the Gold Coast mentions that she had a very pretty little African maid, called Jessie, in Accra, but she was a 'little minx' and too much responsibility to take on tour.

42 J.A. Rogers, *Sex and Race: Negro Caucasian Mixing in All Ages and All Lands*, New York, 1942–44, reprint, Helga M. Rogers, 1972, 3 vols, 1: 148.

43 *Chocolat*, directed by Claire Denis, 1989; See also J. Forbes, 'Hot Chocolate' interview with Claire Denis, 'Wednesday Women' in the *Guardian*, 21 March 1989. Claire Denis was herself brought up in different parts of Africa, including the Cameroons. An interesting insight into racism from the perspective of a Cameroonian houseboy is provided in a fictitious diary form by F. Oyono, *Houseboy*, translated from the French by John Reed, Heinemann, 1966.

44 W.M. Macmillan, *Africa Emergent: A Survey of Social, Political and Economic Trends in British Africa*, London, OUP, 1938, p. 277; J.H. Oldham, *Christianity and the Race Problem*, London, 1924, p. 242; and Sir A. Burns, *Colonial Civil Servant*, London, 1949, p. 28. See also O. Mannoni, *Prospero and Caliban: the Psychology of Colonialism*, New York, Praeger, 1964, pp. 110–16.

45 Callaway, *Gender, Culture and Empire*, pp. 28, 185; O. Mannoni, *Prospero and Caliban: the Psychology of Colonialism*, New York, Praeger, 1964, pp. 110–16.

46 J. Haggis, 'Gendering Colonialism or Colonising Gender? Recent Women's Studies on Approaches to White Women and the History of British Colonialism' in *Women's Studies International Forum*, 13 (1/2): 105–15, 1990, p. 113.

47 M. Perham, *Major Dane's Garden*, London, 1926, p. 340. Perham's novel is based on her personal experience of a bush posting in British Somaliland, where she spent a year with her elder sister who was married to a Major J. Rayne, a DC at Hargeisa.

48 Haggis, 'Gendering Colonialism', pp. 107, 113.

49 F. Bryk, *Dark Rapture*, New York, 1939, p. 65.

50 Haigh, *Nigerian Sketches*, pp. 231–3. See also Oakley, *Treks*, pp. 43, 95–6; and Mills, *Episodes from the Road to Timbuktu*, p. 59.

51 A.C.G. Hastings, *Gone Native* (1928), cited in Callaway, *Gender, Culture and Empire*, p. 55; Wallace, *Sanders of the River*, pp. 169–76; and Rogers *Sex and Race*, vol. 1, pp. 2, 42, 126–7.

52 Duncan-Johnstone, Diaries, 11 December 1934, DJ, 3/4, pp. 4–5; 'Notes on Native Administration, 1936–42', DJ, 5/8, p. 18. For details of 'Circular A', see H. Kuklich, *The Imperial Bureaucrat: The Colonial Administrative Service in the Gold Coast 1920–1939*, Stansford, UCLA Press, 1979, pp. 122–8.

53 Memoirs of colonial officers cited in C. Allen (ed.) *Tales from the Dark Continent*, pp. 18, 45.

54 MacCrone, *Racial Attitudes*, p. 276; Wallace, *Sanders of the River*, pp. 102–4,171–8, 200.

55 P. Hayes, ' "Cocky" Hahn and the "Black Venus": The Making of a Native Commissioner in South West Africa, 1915–46' in *Gender and History*, 1996, 8 (3):

368–88 and 370–9. See also Brigadier General F.P. Crozier, *Five Years Hard: Being an account of the fall of the Fulani Empire and a picture of the daily life of a Regimental Officer among the peoples of the Western Sudan*, London, 1932, pp. 161–5.

'Cocky' Hahn was a colonial officer implicated in a case of gratuitous violence against an African woman in the 1920s, but in the inquiry was represented as manly and heroic and exonerated from blame.

56 M. Vaughan, *Curing their Ills: Colonial Power and African Illness*, Cambridge, Polity Press, 1991, pp. 22–3, 69, 70; M.R. Cutrafelli, *Women of Africa: Roots of Oppression*, London, translated from Italian, 1983, pp. 52, 162–3.

57 Leith-Ross, *Stepping Stones*, pp. 95, 97–8; C. Coquery-Vidrovitch, *African Women: A Modern History*, Boulder, Colorado, Westview Press, 1997, p. 31.

58 J. Van Allen, ' "Sitting on a man": Colonialism and the Lost Political Institutions of Igbo Women' in *Canadian Journal of African Studies*, 1972, VI (ii): 151–179 and 169.

59 S. Leith-Ross, *Stepping Stones*, p. 184. See also Leith-Ross, *African Women: A Study of the Igbo of Nigeria*, London, Faber and Faber, 1939; M.M. Green, *Igbo Village Affairs*, London, Frank Cass, 1947.

Leith-Ross (née Ruxton) was a pioneering colonial wife stationed in northern Nigeria when wives were not allowed without Lugard's permission. After her husband's premature death, she opted to stay on to carry out a pioneer study of Fulani language and made the rare transition from wife to professional woman in the CAS. Leith-Ross' father had been in the West African Slave Patrol and she had met her husband, who was in the West African Frontier Force, when visiting her brother who was serving as one of Lugard's administrators (interview with Leith-Ross, C.Allen (ed.) *Tales from the Dark Continent* pp. 33–9).

60 Hayes, ' "Cocky" Hahn and the "Black Venus" ', pp. 381–2. For Huxley's general observations on gender in African societies, see Elspeth Huxley, *Four Guineas: A Journey Through West Africa*, London, The Reprint Society, 1955, first published in 1954. Also relevant are Princess Marie Louise's descriptions and snapshots of women in the 'backward' Northern Territories of the Gold Coast in *Letters from the Gold Coast*, pp. 47–8.

61 Coquery-Vidrovitch, *African Women*, p. 59; M. Perham, *Ten Africans*, Cambridge, 1936, pp. x–xii; T.O. Ranger, 'The Invention of Tradition in Colonial Africa' in E. Hobsbawm and T.O. Ranger (eds) *The Invention of Tradition*, London, 1983, pp. 258–9.

62 Leith-Ross, *Stepping Stones*, p. 88.

63 N.E. Mba, *Nigerian Woman Mobilised: Women's Political Activity in Southern Nigeria, 1900–1965*, Berkeley, University of California Press, 1982, p. 135; Hailey, *African Survey*, p. 1187.

Adelaide Casely-Hayford was married to the Gold Coast lawyer and political activist, J.E. Casely Hayford. Adelaide Casely-Hayford was born in 1904 in Sierra Leone of Fanti/English ancestry and was a complex and energetic woman whose life spanned the whole colonial era in Africa. She pioneered a girls' vocational school in Freetown in 1926, and corresponded regularly with Anna Melissa Graves. (A.M. Cromwell, *An African Victorian Feminist: The Life and Times of Adelaide Smith Casely-Hayford, 1868–1960*, London, Frank Cass, 1986; Graves, *Benvenuto*, pp. 44, 76–7, 90–1.)

64 Haig, *Nigerian Sketches*, pp. 238–41.

65 Princess Marie Louise, *Letters from the Gold Coast*, pp. 69–70. H.H. Egerton, *British Colonial Policy in the Twentieth Century*, London, Methuen & Co., 1922, pp. 212–26.

66 Lugard, *Political Memoranda*, pp. 307–1. See also Coquery-Vidrovitch, *African Women*, pp. 35–8; Princess Marie Louise, *Letters from the Gold Coast*, pp. 37–8.

67 Huxley, *Four Guineas*, pp. 37–8.

Palaver comes from the Portuguese word, *palabra*, reflecting early Portuguese trading in the region. In the more 'civilised' northern Nigeria, durbars, based on the spectacular Indian durbars, were introduced by Lugard.

68 Captain, St J. Eyre Smith to Princess Marie Louise, July 1926, *Letters From the Gold Coast*, p. 106; ibid., pp. 24–5. See also Ranger, 'The Invention of Tradition in Colonial Africa' in E. Hobsbawm and T.O. Ranger (eds.) *The Invention of Tradition*, pp. 220–4.

69 'Chief of Lawra to Her Highness, Princess Marie Louise', in *Letters from the Gold Coast*, pp. 216–7. See also, 'The chairmen and members of the Victoria Park Committee, Accra, to Princess Marie Louise', ibid., June 1926, p. 225.

70 F. Fanon, *The Wretched of the Earth*, New York, 1966, first published in Paris, 1961, pp. 203–4; Chief A. Enahoro, *Fugitive Offender: The Story of a Political Prisoner*, London, 1965, p. 83.

71 Lugard, *Political Memoranda*, pp. 130–6.

72 Open letter, marked 'For private circulation only', signed A.G. Fraser, London, April 1935, p.4, Winifred Holtby Papers 4/9;. Hailey, *An African Survey*, p. 1177. See also Lugard, *Political Memoranda*, pp. 130–6.

73 I. Wilkes, *One Nation, Many Histories, Ghana Past and Present*, Accra, Ghana Universities Press, 1996, p. 6. See also A.G. Fraser to W. Holtby, 8 December 1933, Winifred Holtby Papers 4/14.

74 C.R. Buxton to W. Holtby, 11 November 1934, WH, Winifred Holtby Papers, 4/9; R. Furse, *Aucuparious: Recollections of a Recruiting Officer*, London, OUP, 1962, p. 124.

75 Cardinall, *The Gold Coast*, p. 200. See also Princess Marie Louise, *Letters from the Gold Coast*, pp. 128, 213.

76 E. Waugh, *When the Going Was Good*, London, Penguin, 1968, first published by Duckworth in 1946, pp. 141–2; A. Warren, 'Citizens of the Empire: Baden Powell, Scouts and Guides and an Imperial ideal, 1900–40' in J. M. Mackenzie (ed.) *Imperialism and Popular Culture*, Manchester MUP 1986, pp. 233–53 and 250–1.

77 Duncan-Johnstone, Diaries, 23 April 1928, 24 May 1930, DJ, 1/4, p. 3 and 1/11, pp. 21–2.

78 Princess Marie Louise, *Letters from the Gold Coast*, p. 22.

79 R.L. Buell, *The Native Problem in Africa*, New York, 1928, 2 vols, 2, p. 829.

80 Buell, *The Native Problem*, 2, pp. 829–30.

81 Crocker, *Nigeria*, pp.128, 22, 203–5; Gorer, *Africa Dances*, pp. 276–7.
 'Wog' is twentieth century slang for a non-white foreigner whose origin is unknown (*Oxford Etymological Dictionary*).

82 Coquery Vidrovitch, *African Women*, pp.152–3; Greene, *Journey Without Maps*, p. 34.

83 B. Freund, *The Making of Contemporary Africa: The Development of African Society since 1800*, London, Macmillan, 1984, pp. 156–7; M. Perham, 'Nigeria Today' in *The Times*, December 1932, cited in *Colonial Sequence, 1930–1949: A Chronological Commentary upon British Colonial Policy, Especially in Africa*, London, Methuen & Co. Ltd., 1967, p. 64.

84 W.M. Macmillan to N. Leys, 27 April 1935, W.M. Macmillan File, 1935; For the CO view, see C. Parkinson, *The Colonial Office From Within 1909–1945*, London, 1947, p. 105.

85 Sir A. Burns, *Colour Prejudice: with Particular Reference to the Relationship between Whites and Negroes*, London, 1948, pp. 71–4. See also J. Flint, 'Scandal at the Bristol Hotel: Some Thoughts on Racial Discrimination in Britain and West Africa and its Relationship to the Planning of Decolonisation, 1939–1947' in *Journal of Imperial and Commonwealth History*, October 1983, 12 (1): 76–91 and 80–1.
 Sir Alan Burns served in the CAS in the Caribbean and Nigeria in the 1920s and 1930s before becoming Governor of Nigeria in 1941.

86 Duncan-Johnstone, Diaries, 4 May 1940, DJ, 3/6, p. 26; C. Parkinson, *The Colonial Office From Within 1909–1945*, London, 1947, p.105. See also Leith-Ross, *Stepping Stones*, p. 135.

87 Mercedes Mackay, the wife of a colonial officer who went out to Nigeria in the 1940s, cited in C. Allen, *Tales from the Dark Continent*, pp. 162–3.

88 Oral Testimonies, C. Allen, *Tales from the Dark Continent*, pp. 51, 148–59, 160–3, 180; Leith-Ross, *Stepping Stones*, p. 127. For general changes during this period, see Cohen, *British Policy*, pp. 73–6.
89 These complex dialectics are expressed in O. Mannoni, 'The Decolonisation of Myself' in *Race*, April 1966, 7 (4): 127–38, which revised his psychoanalytical analysis made as a French official in Madagascar (Malagassy) to account for the resistance of the colonised.

4 'Whose dream was it anyway?' Anti-colonial protest in West Africa, 1929–45

1 M. Crowder, ' "Whose Dream was it Anyway?" Twenty-Five Years of African Independence' in *African Affairs*, 1986, 342(2): 7–20.
2 R. Lynd, 'Preface to N.F. Dryhurst' in *Nationalities and the Subject Races: Report of a Conference held at Caxton Hall*, Westminster, June 28–30, 1916, London, P.S. King and Son, 1919, cited in F. Furedi, *The New Ideology of Imperialism: Renewing the Moral Imperative*, London, Pluto Press, 1995, p.10; Governor Jardine to Secretary of State for Colonies, M. MacDonald, 2 June 1939, CO 267 672 32254/1.
3 MacDonald, *Hansard*, (Commons), vol. 349, col. 419, 28 September 1939. See also M. Perham, *Colonial Sequence, 1930–1949: A Chronological Commentary upon British Colonial Policy, Especially in Africa*, London, Methuen & Co. Ltd., 1967, pp. 24–5.
4 B. Davidson, *Africa in Modern History: The Search for a New Society*, London, 1979, p. 51; C. Achebe, *Things Fall Apart*, London, Heinemann, 1962.
5 The classic test for this period is M. Crowder (ed.) *West African Resistance: The Military Response to Colonial Occupation*, New York, 1971. For a general overview of the development of resistance, see J.B. Webster, A.A. Boahen and M. Tidy, *The Revolutionary Years: West Africa since 1800*, London, Longman, 1981.
6 H. Campbell, 'Pan-Africanism and African Liberation' in S. Lemelle and R.D.G. Kelley, *Imagining Home: Class, Culture and Nationalism in the African Diaspora*, London, Verso, 1994, p. 292. See also Sir A. Burns, *Colour Prejudice: with Particular Reference to the Relationship between Whites and Negroes*, London, 1948, p. 93; Chief A. Enahoro, *Fugitive Offender: The Story of a Political Prisoner*, London, 1965, p. 9; A. Ajayi, 'The Continuity of African Institutions under Colonialism' in T.O. Ranger (ed.) *Emerging Themes on African History*, London, 1968, pp. 179–80, 189.
7 W. Beinart and C. Bundy, *Hidden Struggles in Rural South Africa: Politics and Popular Movements in the Transkei and Eastern Cape*, London, James Currey, 1987, pp. 28–9.
8 E. Akyeampong, 'What's in a Drink? Class Struggle, Popular Culture and the Politics of *Akpeteshie* (Local Gin) in Ghana, 1930–67' in *Journal of African History*, 1996, 37: 215–36 and 224; C. Coquery-Vidrovitch, *African Women: A Modern History*, Boulder, Colorado, Westview Press, 1997, pp. 172–3 and Chapter 15, 'Women and Politics: Resistance and Action in West Africa'.
9 E. Burns, *British Imperialism in West Africa*, London, 1927, p. 5; L. Woolf, *Empire and Commerce in Africa: A Study of Economic Imperialism*, London, Hogarth Press, 1920, pp. 7, 18, 318. For the pro-colonial view, see Sir W. Geary, *Nigeria Under British Rule*, London, 1927, pp. 272–3; A. McPhee, *The Economic Revolution in West Africa*, London, 1926, p. 64.
10 Lord Hailey, *An African Survey: A Study of Problems Arising in Africa South of the Sahara*, revised in 1956, London, OUP, 1957, pp. 732–5, 1531–3. For vested interests of politicians, see S. Haxey, *Tory M.P.*, Left Book Club Edition, London, Gollancz, 1939. For instance, Leo Amery, an influential imperialist politician who was a Secretary of State for Colonies during the 1920s, was the director of a company working in the Gold Coast and had mining interests in South Africa (p. 108).
11 For a comprehensive, if predominantly Eurocentric, study of Multinationals operating in West Africa, see D.K. Fieldhouse, *Unilever Overseas: The Anatomy of a Multinational*,

1895–1956, London, Croom Helm, 1978; *Merchant Capital and Economic Decolonisation: The United Africa Company, 1929–1987*, Oxford, Clarendon Press, 1994. Also relevant is P.N. Davies, *The Trade Makers: Elder Dempster in Africa, 1852–1972*, London, 1973; Sir F. Pedler and A. Burns, *The Lion and the Unicorn in Africa: A History of the United Africa Company, 1787–1931*, London, Heinemann, 1974; and, for 'oligopolism' of multinationals, see R. Howard, *Colonialism and Underdevelopment in Ghana*, London, 1978.

12 A.W. Cardinall, *The Gold Coast*, Accra, Government Printer, 1932, pp. 84–8, 92, 242. For social and cultural change and its impact on class formation in Ghana, see P. Hill, *The Migrant Cocoa Farmers of Southern Ghana*, Oxford, James Curry, 1997, first published in 1963.

13 B. Freund, 'Introduction' in *The African Worker*, Cambridge, CUP, 1988. See also C. Newberry, 'The Imperial Workplace: Competitive and Coerced Labour Systems in New Zealand, Northern Nigeria, and Australian New Guinea' in S.M. Marks and P. Richardson (eds) *Studies in International Labour Migration*, London, 1983, pp. 187–215, 221; Hailey, *An African Survey*, p. 1405. For a fuller analysis of proletarianisation, see B. Freund, *Capital and Labour in the Nigerian Tin Mines*, London, 1981 and 'Class, Culture and Social Change in Colonial Africa, 1900–1940' in *The Making of Contemporary Africa: The Development of African Society since 1800*, London, Macmillan, 1984.

14 Cardinall, *The Gold Coast*, pp. 170–5, 122. See also R.L. Buell, *The Native Problem in Africa*, New York, 1928, 2 vols, vol 1, pp. 781–2.

15 Hailey, *An African Survey*, pp. 792–3; E. Hobsbawm, *The Age of Extremes: The Short Twentieth Century: 1914–1991*, London, Michael Joseph, 1994, pp. 172–5; Cardinall, *The Gold Coast*, pp. 114–5.

16 *An Economic Survey of the Colonial Empire, 1936*, 1936, London, HMSO, pp. 45–9. See also G. Greene, *Journey Without Maps*, London, 1962, first published in 1936, p. 41. For general trends during this period, see A.G. Hopkins, *An Economic History of West Africa*, London, 1973, pp. 208–19.

17 Circular No. 124, Labour Party Advisory Committee on Imperial Questions, International Department marked 'Private and Confidential', enclosed in W.H. Gillies to Holtby, 10 November 1933, Winifred Holtby Papers, WH, 4/15. See also Hobsbawm, *The Age of Extremes*, p. 92. For the impact on peasant producers, see C.J. Shephard, *Report on the Economics of Peasant Agriculture in the Gold Coast*, Accra, 1936.

18 J.D. Hargreaves, *Decolonisation in Africa*, London, 1996, p. 40; 'Extract from a Report on the General Situation in the Gold Coast, West Africa', 27 November 1937, annotated by I.T.A. Wallace Johnson, Arthur Creech Jones Papers (ACJ) 18/3, pp. 31–4; Duncan-Johnstone, Diaries, 22 November 1937, Duncan-Johnstone Papers, (DJ), 3/6.

19 *Report of the Commission on the Marketing of West African Cocoa*, Cmd. 5845, HMSO, London, 1938, pp. 3–5. See also Hailey, *African Survey…1956*, pp. 830, 1473.

20 G. Padmore, *Africa: Britain's Third Empire*, New York, Negro Universities Press, 1969, first published in 1949, pp. 83–4; Hopkins, *An Economic History of West Africa*, p. 254.

21 Wallace Johnson, 'Extract from a Report on … the Gold Coast'; ARPS, 'Gold Coast Grievances', p. 26, enclosed in ACJ, 18/3. See also Ruby Quartey-Papafio, headmistress to the government girls' school, in Accra, to A.M. Graves, 1 December 1931, in A.M. Graves (ed.) *Benvenuto Cellini had no prejudice Against Bronze: Letters from West Africans*, Baltimore, privately published, 1943, p. 31; and G. Padmore, *The Life and Struggles of Negro Toilers*, London, RILU, 1931, p. 97.

22 'Notes on Native Administration', 1936, DJ, 3/7, pp. 16–21.

23 Buell, *The Native Problem*, 1, pp. 96–8; *A Report of Proceedings and Decisions of the First International Conference of Negro Workers at Hamburg, Germany, July 1930*, pp. 21–3, 40. See also E. Hobsbawm, 'Taming the Wild Beasts of the Forest' in *Age Of Empire*, London, Weidenfeld & Nicolson, 1988.

24 Padmore, *Negro Toilers*, p. 94. For details of disturbances, reflected in the concern of the imperial parliament, see W.T. Lunn (Lab), *Hansard*, vol. 232, col. 1410–11, 27

November 1929; questions raised by J. Horrabin (Lab) and W.T. Brown (Lab), *Hansard*, vol. 232, col. 486–7, 1657, 20 and 28 November 1929.

25 J. McCulloch, *Colonial Psychiatry and the African Mind*, Cambridge, Cambridge University Press, 1995, p. 3.

26 Hailey, *An African Survey*. . .1956, p. 1130; Akyeampong, 'What's in a Drink?', p. 222–3.

   In 1931, there were nineteen towns over 5,000 populations in the Gold Coast, as opposed to only seven in 1921 (Cardinall, *The Gold Coast*, pp. 200–201)

27 Cardinall, *The Gold Coast*, pp. 75–82, 158–9, 203, 243–7. See also *Report by the Hon. W.G.A. Ormsby-Gore (Parliamentary Under Secretary of State for Colonies) on his visit to West Africa in 1926*, Cmd. 2744, London, HMSO, 1926.

   In 1931, there were 196,283 French West Africans, 67,783 Nigerians and 2,808 Sierra Leonians in the Colony.

28 Unsigned letter from Prestea mines to Wallace Johnson (IASB), 11 January 1938, ACJ, 18/3; Princess Marie Louise, *Letters from the Gold Coast*, London, Methuen & Co. Ltd., 1926, pp. 193–4.

29 See, for instance, C.R. Buxton, 'An Onlooker in West Africa', Part 2, in *Labour*, March 1935, enclosed in C. Roden Buxton Papers, 5/4, p. 44; letter marked 'For Private Circulation Only', signed by A.G. Fraser, London, April 1935, WH, 4/9; Buell, *The Native Problem*, vol. 1, p. 781. For fuller details of conditions in the mines, see Cardinall, *The Gold Coast*, pp. 204, 245–6.

30 I.T.A. Wallace Johnson (IASB) to Arthur Creech Jones, 2 February 1938, ACJ, 18/3, p. 58; P. Cunliffe-Lister, *Hansard*, vol. 283, col. 1977–9, 14 November 1934; Duncan Johnson, Diaries, 20 July 1934, DJ, 3/3, p.72.

31 N. Leys, 'Politics on the Gold Coast', Labour Party Advisory Committee on Imperial Questions, International Department, no. 189, November 1937, marked 'Private and Confidential', enclosed in ACJ 18/3, p. 57; Questions raised by Creech Jones (Lab) and Sorensen (Lab), *Hansard*, vol. 345, col. 402, 15 March 1939; vol. 348, col. 2250–1, 21 June 1939.

   Conservative MPs also had shares in the Ashanti Gold Fields (Hargreaves, *Decolonisation in Africa*, p. 131).

32 J.N. Marbell, Prestea, to Wallace Johnson, 11 January 1938, ACJ 18/3, p. 60; Wallace Johnson to Creech Jones, 2 February 1938, ACJ, 18/3, p. 58; Duncan-Johnstone, Diaries, 4 October 1934, DJ, 3/1, p. 81; 20 August 1934, DJ, 3/3, p. 72.

33 Duncan-Johnsone, Diaries, 20 July 1938, DJ, 3/8, p. 22; 'Extract from a Report on the Gold Coast' enclosed in Wallace Johnson to Creech Jones, 2 February 1938, ACJ, 18/3, p. 60.

   'Progressive factions' in the ARPS had held a Youth Conference at Achimota College in 1930, which had pushed the nationalist movement in a more radical direction, and the ARPS became a constant thorn in the flesh of the colonial officers.

34 Letter from a Sierra Leone correspondent to IASB, enclosed in Wallace Johnson to Creech Jones, 9 March 1938, ACJ 18/3, pp. 62–3, 65; question raised by Sorensen, *Hansard*, vol. 347, col. 2316–7, 24 May 1939; W.R. Miller, *Have We Failed in Nigeria?*, London and Redhill, United Society for Christian Literature, Lutterworth Press, 1947, pp. 11, 17; 22–30.

35 '*African Standard* Report' in *Colonial Information Bulletin*, 15 May 1939, 3 (2): 2.

36 MacDonald, *Hansard*, vol. 348, col. 2250–1, 28 June 1939. See also correspondence between Polak, Bridgeman and Creech Jones, 17 June – 7 July 1939, ACJ, 18/7, pp. 178–97.

37 'Trinidad and After: A. Creech Jones, MP, Defines Some Labour Problems in the Colonies' in *African Sentinel*, Nov. – Dec., 1937, pp. 2 and 15, ACJ, 9/2, item 6. See also MacDonald, *Hansard*, (Commons), vol. 304, col. 2059–60, 25 July 1935.

38 J.I. Roper, *Labour Problems in West Africa*, London, 1958, pp. 25–9. See also MacDonald to Paling (Lab) *Hansard*, vol. 347, col. 2316–7, 24 May 1939; vol. 350, col. 1043–4, 24 July 1939; 'Trinidad and After', p. 5.

39 Duncan-Johnstone, Diaries, 9 May 1938, DJ, 3/6, pp. 29–31. See also 'Notes on Native Administration', 1936, DJ, 4/2, pp. 1–4, 22, 23.

40 B.N. Azikiwe, 'Murdering Women in Nigeria' in *The Crisis*, May 1930, 37: 163–6 and 164–5; 'A brief summary of some of the main grievances voiced by the Gold Coast ARPS', enclosed in a circular letter from R. Kidd, NCCL, 8 July 1936, ACJ, 18/3, pp. 9–10, 24.

41 Duncan-Johnstone to Colonial Secretary, 12 June 1936, DJ, 4/2, p. 35; G. Gorer, *Africa Dances*, London, 1935, pp. 274–6; For the African viewpoint, see Dinneford Smith, 'Reflections on Mr C.R. Buxton's Impressions of West Africa' in *Daily Guardian*, Freetown, 6 March 1935, p. 5, enclosed in Charles Roden Buxton Papers 5/4.

42 Shenton Thomas (Governor of the Gold Coast) to A. Fiddian, 27 February 1934, CO 96 714/21639/3. For more general background to the African press, see F.I.A. Omu, *Press and Politics in Nigeria 1880–1937*, London, 1978; F. Barton, *The Press of Africa: Persecution and Perseverance*, London, 1978.

43 Shenton Thomas to Cunliffe-Lister, 13 June 1934, CO 96 717/21750/1; Duncan-Johnstone, Diaries, 14 December 1929, DJ, 1/7, p.63; secret memo to Clausen, 13 October 1930, CO/3718 (Intelligence); memo from Governor Thompson marked 'Secret', 23 April 1930; 'Northern Provinces, Nigeria Police Intelligence Report for Quarter Ending March 1930/June 1930', enclosed in secret despatch from Thompson to Passfield, 13 August 1930; memo, J.J. Spencer, (ACP, Police Intelligence Bureau), 4 March 1930, CO 583, 174/864/7.

Intelligence reports concluded that the 'Tunisians' were probably 'intellectuals of Egyptian Soudanese origin' who were 'not infrequently found intriguing against the British in Africa'.

44 Governor Thompson to Passfield (marked 'Confidential A'), 15 August 1930; memo by G.L.M. Clausen, 6 October 1930, enclosed in CO 583, 174/864/7.

45 A. Burns (Governor's deputy) to P. Cunliffe-Lister, 5 December 1933; report by A. Fiddian, 10 January 1934, and attached CO memos CO 383 195/21029. The complaints were handled by Alex Fiddian, senior assistant secretary in charge of the West African department at the CO. See also *The Negro Worker*, 15 June 1932, 2 (6): 1, 14–17.

46 Cunliffe-Lister, *Hansard*, vol. 289, col. 1300 and col. 1746–7, 2 May 1935; W.M. Macmillan to W. Holtby, 23 November 1933, Winifred Holtby Papers, 4/13; Shenton Thomas to Cunliffe-Lister, 20 January 1934 (marked 'Confidential'), telegram from Shenton Thomas to the Secretary of State for Colonies, 26 March 1934, enclosed in correspondence between A. Fiddian and G. Creasy, March – April 1934, CO 96 714/21639. For initial CO caution, see memo by A. Fiddian, annotated by A. Duncan, 1 March 1934, enclosed in CO 96 714/21639.

47 Report by A. Fiddian, 10 January 1934, CO 96 714/21639; attached 'Enclosure 2'; *Gold Coast Gazette Extraordinary*, published by Authority, Wednesday, 21 February 1934.

48 Gorer, *Africa Dances*, p. 227. ARPS, 'Gold Coast Grievances', p. 28, enclosed in ACJ, 1813; NCCL Annual Report and Balance Sheet' in National Council of Civil Liberties (NCCL) Papers, 1934, p. 24.

49 Letter from the French Secretary for Native Affairs with Duncan-Johnstone's annotated comments, enclosed in Diaries, 18 December 1934, DJ, 3/3; exchange of information between the French authorities and Gold Coast administrators, CO 96 717/217861, 1934–5; Duncan-Johnstone, Diaries, 4 October 1934, DJ, 3/1, p. 81.

50 Telegram from Shenton Thomas to the Secretary of State for Colonies, 26 March 1934; letters of protest from WASU and other organisations, enclosed in correspondence between A. Fiddian and G. Creasy, March – April 1934, CO 96 714/21639. See also 'Notes on the Gold Coast issued by the National Council of Civil Liberties

(1934)', enclosed in the papers of the London Group on African Affairs (LGAA), file 5, pp. 1–6.

51 'Aborigines Petition to his Majesty, November, 1934'; Gold Coast Grievances, no. 9, ACJ, 18/3, pp. 24–6. For an in-depth analysis of the delegation, see S. Rhodie, 'The Gold Coast Aborigines Abroad' in *Journal of African History*, 1965, 4 (3): 389–408.

52 Minute by Fiddian, 15 December 1934, CO 96 718/21752; minute by Gerald Creasy, 12 July 1934, CO 96 717/121750.

53 Minute by Creasy, 6 August 1936, CO 96 723/31135/2; 'The Gold Coast Aborigines Protection Society: Delegation to the Colonial Office' (materials for the Colonial Office debate, 9 July 1936), ACJ, 18/3, pp. 8–9. For criticisms of CO attitudes, see W.T. Lunn, *Hansard*, (Commons), vol. 304, col. 2065–6, 25 July 1935.

54 R. Kidd, NCCL, to Creech Jones, 8 July 1936, ACJ, 18/3, pp. 9–10. For extension of the ordinances, see 'Seditious Ordinances Bill for Southern Rhodesia (transmitted to the Legislative Assembly by his Excellency the Governor, 1936)', enclosed in CRB, 6/2, pp. 16–19.

55 Shenton Thomas to A. Fiddian, 27 February 1934, CO 96 717/21639. See also N. Azikiwe, *My Odyssey: An Autobiography*, London, 1970, pp. 256–9 and information from editorials in the *West African Pilot*, Lagos, 1937.

Wallace Johnson was born in 1895 near Freetown of poor Creole parents and received a modest Methodist education. He worked for the municipal council, but was fired in 1926 when he left the colony and became involved with the Comintern. After a spell at sea, he returned to West Africa and from 1929–30 was a clerk at Sekondi in the Gold Coast. He became involved in trade unionism and developed his journalistic talents, writing regularly for the *Negro Worker*. During 1930–1, he attended the People's University of the East in Moscow and on his return to West Africa he became a full-time political activist (J.A. Rogers, *The World's Great Men of Colour*, New York, 1947, pp. 270–4).

56 Minute by Maclennan, 15 June 1936, CO 96 731/3123/1; Minute by Gerald Bushe, n.d., ibid.; R. Kidd (NCCL) to Creech Jones, 8 July 1936, ACJ, 18/3, p. 10.

57 MacDonald to Creech Jones, 5 July 1938; 9 July 1938, ACJ, 18/3, pp. 77–83 and 'Private Notes', ACJ, 18/3, p. 76; 'NCCL Annual Balance Sheet, 1938–9', NCCL Papers.

58 Brief prepared by O.G.R. Williams for MacDonald's meeting with the Sierra Leone Deputation, CO 267 637 32254/8, 1939 ('Deputation, Sedition, Undesirable Literature, Trade Unions and Trade Dispute Legislation'). For fuller details of Wallace Johnson's involvment in WAYL, see L. Spitzer and L.R. Denzer, 'I.T.A. Wallace Johnson and the West African Youth League' in *The International Journal of African Historical Studies*, parts 1 and 2, 1973, 4(3/4): 431–63 and 565–60.

59 R. Ridd to A. Creech Jones, 14 May 1938; A. Creech Jones to M. MacDonald, 5 July 1938; M. MacDonald to A. Creech Jones, 9 July 1938, ACJ, 18/3, pp. 77–83. See also the cable from the Freetown 'Civil Liberties League', which is enclosed in NCCL, 52/2.

60 C.A. Davis (Sierra Leone) to S. Pankhurst, 28 May 1939, ACJ, 18/7. See also 'Miscellaneous Representations', CO 267 762/32254/1,1939 and correspondence between Pankhurst, MacDonald, Creech Jones and other reformist critics, September 1939 – June 1946, ACJ, 18/7, pp. 160–92.

61 Enclosure no. II and no. III, Sierra Leone no. 325, 31 June 1939 (photos); Meeting of the Women's Auxiliary of the Youth League, 3 June 1939, 'Meeting of Civil Liberties and Native Defence League, incorporating WAYL' (Enclosure A), 15 June 1939, CO 267 763 32254/8. For Jardine's attitudes, see Jardine to MacDonald, 2 June 1939, CO 267 672 32254/1 (letter enclosed from M. Wyndam, 'Liberated Africans Co-operative Labour Union', Freetown, 27 April 1939, which he dismissed as 'unintelligible', although it is perfectly legible and in good English); Jardine to O.R.G. Williams, 27 November 1939, CO 267 763 32254/8.

62 'Copy of Minutes' from Acting Superintendent of Prisons, Officer in Charge of Internment Camp, 28 January 1940, CO 267, 678/32254/8. Details of the appeal are contained in correspondance between G. Creasy, Colonial Office, M. MacDonald, Colonial Secretary, A. Creech Jones, H. S. Polak (NCCL) and Burchell's (Solicitors to the Crown Agents), January – May 1939, ACJ, 18/3.

63 Internal memo to Cosmo Parkinson, dated November1939, with MacDonald's annotations, CO 267 672/32254/1; Minutes of the Sierra Leone Deputation, 1939, CO 267 763 32254/8.

Deputation members included Dr Harold Moody, President of the LCP who acted as leader, Peter Blackman (LCP), Lapido Solake (WASU), the Reverend Ejesa Osora and H.J. Williams (Sierra Leone), Reginald Bridgeman and Ronald Kidd (NCCL) and Sylvia Pankhurst. The deputation was introduced by the Labour MP, Arthur Creech Jones.

64 Exchanges between Creech Jones, Paling and MacDonald in *Hansard* (Commons), vol. 332, col. 857–8; col, 1383–4, 18, 25 November 1939.

65 S.R. Wood, Secretary of the Gold Coast Aborigines' Rights Protection Society, General Secretary of National Congress of British West Africa, 'The Gold Coast Deputation: Its Message to the British and the African' in *The Keys*, January – March 1936, 3 (3): 35–6.

66 H. Adi, 'The Communist Movement in West Africa' in *Science and Society*, 1997, 61 (1): 96; J. Ford, 'Negro Seamen and the Revolutionary Movement in Africa' in *Negro Worker*, April –May 1931, 1 (4/5); Padmore, *Africa: Britain's Third Empire*, p. 10. For Comintern attitudes, see *The Revolutionary Movement in the Colonies: Theses ... Adopted at the Sixth World Congress of the Communist International*, London, 1929, pp. 56–8.

67 F. Furedi, *The New Ideology of Imperialism: Renewing the Moral Imperative*, London, Pluto Press, 1995, p. 124.

68 *The Nigerian Pioneer*, 17 February 1922, 9 (364); *Report by the Honorable W.G.A. Ormsby-Gore*, pp. 25–8; Buell, *The Native Question*, vol. 2, pp. 742, 843–4. For general information on early nationalism, see H.J. Wilson, *The Origins of West African Nationalism*, London: Macmillan, 1969.

69 J. Cary, *A Case for African Freedom*, London, 1941, pp. 20–1. For Garveyite influence on nationalist leaders, see Azikiwe, *My Odyssey*, pp. 34–5,138–9; *Ghana; the Autobiography of Kwame Nkrumah*, New York, 1957, pp. 14, 45. For general background, see G.O. Olusanya, 'Garvey and Nigeria' and A. Hughes, 'Africa and the Garvey Movement' in R. Lewis and M. Warner-Lewis (eds.) *Garvey, Africa, Europe, the Americas*, Kingston, 1986, pp. 111–35, 137–51.

70 Enahoro, *Fugitive Offender*, pp. 90, 100–1; For comments on Fortes, see Perham, 'Problems of Indirect Rule' in *Colonial Sequence*, pp. 104, 115.

71 Duncan-Johnstone, Diaries, 4 August 1928, DJ, 1/5, pp. 5–6; J. Ayo Langley, Introduction to Sekyi's play, *The Blinkards: A Comedy*, London, 1974; J.K. Sekyi, 'White Manning in West Africa' and 'Extracts from the Anglo-Fanti' in *Negro Anthology made by Nancy Cunard 1931–1933*, published by Nancy Cunard, London, Wishart & Co., 1934, pp. 76, 770–4.

72 Father S.B. Yudé Sié to Anna Graves, 6 September 1935, 27 June 1936, 10 May 1938 in Graves, *Benvenuto*, pp. 123–6, 130, 135, 138. For the impact of the invasion on nationalist leaders, see Nkrumah, *Ghana*, p. 27; Enahoro, *Fugitive Offender*, p. 45; Azikiwe, *My Odyssey*, pp. 218–9. For a more in-depth analysis, see S.K.B. Asante, *Pan-African Protest: West Africa and the Italo-Ethiopian Crisis, 1934–1941*, London, 1977.

73 Cary, *A Case for African Freedom*, pp. 20–1; M. Perham and L.D. Curtis, *The Protectorates of South Africa: The Question of their Transfer to the Union*, London, 1935, pp. 95–6; E. Goode Robeson, *African Journey*, p. 24.

74 Lapido Solanke, M.A. 'Life and Conditions in West Africa', in *The Black Man*, July – August 1936, 2 (2): 12–4. For general background to WASU, see H. Adi, *West Africans in Britain 1900–1960: Nationalism, Pan-Africanism and Communism*, London, Lawrence &

Wishart,1998. The organisation published a magazine, *WASU*, which charted the development of race and political consciousness in West Africa and Britain.

75 W.M. Macmillan, *The Road to Self-Rule: A Study in Colonial Evolution*, London, 1959, p. 217; Enahoro, *Fugitive Offender*, pp. 66–7, 90–92.

76 Hailey, *An African Survey*. . .1956, p. 257. See also Sir M. Hailey, 'Nationalism in Africa' in *Journal of the Africa Society*, April 1937, 36: 134–47; Furedi, *The New Ideology of Imperialism*, pp. 5–7, 41.

77 Padmore, *Africa*, pp. 204–11; Nkrumah *Ghana*, pp. 43, 63. See also Azikiwe, *My Odyssey*, pp. 32–5, 66–8, 121–2, 228, 274–9 and *Renascent Africa*, Accra, 1937, 2nd edn, London, 1966.

    Azikiwe was educated at a missionary school in Ontisha and studied at the all black Howard University, Washington, D.C. He became an important newspaper proprietor in the late 1930s, but also became involved in some dubious financial scams in the 1940s and 1950s.

78 Padmore, *Africa*, p. 208; Azikiwe, *My Odyssey*, p. 24

79 D. Killingray and R. Rathbone (eds) *Africa and the Second World War*, London, Macmillan, 1986, pp. 11–15, 17. See also R. Lambo, 'Achtung! The Black Prince: West Africans in the Royal Air Force, 1936–46' in D. Killingray (ed.) *Africans in Britain*, Frank Cass, 1994, pp. 145–64; A.M. Israel, 'Measuring the War Experience: Ghanaian Soldiers in World War II' in *Journal of Modern African Studies*, 1987, 251 (1): 159–68.

80 S. Leith-Ross, *Stepping Stones: Memoirs of Colonial Nigeria, 1907–1960*, edited by M. Crowder, London and Boston, Peter Owen, 1983, pp. 111, 114.

81 H. Adi, 'Introduction' in H. Adi and M. Sherwood, *The 1945 Manchester Congress Revisited*, London and Port of Spain, New Beacon Books, 1995, pp. 21–2. For developments during the war, see *Report on Labour Conditions in West Africa by Major G. St. J. Orde Brown; 1940–41*, Cmd. 6277, London, HMSO, 1941.

82 *Report of the Commission of Inquiry into Disturbances in the Gold Coast 1948*, HMSO, 1948. See also 'Strikes and Disturbances; Riots After Parade of Ex-servicemen in Accra. Report of the Commission of Enquiry', CO 96 796/31312/2D/1. Much of the correspondence about the unrest between Creasy and the CO has been destroyed under statute.

    Nkrumah (1909–72) was educated at Achimota College, the US and Britain, but his period of most intense politicisation was during his stay in Britain from 1945–7 (M. Sherwood, *Kwame Nkrumah: the years abroad, 1935–1947*, Legon, Ghana, Freedom Publications, 1996). For general background to the nationalist movement in the Gold Coast, see F.M. Bourret, *The Road to Independence 1919–1957 The Gold Coast*, London, 1960.

83 *The Colonial Territories, 1948–1949*, HMSO, marked 'Confidential: final revise', p. 89–90; Miller, *Have We Failed in Nigeria?*, pp. 35–7, 57.

84 Hailey, *An African Survey... 1956*, pp. 1235–6, 1949–50; Leith-Ross, *Stepping Stones*, pp. 117–8, 125, 130.

85 *The Colonial Territories, 1948–1949*, HMSO, Marked 'Confidential: final revise', p. 89–90.

86 *Proposals for the Revision of the Constitution of Nigeria, 1944–45*, Cmd. 6599, London, HMSO, 1945, p. 2. For general background, see J.D. Hargreaves, *The End of Colonial Rule in West Africa*, London, Longman, 1976.

87 V. Brittain, 'Ghana's Precarious Revolution' in *New Left Review*, 1983, 140, pp. 51–61; W. de Graf, *The Nigerian State: Political Economy, State, Class and Political System in the Post-Colonial Era*, 1989; E. Osaghae, *The Crippled Giant; Nigeria Since Independence*, Hurst & Co., London, 1998. For more detail of nationalist movements, see J.S. Coleman's classic study, *Background to Nationalism in Nigeria*, Berkely, University of California Press, 1958. For general background, see A Mazrui (ed.) *Africa Since 1935*, London, Heinemann, 1993.

88 P.G. Lauren, *Power and Prejudice: the Politics and Diplomacy of Racial Discrimination*, New York, Westview Press, 1996, 2nd edn, p. 221.

89 L. Vail, 'Introduction' in L. Vail (ed.) *The Creation of Tribalism in Southern Africa*, London, James Currey, 1989, pp. 10–11; Hailey, *An African Survey... 1956*, pp. 205, 253–4.

90 Hailey, *An African Survey. . .1956*, pp. 204–6.

91 Coquery-Vidrovitch, *African Women*, pp. 168–75. Also relevant is P.K. Uchendu, *The Role of Nigerian Women in Politics: Past and Present*, Enugu, 4th Dimension Publishing Co., 1993; A.A. Ayoade, *et al. Women and Politics in Nigeria*, Lagos, Malthouse, 1992.

92 Mabel Dove-Danquah was the editor of the Accra *Evening News*. In 1952, she was the first woman to be elected to a colonial legislative assembly. (M. Busby, *Daughters of Africa*, London, Frank Cass, 1991, pp. 154, see Chapter three, FN 63, for information about Adelaide Casely-Hayford.)

93 See, for example, A. Smith, *State and Nation in the Third World: The Western State and African Nationalism*, London, 1983; 'Nationalism in Africa' in E. Kedourie, *Nationalism in Asia and Africa* 1971; J.D. Hargreaves, *Decolonisation in Africa*, London, Longman, 2nd edn, 1996; H.S. Wilson, *African Decolonisation*, London, Edward Arnold, 1994. For a survey of current debates over nationalism, see A. Heywood, *Political Ideologies: An Introduction*, London, Macmillan, 1992, pp. 159–63; J. Hutchinson and A.D. Smith (eds) *Nationalism*, Oxford, Oxford University Press, 1994, particularly sections 2 and 5. The most challenging critiques of 'third-world' nationalism have come from South Asian subaltern studies, exemplified in Partha Chatterjee's *Nationalist Thought and the Colonial World: A Derivative Discourse*, London, Zed, 1986; *The Nation and its Fragments,*, Princeton, NJ, Princeton University Press, 1993. There has been no comparative development in African studies, although the state has received considerable attention.

94 T. Hodgkin, *Nationalism in Colonial Africa*, London, Muller, 1956, pp. 21–3.

95 R. Hinden, *Plan for Africa: A Report Prepared for the Colonial Bureau of the Fabian Society*, London, Allen & Unwin Ltd., 1941. Broader economic problems are discussed in D.K. Fieldhouse, *Black Africa, 1945–1980: Economic Decolonisation and Arrested Development*, London, Hyman, 1986 and, for a more radical perspective, see S. Amin *Neo-Colonialism in West Africa*, London, 1973. For the failure of nationalism, see also B. Davidson *The Black Man's Burden: Africa and the Curse of the Nation State*, London, James Currey, 1992.

96 M. Ferro, *Colonisation: A Global History*, London and New York, Routledge, 1997, p. 336.

5 Forging the racist state: imperialism, race and labour in Britain's 'white dominion'

1 Poem by A.W.G. Champion in *Mhelomadala*, 1928, Champion Papers, box 2, 3/22; Poem cited in 'Literature and Resistance in South Africa', an ANC document published in the ANC's *Senchaba*, 1, 6, June 1967, reproduced in A. de Braganca and I. Wallerstein, (eds) *The African Liberation Reader*, London, Zed Press, 1982, 3 vols, vol. 1, p. 184.

2 D.G. Wolton, *Whither South Africa*, London, 1947, p.139; M. Mamdani, *Citizen and Subject: Contemporary Africa and the Legacy of Late Colonialism*, Princeton, Princeton University Press, 1996, p. 8.

3 I.L. Evans, *Native Policy in Southern Africa; An Outline*, Cambridge, CUP, 1934, pp. iii, 63.
    A fellow of St John's College, Cambridge, Evans had studied 'the problems confronting Britain in the African tropics'.

4 F.D. Tothill, 'White Man's Country: An Aspect of Mid-twentieth century Australia' in *Kleio*, 1995, XXVII: 165–95.

5 L. Woolf, *Imperialism and Civilisation*, London, Hogarth Press, 1928, p.108.

6 J. Barrett, 'South Africa in a Changing World' in E. Hellman and H. Lever (eds) *Race Relations in South Africa*, London and Basingstoke, Macmillan, 1980, first published in 1979, p. 214; C.W. de Kiewiet, *The Imperial factor in South Africa*, London, Frank Cass, 1967, pp. 1 and 5, first published 1937.

7 Key works by Macmillan include *Bantu, Boer and Briton: The Making of the South African Native Problem*, London, 1928 and *Complex South Africa: An Economic Footnote to History*, London, 1930. The importance of Macmillan in challenging orthodoxy on South Africa is discussed in P. Rich, 'W.M. Macmillan, South African Race Segregation and Commonwealth Race Relations, 1919–1938' in H. Macmillan and S. Marks (eds) *Africa and Empire: W.M. Macmillan, Historian and Social Critic*, London, Temple Smith, 1989, pp. 192–212, p. 211.

8 For useful overviews of historical research for the inter-war period, see N. Worden, *The Making of Modern South Africa*, Blackwell, 1994; W. Beinart, *Twentieth Century South Africa*, Oxford and New York, OUP, 1994. Current historiographical debates are lucidly summarised in the introduction to W. Beinart and S. Dubow (eds) *Segregation and Apartheid in Twentieth Century South Africa*, London, Routledge, 1995.

9 F. Brett Young, *In South Africa*, London, William Heinemann Ltd., 1952, p. 13.

10 Beinart and Dubow, *Segregation and Apartheid*, p. 5.

11 Sol T. Plaatje, *Native Life in South Africa*, Raven Press, Johannesburg, 1982, first published in 1922, with an introduction by B. Willan, p. 155.

12 Evans, *Native Policy*, p. 11; T. Keegan, *Colonial South Africa and the Origins of the Racial Order*, London, Leicester University Press, 1996; M. Legassick, 'British Hegemony and the Origins of Segregation in South Africa, 1901–14' in Beinart and Dubow, *Segregation and Apartheid*, pp. 43–60; B. Magubane, *The Round Table Movement*, London, Sapes, 1994, p. 6.

13 Sol T. Plaatje, *Mhudi*, edited by S. Gray with an introduction by T. Couzens and woodcuts by Cecil Skotness, London, Heinemann, 1978, first published by Lovedale Press in 1930.

14 D. Cammack, *The Rand At War, 1899–1902: The Witwatersrand and the Anglo-Boer War*, London, James Currey 1990, p. 11. The extent of British finance capitalism in South Africa was exposed in the British liberal and anti-imperialist J.A. Hobson's classic work, *Imperialism: A Study*, London, 1988, edited and with an introduction by J. Townshend, first published in 1902.

15 R.F. Selope Thema, L.T. Moabaza, East Dulwich, London, to the Rt. Hon. Viscount Milner, Secretary of State for Colonies, 22 May 1919, Smuts Papers, Union Archives, Pretoria, A1, band 115, vol. 35, F1, 17. See also Sol T. Plaatje, *Mafeking Diary: A Black Man's View of a White Man's War*, London, James Currey, 1990, first published in 1901. For an Afrikaner perspective on the war, see D. Reitz, *Commando*, London, Faber & Faber, 1938.

Reitz fought with Smuts and, like many others, went into voluntary exile after the war (in Reitz' case to Madagascar) until he was encouraged by Smuts to return and devote himself to promoting unity between the Boers and the British (D. Reitz, *No Outspan*, London, Faber & Faber, 1943, pp. 23–5).

16 S. Marks and S. Trapido, 'Lord Milner and the South African State' in *History Workshop Journal*, 1979, 2: 70; Legassick, 'British Hegemony and the Origins of Segregation', p. 44; Magubane, *The Round Table Movement*, p. 5.

17 Plaatje, *Native Life in South Africa*, p. 19. For Abdurahman's negative impressions of Britain, see interview between M. Hodgson and Abdurahman, M. Hodgson, Diaries, January 1930, V.M. Ballinger (née Hodgson) Papers, A. 2.

Terminology relating to race in South Africa is a minefield. I use the term 'Coloured' here as it is still used in South Africa today, although it has negative connotations in other contexts.

18 Evans, *Native Policy*, p. 29. For a fuller analysis of the complexities of the Land Act, see H.M. Feinberg, 'The 1913 Natives Land Act in South Africa: Politics, Race and

Segregation in the Early 20th Century' in *The International Journal of African Historical Studies*, 1993, 26 (1) 65–109.

19 H. Egerton, *British Colonial Policy in the Twentieth Century*, London, Methuen & Co., 1922, pp. 51–2; Plaatje, *Native Life in South Africa*, pp. xi, 19, 38–9.

20 R.L. Buell, *The Native Problem in Africa*, New York, 1928, vol. 2, pp. 123–4. See also Plaatje, *Native Life in South Africa*, p. 151.

21 J. Harris (ASAPS) to R.B. Stewart, Private Secretary to the High Commission, 10 April 1919, Smuts Papers A1, band 115, vol. 35, F1, nos. 6, 8; Plaatje, *Native Life in South Africa*, pp. 8, 19, 151. For biographical detail about Plaatje and details of the early ANC, see B. Willan, *Sol Plaatje: South African Nationalist 1876–1932*, London, Heineman, 1984.

22 Reitz, *No Outspan*, p. 25. Reitz helped Smuts suppress the rebellion which underscored the deep splits between Afrikaners over relations with Britain and British South Africans. For general background to African involvement in the war, see A. Grundlingh, *Fighting their Own Wars: South African Blacks and the First World War*, Johanesburg, Raven Press, 1987.

23 SANNC Memorial, Johannesburg, 16 December 1918, signed S.A. Makgatho, President, and I. Bud-M'Belle, General Secretary, enclosed in a letter from Governor-General Buxton, Cape Town, to Milner, South Africa, no. 108, 15 February 1919, Smuts Papers, A1, vol. CXV, Union of South Africa, 1919, 'ANC Delegation to Britain', band 115, 116, vol. 35, nos. 1–34, F1, no. 6.

24 'Mendi Memorial Day', lecture given by H. Selby Msiang to Gamma Sigma Club, Bantu Men's Social Centre, Johannesburg, 'Bantu Men's Social Centre Annual Report, 1933', Champion Papers, box 1, 4.2; 'Friends of Africa Report for Period January to July, 1942', enclosed in V.M. Ballinger Papers, D3.1.

25 SANNC Memorial; R.F. Selope Thema, L.T. Moabaza, East Dulwich, London to Rt. Hon. Viscount Milner, Secretary of State for Colonies, 22 May 1919, Smuts Papers, A1, band 115, vol. 24, F1, no. 4.

26 Selope Thema, *et al.*, to Milner, 23 May 1919; R.W. Msimang, Johannesburg, to the Rt. Hon. W.P. Schreiner, Whitehall, Westminster, 10 January 1919, Smuts Papers, A1, band 115, vol. 24, F1, no. 17; APO statement from A. Abdurahmen, President, and Matt. J. Fredericks, General Secretary, Cape Town, to chairman and members of the Peace Conference, 27 March 1919, Smuts Papers A1, band 115, vol. 15, F1, no. 6.

27 F.S. Malan, Prime Minister's Office, Cape Town, minute no. 225 (addressed to the Governor-General), 14 February 1919; Smuts Papers, A1, band 115, vol. 35, F1, nos. 6, 17. See also J.W. Mushet, Cape Town to J. Harris, London, 21 March 1919; H. Lambert, CO, to R.A. Blankenberg, 14 April 1919; Governor-General Buxton, Cape Town, to Milner, South Africa, no. 108, 15 February 1919, Smuts Papers A1, band 115, vol. 35, F1, nos. 6, 8.

28 South African Native Delegation, 'African Telegraph', London, to Lloyd George, British Embassy, Paris, 4 June 1919; H.C. Thornton, Downing Street, to Botha, 17 May 1919; Report of interview enclosed in H.C. Thornton, Downing Street, to Botha, 17 May 1919; Buxton to Milner, 17 April 1919; copy of cablegram dispatched, 20 May, by Reuters to South African Newspapers; Smuts Papers, A1, band 115, vol. 35, F1, nos. 7, 11. See also general correspondence between Smuts and Milner, Smuts Papers, A1, band 115, vol. 35, F1, nos. 4 to 17.

29 Egerton, citing *Journal of the Parliaments of the Empire* in *British Colonial Policy*, p. 175; R.A. Blankenburg to S. Msimang, 11 April 1919; J. Harris to R.B. Stewart, Private Secretary to the High Commission, 10 April 1919, Smuts Papers, A1, band 115, vol. 35, F1 nos. 6, 8.

30 Buell, *The Native Problem*, 2, p. 124.
    Plaaatje returned to South Africa in 1924 and died in 1932.

31 R.H. Kiernan, *General Smuts*, London, George G. Harrop & Company Ltd., 1943, p. 91. Much has been written on Smuts, but his first biographer was the liberal South

African author, Sarah Gertrude Millin, who was close to Smuts and wrote the hagiographic, *General Smuts*, London, Faber, 1936.

32 W. Holtby, 'Notes on the Way' in *Time and Tide*, 27 October 1934, pp. 18–24; Beinart, *Twentieth Century South Africa*, pp. 133–4.

33 Brett Young, *In South Africa*, pp. 134–5.

34 See, for example, N. Mansergh, *South Africa, 1906–1961*, New York, 1962, pp. 2, 329–33.

35 Reitz, *No Outspan*, p. 81.

36 Ibid., pp. 169, 185. For an incisive study of developments in Afrikaner nationalism, see D. O'Meara, *Volkskapitalisme: class, capital and ideology in the development of Afrikaner nationalism, 1934–1948*, Cambridge, CUP, 1983.

37 A. Rathbone, 'The Problem of African Independence' in *Labour Monthly*, April 1936, 18 (4). For a controversial reassessment of these developments, see P.J. Furlong, *Between Crown and Swastika: The Impact of the Radical Right on the Afrikaner Nationalist Movement in the Fascist Era*, Hanover, NH, University Press of New England, 1992.

38 M. Perham, *African Apprenticeship: An Autobiographical Journey in Southern Africa, 1929*, London, 1974, pp. 138–141.

39 Rathbone, 'The Problem of African Independence', p. 242; R. Ally, *Gold and Empire; The Bank of England and South Africa's Gold, 1889–1926*, Johannesburg, Johannesburg University Press, 1994; D. Lavin, *From Empire to International Commonwealth: A Biography of Lionel Curtis*, Oxford, Clarendon Press, 1995.
      Curtis was a civil servant in Johannesburg before Union and a key member of the Round Table Movement.

40 Woolf, *Imperialism and Civilisation*, p. 102.

41 Senator Tom Visser, 'Speech at Wits University' in *Johannesburg Star*, 28 August 1931, enclosed in Champion Papers, Diaries, box 2, 30/31; S. Dubow, 'The Elaboration of Segregationist Ideology' in Beinart and Dubow, *Segregation and Apartheid*, pp. 151–2; Lord Hailey, *An African Survey; A Study of Problems Arising in Africa South of the Sahara*, London, OUP, 1957, pp. 157–8. For a fuller study of racist thought as articulated by the professional intelligentsia, see S. Dubow, *Scientific Racism in Modern South Africa*, London, CUP, 1995.

42 *The Sjambok*, 6 March 1931, cited in I.D. MacCrone, *Race Attitudes in South Africa: Historical, Experimental and Psychological Studies*, London and New York, OUP, 1937; Buell, *The Native Problem*, 1, pp. 53–5. See also L. Barnes, *Caliban in Africa: An Impression of Colour-Madness*, London, Victor Gollancz, 1930, pp. 232, 302.

43 J.A. Rogers, *Sex and Race: Negro Caucasian Mixing in All Ages and All Lands*, New York, 1942–4, reprint, Helga M. Rogers, 1972, 3 vols, vol. 1, pp. 135, 137–40.

44 R.F.A Hoernlé, *South African Native Policy and the Liberal Spirit*, Lovedale, Lovedale Press, 1940, pp. 265–7, 277–8, 281. For a contemporary liberal insight into the position of the coloured population, see T.S. Marais, *The Cape Coloured People 1652–1937*, London, 1939; S.G. Millin, *God's Step-Children*, London, 1924.

45 G.H. Nicholls, *Bayete? 'Hail to the King'*, London, 1923, pp. 247, 345.

46 H. Lever, 'Changing Racial Attitudes' in Hellman and Lever (eds) *Race Relations in South Africa*, London and Basingstoke, Macmillan, 1980, first published in 1979, pp. 186–213; MacCrone, *Race Attitudes in South Africa*, pp. v, 308.

47 MacCrone, discussion point in Senator Tom Visser, 'Speech at Wits University', 1931.

48 MacCrone, *Race Attitudes*, pp. 273–9, 260–1.

49 Reitz, *No Outspan*; De Kiewiet, *The Imperial Factor*, p. 2; MacCrone, *Race Attitudes*, pp. 114–35, 206. For comparative studies, see H. Lamar and L. Thompson, *The Frontier in History: North America and Southern Africa Compared*, New Haven, 1982; John W. Cell, *The Highest Stage of White Supremacy: The Origins of Segregation in South Africa and the American South*, Cambridge, 1982; G Fredrickson, *White Supremacy: A Comparative Study in American and South African History*, New York, 1981.

50 Keegan, *Colonial South Africa*, pp. 9–10, 26–36, 61–74. Beinart, *Twentieth Century South Africa*, p. 6.
51 Commissioner Lamb, 'Migration Problems in the Empire' in H.E. Harper (ed.) *Empire Problems (Report of the Third Cambridge Empire Conference, 28–30 October 1938)*, London, Frederick Muller Ltd., 1939, p. 20.

Lamb represented the Salvation Army Migration and Settlement Department set up in 1903 to build up the Dominions with people of 'British ideals', including Christianity (Brigadier M. Owen Culshaw, 'Empire Migration and Settlement: Salvation Army Methods and Aims' in ibid.) According to the 1936 census, the European population was 2,003,512 – of which 1.5 per cent were Jewish and over 1,000,000 were Afrikaans-speaking. The majority of the English-speaking population was South African born. The non-white population was over 9,588,665 (MacCrone, *Race Attitudes*, p. 308).
52 Brett Young *In South Africa*, pp. 134–5.
53 Reitz, *No Outspan*, p. 157; J.M. Mackenzie, 'The Natural World and Popular Consciousness in Southern Africa: the European Appropriation of Nature' in P. Kaarsholm (ed.) *Cultural Struggle and Development in Southern Africa*, London, James Currey, 1991, pp. 13–33. Also relevant is W. Beinart and P. Coates, *The Taming of Nature in the USA and South Africa*, London, New York, 1994.
54 Evans, *Native Policy*, pp. 45–50, 60; Egerton, *British Colonial Policy*, p. 45.
55 P. Rich, *State Power and Black Politics in South Africa, 1912–51*, London, Macmillan, 1996, pp. 157–9. For a broader background to economic developments and the migrant labour system, see D. Duncan, *The Mills of God: The State and African Labour in South Africa, 1918–1948*, Johannesburg, University of Witwatersrand Press, 1995; M. Lipton, *Capitalism and Apartheid; South Africa, 1910–1986*, Cape Town and Johannesburg, David Phillips Books; D. Yudelman, *The Emergence of Modern South Africa: State, Capital and the Incorporation of Organised Labour on the South African Goldfields, 1872–1930*, Cape Town and Johannesburg, David Phillips Books, 1982.
56 C. Bundy, *The Rise and Fall of the South African Peasantry*, London, James Currey, 1988; private notes, W.M. Macmillan Papers, File 1936–7.
57 Evans, *Native Policy*, pp. 40–7, 81; Hailey, *An African Survey. . .1956*, pp. 651–2.
58 Brett Young, *In South Africa*,, pp. 63–6.
59 *The Truth About the ICU*, Champion Papers, box 2, 3.2.2, p. 13. See also Hailey, *An African Survey. . .1956*, p. 421; and Evans, *Native Policy*, p. 59 for favourable comments on native policy in the Transkei.
60 Interview between magistrates, Transkei, and M. Hodgson, 12 July 1929 and 16 July 1929; administrator, Transkei, in interview with M. Hodgson, 17 July 1929, M. Hodgson, Diaries, 1929.
61 Interview between magistrates, Transkei, and M. Hodgson, 12 July 1929 and 16 July 1929, M. Hodgson, Diaries, 1929.
62 Interview between M. Hodgson and Transkei magistrate, Lands Department, Umtata, 12 July 1929; interview with native trader/recruiter, magistrate, Transkei, Umtata, 12 July 1929, M. Ballinger Papers, Diaries, 1929. For a wider background to migration, see T. Dunbar Moodie (with V. Ndatshe) *Going for Gold: Men, Mines, and Migration*, Berkeley, UCLA Press, 1994.
63 Interview with a magistrate, Transkei, 12 July 1929; interview with an assistant magistrate, 11 July 1929, M. Hodgson, Diaries, 1929. See also interview with Captain McVeigh, NRC, King Williamstown, 17 July 1929, and Transkei magistrate, Lands Department, Umtata, 12 July 1929; recruiter to M. Hodgson, 11 July 1929, ibid.
64 Reitz, *No Outspan*, p. 81. See also M. Hodgson, 16 July 1929, M. Ballinger Diaries, 1929.
65 W. Beinart and C. Bundy, *Hidden Struggles in Rural South Africa: Politics and Popular Movements in the Transkei and Eastern Cape*, London, James Currey, 1987, pp. 21–5, 227–8. These complexities of rural life are explored more fully in H. Bradford,

A Taste of Freedom: The ICU in Rural South Africa, 1924–1930, Johannesburg, 1987; T. Keegan, *Facing the Storm: Portraits of Black Lives in Rural South Africa,* Athens, Ohio University Press, 1988.

66 M. Hodgson, Diaries, 2 December 1930. See also the interview between M. Hodgson and Merle Davis, September 1931; magistrate to M. Hodgson, 12 July 1929, ibid.

67 E. Goode Robeson, *African Journey,* London, Victor Gollancz, 1946, p. 74; *The Truth About the ICU,* Champion Papers, p.16

68 *The Poor White Problem in South Africa. Report of the Carnegie Committee of Enquiry,* Stellenbosch, 1932, 5 vols.

69 W.M. Macmillan, *Africa Emergent; A Survey of Social, Political and Economic Trends in British Africa,* London, 1938, pp. 178–9; Evans, *Native Policy,* pp. 67–70.

70 M. Hodgson, Diaries, 14 and 23 January 1930.

71 *The Truth About the ICU,* p.16; and for the official view, 'Cheap wine – social abuses', Smuts Papers, B and H, 119, vol. 19, 21 March 1934; Buell, *The Native Problem,* vol. 1, pp. 39–59. For social problems and statistical data on black crimes, including convictions for liquor offences, see R.E. Phillips, *The Bantu in the City: A Study of Cultural Adjustment on the Witwatersrand,* Lovedale, Lovedale Press, 1938, p. 178, *passim.*

72 M. Hodgson, Diaries, 3 January 1930.

73 S. Marks and S. Trapido (eds) *The Politics of Race, Class and Nationalism in Twentieth Century South Africa,* London, Longman, 1987, p. 50. B. Breytenbach, 'Land of Myths' in the 'Sunday Tribune', Durban, 19 August 1990.

The Afrikaner poet, Breytenbach, was a self-imposed exile in Paris after 1960. On his return to South Africa in 1972, he was arrested and sentenced to nine years in prison (M. Chapman, *Southern African Literatures,* London, Longman, 1996, pp. 345–7). His experiences of prison life are recorded in *The True Confessions of an Albino Terrorist,* Johannesburg and London, 1989.

74 Beinart, *Twentieth Century South Africa,* pp. 104–5; L. Vail (ed.) 'Introduction' in *The Creation of Tribalism in Southern Africa,* London, James Currey, 1989, p. 15;

75 Goode Robeson, *African Journey,* pp. 84–7.

76 Senator Tom Visser, 'Speech at Wits University', 1931.

77 'Annual Report: Women's Section of the National Congress; Natal Province, 1948', enclosed in Champion Papers, Diaries, box 4, 9.2.2; R.W. Msimang (SANNC), Johannesburg, to the Rt. Hon. W.P. Schreiner, Whitehall, Westminster, 10 January 1919, Smuts Papers, A1, band 115, vol. 24, F1, no. 17.

78 S. Marks, 'Patriotism, Patriarchy and Purity: Natal and the Politics of Zulu Ethnic Consciousness' in Vail, *The Creation of Tribalism,* p. 229; J. Cock, *Maids and Madams; Domestic Workers Under Apartheid,* London, Women's Press, 1989, pp. 58–65.

79 B. Bozzoli (with the assistance of Mmantho Nkotsoe), *Women of Phokeng: Consciousness, Life Strategy and Migrancy in South Africa, 1900–1983,* London, James Currey, 1991; L. Ngcobo, *And They Didn't Die,* London, Virago,1990; S. Marks, *Divided Sisterhood: Race, Class and Gender in the South African Nursing Profession,* London, Macmillan, 1995.

80 M. Boland, *Woman's Hour,* Radio 4, 25 November 1997. See also D. Stasiulis and N. Yuval-Davis (eds) *Unsettling Settler Societies; Articulations of Gender, Race, Ethnicity and Class,* London, Sage, 1995, 'Introduction' and pp. 13, 31.

An 'epidemic of rape' currently affects an estimated 3,000,000 women, black and white, yearly, which is nearly one in ten, including young girls (Boland, 1997).

81 D. Gaitskell, 'Wailing for purity: prayer unions, African mothers and adolescent daughters, 1918–1936' in S. Marks and R. Rathbone (eds) *Industrialisation and Social Change in South Africa: African Class Formation, Culture and Consciousness, 1870–1930,* London, Longman, 1982, pp. 338–58. See also C. Walker 'Women and Gender in Southern Africa: An Overview' in C. Walker (ed.) *Women and Gender in Southern Africa to 1945,* London, James Currey, 1990, pp. 15–16.

82 Worden, *The Making of Modern South Africa,* pp. 62–3. For African resentment of unfair taxes and police harassment, see Phillips, *The Bantu in the City,* pp. 196–9, 205–7.

83 Wulf Sachs, *Black Hamlet*, edited by S. Dubow and J. Rose, John Hopkins University Press, 1996, first published in 1937; ANC, 'Culture in Chains' in De Braganca and Wallerstein (eds) *The African Liberation Reader*, vol. 1, pp. 143–7.

84 D. Coplan, 'The Emergence of an African Working-Class Culture' in Marks and Rathbone (eds) *Industrialisation and Social Change*, pp. 358–9.

85 Phillips, *The Bantu in the City*, pp. 305–6, 313–4. Also relevant is L.A. Notcutt and G.C. Latham, *The African and the Cinema. An Account of the Work of the Bantu Educational Cinema Experiment During the Period, March 1935 to May 1937*, Johannesburg, 1937.

Early pioneering anthropological studies that addressed 'race relations' included E. Hellman, 'Native life in a Johannesburg slum yard' in *Africa*, 1935, 8: 34–62; E. Hellman, *Rooiyard: A Sociological Survey of an Urban Native Slum Yard*, Cape Town, 1948; I. Shapera (ed.) *Western Civilisation and the Natives of South Africa: Studies in Culture Contact*, London, 1934.

86 Phillips, *The Bantu in the City*, pp. xiii, 305–6, 312–4; *The Bantu are Coming*, London, 1930, pp. 8–9, 58.

Phillips gained his experience as a social worker and through research carried out for his Ph.D.

87 Modiagotla Conan Doyle, Coloured ICU organiser, Cape Town, M. Ballinger Diaries, January 1930. For favourable comments on Phillips, see A.M. Jabavu, brother of Professor D.D.T. Jabavu and a 'close friend' of Clements Kadalie, to A.W.G. Champion, 1930, Champion Papers, Box 2, 3.1, 25/1.

88 E. Hellman, 'Fifty Years of the South African Institute of Race Relations' in Hellman and Lever (eds) *Race Relations in South Africa*, pp. 4–5; S. Dubow, 'The Elaboration of Segregationist Ideology' in Beinart and Dubow (eds) *Segregation and Apartheid*, pp. 151–2.

89 'Bantu Men's Social Centre Information Leaflet', Champion Papers, box 1, 4.2. The Pathfinder Movement was established by the Governor-General in 1918 as a separate scouting movement for native boys, although the initiative was opposed by some whites (A. Warren, Citizens of Empire: Baden Powell, Scouts and Guides and an Imperial. Ideal, 1900–40, in J.M. Mackenzie (ed.) *Imperialism and Popular Culture*, Manchester, MUP, 1987, pp. 249–50).

90 'Bantu Men's Social Centre: Constitution' and 'Bantu Men's Social Centre: Annual Report', 1933, Champion Papers, box 1, 4.2.

91 'Bantu Men's Social Centre: Annual Report' 1933.

92 T. Couzens ' "Moralising Leisure Time": the Transatlantic Connection and Black Johannesburg, 1918–1936' in Marks and Rathbone, *Industrialisation and Social Change*, pp. 314–37, p. 328. See also Bantu Men's Social Institute, 1945, M. Ballinger Papers, A3.22–A3.24; Goode Robeson, *African Journey*, p. 87.

93 Rich, *State Power and Black Politics*, pp. 157–9.

6 'Knocking on the white man's door': repression and resistance

1 L. Woolf, *Imperialism and Civilisation*, London, Hogarth Press, 1928, pp. 102, 110; 'Preface' in *Africans' Claims in South Africa*, Congress Series No. II, Johannesburg, African National Congress, Champion Papers, box 2, 9.3.1.

2 E. Roux, *Time Longer than Rope: A History of the Black Man's Struggle For Freedom in South Africa*, University of Wisconsin Press, 1964; P. Bonner, P. Delius and D. Posel (eds) *Apartheid's Genesis, 1935–1961*, Johannesburg, Witwatersrand University Press, 1993. For a critique of the limitations of earlier resistance studies, see W. Beinart and C. Bundy (eds) *Hidden Struggles in Rural South Africa: Politics and Popular Movements in the Transkei and Eastern Cape*, London, James Curry, 1987, pp. 1–10 and S. Marks and R. Rathbone (eds) *Industrialisation and Social Change in South Africa: African Class Formation, Culture and Consciousness, 1870–1930,*, London, Longman, 1982, pp. 25–7.

3 E. Unterhalter, 'Constructing Race, Class, Gender and Ethnicity: State and Opposition Strategies in South Africa' in D. Stasiulis and N. Yuval-Davis (eds) *Unsettling Settler Societies; Articulations of Gender, Race, Ethnicity and Class*, London, Sage, 1995, pp. 207–41; W. Beinart, *Twentieth Century South Africa*, Oxford and New York, OUP, 1994, p. 107. For the significance of Christianity, see I. Comaroff and J. Comaroff, *Of Revelation and Revolution: Christianity, Colonialism and Consciousness in South Africa*, Chicago, University of Chicago Press, 1991.

4 C. Walker, 'Women, "Tradition" and Reconstruction' in *Review of African Political Economy*, 1994, 61: 19–38; J. Beall, S. Hassim, A. Trades, 'A bit on the Side? Gender Struggles in the Politics of Transformation in South Africa' in *Feminist Review*, 1989, 33: 24–42.

5 C. Coquery-Vidrovitch, *African Women: A Modern History*, Boulder, Colorado, Westview Press, 1997, pp. 189–90; See also B. Bozzoli, *Women of Phokeng: Consciousness, Life Strategy and Migrancy in South Africa, 1900–1983*, London, James Currey, 1991. Other seminal studies include, C. Walker *Women and Resistance in South Africa*, London, 1982; H. Bernstein *For Their Triumphs and for Their Tears* London, International Defence and Aid Fund for South Africa, 1985; I. Berger *Threads of Solidarity: Gender, Race And Labour In South Africa*, London, James Currey, 1992; J.C. Wells, 'The History of Black Women's Struggle Against Pass Laws in South Africa, 1900–1956' in M. May and M. Wright (eds) *African Women and the Law*, Boston, University of Boston Press, 1982, pp. 145–68.

6 Marks and Rathbone, *Industrialisation and Social Change*, pp. 2, 27–30.

7 E.W. Smith, *Aggrey of Africa: A Study in Black and White*, London, 1929, pp. 165–6, 143.

Originally from the Gold Coast, Aggrey spent twenty years in America as a student and a teacher. Miss Caroline Phelps-Stokes had left almost £1m. for the 'education of Negroes' in Africa and the US, and this became an important source of funding of philanthropic initiatives in South Africa in the inter-war years.

8 1919 SANNC Constitution, cited in R.L. Buell, *The Native Problem in Africa*, New York, 1928, 2 vols, vol. 2, pp. 123–4. For a broader overview of the early development of the ANC, see P. Walshe, *The Rise of African Nationalism in South Africa: The African National Congress, 1912–1952*, Berkeley and Los Angeles, UCLA Press, 1971.

9 D.D.T. Jabavu, *The Black Problem*, Lovedale, Lovedale Press, 1920, p. 31.

10 R.A. Hill and G.A. Pirio, ' "Africa for the Africans": the Garvey Movement in South Africa, 1920–1960' in S. Marks and S. Trapido (eds) *The Politics of Race, Class and Nationalism in Twentieth Century South Africa*, London, Longman, 1987, pp. 209–54, pp. 230–8, 240–3.

11 Hill and Pirio, ' "Africa for the Africans" ', p. 209; Marks and Trapido, *The Politics of Race, Class and Nationalism*, p. 38; P. Rich *State Power and Black Politics in South Africa*, London, Macmillan, 1996, pp. 39–43.

12 D. Thwaite, *The Seething African Pot: A Study of Black Nationalism, 1882–1935* London, 1936, pp. 15, 240.

13 G. Heaton Nicholls, *Bayete*, London, 1923, pp. 135, 222–4, 257, 271–3, 365–6.

14 M. Perham, *African Apprenticeship: An Autobiographical Journey in Southern Africa, 1929*, London, 1974, pp. 24–5.

15 D.H. Anthony, 'Max Yergan and South Africa: A Transatlantic Interaction' in S.J. Lemelle and R.D.G. Kelley (eds) *Imagining Home: Class, Culture and Nationalism in the African Diaspora*, London, Verso, 1994, pp. 185–202.

16 Thwaite, *The Seething African Pot*, pp. 189; Perham, *African Apprenticeship*, p.137. See also M.K. Gandhi, *Satyagrapha in South Africa*, Madras, 1928.

17 *The Truth About the ICU*, printed by Roberts Printing Works for the African Workers Club, Durban, Champion Papers, box 2, 3.2.2. Also relevant is C. Kadalie, *My Life and the ICU*, London, 1970, edited with an introduction by S. Trapido. For more general background, see P.L. Wickins' solid, if rather dated, *The Industrial and Commercial Workers Union of South Africa*, Cape Town, 1978.

18 Cited from official Union Government records in Buell, *The Native Problem*, vol. 2, pp. 123–4.

19 Letters to Smuts, 23, 24 March 1922, Smuts Papers, A1, vol. CXV, band 115, 116, vol. 29, vol. 30.

20 Buell, *Native Policy in South Africa*, vol. 2, pp. 39, 58, 118.

21 Roux, *Time*, pp. 137–40, 263. For further background, see S. Johns, *Raising the Red Flag: The International Socialist League and the Communist Party of South Africa, 1914–1932*, Belleville, Cape Town, Mayibuye Books, University of Western Cape, 1995 and B. Hirson and G.A. Williams, *The Delegate for Africa: David Ivon Jones, 1883–1924*, Johannesburg, Core Publications, 1995.

22 C. Kadalie to A.W.G. Champion, 21 September 1925, Champion Papers, box 2, 3.2.2.

23 M. Hodgson (Ballinger), Diaries, 27 January 1930, V. M. Ballinger Papers, A2, 5. See also W.M. Macmillan, *Africa Emergent: A Survey of Social, Political and Economic Trends in British Africa*, London, 1938, pp. 180–1.

24 H.J. and R.E. Simons, *Class and Colour in South Africa, 1850–1950*, London, 1969, pp. 459, 465. See also T. Jackson, 'South African Negro Workers on Dingaan's Day' in *Negro Worker*, December 1931, 1 (1): 4–5; *Daily Worker*, 6 May 1930, pp. 3, 30; A.T. Nzula, I.I. Potekhin and A.Z. Zusmanovitch, *Forced Labour in Colonial Africa*, edited with an introduction by R. Cohen, London, Zed Press, 1979, first published in Moscow in 1933, pp. 123–4, 211.

25 'Notes on East London, 1933–1935'; M. Hodgson, Diaries, 23 June 1930, V. M. Ballinger Papers, A2, 5; W. Ballinger to W. Holtby, 2 April 1932, Winifred Holtby Papers, 4/10.

26 Perham, *African Apprenticeship*, pp. 192–3; Poster advertising 'kaffir beer boycott', 15 April 1930 and additional information relating to the unrest in Durban, Champion Papers, File 3, 3.4.1; 'The Union, The Nation and the Talking Crow: the Ideology and Tactics of the Independent ICU in East London' in Beinart and Bundy, *Hidden Struggles*, pp. 270–321.

27 Interview between Margaret Hodgson and Abdurahman, January 1930 and annotated comments, M. Hodgson, Diaries, 1930. See also 'Report of the Proceedings and Resolutions of the Non-European Conference' in the *Cape Times*, 4–6 January 1930 (extracts) in T. Karis and G.M. Carter (eds) *From Protest to Challenge: A Documentary History of African Politics in South Africa, 1882–1964*, Stansford, 1972–7, 4 vols, vol. 1, document 45, pp. 268–72.

28 I. Goldin, 'Coloured Identity and Coloured Politics in the Western Cape region of South Africa' in L. Vail (ed.) *The Creation of Tribalism in Southern Africa*, London, James Currey, 1989, pp. 241–55, pp. 248–51.

29 W. Ballinger to W. Holtby, 21 November 1930, W. Holtby Papers, 4/11.
   A Cape Town branch of the British Fabian Society was established in 1930.

30 'Speech of Comrade T. Jackson, delegate from South Africa to the International Labour Defence' in *Negro Worker*, February – March 1933, 3 (2/3): 5–7; Cohen, 'Introduction' in Nzula, *et al.*, *Forced Labour*, pp. 8–9. See also *Umvikeli Thebe (The African Defender)*, January 1935, 1: 1–2 and for more details of these developments, Nzula, *et al.*, *Forced Labour*, pp. 131–7, 158–9, 167, 209; H.J. and R.E.Simons, *Class and Colour*, pp. 417–9.

31 *A Report of Proceeding and Decisions of the First International Conference of Negro Workers at Hamburg, Germany, July, 1930*, Hamburg, ITUC-NW, 1930, pp. 11–15, 30–32 and Part 4, 'Resolutions'. For a fuller analysis of these developments, see M. Legassick, *Class and Nationalism in South African Protest: The South African Communist Party and the 'Native Republic', 1928–1934*, New York, 1973.

32 A. Drew, 'Writing South African Communist History' in *Science and Society*, 1997, 61 (1):107–13.

33 B. Weinbren to E. Roux, 27 April 1929, Roux Papers. See also Cohen, 'Introduction' in Nzula, *et al.*, *Forced Labour*, pp. 3–6.
34 M. Hodgson, Diaries, November 1930.
35 *The Truth About the ICU*, pp. 9–10, 25–6.
36 S. Marks, 'Patriotism, Patriarchy and Purity: Natal and the Politics of Zulu Ethnic Consciousness' in Vail (ed.) *The Creation of Tribalism*, pp. 216–7; S. Marks, *The Ambiguities of Dependence in South Africa; Class, Nationalism and State in Twentieth Century Natal*, Baltimore and Johannesburg, 1986.
37 Beinart, *Twentieth Century South Africa*, pp. 104–5; Perham, *African Apprenticeship*, pp 192–3, 200.
38 *The Truth About the ICU*, pp. 7, 24; W. Ballinger to W. Holtby, 14 January 1931, W. Holtby Papers 4/10. Additional biographical detail from UNISA Documentation Centre for African Studies.
39 M. Hodgson, Diaries, September 1929; Letter from Champion to Abdurahman, 1930, V. M. Ballinger Papers.
40 Kadalie to Champion, 5 June 1928; Champion to Kadalie, 1928 enclosed in Champion Papers, box 2, 3.2.2.
41 Beinart and Bundy, 'The Union, the Nation and the Talking Crow', pp. 291–4.
42 *Mehlomadala*, pp. 21–3; *The Truth About the ICU*, p. 7.
43 Town Clerk, Durban, to Champion, 6 October 1934, Champion Papers 3/20. Biographical data from UNISA Documentation Centre for African Studies.
44 M. Macmillan to B. Bush, 30 April 1983. See also Kadalie to W. Ballinger, 3 January 1931; W. Ballinger to N. Leys, 2 January 1933, W. Holtby Papers, 4/6.
45 Beinart and Bundy, *Rural Struggles*, pp. 24, 38–9; H. Bradford, *A Taste of Freedom: The ICU in Rural South Africa, 1924–1930*, Johannesburg, 1987. For general difficulties of organising mineworkers, see Nzula, *et al.*, *Forced Labour*, pp. 131–7.
46 Roux, *Time*, pp. 274–5;
47 H.J. and R.E. Simons, *Class and Colour*, p. 510; 'Lynching in South Africa' in *Colonial Information Bulletin*, 20 September 1937, 1 (12): 2–3.
48 Phillips, *The Bantu in the City*, pp. 196, 258–9, 275–6.
49 Lord Hailey, *An African Survey: A Study of Problems Arising in Africa South of the Sahara (Revised, 1956)*, London, OUP, 1957, pp. 159–62.
50 Presidential address by Professor D.D.T. Jabavu, AAC, 29 June 1936; The All African Convention: Proceedings and Resolutions of the AAC, 15–18 December 1935; 'The Constitution of the AAC, 1937' in Karis and Carter, *From Protest to Challenge*, vol. 2, documents 9, 11, 15, pp. 31–41, 4, 52–3.
51 Reverend Mahabane, cited in 'The All African Convention: Proceedings and Resolutions of the AAC, 15–18 December 1935' in ibid., document 9, pp. 37–8.
52 Presidential Address by the Reverend J.A. Calata, Cape African Congress, 14 July 1938; Presidential Address of Professor D.D.T. Jabavu, AAC, 29 June 1936; Proceedings and Resolutions of the AAC, 29 June – 2 July 1936, ibid., document 11, pp. 51, document 12, p. 56, document 16, p. 74.
53 Italo-Abyssinian War: Anglo-French Peace Proposals, Secret and Unparaphrased: Minister of State for External Affairs to Secretary of State, Dominions, 20 December 1935, Smuts Papers, band 112, vol. 28. See also *Umvikeli Thebe*, April 1936, p.3 and general coverage for 1936.
54 M. Ballinger to W.M. Macmillan, 13 July 1936, 20 December 1936, William Macmillan Papers, File May – December 1936.
55 'Resolution on Clause One of the Native Representation Bill (Franchise) placed by Selby Msimang' and 'The All African Convention: Proceedings and Resolutions', documents 8, 9 in Karis and Carter (eds) *Protest and Challenge*, pp. 33, 37, 42, 104.
56 I.B. Tabatu, *The All African Convention: The Awakening of a People*, Johannesburg, People's Press, 1950, pp. 4–5, 40–4; Letter from Yergan attached to 'Minutes of AAC, Dec. 1937', reproduced in ibid., pp. 24–5.

57 H.J. Simons and R.E. Simons, *Class and Colour*, p. 552; Roux, *Time*, pp. 322, 375–6; Phillips, *Bantu in the City*, pp. 343–4.

58 Tabatu, *The All African Convention*, pp. 35–6.

59 Perham, *African Apprenticeship*, pp. 53–4,132–3.
   Jabavu was undoubtedly one of the foremost black leaders and intellectuals of the period. A recent biography has described him as a fascinating and controversial figure who skilfully navigated between black and white cultures (C. Higgs, *The Ghost of Equality: The Public Lives of D.D.T. Jabavu of South Africa, 1885–1959*, Johannesburg, David Phillips, 1997.)

60 Perham, *African Apprenticeship*, p. 45; Macmillan, *My South African Years*, pp. 227–8.

61 Hailey, *An African Survey*, p. 1140. For South African propaganda, see *The Royal Visit to South Africa, 1947*, Pretoria, South African Railways, 1947.

62 Roux, *Time*, pp. 337–8.

63 'Introduction' in Vail, *The Creation of Tribalism*; Marks and Rathbone, 'Introduction' in *Industrialisation and Social Change*, p. 2.

64 'Introduction' in Marks and Rathbone, *Industrialisation and Social Change*, p. 27; C. van Onselen, 'Worker Consciousness in Black Miners: Southern Rhodesia, 1900–1920' in *Journal of African History*, 1973, XIV (2): 237–56. For an excellent summary of recent debates relating to problems of ethnicity, political consciousness and violence and their links with the Apartheid past, see M. Szeftel, 'Ethnicity and Democratisation in South Africa' in *Review of Political Economy*, 1994, 21 (61): 185–99.

65 E. Goode Robeson, *African Journey*, London, Victor Gollancz Ltd., 1946, pp. 49, 66.
   Essie Robeson spent several weeks in South Africa in 1936. She was met at the boat by the anthropologist, Irving Shapera, and travelled around with black leaders, including Max Yergan, meeting a wide cross section of the black population.

66 For ANC activities, see F. Meli, *South Africa Belongs to Us: A History of the ANC*, London, James Currey, 1989. For general developments in trade unionism, see B. Hirson, *Yours for the Union: Class and Community Struggles in South Africa, 1930–1947*, Johannesburg, Witwatersrand University Press, 1990. Developments in the ICU are recalled in H.M. Basner, *Am I an African? The Political Memoirs of H.M. Basner*, with a foreword by T. Lodge and M. Basner, Johannesburg, Johannesburg University Press, 1993.

67 D.D.T. Jabavu to M. Ballinger, 4 December 1943, M. Ballinger Papers, BC 345, A3, 58. See also T.R. White, 'Z.K. Matthews and the formation of the ANC Youth League at the University College of Fort Hare' in *Kleio*, 1995, XXVIII: 124–44.

68 *Africans' Claims in South Africa*, Congress Series no. II, Johannesburg, African National Congress, Champion Papers, 9.3.1, preface.

69 For fuller details of the wartime government, see D. Reitz, *No Outspan*, London, Faber and Faber, 1943, pp. 243–6. See also Beinart, *Twentieth Century South Africa*, p. 134.
   Reitz was deputy Prime Minister and Minister of Native Affairs.

70 R.H. Godlo, member of the Native Representation Council and executive member of the ANC, to M. Ballinger, 21 March 1941. See also M. Ballinger to Smuts, 21 March 1941; telegram from Godlo to Smuts, Assembly, Cape Town, 13 March 1941, M. Ballinger Papers, BC 435, A3 33, 34.

71 L. Grundlingh, 'The Recruitment of South African Blacks for Participation in the Second World War' in D. Killingray and R. Rathbone (eds) *Africa and the Second World War*, London, 1986, pp. 181–203. See also M. Roth, ' "If you give us rights we will fight": Black involvement in the Second World War', *South African Historical Journal*, 1983, XV, pp. 85–104.

72 White, 'Z.K. Matthews and the formation of the ANC Youth League at the University College of Fort Hare' in Kleio, 1995, XXVIII, pp. 129–44, 133.

73 Bernard Magubane, *The Ties that Bind*, Trenton, Africa World Press, 1987, pp. 123–4.

74 Rich, *State Power*, p. 117. For details of South African representation at the 1945 congress, see the report of the session on 'Oppression in South Africa' in H. Adi and

M. Sherwood, *The 1945 Manchester Congress Revisited*, London and Port of Spain, New Beacon Books, 1995, pp. 84–6.

Abrahams (the author of *Mineboy*, London, Heineman, 1963, first published in 1946), went to live in Jamaica, which he believed had outlived its 'multiracial problems'. South Africa, in contrast, was so 'riddled with hate' that only a 'terrible and bloody' solution seemed possible (P. Abrahams, *Jamaica: An Island Mosaic*, London, HMSO, 1957, p. 261).

75 Beinart, *Twentieth Century South Africa*, p. 131.

7 'Fighting for the underdog': British liberals and the South African 'native question'

1 *Racial Problems in South Africa: Report by a Deputation from the Society of Friends, 1938*, London, Society of Friends, 1938, p. 4.

2 V. Brittain, *Testament of Friendship: The Story of Winifred Holtby*, London, 1941, p.184. For an articulation of the key values that reformist socialists shared with liberals, see 'Subject Races Within the Empire: Report of the Study Group set up by the Cambridge University Labour Club, October, 1927', pp. 6–8, Roux Papers.

3 P. Rich, *White Power and the Liberal Conscience: Racial Segregation and South African Liberalism, 1921 to 1960*, Manchester, MUP, 1984; R. Elphick, 'Missionary Activity and Inter-War Liberalism' in J. Butler, R. Elphick, D. Welsh, (eds) *Democratic Liberalism in South Africa: Its History and Prospect*, Cape Town and Johannesburg, Wesleyan University Press, 1987, pp. 64–80. Also relevant is P. Rich, *Hope and Despair: English Speaking Intellectuals and South African Politics, 1896 to 1976*, London, British Academic Press, 1993, and for an influential study on the complexities of liberalism in the preindustrial era, S. Trapido, 'The Friends of the Natives: merchants, peasants and the political and ideological structure of liberalism in the Cape' in S. Marks and A. Atmore (eds) *Economy and Society in Pre-Industrial South Africa*, London, Longman, 1980, pp. 247–84.

4 W.M. Macmillan, *Africa Emergent: A Survey of Social, Political and Economic Trends in British Africa*, London, 1938, pp. 180–1; L. Barnes, *Caliban in Africa: An Impression of Colour-Madness*, London, 1930, p. 95. See also *Africana*, newsletter of the LGAA, December 1931, p. 2, Winifred Holtby Papers WH, 4/23.

5 W. Holtby to V. Brittain, 20 April 1926, June 1926, WH, drawer 6, file 1926–7; V. Brittain, *Testament of Friendship: The Story of Winifred Holtby*, London, 1941, pp. 131, 161.

Holtby's initial connection with South Africa came through her close friend, Jean MacWilliam, the head of Pretoria High School, whom she met in France during the war while serving in the Women's Army. Other Joint Council contacts included Ethelreda Lewis, the wife of a mining magnate, and Mabel Palmer (see note 9).

6 A. Creech Jones to C. Kadalie, 21 October 1927; 15 September 1927; 8 November 1927; C. Kadalie to A. Creech Jones, 21 March 1928, WH, 11/50; F. Brockway to A. Creech Jones, 19 August 1927, Arthur Creech Jones Papers (ACJ), Rhodes House, Oxford, 6/1.

7 A. Creech Jones to W. Holtby, 7 February 1928; 13 February 1928, WH, 4/6. Details of funding arrangements are discussed in letters between Creech Jones and Holtby, April 1929, WH, 6.

8 M. Hodgson, Diaries, 29 January 1930, V.M. Ballinger Papers, A2, 2; W. Holtby to A. Creech Jones, 16 October 1928, WH, 11/50. See also 'ICU advisor makes his debut' in *Natal Mercury*, 19 July 1928, enclosed in WH, 4/6. For black criticisms, see C. Kadalie, *My Life and the ICU*, London, 1970, edited and with an introduction by Stanley Trapido, pp. 177–80; *Mehlomadala*, Champion Papers, box 2, 3.2.2.

9 W. Beinart and C. Bundy, *Hidden Struggles in Rural South Africa: Politics and Popular Movements in the Transkei and Eastern Cape*, London, James Curry, 1987, p. 318;

M. Palmer to A.W.G. Champion, 13 February 1930. For further discussion of Mabel Palmer's activities in South Africa, see S. Marks, 'Mabel Palmer, Feminism and Black Education', unpublished paper given at the Institute of Commonwealth Studies, Postgraduate Seminar Series, 1997–8, 7 May 1998.

10 A.W.G. Champion to M. Palmer, 17 February 1930, Champion Papers, box 2, 3.1.8, 3.1.9.

11 W. Ballinger to W. Holtby, 18 February 1931; H. Pim to W. Holtby, 31 March 1931; A. Hlubi to W. Holtby, 1931; F. Livie-Noble to W. Holtby, 27 June 1931, WH, 4/10, 4/13,4/18.
    Fircroft had an international studentship and allegedly 'no race prejudice' (P.G. Mockerie, *An African Speaks for his People*, London, 1934, pp. 11–12, 17–19).

12 For white assessment of the splits and antagonisms in the ICU, see A. Creech Jones to W. Holtby, 17 September 1930, 21 November 1930, 30 May 1933, and 28 November 1933, WH, 4/6.

13 J. Harris to Mrs Pethwick-Lawrence, 1 August 1930, Anti Slavery and Aborigines Protection Society Papers, Rhodes House, Oxford (ASAPS), G 19; M. Perham, *African Apprenticeship: An Autobiographical Journey in Southern Africa, 1929*, London, 1974, pp. 137, 170.

14 M. Hodgson, Diaries, 12 January 1930 and 22 January 1930. See also M. Hodgson to N. Leys, 28 December 1932, WH, 4/9.

15 W.M. Macmillan to N. Leys, 21 January 1935, WH, 4/9; M. Hodgson to W. Holtby, 12 October 1932, WH, 4/11.

16 H. Bradford, *A Taste of Freedom: The ICU in Rural South Africa, 1924–1930*, Johannesburg, 1987, pp. 167–8; F.A. Mouton, *Voices in the Desert*, Johannesburg, Benedict Books, 1997.

17 W. Ballinger to W. Holtby, 25 March 1931; M. Hodgson to W. Holtby, 21 September 1932; H. Pim to W. Holtby, 12 July 1933, 6 December 1933 and 18 October 1933, WH, 4/10, 4/11, 4/12. Problems of administering the Ballinger Fund on a routine day-to-day basis are covered in correspondence between Holtby and Pim, 1930–3, WH, 4/14.

18 F.A. Mouton, '"A cusser when crossed": the turbulent career of William Ballinger', *Kleio*, 1995, XXVII: 145–64, 147, 158.

19 E. Hellman, 'Fifty Years of the South African Institute of Race Relations', in E. Hellman and H. Lever (eds) *Race Relations in South Africa*, London and Basingstoke, Macmillan, 1980, pp. 4–5; W. Holtby to V. Brittain, June 1926, WH, drawer 6, file 1926; Macmillan, *My South African Years: An Autobiography*, Cape Town, 1975, pp. 160–1.

20 Mosa Anderson to W. Holtby, 21 November 1929, WH, 4/12; Perham, *African Apprenticeship*, pp. 145–6. For details of the UK appeal, see H. Pim to W. Travers Buxton, 4 March 1927; J.D. Rheinallt Jones to J. Harris, 25 January 1927, Anti-Slavery and Aborigines Protection Society (ASAPS) Papers, D2/21, G194.

21 Prominent members included Frederick Livie-Noble, the Secretary, who had been involved in the Bantu Men's Social Clubs and the Pathfinder Scouts in the 1920s, Leonard Barnes, Julian Huxley, Charles Roden Buxton, Arthur Creech Jones, Norman Leys, Dr Harold Moody, Julius Lewin, Drummond Shiels, Dorothy Woodman (Union of Democratic Control), Henry Polak (who later joined the NCCL), Ellen Wilkinson, MP, and Leonard Woolf. Fabian influence was reflected in the emphasis on research, publicity and pressure for mild reforms. LGAA publicity pamphlet and membership list, 1931, WH, 4/13.

22 See, for instance, H. Macmillan and S. Marks (eds) *Africa and Empire: W.M. Macmillan, Historian and Social Critic*, London, Temple Smith, 1989. See also M. Hodgson to W. Holtby, 12 October 1932, WH, 4/1 and for British contacts, see correspondence between N. Leys, L. Curtis and W.M. Macmillan, WMM, files 1926–30.

Macmillan was born in Aberdeen in 1885, moved to South Africa when he was six and became a Rhodes scholar at Oxford before the First World War (*My South African Years*, p.124).

23 M. Hodgson to W. Holtby, 9 September 1933, WH, 4/11; Mona Macmillan, interview, 11 March 1982; W.M. Macmillan to L. Curtis, 12 July 1929, WMM, file 1929–30.

Lewin subsequently became Associate Professor of African History at Cape Town University.

24 W.M. Macmillan to M. Ballinger, 23 February 1965, V.M. Ballinger Papers, 345, A3, 71. See also H. Macmillan, ' "Paralysed Conservatives": W.M. Macmillan, the Social Scientist and the Common Society, 1923–48' in Macmillan and Marks (eds) *Africa and Empire*, pp. 72–91, p. 87.

25 W. Ballinger to W. Holtby, 11 September 1934, WH, 4/10.

26 J. Goody, *The Expansive Moment: Anthropology in Britain and Africa, 1918–1970*, Cambridge, CUP, 1995, pp. 154–7. Also relevant is J.D. Rheinnalt Jones, 'Native Studies in our Universities' in Reverend Dexter Taylor (ed.) *Christianity and the Natives of South Africa*, Lovedale, Lovedale Press, 1928, pp. 152, 155–8.

27 W.M. Macmillan to Mona Tweedie, 25 November 1931, 26 October 1931, WMM, file 1931–2. See also Perham, *African Apprenticeship*, pp. 190–1.

28 W. Ballinger to W. Holtby, 31 January 1934, WH, 4/11; W.M. Macmillan to Mona Tweedie, 15 September,1932, WMM, file 1931–2. See also M. Hodgson to W. Holtby, 12 October 1932, 17 November 1933, WH, 4/11, 4/10.

29 W. Ballinger to W. Holtby, 25 March 1931, WH, 4/10.

30 H.R. Raikes to W.M. Macmillan, 10 November 1932; W.M. Macmillan to Mona Tweedie, 15 September 1932, WMM, file 1931–2. See also Macmillan, *My South African Years*, p. 205; Perham, *African Apprenticeship*, p. 151.

Raikes maintained that he had a 'keen interest in the native'.

31 Mona Macmillan to B. Bush, 30 April 1983. For details of Macmillan's difficulties in England, see *My South African Years*, pp. 242–6, and relevant correspondence in WMM, file 1933–4.

Macmillan's first wife, Jean, was a mild liberal who was reputably perturbed by his increasing social and political isolation. In 1930, he married Mona Tweedie, daughter of Vice Admiral Hugh Tweedie, who was based at Simonstown (Mona Macmillan, interview, 11 March 1982).

32 W. Ballinger to W. Holtby, 12 April 1933, WH, 4/10.

33 Barnes, *Caliban*, p.131; W.M. Macmillan to Mona Tweedie, n.d., WMM, file 1931–2.

34 R.E. Phillips, *The Bantu in the City: A Study of Cultural Adjustment on the Witwatersrand*, Lovedale, 1938, pp. 348–50; J. Harris to Mrs Pethwick-Lawrence, 1 August 1930, ASAPS, G, 194.

35 M. Hodgson and W. Ballinger to W. Holtby, 31 January 1934, WH, 4/11; M. Hodgson to W. Holtby, 18 December 1932, 12 October 1932, WH, 4/10. For Ballinger's comments on equal rights, see W.G. Ballinger, *Race and Economics in South Africa*, Day-to-day pamphlets, no. 21, London, 1934, p. 47.

36 Sir M. Hailey, *An African Survey*, London, OUP, 1957, p. 1461; Rich, *White Power*, p. 36.

Ross was described by Holtby as 'working hard for the natives'. She had started a library at the Pretoria Location and was trying to raise money for a native swimming pool (J. Macmillan to W. Holtby, 3 March 1931, WH, 4/15).

37 Hailey, *An African Survey*, p. 504; Perham, *African Apprenticeship*, pp. 129–31.

38 *Financial and Economic Position of the Bechuanaland Protectorate: Report of the Commission Appointed by the Secretary of State for Dominion Affairs, March, 1933*, London, HMSO, 1933, pp. 18–22, 30–1; I.L. Evans, *Native Policy in Southern Africa: An Outline*, Cambridge, CUP, 1934, pp. 90–2. Also relevant is Barnes, *The New Boer War*, London,

Hogarth, 1932, Section 2; V.M. Hodgson and W.G. Ballinger, *Britain in South Africa, no. 2: The Bechuanaland Protectorate*, Lovedale, 1931–2, pp. 33–63.

39 Evans, *Native Policy*, pp. 79, 100–102; Sir A. Pim, *Report on the Financial and Economic Situation in Swaziland, 1932*, London, HMSO, 1932, p. 18. For conditions in Basutoland, see 'Report on Basutoland' by Mrs Ross of Pretoria, 1931, enclosed with a letter from J. Macmillan to W. Holtby, 3 March 1931, WH, 4/15.

40 Cited in Hodgson and Ballinger, *Britain in South Africa*, pp. 24–9.

41 L. Barnes, *The New Boer War*, London, Hogarth, 1932, pp. 21–5; M. Ballinger, *Diaries*, 26 January 1930; M. Hodgson to N. Leys, 14 January 1931; L. Barnes to W. Ballinger, 3 January 1931, WH, 4/11, 4/10.

42 B. Weinbren to E. Roux, 7 June 1929, Roux Papers. For anti-communist sentiments, see C. Parkinson to W.H. Thomas, 25 July 1933, *Hansard*, vol. 280, cols 2391–2.

43 J. Harris (ASAPS) to Dominions Office, 30 August 1932; Under Secretary of State, Dominions Office, to J. Harris, 5 September 1932, ASAPS, D6/3.

44 J.H. Thomas to C. Parkinson, 25 July 1933, *Hansard*, (Commons), vol. 280, cols 2391–2; W. Ballinger to W. Holtby, 21 March 1931, 21 June 1933, WH, 4/10.

45 W. Ballinger to W. Holtby, 11 March 1931; M. Hodgson to N. Leys, 21 January 1931, WH, 4/10.

46 Evans, *Native Policy*, p. 102.

47 A. Rathbone, 'The Problem of African Independence', *Labour Monthly*, April 1936, 18 (4): 242; Barnes, *Caliban*, pp. 222–3.

48 J.H. Thomas, 29 March 1938, *Hansard*, vol. 303, col. 593; vol. 333, cols 1807–12.

49 M. Crowder, *The Flogging of Phinehas McIntosh: A Tale of Colonial Folly and Injustice, Bechuanaland, 1933*, New Haven and London, Yale University Press, 1988, pp. 40–4, 86.

50 L. Barnes, 'Memorandum on the Tshekedi Case', October 1933, LGAA, file 4, ff. 14–29.

51 Crowder, *The Flogging of Phinehas McIntosh*, p. 51, 86, 110.

52 E. Goode Robeson, *African Journey*, London, Victor Gollancz Ltd., 1946, p. 33; W. Ballinger to W. Holtby, 11 March 1931, 10 September 1933, 4/10. For additional biographical data, see Crowder, *The Flogging of Phinehas McIntosh* and M. Benson, *Tshekedi Khama*, London, 1960.

53 W.H. Thomas in reply to C. Parkinson, 13 December 1933, *Hansard*, vol. 284, cols 182–3; T. Khama to C. Roden Buxton, 7 August 1933, Charles Roden Buxton Papers (CRB), 6/6; T. Khama, *A Statement to the British Parliament and People*, London, 1934, and *A Reply to the Propaganda of the Incorporation of the Bechuanaland Protectorate Within the Union*, London, 1933. The pamphlets are enclosed in CRB 5/1, 'South Africa and the Protectorates, 1909–1938', which includes letters from Tshekedi and other liberals who supported his case.

54 T. Khama to C. Roden Buxton, 6 November 1933, CRB, 6/6. For the British campaigns, see L. Barnes, 'Memorandum on the Tshekedi Case', October 1933, LGAA, file 4, ff. 14–29; F. Livie-Noble to W. Holtby, 27 October 1933; J.F. Horrabin to W. Holtby, 6 October 1933, WH, 4/14. For general correspondence between Livie-Noble, Holtby, J.H. Thomas and others, July – December 1933, see LGAA, file 4, ff. 1–123.

55 J.H. Thomas to W.T. Lunn, 14 November 1933, *Hansard*, vol. 281, cols 730–2; J.H. Thomas, 20 June 1935, ibid., vol. 303, col. 620, 20 June 1935.

56 P. Kerr, 'Preface' in A.S. Cripps, *An Africa for the Africans: A Plea on Behalf of Territorial Segregation Areas and of their Freedom in a South African Colony*, with a preface by Philip Kerr, Secretary of the Rhodes Trust, New York, 1969, first published in London in 1927, pp. viii–ix.

57 W. Ballinger to W. Holtby, 11 March 1931, 10 September 1933, 26 June 1933; W. Hodgson to N. Leys, 21 January 1931, W. Hodgson to W. Holtby, 9 March 1933, WH, 4/10, 4/11.

58 M. Hodgson to W. Holtby, 21 August 1934, WH, 4/11; A. Creech Jones to W. Holtby, 19 January 1933, 14 February 1933, WH, 4/6, 4/8, 4/13; W. Holtby to A. Creech Jones, 17 January 1933, ACJ, 6/1. For reservations about Barnes and Ballinger, see F. Livie-Noble to W. Holtby, 20 January 1932; A. Hoernle to A. Creech Jones, 6 June, 1933; N. Leys to Sir James Rose Innes, 2 May, 1933.

59 'Minutes of Meeting held at Glebe Place, SW3 on September 27th 1934', 1 October 1934, WH, 4/6; W. Ballinger to J. Lewin, 14 January 1935, ACJ, 6/1; J Lewin to W.M. Macmillan, 26 October 1934, WMM, 1934.

60 V. Brittain to Miss Stohr (South Africa), 14 March 1940, V.M Ballinger Papers, A410/F2/card 20, 21; 'Friends of Africa Minutes (South Africa)' Sept.–Dec. 1936, and 'Friends of Africa Industrial Report', Oct–Dec. 1936, W. Ballinger Papers, A410/F2/card 20; 'Memorandum' enclosed in ibid., AC410/C2/card 12.

61 Mouton, 'A cusser when crossed', p. 160; 'Friends of Africa Correspondence' and 'Friends of Africa Minutes', Jan–Dec. 1940, V.M. Ballinger Papers, A410/F2/card 20, 21.

62 I. Schapera, *Migrant Labour and Tribal Life; A Study of Conditions in the Bechuanaland Protectorate*, London, OUP, 1947, pp. 20–1; Hailey, *An African Survey*, p. 1461.

63 Creech Jones, 'Notes and Typescript of a Speech on Race Relations in Africa following Dr Malan's demand for the Protectorates', 1946, ACJ, 9/6; G. Padmore, *Africa: Britain's Third Empire*, New York, Negro Universities Press, 1969, first published in 1949, pp. 34–7.

64 T. Khama to E. Roux, 5 April 1950, Roux Papers. For more general background to these controversies, see T. Tlou, N. Parsons and W. Henderson, *Seretse Khama, 1921–1986*, Bloemfontein, Macmillan, South Africa, 1995.

65 W. Stanford, Speaker of the Basutoland National Council, to M. Ballinger, 10 June 1961, Ballinger Papers, BC 345, A3131; S. Howe, *Anti-colonialism in British Politics: The Left and the End of Empire, 1918–1964*, Oxford, Clarendon Press, 1993, pp. 174, 196–7.

66 Barnes, *Caliban*, pp. 6, 233; M. Ballinger, Banbury, Oxford, to 'Jannie' Smuts, 26 November 1930, V.M. Ballinger Papers, A1 930, vol. 44, no. 209.

67 M. Hodgson (Ballinger) to W. Holtby, 31 January 1934, WH, 4/11; Barnes, *Caliban*, p. 233.

68 M. Ballinger to W.M. Macmillan 13 July 1936, 20 December 1936, WMM file, March–December 1936; M. Hodgson to W. Holtby, 21 November 1931, 9 March 1933; H. Pim to W. Holtby, 13 April 1932, WH, 4/11, 4/13.

69 Rich, 'W.M.M. Macmillan as a Critic of Empire: The Impact of an Historian on Colonial Policy' in Macmillan and Marks, *Africa and Empire*, p. 21; H. Pim to W. Holtby, 1 March 1933; WH, 4/15.

70 H.J. Simons and R.E. Simons, *Class and Colour in South Africa, 1850–1950*, London, 1969, p. 122. See also D. Wolton to E. Roux, 23 May 1928; B. Weinbren to E. Roux, 27 April 1929, Roux Papers; G. Hardy, *Those Stormy Years*, London, 1956, p.105.

After Roux 's expulsion from the CPSA, he moved towards a closer relationship with liberals.

71 Mouton, 'A cusser when crossed', p. 160; 'Friends of Africa Minutes', Jan–Dec. 1940, Ballinger Papers, A410/F2/card 20; M. Ballinger to D.T.T. Jabavu, 4 December 1943, M. Ballinger Papers, BC 345 A 358.

72 Typescript copy of 'The Voice of a Million' in *Milady*, n.d.; draft article by Ellen Hellman for the South African University Women's Magazine, *The Blue Stocking*, 1946, enclosed in V.M. Ballinger Papers, BC 345, A5.4.

Born in 1894, Margaret Ballinger was brought up in the Eastern Cape in the liberal tradition and, unlike Ballinger, had no party affiliations. She met Ballinger through their shared 'native work'. Both were of Scottish origin, from respectable working-class backgrounds and were 'outsiders' in the wealthy liberal milieu. Their marriage in 1934, however, precipitated an additional financial crisis as Hodgson was obliged to give up her university lectureship in History in accordance with regulations forbidding the employment of married women (Perham, *African Apprenticeship*, pp. 130–1; M. Ballinger, *From Union to Apartheid: A Trek to Isolation*, Folkestone, 1969, pp. 37–8).

73 G. Phillips to M. Ballinger, 10 November 1961, M. Ballinger Papers, BC345, A3, 84.
74 W.M. Macmillan to M. Ballinger, 23 February 1965, M. Ballinger Papers, BC 345. A3, 84.
75 M. Ballinger to W.M. Macmillan, 6 January 1936, WMM, file May–December 1936; W.M. Macmillan to M. Hodgson, 22 December 1933, WH, 4/11; W. Holtby to W. Ballinger, 3 July 1934, WH, 4/11; W.M. Macmillan, *Africa Emergent: A Survey of Social, Political and Economic Trends in British Africa*, London, 1938, p. 93.
76 M. Ballinger to W. Holtby, 13 February 1935, WH, 4/11; Ballinger, *From Union to Apartheid*, pp. 27–8, 143.
77 R. Reynolds, *Beware of Africans: A Pilgrimage from Cairo to the Cape*, London, 1955, pp. 268–9; *Racial Problems in South Africa*, pp. 11, 21, 81, 122.
78 Barnes, *Caliban*, p. 196.
79 M. Scott, *A Time to Speak*, London, 1958, p. 36.
80 C. Kadalie to A. Creech Jones, ACJ, 2 September 1927.
81 A. Creech Jones to C. Kadalie, 15 September 1927, 8 November 1927 and A. Creech Jones to W. Holtby, 18 November 1927, 7 February 1928, WH, 4/6, 11/50. For comments on Kadalie's offending behaviour, see J. Harris to W.M.M. Macmillan, 24 August 1927, WMM, file 1927. A 'Miss Sidolph' offered to go out to South Africa as Kadalie's secretary, but Creech Jones maintained that she was too inexperienced. By 1928, Kadalie had dropped the idea of secretarial help.
82 D.D.T. Jabavu, 'Native Disabilities in South Africa', July 1932, in T. Karis and G.M. Carter (eds) *From Protest to Challenge: A Documentary History of African Politics in South Africa, 1882–1964*, Stansford, 1972–7, 4 vols, vol. 2, document 47, p. 288.
83 A. Memmi, *The Coloniser and the Colonised*, London, Earthscan, 1990, first published in 1957, pp. 116–7.
84 See, for instance, Mosa Anderson (Charles Roden Buxton's secretary) to Holtby, 18 November 1932, WH, 4/12.
Anderson admitted that her mother 'paid for things she couldn't have done otherwise' with her South African investments.
85 V. Bartlett, *The Colour of Their Skins*, London, Chatto & Windus, 1969, pp. 103–4. For feelings of impotence, see H. Pim to W. Holtby, 1 March 1933 and J. MacWilliam (Headmistress of Pretoria Girls' High School) to W. Holtby, 3 March 1931, WH, 4/14, 4/15.
86 Reynolds, *Beware of Africans*, pp. 295–6; P. Rich, *State Power and Black Politics in South Africa*, London, Macmillan, 1996, p. 59. For developments in South African liberalism, 1938–48, see P. Lewsen, *Voices of Protest*, Johannesburg, A.D. Donker, 1988.
87 R. Vigne, *Liberals Against Apartheid: A History of the Liberal Party of South Africa, 1953–86*, London, Macmillan, 1997; Macmillan, 'Paralysed Conservatives' in H. Macmillan and S. Marks (eds) *Africa and Empire: W.M. Macmillan, Historian and Social Critic*, London, Temple Smith, p. 89.
88 F. Brett Young, *In South Africa*, London, William Heinemann Ltd., 1952, pp. 169–70; Padmore, *Africa: Britain's Third Empire*, p. 39.
89 Bartlett, *The Colour of their Skins*, pp. 118–9; *Their Majesties, the King and Queen, and their Royal Highnesses, the Princess Elizabeth and the Princess Margaret, in the Union of South Africa, February to April, 1947*, Pretoria, South African Railways, 1947; W.M. Macmillan, *Africa Beyond the Union*, Johannesburg, SAIRR, 1949, p. 76.
90 Macmillan, *Africa Emergent*, p. 359.

8 Into the heart of empire: black Britain

1 'Memorandum on Distressed Seamen at Cardiff and Elsewhere', n.d., London Group on African Affairs Papers (LGAA), 2/6; 'Joint Council Annual Report', 1 May 1933, pp. 3–4, Winifred Holtby Papers, 4/21.
2 E. Walrond, 'The Negro in London' in *The Black Man*, late December 1935, 1 (11): 9–10.

   Walrond was born in British Guiana in 1898. Educated in Barbados, he became involved in the Harlem Renaissance in the 1920s and worked on the iconoclastic journal, *Fire*, with Langston Hughes, Claude McKay and Zora Neale Hurston. In Britain, he was cultivated in white literary circles and his published works include a sadly forgotten collection of short stories, *Tropic Death* (1926), which depicts fragments of life in the Caribbean in the early twentieth century, including the experiences of migrant labour working on the Panama Canal.
3 For general background to these developments, see P. Fryer, *Staying Power: The History of Black People in Britain*, London, Pluto, 1984; R. Lotz and D. Pegg (eds) *Under the Imperial Carpet: Essays in Black History 1780–1950*, London, 1986; D. Killingray (ed.) *Africans in Britain*, London, Frank Cass, 1994; C. Holmes, *John Bull's Island: Immigration and British Society 1871–1971*, London, Macmillan, 1988.
4 S. Howe, 'Preface' in *Anti-Colonialism in British Politics: The Left and the End of Empire; 1918–1964*, Oxford, Clarendon Press, 1993.
5 S. Bourne, *Black in the British Frame: Black People in British Film and Television, 1896–1996*, London, Cassell, 1998, Ch. 4, 'Harlem Comes to London'. See also R. Makonnen, *Pan-Africanism from Within*, as recorded and edited by Kenneth King, London, 1973, pp. 123–5; E. Marke, *Old Man Trouble*, London, 1975, pp. 102–6. Information about Len Johnson came from the late Eddie Frau of the Working-Class Movement Library, Manchester. Monolulu was in reality a West Indian named Mackay, while Knight was from British Guiana and had served in the First World War.
6 *Report of a Committee on Distressed Colonial and Indian Subjects, 1910*, Cmd 5133, London, HMSO, 1910. Correspondence relating to a 1913 conference organised by the African Society and the Anti-Slavery and Aborigines Protection Society, Anti-Slavery and Aborigines Protection Society Papers (ASAPS), D6/1, 1–115 ff.; L. Woolf, *Imperialism and Civilisation,*, London, Hogarth Press, 1928, p. 187. For general background, see   K. Lunn (ed.) *Hosts, Immigrants and Minorities: Historical Responses to Newcomers in British Society, 1870–1914*, London, William Dawson & Sons, 1980.
7 Travers Buxton to the Rt. Hon. E. Shortt, His Majesty's Principal Secretary of State, Home Office, 17 June 1919, ASAPS, D6/2; *Directorate of Intelligence, Special Report No. 10: Unrest Among the Negroes, Oct. 7, 1919*, reproduced in W.F. Elkins, 'Unrest Among the Negroes: A British Document of 1919' in *Science and Society*, 1968, 32 (1): 68–74. For a fuller analysis of the riots see J. Jenkinson, 'The 1919 Riots' in P. Panjayi (ed.) *Racial Violence in Britain in the Nineteenth and Twentieth Centuries*, Leicester, Leicester University Press, London, 1996, pp. 90–114.
8 Dr M. Hirschfeld, *The Sexual History of the World War*, New York, 1937, pp. 367–8; R.C. Reinders, 'Racialism on the Left: E. D. Morel and the "Black Horror" on the Rhine' in *International Review of Social History*, 1968, 13 (3): 5, 6, 7–8.
9 Edward Shortt, Home Secretary, *Hansard* (Commons), vol. 117, col. 327, 26 June 1919; Background to 'Aliens Restriction Bill (House of Lords) Session 1927', enclosed in CRB, 2/5; I.R.G. Spencer 'The Open Door: Labour Needs and British Immigration Policy, 1945–55' in *Immigrants and Minorities*, 1996, 15 (1): 22–4.
10 C.R. Buxton, annotated comments on 'Aliens Restriction (Amendment) Act, 1919; 1927', enclosed in Charles Roden Buxton Papers (CRB), 2/5; N. Evans, 'Across the Universe: Racial Violence and the Post-war Crisis in Imperial Britain, 1919–25', in D. Frost (ed.) *Ethnic Labour and British Imperial Trade: A History of Ethnic Seafarers in the UK*, London, Frank Cass, 1995, pp. 59–89, p. 59.

11 L. Tabili, *We Ask for Justice: Workers and Racial Difference in Late Imperial Britain*, Ithaka, Cornell University Press, 1994, Ch. 6; T. Lane 'The Political Imperatives of Bureaucracy and Empire: The Case of the Coloured Alien Seamen Order, 1925' in Frost (ed.) *Ethnic Labour*, pp. 104–30.

12 J.R. Clynes, *Hansard* (Commons), vol. 238, cols. 1042–3, 1065–8, 7 May 1930, vol. 240, col. 1328, 26 June 1930, vol. 236, col. 2309, 21 April 1930. See also questions to the Home Secretary, ibid., vol. 236, col. 265–6, 4 March 1930, vol. 237, col. 2386, 10 April 1930, and interchanges between MPs and the Home Secretary, ibid., vol. 260, col. 398–9, 25 November 1931, col. 1957–8, 9 December 1931, vol. 270, col. 242–3, 8 November 1932, col. 142, 7 November 1932.

13 'Report of the LGAA Sub-committee appointed to Investigate and Report on the Conditions Prevailing Among Coloured Seamen in the British Ports and to make Recommendations on this Subject', dated 21 April 1931, Winifred Holtby Papers WH, 4/23.

14 R. Kidd (NCCL) to J. McGovern, MP, 3 July 1935, National Council for Civil Liberties Papers (NCCL), 92/1. Additional information relating to individual 'aliens' may be found in NCCL, 8/1.

15 G.W. Brown, 'The Investigation of Coloured Colonial Seamen in Cardiff' in *The Keys*, October – December 1935, 3 (2): 18–22. For a fuller background, see N. Evans, 'Regulating the Reserve Army: Arabs, Blacks and the Local State in Cardiff, 1919–1945' in *Immigrants and Minorities*, 1985, 4 (2): 21–39.

16 Rev. G.F. Dempster, cited in 'Report of the Deputation from the Welfare Committee on Africans in Europe and Various other Societies in the Ports of Great Britain to the Parliamentary Under-Secretary of State, Home Office, 28 July 1936'; Welfare of Africans in Europe War Fund (Surplus) – 'Report for the Year ending 31st May 1936', ASAPS, H2/76.

17 See, for instance, questions by Captain A. Evans and H. White, *Hansard*, (Commons), vol. 317, col. 853–4, col. 1025–26, 11 and 12 November 1936.

18 R. Sandeman Allen and C. Ammon to E. Brown, 12 November 1936 *Hansard* (Commons), vol. 317, col. 1025–6; A. Runciman, President, Board of Trade to W. Ormsby-Gore, ibid., vol. 317, col. 1025–6, 12 November 1936; E. Shinwell and C. Ammon to A. Runciman, ibid., col. 1483–4, 11 November 1936; Captain A. Evans to Ormsby-Gore, ibid., vol. 317, col. 853–4, 11 November 1936; interchange between A. Evans and Ormsby-Gore, ibid., vol. 317, col. 853, 854, 11 November 1936; 17 February 1937, ibid., vol. 320, col. 1167–8.

19 Mr W. John (Lab. Rhonda West) to E. Brown, *Hansard* (Commons), vol. 326, col. 1087, 13 July 1937; R. Sorensen (Labour) to Brown, ibid., col. 1516–7, 15 July 1937; W. Gallagher to Brown and G. Hall to Brown, ibid., vol. 346, col. 1283–4, 27 April 1939. See also, 'Report of a Deputation to the Chief Constable, Cardiff, 8 April, 1937', enclosed in 'Colour Bar – Seamen, 1934–1943' in NCCL, 92/1; D. Caradog Jones, *The Economic Status of Coloured Families in the Port of Liverpool*, Liverpool Association for the Welfare of Coloured People, Liverpool, 1940, p. 2.

20 Tabili, *'We Ask for Justice'*, pp. 132–3; *British Nationality Bill: Summary of Main Provisions, 1947–48*, Cmd. 7326, London, HMSO, 1948.

21 N. Sharp, 'Cardiff's Coloured Population' in *The Keys*, January 1934, 1 (3): 45–6; I. Law and J. Humphrey (eds) *A History of Race and Racism in Liverpool, 1666–1950*, Liverpool, CRE, 1981, p. 30.

22 Sharp, 'Cardiff's Coloured Population'; A.M.E. Huggins to F. Livie-Noble (LGAA), 27 November 1930, WH, 4/13. See also F. Livie-Noble to A.M.E. Huggins, 16 November 1930.

23 Tabili, *We Ask for Justice*, pp. 144–59; K. Little, *Negroes in Britain: A Study of Race Relations in English Society*, London, Routledge, Kegan & Paul, 1948, p. 245.

24 F. Livie-Noble to Susan Lawrence, MP, 3 March 1931, LGAA, 2/6.

25 M. Sherwood, *Pastor Ekarte and the African Churches Mission, Liverpool 1932–64*, London, Savannah Press, 1994, p. 105. See also 'Liverpool's Coloured Centre' by Pastor Ekarte in *The Keys*, January – March 1937, 4 (3): 34. The mission was opened in July 1931 by the Bishop of Liverpool. For details of the 'Sons of Africa', see Little, *Negroes in Britain*, pp. 108–9, 193 and M. Banton, *The Coloured Quarter*, London, 1955, pp. 217–8.

26 Little, *Negroes in Britain*, p. 78 and personal information from anonymous informants.
    Marke was from a petit-bourgeois Creole family in Freetown and led a colourful life, mixing with wealthy whites. He provided one of the rare written memories of the riots from the black perspective, see *Old Man Trouble*, pp. 26–34, 51–3 and Val Wilmer, 'Ernest Marke: Witness to the Wild Side', Obituary in *The Guardian*, 16 September 1995.

27 N.M.C. Sinclair *The Tiger Bay Story*, Cardiff, Butetown History and Arts Project, 1993, pp. 31–5, 64, 89–93, 103–7.

28 M. Banton, 'The Black Man in London in the Early 1930s: A Note on Some Novels' in *Immigrants and Minorities*, 1995, 14 (2): 195–9; letter from Cunard to Azikiwe, cited in N. Azikiwe, *My Odyssey: An Autobiography*, London, 1970, p. 197. See also M. Sherwood in H. Adi and M. Sherwood (eds) *The 1945 Manchester Pan-African Congress Revisited*, Port of Spain, New Beacon Books, 1995, p. 135.
    'Spade' was the popular *avant-garde* term for 'black', which was still used in the 1950s by the 'beat' generation.

29 E. Waugh, 13 June, 1930, in M. Davie, ed. *The Diaries of Evelyn Waugh*, London, Penguin, 1976, 314; *Piccadilly*, Great Britain, 1929, Directed by the German director, E. A. Dupont, script (and subsequent novel) by Arnold Bennett.

30 J. Maycock, 'Drop the Dead Honky' in *The Guardian*, Friday Review, 31 October 1997 (which addresses the 'long strange history' of white niggers or 'wiggers'); E. Pilkington, *Beyond the Mother Country: West Indians and the Notting Hill White Riots*, London, I.B. Taurus & Co. Ltd., 1988, p. 65, 93.

31 Waugh, 28 February 1928, 9 December 1927, *The Diaries of Evelyn Waugh*, pp. 241, 293; E. Waugh, *Decline and Fall*, London, 1928, pp. 90–4; W. Holtby, *Mandoa, Mandoa: A Comedy of Irrelevance*, London, 1933, pp. 270–3, 317.
    In the 1930s, Leslie 'Jiver' Hutchinson played in the 'West Indian Swing' band, led by Ken 'Snake Hips' Johnson, who was killed when the band was playing at the Café de Paris during the London Blitz in 1941 (S. Voce, 'Obituary: Carl Barriteau' in the *Independent*, 31 August 1998). Barriteau was a Trinidadian clarinettist in the band.

32 J.A. Rogers, *Sex and Race: Negro Caucasian Mixing in All Ages and All Lands*, New York, 1942–4, reprint, Helga M. Rogers, 1972, 3 vols, vol. 1, pp. 214–17; M. Garvey's comments on 'Coloured Men Who Attract White Girls' in *News Chronicle*, 15 April 1937, *The Black Man*, March – April, 1937, vol. 2 (6): 15–17; ibid., late July, 1935, 3 (7): 10. For a gossipy, modern interpretation of the 'Mountbatten scandal', which has Paul Robeson as the lover, see S. Mackenzie, 'Life Stories; Edwina Mountbatten: the Richest Heiress of her Generation' in *Marie Claire*, February 1994, pp. 239–42.
    Edwina Mountbatten was also romantically connected with the Indian nationalist leader, Pandit Nehru.

33 D. Garland Anderson, *Nigger Lover*, London, 1936, pp. 245–7 and review, *The Keys*, April – June, 1938, 5 (4): 92; N. Cunard, *Black Man and White Ladyship: An Anniversary*, Toulouse, privately printed in 1931, marked 'Not for Sale', p. 10; R. Michelet, 'Nancy Cunard' in H. Ford (ed.) *Nancy Cunard: Brave Poet, Indomitable Rebel, 1896–1965*, New York, 1968, pp. 130–1. The Man Ray photograph is reproduced in D. Fielding, *Emerald and Nancy: Lady Cunard and her Daughter*, London, 1968, p. 74. For additional biographical detail, see A. Chisholm, *Nancy Cunard*, London, 1996.

34 Makonnen, *Pan-Africanism from Within*, p. 147; M. Perham, *The Colonial Reckoning, from the Reith Lectures, 1961*, London, 1961, p. 28.

35 Interview with Horace Ove, 17 January 1988, cited in Pilkington, *Beyond the Mother Country*, pp. 64–5; C.E. Moore and S.R. Wood, 'What Moore and Wood Think of the English' in *The Black Man*, July 1935, 1 (7): 14–15. See also Makonnen, *Pan-Africanism from Within*, p. 132; K. Nkrumah, *Ghana: the Autobiography of Kwame Nkrumah*, New York, 1957, p. 56.
36 W. Holtby to V. Brittain, 23 September 1934, WH, drawer 6, file 1934.
37 P. Robeson with L.L. Brown, *Here I Stand*, Boston, Beacon Press, 1988, first published, 1958, p. 41; Azikiwe, *My Odyssey*, p. 197. For white comments on the favoured status of black Americans, see Garland Anderson, *Nigger Lover*, p. 89; C. Roden Buxton, MP, *The Race Problem in Africa*, London, 1931, p. 52.
38 Bourne, *Black in the British Frame*, pp. 74–6; Waugh, 22 September 1926. For Waugh's comments on a visit to see the *Blackbirds Revue* and the party he attended, see diary entries for 22 September 1927, 13 June 1927 in *The Diaries of Evelyn Waugh*, pp. 265, 314. For additional comments relevant to the Blackbirds, see entries for 28 February 1927, 7 March 1927, 10 March 1927, ibid.
39 Robeson, *Here I Stand*, pp. 40–1; L.L. Brown, *The Young Paul Robeson: 'On My Journey Now'*, Boulder, Colorado, Westview Press, 1997, p. 124.
       Waugh went to see *Emperor Jones* and *Othello*, which he thought was a 'hopeless production', but thought Robeson's role was 'convincing'. Waugh met Robeson several times at parties and on one such occasion in a country house he recorded that Robeson had 'passed out' (15 September 1925; 25 May 1930, 12 June 1930 in *The Diaries of Evelyn Waugh*, pp. 221, 311, 314).
40 E. Goode Robeson, *African Journey*, London, Victor Gollancz Ltd., 1946, pp. 17, 166–74.
       Robeson married Eslanda in 1922. Unlike Robeson, she came from the 'near white' coloured aristocracy. According to Brown, it was Eslanda's drive and ambition that pushed Robeson towards his acting and singing career (L.L. Brown, *The Young Paul Robeson*, p. 118).
41 *Negro Anthology Made by Nancy Cunard, 1931 to 1933*, published by Nancy Cunard at Wishart and Co., London, 1934, p. 11.
       This unique and path-breaking anthology was heavily influenced by black cultural movements like the Harlem Renaissance, and included contributions by black writers and activists, English and French anthropologists and *avant garde* writers. Covering Africa and the African Diaspora, the anthology was strongly anti-imperialist and designed to counteract race prejudice, embracing contributions on 'Negro' history, art and culture as well as political themes.
42 E. Walrond, 'The Negro in London'; E. Smilowitz, 'Una Marson: Woman Before Her Time' in *Jamaica Journal*, May 1993, p. 68. See also A. Ade Ademola, B.A. Hons. Cantab., 'Colour Bar in Great Britain' in *Negro Anthology*; G. Padmore, 'Race Prejudice in Britain', *Negro Worker*, vol. 2, no. 3, March 1932, pp. 2–3; H. Moody, 'Race Prejudice' in *The Keys*, January–March 1936, pp. 29–30. For further information about Marson, see D. Jarrett Macauley, 'Exemplary Women' in D. Jarrett Macauley (ed.) *Reconstructing Womanhood, Reconstructing Feminism*, London, Routledge, 1996, pp. 38–51.
43 R. Sorensen to Home Secretary, *Hansard*, vol. 231, col. 1544–5, 14 February 1938; 'Joint Council Annual Report', 1 May 1933, pp. 3–4, WH, 4/21; LCP report enclosed, ibid.
44 W. Holtby to V. Brittain, 4 October 1925, WH, drawer 6, file 1925; Little, *Negroes in Britain*, p. 2.
45 T. Buxton to L. Amery, Secretary of State (Dominions), 8 April 1929; J. Fletcher to the Belgian Ambassador, London, 2 January 1934; 21 December 1933; J. Harris to the Commissioner of Police, London, 22 December 1933, ASAPS, D6/3.
46 M. Garvey, *The Black Man*, January 1937, 2 (5): 16; ibid., July 1938, 3 (10): 16–18; Lapido Solanke, WASU, cited in H. Adi, *West Africans in Britain, 1900–1960*,

Nationalism, Pan-Africanism and Communism, London, Lawrence & Wishart, 1998, pp. 24–7.

47 Interview with Ernest Marke in Adi and Sherwood, *The 1945 Manchester Pan-African Congress Revisited*, p. 38. See also Sinclair, *The Tiger Bay Story*, pp. 24–5, 40–7 and for more detailed discussion, 'A guinea a day; film extras and bit players' in Bourne, *Black in the British Frame*, Ch. 3.

48 Bourne, *Black in the British Frame*, p. 20; M. Garvey, 'Editorial' in *The Black Man*, Aug. 1935, 1 (7): 9; ibid., Aug–Dec. 1935, 1 (9): 10; M. Garvey to J. Harris, 5 November 1936, ASASP, D/73. See also M.B. Duberman, *Paul Robeson*, London, Bodley Head, 1989, p. 68.

49 Robeson, *Here I Stand*, pp. 34, 56–7; Goode Robeson *African Journey*, p. 49; H. Adi, *A Celebration of the Life of Paul Robeson, 1898–1976*, SOAS, 1998, p. 16.

50 T. Cripps, *Slow Fade to Black: The Negro in American Film, 1900–1942*, Oxford, OUP, 1977, pp. 309–11; News Item 71, *The Keys*, 1938, 5 (4).

Robeson had first visited Welsh miners in the late 1920s in response to poverty appeals, and was reputedly a frequent visitor to Tiger Bay, where his uncle by marriage, Aaron Mossell, a black American communist who had also lived in South Africa, was resident. Mossell represented the Coloured and Colonial Association at the 1945 Pan-African Congress (Sinclair, *The Tiger Bay Story*, p. 42).

51 Goode Robeson, *African Journey*, pp. 63–4, 153. E. Goode Robeson to W. Holtby, 1935, WH, 4/15. See also M. Edwards, *Paul Robeson, Honorary Welshman*, Treorchy, Rhondda, Paul Robeson Exhibition, n.d.

52 *Colonial Information Bulletin*, 15 Oct. 1937, 1 (13): 12; L.L. Brown, *The Young Paul Robeson: 'On My Journey Now'*, Boulder, Colorado, Westview Press, 1997, pp. 120–5. More details of Robeson's political activities may be found in *Paul Robeson: Writing, Speeches and Interviews, 1919–1947*, edited and with an introduction by P.S. Foner, London, 1978.

53 Adi, *West Africans in Britain*, pp. 2–4; J. Langley, 'Introduction' in Kobina Sekyi, *The Blinkards: A Comedy*, London, 1974, pp. 3–4; Goode Robeson, *African Journey*, pp. 63–4. For more details of the problems of students, see I.G. Cummings, 'Students of African Descent in the United Kingdom' in H.E. Harper (ed.) *Empire Problems*, London, 1939, Appendix 1, pp. 187–90.

54 See, for instance, Adi, *West Africans in Britain*, ch 1, pp. 6–22 and Fryer, *Staying Power*.

55 C. Coquery-Vidrovitch, *African Women: A Modern History*, Boulder, Colorado, Westview Press, 1997, p. 175.

56 George Padmore was a Trinidadian, born Malcolm Ivan Meredith Nurse in 1902. He was educated in the US, where he joined the Communist Party in 1927. From 1935–57 he was resident in London, where he developed his pan-African philosophy. He was a prolific writer, publishing a number of seminal books and articles (W.M. Warren, 'Introduction' to G. Padmore, *Africa and World Peace*, London, Frank Cass, 1972, first published, 1937, pp. v–xv).

57 M. Garvey, 'The Rise of African Sentiment' in *The Black Man*, October, 1938, 3 (10): 4–5; 'A Bare-Faced Coloured Leader' (criticism of W.E.B. Dubois) ibid., late July 1935, 1 (8): 5–6; Robeson, *Here I Stand*, pp. 40–5, 61, 90; J. Hooker, 'Introduction' in *Black Revolutionary: George Padmore's Path From Communism to Pan-Africanism*, London, 1967. For deeper insight into these debates, see C.J. Robinson, *Black Marxism: The Making of the Black Radical Tradition*, London, Zed, 1984.

58 C.L.R. James, 'A History of Negro Revolt' in *Fact*, September 1938, 18: 1–72, 24. For James' impact today, see M. Busby, 'Context' in *The Guardian*, 3 August 1996, pp. 29–30 and for his political thought, A. Bogues, *Caliban's Freedom: The Early Political Thought of C.L.R. James*, London, Pluto, 1997; C.L.R. James and A. Grimshaw, *The C.L.R. James Reader*, London, Blackwell, 1992.

59 Mannin, *Comrade O Comrade*, p. 139; M. Garvey, 'Communism and the Negro' in *The Black Man*, May–June 1936 2 (1): 2–3; 'Let the Negro Accumulate Wealth: It will

bring him power', ibid., late July 1935, 1 (8): 4; 'Editorial' in ibid., October – November 1937, 2 (2): 11–12.

Garvey had been in England before the First World War, but arrived back in 1927. For fuller background to developments in Garveyism, see also A. Jacques Garvey (ed.) *The Philosophy and Opinions of Marcus Garvey*, reproduction, London, Frank Cass, 1967.

60 G. Padmore, *Pan-Africanism or Communism? The Coming Struggle for Africa*, with a foreword by Richard Wright, London, 1956, pp. 138–9.

61 See, for instance, Rita Fleming Gyll (an Englishwoman), 'Why I Joined the League of Coloured Peoples' in *The Keys*, January–March 1937, 6: 48–50.

62 General information from *The Keys*, 1933–7; 'Report of the Annual Conference', *The Keys*, October – December 1934, 4: 21. For a fuller background, see D.A. Vaughn, *Negro Victory: the Life Story of Dr Harold Moody*, London, 1950, pp. 50–5.

63 Padmore, 'Race Prejudice' in *Negro Anthology*, p. 555; R. Moody, *The Keys*, October 1933, 1 (2): 24.

64 'Editorial' in *The Keys*, April – June 1935, 2 (4): 69; H. Adi, *West Africans in Britain*, pp, 57–67. See also *The Truth About Aggrey House: An Exposure of the Government Plan for the Control Of African Students in Great Britain*, London, WASU, 1934; 'African Defence Committee' in *Labour Monthly*, March 1934, 16 (3): 126; Moody, 'Statement re: Aggrey House' in *The Keys*, April–June 1934, 1 (4); 'The President's Message', ibid., October–December 1934; pp. 3–4.

65 See, for instance, Cummings' participation in the forum reported in Harper (ed.) *Empire Problems* which is discussed in chapter ten.

66 'Activities of the Colonial Defence Association, Cardiff' in *Colonial Information Bulletin*, 15 November 1937, 2 (14): 2; Letter from Arnold Ward, ibid., September–October 1932, 2 (9/10): 22.

The CDA leader, Harry O' Connell, was a seaman from British Guiana.

67 E. Mannin to B. Bush (personal correspondence), 3 June 1980; Tabili, *We Ask for Justice*, p. 81. See also Chris Jones 'Britain's Coloured Seamen' in *The Keys*, March – July 1937, 5 (1): 17–18.

68 'Editorial' in *The Keys*, January–March, 1936, 3 (3),: 3; R.O. Thomas, 'Revolt in the West Indies', and C.L.R. James, 'Abyssinia and the Imperialists' in ibid., pp. 31–8; E. Walrond, 'Fascism and the Negro' in *The Black Man*, March–April, 1937, 2 (6): 8–12. See also 'A Right Royal Welcome' in the *New Times and Ethiopian News* 13 June 1936, p. 3.

69 M. Kenyatta, 'Hands off Abyssinia' in *Labour Monthly*, September 1935, 17 (9): 232–6.

70 Makonnen, *Pan Africanism from Within*, p. 148; IASB publicity handout, Arthur Creech Jones Papers, 17/2.

71 P.G. Lauren, *Power and Prejudice: the Politics and Diplomacy of Racial Discrimination*, New York, Westview Press, 1996, pp. 145–6.

72 Spencer, 'The Open Door', p. 37; N. Leys, *The Colour Bar in East Africa*, London, 1941, p. 150.

73 Sir A. Burns, *Colour Prejudice: with Particular Reference to the Relationship between Whites and Negroes*, London, 1948, pp. 13, 16–17; G. Smith, *When Jim Crow met John Bull: Black American Soldiers in World War 11*, London, I.B. Taurus, 1986; J. Toole, 'GIs and the Race Ban in Wartime Warrington' in *History Today*, July 1993, 43: 7, 22–5. For further detail of wartime developments, see M. Sherwood, *Many Struggles: West Indian Workers and Service Personnel in Britain 1939–1945*, London, Karina Press, 1985; B. Bousquet and C. Douglas, *West Indian Women at War: British Racism in World War Two*, London, 1990; J. Gardiner, *'Over Here': the GIs in Wartime Britain*, London, 1992.

74 R. Macdonald, 'Dr Harold Moody and the League of Coloured Peoples, 1931–1947: A Retrospective View' in *Race*, 1973, 14, (3): 30; Fryer, *Staying Power*, pp. 364–7.

75 Nkrumah, *Ghana*, pp. 54–8, 60–1; Marke, *Old Man Trouble*, pp. 134–6.

76 G. Padmore (ed.) *Colonial and ...Coloured Unity; History of the Pan African Congress* (reprint of the *Report of the 1945 Pan African Congress*, Manchester, 1947), second edition with new material, London, The Hammersmith Bookshop Ltd., 1963, p. 28, pp. v, 11–13, 37–46, 55–61.

    Ras Makonnen was a British Guianian who, after studying in the US and Denmark, had arrived in London in 1937. He owned two restaurants and a Pan-African Publishing Company in Manchester. For a fuller background to the conference, see G Padmore (ed.) *The Voice of Coloured Labour*, London, Pan-African Federation, 1945, pp. 3–5.

77 *History of the Pan African Congress*, pp. 27–9, 30–5, 63–4. For the wider impact of the Atlantic Charter, see M. Sherwood, ' "Diplomatic Platitudes": The Atlantic Charter, The United Nations and Colonial Independence' in *Immigrants and Minorities*, 1996, 15 (2): 135–50.

78 P. Abrahams, *Jamaica: An Island Mosaic*, London, HMSO, 1957, p. 102; Sherwood, in A. Adi and M. Sherwood, *The 1945 Manchester Congress Revisited*, London and Port of Spain, New Beacon Books, 1995, pp. 9, 46–8.

79 This vital formative period in contemporary black and white British identities remains under-researched. However, seminal studies include C. Waters, ' "Dark Strangers", in Our Midst; Discourses of Race and Nation in Britain, 1947–1963' in *The Journal of British Studies*, 1997, 36: 208–32; B. Schwartz, ' "The Only White Man in There": the Re-racialisation of England, 1956–1968' in *Race and Class*, 1996, vol. 38; W. Webster, *Imagining Home: Race Class and National Identity, 1945–64*, London, UCL Press, 1997. Also relevant is B. Bush, 'The Dark Side of the City: Representations of Black London in the 1950s', conference paper in *City Limits Conference*, Staffordshire University, 11–14 September 1996, which reflects my own 'research in progress'.

80 Evans, 'Across the Universe', p. 84. For more detail of Jones, who came to Britain in the late 1940s after she was deported for 'un-American activities' from the US (where she had lived from the 1920s), see B. Johnson, *I think of My Mother: Notes on the Life and Times of Claudia Jones*, London, Karia Press, 1985.

81 Makonnen, *Pan Africanism from Within*, pp. 123–4, 179; Padmore, *Pan-Africanism or Communism?*, p. 201.

9 Into the heart of empire: the 'race problem'

1 K. Little, *Negroes in Britain: A Study of Race Relations in English Society*, London, Routledge, Kegan & Paul, 1948, p. 205; C. Mackay, *A Long Way From Home: An Autobiography*, with an introduction by St Clair Drake, New York, 1970, pp. 68–70.

    Claude Mackay, a Jamaican writer who worked on the *Workers Dreadnought* with Sylvia Pankhurst immediately after World War One, became quickly disillusioned by the 'obtuse prejudices' that surfaced even on the reformist Left and questioned the motives of liberals. He went to live in New York, where he participated in the 'Harlem Renaissance', and travelled with Langston Hughes in Europe, North Africa and the Soviet Union (K.J. Ogren, 'African Strategies in the Harlem Renaissance' in S.J. Lemelle and R.D.G. Kelley (eds) *Imagining Home: Class, Culture and Nationalism in the African Diaspora*, London, Verso, 1994, p. 27.

2 E. Barkan, *The Retreat from Scientific Racism: The Changing Concepts of Race in Britain and the United States between the World Wars*, Cambridge, CUP, 1992, pp, 58–63. See also P. Rich, *Race and Empire in British Politics, 1890–1960*, Cambridge, Cambridge University Press, 1986.

3 *Record of the Proceedings of the First Universal Races Congress held at the University of London 1911'*, published for the Executive Council, London, 1911, pp. 3–6.

    The Quakers themselves had originally been persecuted in the seventeenth century for their beliefs – hence their commitment to the underdog, the 'oneness' of humanity and their emphasis on moral obligation and 'racial equality'.

4 'Summary of Receipts and Payments from June 1st, 1921 to May 31st, 1922' in the Anti-Slavery and Aborigines Protection Society Papers, ASAPS, H2/76.

5 'Welfare of Africans in Europe War Fund Accounts' in 'Annual Reports of the Welfare of Africans in Europe War Fund (Surplus), 1928–1939', ASAPS, H2/76. See also J. Harris to Pastor Ekarte, 5 September 1933, ibid.

6 J. Harris to J. Bruce, 13 December 1933; J. Harris to Private Secretary, Union High Commissioner, 9 November 1931; J. Harris to D. Shiels, Under Secretary of State for Colonies, 18 February 1930, ASAPS, D6/3.

7 J. Harris to Sir Kitoya Ajasi, Lagos, 1933, ASAPS, H1/20.

8 Reading solicitor to Mr S.H. Pearce, Lagos, 1 February 1933, ASAPS, H1/20; 'Report for the year ending 31st May, 1934', ASAPS, H2/76.

9 J. Harris to Harold Donell, Crown Agents for the Colonies, 23 June 1933, ASAPS, D6/3.

10 See, for instance, J. Harris to Commissioner of Police, London, 22 December 1933, ASAPS, D6/3.

11 'Report for the Year ending 31st May, 1934' and other relevant annual reports, ASAPS, H2/76.

12 'Report for the Year ending 31st May, 1939'; 'Report for the Year ending 31st May, 1936', ASAPS, H2/76. The committee received some 850 letters during 1938–9.

13 Norman Angell and Charles Roden Buxton, cited in 'Report on the Inaugural Public Meeting', Friends' House, London, 24 April 1931, Winifred Holtby Papers WH, 4/21; Circular letter on the 'Proposed Joint Council' inviting people to an inaugural meeting, signed by J. Fletcher, ASAPS, 6 January 1931; Minutes of the Executive Committee, 20 March 1931; Joint Council publicity handout, WH, 4/21.

   Prominent members of the Joint Council included Henry Polak of the National Council of Civil Liberties (chairman) the Quaker, John Fletcher, of the ASAPS and of the Friends' Service Council (secretary) and Dr Harold Moody (vice-chairman). Other executive members included Arnold Ward of the Negro Workers Association, Winifred Holtby and Charles Roden Buxton.

14 'Notes on an Inquiry into the Colour Bar Conditions in the Universities', enclosed in the Minutes of the Executive Committee, 10 February 1931; Joint Council Minutes, 20 March 1931, WH, 4/21.

15 Arnold Ward (NWA), *Negro Worker*, September–October 1932, 2 (9 & 10): 22. See also Joint Council Executive Minutes and Annual Reports, 1931–3, WH, 4, 21.

16 The London Group on African [Native] Affairs circular appeal to raise funds for Willam Ballinger's work in South Africa, signed Frederick Livie-Noble, WH, drawer 4, 1/23. The 'Native' in the title was quickly dropped.

17 F. Livie-Noble to W. Holtby, 14 March 1930, WH, 4/13. LGAA publicity pamphlet and membership list, 1931, WH 4/2.

18 F. Livie-Noble to W. Holtby, 25 November 1930, WH, 4/13.

19 Mrs Paul Robeson to F. Livie-Noble, 24 March 1931, WH, 4/23; Minutes of a meeting of the LGAA, 11 July 1931; 'Report of the Sub-committee Appointed to Investigate and Report on the Conditions Prevailing Amongst the Coloured Seamen in the British Ports and then Make Recommendations on this Subject' (1931), Papers of London Group on African Affairs (LGAA), 2/6.

20 Joint Council Annual Report, 1 May 1935, p. 8, WH, file 21. See also 'Memorandum on Distressed Seamen at Cardiff and Elsewhere', n.d., LGAA, 2/6.

21 D. Shiels to W. Holtby, 3 March 1932, Bridgeman File.

22 J. Fletcher to W. Holtby, 16 November 1933, WH 4/21.

23 W. Holtby, *Mandoa, Mandoa: A Comedy of Irrelevance*, London, Collins, 1933, pp. 247–9. For comments on Holtby, see A. Creech Jones to W. Holtby, 19 January 1933, N. Leys to W. Holtby, 19 March 1931, WH, 4/8. For fuller discussion of female activism, see B. Bush, 'Britain's Conscience on Africa: White Women, Race and Imperial Politics

in Inter War Britain' in C. Midgley (ed.) *Gender and Imperialism*, Manchester, MUP, 1997.

24 See correspondence between Holtby and individual students, WH, 4/18. Also relevant is correspondence between Holtby and F. Livie-Noble, 1930–2, WH, 4/13.

25 Holtby, *Mandoa*, pp. 18, 117, 258–9, 275–7. For responses from Holtby's circle, see letters of congratulation from Arthur Creech Jones, Livie-Noble, Janey Leys (Norman Leys' wife), Roden Buxton and Vera Brittain, WH, 2/47.

26 W. Holtby to V. Brittain, 19 October 1934, WH, drawer 6. For insight into Leys' politics, see Leys to Duncan and Erica Leys (son and daughter-in-law), 19 February 1934, WH, 4/9.

27 Lady Rhondda, editor of the feminist periodical, *Time and Tide*, cited in V. Brittain, *Testament of Friendship: The Story of Winifred Holtby*, London, 1941, p. 110.

28 'Minutes of the Joint Council of White and Coloured', 11 March 1931, item 58, 'Mixed Marriages', WH, 4/21; C.R. Buxton, MP, *The Race Problem in Africa*, London, 1931, pp. 50–2.

Buxton, who was educated at Harrow and Cambridge, came from a family that had a tradition of public service and involvement in Africa. Although he broke with his family's liberal traditions in 1917 when he joined the Independent Labour Party, he remained strongly influenced by Quakerism, led a frugal, austere life that belied his upper middle-class origins and believed that he had a vocation to 'help' Africans (Victoria De Bunsen, *Charles Roden Buxton: A Memoir*, London, 1948, pp. 10, 27, 39–49, 83–7, 133).

29 G. Padmore, 'Race Prejudice' in *Negro Anthology Made by Nancy Cunard, 1931–33*, London, 1934, published privately, p. 555; H. Rathbone, 'The Problems of African Independence' in *Labour Monthly*, March–April 1936, 18 (3 & 4): 167. See also W.M. Macmillan, 'A Student of British Africa looks at America', Notes, William Macmillan Papers, file 1935.

30 L. Hughes, 'Goodbye Christ', cited in C. Dover, *Half-Caste*, London, 1939, p. 235; M. Garvey, 'Editorial' in *The Black Man*, late July 1935, 1, (7): 3.

31 E. Gordon 'Blacks turn Red' in *Negro Anthology*, p. 237.

32 *National and Colonial Questions (Theses adopted by the Second Congress of the Communist International*, Moscow, August 1920) with an introduction by the Executive Committee of the CPGB, London, CPGB, 1920, p. 1. For general developments in this period, see S. Macintyre, *A Proletarian Science: Marxism in Britain, 1917–1933*, London, OUP, 1979. The most recent study of CP involvement in anti-colonialism is J. Jones, 'The Anti-Colonial Politics and Policies of the Communist Party of Great Britain', Ph.D. Thesis, Wolverhampton, 1997.

33 Report of the Commission on the National and Colonial Questions, July 26 (the Second Congress to the Communist International, July 19–August 7, 1920), London, CPGB, 1920, p. 2.

34 T.A. Jackson, *What is the British Empire to You?*, London, CPGB, 1925, p. 9.

35 *Report of the Seventh Annual Congress of the CPGB, May 30–June 1st, 1925*, London, CPGB, 1925, pp. 67, 71, 194–6.

36 *British Imperialism: An Outline of Workers' Conditions in the Colonies*, research by LRD with an introduction by Harry Pollitt, London, National Minority Movement, 1930; *Resolutions of the 11th Congress of the CPGB, 1929*, London, CPGB, 1929, pp. 9–10, 42; *The New Line: Documents of the Tenth Congress of the CPGB, held at Bermondsey, London, on Jan. 19–22, 1929*, London, CPGB, 1929, pp. 5–6.

37 *Resolutions of the Fourth World Congress of the RILU*, London, RILU, 1928, pp. 23, 28, 70, 99; *Resolutions of the Fifth World Congress of the RILU, Moscow, Aug. 1931*, London, Minority Movement, 1931, pp. 113–4, 159–64.

38 Comrade Arnot, 'The British Minority Movement and its Tasks in the Field of Colonial Work' in *RILU Magazine*, February 1932, 2 (3): 207. See also *Resolutions of the Fifth World Congress of the RILU*, p. 162. For communist involvement in the 1930 'Arab

riots', see K. Lunn, 'Race Relations or Industrial Relations? Race and Labour in Britain, 1880–1950' in K. Lunn (ed.) *Race and Labour in Twentieth Century Britain*, London, Frank Cass, 1985, p. 15.

39 'Report of the 1929 LAI meeting in Cologne attended by Arthur Cook, Pollitt and Alex Gossip, etc.' in *International Press Correspondence (Imprecorr)*, English edition, 18 January 1929, Vienna, 9 (4): 77; *Resolutions of the 11th Congress of the CPGB, 1929*, London, CPGB, 1929, pp. 58–9.

40 A. Clegg to B. Bush, 21 March 1983. See also J. Saville, 'Reginald Bridgeman: Anti-Imperialist' in J. Saville and J. Bellamy (eds) *Dictionary of Labour Biography*, London, 1972–84, 7 vols, 7: 26–36.

Bridgeman had worked in the Foreign Office before the First World War and in 1920 was a diplomat in Tehran. Between 1919–22 he became a left-wing socialist who retained his upper-class mannerisms and his colleagues recall him as somewhat of a 'dandy' who wore Saville Row shirts (Arthur Clegg to B. Bush, 21 March 1983). He was a regular contributor to *Labour Monthly* and other Left publications and lectured at the Marx Memorial Library Workers' Summer Schools in 1936–7 (*Labour Monthly*, May 1937, 19 (5): 316). In 1940, he withdrew from active politics, but remained a member of the Royal Institute of International Affairs, NCCL, Coloured Film Artistes Association and the ASAPS (Saville and Bellamy).

41 Interview with Fenner Brockway, 16 April 1980. For insider insight into these splits in the ILP and general ILP involvement in anti-imperialism, see. F. Brockway, *Inside the Left: 30 Years of Platform, Press, Prison and Parliament*, London, 1942.

42 *Daily Worker*, 26 November 1934, p. 2. See also H. Adi, 'The Communist Movement in West Africa' in *Science and Society*, special issue titled, 'Communism in Britain and the British Empire', 1997, 61 (1): 94–9; *Report of the National Conference of the League Against Imperialism (British Section), February 1931*, pp. 3–5, 20–1.

43 W. Gillies to A.L. Scott, 7 July 1935, Bridgeman File. See also J. Fletcher to W. Holtby, 16 November 1933, WH, file 2.

44 *The Colonial Question: A Study Syllabus for Worker*, London, CPGB, 1930, pp. 11, 18.

45 Conrad Noel, draft of 'Empire Day' pamphlet, 1930, Conrad Noel Papers, 2/4; G. Padmore, 'What is Empire Day?' in *Negro Worker*, 15 June 1932, 2 (6).

46 *The Colonial Question*, p. 18; H.G. Wells, 'What is the Empire worth to mankind?' in the *Sunday Express*, September 1927, enclosed in Conrad Noel Papers, 2/4. For campaigns, see 'Children's Corner' in *Daily Worker*, 15 May 1930, p .4; R. Bridgeman to Sir Charles Trevelyan, President of the Board of Education, 10 April 1930, Conrad Noel Papers, 2/4; R. Bridgeman to C. Noel, 16 April 1930.

47 For background to the campaign and details of the Scottsboro Defence Committee, see *We Were Framed: The First Full Story of the Scottsboro Case*, London, Scottsboro Defence Committee, 4 Paton Street, WCL, June 1934, pp. 1–18; *The Keys*, January 1934, 1 (3): 42, 62.

48 *Negro Worker*, 15 June 1932, 2 (6): 9–11; *Daily Worker*, 2 May 1933, p. 1.

49 F. Renshaw and K.A. Miller, *Scottsboro: The Firebrand of Communism*, Alabama, Montgomery Brown Printing Co., 1936. See also *Stop 'Legal Lynching' of Nine Negro Boys: Rush Your Protests* London, ILD, n.d.

50 R. Makonnen, *Pan-Africanism from Within*, as recorded and edited by Kenneth King, London, 1973, pp. 124–5.

51 'The Council for Promoting Equality of Civil Rights Between White and Coloured People', circular, November 1933, WH, file 21; G. Padmore, *Pan-Africanism or Communism? The Coming Struggle for Africa*, with a foreword by Richard Wright, London, 1956, p. 330.

52 J. Gillies, Labour Party International Department, to A.L. Scott, 7 August 1935, Bridgeman File. For CP attitudes, see 'Summary of Discussions on Fascism and War: Conference on Trade Union Problems and Policy, Bermondsey Town Hall, August,

24–5' in *Labour Monthly*, October 1935, 17 (10): 639–44; E. Burns, *Abyssinia and Italy*, London, Left Book Club, 1936.

53   R. Palme Dutt, 'Notes of the Month' in *Labour Monthly*, 1 October 1935, 17 (10): 589. For black reactions, see G. Padmore, *How Britain Rules Africa*, London, 1936, pp. 15, 16.

54   'NCCL Membership and Constitution' in the National Council of Civil Liberties Papers (NCCL), 75/1. Also of interest is *A Potted History of the National Council of Civil Liberties*, pamphlet, c.1942, enclosed in ibid., 77/7. The stimulus for the foundation of the NCCL was the 1934 Incitement to Disaffection Act (see *The Incitement to Disaffection Act – How it Stands*, pamphlet, NCCL, 1934).

55   'Accusations of Communism in the NCCL, 1939–1941' in NCCL, 76/2; See also Pastor Ekarte (African Churches Mission, Liverpool) to Kidd, 12 February 1941 asking for advice about African seamen on the Elder Dempster line on Padmore's recommendation, NCCL, 92/1.

56   *Labour Monthly*, March 1937, 19 (3): 192–8, 199; See also B. Bradley, *Colonies, Mandates and Peace*, London, Peace Library, n.d., pp. 5–7, 21–4.

57   'Report of the Peace and Empire Conference Chaired by Jawaharlal Nehru' in *Colonial Information Bulletin*, 1 August 1938, 2 (2): 3–4.

58   J. Lewin to Professor J. Saville, 30 October 1980, Bridgeman File.

59   'World Assembly Against Racialism and Anti-Semitism', NCCL, 44/2, 44/3; *Colonial News* (Monthly Bulletin of the International Secretariat of the LAI), May 1937; *Colonial Information Bulletin*, September 1938, 1 (11): 8. The LAI line post-1935 is outlined in *The British Empire*, London, LAI, 1936.

60   Padmore, *Pan-Africanism or Communism?*, p. 124; S. Howe, *Anti-Colonialism in British Politics: The Left and the End of Empire, 1918–1964*, Oxford, Clarendon Press, 1993, p. 127; Adi, 'The Communist Movement in West Africa', p. 96. Marika Sherwood's research indicates that the British Government continues to hold all files on Padmore after 1935 'for reasons of national security' (Sherwood in H. Adi and M. Sherwood, *The 1945 Manchester Pan-African Congress Revisited*, London and Port of Spain, New Beacon Books, 1995, p. 10).

61   N. Cunard and G. Padmore, *The White Man's Duty*, London, 1942, pp. 2–4.

62   A. Clegg to B. Bush, 21 March 1983.
     Blackman was a Barbadian who came to Britain to study for the church, but was so appalled by racism that he became a Communist (talk by P. Blackman, Charles Wotten Centre, Liverpool, 12 September 1983).

63   Brockway, personal information, interview, 16 April 1980; *Inside the Empire Quarterly*, London, CIB, 1945 – February 1940, 1 (1) (price: 2 d.). For a wider background to the development of the CPGB in this period, see N. Branson, *History of the Communist Party of Great Britain, 1941–1951*, London, Lawrence & Wishart, London, 1997, and for a fuller, less subjective study of the early war years, see K. Morgan, *Against Fascism and War: Ruptures and Continuities in British Communist Politics, 1935–1941*, Manchester and New York, Manchester University Press, 1989. For the Movement for Colonial Freedom, see Howe, *Anti-colonialism*, pp. 178–82 and for a personal account, see F. Brockway, *The Colonial Revolution*, London, 1973, pp. 42–5, 245–81.

64   For this information, I am indebted to an anonymous informant who was a party activist in the 1930s and was involved in the 1950s with the World Federation of Trade Unionists, which had extensive connections with colonial activists (personal interview, conducted at the Working-class Movement Library, 23 September 1982). See also 'Questionnaire on War' in *Labour Monthly*, August 1934, 16 (8): 465–71.

65   G. Padmore, *Africa and World Peace*, London, Frank Cass, 1972, first published in 1937, p. 7.

66   *The Communist Review*, Dec. 1932, 4 (12) p. 279. For details of harassment and general background to the inter-war CP from the inside, see H. Pollitt, *Serving My Time: An Apprenticeship to Politics*, London, 1940, pp. 210–12, 248, 256–7.

67 Howe, *Anti-colonialism in British Politics*, p. 67. See also Makonnen, *Pan-Africanism from Within*, pp. 101–103; Padmore, *Pan-Africanism or Communism*, p. 329; talk by Blackman, Charles Wotten Centre, Liverpool, 12 September 1983.
68 A. Clegg to B. Bush, 21 March 1983; Padmore, *Pan-Africanism or Communism?*, pp. 148, 314, 320–2. See also Padmore, *How Russia Transformed Her Colonial Empire: A Challenge to the Imperialistic Powers*, London, Dobson, 1946.
69 Cited in I.R.G. Spencer, 'The Open Door: Labour Needs and British Immigration Policy, 1945–55' in *Immigrants and Minorities*, 1996, 15 (1): 22–42, p. 41. See also Adi, 'The Communist Movement in West Africa', pp., 97 and *West Africans in Britain 1900–1960: Nationalism, Pan-Africanism and Communism*, London, Lawrence & Wishart, 1998, pp. 128–31; *We speak for Freedom: Report of the Conference of the CPs of the British Empire, held on Feb. 26 – March 2, 1947*, with a foreword by H. Pollitt, political report by R. Palme Dutt and supplement on Africa and the West Indies by Desmond Buckle, London, CPGB, 1947.
70 J.R.N. Pietersie, *Empire and Emancipation: Power and Liberation on a World Scale*, London, Pluto Press, 1990, p. 255; R. Miles, *Racism after Race Relations*, London, Routledge, 1994, p. 50; F. Anthias and N. Yuval Davis, *Racialised Boundaries: Race, Nation, Gender, Colour and Class and the Anti-Racist Struggle*, London, Routledge, 1992.
71 This point was forcefully made by C.L.R. James in an interview with Leon Trotsky, 5 April 1939, Coyoacan, Mexico. See Leon Trotsky, *Leon Trotsky on Black Nationalism and Self Determination*, edited and with an introduction by George Breitman, New York and Toronto, 1978, p. 73. See also P. Gilroy, *The Black Atlantic: Modernity and Double Consciousness*, London, Verso, 1993; C. Robinson, *Black Marxism: The Making of the Black Radical Tradition*, London, Zed, 1984, pp. 1–6.
72 L. Tabili, 'Labour Migration, Racial Identity and Class Identity. Some Reflections of the British Case' in *North West Labour History*, 1995/96, issue no. 20, pp.16–36, p. 18.
73 For a summary of contemproary debates, see Miles, *Racism after Race Relations*, pp. 39–44.
74 L. Tabili, *We Ask for Justice: Workers and Racial Difference in Late Imperial Britain*, Cornell University Press, 1994, pp. 132–3; K. Malik, *The Meaning of Race: Race, History and Culture in Western Society*, London, Macmillan, 1996, p. 170; C. Holmes, *John Bulls' Island: Immigration and British Society, 1871–1971*, London, Macmillan,1987, p. 229. For an overview of these developments, see I.G. Spencer, *British Immigration Policy since 1939: The Making of Multiracial Britain*, London, Routledge, 1997.
75 Miles, *Racism after Race Relations*, p. 35. See also S. Patterson, *Dark Strangers: A Study of West Indians in London*, London, Tavistock, 1962; E. Huxley, *Back Streets, New Worlds: A Look at Immigrants in Britain*, London, Chatto & Windus, 1964. Other works in a similar genre include A.H. Richmond, *Colonial Prejudice in Britain: A Study of West Indian Workers in Britain, 1942–1954*, London, RKP, 1954; M. Banton, *The Coloured Quarter: Negro Immigrants in an English City*, London, Jonathan Cape, 1955. For post-war welfare initiatives, see S. Ruck (ed.), *The West Indian Comes to England*, London, Routledge, Kegan & Paul, 1960.
76 Patterson, *Dark Strangers*, pp. 19–20; Malik, *The Meaning of Race*, pp. 30–34.
77 Miles, *Racism after Race Relations*, pp. 6–7. For background to developments in the IRR, see A. Sivanandan, *Race and Resistance: The IRR Story*, London, IRR, 1974.
78 D.T. Goldberg, *Racist Culture; Philosophy and the Politics of Meaning*, Oxford, Blackwell, 1993, p. 27; I. Katznelson, *Black Men, White Cities: Race, Politics and Migration in the United States, 1900–1930 and Britain, 1948–68*, London, 1984.
79 Padmore, *Pan-Africanism or Communism*, p. 365; Makonnen, *Pan-Africanism from Within*, pp. 181–2.

10 The winds of change: towards a new imperialism in Africa?

1 H.E. Harper (ed.) *Empire Problems (Report of the Third Cambridge Empire Conference, 28–30 October, 1938)*, London, Frederick Muller Ltd., 1939, p. 6; E. Goode Robeson, *African Journey*, London, Victor Gollancz Ltd., 1946, p. 9; 'Notes and Typescript on race relations in Africa following Dr Malan's demand for the Protectorates', n.d., Arthur Creech Jones Papers (ACJ), 9/6.

2 This term was used by Smith and Bull to describe Margery Perham (A. Smith and M. Bull (eds) *Margery Perham and British Rule in Africa*, London, Frank Cass, 1991, Introduction, p. 1). However, it aptly encapsulates the role played by the wider constituency of liberal and reformist critics.

3 S. Howe, *Anti-colonialism in British Politics: The Left and the End of Empire, 1918–1964*, Oxford, Clarendon Press, 1993, pp. 2–3.

4 N. Leys to C. Roden Buxton, 17 October 1930, Winifred Holtby Papers WH, 4/8; Howe, *Anti-colonialism*, pp. 47–51.

5 C. Roden Buxton to W. Macmillan, 24 March 1926, William Macmillan Papers (WMM), file 1926.
   Buxton was a member of the Labour Party Imperial Committee from 1923 until his resignation from the party in 1926.

6 ASAPS correspondence, 1916–26, Anti-Slavery and Aborigines Protection Society Papers (ASAPS), D6/2.

7 'Subject Races Within the Empire: Report of the Study Group set up by the Cambridge University Labour Club, October 1927' in Roux Papers; L. Woolf, *Imperialism and Civilisation*, London, Hogarth Press, 1928, p. 133.

8 T. Buxton, J. Harris and C. Roberts (President of the ASAPS) to the Prime Minister, R. MacDonald, 25 September 1930, ASAPS, D6/3.

9 J. Harris to P. Cunliffe Lister, 30 March 1932; ASAPS to J. H. Thomas, 4 March 1932, ASAPS, 6/3; D. Shiels to W. Holtby, 3 March 1932, Bridgeman File; WH, 4/15.

10 D. Woodman to W. Holtby, 14 March 1931, WH, 4/21; 'The Work of the Union of Democratic Control, 1932' in the Union of Democratic Control Papers (UDC), 5/288.
   The UDC was founded in 1914 by E.D. Morel, Charles Roden Buxton and other 'outstanding champions' of 'democratic control' of foreign policy (E.D. Morel, *The African Problem and the Peace Settlement*, London, UDC, 1917, pp. 1–3).

11 W. Gillies to W. Holtby, 3 October 1933, WH, 4/15. For details of pressure groups on Indian Affairs, see Howe, *Anti-Colonialism*, p. 130.

12 Lord Hailey, *An African Survey*, London, OUP, 1957, pp. 191–2. For pro-settler parliamentary support, see Sir Edward Grigg, *Hansard* (Commons), vol. 304, cols, 2061–3, 25 July 1935, and for criticisms, see C. Roden Buxton, 'The Black Man's Friend' in *New Leader*, 6 January 1928, p. 5; N. Leys, *A Last Chance in Kenya*, London, 1927. For a fuller background to imperialism in East Africa, see E.A. Brett, *Colonialism and Underdevelopment in East Africa*, London, Gregg Revivals, 1992.

13 F. Livie-Noble to W. Holtby, 12 November 1930, WH, 4/13; 'Draft of a long letter to the Press'; N. Leys and W. Holtby to W. Elliot, 1 October 1930, 12 October 1930, WH, 4/24; Walter Elliot, 'BBC Pamphlet on Africa', WH, 4/9.

14 Julian Huxley in a foreword to P.G. Mockerie, *An African Speaks for his People*, London, 1934, pp. 11–12, 17–19. See also J. Harris to D. Shiels, 18 December 1930; J. Harris and T. Buxton to the Rt. Hon. Stanley of Alderley, chairman of the Joint Parliamentary Committee Upon Closer Union in East Africa, 17 February 1931, ASAPS, D6/3; D. Woodman to W. Holtby, 3 January 1931, WH, file 21.

15 R. Nicholson to W. Macmillan, 17 March 1933, WMM, file 1932–3.

The main aim of the Royal Empire Society was to 'maintain unbroken the links of United Empire' and the Royal African Society had a similar 'empire strengthening' mission (Royal African Society publicity pamphlet, enclosed in WMM, file 1932–3.

16 N. Leys to W. Holtby, 9 November 1933, WH, 4/9; W. Holtby to A. Creech Jones, 29 August 1931, ACJ, 6/1.

17 J. Harris, 'Report on the Conference of African Groups', 20 October 1936, ASP, G433; G. Dawson to W. Macmillan, 1 May 1932, WMM, file 1931–2.

18 Sir Geoffrey Huggins, the Southern Rhodesian Premier and Minister for Native Affairs at a meeting in Bulawayo in 1938, cited in G. Padmore, *Africa: Britain's Third Empire*, New York, Negro Universities Press, 1969, first published in 1949, p. 41. See also N. Leys to W. Ballinger, 27 February 1935, WH, 4/8.

19 *Africana: A Bulletin of Books on African Affairs*, December 1931, 1: 3, WH, 4/23.

20 *The Protection of Colonial Peoples: A Study in British Colonial Policy*, London, New Fabian Research Bureau, n.d., pp. 3–5, 10, 32–5, 45–51. See also L. Barnes, *Duty of Empire*, London, 1935, p. 285; *The Colonial Empire*, London, Labour Party, 1933, p. 12.

21 M. Perham, *The Colonial Reckoning, from the Reith Lectures, (1961)*, London, 1963, pp. 29–9; Barnes, *Duty of Empire*, pp. 89, 98, 301–7.

22 C. Gertzel, 'Perham's View of Africa' in Smith and Bull (eds) *Margery Perham*, pp. 31–4. See also M. Perham, 'Black and White in Africa' in *The Listener*, 28 March 1934; 'Our Task in Africa' from *The Times*, 10, 11, 12 February 1936, reproduced in M. Perham, *Colonial Sequence, 1930–1949: A Chronological Commentary upon British Colonial Policy, Especially in Africa*, London, Methuen & Co. Ltd., pp. 83–90, 91–119, 140–52.

23 J. Harris, 'Report of the Conference on African Groups', 26 October 1936; 'African Conference Correspondence', 1936–8, ASAPS, G433; 'Papers of the Consultative Committee', LGAA, 3/3. See also Perham, 'Some Problems of Indirect Rule in Africa', 8 May 1934, reproduced in *Colonial Sequence*, pp. 91–119, 140–52.

24 W. Macmillan to N. Leys, 21 January 1935, WH, 4/9.

25 Macmillan, *Africa Emergent*, pp. 23; 'The Oldest British Colony: A Study of Poverty' in *Labour Monthly*, June 1936, 18 (6), pp. 380–81. See also *Report of the West India Royal Commission into the Disturbances in the West Indies, 1939–40*, Moyne Report, Cmd. 6174, London, HMSO, 1940.

26 'Memoranda of the Advisory Committees on International and Imperial Questions, 1934–9', ACJ, 17/1; 'Colonies, 1937–8', ACJ, 14/3. For a detailed discussion of these developments in reformist discourse, see Howe, *Anti-colonialism*.

27 Perham, *Colonial Sequence*, pp. xiii–xiv; Howe, *Anti-colonialism*, pp. 19–21.

28 H. Rathbone, 'The Problem of African Independence' in *Labour Monthly*, March – April 1936, 18 (3 & 4): 164, 248–9; Perham, 'Our Task in Africa', p. 146–51; E. Grigg to W. Lunn, *Hansard* (Commons), vol. 304, col. 2069–70, 25 July 1935. Sir Edward Grigg was a Liberal MP from 1922–5 and a Conservative from 1933–45.

29 This term is associated with contemporary Left critics. See, for instance, 'Empire Strengthening' in *Colonial Information Bulletin*, 15 July, 1937, 1 (7).

30 In 1935, Stanley Baldwin took over from Ramsay MacDonald as Prime Minister of the Coalition Government and Malcolm MacDonald became Secretary of State for Dominions with J.H. Thomas, Secretary of State for Colonies. In 1936, Thomas was replaced by Ormsby-Gore who, in turn, was supplanted in 1938 by Malcolm MacDonald who remained in office until mid-1940.

31 Perham 'Our Task in Africa', p. 151.

32 P.J. Cain and A.G. Hopkins, *British Imperialism: Crisis and Deconstruction, 1914–1990*, London, Longman, 1993, pp. 227–8.

33 W.M. Macmillan, 'The Tragedy in Abyssinia and the Future of Africa' rough draft notes, WMM, file 1936; W. Macmillan to N. Leys, 21 January 1935, WH, 4/9; E. Waugh, *Waugh in Abyssinia*, London, Longmans Green, 1936, pp. 21–3.

34 R. Coupland, *The Empire in These Days*, London, 1935, pp. 15–17, 21.

35 E. Rathbone, *Hansard* (Commons), col. 2380, 29 May 1936; ibid., vol. 309, 24 April 1936, col. 64–173, 105 (L. Amery), 169, (J. McGovern), and 172–3 (W. Gallacher); A. Eden, 22 April 1936, vol. 311, col. 130–1; Baldwin, ibid., 11 May 1936, vol. 312, col. 2380, 29 May 1936.

36 Exchange between A. Henderson (Lab) and Sir A. Wilson, *Hansard* (Commons), vol. 309, col. 102, 113–4, 144–5, 7 May 1936; P.G. Lauren, *Power and Prejudice: the Politics and Diplomacy of Racial Discrimination*, New York, Westview Press, 1996, second edition, p. 172.

    Wilson (Conservative, Hitchen 1933–40) had a reputation as a supporter of fascist regimes.

37 M. Perham, 'War and the Colonies', reproduced from *The Spectator*, 6 October 1941 in *Colonial Sequence*, pp. 208–18; A. Sbacchi, *Ethiopia Under Mussolini: Fascism and the Colonial Experience*, London, 1985, pp. 1–3. Also relevant is A. Martin, 'Old Ally renews Ethiopian Courtship' in the *Guardian*, Tuesday, 4 June 1996, which refers to long-standing trade links and the Sandford English School established in 1946.

38 Fuller details about the fund are enclosed in LGAA, box 5/1.

    Livie-Noble of the LGAA was the Honorary Secretary of the Relief Fund.

39 *Peace and the Colonial Problem*, London, National Peace Council, 1935, pp. 1, 19, 51.

40 L.S. Amery, *The German Colonial Claim*, London and Edinburgh, W. & R. Chambers Ltd., 1939, pp. 86–7, 125.

41 L. Barnes, *Empire or Democracy: A Study of the Colonial Question*, London, 1939, pp. 27–9, 102–3. See also M. MacDonald, Colonial Secretary, *Hansard* (Commons), vol. 342, col. 1244–6, 7 December 1938, col. 2493–3494, 19 December 1938; E. Grigg, ibid., vol. 304, col. 2071, 25 July 1935.

42 M. MacDonald, *Hansard* (Commons), vol. 341, col. 1006, 6 December 1938, vol. 342, col. 1231, 1239, 7 December 1938, col. 2640, 20 December 1938; P. Noel Baker, ibid., vol. 342, col. 1119, 1205–6, 7 December 1938.

43 G. Padmore, 'The British Empire is the Worst Racket Yet Invented By Man' in *New Leader*, 15 December 1939.

    The *New Leader* was the ILP paper.

44 Amery, *The German Colonial Claim*, pp. 22–3; Hailey, *An African Survey*, pp. 171, 244. For details of the Colonial League, see S. Haxey, *Tory MP*, Left Book Club Edition, London, Gollancz, 1939, p. 228–9.

45 L. Barnes, *The Future of the Colonies*, London, 1936, p. 20; 'NRFB's Weekend Conference on Labour's Foreign Policy, 27–28 June 1936', ACJ, 17/1, pp. 27–8; A. Creech Jones *Hansard* (Commons), vol. 342, col. 1236–7, 1254–6, 1 December 1938; *The Demand for Colonial Territories and Equality of Economic Opportunity*, London, Labour Party, 1937, p. 48.

46 Barnes, *Empire or Democracy*, pp. 192, 255–60. For comments on Empire Day see Barnes to C. Noel, 7 November 1929, Conrad Noel Papers.

    Barnes was born in London in 1885 and educated at St Paul's School. He graduated in classics from Oxford and after the First World War followed his father into the CO. He soon left the service and went to South Africa in 1925, where he acquired his expertise on African problems as a journalist. He returned to England in 1932, became a protégé of Leys and was an unsuccessful Labour candidate for Derby in 1935 (Leys was chairman of the Derby Labour Party). He became a lecturer in Education at Liverpool University in 1936 (N. Leys to G. Catlin, Vera Brittain's husband, 11 January 1935, WH, 4/9, Barnes Papers).

47 Cain and Hopkins, *British Imperialism* pp. 227–8; Howe, *Anti-colonialism*, pp. 106–7. For the German perspective, see H. Pogge Von Strandmann, 'Imperialism and Revisionism in Interwar Germany' in W.J. Mommsen and J. Osterhammel (eds) *Imperialism and After: Continuities and Discontinuities*, London, 1986, pp. 90–119, 100–101.

48 R. Kidd (NCCL) to A. Creech Jones, 8 July 1936, ACJ, 18/3; *International African Opinion*, 7 January 1938, enclosed in ACJ, 17/2; Barnes, *Empire of Democracy*, p. 169;

M. Havinden and D. Meredith, *Colonialism and Development: Britain and its Tropical Colonies, 1850–1960*, London, 1993, pp. 191–5, p. 193.

For black protest, see, 'Resolutions of WASU condemning any deals with Germany over the colonies, 19 November 1938', ACJ, 16/1; I.T.A. Wallace Johnson (IASB) to John Parker, MP, 17 June 1937, ACJ, 17/2; *The Keys*, January–March 1937, 4 (3): 21.

49 D. Lamb, Commissioner, Salvation Army, 'Migration Problems in the Empire' in Harper (ed.) *Empire Problems*, p. 98. See also Mrs Hugo Harper, 'Disintegrating Problems within the Empire' in ibid., pp. 3–4, 13, 20–21.

Lamb was a member of the Royal Empire Society and Director of the Emigration Department, South Africa, 1903–30. The Cambridge branch of the Royal Empire Society was centred on Harper House, founded in 1919 in the memory of Major Hugo Alfred Harper, who was killed in action in France, as a centre dedicated to promoting 'Empire Studies' in schools and universities in Britain and the Empire. It was intended that Harper House should play the same part in Cambridge as Rhodes House played in Oxford, and it boasted the largest empire library after that of the Royal Empire Society, which was reputedly the largest in the world. The warden was Mrs Hugo Harper, who had convened the conference (information from ibid.).

50 D. Cannadine, 'The British Monarchy, *c.*1820–1977' in E. Hobsbawm and T. Ranger (eds) *The Invention of Tradition*, London, 1983, pp. 143–4, 149; Cain and Hopkins, *British Imperialism*, p. 229.

51 M. MacDonald *Hansard* (Commons), vol. 342, col. 1246–7, 7 December 1938; M. Hailey, 'Nationalism in Africa' in *Journal of the African Society*, April 1937, 36: 146. See also R.D. Pearce, *The Turning Point in Africa: British Colonial Policy 1938–1948*, London, Frank Cass, 1982.

52 W. Macmillan to J. Lewin, 18 January 1935, WMM, file 1935; A.D. Roberts, *The Colonial Moment in Africa: Essays on the movement of minds and materials, 1900–1940*, Cambridge, CUP, 1986, p. 49. For background to the survey, see Lord Lothian's preface to Sir M. Hailey, *An African Survey*, Oxford, OUP, 1938.

The fact that Lord Lothian, with whom Macmillan had crossed swords over South Africa in the early 1930s, was instrumental in getting the survey off the ground may also have been significant in Macmillan's rejection. After visiting West Africa, he published *Africa Emergent* in 1938, but Hailey's *African Survey*, published in the same year (with a revised edition in 1957), had the most impact in official circles at home and abroad.

53 Hailey, *An African Survey*. . .1956, pp. 44, 50.

54 Pearce, *The Turning Point in Africa*, p. 114; A.D. Roberts, *The Colonial Moment in Africa: Essays on the movement of minds and materials, 1900–1940*, Cambridge, CUP, 1986, p. 49, 73.

55 Sir Andrew Cohen, *British Policy in Changing Africa*, London, Routledge & Kegan Paul, 1960, p. 6; Sir Cosmo Parkinson, *The Colonial Office From Within 1909–1945*, London, 1947, pp. 121–2. See also W. Macmillan to W. Holtby, 7 August 1935, WH, 4/14.

56 Hailey, *An African Survey*. . .1956, p. 202.

57 The Hailey Papers, OURCP, Rhodes House, contain useful pamphlets, papers, reports, etc., connected with the *African Survey*. In addition to his 1938 and 1956 *African Surveys*, he also produced *Native Administration in the British African Territories*, London, 1951.

58 See, for example, MacDonald, *Hansard* (Commons), vol. 333, col. 968, 22 November 1938; E. Evans, ibid., vol. 342, col. 1230, 7 December 1938; J. Maxton, ibid., vol. 348, col. 440–2, 7 June 1939. See also J. Flint, 'Macmillan as a Critic of Empire' in H. Macmillan and S. Marks (eds) *Africa and Empire: W.M. Macmillan, Historian and Social Critic*, London, Temple Smith, 1989, p. 222.

59 K. Malik, *The Meaning of Race: Race, History and Culture in Western Society*, London, Macmillan, 1996, p. 19.

60 Policies are summarised in R. Hinden, *Plan for Africa: A Report Prepared for the Colonial Bureau of the Fabian Society*, London, Allen & Unwin Ltd., 1941. For dialogue with Africans, see a report of a meeting organised by the FRB, which was also attended by government officials, in *The WASU*, May 1943, 10 (1): 18.

61 J. Goody, *The Expansive Moment: Anthropology in Britain and Africa, 1918–1970*, Cambridge, CUP, 1995, pp. 69–71. Personal information, Mona Macmillan, 17 March 1983; M. Perham, 'African Facts and American Criticisms' in *Foreign Affairs*, April 1944, 22 (3); 'The Colonial Dilemma' in *The Listener*, 15 July 1949, reproduced in *Colonial Sequence*, pp. 251–62, pp. 333–40.

   Richards was director of the East African Institute of Social and Economic Research, became a Smuts reader at Cambridge in 1939 and subsequently became director of the African Studies Centre, which pioneered interdisciplinary studies in the postwar years. Both Evans Pritchard and Fortes were obviously threatened by Richard's academic success and possibly her influential friends (she was close to Ruth Cohen, principal of Newnham College, Cambridge, and sister to Andrew Cohen). Evans Pritchard was particularly vitriolic and misogynistic, arguing that women should stick to 'welfare work' and their intrusion into anthropological field work was 'undesirable'; if he had 'poked' Audrey when he had the opportunity, it would have 'settled her' (Evans Pritchard to Fortes, 1937, cited in Goody pp. 69–70).

62 D.J. Morgan, *The Official History of Colonial Development*, London, 1980, 5 vols, vol.1, *The Origins of British Aid Policy, 1924–45*, p. xvii; Havinden and Meredith, *Colonialism and Development*, p. 25. For general background, see J.M. Lee and M. Petter, *The Colonial Office, War and Development Policy: Organisation and the Planning of a Metropolitan Initiative, 1939–45*, London, Maurice Temple Smith, 1982, pp. 156–9.

63 Hailey, *An African Survey. . .1956*, p. 203.

64 Padmore, *Africa: Britain's Third Empire*. pp. 9, 158–62,180–1. See also V. Bartlett, *The Colour of Their Skins*, London, Chatto & Windus, 1969, p. 191.

65 J. Lewin, 'Leonard Barnes: The Man and his Books', review article in *African Affairs*, October 1975, 74 (297): 484.

   For details of threats to ban *Soviet Light*, see Dr G.M. Thomas (University of Kent) to L. Barnes, 6 September, 1 November 1971, Barnes Papers, box 25.

66 'A Minimum Programme of Civil Liberties in the Colonial Territories', 15 July 1941, NCCL, 52/2; Sir A. Burns, *Colour Prejudice with Particular Reference to the Relationship between Whites and Negroes*, London, 1948, pp. 48–50, 90–5, 140–4.

67 E. Pilkington, *Beyond the Mother Country: West Indians and the Notting Hill White Riots*, London, I.B. Taurus & Co. Ltd., 1988, p. 86; Perham, 'Capital, Labour and the Colour Bar' in *The Times*, 14 March 1942; information about Guy Gibson from Petwood Hotel, Woodhall Spa, Lincolnshire, where the dambusters were based.

68 H. Banda to A. Creech Jones, 26 July 1945, ACJ, 7/1. See also, Perham, 'Education for Self-Government' in *Foreign Affairs*, October 1945, reproduced in *Colonial Sequence*, p. 273. Banda was practising medicine in South Shields at the time.

69 Lauren, *Power and Prejudice*, pp. 148, 163–4, 172, 191–2.

70 Padmore, *Africa: Britain's Third Empire*, pp. 2, 9, 188; Pearce, *The Turning Point*, pp. 98–9, 116; Perham 'The Colonial Dilemma' in *The Listener*, 15 July 1949, reproduced in *Colonial Sequence*, pp. 335, 338; 'Notes and Typescript on race relations in Africa', 1946, ACJ, 7/1.

   Creech Jone's socialism stemmed from Christianity rather than 'intellectually conceived economic theory'. His interest in Africa had been initially generated by the atrocities in the Congo, which were exposed by E.D. Morel and Roger Casement, and he retained a liberal, international faith reflected in his membership of the executive of the Anti-Slavery Society (Pearce, *The Turning Point*, p. 98).

71 J. Kent, *British Imperial Strategy and the Origins of the Cold War, 1944–49*, London, Leicester UP, 1993, pp. 148–51; W. Churchill 'Great Design in Africa' in *The Times*, London, 11 November 1942.

72 F. Cooper, *The Decolonisation of African Society: The Labour Question in French and British Africa*, Cambridge, CUP, 1997; M. Butler, *Industrialisation and the British Colonial State: West Africa, 1939–51*, London, Frank Cass, 1997; R. Hyam 'Africa and the Labour Government, 1945–1951' in *Journal of Imperial and Commonwealth History*, 1988, 16 (2): 149–56.

73 Hailey, *An African Survey. . .1956*, pp. 110–11, 1612.

74 Kent, *British Imperial Strategy*, pp. 6, 152 and Ch. 5 and *The Internationalisation of Colonialism: Britain, France and Black Africa, 1939–1956*, London, 1992; *The Colonial Territories, 1948–1949*, marked 'Confidential: Final revise', London, HMSO, 1949, pp. 2, 120–21.

75 Perham, 'African Facts and American Criticisms' in *Foreign Affairs*, April 1944, 22 (3), reproduced in *Colonial Sequence*, pp. 251–62 and, for earlier criticisms, 'America and the Empire' in *The Times*, 20, 21 November 1942 in ibid., pp. 235–7.

76 J. Nederveen Pietersie, *Empire and Emancipation*, London, Pluto Press, 1990, pp. 262, 282; Cohen, *British Policy in Changing Africa*, pp. 113–4. W.R. Louis and R. Robinson, 'The Imperialism of Decolonisation' in *Journal of Imperial and Commonwealth History*, 1994, 22 (3): 462–511, 464; For wider background see A. Orde, *The Eclipse of Great Britain: The United States and British Imperial Decline, 1895–1956*, London, Macmillan, 1996; and W. R. Louis classic text, *Imperialism at Bay: The United States and the Decolonisation of the British Empire, 1941–1945*, Oxford, OUP, 1977.

77 J.M. Mackenzie (ed.) *Imperialism and Popular Culture*, Manchester, MUP, 1987, pp. 165–89, 173–7; Kent, *British Imperial Strategy*, p. 211.

78 D. Cannadine, 'The British Monarchy', p. 145. See also *Their Majesties, the King and Queen, and their Royal Highnesses, the Princess Elizabeth and the Princess Margaret, in the Union of South Africa, February to April, 1947*, Pretoria, South African Railways, 1947.

79 W. Webster, *Imagining Home: Gender, Race and National Identity, 1945–65*, London, UCL Press, 1997, pp. 47–52. Huxley's writings include, *White Man's Country: Lord Delamere and the Making of Kenya*, 2 vols, London, Chatto & Windus, 1956, first published in 1935; *The Flame Trees of Thika: Memories of An African Childhood*, London, Chatto & Windus, 1959, filmed for Thames TV in 1981, part one of her three part auto-biographical trilogy.

80 D. Birkett, 'The Great Pretender' in *Guardian Weekend*, 13 December 1997, pp. 14–23; *Arthur Mee's Book of the Flag: Island and Empire*, London, Hodder & Stoughton Ltd, 1941, p. 219; P.R. Gawthorne, *Empire Youth Annual*, London, P.R. Gawthorn Ltd., 1947 (with a foreword by General Smuts).
    The annual was possibly started in 1946 as the editorial by Percy Gawthorne mentions the 'wonderful reception' of the last edition.

81 Howe, *Anti-colonialism*, pp. 178–82, 234.

82 Obituary, *The Times*, 19 March 1977; A. McAdam, Letter to *The Times*, 27 March 1977; J. Lewin, 'Leonard Barnes: The Man and his Books', review article in *African Affairs*, 1975, 74 (297): 484, Barnes Papers, box 25. In 1975, on Barnes' eightieth birthday, a collective tribute was organised by Colin Leys, Julius Lewin, John Rex, Victor Kiernan, Martin Legassick, Ruth First, Shula Marks, George Shepperson, Stanley Trapido, Ronald Robinson and Thomas Hodgkin. In 1966, Barnes became consultant to the UN and *African Renaissance* (1969) and *African Eclipse* (1971) deal with the problems of independence.

83 Cohen, *British Policy in Changing Africa*, pp. 13, 113–4. See also Perham, 'African Facts', p. 260; J.D. Hargreaves, *De-colonisation in Africa*, London, Longman, 1996, second edition, p. 3.

84 E. Hobsbawm, *The Age of Extremes: The Short Twentieth Century: 1914–1991*, London, Michael Joseph, 1994, pp. 15–16, 52–3, 207.

Retrospective: Africa and the African diaspora in a 'post-imperial' world

1   Resist Recolonisation! General declaration by the delegates and participants of the 7th Pan-African Congress in S.J. Lemelle and R.D.G. Kelley (eds) *Imagining Home: Class, Culture and Nationalism in the African Diaspora*, London, Verso, 1994, Appendix. B, p. 365; J. Nederveen Pietersie, *Empire and Emancipation: Power and Liberation on a World Scale*, London, Pluto Press, 1990, p. 381.

2   M.J. Herskovits, *The Human Factor in Changing Africa*, London and New York, Routledge, Kegan and Paul, 1962, p. 8.

3   G. Padmore, *Africa: Britain's Third Empire*, New York, Negro Universities Press, 1969, first published in 1949, p. 261.

    One of the main organisers of Jubilee 2000 is Martin Dent, a lecturer at Keele University and the great, great grandson of Thomas Fowell Buxton, the 'liberator' of the slaves (M. Dent, 'Jubilee 2000: A New Start for the Debt-Ridden Developing World', Ray Jenkins Memorial Lecture, Staffordshire University, 8 May 1998).

4   Andrew Kopkind writing in the *Boston Phoenix*, 1972, cited in his obituary by Alexander Cockburn in *The Guardian*, 29 October 1994.

5   J. Cary, *A Case for African Freedom*, London, Secker & Warburg, 1944, first published in 1941.

6   A Zimbabwean academic, speaking on Peter Jay's recent series, 'Empire', BBC Radio 4, January 1998.

7   B. Warren, *Imperialism: Pioneer of Capitalism*, Cambridge, CUP, 1984, pp. 9, 47.

8   M. Mamdani, *Citizen and Subject: Contemporary Africa and the Legacy of Late Colonialism*, Princeton, Princeton University Press, 1996; S.P. Riley, 'The Political Economy of Anti-Corruption Strategies in Africa' in *European Journal of Development Research*, 1998, 10 (1): 129–43, p. 131; J.F. Bayart, *The Politics of the Belly: The State in Africa*, London, Longman, 1993.

9   R. Klitgaard, *Tropical Gangsters: One Man's Experience with Development and Decadence in Deepest Africa*, London, 1996. See also L. Cliffe and D. Seddon, 'Africa in a New World Order' in *Review of African Political Economy*, 1991, 50: 3–12.

    Klitgaard, a World Bank representative was one of these 'tropical gangsters'.

10 Bayart, *The Politics of the Belly*, p. 5. See also D. Hellinger, 'US Aid Policy in Africa; No Room for Democracy' in *Review of African Political Economy*, 1992, no. 55.

11 D. Hickey and K.C. Wylie, *An Enchanting Darkness: the American Vision of Africa in the Twentieth Century*, East Lansing, Michiegan State University, 1993; Pietersie, *Empire and Emancipation*, p. 285.

12 R. Stam and E. Shohat, 'Contested Histories: Eurocentricism, Multiculturalism, and the Media' in D.T. Goldberg (ed.) *Multiculturalism: A Critical Reader*, Oxford, Blackwell, 1994, pp. 296–324, pp. 296–304; Ngugi Wa Thiongo, *Moving the Centre: The Struggle for Cultural Freedoms*, Oxford, James Currey, 1993; Ngugi Wa Thiongo, *De Colonising the Mind*, Oxford, James Currey, 1986.

13 P.R. Schmidt and R.M. McIntosh (eds.) *Plundering Africa's Past*, Bloomington, In, Indiana University Press; London, 1996, Introduction.

14 D. Richards, 'The Man died in *africa95*' in *Review of African Political Economy*, 1996, 68 (23): 139–47, p.141; W. Januszczak, 'Condescending Colonialism' in the *Sunday Times*, 8 October 1995, p. 13. I attended a private preview of the Royal Academy exhibition, where we were impatiently rushed around. There was no sense of the vitality of contemporary African culture and African guests gazed upon sterile and ethnographic representations of the African past.

15 H. Louis Gates Junior, 'Goodbye, Columbus?: Notes on the Culture of Criticism' in Goldberg (ed.) *Multiculturalism*, pp. 192–217, pp. 209–11.

16 A. Campbell, *Empire in Africa*, London, Gollancz, 1944, p. 34.

17 M. Ignatiev, 'Guardians of Chaos', *BBC 2*, 17 October 1995.

18 P. Chabal, 'The African Crisis: Context and Interpretation' in a conference discussion paper on 'African Research Futures: Postcolonialism and Identity', SCUSA Annual Conference, Manchester, 13–16 May 1994; M. Barratt Brown, *Africa's Choices After Thirty Years of the World Bank*, Boulder Colorado, Westview Press, 1997.

19 See, for example, R. Rhodes James, 'Now that the sun has gone down' in *The Times*, 4 September 1995. Recent popular appraisals of empire include Peter Jay's, 'Empire', BBC Radio 4, January 1998 and L. James (ed.) *The British Empire 1497–1997: 500 Years that Shaped the World*, London, Telegraph Group, 1997.

20 B. Flynn, 'The Survivor' in the *Guardian*, 11 October 1996; 'Deadly Voyage', BBC 2, 12 October 1996.

21 S. Hall, 'Racism and Reaction' in *Five Views of Multiracial Britain*, London, Commission for Racial Equality, 1978, p. 25. For the Stephen Lawrence case, see D. Pallister, 'The Shadow of Justice' in the *Guardian*, 11 June 1998. For European attitudes to black minorities, see D. Cesarini (ed.) *Citizenship, Nationality and Migration in Europe*, London, Routledge, 1995.

22 J. Hanlon, *Mozambique: Who Calls the Shots*, Oxford, James Currey, 1991, p. 243; J. Pilger, 'Freedom Next Time' in the *Guardian Weekend*, 11 April 1998, pp. 14–28. For a more in-depth analysis of the South African economy, see B. Fine and Z. Rustomjee, *The Political Economy of South Africa*, Boulder Colorado, Westview Press, 1997.

23 L.A. Swatuk and R.D. Black (eds) *Bridging the Rift: The New South Africa in Africa*, Boulder Colorado, Westview Press, 1997.

24 T.A. Zack-Williams, 'African Development and African Diaspora: Separate Concerns?' in *Review of African Political Economy*, 1995, 22 (65): 349–59.

25 N.J. Savishinsky, 'Transnational Popular Culture and the Global Spread of the Jamaican Rastafarian Movement' in *New West India Guide/Neue West-Indische Gids*, 1994, 68 (3 & 4): 259–28; H. Campbell, 'Pan-Africanism and African Liberation' in Lemelle and Kelley (eds) *Imagining Home*, pp. 285–387, p. 302.

Bibliography

Unpublished sources

CHABAL, P, 'The African Crisis: Context and Interpretation', SCUSA Annual Conference, Manchester 13–16 May, 1994.

JONES, J., 'The Anti-Colonial Politics and Policies of the Communist Party of Great Britain', Ph.D. Thesis, Wolverhampton, 1997.

BUSH, B, 'The Dark Side of the City; Representation of Black London in the 1950s', conference paper in *City Limits Conference*, Staffordshire University, 11–14, September 1996.

Government records

Colonial Office Records, Public Record Office, London.

Private collections of individuals and organisations

A.F.L. Wilkinson Papers, OUCRP, Rhodes House, Oxford

A.W.G. Champion Papers, University of South Africa Documentation Centre for African Studies, Pretoria, RSA.

Arthur Creech Jones Papers, Rhodes House, Oxford

V.M. Ballinger Papers, University of Cape Town, Cape Town, RSA.

W. Ballinger Papers, SOAS Microfilm, SOAS, London

Bridgeman File, Hull University Library, UK

British and Foreign Anti-Slavery and Aborigines Protection Society Papers, Rhodes House, Oxford.

CARR, F.B., 'Reminiscences', unpublished manuscript describing his Nigerian service, 1919–49, OUCRP, Rhodes House, Oxford

Charles Roden Buxton Papers, Rhodes House.

Conrad Noel Papers, Hull University Library.

Leonard Barnes Papers, SOAS, London

London Group on African Affairs Papers, Rhodes House, Oxford

W.M. Macmillan Papers, in private possession.

National Council of Civil Liberties Papers, Hull University Library.

Papers of Lieutenant Colonel A.C. Duncan-Johnstone, OUCRP, Rhodes House.

Roux Papers, Institute of Commonwealth Studies, London

J.S. Smuts Papers, National Archives, Pretoria, RSA.
Union of Democratic Control, Collected Records, Hull University Library, UK
Winifred Holtby Papers, Hull City Libraries UK

Oral testimonies

P. Blackman
Fenner Brockway
Arthur Clegg
Mona Macmillan
Ethel Mannin
Eddie Frow

Film, radio and television productions

Boland, M., *Woman's Hour* BBC Radio 4, 25 November 1997.
Brook, Peter, 'Beyond the Blue Horizon' BBC Radio 4, 3 March 1994.
'The Coca-Cola conquest' on *Channel 4 Television*, 6 August 1998.
Coup de Torchon, 1981, Director Bernard Tavernier.
Jay, Peter, *Empire* , BBC Radio 4 (Series) January 1998.
Sanders of the River, London Film Productions, 1935, producer Alexander Korda, directed by Zoltan Korda.
Chocolate, 1989, Director Claire Denis.

Published sources

Government Publications

'*Aide Memoire* handed to the Prime Minister of the Union of South Africa by the Secretary of State for Dominion Affairs on 15 May 1935: 1934–5', Cmd. 4948, London, HMSO, 1935.
An Economic Survey of the Colonial Empire, 1932, London, HMSO, 1934.
An Economic Survey of the Colonial Empire, 1936, London, HMSO, 1936.
'British Nationality Bill: Summary of Main Provisions, 1947–48', Cmd. 7326, London, HMSO, 1948.
'Colonial Office Conference, 1930: Summary of Proceedings, 1929–30', Cmd. 3628, London, HMSO, 1930.
'Correspondence Relating to the Welfare of Women in Tropical Africa, 1935–37: 1937–38', Cmd. 5784, London, HMSO, 1938.
'Despatch from the Secretary of State to the Colonial Governments Regarding Certain Aspects of Colonial Wartime Policy, 1940–41', Cmd. 6299, London, HMSO, 1941.
'Financial and Economic Position of the Bechuanaland Protectorate: Report of the Commission Appointed by the Secretary of State of Dominion Affairs, March 1933', Cmd. 4113, London, HMSO, 1933.
'First Interim Report of the Colonial Development Advisory Committee, August 1929 – February 1930: 1929–30', Cmd. 3540, London, HMSO, 1930.
Hansard, House of Commons Debates, 5th series.

'Memorandum by the Advisory Committee on Native Education in the British Tropical African Dependencies, 1924–1925', Cmd. 2374, London, HMSO, 1925.

'Proposals for the Revision of the Constitution of Nigeria, 1944–45', Cmd. 6599, London, HMSO, 1945.

'Report by the Hon. W.G.A. Ormsby-Gore, Parliamentary Under Secretary of State for the Colonies in his visit to West Africa in 1926', Cmd. 2744, London, HMSO, 1925. – or 1926.

'Report of the Commission on Closer Union of the Dependencies in Eastern and Central Africa, 1928–29', Cmd. 3234, London, HMSO, 1929.

'Report of a Commission of Inquiry into the Disturbances at Aba and other Places in South Eastern Nigeria in November and December 1929, 1929–31', Cmd. 3784, London, HMSO, 1931.

'Report of the Commission on the Marketing of West African Cocoa; 1937–38', Cmd. 5845, London, HMSO, 1938.

'Report of a Committee on Distressed Colonial and Indian Subjects, 1910', Cmd. 5133, London, HMSO, 1910, and 'Evidence and Appendices', 1910, Cmd. 5134.

'Report on the Financial and Economic Situation in Swaziland, 1932', Cmd. 4132, London, HMSO, 1932.

'Report on Labour Conditions in West Africa by Major G. St J. Orde Brown; 1940–41', Cmd. 6277, London, HMSO, 1941.

'Report of a Committee on the System of Appointment in the Colonial Office and the Colonial Service, 1929–30', Cmd. 3540, London, HMSO, 1930.

'Report of the West India Royal Commission into the Disturbances in the West Indies, 1939–40', Cmd. 6174, London, HMSO, 1940.

'Report of the Colonial Films Committee, 1929–30', Cmd. 3630, London, HMSO, 1930.

'Statement of Policy on Colonial Development and Welfare 1939–40', Cmd. 6175, London, HMSO, 1940.

'The Colonial Territories, 1948–1949', marked 'Confidential: Final Revise', London, HMSO, 1949.

Newspapers and periodicals

Anti-Imperialist Review, organ of the International Secretariat of the LAI, Berlin, 1929–31 (erratic).

Colonial Information Bulletin, London, CIB, 1937–9.

The Communist Review and Communist, Moscow and London, 1921–33.

Daily Worker, London, CPGB.

Inside the Empire: A Monthly Review, CIB, 1940, later changed to a quarterly format.

International Press Correspondence, Imprekorr, Vienna, English edition (weekly), 1920.

The Black Man: A Monthly Magazine of Negro Thought and Opinion, 1933–1939, compiled with an introductory essay by Robert A. Hill, N.Y., Kraus Thompson, 1975.

The Keys: The Offical Organ of the League of Coloured Peoples, with an introductory essay by Roderick J. MacDonald., N.Y., Kraus-Thompson, 1967.

The Labour Monthly: A Magazine of International Labour

The Negro Worker (L'Ouvriér Négre), organ of the International Committee of Negro Workers, Hamburg, published monthly, often semi-monthly, 1928–37.

The New Times and Ethiopia News Weekly, 1936–56, Woodford Green, London.

The Nigerian Pioneer, Lagos, 1913–.

The West African Pilot, Lagos.
Umvikeli Thebe (The African Defender), organ of Ikaka Labasebenzi, South African Labour Defence, Johannesburg, January–July 1936.
WASU, Organ of the WASU, London, 1926–.

Pamphlets, reports and minutes

A Report of Proceedings and Decisions of the First International Conference of Negro Workers at Hamburg, Germany, July 1930, Hamburg, ITUC-NW, 1930.
'Annual Conference and Congress Reports of the CPGB', 1922–39, Marx Memorial Library, London and Working Class Movement Library, Manchester.
'Annual Conference Reports of the ILP, 1922–30', Marx Memorial Library, London and Working Class Movement Library, Manchester.
BALLINGER, W.G., *Race and Economics in South Africa*, day-to-day pamphlets, no. 21, London, 1934.
BRADLEY, B., *Colonies, Mandates and Peace*, London, Peace Library, n.d.
BRAILSFORD, H.N., *Towards a New League of Nations*, London, New Statesman, 1936.
British Imperialism: An Outline of Workers Conditions in the Colonies, London, National Minority Movement, 1930.
British Imperialism in East Africa, prepared by the Labour Research Department, Colonial Series no.1, London, LRD, 1926.
BROCKWAY, F. *How to End War – The I.L.P. view on Imperialism and Internationalism*, London, I.L.P. Publication Department, Nov. 1922, pamphlet.
BURNS, E., *British Imperialism in West Africa*, London, LRD, 1927, Colonial Series No. 4.
BURNS, E., *Abyssinia and Italy*, London, Left Book Club, 1936.
BUXTON, C.R., MP, *The Race Problem in Africa*, London, 1931.
CARADOG JONES, D., 'The Economic Status of Coloured Families in the Port of Liverpool', Liverpool Association for the Welfare of Coloured People, Liverpool, 1940.
CUNARD, N., *Black Man and White Ladyship: An Anniversary*, Toulouse, 1931, privately printed, marked 'Not for Sale'.
Education in Africa, Report of Africa Education Committee, New York, Phelps Stoke Fund, 1920.
Empire Day, London, LAI, n.d.
FLETCHER, M.E., *Report on the Investigation into the Colour Problem in Liverpool and Other Ports*, Liverpool, 1930.
HARPER, H.E. (ed.) *Empire Problems, Report of the Third Cambridge Empire Conference, 28–30 October 1938*, London, Frederick Muller Ltd., 1939.
HINDEN, R., *Plan for Africa: A Report Prepared for the Colonial Bureau of the Fabian Society*, London, Allen & Unwin Ltd., 1941.
HODGSON, M.L., BALLINGER, W.G., *Britain in South Africa, no. 2: Bechuanaland Protectorate*, Lovedale, 1931–2.
JACKSON, T.A., *The British Empire*, London, CPGB, 1922.
JACKSON, T.A., *What is the British Empire to You?*, London, CPGB, 1925.
KHAMA, T., *A Statement to the British Parliament*, London, ASAPS, 1934.
KHAMA, T., *A Reply to the Propaganda for the Incorporation of the Bechuanaland Protectorate within the Union*, London, ASAPS, 1933.

'League Against Imperialism and for National Independence: Resolutions passed at the session of the General Council held in Brussels, 9th, 10th, 11th, Dec. 1927', Berlin, 1927.

'Peace Conference: British Empire Delegation', 5, minutes of the meeting held at the Hotel Majestic, Paris, on Thursday, 28 January 1919.

'Peace Conference: British Empire Delegation', 1, minutes of the meeting, held at the Hotel Majestic, Paris, 13 January 1919.

'Memorandum on Projected Legislation Affecting Rights and Liberties of Africans in Southern Rhodesia and Kenya', London, LGAA, 1936.

'Memorandum on the Rights and Liberties of Africans: South African Native Policy', London, LGAA, 1937.

MOREL, E.D., *The African Problem and the Peace Settlement*, London, U.D.C, 1917.

National and Colonial Questions, Theses Adopted by the Second Congress of the Communist International, Moscow, August 1920, with an introduction, London, CPGB, 1920.

NOEL, C., Vicar of Thaxted, *The Meaning of Imperialism*, London, LAI, 1930.

PADMORE, G. (ed.) *Colonial and ... Coloured Unity; History of the Pan-African Congress*, reprint of the 'Report of the 1945 Pan-African Congress*, Manchester, 1947, second edition with new material, London, The Hammersmith Bookshop Ltd., 1963.

PADMORE, G., *Negro Workers and the Imperialist War – Intervention in the Soviet Union*, Hamburg, ITUC-NW, 1931.

PALME DUTT, C., *Labour and the Empire*, London, CPGB, n.d.

PALME DUTT, R., *Empire Socialism*, London, CPGB, 1926.

PALME DUTT, R., *Free the Colonies* London, Minority Movement, n.d.

Peace and the Colonial Problem, London, National Peace Council, 1935.

PLAATJE, S.T., *The Mote and the Beam. An Epic on Sex Relationships? twixt White and Black in British South Africa*, New York, 1921.

PLAATJE, S.T., *Some of the Legal Disabilities Suffered by the Native Population of the Union of South Africa and Imperial Responsibility*, London, 1919.

Racial Problems in South Africa: Report by a Deputation from the Society of Friends, in Great Britain and America to South Africa, 1938, London, Society of Friends, 1938.

Record of the Proceedings of the First Universal Races Congress held at the University of London, 1911, published for the Executive Council, London, 1911.

Report of the Fourth Congress of the RILU, London, RILU, 1928.

Report of the 5th Congress of the RILU, London, CPGB, 1930.

Report of the National Conference of the League Against Imperialism, British Section, February 1931, London, LAI, 1931.

Report of the Select Committee on Aborigines, 1837, London, APS, 1837.

Resolutions of the Fifth World Congress of the RILU, Moscow, Aug. 1930, London, Minority Movement, 1931.

RUCK, S.K. (ed.) *The West Indian Comes to England: A Report Prepared for the Trustees of the London Parochial Charities by the Family Welfare Association, London*, London, Routledge, Kegan and Paul, 1960

SHEPHERD, C.T., *Report on the Economics of Peasant Agriculture in the Gold Coast*, Accra, Government Printing Office, 1936.

Socialism and the Empire: Report of the ILP Empire Policy Committee submitted to the Annual Conference of the Party, 1926, London, ILP, 1926.

Stop 'Legal Lynching' of Nine Negro Boys: Rush Your Protests, London, International Labour Defence, Brit. Section., n.d.

The British Empire, London, LAI, n.d.

The Colonial Empire, London, Labour Party, 1933.

The Colonial Question: A Study Syllabus for Workers, London, CPGB, 1930.

The Demand for Colonial Territories and Equality of Economic Opportunity, London, Labour Party, 1937.

The Incitement to Disaffection Act – How it Stands, London, NCCL, 1934.

The Poor White Problem in South Africa:, Report of the Carnegie Committee of Inquiry, Stellenbosch, 1932. 5 vols.

The Protection of Colonial Peoples: A Study in British Colonial Policy, London, New Fabian Research Bureau, n.d.

The Revolutionary Movement in the Colonies: Theses on the Revolutionary Movement in the Colonies and Semi-Colonies, Adopted by the Sixth World Congress of the Communist International, 1928, Foreword by J. R. Campbell, London, 1929.

The Truth About Aggrey House: An Exposure of the Government Plan for the Control of African Students in Great Britain, Publication of the West African Student's Union of Great Britain and Northern Ireland, London, 1934.

The War Danger Over Abyssinia, London, LAI, n.d.

TRAPIDO, S., 'The Friends of the Natives: merchants, peasants and the political and ideological structure of liberalism in the Cape' in S. Marks and A. Atmore (eds) *Economy and Society in Pre-Industrial South Africa*, London, Longman, 1980.

United West Africa, or Africa at the Bar of Nations, London, WASU, 1927.

We Speak for Freedom: Report of the Conference of the CPs of the British Empire, held on Feb. 26 – March 2, 1947, London, London, CPGB, 1947.

'We Were Framed' – The First Full Story of the Scottsboro Case, Scottsboro Defence Committee, 4 Paton St., WC1, June, 1934.

WYNDHAM, H.A., *Problems of Imperial Trusteeship: The Atlantic and Emancipation by H. A. Wyndham*, A Report in the Study Group Series of the Royal Institute of International Affairs, London, 1937.

Books

ABRAHAMS, P., *Jamaica: An Island Mosaic*, London, HMSO, Corona Library, 1957.

ABRAHAMS, P., *Mineboy*, London, Heinemann, 1963, first published in 1946.

ACHEBE, C., *Things Fall Apart*, London, Heinemann, 1962.

ADI, H., *West Africans in Britain 1900–1960: Nationalism, Pan-Africanism and Communism*, London, Lawrence & Wishart, 1998.

ADI, H., *A Celebration of the Life of Paul Robeson, 1898–1976*, SOAS, 1998.

ADI, H. and SHERWOOD, M., *The 1945 Manchester Pan-African Congress Revisited*, London and Port of Spain, New Beacon Books, 1995.

AHIRE, P., *Imperial Policing: The Emergence of the Police in Colonial Nigeria, 1860–1960*, Milton Keynes, Open University Press, 1991.

AHRIN, K (ed.) *The Life and Work of Kwame Nkrumah*, Trenton, Africa World Press, 1993.

AKYEAMPONG, E. K *Drink, Power and Cultural Change: A Social History of Alcohol in Ghana C. 1800 to Recent Times* Oxford, James Currey, 1996

ALLEN, C., (ed.) *Tales from the Dark Continent: Images of British Colonial Africa in the Twentieth Century*, London, Futura, 1979, first published in 1979 in conjunction with the BBC.

ALLY, R., *Gold and Empire: The Bank of England and South Africa's Gold, 1889–1926*, Johannesburg, Johannesburg University Press, 1994.

AMERY, L.S., *The German Colonial Claim*, London and Edinburgh, W. & R. Chambers Ltd., 1939.

AMIN, A., *Neo-colonialism in West Africa*, Harmondsworth, Penguin, 1973.

AMIN, S., *Eurocentricism*, London, Zed, 1990.

ANDERSON, D.A. and KILLINGRAY, D. (eds) *Policing the Empire: Government, Authority and Control, 1830–1940*, Manchester, MUP, 1991.

ANDERSON, G.D., *Fascists, Communists and the National Government, Civil Liberties in Great Britain 1931–1937*, Columbia and London, Universtiy of Missouri Press 1983.

ANGELL, N., *The Defence of the Empire*, London, Hamish Hamilton 1937.

ANSPREGER, F., *The Dissolution of Colonial Empires*, London, Routledge, 1989.

ANTHIAS, F. and DAVIS, N.Y., *Racialised Boundaries: Race, Nation, Gender, Colour and Class and the Anti-Racist Struggle*, London, Routledge, 1992.

ARNGROVE, R.F. (ed.) *Philanthropy and Cultural Imperialism: The Foundations at Home and Abroad*, Boston, Mass., G.K. Hall 1980.

ARRIGHI, G., *The Long Twentieth century: Money, Power and the Origins of Our Times*, London, Verso, 1994.

ASANTE, S.K.B., *Pan-African Protest: West Africa and the Italo-Ethiopian Crisis, 1934–1941*, London, Longman 1977.

AXFORD, B., *The Global System*, London, Polity Press, 1995.

AYOADE, A.A., *et al.*, *Women and Politics in Nigeria*, Lagos, Malthouse, 1992.

AZIKIWE, N., *Renascent Africa*, Accra, 1937, 2nd edn., London, 1966.

BAK RASMUSSEN, A.M., *A History of the Quaker Movement in Africa*, London, British Academic Press, 1994.

BALLINGER, W.G. and HODGSON, M.L., Bechmanaland Protectorate, *Britain in South Africa*, Lovedale, Lovedale Press, 1935.

BANTON, M., *The Coloured Quarter: Negro Immigrants in an English City*, London, Jonathan Cape, 1955.

BARKAN, E., *The Retreat from Scientific Racism: The Changing Concepts of Race in Britain and the United States between the World Wars*, Cambridge, CUP, 1992.

BARNES, L., *Africa in Eclipse*, London, Gollancz 1971.

BARNES, L., *African Renaissance*, London, Gollancz 1969.

BARNES, L., *Soviet Light on the Colonies*, London, Penguin, 1944.

BARNES, L., *Empire or Democracy: A Study of the Colonial Question*, London, Victor Gollancz Ltd., 1939.

BARNES L., *The Future of the Colonies*, London, 1936.

BARNES, L., *Duty of Empire*, London, 1935.

BARNES, L., *Caliban in Africa: An Impression of Colour-Madness*, London, Victor Gollancz, 1930.

BARNES, L., *The New Boer War*, London, Hogarth, 1932.

BARRATT BROWN, M., *Africa's Choices After Thirty Years of the World Bank*, Boulder Colorado, Westview Press, 1997.

BARTLETT, V., *The Colour of Their Skins*, London, Chatto & Windus, 1969.

BARTON, F., *The Press of Africa: Persecution and Perseverance*, London, Macmillan 1979.

BAYART, J.F., *The Politics of the Belly: The State in Africa*, London, Longman, 1993.

BEER, G.L., *African Questions at the Paris Peace Conference*, edited and with an introduction, annexes and additional notes by Louis Herbert Gray, London, Dawsons of Pall Mall, 1968, first published in 1923.

BEINART, W. and BUNDY, C., *Hidden Struggles in Rural South Africa: Politics and Popular Movements in the Transkei and Eastern Cape*, Oxford, James Curry, 1987.

BEINART, W. and COATES, P., *The Taming of Nature in the USA and South Africa*, London, New York, 1994.

BEINART, W. and DUBOW, S. (eds) *Segregation and Apartheid in Twentieth Century South Africa*, London, Routledge, 1995.

BEINART, W., *Twentieth Century South Africa*, Oxford and New York, OUP, 1994.

BENSON, M., *The African Patriots: The Story of the ANC of South Africa*, London, Faber and Faber 1963.

BENSON, M., *Tshekedi Khama*, London, Faber and Faber 1960.

BERGER, I., *Threads of Solidarity: Gender, Race And Labour In South Africa*, Oxford, James Currey, 1992.

BERMAN, M., *All That is Solid Melts into Air: The Experience of Modernity*, London, Verso, 1983.

BERNSTEIN, H., *For Their Triumphs and for Their Tears*, London, International Defence and Aid Fund for South Africa, 1985.

BERRY, E., *Mad Dogs and Englishmen*, London, Michael Joseph, 1941.

BHABHA, H., *The Location of Culture*, London, Routledge, 1994.

BHABHA, H., *Nation and Narration*, London, Routledge, 1990.

BIRMINGHAM, D., *The Decolonisation of Africa*, London, UCL Press, 1995.

BLIXEN, K, *Out of Africa*, London, 1937.

BOAHEN, A.A., *Africa Under Colonial Domination, 1880–1935*, Oxford, James Curry, 1990.

BOAHEN, A.A., *African Perspectives on Colonialism*, Oxford, James Curry, 1989.

BOERSNER, D., *The Bolsheviks and the National and Colonial Question, 1917–1928*, Geneva, Librarie E. Droz 1957.

BOGUES, A., *Caliban's Freedom: The Early Political Thought of CLR James*, London, Pluto, 1997.

BONNER, P., DELIUS, P. and POSEL, D., *Apartheid's Genesis, 1935–1961*, Johannesburg, Witwatersrand University Press, 1993.

BOURNE, S., *Black in the British Frame: Black People in British Film and Television, 1896–1996*, London, Cassell, 1998.

BOURRET, F.M., *Ghana: The Road to Independence 1919–1957*, London, Oxford Universtiy Press, 1960.

BOUSQUET, B. and DOUGLAS, C., *West Indian Women at War: British Racism in World War Two*, London, Lawrence and Wishart, 1990.

BOZZOLI, B., *Women of Phokeng: Consciousness, Life Strategy and Migrancy in South Africa, 1900–1983*, Oxford, James Currey, 1991.

BRADFORD, H., *A Taste of Freedom: The ICU in Rural South Africa, 1924–1930*, New Haven, Yale UP, 1987.

BRADLEY, K., *Once a District Officer*, London, Macmillan, 1966.

BRADLEY, K., *The Diary of a District Officer*, London, Harrap & Co. 1943.

BRAILSFORD, H.N., *The War of Steel and Gold: A Study of the Armed Peace*, London, G. Bell & Sons, 1914.

BRANSON, N., *History of the Communist Party of Great Britain, 1941–1951*, London, Lawrence & Wishart, London, 1997.

BRETT, E.A., *Colonialism and Underdevelopment in East Africa*, London, Gregg Revivals, 1992.

BRIFFAUT, R., *The Decline and Fall of the British Empire*, New York, Simon and Schuster, 1938.

BRITTAIN, V., *Testament of Friendship: The Story of Winifred Holtby*, New York, The Macmillan Company, 1940.

BRYK, F., *Dark Rapture*, New York, 1939.

BROCKWAY, F., *The Colonial Revolution*, London, 1973.

BROOKES, E.H., *R-J: In Appreciation of the Life of David Rheinhallt Jones and his work for the betterment of Race Relations in Southern Africa*, Johannesburg, Institute of Race Relations, 1953.

BROOKES, E.H., *The Colour Problems of South Africa*, Lovedale, Lovedale Press, 1934.

BROOKES, E.H., *The History of Native Policy in South Africa from 1830 to the Present Day*, Pretoria, second revised edition, J.L. Van Schaik, 1927.

BROWN, L.L., *The Young Paul Robeson: 'On My Journey Now'*, Boulder, Colorado, Westview Press, 1997.

BUELL, R.L., *The Native Problem in Africa*, New York, 2 vols, Macmillan Co 1928.

BUNDY, C., *The Rise and Fall of the South African Peasantry*, Oxford, James Currey, 1988.

BURNS, Sir A., *Colour Prejudice: with Particular Reference to the Relationship between White and Negroes*, London, George Allen & Unwin, 1948.

BUSBY, M., *Daughters of Africa*, London, Frank Cass, 1991.

BUTLER, J., ELPHICK, R. and WELSH, D. (eds) *Democratic Liberalism in South Africa: Its History and Prospect*, Cape Town and Johannesburg, Wesleyan University Press, 1987.

BUTLER, M., *Industrialisation and the British Colonial State: West Africa, 1939–51*, London, Frank Cass, 1997.

BUXTON, C.R. (ed.) *Labour's Way With the Commonwealth*, London, Methuen & Co Ltd, 1935.

CAIN, P.J. and HOPKINS, A.G., *British Imperialism: Crisis and Deconstruction, 1914–1990*, London, Longman, 1993.

CALLAWAY, H., *Gender, Culture and Empire: European Women in Colonial Nigeria*, London, Macmillan, 1987.

CAMMACK, D., *The Rand At War, 1899–1902: The Witwatersrand and the Anglo-Boer War*, Oxford, James Currey, 1990.

CAMPBELL, A., *Empire in Africa*, London, Gollancz, 1944.

CARDINALL, A.W., *The Gold Coast, 1931, based on figures and facts collected by the chief census officer of 1931*, Accra, Government Printer, 1932.

CARR, E.H., *The Twilight of the Comintern, 1930–1935*, London, Macmillan 1982.

CARSON, C., *Last Night's Fun: A Book About Irish Traditional Music*, London, Jonathan Cape, 1996.

CARY, J., *A Case for African Freedom*, London, Secker & Warburg, 1944, first published in 1941.

CARY, J., *Mister Johnson*, London, Methuen, 1939.

CASTLE, K., *Britannia's Children: Reading Colonialism through Children's Books and Magazines*, Manchester, MUP, 1996.

CELL, J.W., *The Highest Stage of White Supremacy: The Origins of Segregation in South Africa and the American South*, Cambridge, CUP, 1982.

CESARINI, D. and FULBROOK, M. (eds) *Citizenship, Nationality And Mirgration in Europe*, London, Routledge, 1995.

CHABAL, P., *Power in Africa: An Essay in Political Interpretation*, London, Macmillan, 1994, First published, 1992.

CHATTERJEE, P., *The Nation and its Fragments*, Princeton, NJ, Princeton University Press, 1993.

CHATTERJEE, P., *Nationalist Thought and the Colonial World: A Derivative Discourse*, London, Zed, 1986.

CHAUDHURI, N. and STROBEL, M. (eds) *Western Women and Imperialism: Complicity and Resistance*, Bloomington, IN, Indiana University Press, 1992.

CHISHOLM, A., *Nancy Cunard*, London, 1996.

CLAYTON, A., *The British Empire as a Superpower, 1919–1939*, London, Macmillan, 1989.

CLOSE, E., *A Woman Alone in Kenya, Uganda and the Belgian Congo*, London, Constable & Co. 1924.

COCK, J., *Maids and Madams: Domestic Workers Under Apartheid*, London, Women's Press, 1989.

COHEN, Sir A., *British Policy in Changing Africa*, London, Routledge & Kegan Paul, 1960.

COHEN, R., *Global Diasporas: An Introduction*, London, UCL Press, 1997.

COLEMAN, J.S., *Nigeria: Background to Nationalism*, Berkeley, University of California Press, 1971, First published, 1958.

COMAROFF, I., and COMAROFF, J., *Of Revelation and Revolution: Christianity, Colonialism and Consciousness in South Africa*, Chicago, University of Chicago Press, 1991.

COOMBES, A.E., *Reinventing Africa: Museums, Material Culture and Popular Imagination in Late Victorian and Edwardian England*, New Haven and London, Yale University Press, 1994.

COOPER, F., *The Decolonisation of African Society: The Labour Question in French and British Africa*, Cambridge, CUP, 1997.

COQUERY-VIDROVITCH, C., *African Women: A Modern History*, Boulder, Colorado, Westview Press, 1997, first published in French in 1994.

COTY, F., *Centre le Communism: le Peril Rouge En Pays Noirs*, Paris, 1930.

COUPLAND, R., *The Empire in These Days: An Interpretation*, London, Macmillan & Co.,1935.

CRIPPS, A.S., *An Africa for the Africans: A Plea on Behalf of Territorial Segregation Areas and of their Freedom in a South African Colony*, with a preface by Philip Kerr, Secretary of the Rhodes Trust, New York, 1969, first published in London in 1927.

CRIPPS, T., *Slow Fade to Black: The Negro in American Film, 1900–1942*, Oxford, OUP, 1977.

CROCKER, W.R., *Nigeria: A Critique of British Colonial Administration*, London, George Allen & Unwin, 1936.

CROMWELL, A.M., *An African Victorian Feminist: The Life and Times of Adelaide Smith Casely Hayford, 1868–1960*, London, Frank Cass, 1986.

CRONIN, D.E., *Black Moses: The story of Marcus Garvey and the Universal Negro Improvement Association*, Madison, University of Wisconsin Press, 1955.

CROSS, C., *The Fall of the British Empire, 1918–1968*, London, Hodder & Stoughton, 1969.

CROWDER, M, *The Flogging of Phinehas McIntosh: A Tale of Colonial Folly and Injustice, Bechuanaland, 1933*, New Haven and London, Yale University Press, 1988.

CROWDER, M. (ed.) *West African Resistance: The Military Response to Colonial Occupation*, London, Hutchinson, 1971.

CROWDER, M., *West Africa Under Colonial Rule*, London, Hutchinson, 1968.

CROZIER, Brigadier General. F.P., *Five Years Hard: Being an account of the fall of the Fulani Empire and a picture of the daily life of a Regimental Officer among the peoples of the Western Sudan*, London, Jonathon Cape, 1932.

CUNARD, N., *Negro Anthology made by Nancy Cunard 1931–1933*, published by Nancy Cunard at Wishart & Co., London, 1934.

CUNARD, N. and PADMORE, G., *The White Man's Duty*, London, 1942.

CURRAN, J. and PORTER, V. (eds) *British Cinema History*, London, Wiedenfeld & Nicholson, 1983.

CUTRAFELLI, M.R., *Women of Africa: Roots of Oppression* (trans. from Italian), London, Zed Press, 1988.

DARBY, P., *Three Faces of Imperialism, British and American Approaches to Asia and Africa, 1870–1970*, Yale, Yale UP, 1987.

DAVIDSON, B., *The Search for Africa: History, Culture, Politics*, Oxford, James Currey, 1994.

DAVIDSON, B., *The Black Man's Burden: Africa and the Curse of the Nation State*, Oxford, James Currey, 1992.

DAVIDSON, B., *Africa in Modern History: The Search for a New Society*, London, Allen Lane 1979.

DAVIDSON, B., *The African Awakening*, London, Cape, 1955.

DAVIE, M. (ed.) *The Diaries of Evelyn Waugh*, London, Penguin, 1976.

DAVIES, P.N., *The Trade Makers: Elder Dempster in Africa, 1852–1972*, London, 1973.

DAVIS, D.B., *Slavery and Human Freedom*, London and Harvard, Yale UP, 1986.

DE BUNSEN, V., *Charles Roden Buxton: A Memoir*, London, George Allen and Unwin, 1948.

DE BRAGANCA, A. and WALLERSTEIN, I., *The African Liberation Reader*, London, Zed Press, 3 vols, 1982.

DE KIEWIET, C.W., *The Imperial factor in South Africa*, London, Frank Cass, 1965, first published, 1937.

DE KIEWIET, C.W. *A History of South Africa; Social and Economic*, Oxford, Claredon Press, 1941.

DE GRAF, W., *The Nigerian State: Political Economy, State, Class and Political System in the Post-Colonial Era*, London, James Currey, 1988.

DIGRE, B., *Imperialism's New Clothes: The Reparation of Tropical Africa, 1914–1919*, New York, Peter Lang, 1990.

DOVER, C., *Half-Caste*, London, 1939.

DOVER, C., *Know This of Race*, London, Secker and Warburg M. Secker and Warburg Ltd, 1937.

DRACHLER, J. (ed.), *Black Homeland: Black Diaspora: Cross Currents of the African Relationship*, London, Kennikat Press, 1975.

DUBERMAN, M.B., *Paul Robeson*, London, Bodley Head, 1989.

DUBOIS, W.E.B., *The Souls of Black Folk*, essays and sketches first published in Chicago in 1903 with a new introduction by Herbert Aptheker, New York, Kraus-Thompson Organisation Ltd., 1973.

DUBOIS, W.E.B., *The World and Africa: An inquiry into the part which Africa has played in world history*, New York, Internation Publishers, 1965, first published in 1946–7.

DUBOW, S., *Scientific Racism in Modern South Africa*, Cambridge, CUP, 1995.

DUNBAR MOODIE, T. (with V. Ndatshe), *Going for Gold: Men, Mines, and Migration*, Berkeley, UCLA Press, 1994.

DUNCAN-JOHNSTONE, A.C. and BLAIR, H.A., *Inquiry into the Constitution and Organisation of the Dagbon*, Accra, Government Printer, 1932.

DUNCAN, D., *The Mills of God: The State and African Labour in South Africa, 1918–1948*, Johannesburg, University of Witwatersrand Press, 1995.

ECCLESHALL, R., *et al.*, *Political ideologies: An Introduction*, London, Hutchinson, 1986.

EDWARDS, N., *Cadbury on the Gold Coast*, Bourneville, 1955.

EDWARDS, M., *Paul Robeson, Honorary Welshman*, Treorchy, Rhondda, Paul Robeson Exhibition, n.d.

EGERTON, H.E., *British Colonial Policy in the Twentieth Century*, London, Methuen & Co., 1922.

ENGELS, D., and MARKS, S. (eds) *Contesting Colonial Hegemony: State and Society in Africa and India*, London and New York, British Academic Press, 1994.

EVANS, I.L., *Native Policy in Southern Africa: An Outline*, Cambridge, CUP, 1934.

FAGE, J.D., *A History of West Africa: An Introductory Survey*, Cambridge, CUP, 1969.

FAGE, J.D., *Ghana: A Historical Interpretation*, Madison, University of Wisconsin Press, 1961.

FANON, F., *Black Skin White Masks*, translated by Charles Lam Markham, London, Pluto Press, 1993, first published in 1967.

FANON, F., *The Wretched do the Earth*, New York, 1966, First published, Paris, 1961, Trans. Constance Farrington, preface by Jean-Paul Sartre.

FEDOROWICH, K., *Reconstruction and Soldier Settlement in the Empire Between the Wars*, Manchester, MUP, 1995.

FERRO, M., *Colonisation: A Global History*, London and New York, Routledge, 1997.

FIELDHOUSE, D.K, *Merchant Capital and Economic Decolonisation: The United Africa Company, 1929–1987*, Oxford, Clarendon Press, 1994.

FIELDHOUSE, D.K.., *Black Africa, 1945–1980: Economic Decolonisation and Arrested Development*, London, Allen & Unwin, 1986.

FIELDHOUSE, D.K., *Colonialism, 1870–1945 An Introduction*, London, Allen & Unwin Weidenfield & Nicholson, 1981.

FIELDHOUSE, D.K., *Unilever Overseas: The Anatomy of a multinational, 1895–1956*, London, Croom Helm, 1978.

FIELDING, D., *Emerald and Nancy: Lady Cunard and Her Daughter*, London, Eyre & Spottiswoode, 1968.

FINE, B. and RUSTOMJEE, Z., *The Political Economy of South Africa: From Minerals Energy Complex to Industrialisation*, Boulder Colorado, Westview Press, 1997.

FORD, H. (ed.) *Nancy Cunard: Brave Poet, Indomitable Rebel, 1896–1965*, New York, Chilton Book Co. 1968.

FOUCAULT, M., *The History of Sexuality*, trans. from French by Robert Hurley, London, 1978–1979, first published, Paris, 1976, vol. 1, *An Introduction*.

FOWLER-LUNN, K., *The Gold Missus: A Woman Prospector in Sierra Leone*, New York, W. W. Norton & Co., inc., 1938.

FOX, J., *White Mischief*, London, Jonathan Cape,1982.

FREDRICKSON, G., *White Supremacy: A Comparative Study in American and South African History*, New York, 1981.

FREUND, B., *Capital and Labour in the Nigerian Tin Mines*, London, Longman, 1981.

FREUND, B., *The African Worker*, Cambridge, CUP, 1988.

FREUND, B., *The Making of Contemporary Africa: The Development of African Society since 1800,*, London, Macmillan,1984.

FROST, D. (ed.) *Ethnic Labour and British Imperial Trade: A History of Ethnic Seafarers in the UK*, London, Frank Cass, 1995.

FRYER, P., *Staying Power: The History of Black People in Britain* London, Pluto, 1984.

FUREDI, F., *The Silent War: Racism, Imperialism and Ideology in the Twentieth Century*, London, Pluto, 1998.

FUREDI, F., *The New Ideology of Imperialism: Renewing the Moral Imperative*, London, Pluto Press, 1995.

FURLONG, P.J., *Between Crown and Swastika: The Impact of the Radical Right on the Africaner Nationalist Movement in the Fascist Era*, Boston, University Press of New England, 1992.

FURNIVAL, J.S., *Colonial Policy and Practice*, New York, New York University Press, 1956.

FRANKEL, S., *Capital Investment in Africa*, London, 1938.

FYFE, C., *Sierra Leone Inheritance*, Oxford, OUP, 1964.

GANDHI, M.K., *Satyagrapha in South Africa*, Madras, 1928.

GANN, L.H. and DIUGNAN, P. (eds) *Burden of Empire: An Appraisal of Western Colonialism in Africa South of the Sahara*, London, Pall Mall, 1968.

GANN, L.H. and DIUGNAN, P. (eds) *Colonialism in Africa, 1870–1960*, Cambridge, CUP, 3 vols., 1970.

GARDINER, J., *'Over Here': the GIs in Wartime Britain*, London, Collins and Brown,1992.

GARLAND ANDERSON, D., *Nigger Lover*, London, L.N. Fowler & Co Ltd, 1938.

GARVEY, A. (ed.) *The Philosophy and Opinions of Marcus Garvey*, reproduction, London, Frank Cass, 1967.

GAWTHORNE, P.R. (ed.) *Empire Youth Annual*, London, P.R. Gawthorne Ltd., 1947.

GEARY, Sir W., *Nigeria Under British Rule*, London, Frank Cass, 1965, first printed in 1927.

GEISS, I., *The Pan-African Movement: A History of Pan-Africanism in America, Europe and Africa*, London, Methuen, 1974.

GIBBS, H., *The Spectre of Communism*, London, 1938.

GIFFORD, P. and LOUIS, W.R. (eds.) *France and Britain in Africa: Imperial Rivalry and Colonial Rule*, New Haven and London, Yale University Press, 1971.

GILROY, P., *The Black Atlantic: Modernity and Double Consciousness*, London, Verso, 1993.

GODDEN, G.M., *Communist Attack on the People of Great Britain: International Communism at Work*, London, Burns, Oats & Co. 2nd Edition, 1938.

GOLDBERG, D.T. (ed.) *Multiculturalism: A Critical Reader*, Oxford, Blackwell, 1994.

GOLDBERG, D.T., *Racist Culture: Philosophy and the Politics of Meaning*, Oxford, Blackwell, 1993.

GOODE ROBESON, E,, *African Journey*, London, Victor Gollancz Ltd., 1946.

GOODY, J., *The Expansive Moment: Anthropology in Britain and Africa, 1918–1970*, Cambridge, CUP, 1995.

GORER, G., *Africa Dances: A book about West African Negroes*, London, Faber and Faber, 1935.

GREEN, M.M., *Igbo Village Affairs*, London, Frank Cass, 1947.

GREENE, G., *Journey Without Maps*, London, Penguin 1971, first published, 1936.

GRUNDLINGH, A., *Fighting their Own Wars: South African Blacks and the First World War*, Johannesburg, Raven Press, 1987.

GUPTA, P.S., *Imperialism and the British Labour Movement, 1914–1964*, London, Macmillan, 1975.

HABERMAS, J., *The Philosophical Discourse on Modernity*, Cambridge, Polity Press, 1987.

HADEN-GUEST, L., *The Labour Party and the Empire*, London, 1926.

HAIG, E.F.G., *Nigerian Sketches*, London, George Allen and Unwin Ltd, 1931.

HAILEY, *An African Survey: A Study of Problems Arising in Africa South of the Sahara, Revised, 1956.*, London, OUP, 1957, issued under the auspices of the Royal Institute of International Affairs.

HAILEY, Sir M., *Native Administration in the British African Territories*, London, HMSO, 1951.

HAILEY, Sir M., *An African Survey: A Study of Problems Arising in Africa South of the Sahara*, London, OUP, 1938.

HALL, S., *et al.*, (eds) *Formations of Modernity*, London, Polity Press, 1992.

HANLON, J., *Mozambique: Who Calls the Shots?* Oxford, James Curry, 1991.

HARGREAVES, J.D., *Decolonisation in Africa*, second edition, London and New York, Longman, 1996.

HARGREAVES, J.D., *The End of Colonial Rule in West Africa: Essays in Contemporary History*, London, Macmillan, 1979.

HARVEY, D., *The Condition of Post-Modernity: An Inquiry into the Origins of Cultural Change*, Oxford, Blackwell, 1990.

HAVINDEN, M. and MEREDITH, D., *Colonialism and Development: Britain and its Tropical Colonies, 1850–1960*, London, 1993.

HAXEY, S., *Tory MP*, Left Book Club Edition, London, Gollancz, 1939.

HAYFORD, J.E.C., *Ethiopia Unbound: Studies in Race Emancipation*, London, 1911.

HEGEL, G.W.F, *The Philosophy of History*, with an introduction by C.J. Friedrich and translated by J. Sibree, New York, Dover Publications Ltd., 1956.

HEGEL, G.W.F., *The Phenomenology of Mind*, 2nd edn, translated with introduction and notes by J.B. Baillie, London, Allen and Unwin1949.

HELD, D., *Models of Democracy*, London, Polity, 1987.

HELLMAN, E. and LEVER, H. (eds) *Race Relations in South Africa*, London and Basingstoke, Macmillan, 1980.

HELLMAN, E., *Rooiyard: A Sociological Survey of an Urban Native Slum Yard*, Cape Town, OUP for Rhodes-Livingstone Institute, Livingstone, Northern Rhodesia, 1948.

HERSKOVITS, M.J., *The Human Factor in Changing Africa*, Routledge, Kegan & Paul, 1962.

HETHERINGTON, P., *British Paternalism and Africa, 1920–1940*, London, Frank Cass 1978.

HEUSSLER, R., *Yesterday's Rulers: The Making of the British Colonial Service*, Syracuse, Syracuse UP, 1963.

HEYWOOD, A., *Political Ideologies: An Introduction*, London, Macmillan, 1992.

HICKEY, D., WYLIE, K.C., *An Enchanting Darkness: the American Vision of Africa in the Twentieth Century*, East Lansing, Michigan State University, 1993.

HIGGS, C., *The Ghost of Equality: The Public Lives of D.D.T. Jabavu of South Africa, 1885–1959*, Johannesburg, David Phillips, 1997.

HILL, P., *The Migrant Cocoa Farmers of Southern Ghana*, Oxford, James Curry, 1997, first published in 1963.

HILL, R.A and BAIR, B. (eds.) *Marcus Garvey: Life and Lessons*, Berkeley, California, UCLA Press, 1987.

HINDEN, R. (ed.) *Fabian Colonial Essays*, London, Allen and Unwin, 1945.

HIRSCHFELD, M., *The Sexual History of the World War*, New York, 1937.

HIRSCHFELD, M., *Racism*, translated and edited by Eden and Cedar Paul, London, V. Gollancz Ltd, 1938.

HIRSON, B., *Yours for the Union: Class and Community Struggles in South Africa*, Johannesburg, Witwatersrand University Press, 1990.

HIRSON, B. and WILLIAMS, G.A., *The Delegate for Africa: David Ivon Jones, 1883–1924*, Johannesburg, Core Publications, 1995.

HOARE, Q. and NOWELL SMITH, G. (ed.) *Selection from the Prison Notebook of Antonio Gramsci*, London, Lawrence & Wishart, 1971.

HOBSBAWM, E., *Age Of Empire*, London, Weidenfeld & Nicolson, 1988.

HOBSBAWM, E. and RANGER, T.O. (eds) *The Invention of Tradition*, Cambridge, CUP, 1996, first published in 1983.

HOBSBAWM, E., *The Age of Extremes: The Short Twentieth Century: 1914–1991*, London, Michael Joseph, 1994.

HOBSON, J.A., *Imperialism: A Study*, edited and with introduction by J. Townshend, London, Allen & Unwin, 1988, 3rd Edition, first published in 1902.

HODGKIN, T., *Nationalism in Colonial Africa*, London, Muller, 1956.

HOERNLE, R.F.A., *South African Native Policy and the Liberal Spirit*, Lovedale, Lovedale Press, 1940.

HOLMES, C., *John Bulls' Island: Immigration and British Society, 1871–1971*, London, Macmillan,1987.

HOLTBY, W., 'Notes on the Way' in *Time and Tide*, 27 October 1934, pp. 18–24.

HOLTBY, W., *Mandoa, Mandoa: A Comedy of Irrelevance*, London, Collins, 1933.

HOOKER, J.K., *Black Revolutionary: George Padmore's Path from Communism to Pan-Africanism*, London, Pall Mall Press, 1967.

HOPKINS, A.G., *An Economic History of West Africa*, London, Longman, 1973.

HOWARD, R., *Colonialism and Underdevelopment in Ghana*, London, Croom Helm, 1978.

HOWE, S., *Anti-colonialism in British Politics: The Left and the End of Empire, 1918–1964*, Oxford, Clarendon Press,1993.

HOYNINGEN-HUENE, G., *African Mirage: The Record of a Journey*, London, B.T. Batsford, 1938.

HUTCHINSON, J. and SMITH, A.D. (eds) *Nationalism*, Oxford, Oxford University Press, 1994.

HUTTENBACK, R., *Racism and the Empire : While settlers and coloured Immigrants of the British Self Governing Colonies, 1830–1910*, Ithaka & London, Cornell UP, 1978.

HUXLEY J. and HADDON, A.C. (eds) *We Europeans: A Survey of Racial Problems, With a Chapter on Europe Overseas, by A.M. Carr Saunders*, London, Jonathon Cape, 1935.

HUXLEY, E., *Back Streets, New Worlds: A Look at Immigrants in Britain*, London, Chatto & Windus, 1964.

HUXLEY, E., *The Flame Trees of Thika: Memories of An African Childhood*, London, Chatto & Windus, 1959.

HUXLEY, E., *East Africa*, London, published for the Penns in the Rock Press by William Collins, 1941.

HUXLEY, E., *White Man's Country: Lord Delamere and the Making of Kenya*, 2 vols, London, Chatto & Windus, 1956, first published in 1935.

HYAM, R., *Empire and Sexuality: The British Experience*, Manchester, MUP, 1990.

JABAVU, D.D.T., *The Black Problem*, Lovedale, Lovedale Press, 1920.

JAMES, C.L.R., *A History of Pan-African Revolt*, London, M. Secker and Warburg, 1938.

JAMES, C.L.R., *World Revolution, 1917–1936: The Rise and Fall of the Communist International*, London, M. Secker and Warburg, 1937.

JAMES, C.L.R.and GRIMSHAW, A., *The C.L.R. James Reader*, London, Blackwell, 1992.

JAMES, L., *The Rise and Fall of the British Empire*, London, Little, Brown, 1994.

JAMES, L. (ed.) *The British Empire, 1497–1997: 500 Years that Shaped the World*, London, Telegraph Group, 1997.

JAYWARDENA, K., *The White Woman's Other Burden*, London, Routledge, 1995.

JEFFRIES, C., *The Colonial Empire and Its Civil Service*, with a foreword by the Rt Hon. Lord Harlech, Cambridge, CUP, 1938.

JEFFRIES, C., *The Colonial Office*, London, George Allen & Unwin, 1956.

JOHNS, S., *Raising the Red Flag: The International Socialist League and the Communist Party of South Africa, 1914–1932*, Belleville, Cape Town, Mayibuye Books, University of Western Cape, 1995.

JOHNSON, B., *I think of My Mother: Notes on the Life and Times of Claudia Jones*, London, Karia Press, 1985.

JOHNSTON, Sir H.H., *The Black Man's Part in the War*, London, Simkin, Marshall, Hamilton Kent & Co., 1917.

JONES, G.S., *Languages of Class; Studies in English working-class history, 1832–1982*, Cambridge, CUP, 1983.

JUDD, D., *Empire: The British Imperial Experience from 1765 to the Present*, London, Harper Collins, 1996.

JULY, R., *The Origins of Modern African Thought: Its Development in West Africa During the Nineteenth and Twentieth Centuries*, London, Faber, 1968.

KAARSHOLM, P. (ed.) *Cultural Struggle and Development in Southern Africa*, Oxford, James Currey, 1991.

KATZNELSON, I., *Black Men, White Cities: Race Politics and Migration in the United States, 1900–30 and Britain, 1948–68*, London, OUP, 1984.

KEDOURIE, E (ed.), *Nationalism in Asia and Africa*, London, Weidenfeld and Nicholson, 1971.

KEEGAN, T., *Colonial South Africa and the Origins of the Racial Order*, London, Leicester University Press, 1996.

KEEGAN, T., *Facing the Storm: Portraits of Black Lives in Rural South Africa*, Athens, Ohio University Press, 1988.

KENT, J., *British Imperial Strategy and the Origins of the Cold War, 1944–49*, London, Leicester UP, 1993.

KENT, J., *The Internationalisation of Colonialism: Britain, France and Black Africa, 1939–1956*, London, 1991.

KEYLOR, W.R. (ed.) *The Legacy of the Great War: Peacemaking, 1919*, Boston, New York, Houghton Mifflin, 1998.

KIDD, R., *British Liberty in Danger: An Introduction to the Study of Civil Rights*, with a foreword by Henry W. Nevinson, London, 1940.

KIERNAN, R.H., *General Smuts*, London, George G. Harrop & Company Ltd., 1943.

KIERNAN, V.G., *Imperialism and Its Legacies*, London and New York, Routledge, 1995.

KILLINGRAY, D.A. (ed.) *Africans in Britain*, London, Frank Cass, 1994.

KILLINGRAY, D.A. and RATHBONE, R. (eds) *Africa and the Second World War*, London, Macmillan, 1986.

KIMBLE, D., *A Political History of Ghana: the Rise of Gold Coast Naturalism, 1850–1928*, London, Clarendon Press,1963.

KLITGAARD, R., *Tropical Gangsters: One Man's Experience with Development and Decadence in Deepest Africa*, London, 1996.

KOHN, M., *The Race Gallery, The Return of Racial Science*, London, Cape, 1996.

KUKLICH, H., *The Imperial Bureaucrat: The Colonial Administrative Service in the Gold Coast 1920–1939*, Stansford, UCLA Press, 1979.

KUKLICH, H., *The Savage Within: The Social History of British Anthropology, 1885–1945*, Cambridge, CUP, 1991.

LACLAU, E., *Politics and Ideology in Marxist Theory: Capitalism, Facism and Populism*, London, NLB, 1977.

LAMAR, H. and THOMPSON, L., *The Frontier in History: North America and Southern Africa Compared*, Yale, Yale UP, 1982.

LANGLEY, J.A., *Pan-Africanism and Nationalism in West Africa 1900–1945*, Oxford, OUP, 1973.

LANSBURY, G. (ed.) *Labour's Way with the Commonwealth*, London, 1935.

LATOUCHE, S., *The Westernisation of the World: The Significance, Scope and Limits of the Drive Towards Global Conformity*, London, Polity Press, 1996.

LAUREN, P.G., *Power and Prejudice: the Politics and Diplomacy of Racial Discrimination*, 2nd edn, New York, Westview Press, 1996.

LAVIN, D., *From Empire to International Commonwealth: A Biography of Lionel Curtis*, Oxford, Clarendon Press, 1995.

LAW, I. and HUMPHREY, J. (eds) *A History of Race and Racism in Liverpool, 1666–1950*, Liverpool, CRE, 1981.

LAZERSON, J.N. *Against the Tide: Whites in the Struggle Against Apartheid*, Boulder, Westview, 1994.

LEE, J.M. and PETTER, M., *The Colonial Office, War and Development Policy: Organisation and the Planning of a Metropolitan Initiative, 1939–45*, London, Maurice Temple Smith, 1982.

LEGASSICK, M., *Class and Nationalism in South African Protest: The South African Communist Party and the 'Native' Republic, 1929–1934*, Syracuse, Syracuse UP, 1973.

LEITH-ROSS, S., *African Women: A Study of the Igbo of Nigeria*, London, Faber & Faber, 1939.

LEITH-ROSS, S., *Stepping Stones: Memoirs of Colonial Nigeria, 1907–1960*, edited by M. Crowder, London and Boston, Peter Owen, 1983.

LEMELLE, S.J. and KELLEY, R.D.G. (eds) *Imagining Home: Class, Culture and Nationalism in the African Diaspora*, London, Verso, 1994.

LENIN, V.I., *Imperialism: The Highest Stage of Capitalism: A Popular Outline*, New York, International Publishers, 1939 first published in 1916.

LERUMO, A., *Fifty Fighting Years – The Communist Party of South Africa, 1921–1971*, London, Inkululeko, 1971.

LEWIS, R. and WARNER-LEWIS, M. (eds) *Garvey, Africa, Europe, the Americas*, Kingston, 1986.

LEWSEN, P., *Voices of Protest*, Johannesburg, A.D. Donker, 1988.

LEYS, N., *The Colour Bar in East Africa*, London, Hogarth Press,1941.

LEYS, N., *A Last Change in Kenya*, London, L & V. Woolf, 1931.

LIPTON, M., *Capitalism and Apartheid: South Africa, 1910–1986*, Cape Town and Johannesburg, David Phillips Books, 1990.

LITTLE, K., *Negroes in Britain: A Study of Race Relations in English Society*, London, Routledge, Kegan & Paul, 1948.

LLOYD. T.O., *The British Empire, 1558–1995*, 2nd edn, Oxford, OUP, 1996.

LORAM, C.T., *The Education of the South African Native*, London, Longmans & Co, 1917.

LOTZ, R., and PEGG, D. (eds) *Under the Imperial Carpet: Essays in Black History 1780–1950*, London, Rabbit Press, 1986.

LOUIS, W.R., *Imperialism at Bay: The United States and the Decolonisation of the British Empire, 1941–1945*, Oxford, OUP, 1977.

LUGARD, F.C.D. *Political Memoranda: Revision of Instructions to Political Officers on Subjects Chiefly Political and Administrative, 1913–1918*, edited with an introduction by A.H.M. Kirk-Greene, London, Frank Cass, 1970.

LUGARD, Sir F.D., *The Dual Mandate in British Tropical Africa*, Edinburgh and London, William Blackwood & Sons, 1922.

LUNN, K., (ed.) *Race and Labour in Twentieth Century Britain*, London, Frank Cass, 1985.

LUNN, K. (ed.) *Hosts, Immigrants and Minorities: Historical Responses to Newcomers in British Society, 1870–1914*, London, William Dawson & Sons, 1980.

MACAULEY, D. J. (ed.) *Reconstructing Womanhood, Reconstructing Feminism*, London, Routledge, 1996.

MACINTYRE, S., *A Proletarian Science: Marxism in Britain 1917–1933*, London, OUP, 1979.

MACKENZIE, J.M. (ed.) *Imperialism and Popular Culture*, Manchester, MUP, 1987.

MACKENZIE, J.M., *The Empire of Nature: Hunting, Conservation and British Imperialism*, Manchester, MUP, 1988.

MACKENZIE, J.M., *Propaganda and Empire: The Mainpulation of British Public Opinion, 1880–1960*, Manchester, MUP, 1988.

MACKIE, L., *The Great Marcus Garvey*, London, Hansib Publishers, 1987.

MACMILLAN, H, and MARKS, S. (eds) *Africa and Empire: W.M. Macmillan, Historian and Social Critic*, London, Temple Smith, 1989.

MACMILLAN, W.M., *The Road to Self-Rule: A Study in Colonial Evolution*, London, Faber, 1959.

MACMILLAN, W.M., *Africa Beyond the Union*, Johannesburg, SAIRR, 1949.

MACMILLAN, W.M., *Democratise the Empire: A Policy of Colonial Reform*, London, Kegan Paul & Co., 1941.

MACMILLAN, W.M., *Africa Emergent: A Survey of Social, Political and Economic Trends in British Africa*, London, Faber & Faber, 1938.

MACMILLAN, W.M., *Warning from the West Indies: A Tract for Africa and the Empire*, London, Faber & Faber, 1936.

MACMILLAN, W.M., *Complex South Africa: An Economic Footnote to History*, London, Faber & Faber, 1930.

MACMILLAN, W.M., *Bantu, Boer and Briton: The Making of the South African Native Problem*, London, Faber & Gwyer, 1929.

MACMILLAN, W.M., *The Cape Colour Question: A Historical Survey*, London, Faber & Gwyer, 1927.

MACMILLAN, W.M., CHARLES, K., *et al.*, *Europe and West Africa: Some Problems and Adjustments*, Oxford, OUP, 1940.

MAGUBANE, B.M., *The Political Economy of Race and Class in South Africa*, New York, Monthly Review Press, 1979.

MAGUBANE, B.M., *The Round Table Movement: Its Influence on the Historiography of Imperialism*, Harare, Sapes, 1994.

MAGUBANE, B.M., *The Ties that Bind*, Trenton, Africa World Press, 1987.

MAIR, L., *Primitive Government*, London, Peter Smith, 1962.

MAIR, L., *Native Policies in Africa*, London, Routledge and Kegan Paul, 1936.

MALIK, K., *The Meaning of Race: Race, History and Culture in Western Society*, London, Macmillan, 1996.

MAMDANI, M., *Citizen and Subject: Contemporary Africa and the Legacy of Colonialism*, Princeton, Princeton University Press, 1996.

MANGAN, J. (ed.) *Benefits Bestowed? Education and British Imperialism*, Manchester, MUP, 1988.

MANNIN, E., *'Comrade O Comrade' or Low-down on the Left*, London, Jarrolds Ltd., 1947.

MANNONI, O., *Prospero and Caliban: The Psychology of Colonisation*, translated by P. Powesland, New York, Praeger, 1964.

MANSERGH, N., *South Africa, 1906–1961*, London, Allen & Unwin, 1962.

MANSERGH, N., *Survey of British Commonwealth Affairs: Problems of External Policy; 1931–1939*, London, Allen & Unwin, 1952.

MARAIS, J.S., *The Cape Coloured People 1652–1937*, London, Longmans, 1939.

MARKS, S. and RATHBONE, R. (eds) *Industrialisation and Social Change in South Africa: African Class Formation, Culture and Consciousness, 1870–1930*, London, Longmans, 1982.

MARKS, S. and TRAPIDO, S. (eds) *The Politics of Race, Class and Nationalism in Twentieth Century South Africa*, London, Longmans, 1987.

MARKS, S., *Divided Sisterhood: Race, Class and Gender in the South African Nursing Profession*, London, Macmillan, 1995.

MARKS, S., *The Ambiguities of Dependence in South Africa: Class, Nationalism and State in Twentieth Century Natal*, Baltimore and London, John Hopkins University Press, 1986.

MARSHALL, P.J., (ed.) *The Cambridge Illustrated History of the British Empire*, Cambridge, CUP, 1996.

MARWICK, B.A., *The Swazi: An Ethnographic Account of the Natives of the Swaziland Protectorate*, Cambridge, CUP, 1940.

MATTHEWS, B., *Consider Africa*, London, The Livingstone Press, 1935.

MATTHEWS, B., *The Clash of Colour: A Study in the Problem of Race*, London, Edinburgh House Press, 1936, first published 1924.

MAY, M., and WRIGHT, M. (eds) *African Women and the Law*, Boston, University of Boston Press, 1982.

MAZRUI, A. (ed.) *Africa Since 1935: From About 1935 to the Present*, London, Heinemann, 1993.

MAZRUI, A. and TIDY, M., *Nationalism and the New States in Africa*, London, Heinemann, 1984.

MBA, N.E., *Nigerian Woman Mobilised: Women's Political Activity in Southern Nigeria, 1900–1965*, Berkeley, University of California Press, 1982.

McCLINTOCK, A., *Imperial Leather: Race, Gender and Sexuality in the Colonial Contest*, London, Routledge, 1995.

MacCRONE, I.D., *Race Attitudes in South Africa: Historical, Experimental and Psychological Studies*, London and New York, OUP, 1937.

McCULLOCH, J., *Colonial Psychiatry and the African Mind*, New York and Cambridge, CUP, 1995.

McKENZIE, K.E., *The Comintern and World Revolution 1928–1943: The Shaping of Doctrine*, London and New York, Columbia University Press, 1964.

McPHEE, A., *The Economic Revolution in British West Africa*, London, Frank Cass, 1971, first published 1926.

MEADE, T. and WALKER, M., *Science, Medicine and Cultural Imperialism*, London, Macmillan, 1991.

MELI, F., *South Africa Belongs to Us: A History of the ANC*, Oxford, James Currey, 1989.

MEMMI, A., *The Coloniser and the Colonised*, London, Earthscan, 1990, first published in 1957.

MERLE DAVIS, J. (ed.) *Modern Industry and the African*, London, 1933.

MIDGLEY, C. (ed.) *Gender and Imperialism*, Manchester and New York, Manchester University Press, 1998.

MILLIN, S.G., *General Smuts*, London, Faber and Faber, 1936.

MILLIN, S.G., *God's Step-Children*, London, Faber and Faber, 1924.

MILES, R., *Racism after Race Relations*, London, Routledge, 1994.

MILLER, W.R., *Have We Failed in Nigeria?* London and Redhill, United Society for Christian Literature, Lutterworth Press, 1947.

MILLS, Lady D., RM., *Episodes from the Road to Timbuktu: The Record of a Woman's Adventurous Journey*, London, Duckworth, 1927.

MILLS, Lady D., RM., *The Golden Land: A Record of Travel in West Africa*, London, Duckworth, 1929.

MILLS, S., *Discourses and Difference: An Analysis of Women's Travel Writing and Colonialism*, London, Routledge, 1991.

MOCKERIE, P.G., *An African Speaks for his People*, with a foreword by Professor Julian Huxley, London, L. & V. Woolf, 1934.

MOLEAH, A.T., *South Africa: colonialism, apartheid and African dispossession*, Wilmington, Dice Press, 1993.

MOMMSEN, W.J. and OSTERHAMMEL, J. (eds) *Imperialism and After: Continuities and Discontinuities*, London, German Historical Institute, 1986.

MOREL, E.D., *The Black Man's Burden*, Manchester and London, National Labour Press, 1920.

MORGAN, D.J., *The Official History of Colonial Development*, London, Macmillan, 5 vols, 1980.

MORTON, J.M., *The Best of Beachcomber*, selected and introduced by Michael Frayn, London, Penguin, 1966.

MOSES W.J., *The Golden Age of Black Nationalism, 1850–1925*, New York, 1978.

MOUTON, F.A., *Voices in the Desert: Margaret and William Ballinger: a bibliography*, Pretoria, Benedict Books, 1997.

MUDIMBE, V.Y., *The Idea of Africa*, Oxford, James Currey, 1995.

MUMFORD, W.B., and ORDE BROWN, G.St.T., *Africans Learn to be French: A Review of Educational Activities in the Seven Federated Colonies of French West Africa, Based on a Tour of French West Africa Undertaken in 1935*, London, Evans Bros., 1937.

NANDY, A., *The Intimate Enemy: Loss and Recovery of Self Under Colonialism*, London and Delhi, OUP, 1988.

NGCOBO, L., *And They Didn't Die*, London, Virago, 1990.

NGUGI, Wa Thiongo, *De-Colonising the Mind*, Oxford, James Currey, 1986.

NGUGI, Wa Thiongo, *Moving the Centre: The Struggle for Cultural Freedoms*, Oxford, James Currey, 1993.

NICHOLLS, G.H., *The Problem of the Native in South Africa*, Pretoria, Government Printer, 1937.

NICHOLLS, G.H., *Bayete? 'Hail to the King'*, London, G. Allen & Unwin, 1923.

NICHOLSON, I.F., *The Administration of Nigeria 1900–1960: Men, Methods and Myths*, Oxford, OUP, 1969.

NORTON, A.J., *Dark Rapture: The Sex Life of the African Negro*, New York, Walden Publication, 1939.

NOTCUTT, L.A. and LATHAM, G.C., *The African and the Cinema. An Account of the Work of the Bantu Educational Cinema Experiment During the Period, March 1935 to May 1937*, London, 1937.

NZULA, A.T., Potekhin, I.I., Zusmanovitch, A.Z., *Forced Labour in Colonial Africa*, ed. and intro by R. Cohen, Zed Press, London, 1979, first published in Moscow in 1933.

OAKE, M.E., *No Place for a White Woman*, London, Duckworth, 1933.

OAKLEY, R., *Treks and Palavers*, London, Seeley, Service & Co., 1938.

OLDHAM, J.H. and GIBSON, B.D., *The Remaking of Man in Africa: On Christian Education in Africa*, London, OUP, 1931.

OLDHAM, J.H., *Christianity and the Race Problem*, London, Student Christian Movement, 1924.

OLIVER, R. and FAGE, J.D., *A Short History of Africa*, London, Penguin, 1988, sixth edition.

OLIVIER, S., *White Capital and Coloured Labour*, London, Hogarth Press, 1929.

OLIVIER, S., *Anatomy of African Misery*, London, Hogarth Press, 1927.

O'MEARA, D., *Volkskapitalisme: class, capital and ideology in the development of Afrikaner nationalism, 1934–1948*, Cambridge, CUP, 1983.

OMISSI, D.E., *Air Power and Colonial Control: The Royal Airforce, 1919–39*, Manchester, MUP, 1990.

OMU, Fred I.A., *Press and Politics in Nigeria, 1880–1939*, London, Longmans, 1978.

ORDE, A., *The Eclipse of Great Britain, the United States and British Imperial Decline, 1895–1956*, London, Macmillan, 1996.

ORDE-BROWN, G., St John, *Labour Conditions in the West Indies: Report by Major G. St. J. Orde Brown Presented by the Sec. of State for the Colonies to Parliament by Command of His Majesty,*, London, HMSO, 1939.

ORDE-BROWN, G., St John, *The African Labourer*, London, 1933.

OSAGHAE, E., *The Crippled Giant: Nigeria since Independence*, London, Hurst & Co., 1998.

OYONO, F., *Houseboy*, translated from the French by John Reed, London, Heinemann, 1966.

PADMORE, G., *Pan-Africanism or Communism? The Coming Struggle for Africa*, with a foreword by Richard Wright, London, Dennis Dobson, 1956.

PADMORE. G., *Africa: Britain's Third Empire*, New York, Negro Universities Press, 1969, first published, 1949.

PADMORE, G., *How Russia Transformed Her Colonial Empire: A Challenge to the Imperialistic Powers*, London, Dobson, 1946.

PADMORE, G. (ed.) *The Voice of Coloured Labour*, London, Pan -African Federation, 1945.

PADMORE, G., *Africa and World Peace*, London, Frank Cass, 1972, first published in 1937.

PADMORE, G., *How Britain Rules Africa*, London, Wishart Books, 1936.

PADMORE, G., *The Life and Struggles of Negro Toilers*, London, 1931.

PAGE, M. (ed.) *Africa and the First World War*, London, Macmillan, 1987.

PAKENHAM, T., *The Scramble for Africa, 1876–1912*, London, Abacus, 1992.

PANJAYI, P. (ed.) *Racial Violence in Britain in the Nineteenth and Twentieth Centuries*, Leicester, Leicester University Press, 1996.

PANJAYI, P., *Immigration, Ethnicity and Racism, 1890–1948*, London, MUP, 1994.

PARKINSON, C., *The Colonial Office From Within 1909–1945*, London, Faber & Faber, 1947.

PATON, A. *Cry, the Beloved Country: A Story of comfort in desolation* London, Penguin, 1944.

PATTERSON, S., *Dark Strangers: A Study of West Indians in London*, London, Tavistock,1962.

PEARCE, R.D.,*The Turning Point in Africa: British Colonial Policy 1938–1948*, London, Frank Cass,1982.

PEDLAR, Sir F. and BURNS, A., *The Lion and the Unicorn in Africa: The United Africa Co. 1787–1931*, London, Heinemann, 1974.

PERHAM, M., *Colonial Sequence, 1930–1949: A Chronological Commentary upon British Colonial Policy, Especially in Africa*, London, Methuen & Co. Ltd., 1967.

PERHAM, M., *The Colonial Reckoning from the Reith Lectures*, London, Collins, 1961.

PERHAM, M.,*Native Administration in Nigeria*, London, OUP, 1937.

PERHAM, M. (ed.) *Ten Africans*, London, Faber & Faber, 1936.

PERHAM, M., *Major Dane's Garden*, London, Rex Collins, 1970, first published in 1926.

PERHAM, M., and CURTIS, L., *The Protectorates of South Africa: the Question of Their Transfer to the Union*, London, OUP, 1935.

PHILLIPS, A., *The Enigma of Colonialism: An Interpretation of British Policy in West Africa*, Oxford, James Currey, 1990.

PHILLIPS, R.E., *The Bantu are Coming*, New York, Student Christian Movement Press, 1930.

PHILLIPS, R.E., *The Bantu in the City: A Study of Cultural Adjustment on the Witwatersrand*, Lovedale, Lovedale Press, 1938.

PIETERSIE, J.R.N., *White on Black: Images Of Africa And Blacks In Western Popular Culture*, New Haven and London, Yale University Press, 1992.

PIETERSIE, J.R.N., *Empire and Emancipation: Power and Liberation on a World Scale*, London, Pluto Press, 1990.

PILKINGTON, E., *Beyond the Mother Country: West Indians and the Notting Hill White Riots*, London, I.B Taurus & Co. Ltd., 1988.

PIMLOTT, B., *Labour and the Left in the 1930s*, Cambridge, CUP, 1977.

PLAATJE, S.T., *Native Life in South Africa*, Raven Press, Johannesburg, 1982, first published in 1922. With and Introduction by Brian William.

PLAATJE, S.T., Mhudi: and epic of Native Life a hundred years ago, London, Heinemann, 1978. First published in 1930.

PLAATJE, S., *Mafeking Diary: A Black Man's View of a White Man's War*, Oxford, James Currey, 1990, first published in 1901.

PORTER, B., *The Lion's Share: A Short History of British Imperialism, 1850–1995*, 3rd edn, London, Longman, 1996.

PORTER, B., *Critics of Empire: British Radical Attitudes to Colonialism in Africa, 1895–1914*, London, Macmillan, 1968.

PRAKASH, G. (ed.) *After Colonialism: Imperial Histories and Post Colonial Displacements*, Princeton, Princeton University Press, 1995.

PRATT, M.L., *Imperial Eyes: Travel Writing and Transculturation*, London, Routledge, 1992.

PULESTON, F., *African Drums*, London, Victor Gollancz, 1930.

QUIGLEY, C., *The Anglo-American Establishment: From Rhodes to Cliveden*, New York, Books in Focus, 1981.

RATTRAY, R.S., *Ashanti Laws and Constitutions*, Oxford, OUP, 1929.

RATTRAY, R.S., *Religion and Art in Ashanti*, Oxford, OUP, 1927.

RATTSANI, D. and A. (eds) *Race, Culture and Difference*, London, Sage, 1992.

REITZ, D., *No Outspan*, London, Faber & Faber, 1943.

REITZ, D., *Commando*, London, Faber & Faber, 1938.

RENSHAW, F. and MILLER, K.A., *Scottsboro: The Firebrand of Communism*, Montgomery, Alabama, Brown Printing Co., 1936.

REYNOLDS, R., *Beware of Africans: A Pilgrimage from Cairo to the Cape*, London, Jarrolds, 1955.

RICH, P., *State Power and Black Politics in South Africa,1912–51*, London, Macmillan, 1996.

RICH, P., *Hope and Despair: English Speaking Intellectuals and South African Politics, 1896–1976*, London, British Academic Press, 1993.

RICH, P., *Race and Empire in British Politics, 1890–1960*, Cambridge, Cambridge University Press, 1986.

RICH, P., *White Power and the Liberal Conscience: Racial Segregation and South African Liberalism, 1921 to 1960*, Manchester, MUP, 1984.

RICHARDS, J. (ed.) *The Age of the Dream Palace: cinema and society in Britain, 1930–1939*, London, Routledge & Kegan Paul, 1984.

RICHMOND, A.H., *Colour Prejudice in Britain: A Study of West Indian Workers in Britain, 1942–1954*, London, RKP, 1954.

ROBERTS, A.D. (ed.) *The Colonial Moment in Africa: Essays on the movement of minds and materials, 1900–1940*, Cambridge, CUP, 1986.

ROBERTS, B.C., *Labour in the Tropical Territories of the Commonwealth*, London, Hutchinson, 1962.

ROBINSON, C.J., *Black Marxism: The Making of the Black Radical Tradition*, London, Zed, 1984.

ROBINSON, K. *The Dilemmas of Trusteeship: aspects of British colonial policy between the wars*, London, OUP, 1965.

ROBINSON, R., *The Dilemmas of Trusteeship: Aspects of British Colonial Policy between the Wars*, London, OUP, 1965.

RODNEY, W., *How Europe Underdeveloped Africa*, London, Bogle l'ouverture, 1975.

ROGERS, J.A., *Sex and Race: Negro Caucasian Mixing in All Ages and All Lands*, 3 vols, New York, 1942–4, reprint, Helga M. Rogers, 1972. Also entitled *Sex and Race: A History of White, Negro and Indian Miscegenation in the Two Americas*, 1944 edition.

ROGERS, J.A., *The World's Great Men of Colour*, New York, J.A. Rogers, 1946.

ROPER, J.I., *Labour Problems in West Africa*, London, Penguin Books, 1958.

ROTBERG, R. and MAZRUI, A.A. (eds) *Protest and Power in Black Africa*, Harmondsworth, Penguin Books, 1970.

ROTBERG, R.J., *A Political History of Tropical Africa*, London, OUP, 1965.

ROTHERMUND, D., *The Global Impact of the Great Depression, 1929–1939*, London, Routledge, 1996.

ROUX, E., *Time Longer Than Rope: A History of the Black Man's Struggle for Freedom in South Africa*, Madison, University of Wisconsin Press, 1964, first published in London in 1948.

RUTHERFORD, J., *Forever England: Reflections on Race, Masculinity and Empire*, London, Lawrence & Wishart, 1997.

RYAN, J.R., *Picturing Empire: Photography and the Visualisation of the British Empire*, London, Reaktion Books, 1997.

SACHS, W., *Black Hamlet: The Mind of an African Negro Revealed by Psychoanalysis*, edited by S. Dubow and J. Rose, John Hopkins University Press, 1996, first published in 1937.

SAID, E.W., *Culture and Imperialism*, London, Vintage, 1993.

SARDAR, N., NANDY, A., WYNN DAVIES, M., *Barbaric Others: A Manifesto on Western Racism*, London and Boulder, Colorado, Pluto Press, 1993.

SBACCHI, A., *Ethiopia under Mussolini: Fascism and the Colonial Experience*, London, Zed, 1985.

SCHAPERA, I. (ed.) *Western Civilisation and the Natives of South Africa: Studies in Culture Contact*, London, Routledge and Sons Limited, 1934.

SCHAPERA, I., *Migrant Labour and Tribal Life: A Study of Conditions in the Bechuanaland Protectorate*, London, OUP, 1947.

SCHMIDT, P.R. and MCINTOSH, R.M. (ed.) *Plundering Africa's Past*, Bloomington, IN, Indiana University Press, 1996.

SCHWARTZ, B. (ed.) *The Expansion of England: Race, Ethnicity and Cultural History*, London, Routledge, 1996.

SEGAL, R., *The Race War: The World Wide Clash of White and Non-White*, New York, Bantam, 1967.

SEKYI, K., *The Blinkards: A Comedy*, with a foreword by H.V.H. Sekyi and an introduction by J. Ayo Langley, London, Heinemann Educational, 1974.

SHARP, A., *The Versailles Settlement: Peacemaking in Paris, 1919*, London, St Martin's Press, 1991.

SHERWOOD, M., *Kwame Nkrumah: The Years Abroad, 1935–1947*, Legon, Ghana, Freedom Publications, 1996.

SHERWOOD, M., *Pastor Ekarte and the African Churches Mission, Liverpool 1932–64*, London, Savanah Press, 1994.

SHERWOOD, M., *Many Struggles: West Indian Workers and Service Personnel in Britain 1939–1945*, London, Karina Press, 1985.

SIMONS, H.J. and R.E., *Class and Colour in South Africa, 1850–1950*, Harmondsworth, Penguin Books, 1969.

SINCLAIR, N.M.C., *The Tiger Bay Story*, Cardiff, Butetown History and Arts Project, 1993.

SIVANANDAN, A., *Race and Resistance: The IRR Story*, London, Race Today Publications, 1973.

SKLAR, R., *Nigerian Political Parties*, Princeton, Princeton UP, 1963.

SMITH, A. and BULL, M. (eds) *Margery Perham and British Rule in Africa*, London, Frank Cass, 1991.

SMITH, A., *State and Nation in the Third World: The Western State and African Nationalism*, Brighton, Wheatsheaf, 1983.

SMITH, E.W., *Aggrey of Africa: A Study in Black and White*, London, Student Christian Movement, 1929.

SMITH, G.A., *When Jim Crow met John Bull: Black American Soldiers in World War II*, London, IB Taurus, 1986.

SMITH, R.S., *Warfare and Diplomacy in Pre-Colonial West Africa*, Madison, University of Wisconsin Press, 1989.

SMITH, T., *The Pattern of Imperialism: The United States, Great Britain and the Late Industrialising World since 1915*, Cambridge, CUP, 1981.

SMUTS, J.C., *Africa and Some World Problems*, Oxford, The Claredon Press, 1930.

SOWELL, T., *Race and Culture: A World View*, New York, Basic Books, 1994.

SPENCER, I.R.G., *British Immigration Policy Since 1939: The Making of Multiracial Britain*, London, Routledge, 1997.

STASIULIS, D. and YUVAL-DAVIS, N. (eds) *Unsettling Settler Societies: Articulations of Gender, Race, Ethnicity and Class*, London, Sage, 1995.

STODDARD, L., *Clashing Tides of Colour*, New York and London, C. Scribner's Sons, 1935.

STODDARD, L., *The Rising Tide of Colour Against White World Supremacy*, London, 1935, first published in 1921.

STOLER, L.A., *Race and the Education of Desire: Foucault's History of Sexuality and the Colonial Order of Things*, London and Durham, Carolina, Duke University Press, 1995.

STRICHTER, S. and HAY, J., *African Women South of the Sahara*, London, Longman, 1984.

STROBEL, M., *European Women and the Second British Empire*, Bloomington, Indiana U.P., 1991.

SWATUK, L.A. and BLACK, R.D. (eds) *Bridging the Rift: The New South Africa in Africa*, Boulder Colorado, Westview Press, 1997.

TABATU, I.B., *The All African Convention: The Awakening of a People*, Johannesburg, People's Press, 1950.

TABILI, L., *We Ask for Justice: Workers and Racial Difference in Late Imperial Britain*, Ithaka, NY, London, Cornell U.P., 1994.

TATTERSALL, N., *The Forgotten Trade: Comprising the Log of Daniel and Henry of 1700 and Accounts of the Slave Trade from the Minor Ports of England, 1698–1725*, London, Jonathan Cape, 1991.

TATZ, C.M., *Shadow and Substance in South Africa: A Study in Land and Franchise Policies affecting Africans, 1910–1960*, Pietermaritzburg, University of Natal Press, 1962.

TAYLOR, P.M., *The Projection of Britain: British Overseas Publicity and Propaganda, 1919–1939*, Cambridge, CUP, 1981.

THOMAS, N., *Colonialism's Culture: Anthropology, Travel and Government*, London, Polity, 1994.

THOMPSON, V.B., *Africa and Unity: The Evolution of Pan-Africanism*, with a foreword by Basil Davidson, London, Longmans, 1969.

THORNTON, A.P., *The Imperial Idea and Its Enemies: A Study in British Power*, London, Macmillan, 1963.

THWAITE, D., *The Seething African Pot: A Study of Black Nationalism, 1882–1935*, London, Constable & Co., 1936.

TINKER, H., *Race, Conflict and the International Order*, London, Macmillan, 1979.

TLOU, T., PARSONS, N., and HENDERSON, W., *Seretse Khama, 1921–1986*, Bloemfontein, Macmillan, South Africa, 1995.

TOMLINSON, J., *Cultural Imperialism: A Critical Introduction*, London, Pinter Publishers, 1991.

TOYNBEE, A.J., *A Study of History*, 2nd edn, 3 vols, vol. 2, London, 1935.

UCHENDU, P.K., *The Role of Nigerian Women in Politics Past and Present*, Enugu, 4th Dimension Publishing Co., 1993.

VAIL, L. (ed.) *The Creation of Tribalism in Southern Africa*, Oxford, James Currey, 1989.

VAUGHAN, M., *Curing their Ills: Colonial Power and African illness*, Cambridge, Polity Press, 1991.

VAUGHN, D.A., *Negro Victory: The Life Story of Dr Harold Moody*, London, 1950.

VIGNE, R., *Liberals Against Apartheid: A History of the Liberal Party of South Africa, 1953–68*, London, Macmillan, 1997.

VON LAUE, T.H., *The World Revolution of Westernisation; The Twentieth Century in Global Perspective*, London, 1989.

WALKER, C. (ed.) *Women and Gender in Southern Africa to 1945*, Oxford, James Currey, 1990.

WALKER, C., *Women and Resistance in South Africa*, London, Onyx Press, 1982.

WALLACE, E., *Sanders of the River*, London and Melbourne, Ward, Lock & Co., n.d.

WALLERSTEIN, I., *Historical Capitalism with Capitalist Civilisation*, London, Verso, 1996.

WALROND, E., *Tropic Death*, New York, Boni & Liveright, 1926.

WALSHE, P., *The Rise of African Nationalism in South Africa: The African National Congress 1912–1952* Berkeley and Los Angeles, UCLA Press, 1971.

WALVIN, J., *Black and White: The Negro in English Society, 1555–1945*, London, Allen Lane, 1973.

WARE, V., *Beyond the Pale: White Women, Racism and History*, London, Verso, 1992.

WARREN, B., *Imperialism: Pioneer of Capitalism*, Cambridge, CUP, 1984.

WAUGH, E., *The Diaries of Evelyn Waugh*, edited by Michael Davie, London, Penguin, 1976.

WAUGH, E., *When the Going Was Good*, London, Penguin, 1968, first published by Duckworth in 1946.

WAUGH, E., *Waugh in Abyssinia*, London, Longmans Green, 1936.

WAUGH, E., *Black Mischief*, London, Chapman and Hall, 1948. First published in 1933.

WAUGH, E., *Decline and Fall*, London, 1928.

WEBSTER, J.B., BOAHEN, A.A. and TIDY, M., *The Revolutionary Years: West Africa since 1800*, London, Longman, 1981.

WEBSTER, W., *Imagining Home: Race, Class and National Identity, 1945–64*, London, UCL Press, 1997.

WELLOCK, W., *India's Awakening: Its National and World Wide Significance*, London, Labour Publishing Co.,1922.

WELLS, H.G., *Imperialism and the Open Conspiracy*, London, Faber & Faber, 1929.

WESSERLING, H., *The Partition of Africa, 1880–1914*, translated by A.J. Pomerans, London and Westport Conn., Praeger, 1996.

WESTERMANN, D., *The African Today*, New York and London, International African Institute, OUP, 1934.

WICKINS, P.L., *The Industrial and Commerical Workers' Union of South Africa*, Cape Town, OUP, 1978.

WILKES, I., *One Nation, Many Histories, Ghana Past and Present*, Accra, Ghana Universities Press, 1996.

WILLAN, B., *Sol Plaatje: South African Nationalist 1876–1932*, London, Heinemann, 1984.

WILLIAMS, P., *Seeing a Colour Blind Future*, London, Virago, 1997.

WILSON, E.T., *Russia and Black Africa Before World War II*, London and New York, Holmes and Meier Publishers Ltd, 1976.

WILSON, H.S. *African Decolonisation*, London, Edward Arnold, 1994.

WILSON, H.J., *The Origins of West African Nationalism*, London, Macmillan, 1969.

WINKS, R., *The Imperial Revolution: Yesterday and Tomorrow*, London, Clarendon Press, 1994.

WOLPE, H., *Race, Class and the Apartheid State*, Oxford, James Currey, 1988.

WOLTON, D.G., *Whither South Africa*, London, Lawrence & Wishart, 1947.

WOOLF, L., *Empire and Commerce in Africa – A Study in Economic Imperialism*, London, Labour Research Department, George Allen & Unwin, 1920.

WOOLF, L., *Imperialism and Civilisation*, London, Hogarth Press, 1928.

WORDEN, N., *The Making of Modern South Africa*, London, Blackwell, 1994.

YOUNG, F.B., *In South Africa*, London, William Heinemann Ltd., 1952.

YOUNG, J.W., *Britain and the World in the Twentieth Century*, London, Arnold, 1997.

YOUNG, R.J.C, *Colonial Desire: Hybridity in Theory, Culture and Race*, London, Routledge, 1992.

YOUNG, R.J.C., *White Mythologies: Writing History and the West*, London, Routledge, 1990.

WRIGHT, S.P., *Living in an Old Country: The National Past in Contemporary Britain*, London, Verso, 1995.

YUDELMAN, D., *The Emergence of Modern South Africa: State, Capital and the Incorporation of organised Labour on the South African Goldfields, 1872–1930*, Cape Town and Johannesburg, David Phillips Books, 1983.

Autobiographies, memoirs and letters

AWO: The Autobiography of Chief Obafemi Awolowo, Cambridge, CUP, 1960.

AZIKIWE, N., *My Odyssey: An Autobiography*, London, G. Hurst, 1970.

BALLINGER, Margaret, *From Union to Apartheid: A Trek to Isolation*, Folkestone, Bailey Bros and Swinfen Ltd, 1969.

BASNER, H.M., *Am I an African? The Political Memoirs of H.M. Basner*, with a foreword by T. Lodge and M. Basner, Johannesburg, Johannesburg University Press, 1993.

BRITTAIN, V. and HANDLEY-TAYLOR, G. (eds) *Selected Letters of Winifred Holtby and Vera Brittain, 1920–1935*, London, A. Brown, 1960.

BROCKWAY, Fenner, *Inside the Left: 30 Years of Platform, Press, Prison and Parliament*, London, G. Allen & Unwin, 1942.

BURNS, Sir A., *Colonial Civil Servant*, London, G. Allen & Unwin, 1949.

CAMERON, Sir D., *My Tanganyika Service and Some Nigeria*, London, G. Allen & Unwin, 1939.

ENAHORO, Chief A., *Fugitive Offender: The Story of a Political Prisoner*, London, Cassell, 1965.

FURSE, Major Sir R., *Aucuparius: Recollections of a Recruiting Officer*, Oxford, OUP, 1962.

GRAVES, A.M. (ed.) *Both Deeper than and above the Mêlée – Letters from Europeans*, Baltimore, privately printed in 1945.

GRAVES, A.M. (ed.) *Benvenuto Cellini Had No Prejudice Against Bronze: Letters from West Africans*, Baltimore, privately printed in 1943.

HARDY, G., *Those Stormy Years*: Memories of the fight for freedom on five continents, London, Lawrence & Wishart, 1956.

KADALIE, C., *My Life and the ICU*, edited with an introduction by S. Trapido, London, Frank Cass, 1970.

LASSON, F. (ed.) *Isak Dinesen: Letters from Africa, 1914–1931*, London, Pan, 1981.

MACKAY, C., *A Long Way From Home: An Autobiography* with an introduction by St Clair Drake, New York, 1970.

MACMILLAN, W.M., *My South African Years: An Autobiography*, Cape Town, David Philips, 1975.

MAKONNEN, R., *Pan-Africanism from Within*, as recorded and edited by Kenneth King, London, OUP, 1973.

MARKE, E., *Old Man Trouble*, London, Wiedenfeld and Nicholson, 1975.

NKRUMAH, K., *Ghana; the Autobiography of Kwame Nkrumah*, London, Thos. Nelson and Sons,1957.

NOEL, C., *An Autobiography*, London, J. M. Dent & Sons, 1945.

PERHAM, M., *African Apprenticeship: An Autobiographical Journey in Southern Africa, 1929*, London, Faber, 1974.

POLLITT, H., *Serving My Time: An Apprenticeship to Politics*, London, Lawrence & Wishart, 1940.

PRINCESS MARIE LOUISE, *Letters from the Gold Coast*, London, Methuen & Co. Ltd., 1926.

ROBESON, P. with L.L. Brown, *Here I Stand*, Boston, Beacon Press, 1988, first published in 1958.

Paul Robeson: Writing, Speeches and Interviews, 1919–1947, edited and with an introduction by P.S. Foner, London, 1978.

ROUX, E.W., *Rebel Pity: the Life of Eddie Roux*, London, Rex Collings, 1970.

SAVILLE, J. and BELLAMY, J. (eds) *Dictionary of Labour Biography*, 9 vols, London, Macmillan, 1972–93.

SCOTT, M., *A Time to Speak*, London, Doubleday, 1958.

Document collections

ASHTON, S.R. and STOCKWELL, S.E. (eds) *British Documents on the End of Empire*, volume 1: *Imperial Policy and Colonial Practice, 1925–1945*, Part 2, London, HMSO and Institute of Commonwealth Studies, 1996.

KARIS, T. and CARTER, G.M.. (eds) *From Protest to Challenge: A Documentary History of African Politics in South Africa, 1882–1964*, 4 vols, Stansford, California, Hoover Institution Press, 1972–7.

LANGLEY, J.A., *Ideologies of Liberation in Black Africa, 1856–1970; Documents on Modern African Political Thought from Colonial Times to the Present*, London, R. Collings, 1979.

MANSERGH, N. (ed.) *Documents and Speeches on British Commonwealth Affairs, 1931–1952*, 2 vols, London, OUP, 1953.

Articles

ADI, H., 'The Communist Movement in West Africa' in *Science and Society*, special issue titled, 'Communism in Britain and the British Empire', 1997, 61 (1): 94–9.

ADI, H., 'West African Students in Britain 1900–60: The Politics of Exile' in *Immigrants and Minorities*, 1993, 12 (3): 28–41.

AKYEAMPONG, E., 'What's in a Drink? Class Struggle, Popular Culture and the Politics of *Akpeteshie* (local gin), in Ghana, 1930–67' in *Journal of African History*, 1996, 37: 215–36.

AJAYI, A., 'The Continuity of African Institutions under Colonialism' in T.O. Ranger (ed.) *Emerging Themes on African History*, London, 1968.

ALI, J., 'Racism, Colonialism and the Cinema' in *Screen*, January – February 1983, 24 (2): 89–107.

ARNOT (Comrade), 'The British Minority Movement and its Tasks in the Field of Colonial Work' in *RILU Magazine*, February 1932, 2 (3): 207.

ASECHEMIE, D.P.S., 'African Labour Systems, Maintenance Accounting and Agency Theory' in *Critical Perspectives on Accounting*, 1997, 8: 373–92.

AZIKIWE, B.N., 'Murdering Women in Nigeria' in *The Crisis*, May 1930, 37: 163–6.

BANK, Andrew, 'The Great Debate and the Origins of South African Historiography' *Journal of African History*, 1997, 38; 261–281

BANTON, M., 'The Black Man in London in the Early 1930s: A Note on Some Novels' in *Immigrants and Minorities*, 1995, 14 (2): 195–9.

BARRATT BROWN, M., 'An African Road for Development: Are We All Romantics?' in *Leeds African Studies Bulletin*, December 1997, 62: 13–41, 30.

BEALL, J., HASSIM, S. and TRADES, A., 'A bit on the Side? Gender Struggles in the Politics of Transformation in South Africa' in *Feminist Review*,1989, 33: 24B. Bush, 'The Dark Side of the City: Representations of Black London in the 1950s', conference paper in *City Limits Conference*, Staffordshire University, 11–14 September 1996.

BELOFF, M., 'The British Empire' in *History Today*, February, 1996, 46 (2).

BIRKETT, D., 'The Great Pretender' in the *Guardian Weekend*, 13 December 1997.

BOURNE, J., 'Ombudsmen and Cheerleaders, the Sociology of Race Relations in Britain' in *Race and Class*, Spring 1980, 21 (4): 331–53.

BRITTAIN, V., 'Ghana's Precarious Revolution' in *New Left Review*, 1983, 140: 51–61.

BUSH, B., 'History, Memory, Myth? Reconstructing the History (or Histories) of Black Women in the African Diaspora' in S. Newell (ed.) *Images of African and Caribbean Women: Migration, Displacement, Diaspora*, Centre for Commonwealth Studies, University of Stirling, Occasional Paper, November, 1992, no. 4.

BUSH, B., 'Britain's Conscience on Africa': White Women, Race and Imperial Politics in Inter War Britain' in C. Midgley (ed.) *Gender and Imperialism*, Manchester, MUP, 1997.

CLAYTON, A., Review of *The New Ideology of Imperialism* in the *Journal of Imperial and Commonwealth History*, 1995, 23: 185–7.

CLIFFE, L. and SEDDON, D., 'Africa in a New World Order' in *Review of African Political Economy*, 1991, 50: 3–12.

COOPER, W. and REINDERS, R.C., 'Black Britain Comes "Home": Claude Makay in England, 1920' in *Race*, July 1967, 19 (1): 67–85.

CROWDER, M., 'Whose Dream was it Anyway? Twenty-Five Years of African Independence' in *African Affairs*, 1986, 342 (2): 7–20.

DARBY, P., 'Taking Fieldhouse Further: Post-Colonising Imperial History' in *Journal of Imperial and Commonwealth History*, 1998, vol. (2): 323–50.

DARBYSHIRE, N., 'Darkness over empire' in *Daily Telegraph*, 26 August 1997.

DREW, A., 'Writing South African Communist History' in *Science and Society*, 1997, 61 (1):107–13.

DUFFIELD, I., 'Review Article: Pan-Africanism, Rational and Irrational' in *Journal of African History*, 1977, 18 (4): 597–620.

ELKINS, N.F., 'Unrest Among the Negroes: A British Document of 1919' in *Science and Society*, 1968, 32 (1): 66–79.

ELLIOT, W., 'Impressions of a Tourist in West Africa' in *Empire Review*, 1928, 48: 169–76.

EVANS, N., 'Regulating the Reserve Army: Arabs, Blacks and the Local State in Cardiff, 1919–1945' in *Immigrants and Minorities*, 1985, 4 (2).

FEINBERG, H.M., 'The 1913 Natives Land Act in South Africa: Politics, Race and Segregation in the Early 20th Century' in *The International Journal of African Historical Studies*, 1993, 26 (1): 65–109.

FERRIS, J.R., 'The Greatest Power on Earth: Great Britain in the 1920s' in *International History Review*, 1991, 14 (4): 739–52.

FLINT, J., 'Scandal at the Bristol Hotel: Some Thoughts on Racial Discrimination in Britain and West Africa and its Relationship to the Planning of Decolonisation, 1939–1947' in *The Journal of Imperial and Commonwealth History*, 1983, 12 (1): 74–93.

GARIGUE, P., 'The West African Student's Union: A Study in Culture Contact' in *Africa*, 1953, 23 (1): 55–79.

GOULBOURNE, H., 'Black Workers in Britain' in *The African Review*, 1977, 7(2): 63–75.

HAGGIS, J., 'Gendering Colonialism or Colonising Gender? Recent Women's Studies Approaches to White Women and the History of British Colonialism' in *Women's Studies International Forum*, 1990, 13(1/2): 105–15.

HAILEY, Sir M., 'Nationalism in Africa' in *Journal of the Africa Society*, April 1937, 36: 134–47.

HALL, C., 'The ruinous ghost of empire past' in *The Times Higher*, 18 March 1996.

HALL, S., 'Racism and Reaction' in *Five Views of Multiracial Britain*, London, Commission for Racial Equality, 1978

HAYES, P., ' "Cocky" Hahn and the "Black Venus": The Making of a Native Commissioner in South West Africa, 1915–46' in *Gender and History*, 1996 (8) 3.

HELLINGER, D., 'US Aid Policy in Africa: No Room for Democracy' in *Review of African Political Economy*, 1992, 55.

HOBSBAWM, E., 'To see the future look at the past' in *The Guardian*, 7 June 1997.

HOOKS, B., 'Representing Whiteness in the Black Imagination' in L. Grossberg, C. Nelson, P.A. Treichler (eds) *Cultural Studies*, London and New York, Routledge, 1992, pp. 338–46, p. 339.

HOPKINS, A.G., 'Big Business in African Studies' in *The Journal of African History*, 1987, 28 (2): 119–40.

HOWE, S., 'David Fieldhouse and Imperialism: Some Historiographical Revisions' in *Journal of Imperial and Commonwealth History*, 1998, vol., (2): 213–32.

HYAM, R., 'Africa and the Labour Government, 1945–1951' in *Journal of Imperial and Commonwealth History*, 1988, 16 (2): 149–56.

ISRAEL, A.M., 'Measuring the War Experience of Ghanaian Soldiers in World War II' in *Journal of Modern African Studies*, 1987, 25 (1): 159–68.

JAMES, C.L.R., 'A History of Negro Revolt', in *Fact*, September 1938, 18: 1–72.

JEWSIEWICKI, B. and MUDIMBE, V.Y. 'Africans' Memories and Contemporary History of Africa' in *History and Theory*, 1993 32 (4).

JOHNSTON, Sir H.H. 'Africa and South America' in *The Nineteenth Century and After*, July, 1918, XXV: 181–94, 187.

KAYE, H.J., 'Imperialism and its legacies' in the introduction to V.G. Kiernan, *Imperialism and Its Legacies*, London and New York, Routledge, 1995.

KENNEDY, D., 'Imperial history and post-colonial theory' in *Journal of Imperial and Commonwealth History*, September 1996, 24 (3).

KILLINGRAY D.A., 'A Swift Agent of Government: Air power in British Colonial Africa, 1916–1939' in *Journal of African History*, 1984, 25 (2): 125–48.

KING, A., 'Pride and a fall in knowledge of empire', *Daily Telegraph*, 26 August 1997.

KIRK-GREENE, A., 'Sanders of the River' in *New Society*, 1977, 788 (42): 308–9.

LEGASSICK, M., 'Race, Industrialisation and Social Change in South Africa: the Case of R.F.A. Hoenlé' in *African Affairs*, 1975–6, 74, (293): 48–67.

LEVINE, M.J.O., 'Communism and South African Native: A French View' in *African Observer*, October 1935, 3 (6): 29–33.

LEWIN, J., 'Leonard Barnes: The Man and His Books, Review Article' in *African Affairs*, October 1975, 74 (292): 485–84.

LEYS, N., 'The Tropics and the League of Nations' in *Socialist Review*, Jan.–March 1921, 2 (1): 28–35.

LOUIS, W.R. and ROBINSON, R., 'The Imperialism of Decolonisation' in *Journal of Imperial and Commonwealth History*, 1994, 22 (3): 462–511.

MACDONALD, R.J., 'Dr Harold Arundel Moody and the League of Coloured Peoples, 1931–1947: A Retrospective View' in *Race*, 1973, 14 (3): 291–310.

MAIR, L., 'A Science of Colonial Government' in *Contemporary Review*, January 1934, 145: 8–88.

MANNONI, O., 'The Decolonisation of Myself' in *Race*, 1966, 7 (4): 327–45.

MARKS, S., 'History, the Nation and Empire – Sniping from the Periphery' in *History Workshop*, Spring 1990, 29: 111–19.

MARX, K. and ENGELS, F., 'The manifesto of the communist party' in *Selected Works in One Volume*, London, 1968.

MARKS, S. and TRAPIDO, S., 'Lord Milner and the South African State' in *History Workshop Journal*, 1979, 2: 70.

MARTIN, A., 'Old Ally renews Ethiopian Courtship' in the *Guardian*, Tuesday, 4 June 1996.

MARTIN, T., 'C.L.R. James and the Race/Class Question' in *Race*, 1972, 14(2): 183–93.

MATTHEWS, S.K., 'An African View of Indirect Rule in Africa' in *Journal of the Royal African Society*, 1937, 36 (145): 433–37.

MAY, R. and COHEN, R., 'The Interaction between Race and Colonialism: A Case Study of the Liverpool Race Riots of 1919' in *Race and Class*, 1974, 26 (3): 276–281.

McKERCHER, 'Great Britain Pre-eminent in the 1930s' in *International History Review*, 1991, 14 (4): 751.

MEISENHELDER, T., 'Marx, Engels, and Africa' in *Science and Society*, Summer 1995, 59 (2): 197–205.

MOUTON, F.A., ' "A cusser when crossed": the turbulent career of William Ballinger' in *Kleio*, 1995, XXVII, pp. 145–64.

MUNZENBERG, W., 'The Frankfurt Conference of the LAI' in *Imprecorr*, 9 August 1929, 9 (38): 813–15.

NEWBERRY, C., 'The Imperial Workplace: Competitive and Coerced Labour Systems in New Zealand, Northern Nigeria, and Australian New Guinea' in S.M. Marks and P. Richardson (eds) *Studies in International Labour Migration*, London, 1983.

NICHOLSON, D., 'Nostalgia for Empire: Decolonisation of a British Empire of the Mind' in *The Listener*, 16 December 1972, 87: 119–29.

NORA, P., 'Between Memory and History: *Les Lieux de Memoire*' in *Representations*, Spring 1989, 26: 7–24.

OKONKWO, R.L., 'The Garvey Movement in British West Africa' in *Journal of African History*, 1980, 21(2): 105–17.

OLUKOJU, A., 'Race and Access to Liquor: Prohibition as Colonial Policy in Northern Nigeria, 1919–45' in *The Journal of Imperial and Commonwealth History*, 1996, 24 (2): 218–43.

OMU, F.I.A., 'The Dilemma of Press Freedom in Colonial Africa: the West African Example' in *Journal of African History*, 1968, 9 (2): 280–98.

PADMORE, G., 'The British Empire is the Worst Racket Yet Invented by Man' in *New Leader*, 15 December 1939, p. 3.

PADMORE, G., 'Race Prejudice in Britain' in *Negro Worker*, March 1932, 2 (3): 2–3.

PADMORE, G., 'Africans Harassed by Imperialists' in *Negro Worker*, May 1929, 2 (2): 3.

PALLISTER, D., 'The Shadow of Justice' in the *Guardian*, 11 June 1998.

PERHAM, M., 'African Facts and American Criticisms' in *Foreign Affairs*, April 1944, 22 (3).

PERHAM, M., 'Black and White in Africa' in *The Listener*, 28 March 1934.

PINES J., 'British Cinema and Black Representation' in R. Murphy (ed.) *The British Cinema Book*, London, British Film Institute Publishing, 1997.

REINDERS, R.C., 'Racialism on the Left: E.D. Morel and the 'Black Horror' on the Rhine' in *International Review of Social History*, 1968, 13 (1): 1–24.

RHODES JAMES, R. 'Now that the sun has gone down' in *The Times*, 4 September 1995.

RHODIE, S., 'The Gold Coast Aborigines Abroad' in *Journal of African History*, 1965, 4 (3): 389–408.

RICHARDS, D., 'The Man died in africa95' in *Review of African Political Economy*, 1996, 68 (23): 139–47.

RILEY, S.P., 'The Political Economy of Anti-Corruption Strategies in Africa' in *European Journal of Development Research*, 1998, 10 (1): 129–43.

ROBERTS, A. 'Africa on Film to *c.*1940' in *History in Africa*, 1987, 14 (2): 189–227.

ROBINSON, R., 'The Moral Disarmament of the African Empire, 1919–1947' in *Journal of Imperial and Commonwealth History*, 1979, 8 (2): 86–104.

ROTH, M., ' "If you give us rights we will fight": Black involvement in the Second World War' in *South African Historical Journal*, 1983, XV: 85–104.

SAVISHINSKY, N.J., 'Transnational Popular Culture and the Global Spread of the Jamaican Rastafarian Movement' in *New West India Guide/Neue West-Indische Gids*, 1994, 68 (3 & 4): 259–28.

SCHWARTZ, B., ' "The Only White Man in There": the Re-racialisation of England, 1956–1968' in *Race and Class*, 1996, vol. 38.

SHALOFF, S., 'Press Controls and Sedition Proceedings in the Gold Coast, 1933–39' in *African Affairs*, 1972, 71: 241–63.

SHERWOOD, M., 'Diplomatic Platitudes: The Atlantic Charter, The United Nations and Colonial Independence' in *Immigrants and Minorities*, 1996, 15 (2): 135–50.

SMILOWITZ, E., 'Una Marson: Woman Before Her Time' in *Jamaica Journal*, May 1993.

SPENCER, I.R.G., 'The Open Door: Labour Needs and British Immigration Policy, 1945–55' in *Immigrants and Minorities*, 1996, 15 (1): 22–40.

SPITZER, L. and DENZER, L.R., 'I.T.A. Wallace-Johnson and the West African Youth League' in *The International Journal of African Historical Studies*, 1973, pts.1 & 2, 4 (3 & 4): 431–63, 565–601.

STOLER, A.L., 'Rethinking colonial categories: European communities and the boundaries of rule' in *Comparative Studies in Society and History*, 1989, 31: 135–6.

SZEFTEL, M., 'Ethnicity and Democratisation in South Africa' in *Review of Political Economy*, 1994, 21 (61): 185–99.

TABILI, L., 'Labour Migration, Racial Identity and Class Identity. Some Reflections of the British Case' in *North West Labour History*, 1995/96, 20: 16–36.

TOOLE, J., 'GIs and the Race Ban in Wartime Warrington' in *History Today*, July 1993, 43, p. 7, 22–5.

TOTHILL, F.D., 'White Man's Country: An Aspect of Mid-twentieth century Australia' in *Kleio*, XXVII, 1995, pp. 165–95.

VAN ALLEN, J. ' "Sitting on a man": Colonialism and the Lost Political Institutions of Igbo Women' in *Canadian Journal of African Studies*, 1972, VI (ii): 151–79.

VAN ONSELEN, C., 'Worker Consciousness in Black Miners: Southern Rhodesia, 1900–1920' in *Journal of African History*, 1973, XIV (2): 237–56.

WALKER, C., 'Women, "Tradition" and Reconstruction' in *Review of African Political Economy*, 1994, 61: 51–63.

WARE, V., ' "Moments of Danger: Race, Gender and Memories of Empire" in *History and Theory*, 1992, 31(4): 123–4.

WATERS, C., ' "Dark Strangers", in Our Midst: Discourses of Race and Nation in Britain, 1947–1963' in *The Journal of British Studies*, 1997, 36: 208–32.

WATKINS, W.A., 'Pan-Africanism and the politics of education' in Lemelle and Kelley (eds) *Imagining Home*.

WINTER, J.M., 'The Webbs and the non-white world: a Case of Socialist racialism' in *Journal of Contemporary History*, 1974, 9(1): 181–204.

YEARWOOD, P.J., 'The Expatriate Firms and the Colonial Economy of Nigeria in the First World War' in *The Journal of Imperial and Commonwealth History*, 1998, 26 (1): 49–71.

ZACK-WILLIAMS, A., 'African Development and African Diaspora: Separate Concerns?' in *Review of African Political Economy*, 1995, 65 (22): 349–58.

Index

Abdurahman, Dr. A. 135, 149, 165, 169
Abrahams, P. 155, 177, 318 n74
Abysinnian Association 222
Abysinnian Refugees Relief Fund 258
Abyssinia 3, 43, 256, 258; *see also* Ethiopia
Accountancy 33, 153, 185, 231; African
  systems of 185; colonial 65
Accra 59, 75, 78, 109
Achimota College, Gold Coast, 78, 97–8,
  120
Achebe, Chinua 101
Act of Union (South Africa) 1910; 133
Adi, H. 119, 217, 221, 239, 242, 243
Africa; alcohol in 39–40, 51, 60, 66, 149,
  164–5; investment in 23, 49; Islam in
  59, 114; western conceptions of 5,
  28–33, 38–40, 82, 254, 268, 274–5; in
  British popular culture 31–3, 50–2, 74,
  268; white mythologies of 29; *see also*
  West Africa, South Africa
Africa House Defence Committee 221
African; crisis 273; culture 53, 68–9, 95,
  210, 216, 274–5; development 192,
  193–5, 249, 253–5, 259–67, 269,
  272–3, 275; grievances 34, 104–20,
  135, 137–8, 143, 150, 176, 187, 191,
  195, 261, 263, 269; oral traditions and
  history 53–4; patriarchy 90–1, 151,
  192; secret societies 68, 90; states 125
African Churches Mission 210, 230
African diaspora 5, 7, 9, 14–15, 18, 43,
  102, 121, 161, 176, 206, 211, 214, 220,
  227, 236, 239, 254, 257, 266, 271–7; in
  Britain 205–27;
African Education Commission 159
African intelligentsia, 34–5, 103, 114,
  120–2, 174, 215, 254–5
African labour 33–4, 55, 56, 98, 104–14,
  140, 176, 266–7; convict 63; female 63;

forced 104, 123; and labour unrest 255,
  267; peasant producers 34, 102, 104–8,
  132, 146, 191; and proletarianisation of
  104–5, 132, 155
African Monroe Doctrine 41, 201
African Morning Post 117
African National Congress (ANC) 149,
  150, 151, 152, 154, 157, 159–160, 161,
  163–5, 167, 169, 171–4, 176–9, 216;
  delegations to Britain 138, 154, 230;
  Youth League 176; women's section
  150 *see also* South African Native
  National Congress
African nationalism and nationalists 2, 5,
  34, 102, 111–12, 119–22, 125–6, 176,
  195, 200, 211, 219, 221, 225, 243–4,
  247, 249, 254–6, 261, 264, 266–9; in
  Britain 211, 221, 243, 264; in West
  Africa 95, 102, 104, 108, 120–8
African Peoples Organisation (APO)
  135–7, 165
African renaissance 6, 198
African Sentinel 112, 118
African women 72–3, 78, 88–93, 103,
  150–1, 158, 175, 254, 273; contribution
  to urban culture 140–2; grievances 64,
  150, 174; impact of colonial rule upon
  89–92, 94; and nationalism 126, 150,
  175; and resistance 64–5, 90, 92, 103,
  148, 158, 164; West African market
  women 94, 78, 90, 92, 103; white
  representations of 79, 87–9, 143, 145,
  263
African Workers Club (Durban) 167–8
Africanisation 97–8, 265
Africanism 158, 160, 165, 169, 200
Africanists 253, 269; networks in Britain
  252; and African studies 21, 35–6, 187
Afrikaner(s) 131, 134, 140–2, 144, 196,

199–200; ethnicity; 140; expansionism 191; nationalism 42, 140, 161–2, 175, 176–7, 201; and 'Purified' Nationalists 140, 179 (*see also* Malan, D. F.); republics and republicanism 133–4, 138, 182
Afrikaner Broederbond 140
Afrikaner National Party (NP)140, 161, 192, 196
Aggrey House, London 220–1, 232, 239; and WASU 220–1
Aggrey, Dr. Kwegyir 97–8, 159, 220
Ajayi, A. 102
Akyeampong, E. 39, 66, 103
Aliens Order, 1905; 207
Aliens Registration Scheme 239
Aliens Restriction Order; 1919, 1920; 207
All African Convention (AAC) 172–3, 175, 176; involvement of African women 175; and 'Sons of Young Africa' 176
Allen, C. 49
Amalaita 150, 167 *see also* Zulu
American Board Mission, 153
American Communist Party; and anti-lynching campaigns 239; and Black Republic 166; and Scottsboro Affair 239–40
Amery, Leo 259
Anderson, D. ('Mrs Garland Anderson); and interracial marriages 212
Anglo-American cooperation 40–2, 267 *see also*, Round Table Movement
Anglo-Asante Wars 65, 93
anglosaxonism 4, 11, 21, 23, 34
Anthias, F. 7–8, 79, 151, 244
Anthony, D. 160–1
anthropology and anthropologists 6, 10, 13 35–8, 60, 69, 78, 120, 216, 229, 246, 265; British School of 35–7, 188; and cultural relativism 10–11; colonial officers as 36, 60; and gentlemanly order 37; popular; 37–8; in South Africa 37, 141, 152, 188; in United States 37; women's involvement in 36–8, 81, 90, 265, 340 n61
anti-colonialism and anti-colonial activists16, 121, 195, 198, 248, 255, 268–9; and nationalism 5, 11–12, 43, 101–2, 211, 217, 225, 261, 272
anti-communism 24, 181–3, 186, 234–5, 238, 258, 261, 267
anti-fascism 43, 240–1
anti-imperialism 2, 7, 12, 16, 38, 42, 43–6,

228, 237–9, 244, 247, 250, 272; in Africa 123–7, 176, 193, 261; in Britain 123, 236–44, 255
Anti-Imperialist Review 241
anti-racism 12, 43–6
anti-semitism 28, 242
anti-slavery 30–1, 39, 235, 272
anti-westernism 22, 43
Apartheid 131–3, 150–1, 157, 161, 165, 171, 179–80, 195, 201, 275–6 (*see also* segregation)
appeasement 258–61
Ariston Gold Mines Ltd. 111–12
Arrighi, G. xiii, 3
Ashanti Gold Fields Corporation, 67, 110–11
Ashcroft, Peggy 212
Asians in Britain 205; Chinese 211, 232
assimilation 10, 34, 246
Association for European and Bantu Women 197
Atlantic Charter (1941) 123, 225
Australia 132, 182; and Australian miners on the Rand 161
Azikiwe, Nnamdi 113, 117, 112–13, 214, 223; biographical information 306 n77

Bair, B. 15
Ballinger, Margaret V. 173, 176, 187, 195–6; biographical information 197, 323 n72; and South African liberalism 197, 200; (*see also* Hodgson, M.)
Ballinger, William 164, 169, 171, 187–8, 189–90, 191–3, 197–9, 217–18, 250, 253; and Ballinger Fund 186; biographical information 183, 195; as ICU advisor 164, 183–6; and native co-operative development 188–9, 194–5; and the South African Independent Labour Party 185
Banton, M. 246
Bantu Men's Social Centres (BMSC) 153–5, 186–7, 189
Barclays Bank 265
Barkan, E. 27, 37, 229
Barnes, Leonard 58, 187, 189, 194, 196, 198, 241, 253, 259, 261, 265, 269; as Africanist 269, 341–2 n 82; and anti-imperialism 259, 265; biographical information 338–9 n 46
Barratt Brown, M. 38, 275
Basutoland 133, 145, 147–8, 182, 190–1; communism in 191

Bayart, J. F. 273
Bechuanaland 133, 149, 182, 190–2, 195;
    Bangwato peoples 191, 195; migration
    to South Africa; 190, 195; Tshekedi
    incident and British public opinion
    192–4 *see also* British South African
    Protectorates
Beecham, Sir Thomas 212
Beer, G. L. 20, 38–40, 51
Beinart, W. 102, 139, 144, 148, 158, 164,
    171, 176, 184
Beloff, M. 2
Bennett, Arnold 211; and film Piccadilly
    (1929) 211
Berman, M. 13
Berry, Erick 72–4
Bhabha, H. 6, 226
Biafra 2, 125
Birkett, D. 81, 268
black; culture 6, 211–12, 216; grievances
    10–12, 219–23; imperialism 219;
    intellectuals 7, 12, 213, 219, 225;
    nationalism 14–15, 18, 43; 'peril' 160;
    Zionism 6
Black (African) Americans 99, 122, 150,
    216, 239–40, 276; in Britain 214, 212,
    216, 225, 240; as entertainers 206, 211,
    214; as GIs 223, 225; and communism;
    45; and South Africa 155, 159–61, 177
    (*see also* Yergan, Max)
Black Atlantic, 6, 280 n16
black community in Britain 205–27;
    (colonial) workers and seamen 205–11,
    221, 225, 229–31, 233, 237–8; women
    215, 219; impact of economic
    depression upon 207–8; problems of
    nationality 207–9; responses to racism;
    210–11, 215–19; social and economic
    conditions of 207–10
black consciousness 5–7, 17, 131, 157,
    159–61, 179, 225, 234, 247; in Britain
    226, 233; and divided consciousness
    174; fragmentation of in South Africa
    165, 174–5; in West Africa 103, 120–6
    see also race consciousness; double
    consciousness
black identities; in Britain 205–6, 210–11;
    and identity politics 7
black organisations (in Britain) 210, 220–3;
    and self help 210, 222–3
Blackman, Peter 222, 242
Boahan, A. A. 104
Bolshevism and Bolshevist agitators 41,

43–4, 74, 159, 206, 259; and 'red peril'
    160; as threat to imperialism 113–14,
    239; 'Zulu Bolshevists' 183 (*see also*
    communism)
Bonner, P. 157
Botswana 196 *see also* Bechunaland
Bourdillon, Sir B. 265
Bourne, S. 216
Bozzoli, B. 151, 158
Bradford, H. 171, 185
Bradley, K. 58, 61, 69
Bradley, Ben 242
Braithewaite, Chris (alias 'Jones') 211, 222,
    240, 242 *see also* Colonial Seaman's
    Union
Brazil; connections with West Africa, 53
Breytenbach, B. 150, 312 n73
Bridgeman, Reginald 238–42, 247, 258;
    biographical information 333 n40 *see
    also* LAI
British Advisory Committee on Native
    Education in Tropical Africa 35
British (national) identities 1–3, 7, 24, 52,
    79, 261–2, 264, 268, 275; immigration
    policy; 201, 205, 207–9, 215, 226, 237
British Parliament and MPs; 63–5, 248,
    250–1, 254, 258–9, 265
British Board of Trade 208
British Broadcasting Corporation (BBC)
    24–5, 49, 216, 251–2, 254, 262, 264,
    267; and controversial series on East
    Africa 251–2; Empire Service 24–5
British Conservative Party 250; and
    Conservative MPs 10, 24, 104, 207–8,
    258; financial interests in Empire 20, 24
British Co-operative Movement 190, 242
British Co-operative Wholesale Society
    194
British Council 267
British Empire 1–2, 20–2, 26, 40, 44, 55,
    103, 132–3, 137, 139–40, 248, 258–61,
    267–8
British Empire Exhibitions 24, 31, 60
British Empire Parliamentary Association,
    140
British and Foreign Anti-Slavery and
    Aborigines Protection Society (ASAPS)
    63, 137–8, 181–3, 187, 188, 191, 193,
    195, 215, 229–30, 232, 250–1, 258
British (Imperial) Government 44, 135–7,
    191, 194, 241, 251, 256–60, 270
British High Commission Territories 174,

182, 191, 195 *see also* British South
  African Protectorates
British High Commission, Union of South
  Africa 135, 137–8, 148, 182, 183, 191,
  193
British Labour Movement 28, 183, 208,
  228, 250–1, 253
British Labour Party and MPs;
  involvement in race and colonial issues
  6, 24, 107, 111, 115, 118, 144, 122,
  181–2, 207–8, 215, 235, 238, 239, 243,
  250–1, 255, 257–9; and Labour
  Governments 251, 266; Labour
  imperialists 24, 259–60, 263; *see also*
  Fabian socialism; reformist socialism
British Left; involvement in race and
  colonial issues; 115, 122, 140–1, 192–3,
  195, 213, 222, 236–44
British liberalism and liberals 133–9,
  205–8, 213, 220; as 'champions of the
  oppressed' 234–6, 272; attitudes to
  Africans 174, 234–6; attitudes to race;
  199; initiatives on race problems in
  Britain 208, 213–14, 220, 229–34, 245;
  interventions in the South African
  'native problem' 133, 174, 181–201;
  and pan-liberal links 181–2, 196–7
British monarchy; and imperialism 24, 75,
  93–5, 261–2, 268 *see also* Princess
  Marie-Louise
British Nationality Act, 1948 209
British Shipping Assistance Act, 1935 208
British South Africa Company 193
British South African Protectorates 6, 41,
  121, 133, 172, 182, 190–6, 225
  controversy over proposed transfer to
  South Africa 192, 195–6; imperial
  neglect; social and economic conditions
  in 183–4, 190–1 *see also* British High
  Commission Territories
British Trade Union Movement and trade
  unionists 181, 183, 207, 242
Brittain, Vera 181–2, 183, 241
Brockway, Fenner 238, 242, 247
Brown, L. L. 214, 217
Buckle, J. Desmond 242
Buell, R. 35, 88, 105, 109–10, 142, 149
Bundy, C. 102, 146, 148, 164, 171, 184
Bunting, S 163, 166, 185
Burns, Sir A. 28, 86, 99, 102, 223, 265
Butler, M. 266

Cadbury Brothers 76, 104; and Cadbury
  World, 3
Cain, P. 4, 5, 23–4, 58, 256, 259–60, 262
Callaway, H. I. 79–80, 86–7
Cameron, Sir D. 63
Cammack, D 134
Campbell, A. 274
Campbell, H. 276
Cannadine, D. 262, 268
Cape and Capetown 133, 143–4, 146,
  149–50, 159, 164, 165, 169, 172, 189,
  193, 215, 268; abolition of slavery,
  1838, 133;Cape Coloured community
  132, 142, 165; Cape Constitution, 1853
  133, 172; Cape (non-white) franchise
  141, 172–3, 197; Cape liberalism 133,
  139, 181–2, 186, 196; Cape Malays
  132; Cape Times 187; University of
  Capetown 188
capitalism 4, 7–8, 11, 13, 21, 45, 54, 103,
  143–4, 155, 157, 159, 192, 219, 237,
  246, 257, 269, 272–3, 277; black 169,
  220; 'gentlemanly', 58
Cardiff 215, 216–17, 221–2, 230, 231;
  'race riots' in 206, 208, 210; Arab
  seamen 222; black community 209–11;
  League of Goodwill 230; Missions to
  Seamen 209: welfare organisations 231
Cardinall, A. W. 53, 64, 66, 97, 105–7,
  109, 111
Caribbean 1, 4, 6, 58, 232, 246, 254 *see also*
  West Indies
Carnegie Foundation 149, 153, 188, 263
  see also philanthropy
Cary, J. 21, 69, 120–1, 272
Casely-Hayford, Adelaide 92, 126;
  biographical information 298n59
Castle, K. 31–3
Chabal, P. 275
Champion, A. W. G. 131, 164–5, 167–70,
  183–5 (*see also* ICU) 131, 154
Chatterjee, P. 9
Chocolat; and director, Claire Denis, 86,
  297 n43
Christianity 122, 273; in Africa 92, 102,
  152, 157, 159, 160, 169; and African
  women 89–90, 151–2; influence
  amongst liberal humanitarians 186,
  188, 199 *see also* missionaries; Quakers
Churchill, Winston 1–2, 41, 212, 266
cinema 25, 31–3; black actors in the
  British cinema 214, 215–16; racism in,
  31–3, 215–16

citizenship 12, 98, 121, 153, 172, 176, 206, 216, 233, 246

civil liberties 123, 222, 241, 265 and colonial grievances; 103, 114–20, 261 *see also* NCCL

civilisation 2, 30, 34, 39–40, 78, 141–2, 253, 272; and 'civilising mission' 28–9, 41, 78–9, 268; and 'civilisation test' 10, 214, 220

'civilised' labour policies 112, 49, 149, 161, 163, 208–9

class 7, 92, 93, 102, 132, 167, 179, 200, 206, 217–19, 221, 228, 238, 244; African working class 104, 109–13, 159, 175, 266; black working class in Britain 206–11, 219, 221, 225, 245; British working classes, 8, 24, 119, 210, 217, 238–9, 243, 245; class consciousness 173, 175; class differences among white colonial critics 182, 186, 199; *see also* race and class

Clegg, Arthur 242

Coalition for Jubilee 2000 272

Cocoa Marketing Board (Gold Coast) 108

Cohen, R. 30, 65, 71, 165, 266–7

Cohen, Sir A. 30, 65, 71, 266

Cold War 124, 179, 242, 267

collaboration see resistance

Colley, L. xii

Colonial Administrative Service (CAS) 20–1, 23, 57; and courses in administration 57, 248; and reorganisation of Colonial African Service 57

Colonial African Service 56–61, 73–9, 88, 99; class distinctions in 58, 75; relations with business community 54, 75–6; structure of 57–9; women employees 57, 81, 92

Colonial Defence Association, Cardiff 221

colonial development and welfare 59, 99, 165, 249, 253 263–7; and 'partnership' with Africans 99, 249, 263, 265, 267

Colonial Development and Welfare Act, Film Committee 216; Welfare Act, 1940; 265

Colonial (Commonwealth) Development Corporation 265

Colonial Film Unit 25

Colonial Information Bulletin 242

Colonial Information Bureau (CIB) 241–2

Colonial League 259

Colonial Office 21, 55, 57, 81, 99, 112, 114, 191, 208, 222–3, 238–9, 254, 261, 263, 265–7; changes within during the Second World War 265–7; Film Committee 216

colonial officers; in West Africa; 34, 56–72, 73–6; conditions of service 57–8, 60–1; and gentlemanly diaspora and order 23, 58–9, 73, 79; and imperial masculinities 51, 56–7, 72, 79, 84, 87; and marriage 81–4, 87; motivations of; 56–7

Colonial Seamans Union (CSU) 222, 240–1

Colonial Social Science Research Council 264

colonial; administrations 13, 16, 55–71; censuses 60, 81, 104; 'chartism' 261; economies 34, 54–5, 58, 102–3, 104–14.127, 146; intelligentsia 34–5, 103, 114, 120–2, 174, 215, 217, 254–5; policing, 43, 70; propaganda 267; reforms 253, 264–7, 270; repression and oppression 68–71, 112–13, 114–20, 251, 254, 261, 269, 272; seamen 205–11, 221, 225; society 49–50; soldiers 205, 209, 231, 233; spectacle 215–16, 274; subjects 92, 120–1, 206, 206–9, 216, 262, 265, 268

colonial mandates (see League of Nations)

colonialism; cultures of 78, 100; internal (South Africa) 133; scientific 36, 60; in West Africa 49–71, 226; in West Africa 49–71 *see also* critics of colonialism; anti-colonialism

colour bar 4, 99, 239, 240, 270; in Britain 223, 225, 229, 238, imperial 23, 34, 223, 225, 232

Coloured Soldiers Association (South Africa) 137

Commonwealth 22, 127, 138, 141, 196, 201, 226, 250, 259, 265, 267–8

Commonwealth Immigration Act, 1962; 209

Commonwealth Relations Office 195 (*see also* Dominions Office)

Communism and Communists 44–5, 118, 158, 182, 200, 226, 234, 240–1, 242, 258–9, 261, 267, 271, 274; in Africa 44–5, 109, 114, 118–19, 159–61, 164, 169, 172, 182–3, 194, 258–9, 261; and communist propaganda; 239, 241–2 influence on African nationalists 244–5;

and race consciousness 223 *see also* Bolshevism

Communist International (Comintern) 16, 44–5, 114, 163, 165–6, 237; and CPGB 237–8, 241–2 *see also* RILU, ITUC-NW

Communist Manifesto 13, 122

Communist Party of Great Britain (CPGB) 44, 197, 206, 221–2, 228, 325, 236–40, 242–3; attitude to black activists 243–4; ethnocentricism of members 237, 242–3; involvement with African nationalists 243–4; Labour Research Department (LRD) 237; membership 243; Minority Movement 237–8; and the Scottsboro Defence Committee 239–40

Communist Party of South Africa (CPSA), 161–7, 172, 179, 185, 191, 197, 237; banning of 179; and 'Black Republic' phase 166, 191; relations between black and white members 166, 185; repression of 163–4

Conference on the African Peoples, Democracy and World Peace, 1939; 241

conservation discourse 40, 144–5

Constantine, Sir Leary 223

Convention Peoples Party (CPP) 123

Cooper, F. 267–8

co-operation and co-operative movements 108, 190, 253; Co-operative Guilds 194, 221 (*see also* British Co-operative Movement and Co-operative Wholesale Society); and credit societies 108, 190; (native) co-operative and industrial development in Southern Africa 188–90, 194–5 (*see also* Ballinger, W.)

Coplan, D, 152

Coquery-Vidrovitch, C. 64, 90, 92, 94, 103, 126, 158

corruption 273

Council for the Defence of Seretse Khama and the Protectorates 195

Council on African Affairs (US) 173

Coupland, R. 23, 257

Couzens, T. 155

Creasy, G 123

Creech-Jones, Arthur, MP 183, 194, 198–9, 241, 247, 251, 259, 264, 266; biographical information 341–2 n70

Cripps, Sir Stafford 238, 241 *see also* Socialist League

Cripps, T. 217

critics of colonialism (white) 5, 12, 16, 28, 35, 42, 99, 103, 187, 192, 223, 250–6, 269 *see also* anti-colonialism, anti-imperialism

Crocker, W. 63, 69

Crowder, Henry 212

Crowder, M. 192–3

Crozier, Brigadier General, 89

cultural imperialism 3, 8–10; 239, 274, 280 n27 and colonial education 239; and cultural oppression 55, 270, 272; problems of definition 8; in South Africa 175; in West Africa, 72–3, 93–100, 124–5

Culture 3, 6, 8–17, 205–6, 210; African; 53, 68–9, 95, 210, 216, 274–5; black; 6, 211–12, 216; of colonialism78, 100; contact 12, 109, 152, 228, 272, 276, 277; and imperialism 2–3, 8–10, 72–100, 200, 206, 243; marabi 151–2; popular, 24–7, 31–3, 50–2, 74, 109, 215–16, 267–8; western 9–11, 59, 102, 122; white expatriate 8, 73–87 *see also* anthropology; race; westernisation

Cummings, Ivor, 221, 223, 261

Cunard, Nancy 211–12, 214, 240, 247; and Negro Anthology 240, 327 n41

Cunliffe-Lister, Sir P. 110, 114–15

Curtis, L. 23, 141, 189, 192

Cutrafelli, M. R. 89–90

Daily Telegraph 5

Darby, P. xii

Davidson, B. 101

De Kiewiet, C. 132, 143

Declaration of Brussels, 1895 39

Declaration of Colonial Peoples 225

decolonisation 1, 5, 262, 264–9, 273, 276; in West Africa 125–8

Delius, P. 157

democracy 9, 12, 95, 120–2, 241, 244, 251, 261, 269, 273

dialectic (of resistance) 17, 244, 271, 277

dialogues; between black activists 217, 219–21, 222–3, 245–7; between pro and anti-colonialists 250, 252–4; diologic exchange; 17 interracial 17, 55, 201, 221, 226, 228, 254–5, 261, 264

diasporas 4–8 and diasporic consciousness, 6; gentlemanly 58–9 imperial, 4 *see also* African diaspora

discourse(s); colonial, 10, 147; conservation 40, 144–5

definition of 10 and ideologies 10; imperial 81, 109, 131; (black); oppositional 9–10; of resistance and liberation 103, 219, 245; of power 9–14, 33–8, 249; race 10–12, 21, 28–43, 72–3, 131, 257; race relations 10, 245–6; segregationist 133, 144, 155, 196;
Dominions Office 191, 195, 263 *see also* white dominions
Dominions Party (South Africa), 140
double consciousness 9, 120 *see also* black consciousness
Dove Danquah, Mabel 126; and biographical information 307 n92
Dover, Cedric 43–4
Drew, A. 166
Dube, Reverend John 167
Duberman, M. B. 216
Dubois, W. E. B xi, 15, 17, 41, 225
Dubow, S. 141
Duncan-Johnstone, A. 57–60, 66–8, 83–4, 88, 108, 110, 113–15, 121, 292 n40
Durban 150, 163, 164–5, 171, 189

East Africa 55, 112, 125, 132, 137, 160, 225, 230, 248, 251–2
economic; exploitation and oppression 42, 254–5, 270, 273, 277; imperialism 28, 194, 256, 258, 260, 265–6, 269–7; development in Africa 10, 49, 263–5; protectionism 20; refugees 275
Eden, Anthony 257
education; in Africa 35, 153, 156, 159, 161, 174, 253, 261, 267; adult education (South Africa) 154–5, 166, 188, 194; of African girls and women 92, 97, 151, 174; 'Bantu' 134, 152–3, 174, 178–9; colonial 95–8, 102, 120–2, 174; missionary (South Africa)134, 137, 146, 160, 172, 174, 187; of West Africans, 95–98
Egerton, H. 22, 93, 138, 145
Egypt; 160, 237; and Egyptian nationalism 43
Ekarte, Pastor Daniels 210, 230
Elder Dempster Shipping Line 52, 56, 112
Elphick, R. 182
emancipation 15–16, 271, 276 *see also* resistance
Empire Day 24, 239, 259, 267, 283 n17; and BBC 25; left protests against in Britain 239; in West Africa 93, 98
Empire Day Movement 25, 267

Empire Film Library 25
Empire Marketing Board 25
Empire Settlement Act, 1922 21
empire; socialists, 24; propaganda 239; strengthening 18, 22–6, 40–3, 249, 252, 256, 262, 265, 269
Enahoro, A. 95, 102, 122
Engels, D. 9
Engels, F.12, 30
Ethiopia 9, 14; 29, 118, 131, 235, 256–8; Italian invasion of (1935) 117–18, 131, 161, 256–8; impact on black consciousness 121, 172–3, 200, 208, 222–3, 236, 240–1, 257; responses of imperial powers to 117–18, 131, 256–8
Ethiopianism 14, 138, 160
ethnicity 38, 125–6, 127, 132, 140, 150, 167, 169, 175, 244, 257, 273; and ethnic consciousness 38, 102, 126, 150, 158; and divisions 175, 276; and identities 104, 135, 165; ethnic nationalisms 125, 158, 175; and violence, 125, 175; white 4, 7
ethnocentricism 2, 37, 90, 236
ethnopsychiatry 109
Eugenics Society 28, 229
eugenics 25–7, 43, 229
eurocenticism 11, 44, 90, 126, 274–5
Europe and European 3–4, 8, 11, 14, 16–17, 20, 22, 27–9, 34, 39–40, 42–5, 73, 76–7, 109, 111, 118, 134, 144, 177, 206–7, 214, 230, 256–9, 275
Evans, N. 207, 226
Evans-Pritchard, E. 265
Evans, I. L. 131, 135–6, 145–6, 149, 190–1, 192

Fabian Colonial Bureau (FCB) 127, 195, 264
Fabian socialism 78, 182, 187, 194, 199, 251, 253, 255, 263–4; and British Fabian Society 28, 184; in Capetown 165, 194; and colonial reform 253, 263–4
fascism 3–4, 12 43, 176, 182, 222, 240–1, 256, 269, 271; fascist threat to African colonies 256–61; and imperialism 240–1, 256–62, 264, 269 (*see also* Ethiopia); and nazism 140; and racism 43–4, 258–9, 261; in South Africa, 140, 171
Fanon, F.71, 95

Federation of Non European Trade Unions (FNETU) 165–6
film 24–5, 248, 267; Colonial Office Film Committee and Film Unit 25, 216; ethnographic 38; censorship in South Africa 152 *see also* cinema
Fircroft College, Birmingham 184 (*see also* Quakers)
First World War 20, 23, 30, 49, 157, 159, 193, 205, 219, 230, 233, 248, 256; impact on black consciousness 43, 159, 205–7; and imperialism 20–2; involvement of black South Africans 137, 143, 155, 177; West African soldiers in 93
Fletcher, J. 183, 232–4
Fletcher, M. E 229
Flint, J. 264
Forced Labour Convention, 1930; 63
Forster E. M. 241
Fort Hare Native College (South Africa) 159, 160, 174, 176, 193
Fortes, M. 36–7, 78, 120
Foucault, M. 9, 25
Fowler-Lunn, Katherine 59
France and the French Empire 20, 30, 38, 45, 84, 256–7, 259, 267; in Algeria 132; colonialism in Africa 34–5, 73, 86, 114–15; use of Senegalese soldiers in Europe 207
Fraser, A. 78, 97
Freemasonary 22
Freetown 56, 59, 118–19
Friends of Africa 194–5, 197, 251–2; South African branch 195
Friends of India 251
Freund, B. 99, 104
Furedi, F. 2, 11, 119–20, 122
Furnival, J. S. 11
Furse, Sir R. 34, 57, 97, 99

Gaitskell, D. 151
Gandhi, Mahatma 123, 161
Garvey, Amy Ashwood 211, 223, 225
Garvey, M 14, 42, 212, 214–16, 219–20, 236; in London 219–20
Garveyism 6, 14–15, 45, 120–2, 148, 159–60, 166, 206, 219–20, 245; and black separatism; in South Africa 159–60; in West Africa 120–2 (*see also* pan-Africanism)
Gates, H. L. 274
Geary, Sir W. 49

Gender 7, 16, 72, 132, 234–5, 244; African gender relations; 92, 151; colonial gender relations (West Africa) 58, 79–93; gender relations and identities in South Africa 151, 145; and imperialism; and resistance 15, 158
General Act and Declaration of Brussels, 1919 39
General Act of Berlin, 1884 39
Germany and Germans 78, 140, 249, 258;colonialism 30, 40; colonial claims 141, 241, 256, 258–61; racial policies 258–9, 261; German South West Africa 41, 137, 139
German Refugee Committee 240
Germany
Gersuiwerde Nasionale Party 140 (*see also* Afrikaner nationalism)
Gertzel, C. 254
Ghana 125, 127 (*see also* Gold Coast)
Gilroy, P. 6–7, 244
globalisation xiii, iv, 3, 269, 273; global; capitalism 273; economy 4, 104, 134; inequalities; instability; order; power relations
Gold Coast Aborigines Rights Protection Society (ARPS) 107–8, 112–13, 222; and African grievances; deputation to London 115–17, 213, 239
Gold Coast and Ashanti 36–7, 49, 59–60, 64–8, 70, 75–86, 93–9, 105–11, 113–18, 123–5, 198, 243, 265, 268; African occupations (statistics) 106–7; Asante politics and culture 53–4, 65–6, 97 cocoa boycotts 108; cocoa production in 76, 104–5, 107–8; Fanti peoples 66, 97; non-African population (statistics) 77; problems of taxation in 66, 108–9; urban popular culture 109; urban protest 108–9; urbanisation and urban conditions 78, 108–9; Wiawso riots 66
Gold Coast Criminal Code Amendment Ordinance, No. 21, 1934 115–17
Gold Coast Gazette 115–16
Goldberg, D.T. 7, 11–12, 17, 78, 247
Goldin, I. 165
Goode-Robeson, E. 37, 53, 79, 91, 121, 149, 150, 155, 175, 215, 216–19, 248–9; visit to South Africa 149–50, 155, 175, 317 n 65, 386 n 61
Goody, J 36–7, 78
Gorer, G. 55, 68, 73, 115

Gramsci, A 9
Graves, Anna, Melissa 78–9; biographical details 296 n25
Greene, Graham 21; impressions of West Africa 55, 59, 73, 75, 78, 98, 105
Green, M, 90
Grigg, Sir Edward, MP 255
Grundlingh, L. 177
Guggisberg, Sir Frederick 76, 95, 108 (*see also* Gold Coast)
Guggisberg, Decima 76, 84–5, 110
Gumede, Joseph 167

Haden-Guest, L 24
Haig, E. W. F 82, 93
Haggis, J. 87
Haile Selassie, Emperor of Ethiopia 222, 241, 256
Hailey, Lord A. 23, 25, 40, 55, 63, 66, 69, 92, 97, 105, 108, 122, 124, 126, 141, 146, 190, 195, 251, 259, 263, 265, 267; and the African Survey 263–4
Haiti 31
Hall, C. 3
Hall, S. 10–11
Hardy, G 197
Hargreaves, J. D. 108, 269
Harrington Stuart, Alice 86
Harris, J. 189, 230–1, 247, 258 *see also* ASAPS
Harvey, D. 3
Havinden, M. 265
Hayes, P 92
Heaton Nichols, G. 142, 160, 167, 196
Hegel, G.W. F. 17, 29–31
hegemony 9, 53, 102, 127
Hellman, E. 197
Herskovits, M. 37, 271
Hertzog, General B. 137, 140, 163, 192, 196, 252, 257
Heussler, R. 57
Hill, R. A. 159–60
Hinden, R. 127, 264
Hirschfeld, M. 44
history and historians 259, 267, 275; African 14, 30–1, 53–4, 274, 276; British business history 4; imperial 2–3, 24, 132; and memory 3, 75, 132, 210, 271; South African 131–2, 184
Hitler, Adolph 258–9
Hlubi, Alex 184–5
Hlubi, Mark Makumalo 177, 216
Hobsbawm, E. xiii, 22, 24, 44, 105, 269

Hobson, J. A. 58, 72, 255
Hodgkin, T. 126
Hodgson, Margaret 147–8, 150, 165, 167, 169, 173, 185, 190, 192, 196–7 *see also* Ballinger, V. M.
Hoernle, A. 188, 197
Hogben, L. 43, 288 n83
Holmes, C. 245
Holtby, Winifred 139, 183–4, 186–7, 194, 198–9, 212, 213–14, 215, 217–18, 233–5, 238, 251; biographical information 234–5; and race relations in Britain 213–14; and South Africa 183, 217–18, 318n5
Home Office 207–8, 223
Hooks, B 53
Hopkins, A. G. 4, 5, 23–4, 54, 58, 108, 256, 259–60, 262
Howe, S. 195, 205, 242–3, 250, 255, 259
Hughes, Langston 236
Huggins, A. M. E. 209
human rights 12, 176, 225, 272–3 *see also* United Nations; Atlantic Charter
humanitarianism 2, 24, 39–40, 183, 186, 190, 196, 198–9, 269, 272–3, 275
Hutchinson, Leslie 'Jiver' 212, 326 n31
Huxley, E. 30–1, 34–5, 53, 90, 94, 246, 268
Huxley, J. 27–8, 252

ICU Yasé Natal 164–5, 167
Ikaka Labasenenzi 166
immigration controls and policy 24, 42; in Britain 201, 205, 207–9, 215, 226, 237 *see also* repatriation
Imperial Institute 25, 229
imperial; conferences 138; consciousness and mentalities 3–4, 12, 24–5, 275–6; culture 2, 72–100, 200, 206, 243; discourse 73, 81, 109, 131; economy 22–3, 34, 49–50, 60, 104–14, 256, 258, 266; exhibitions 24, 60; mission (in West Africa) 12, 72, 50, 54, 56–61, 67, 69, 71, 81; orthodoxy 250, 255, 269
imperialism 2–5, 22, 30–1, 72, 219, 221, 222, 235, 237, 239–41, 248–70; British imperialism in South Africa; 133–41, 190–6, 200–1; informal 22; internationalisation of 38–43, 248–9, 256–9, 269; 'inverse' 206; liberal (progressive) imperialism and imperialists 6, 30, 34–5, 39, 133–4, 138, 192, 194, 220, 250, 252–4, 258,

262–4, 265–6, 269; problems of definition of 3–4; and race 7–10, 23, 39–41, 223, 236–44; sexual 213; and Versailles Peace Settlement 38–43 *see also* cultural imperialism; popular imperialism
independence 1, 123; in Africa 2, 99, 125, 127, 266, 270, 271, 275–6
Independent Industrial and Commercial Workers Union (IICU) 169–71, 184
Independent Labour Party (ILP), Britain 181, 183, 222, 236–7, 238, 241, 242;
India League 251
India Office 208
India and Indians 4, 20, 28, 40, 49, 54, 57, 73–4, 97, 119, 160, 237, 238, 249, 251, 254, 257, 262–4, 266, 275; independence 123; indentured labour (South Africa) 134, 161; nationalism 43, 172, 222, 232–3, 263; (lascar) seamen 208; students in Britain 232
Indian Civil Service (ICS) 12, 57
indirect rule 33–5, 59, 145–8, 190, 192, 194, 249, 253–4, 262, 273; dilemmas of 35, 55–6, 61–71, 113, 125; principles of 49 *see also* Native Administration
Industrial and Commercial Workers Union (ICU) 148–9, 159–60, 161–71, 183–6, 187, 191; involvement of British liberals and reformists in 183–6, 194; splits in 167, 169–71
Inkatha Freedom Party 167
Inkatha kaZulu 167
Institute of Race Relations (IRR) 246
inter-colonial (imperial) co-operation 249, 267
International Africa Opinion 223
International Africa Service Bureau for the Defence of African Peoples and Peoples of African Descent (IASB) 223–4, 242
International African Friends of Abyssinia (IAFA) 222–3, 240
International Institute of African Languages and Culture (International Africa Institute) 36, 60, 78
International Labour Defence 44, 166, 240 (*see also* Comintern)
International Monetary Fund 273
International Trade Union Committee of Negro Workers, (ITUC-NW) 45, 109, 237, 240; members 289 n90
Ireland and the Irish; 237; diaspora; and nationalism 43

interracial; dialogues 17, 55, 17, 55, 201, 221, 226, 228, 245–7; London 211–15; marriages 195, 209–10, 212, 235; sex 25–7, 86–9, 193, 208, 211–13 (*see also* miscegenation); organisations 153–5, 186–90, 220, 232–4, 236 (*see also* Joint Councils, IRR, SAIRR); US interracial councils 186
interracialism 213–14, 221, 229, 236, 243
Italian invasion of Ethiopia, 1935 see Ethiopia
Italy 43 , 173, 249, 25–9

Jabavu, Dr. D. D. T. 159, 164, 165, 172, 174, 230
Jamaica and Jamaicans 206, 212, 219, 220, 225–6, 255
James, C.L.R. 213, 219, 220, 222–3
James, L. 2–3
Japan 20, 41, 43, 249, 258
Jardine, Sir D. 101, 118–19
Jaywardina, K. xii
Jews and Jewish 42, 43–4, 219, 258; diaspora 6–7; migration to Britain 207; women in Britain and solidarity with black cause 213; in South Africa 140, 144, 200
Johannesburg 137, 142, 150, 153–5, 161, 164, 166, 172, 176, 183
Johnson, Len 206
Johnson, Sir H.H. 53
Joint Council to Promote Understanding Between White and Coloured People in Great Britain 205, 215, 229, 232–4, 236; membership 331 n13
Joint Councils of Europeans and Natives (South Africa) 183, 186–90, 232, 233, 236
Joint Parliamentary committee Upon Closer Union in East Africa 230, 252
Jones, David 'Ivon' 163
Jones, Claudia 226
Judd, J. 3
Jung, C. J. 37–8

Kadalie, Clements 161, 164–5, 169–71, 174, 183–4; trip to Europe 169, 184, 199 *see also* ICU, IICU
Katznelson, I. 247
Keegan, T. 133, 144
Kelley, R. 14
Kennedy, D. xii–xiii
Kent, J. 266–7

Kenya 1, 5, 34, 43, 73, 82, 110, 125, 182, 201, 230, 239, 250–2, 255
Kenyatta, Jomo 36, 223, 230, 239–41, 242, 247, 252
Kerr, Philip (Lord Lothian) 23, 40, 258
Kessie, (Prince) Cobina 240

Kidd, R. 241–2
Kikuyu Central Association, 239
Killingray, D. 123–4
Kirke-Greene, A. 34, 51, 69, 71
Kopkind, A. 272
Kotane, Moses 166
Kuklich, H. 36, 57, 59
Kwa Zulu Natal 167, 175 *see also* Natal

Labour Party Advisory Committee on Imperial Questions (LPACIQ) 250–1
Lagos 56, 92, 114, 120, 122, 123, 231
Lane, T. 207
Langley, J.A. 121
Latouche, S. 3
Lauren, P.G. 4, 7, 39, 41, 125, 223, 257
Lavin, D. 79, 141
Lawrence, Stephen 275
League of African Rights 165
League Against Imperialism (LAI) 45, 114, 117, 221, 228, 234; British Branch 238–42
League of Coloured Peoples (LCP) 118–19, 208, 215, 220–3, 223, 223, 225, 232–3, 236, 240–1
League of Nations Union 23, 183
League of Nations 38–40, 41–4, 140, 173, 230, 253, 257–9, 263 Colonial Mandate System 20, 38–40, 253, 259; and principle of trusteeship 38–40 *see also* Permanent Mandates Commission
Legassick, M. 133
Leith-Ross, Sylvia 55, 65, 84, 90, 99–100, 123–4; biographical information 298 n59
Lekhotla-la-Bafo (League of the Poor), 1928 191
Lemelle, S. 14,
Lenin, V. I. 44
Lesotho 196 *see also* Basutoland
Lever Brothers 104
Lewin, J 187, 189, 194, 241, 250
Leys, N. 111, 187, 223, 235, 238, 247, 250, 252–3, 255
liberalism 3–4, 10–11, 30, 134, 161, 182, 199, 236, 244–7, 271–3; academic

liberals 141, 143; and British Empire 6, 30, 34–5, 39, 95, 133–4, 138, 192, 194, 220, 250, 252–5, 258, 262–4, 265–6, 269; Christian liberals 186, 188, 199; conscience on Africa 200, 250–6, 266, 268–9, 272; and liberal dilemma 12, 183, 196–201, 236, 253; and liberal race discourse 7, 10–12, 142, 245–7 *see also* British liberals; multi-racialism; South African liberals
Liberia 31, 257, 265
Little, K. 210, 215, 228
Liverpool 233, 239; black community; 206, 209–10, 221; welfare organisations 210, 229, 230, 231
Liverpool Association for the Welfare of Coloured People 229
Liverpool Association for the Welfare of Half-Caste Children 229
Liverpool Negro Association 221
Livie-Noble, F. 153, 194, 210, 233
Lloyd, T. O. 20
Lloyd Jones, D 40
London Group on African Affairs (LGAA) 187, 205, 208, 210, 220, 233; membership 320 n21; as pressure group on African issues 251–3
London School of Economics (LSE) 36–7, 216
London 7, 36, 41, 43, 102, 115, 123–8, 137, 141, 191, 192 193, 194, 205, 217, 220–1, 222, 225, 226; black London 211–15; interracial clubs 211–12; Notting Hill carnival 226; riots 226
Loram, C. T. 153, 186, 188
Louis, W. R. 38, 267
Lovedale College, South Africa 174, 176, 177, 193,
Lugard, Sir, F. 22–3, 33–4, 51, 54–6, 60–4, 68, 71, 73, 76, 249, 254, 259, 262–3

MacCrone, I. D. 29, 89, 142–3
MacDonald, M. 112, 117–18, 259
Macinnes, C. 212
Mackay, Claude 228, 330 n76
Mackenzie, J.M. 8, 24–5, 144–5, 267
Macmillan, W. M. M. 21, 34, 86, 114, 122, 132, 143, 146, 155, 182, 183, 185, 186–9, 194, 197–201, 236, 250, 252–5; biographical information 187, 320 n22, n31; as pioneering Africanist 187, 252
Magubane, B 133
Mair, L. 36, 258

Makonnen, Ras 223, 225, 240, 330 n76
Malan, Dr. R. 140, 179, 185
Malawi 251 *see also* Nyasaland
Malik, K. 11–12, 245–6, 264
Malinowski, B. 36–7, 265
Mamdani, M. 131, 273
Mandate System *see* League of Nations
Mandela, Nelson 176
Manley, Michael 226
Mannin, Ethel 213, 222, 241, 247
Mannoni, O 86
Marke, Ernest 210, 225; biographical
    information 326 n26
Marks, J. B. 166, 176
Marks, S. 9, 150, 151, 159, 160, 167, 175
Marley, Bob 276
Marshall, P. 2
Marson, Una 214, 215, 219
Marx, K. 13, 30, 226
Marxism 2–4, 7–8, 12, 30, 43–5, 161, 175;
    influence on black intellectuals 122,
    219, 223, 236, 243–5; and resistance
    244 *see also* anti-imperialism, racism
Marxist-Leninism 22–3, 122, 259
masculinities 98; imperial 51, 56–7, 72, 79,
    84, 87 *see also* gender
Mbeki, Govan 161
McIntosh, Phinehas; flogging of 192–3 *see
    also* Bechuanaland
McLaren, P. 11
Mculloch, J 28
media 30, 38, 43, 212, 252; and empire
    24–5, 215, 252 *see also* film, cinema,
    radio
Meek, Charles 60
Meisenhelder, C 30
Memmi, A. 7, 199
Mendi Memorial Day (South Africa), 137
Meredith, D. 265
migrant labour 104, 110, 146–7, 175, 197;
    and culture of migration 147, 150–2;
    and ethnic identification 104, 135;
    gendered nature of 151–2
migrant labour system 146–7, 175, 191,
    195 *see also* South Africa
migration; from Commonwealth to Britain
    209, 226; in South Africa 134–5,
    146–52; in West Africa 104, 109–10;
    white migration to Africa 134, 144,
    144, 311 n51 *see also* immigration
Miles, R. 7–8, 244, 246
Mill, James 12
Miller, W. 112

Millin, S. G. 183
Mills, Florence 211; and Blackbirds Revue
    211
Mills, Lady D. 31, 79–80
Milner, Lord A. 22–3, 40–1, 134–8
mining and mines 23, 60, 104, 112, 150,
    190–1, 193; conditions in the Gold
    Coast 76, 109–11; and Rand mines
    134, 147–9, 190; *see also* migrant labour
miscegenation and anti-miscegenation 25,
    73, 88–9, 209, 213, 214, 229; in South
    Africa 141–5; in Britain 229
missionaries 1, 35–6, 60, 75, 90; and
    mission-educated Africans 59, 98–9,
    134, 137, 146, 160, 172, 174, 187; in
    South Africa 134, 151, 152–3, 172,
    174, 181–2, 188, 190, 194; West Indian
    76
Mitchison, Naomi 240
Mockerie, Parmenas Githendu 252
modernity 9, 12–14, 29–30, 34, 134,
    151–2, 250, 272–3, 276
Mofutsanyana, Edwin 166
Montgomery, Sir Bernard 266
Moody, Dr. Harold 220–1, 225, 232, 241
    (*see also* LCP)
Morel, E. D. 247, 255
Morgan, D. J. 265
Morton, J. B.('Beachcomber') 74
Mountbatten, Lady Edwina 212
Mouton, F. A. 185–6, 195, 197
Movement for Colonial Freedom (MCF)
    242, 268
Msimang, Richard W. 154
multi-culturalism 11–12, 246, 270, 276
multi-racialism 10–11, 186, 229, 232–4,
    236, 244–5, 261, 264, 275 *see also*
    liberalism, interracialism
museums 2–3, 274
Mussolini, Benito 25–8

Nadel, S.F. 60; research in Nigeria 292 n43
Namibia 177 *see also* South West Africa
Natal 132, 153, 134, 140, 142, 147, 161,
    164, 167, 169, 186, 196 *see also* Zulus;
    Kwa Zulu Natal
National Congress of British West Africa
    121
National Council for Civil Liberties
    (NCCL) 115–16, 118–19, 208, 236,
    328, 240–2, 265; and colonial civil
    liberties 115–19, 241, 265; British

Overseas Sub-committee 241; membership and aims 241
National Fabian Research Bureau (NFRB) 251
National Peace Council 258
National Socialism 7, 28
National Union of Seamen (NUS) 222
nationalism; anti-colonial 5, 11–12, 43, 101–2, 211, 217, 225, 261, 272; black 14–15, 18, 43; cultural 14 *see also* African, Indian nationalism
nationality 208–9
Native (Urban Areas) Act (South Africa), 1923 198
Native Administration Act (South Africa), 1927 145, 163
Native Administration 33–6, 93; academic studies of 35–6; in the British South African Protectorates 191–2; in South Africa 6, 145–7, 198; in West Africa 56–6, 65 *see also* indirect rule; taxation
Native Affairs Act (South Africa)1920;145
Native Affairs Department (NAD) South Africa 145–6, 161
Native Laws Amendment Act (South Africa) 1937 152
Native Recruiting Corporation (South Africa) 147
Native Representation Act (South Africa), 1936; 141, 172, 196, 198; and Native Representatives 195
Native Revenue Ordinance (Nigeria)1929; 64
Native Service Contract Act (South Africa) 1932 147
Native Trust and Land Act, (South Africa) 1936 141, 198
Natives Land Act (South Africa) 1913 135–6
Native Welfare Societies (South Africa) 153, 186
Nazi-Soviet Non-Aggression Pact 242
nazism see fascism
Negro Anthology 240, 327 n41
Negro Worker 114, 119
Negro Workers Association (NWA) 117, 221, 238–42, 258
neo-colonialism 273
neo-imperialism 3
New Times and Ethiopian News 222
Ngcobo, L. 151
Ngugi wa Thiongo 274
Nigeria 49, 55–6, 63–4, 68, 73, 76–7, 81, 87, 89–92, 95–6, 104–5, 108, 113–14, 117, 120, 123, 125, 201, 245, 265; 'Women's War' 64–5, 90, 92; Sedition Ordinances 114; trade union protest 123; Yaba Higher College 120 *see also* Lagos
Nigerian Civil War 125
Nigerian Democratic Party (NDP) 120
Nigerian Pioneer 98
Nigerian Townships Ordinance 1917 78
Nkosi, Johannes 164
Nkrumah, K. 122–3, 127, 225, 243–4, 306 n82
Noel Baker, Philip, M.P. 158–9
Noel Buxton Trust 183
Noel, Father Conrad 238 *see also* LAI
Non European Conferences (South Africa) 165
Northern Rhodesia 42, 251
Nowell Report (Gold Coast) 108
Nyasaland 169, 251–2
Nzula, Albert 166, 174 *see also* CPSA

Oakley, R 61, 63, 68
Oldham, Dr. J. H. 35, 86
Olivier, Lord Sidney 30, 40, 52, 72, 250
Olukoju, A. 39
Orde-Brown, St. J. 112
Ormsby-Gore, W. 109, 120
Ossewa Brandung 140

Padmore, George 54, 108, 119, 201, 219, 220, 223, 240, 242–3, 259–60, 265–6, 272; biographical information 328 n56
palavers 93–6, 298–9 n68
Palme Dutt, Rajani 237, 240–1
Palmer, Mabel 184–5, 186
Pan-African Congresses; Second Congress, Paris 1919; 41, 138; Fifth Congress, Manchester 1945 177, 216–17, 225; 7th Congress, Kampala 1994; 271
Pan-African Federation (Britain) 225–6
pan-Africanism 6, 14–15, 43, 102, 118, 120–2, 125, 161, 172–3, 176, 208, 219–20, 223–7, 245, 276; pan-Africanist organisations in Britain 223–5
Pankhurst, Sylvia 118, 222, 247
Paris 38, 41, 43, 138, 211, 242
paternalism 30–1, 33, 232, 234, 236, 246 *see also* indirect rule; trusteeship
Paton, Alan 150
Patterson, Sheila 246

Pearce, R. D. 262–3, 266
peasant commodity production see West Africa, Gold Coast
Perham, M. 20, 28, 30–1, 45, 56, 59, 79, 87, 99, 121, 160, 161, 165, 167, 187, 188, 189, 190, 192, 194, 213, 220, 252, 254–6, 258, 264–6, 269; biographical information 284 n33
Permanent Mandates Commission 38–40, 263 *see also* League of Nations
Phelps-Stokes Foundation 159, 188, 314 n7
philanthropy and philanthropists; in Britain 210, 229, 234, 235, 246; and 'philanthropic racism' 229; in South Africa 152–4, 182, 186, 188; US philanthropic foundations 36, 149, 153, 159, 188
Phillips, A. 75
Phillips, Reverend R. 153, 171–3
Picasso, Pablo 37
Pietersie, J. Nederveen 1, 3, 8, 15–17, 23, 244, 267, 271, 274
Pim, H. 153, 186–8, 191, 194, 196–7
Pim, Sir A.191
Pirio, G. A. 159–60
Pirow, Oswald 163, 193
Plaatje, S. 134–8, 142
Pilkington, E. 212, 213, 265–6
Pines, J. 31
Polak, H. 250
popular imperialism 8, 24–7, 215, 252, 262, 267–8
Porter, B. 20
Posel, D. 157
post-imperial era 271–7
post-colonialism xiii–xiv, 4, 7, 9–10, 29, 55; post colonial problems in Britain 226, 247
post-modernism 10, 274
poverty; in Africa and the Caribbean 253, 255; of blacks in Britain 209, 229–30; in South Africa, 141, 147–8, 151–6, 185, 190
power; global 11, 249; imperial 3, 21, 28, 55, 72, 249, 262, 267; western 271, 276; white 20, 93, 102, 108
Prempeh 11, King of Asante 101
Priestley, J. B. 241
Princess Marie Louise, H. R. H. 49, 54, 60–1, 75–6, 79, 82–6, 93–6, 98, 109–10, 289 n1
Pritt, D. N. 241

proletarianisation see African labour
prostitution 78, 211; and African women 78–90, 149
Proud Valley (1939) 216–17

Quakers 78, 181, 184, 188–9, 198, 229, 232; and international Quaker network 16, 181, 229
Quigley, C. 22–3

race; attitudes 24, 141–4, 196, 198–9; and class 44–5, 134, 145, 166, 217, 219–20, 243–5, 272; and colonial problems 236–44; difference 263; and imperialism 7–10, 23, 39–41, 223, 275; race-mixing (fear of) 142, 235 (*see also* miscegenation); problems; 132, 142–3, 206, 228–47; race ('colour') prejudice 43, 229, 236, 243; in Britain 121, 215, 232, 237; and 'race' riots 43, 206–7, 226, 237, 238; in West Africa 72–100
race consciousness 14–15, 20, 25, 41, 43–4, 113, 121, 155, 159–61, 177, 179, 207, 208, 215–19, 223, 253–4, 257 *see also* black consciousness
race relations 28, 229–30, 232, in Britain 205, 215, 223, 226, 228, 232–3, 245–7; in South Africa 142, 153, 186–90, 198, 201; and US race relations philosophy 155, 186, 188, 236, 246; in West Africa 73, 99–100 *see also* interracialism; multi-racialism
racial; equality 123, 215, 249, 254, 265; exclusion 8, 11, 209; integration 10, 186 (*see also* assimilation); oppression 213, 239, 254, 277; state 206–11; stereotypes 28, 31–3, 143, 215, 266
racism 6–7, 27, 33, 43–4, 141–3, 155, 258, 270, 275–7; in Britain 205–27, 232, 236, 243–7; and capitalism 235, 237, 246; institutional 28, 213, 245–6; inverse 42, in popular culture 31–3, 50–1, 215–16, 266, 268; problems of definition of 7–8; scientific 10, 27–8, 37, 43–4, 141–3, 153; in the United States 27, 39, 172, 182
Radcliffe-Brown, A. 188
radio 1, 24–5 *see also* BBC
Raikes, H. E. 189
Rand Daily Mail 189
Rand Revolt 1922 161
Ranger, T. O. 72, 92, 94
Rastafarianism 14, 276

Rathbone, Eleanor, MP 240, 257
Rathbone, R. 123–4, 159, 175
Rattray, Captain, R. S. 60, 292 n42
re-colonisation 2, 271, 273
Red International of Labour Unions
    (Profintern) (RILU) 44, 237
reformist socialism 40, 161, 171, 179,
    181–2, 183, 187, 193–4, 197–9, 234–5,
    238–9, 243–4, 249, 250–6, 264; as anti-
    communist 181–3, 186, 235, 238 *see also*
    critics of colonialism; Fabian socialism;
    British Labour Party
Reith, Lord 25; and Reith lectures 11 *see
    also* BBC
Reitz, D. 139–40, 308 n15
repatriation 207–8, 215, 233 *see also*
    immigration
resistance 7, 15–17, 35, 126, 219, 244,
    248–9, 255–7, 262, 268–70, 271,
    276–7; of African women 64–5, 90, 92,
    103, 148, 158, 164; cultural 150–2;
    problems of definition, 16, 102; and
    collaboration 6, 16 69, 100, 102,
    133–4, 158, 164, 167, 266; discourses
    of 219, 245; in South Africa 148,
    150–2, 157–80; in West Africa 52,
    59–67, 101–28 *see also* African
    nationalism; anti-colonialism; anti-
    imperialism; black consciousness; pan-
    africanism; race consciousness
Reynolds, Reginald 198, 222, 241–2
Rheinnalt, Jones, D. 186–7 *see also* SAIRR
Rhodes Trust 23, 45 *see also* Round Table
Rhodes, Cecil 23, 34, 186, 266
Rhodesia(s) 5, 41–2, 132, 139, 194 *see also*
    Southern and Northern Rhodesia
Rich, P. 146, 155, 160, 177, 179, 182, 190,
    197, 200, 229
Richards, Audrey 265, 340, n 61
Richards, J. 25
Riley, S. 273
Riotous Assemblies Act, 1914 (South
    Africa) and amendment, 1930 163–4
Roberts, A. 34, 263
Robeson, Paul xi, 31, 37, 51, 155, 173,
    206, 212–19; and Wales 216–17, 328
    n50 *see also* Goode Robeson, Eslanda
Robinson, C. 244
Robinson, K. 11
Robinson, R. 267
Rockerfeller Foundation 57
Roden Buxton, Charles 55, 69, 97, 193,

207, 235, 247, 250, 258; biographical
    information 332 n28
Rodney, W. 272
Rogers, J. A. 44, 88
Rose Innes, Sir James 194
Ross, Jean 190, 321 n36
Round Table 22–3, 38, 40, 42, 133, 252,
    254, 258, 263
Roux, E. 157, 164, 166, 173, 185, 197 *see
    also* CPSA
Royal African Society 252
Royal Empire Society 252; Cambridge
    branch 261, 339 n49
Royal Geographical Society 252
Royal Institute of International Affairs
    141, 246, 263
Royal Society of Arts 254
Russell, Bertrand 241
Ryan, J. R. 40

Sbacchi, A. 257–8
Sachs, W. 152
Said, E. 3, 8, 17, 30
Saklatavla, Shapuri MP 238
Sanders of the River (film and novel) xi,
    31, 38, 50–2, 56–7, 59, 61, 68, 71, 74,
    89, 93–4, 215–16, 290 n7; and
    representations of colonial Africa 50–2;
    and Robeson's repudiation of 216–17
School of Oriental [and African] Studies
    (SOAS) 35–6, 216, 267
Schreiner, Olive 148, 189
Schreiner, Oliver 189
Schwartz. B. xiii
Scott, M.198
Scottsboro Defence Committee (see
    CPGB)
Scouting and Guiding Movement; and
    cultural imperialism 24, 97–8, 239; in
    the Gold Coast 97–8; Pathfinder
    Movement, South Africa 153, 313 n89
Second World War 4, 10–11, 18 75, 119,
    122, 132–3, 139, 175–9, 247, 248–9,
    259, 264–9, 272; black and Coloured
    South African soldiers in 174; impact
    on developments in South Africa
    175–9; as stimulus to African
    nationalism 123–5, 176, 225–6; and
    race relations 87, 98–9, 233, 245–7 as
    stimulus to black consciousness in
    Britain 223–6; and West Africa 123–4
Sedition Ordinances see ARPS; Gold
    Coast; West Africa,

segregation (and separate development) 10,
34–5, 252–3; in South Africa; 131–3,
139–46, 148–52, 154, 159, 161, 166,
196, 198; opposition to 157–8, 171–5,
186–90; origins of 133, 134–5;
segregationist discourse and ideology
133, 144, 155, 196; segregationist
legislation 41, 135, 137, 141, 152, 155,
187; in West Africa 76, 79–100
Sekyi, Kobina 112, 121, 217
self-determination 22, 38, 44, 123, 166,
222, 249, 271
Seme, Pixie 167
Seretse Khama 193, 195; controversy over
marriage to Ruth Williams 195
sexuality 9, 25–6, 86, 89, 211; and racism
86, 143, 207, 209, 216, 226, 213 *see also*
interracial sex
Sharp, A. 40
Sherwood, M. 210, 225
Shiels, Drummond, MP 79, 251
Sierra Leone 49, 52, 59, 75, 112, 117, 219,
221, 231, 233; and colonial civil
liberties 118–20, 305 n63
Simons, J. 173
Sinclair, N. 210–11
Sivanandan, A. 246
slavery 31, 34, 230, 235, 257, 270, 271,
275–6 *see also* anti-slavery
Smith G 223
Smuts, Jan 40–1, 133, 137–40, 153, 161,
165, 175–7, 179, 189, 195, 196, 198,
264
Socialist League (Britain) 238, 241, 242,
252
Society of Friends 181, 183 *see also*
Quakers
Solanke, Lapido 121, 217
Sons of Africa 210
Sorensen, Reginald, MP 112
South Africa 5, 8, 20, 41–3, 55, 73, 104–5,
112, 125, 131–201, 205, 210, 216,
217–18, 222–8, 230, 232, 233–4, 236,
248, 250–2, 257, 259, 263, 272, 275;
American influence in 153–5, 160–1;
beer boycotts 164–5, 167; black
churches 152, 160; black bourgeoisie
135, 159, 167, 174–5, 177, 187; black
organisations (see AAC; ANC;
FNETU; ICU; Non-European
Conferences); 'civilised' labour policies
149, 161, 163; coloured community
132, 135–7, 142, 165; crime 149–50;

English-speaking South Africans 6, 135,
141, 143–5; impact of economic
depression 140, 148–50; Indian
community 134, 173; industrialisation
of 132, 134, 144–5, 157; native reserves
136 (*see also* native administration); pass
laws anti-pass-law campaigns and
134–7, 152, 158, 161, 163–4, 176; poor
white problem 149, 191; race problems
132, 141–3, 155; racial attitudes 141–4,
196, 198–9; racial state 141–55; rural
conditions and struggles 146–8;
repression and oppression of Africans;
131–4, 141, 151–2, 155–6, 157–80;
resistance 157–80; urbanisation
popular struggles 148–52 *see also*
Afrikaner, British imperialism;
migration; mining; Natal; segregation,
trade unions; Transkei
South Africa Act 1909 135, 137–8
South Africa Party (SAP) 139, 140, 163,
196
South African Communist Party see CPSA
South African Independent Labour Party
185
South African Institute of Race Relations
(SAIRR), 142, 154, 186–8, 190, 195,
197, 246
South African Labour Party (SALP) 163,
176, 181, 185
South African Liberal Party 200
South African liberalism and liberals 134,
141–4, 147–8, 152–5, 174, 179, 181–2,
186–90, 231; decline of 196–201;
relations with British liberals , 196–8
South African (Native) National Congress
(SANC) 135–9, 159; and African
grievances 137, 150; deputation to
London 41, 138, 154; as forerunner to
ANC 159
South African ('Boer') War 1899–1902;
134–5
South West Africa, 137, 139, 177, 259 *see
also* Germany
Southern Rhodesia 41–2, 201, 251
Soviet Union, 44–5, 217, 241–3, 265
Sowell, T 7
Special Restriction of Colonial Alien
Seaman's Order, 1925 207–9, 233
Spencer, I. 207, 223,
Stalinism 4, 242
Stasiulis, A. 151
Statute of Westminster 1931 141

Stock, Diana 242, 247
Stockwell, A. J. 2
stokvel 152
Stoler, L. A. 8
Student Christian Association 160
students; African;115, 121–2, 217, 220–1,
    234, 242, 261; colonial; 159, 188, 206,
    211, 217, 230–1, 232–9 *see also* WASU
Swaziland 133, 147, 150, 182, 190–2, 196
Swift, Jonathan, 5

Tabili, L. 207, 209–10, 222, 245
taxation; in the British South African
    Protectorates 191; in West Africa 61–4,
    66, 108–9, 123; resistance to 63–4; of
    South African migrant workers 146,
    148 *see also* Gold Coast; indirect rule
Thaele, James 149, 159
The Black Man 214, 219–20, 222
The Council for Promoting Equality and
    Civil Rights Between White and
    Coloured People 234, 240
The Gambia 49, 63, 94
The Keys 216, 220, 222
The Times 192, 252–4
The West 29, 249, 270, 271–7
Thema, Selope, R.V. 137–8, 154, 174
Thibedi, T. W. 166
Thomas, J. H., M.P, 140, 192, 239
Thomas, Sir Shenton 78, 114–18
Tomlinson, J. 3, 8–9
Toynbee, A. 31
trade unionism; black; 221–2, 225; colonial
    253, 255, in South Africa 161–71, 176,
    (*see also* ICU, IICU, ICU Yase Natal); in
    West Africa 105, 109, 113, 124 *see also*
    British Trade Union Movement
Transkei 145–9, 159–60, 169; co-
    operatives in 190, 195; rural conditions
    and struggles 147–8 *see also* native
    administration
Trapido, S., 151, 160
travelogues 34, 37, 82
Treaty of Versailles 1919 257 (*see also*
    Versailles Peace Conference)
Trotsky, L. 44
Trusteeship Council of the United Nations
    195, 266
trusteeship 11, 17, 22, 29, 33–5, 42, 49,
    145–6, 181, 194, 249–50, 253, 256,
    259, 261–3, 265–6 *see also* imperialism;
    paternalism

Tshekedi Khama 191, 192–4, 195, 240 *see
    also* Bechuanaland
Turner, T. 10

Umsebenzi 165
Umvikele Thebe (African Defender) 172,
    191
Unemployment Assistance Board 209
Union of Democratic Control (UDC) 247,
    251–2, 336 n10
Union of South Africa see South Africa
United Africa Company (UAC) 55, 90,
    104, 125
United Nations (UN) 177, 266, 275; and
    International Trusteeship System 266
United Party (South Africa) 140, 196
United States of America 6, 11, 21, 38–44,
    132, 182, 206, 214, 249, 261, 265–7,
    274, 276; as imperialist power 270, 277;
    philanthropic foundations 36 (*see also*
    Carnegie, Phelps Stokes, Rockerfeller);
    role in Treaty of Versailles 38–43
United Transkeian General Council
    (Bunga), 146–7, 174
Universal Declaration of Human Rights
    157, 166, 255
Universal Negro Improvement Association
    (UNIA) 14, 159, 220 *see also* Garveyism
Universal Race Congress 1911 229
Universal Races Congress 1939 44
University College of Rhodesia and
    Nyasaland 197
Unterhalter, E. 158
urbanisation see Gold Coast; South Africa;
    West Africa

Vail, L. 38, 125–6, 150, 175
Van Onselen, C. 175
Van der Post, Laurens 268
Vaughan, M. 28, 89–90
venereal diseases; in Africa 78, 149, 151,
    190; in Britain; 209
Venn, C. 6
Versailles Peace Conference (and
    Settlement) 20, 38–40, 137–9, 248;
    British Empire Delegation 40, 287 n71;
    and colonial mandates 38–40 *see also*
    League of Nations
Victoria League 261
Vigne, R 200
violence 9, 125, 143, 150–2, 171, 175, 211;
    against African women 89, 151; 'black
    on black' 150; colonial 55, 71, 73, 120;

racial 275; in South Africa 144–5, 150–2, 171, 175, 179
Vischer, Sir H. 35
Von Laue 3

Walker, C. 158
Wallace Johnson, I. T. A. 110, 114, 117–19, 222–3; biographical details 304 n55
Wallace, Edgar 31, 50
Walrond, Eric 205, 215; biographical information 324 n2
Ward, Arnold 221, 238–9, 258
Ware, V. 79, 81
Warren, B. 3, 273
Washington, Booker T. 14–15; and Tuskagee Institute 35, 97
Watkins, W. H. 1
Waugh, Evelyn 31, 58, 73, 97, 211–12, 214, 235, 256–7
Webb, Beatrice 184, 235
Webb, Maurice 188, 189
Webb, Sydney (Lord Passfield) 184, 235
Webster, W. 268
Welch, Elizabeth 214
Welfare of Africans in Europe War Fund 230–2
Wellington Movement (Transkei) 159–60
Wells, H. G. 239, 241
West Africa 5, 8, 36, 39, 49–128, 131, 147, 150–1, 155, 157–8, 192, 194, 198, 250, 253, 266–7; African bourgeoisie 98–9; and 'white mask' 52; African lawyers and press 102, 113, 117–18; and African renaissance 198; British business interests in 54; business community; 73, 75–6, 100; colonial administration 56–71; colonial society 52–3, 72–100; coloured population; 134–7, 150–1; in the English imagination 50–6; impact of economic depression on 64–7, 104–5, 101–10; industrialisation of 266; labour conditions and disturbances 104–14, 267; peasant commodity production 55, 101, 104–5; racial order and racial discrimination 63, 72–100; resistance 52, 59–67, 101–28; seamen 119; Sedition Ordinances 113–20; Syrian population 76–7; trade unions 105, 109, 113, 124; urbanisation and urban unrest 102, 104, 108–9; white expatriate society 72–87, 99–100 *see also*

Nigeria; Gold Coast; Sierra Leone; Gambia
West African National Secretariat (WANS) 243
West African Nursing Service, 75
West African Pilot
West African Student's Union (WASU) 121, 217, 220–1, 240, 264
West African Youth League (WAYL); 112, 118–19, 126; and women members 126
West Africans in Britain 103–4, 115, 121, 217, 221, 228, 239, 242, 234
West Indies and West Indians 76, 99, 112, 205, 211, 219, 223, 254–5; labour disturbances 254–5; in Britain 217, 229
western; culture 9–11, 59, 102, 122; imperialism 38–43, 133, 257–8, 269; media 38; racism 5, 270; power 271, 276 *see also* globalisation; The West
White, T. R. 177
white dominions 4, 20–1, 24, 34, 38, 40–2, 268 *see also* Australia, South Africa
white expatriate society 4, 52, 73–87, 99–100
white settlers; in East and Southern Africa 35, 42, 182, 191–3, 200–1, 206, 225, 250–3, 256, 268, 270, 275; and 'frontier mentality' 133, 143–5, 253
white supremacy 132, 134, 141, 145, 157–8, 175, 182
white women; and black men 84–6, 210–13; and black women 79–81, 87, 90–2, 143, 151; as colonial experts 6, 254 (*see also* Perham, M.); as colonial wives 72, 81–4, 99; in the CAS 57, 81, 90; as liberal and reformist activists 24, 184, 234–5 (*see also* Holtby, Winifred); and racism 86–7; as travellers in Africa 80–2, 84–6; in South Africa 142–3, 151, 248; in West Africa, 72–4, 79–88
whiteness 4, 53, 81, 236, 246–7, 272; and white identities; 17, 29, 261–2
Williams, P. 11
Wilkes, I. 65–6, 97
Wilkinson, A. F. C. 67
Wilkinson, Ellen, MP 251
Wilson, Woodrow 38, 40–1
Witwatersrand University 142–3, 187–8, 189; and Bantu Studies 187–8
Wolton, D. W. 164, 165
women see African women; white women
Wood, S. R. 115, 119
Woodman, Dorothy 247, 251

Woolf, L. 22, 28, 30, 40, 42, 43, 54, 132, 141, 157, 194, 199, 206, 250, 255
Workers Educational Association (WEA) 183, 190
World Bureau of Scouts and Guides 220
World Congress Against Racialism and Anti-Semitism 1939 242

Xuma, A. B. 157, 176–7

Yearwood, P, 54
Yemeni seamen 207

Yergan, Max 160–1, 173, 177
Young Mens' Christian Association (YMCA) 160
Young, J. W. 20
Yuval Davis, N. 7–8, 79, 151, 244

Zack-Williams, A. T. 276
Zambia 251 *see also* Northern Rhodesia
Zimbabwe 251 *see also* Southern Rhodesia
Zulu 196, 216; and Zulu ethnicity 150, 167, 169